THE CAMBRIDGE HISTORY OF
# THE AGE OF ATLANTIC REVOLUTIONS

*

VOLUME III

The Iberian Empires

Volume III covers the Iberian Empires and the important ethnic dimension of the Ibero-American independence movements, revealing the contrasting dynamics created by the Spanish imperial crisis at home and in the colonies. It bears out the experimental nature of political changes, the shared experiences and contrasts across different areas, and the connections to the revolutionary French Caribbean. The special nature of the emancipatory processes launched in the European metropoles of Spain and Portugal is explored, as are the connections between Spanish America and Brazil, as well as between Brazil and Portuguese Africa. It ends with an assessment of Brazil and how the survival of slavery is shown to have been essential to the new monarchy, although, simultaneously, enslaved people began pressing their own demands, just like the Indigenous population.

WIM KLOOSTER is Professor and the Robert H. and Virginia N. Scotland Endowed Chair in History and International Relations at Clark University. He is the (co-)author and (co-) editor of twelve books. His monograph *The Dutch Moment: War, Trade, and Settlement in the Seventeenth Century Atlantic World* won the Biennial Book Award of the Forum on Early-Modern Empires and Global Interactions and the Hendricks Award of the New Netherland Institute.

THE CAMBRIDGE HISTORY OF

# THE AGE OF ATLANTIC REVOLUTIONS

Edited by

WIM KLOOSTER

In three volumes, *The Cambridge History of the Age of Atlantic Revolutions* brings together experts on all corners of the Atlantic World who reveal the age in all its complexity. The Age of Atlantic Revolutions formed the transition from an era marked by monarchical rule, privileges, and colonialism to an age that stood out for republican rule, legal equality, and the sovereignty of American nations. The seventy-one chapters included reflect the latest trends and discussions on this transformative part of history, not only highlighting the causes, key events, and consequences of the revolutions, but also stressing political experimentation, contingency, and the survival of colonial institutions. The volumes also examine the attempts of enslaved and indigenous people, and free people of color, to change their plight, offering a much-needed revision to R. R. Palmer's first synthesis of this era sixty years ago.

*The Cambridge History of the Age of Atlantic Revolutions, Volume I: The Enlightenment and the British Colonies*

EDITED BY WIM KLOOSTER

*The Cambridge History of the Age of Atlantic Revolutions, Volume II: France, Europe, and Haiti*

EDITED BY WIM KLOOSTER

*The Cambridge History of the Age of Atlantic Revolutions, Volume III: The Iberian Empires*

EDITED BY WIM KLOOSTER

# THE CAMBRIDGE HISTORY OF
# THE AGE OF ATLANTIC REVOLUTIONS

*

VOLUME III

The Iberian Empires

WIM KLOOSTER
*Clark University, Massachusetts*

Shaftesbury Road, Cambridge CB2 8EA, United Kingdom

One Liberty Plaza, 20th Floor, New York, NY 10006, USA

477 Williamstown Road, Port Melbourne, VIC 3207, Australia

314–321, 3rd Floor, Plot 3, Splendor Forum, Jasola District Centre, New Delhi – 110025, India

103 Penang Road, #05-06/07, Visioncrest Commercial, Singapore 238467

Cambridge University Press is part of Cambridge University Press & Assessment, a department of the University of Cambridge.

We share the University's mission to contribute to society through the pursuit of education, learning and research at the highest international levels of excellence.

www.cambridge.org
Information on this title: www.cambridge.org/9781108475969

DOI: 10.1017/9781108598248

© Cambridge University Press & Assessment 2023

This publication is in copyright. Subject to statutory exception and to the provisions of relevant collective licensing agreements, no reproduction of any part may take place without the written permission of Cambridge University Press & Assessment.

First published 2023

Printed in the United Kingdom by TJ Books Limited, Padstow, Cornwall

*A catalogue record for this publication is available from the British Library.*

Library of Congress Cataloging-in-Publication Data
NAMES: Klooster, Wim, editor.
TITLE: The Cambridge history of the age of Atlantic revolutions / Wim Klooster.
DESCRIPTION: Cambridge, United Kingdom ; New York : Cambridge University Press, 2023. | Includes bibliographical references and index.
IDENTIFIERS: LCCN 2022058499 (print) | LCCN 2022058500 (ebook) | ISBN 9781108476034 (v. 1 ; hardback) | ISBN 9781108469432 (v. 1 ; paperback) | ISBN 9781108475983 (v. 2 ; hardback) | ISBN 9781108469326 (v. 2 ; paperback) | ISBN 9781108599405 (v. 2 ; eub) | ISBN 9781108475969 (v. 3 ; hardback) | ISBN 9781108469319 (v. 3 ; paperback) | ISBN 9781108598248 (v. 3 ; epub) | ISBN 9781108567671 (v. 1 ; epub)
SUBJECTS: LCSH: Revolutions–History–18th century. | Social change–History–18th century. | Revolutions–History–19th century. | Social change–History–19th century. | History, Modern–18th century. | History, Modern–19th century.
CLASSIFICATION: LCC D308 .C36 2023 (print) | LCC D308 (ebook) | DDC 940.2/7–dc23/eng/20221207
LC record available at https://lccn.loc.gov/2022058499
LC ebook record available at https://lccn.loc.gov/2022058500

ISBN – 3 Volume Set 9781108567817 Hardback
ISBN – Volume I 9781108476034 Hardback
ISBN – Volume II 9781108475983 Hardback
ISBN – Volume III 9781108475969 Hardback

Cambridge University Press & Assessment has no responsibility for the persistence or accuracy of URLs for external or third-party internet websites referred to in this publication and does not guarantee that any content on such websites is, or will remain, accurate or appropriate.

# *Contents*

*List of Figures* viii
*List of Maps* ix
*List of Tables* x
*Contributors to Volume III* xi
*Preface* xiii

Introduction 1
WIM KLOOSTER

PART I
THE SPANISH EMPIRE

1 · The Spanish Empire: General Overview 53
STEFAN RINKE

2 · The Spanish Empire on the Eve of American Independence 79
EMILY BERQUIST SOULE

3 · The Cortes of Cádiz and the Spanish Liberal Revolution of 1810–1814:
Atlantic and Spanish American Dimensions 102
ROBERTO BREÑA

4 · The Constitutional Triennium in Spain, 1820–1823 124
JUAN LUIS SIMAL

5 · Mexico: From Civil War to the War of Independence, 1808–1825 154
JUAN ORTIZ ESCAMILLA

v

*Contents*

6 · Central America  *176*
TIMOTHY HAWKINS

7 · War and Revolution in the Southern Cone, 1808–1824  *205*
JUAN LUIS OSSA SANTA CRUZ

8 · Caribbean South America: Free People of Color, Republican Experiments,
Military Strategies, and the Caribbean Connection on the Path
to Independence  *228*
ERNESTO BASSI

9 · The Southernmost Revolution. The Río de la Plata in the Early
Nineteenth Century  *252*
GABRIEL DI MEGLIO

10 · Royalists, Monarchy, and Political Transformation in the Spanish
Atlantic World during the Age of Revolutions  *277*
MARCELA ECHEVERRI

11 · Africans and their Descendants in the Spanish Empire in the Age
of Revolutions  *304*
JANE LANDERS

12 · Concepts on the Move: Constitution, Citizenship, Federalism,
and Liberalism across Spain and Spanish Atlantic  *325*
JAVIER FERNÁNDEZ-SEBASTIÁN

13 · Patriarchy, Misogyny, and Politics in the Age of Revolutions  *351*
MÓNICA RICKETTS

14 · Impact of the French Caribbean Revolutions in Continental Iberian
America, 1791–1833  *374*
ALEJANDRO E. GÓMEZ

15 · Deferred but not Avoided: Great Britain and Latin
American Independence  *399*
KAREN RACINE

*Contents*

PART II
## BRAZIL, PORTUGAL, AND AFRICA

16 · Overview: The Independence Era in the Luso-Brazilian World   *429*
GABRIEL PAQUETTE

17 · Portugal's Social and Political Change from the *Ancien Régime*
to Liberalism   *450*
NUNO GONÇALO MONTEIRO

18 · Conservative Tracks toward Independence: Transfer of the Court to Rio
de Janeiro, the Porto Revolution, and Brazilian Autonomy   *474*
JURANDIR MALERBA

19 · Building New Brazilian Institutions   *496*
JEFFREY D. NEEDELL

20 · Slaves, Indians, and the "Classes of Color": Popular Participation in
Brazilian Independence   *520*
HENDRIK KRAAY

21 · Brazil and the Independence of Spanish America: Parallel Trajectories,
Linked Processes (1807–1825)   *547*
JOÃO PAULO PIMENTA

22 · Waves of Sedition across the Atlantic: Liberal Politics in Angola in the
Wake of Brazilian Independence (c. 1817–1825)   *567*
ROQUINALDO FERREIRA

*Index   589*

# *Figures*

| | | |
|---|---|---|
| 3.1 | The swearing in of the deputies to the Cortes of Cádiz (1810) | 107 |
| 4.1 | Massacre of the population marching for the Constitution in Cádiz | 127 |
| 4.2 | The failed *coup d'état* of July 1822 | 141 |
| 4.3 | King Fernando VII swears to uphold the Constitution, 9 July 1822 | 142 |
| 5.1 | Indigenous people fighting in 1810 | 161 |
| 5.2 | Insurgents under Morelos capture the fort of Acapulco, 1813 | 164 |
| 6.1 | Cathedral in San Salvador | 178 |
| 7.1 | Battle of Maipú, 5 April 1818, at which San Martín defeated the royalist forces | 220 |
| 9.1 | The capture from British troops of Buenos Aires by Liniers's army in 1806 | 257 |
| 15.1 | The British Arch in Valparaíso, Chile, a modern-day memorial | 418 |
| 15.2 | Monitorial school method | 422 |
| 16.1 | Adoption in Rio de Janeiro in 1821 of the Constitution of Lisbon | 442 |
| 17.1 | Meeting of the provisional Portuguese government, 1 October 1820 | 458 |
| 17.2 | Triumphant Entry of King João VI and his son D. Miguel in Lisbon, 27 May 1823 | 459 |
| 19.1 | Transportation of slaves into Brazil | 502 |
| 19.2 | Emperor Pedro I | 506 |
| 20.1 | *Independência ou Morte*, painting by Pedro Américo Figueiredo de Melo | 521 |
| 20.2 | Indian soldiers fighting Botocudos in São Paulo, c. 1820 | 535 |
| 21.1 | Slave market in Rio de Janeiro | 562 |

# Maps

| | | |
|---|---|---|
| 1.1 | Spanish America in 1800 | 61 |
| 1.2 | The Spanish empire in 1824 | 77 |
| 4.1 | Spain in 1820 | 128 |
| 6.1 | New Spain and New Granada on the eve of the independence period | 180 |
| 8.1 | Caribbean South America | 230 |
| 16.1 | The Portuguese Atlantic World, 1800 | 435 |
| 19.1 | Brazil at independence | 507 |

# Tables

5.1 Military units and territorial demarcation of the royalist army in New Spain and the internal provinces in 1816     169

8.1 Population of late colonial Venezuela (1800)     231

8.2 Population of late colonial Caribbean New Granada     231

# Contributors to Volume III

Ernesto Bassi
Roberto Breña
Marcela Echeverri
Juan Ortiz Escamilla
Roquinaldo Ferreira
Alejandro E. Gómez
Timothy Hawkins
Hendrik Kraay
Jane Landers
Jurandir Malerba
Gabriel di Meglio
Nuno Gonçalo Monteiro
Jeffrey D. Needell
Gabriel Paquette
João Paulo Pimenta
Karen Racine
Mónica Ricketts
Stefan Rinke
Juan Luis Ossa Santa Cruz
Javier Fernández-Sebastián
Juan Luis Simal
Emily Berquist Soule

# *Preface*

I thank Debbie Gershenowitz and Cecelia Cancellaro at Cambridge University Press for the smooth and pleasant collaboration. I would also like to express my gratitude to the three scholars who made up an advisory board that assisted me in choosing the contributors: Rafe Blaufarb, Ben Weider Eminent Scholar in Napoleonic Studies at Florida State University, Patrick Griffin, Madden-Hennebry Professor of History at the University of Notre Dame, and Gabriel Paquette, Professor of History at the Johns Hopkins University. All three have also written a chapter in this book.

About a dozen of the chapters were first presented at the workshop "Black Men and Women in the Age of Revolutions" in January 2020. I thank Yale University for providing an excellent venue for the workshop and Mark Peterson for making arrangements.

Some contributors contracted Covid-19, whereas others were affected by lockdowns. I thank them all for their perseverance. Although a number of invited authors reneged on their contractual promise to write a chapter far into the project, I am confident that the age of Atlantic revolutions has been covered sufficiently in the pages that follow.

**Wim Klooster**

# Introduction

WIM KLOOSTER

Sixty years ago, R. R. Palmer published his two-volume *Age of the Democratic Revolution*, in which he described a "revolution of Western Civilization," that, he argued, had occurred in the years between 1760 and 1800. These decades, Palmer went on, saw numerous agitations, upheavals, and conspiracies on either side of the Atlantic, that arose out of specific or universal conditions, not simply as the result of the French Revolution. What Palmer outlined was what we now call the Age of (Atlantic) Revolutions, a theme that has been and continues to be the inspiration for high-quality publications, in part because this period in history supposedly laid the foundations for the countries shaped in the aftermath of these revolutions, and in part because of the need to explain the unusual political activity and social upheaval on display in this era. Virtually absent from the countless monographs, articles, and edited volumes is an overview of this important period in Atlantic history. Many specialists work within their own subfield, writing and conducting research on, for example, the American Revolution without closely following the newest trends in scholarship on the revolutions in France or Latin America. The aim of this book is to bring together current scholarship for the first reference work dedicated to the age of revolutions. Jointly, the chapters that make up this book will reveal the era in all its complexity. They will reflect the latest trends, discussing more than simply the causes, key events, and consequences of the revolutions by stressing political experimentation, contingency, and the survival of old regime practices and institutions. The time is ripe for analyzing these matters in a way that does justice to both the local nature of the revolts and their much wider Atlantic context.

Most scholars of the Age of Revolutions no longer share Palmer's geographic and temporal frameworks. They include the quarter-century (or more) after 1800 and look beyond western Europe and the United States to Haiti and Latin America. No general agreement exists, however, on the exact start and end dates, nor on its confinement to the Atlantic world. The periodization advocated by C. A. Bayly, who has made a case for the time-frame 1760–1840, is about the same as that adopted in this *Cambridge History of the Age of Atlantic Revolutions*.[1] Like any time limits, these are somewhat arbitrary. One could push the outer boundary to 1848. By that year of revolution, however, so many new factors and forces had emerged on the various national political scenes – including full-fledged liberalism and nationalism, and capitalism's working class – that there is more reason to see them as elements of a new era.

Although the geographic scope of these three volumes is vast, it has been my choice not to include all instances of rebellion, but to focus on coherence. What ties the numerous rebellious movements on either side of the Atlantic basin together in the half-century between the shots fired at Lexington and Concord (1775) and the Spanish loss at the siege of Callao, Peru in 1826 is more than just the, often violent, transitions from old to new regimes. The common glue is what marked these transitions: the questioning of time-honored institutions in the name of liberty; the invention and spread of a politics of contestation at local and national levels; the unprecedented experimentation with new forms of democracy; the abolition of numerous forms of legal inequality; and last but not least the aspiration to universal rights. These were processes in which plebeians, elites, and members of middling groups all participated. These phenomena were not experienced wherever in the world riots and rebellions broke out. They were largely absent, for example, from the Ottoman empire, although it was in great turmoil during the age of revolutions, especially in the years 1806–1808, when two sultans were deposed and thousands of people killed.[2]

What the age of revolutions brought was hope for fundamental change, a scarce good in the early modern world. Any criticism of authorities had previously been forbidden and heavily punished. It was only during periods of unrest that peasants in Europe could express their dissatisfaction without fear of reprisal. In such times, there are also glimpses of the hidden transcript of enslaved men and women throughout the Americas, which reflected the

---

[1] C. A. Bayly, *The Birth of the Modern World, 1780–1914: Global Connections and Comparisons* (Oxford: Oxford University Press, 2004); C. A. Bayly, "The Age of Revolutions in Global Context: An Afterword," in David Armitage and Sanjay Subrahmanyam, eds., *The Age of Revolutions in Global Context, c. 1760–1840* (Houndmills: Palgrave Macmillan, 2010), 209–17: 217.

[2] Ali Yaycioglu, *Partners of the Empire: The Crisis of the Ottoman Order in the Age of Revolutions* (Stanford: Stanford University Press, 2016), 158.

awakening of their hopes.[3] A historian of the Russian Revolution has written that "revolutions disrupt assumptions that the future can only appear along the straight tracks where the present seems to be heading, and so challenge how we understand time and history . . . Utopia is this open disruption of the now, for the sake of possibility, not a closed map of the future. It is the leap not yet the landing."[4] This leap was made time and again by the oppressed. On the eve of the French and Haitian Revolutions, writes **John Garrigus** (Volume II, Chapter 23), many enslaved residents of Saint-Domingue "believed change was possible, whether that came through applying new laws or actively confronting the master class." For the 1790s, no fewer than forty-seven slave revolts and conspiracies have been documented for the Greater Caribbean, a number much larger than ever before or afterwards. Similarly, the years 1789–1802 saw 150 mutinies on single ships and half a dozen fleet-wide mutinies in the British, French, and Dutch navies, which meant that between 67,000 and 100,000 mobilized men were involved in at least one mutiny.[5]

Hope in the American Revolution often took the form of millennial expectations, which were so intense "during the early years of the revolutionary war that numerous patriots foresaw the final destruction of Antichrist and the establishment of the Kingdom of God within the immediate future." One revolutionary on Long Island saw the millennium as "the happy period when tyranny, oppression, and wretchedness shall be banished from the earth; when universal love and liberty, peace and righteousness, shall prevail."[6] The French Revolution aroused hope, both at home and abroad, that tended to be secular in nature. After arriving in France in 1792 as the United States' Minister Plenipotentiary, Gouverneur Morris wrote in a letter that he was delighted to find "on this Side of the Atlantic a strong resemblance to what I left on the other – a Nation which exists in Hopes, Prospects, and Expectations. The reverence for ancient Establishments gone, existing Forms shaken to the very Foundation, and a new Order of Things about

---

[3] Martin Merki-Vollenwyder, *Unruhige Untertanen: Die Rebellion der Luzerner Bauern im Zweiten Villmergerkrieg (1712)* (Luzern: Rex Verlag, 1995), 121–2; James C. Scott, *Domination and the Arts of Resistance: Hidden Transcripts* (New Haven: Yale University Press, 1990).

[4] Mark D. Steinberg, *The Russian Revolution 1905–1921* (Oxford: Oxford University Press, 2017), 292–3.

[5] David Geggus, "Slave Rebellion during the Age of Revolution," in Wim Klooster and Gert Oostindie, eds., *Curaçao in the Age of Revolutions, 1795–1800* (Leiden: KITLV Press, 2011), 23–56: 41–3; Nyklas Frykman, *The Bloody Flag: Mutiny in the Age of Atlantic Revolution* (Oakland: University of California Press, 2020), 10.

[6] Ruth H. Bloch, *Visionary Republic: Millennial Themes in American Thought, 1756–1800* (Cambridge: Cambridge University Press, 1985), 79, 81.

to take Place in which even to the very names, all former Institutions will be disregarded."[7] The imagined new order caused tremendous optimism on the part of enthusiasts for the French Revolution. Norwegian-born Henrik Steffens recalled in his memoirs that when he was sixteen and living with his family in Copenhagen, his father came home one day, deeply impressed by the French Revolution, and told his three sons: "Children, you are to be envied, what a happy time lies ahead of you! If you don't succeed in gaining a free independent position, you have yourselves to blame. All restrictive conditions of status, of poverty will disappear, the least will begin the same struggle with the most powerful, with the same weapons, on the same ground. If only I were young like you!"[8] Steffens experienced the time that followed as not simply a French but a European revolution that was planted in millions of hearts: "The first moment of excitement in history ... has something pure, even sacred, that must never be forgotten. A boundless hope took hold of me, my whole future, it seemed to me, was planted in a fresh, new soil ... From then on my whole existence had taken on a new direction ..."[9]

## Rights

If revolutionaries were guided by ideas emanating from the Enlightenment, did the Enlightenment produce the revolutions? No, answers **Johnson Kent Wright** (Volume I, Chapter 2), at least not in the case of France. "Had 'enlightened' criticism of the Bourbon monarchy been sufficient to have launched the Revolution, it ought to have occurred some two decades earlier than it did." And yet, Wright adds, the French Enlightenment was essential to the way the revolution unfolded. Likewise, enlightened ideas helped steer the revolutions in the Ibero-American world, but, as **Brian Hamnett** argues (Volume I, Chapter 3), the Enlightenment did not lead inevitably or automatically to support for revolution. In New Spain, for example, the outbreak of insurrection in 1810 divided its proponents into hostile camps.

Rights were an essential element of the sometimes baffling transformations that took place during the age of Atlantic revolutions. Rights used to

---

[7] Cited in Philipp Ziesche, "Exporting American Revolutions: Gouverneur Morris, Thomas Jefferson, and the National Struggle for Universal Rights in Revolutionary France," *Journal of the Early Republic* 26:3 (2006), 419–47: 426.

[8] Henrich Steffens, *Was ich erlebte: Aus der Erinnerung niedergeschrieben* (Breslau: Josef Mar und Kompanie, 1840), vol. I, 362–3.

[9] Steffens, *Was ich erlebte*, 364–5.

Introduction

be privileges, granted to someone for the common good. Every male had rights commensurate with his station in life, which thereby confirmed the hierarchical organization of society. They were accompanied by obligations that forced the rights' holders to use their powers for the common good. The new notion that gradually took shape – and remained unfinished – was that humans' own moral power allowed them to stake their claims and relate their own rights to those of others. Rights transcended all structures of authority and were thus common to humankind. Human equality now trumped any differences in rank, nationality, or culture.[10] The US Declaration of Independence – the first revolutionary document to invoke rights – echoed this new idea by positing the existence of a supreme law against which positive law could be measured and, if needed, changed.[11] The French Declaration of the Rights of Man and Citizen served the same function, for which it was criticized by supporters of liberalism as metaphysical.

Once formulated, these catalogs of rights could inspire groups who had not been among the intended beneficiaries to claim parity. Just like Black people could argue that their humanity sufficed to negate their status as slaves, some women pressed for their equal rights. The authors of two Belgian pamphlets, who predicted that the current tide of revolutions would bring an end to "seventeen centuries of masculine abuse," called for a national assembly, half of whose members were to be women. If their demand was ignored by the nation's leaders, women would withdraw from society.[12] Adversaries of such rights, however, used the same language of natural rights to oppose these demands. Woman's nature, male French revolutionaries argued, made her unfit to exercise political power.[13]

The invocation of a higher law coexisted in the age of revolutions with the continued emphasis on ancient positive rights by men and women challenging the social order. In many places across the Atlantic world, as **Stephen**

---

[10] Knud Haakonssen, "From Natural Law to the Rights of Man: A European Perspective on American Debates," in Michael J. Lacy and Knud Haakonssen, eds., *A Culture of Rights: The Bill of Rights in Philosophy, Politics, and Law – 1791 and 1991* (Cambridge: Cambridge University Press, 1991), 19–61: 21, 32, 35–6; Simon Middleton, *From Privileges to Rights: Work and Politics in Colonial New York* (Philadelphia: University of Pennsylvania Press, 2006), 5–6.

[11] Andrew J. Reck, "Natural Law in American Revolutionary Thought," *The Review of Metaphysics* 30:4 (1977), 686–714: 712.

[12] Janet L. Polasky, "Women in Revolutionary Belgium: From Stone Throwers to Hearth Tenders," *History Workshop* 21 (1986), 87–104: 93.

[13] Annelien de Dijn, *Freedom: An Unruly History* (Cambridge, MA: Harvard University Press, 2020), 226.

**Conway** argues in Volume I, Chapter 11, "the events associated with Palmer's 'democratic revolution' began as a conservative reaction to the reforming endeavors of rulers, not as a grassroots desire to extend popular participation." Ireland's Protestants, he shows, were looking backwards "in seeking to reclaim their autonomy." "Most of them were not interested in a democratic transformation of Ireland." **Janet Polasky** (Volume II, Chapter 14) writes that one of the groups challenging Austrian rule in Belgium "wanted to restore the medieval constitutions and reestablish the rule of the three Estates. Instead of natural rights, they referred to 'the eternal rights of man,' meaning something quite different from the enlightenment ideal. Instead of the 'rights of the People,' they referred to the privileges of the 'nation belge.'" In the (Swiss) Helvetic Republic, a document presented to the authorities of Zurich in 1794 that has been labeled the *Stäfner Memorial* demanded both the restoration of old privileges and a constitution that defended individual human rights.[14]

The introduction of rights was no straightforward process, as can be illustrated by the uncertain status of the right to profess one's religious belief. The tone was set by the Virginia Declaration of Rights, which stipulated that "all men are equally entitled to the free exercise of religion, according to the dictates of conscience."[15] Although it has been argued that religious freedom was achievable in Protestant places such as Virginia where tolerance had already been practiced, its adoption was usually a matter of controversy. In Pennsylvania's constitutional debate of 1776, one side – made up of Protestants – opposed religious leniency, which they feared would put them at the mercy of the alien creeds of Islam, Catholicism, and Judaism. Likewise, although Massachusetts' constitution may have guaranteed the exercise of religion in private, it contained an injunction to the legislature to support Protestant teachers.[16] Nor was such intolerance the exclusive domain of elite politicians in the age of revolutions. A series of Catholic relief bills proposed

---

[14] Urte Weeber, "New Wine in Old Wineskins: Republicanism in the Helvetic Republic," in Joris Oddens, Mart Rutjes, and Erik Jacobs, eds., *The Political Culture of the Sister Republics, 1794–1806: France, the Netherlands, Switzerland, and Italy* (Amsterdam: Amsterdam University Press, 2015), 57–64: 62.

[15] Daniel L. Dreisbach, "George Mason's Pursuit of Religious Liberty in Revolutionary Virginia," *The Virginia Magazine of History and Biography* 108:1 (2000), 5–44: 16.

[16] Charles D. Russell, "Islam as a Danger to Republican Virtue: Broadening Religious Liberty in Revolutionary Pennsylvania," *Pennsylvania History: A Journal of Mid-Atlantic Studies* 76:3 (2009), 250–75: 251; Eduardo Posada-Carbó, "Spanish America and US constitutionalism in the Age of Revolution," in Gabriel Paquette and Gonzalo M. Quintero Saravia, eds., *Spain and the American Revolution: New Approaches and Perspectives* (London: Routledge, 2020), 210–23: 217.

## Introduction

by the British government threw into sharp relief the existence of a popular Protestantism that defined itself in opposition to French Catholicism and eventually led to the Gordon Riots (London, 1780).[17]

The antipluralist tendency was, however, stronger in the Catholic world, even in France, where the Catholic faith lost its status as state religion and where Protestants and Jews were emancipated. Political culture proved hard to change.[18] And so it could happen that a small town in Alsace decided in 1794 that the Jews had to shave their beards, and could no longer carry their Decalogues in public or show any other signs of their religion.[19] It was not different in the colonies. When the planters of Saint-Domingue sought protection from the British king in 1793, proposing some articles of government, they insisted on the exclusivity of the Catholic religion.[20] Soon, of course, French revolutionary intolerance went beyond the insistence on Catholicism, when the adoption of the Civil Constitution of the Clergy led to discrimination against the millions of people who clung to the old Church.

The influential constitution of Cádiz stated unambiguously that the religion of the Spanish nation was and would always be the only true Roman Catholic one. When the legislators gathered in Cádiz voted for press freedom in 1810, they followed it up by setting up boards of censorship that would make sure that published works did not threaten religion. Three years later, they went one step further by decreeing the death penalty for anyone suggesting the implementation of a policy of tolerance vis-à-vis non-Catholics.[21] At the same time, as **Roberto Breña** notes (Volume III, Chapter 3), the constitution "tried to control what up to that moment was an almost exclusive role of the Church in public education, publishing, and public discourse." Javier Fernández Sebastián has convincingly argued that "the overwhelming preponderance of Catholicism in the Hispanic world explains how difficult it was to conceive of religion and politics as separate spheres, and the correlative difficulty of regarding 'religion' as an abstract category of a general nature, capable of embracing several 'religions,' in the

---

[17] Brad A. Jones, "'In Favour of Popery': Patriotism, Protestantism, and the Gordon Riots in the Revolutionary British Atlantic," *Journal of British Studies* 52:1 (2013), 79–102.

[18] Bronislaw Baczko, *Politiques de la Révolution française* (Paris: Gallimard, 2008), 62–3.

[19] Claude Muller, "Religion et Révolution en Alsace," *Annales historiques de la Révolution française* 337 (2004), 63–83: 76.

[20] J. Marino Incháustegui, ed., *Documentos para estudio: Marco de la época y problemas del Tratado de Basilea de 1795, en la parte española de Santo Domingo* (Buenos Aires: Academia Dominicana de la Historia, 1957), 640.

[21] Juan Pablo Domínguez, "Intolerancia religiosa en las Cortes de Cádiz," *Hispania* 77:255 (2017), 155–83: 164, 178.

plural." Since Catholicism was the foundation of the nation's identity, tolerance meant "disunion, illegitimacy, even civil war."[22] This sentiment was shared by the priests of central Switzerland when the constitution of the Helvetic Republic was promulgated, which meant that irreligiosity and heresy were no longer punishable.[23]

Residents of the Catholic world would not have viewed religious exclusivity as a form of inequality. As members of the Christian community, every individual enjoyed an equal status by virtue of their baptism. Their ties were governed by brotherly love. At least, that was the case in theory. In practice, it remained an ideal, pursued by Hidalgo and other priests involved in the Mexican uprising of 1810. The early Church fathers rather than Enlightenment *philosophes* were the inspiration for Hidalgo, who stated that his goal was to build a society in which all were recognized as equal children of God.[24] Likewise, the 1797 republican conspiracy in Venezuela, writes **Cristina Soriano** in Volume II, Chapter 28, "argued in favor of social harmony between whites, *pardos*, Indians, and blacks, because all these racial groups were seen as 'brothers in Christ.'"

Not all Catholic leaders were bent on continuing the exclusivity of their religion. Some sought to introduce a measure of tolerance. The difference between tolerance and religious freedom was expressed by the "Jews, settled in France" in a petition to the National Assembly a few months after the Declaration of the Rights of Man and Citizen had been adopted. "The word tolerance," they wrote, "which after so many centuries and so many *intolerant acts* seemed to be a word of humanity and reason, no longer suits a country that wishes to establish its rights on the eternal basis of justice .... To tolerate, indeed, is to suffer what one would have the right to prohibit." Under the new conditions, the dominant religion had no right to prohibit another religion from humbly placing itself by its side.[25] But religious inequality was not to vanish, while tolerance – that typically early modern phenomenon – was still a viable option in Europe and the Americas. The

---

[22] Javier Fernández Sebastián, "Toleration and Freedom of Expression in the Hispanic World between Enlightenment and Liberalism," *Past & Present* no. 211 (May 2011), 159–97: 162–3, 186, 188.

[23] Eric Godel, "La Constitution scandaleuse. La population de Suisse centrale face à la République helvétique," in Andreas Würgler, ed., *Grenzen des Zumutbaren: Erfahrungen mit der französischen Okkupation und der Helvetischen Republik (1798–1803)* (Basel: Schwabe Verlag, 2011), 29–44: 32.

[24] Laura Ibarra García, "El concepto de igualdad en México (1810–1824)," *Relaciones* 145 (2016), 279–314: 287.

[25] "Pétition des juifs établis en France, adressée à l'Assemblée Nationale," 28 January 1790, in *Adresses, mémoires et pétitions des juifs 1789–1794* (Paris: EDHIS, 1968), 17–18.

Polish constitution, writes **Richard Butterwick** (Volume II, Chapter 20), began "with a stirring preamble and an article maintaining the prohibition against 'apostasy' from the Roman Catholic 'dominant and national religion,' while assuring freedom of worship and the protection of government to all creeds." Similarly, the Organic Law that saw the light in Pernambuco, Brazil in 1817 said that the state religion was Roman Catholicism, while the other Christian sects of any denomination were tolerated.[26] In early independent Colombia, a campaign for religious toleration failed to achieve its goal. Foreigners could still not hold Protestant services in public in spite of sustained criticism of the Catholic clergy, which was held responsible for blocking new ideas.[27] The most radical constitution adopted in a Catholic country was that issued by Jean-Jacques Dessalines in 1805. While Toussaint Louverture's constitution of 1801 had declared Catholicism the official state religion, that of Dessalines (although short-lived) introduced religious tolerance.[28]

## Sovereignty and Public Opinion

Many historians have assumed that a form of self-government was already in place in Britain's North American colonies. These are considered to have thrived in a long era of "salutary neglect." When that era ended in the aftermath of the Seven Years' War, a revolution became thinkable. In Volume I, Chapter 6, **Holly Brewer** shows that "salutary neglect" was largely a myth: "The political, legal and economic situations in the colonies were constantly negotiated in a struggle for power that was occurring not only on the level of empire but in England itself ... To the degree that such 'salutary neglect' existed ... it was part of this negotiation and struggle over the meaning and terms of power. While some could escape the power of empire in the short term, it was constantly tugging at their sleeves. One could take up land in the 'wilderness,' for example, ... but the only way one owned it was by getting a legal title – and that demanded negotiation with all the ligaments of colonial authority, from surveyor and courts to secretary of

---

[26] Leonardo Morais de Araújo Pinheiro, "Análise da Lei Orgânica da Revolução pernam-bucana de 1817 à luz dos direitos fundamentais," *Revista Brasileira de História do Direito* 4:2 (2018), 114–34: 130.

[27] David Bushnell, *The Santander Regime in Gran Colombia* (Westport, CN: Greenwood Press, 1970 [1954]), 210, 215.

[28] Lorelle D. Semley, "To Live and Die, Free and French: Toussaint Louverture's 1801 Constitution and the Original Challenge of Black Citizenship," *Radical History Review* 115 (2013), 65–90: 78.

the colony. How one could develop it, and what one could grow, how one could pass it on, were often regulated by laws that might emerge in the colonies but were subject to Royal veto. Other regulations were imposed directly by imperial authorities."

Revolutions are always a struggle for sovereignty. Despite the widely shared support for popular sovereignty, opinions were divided on the people's postrevolutionary political role. A prominent monarchist member of France's National Assembly opined that while all powers emanated from the people, their well-being depended on leaving the exercise of these powers to the king to prevent the chaos of anarchy.[29] In continental British America, **Max Edling** remarks (Volume 1, Chapter 17), the ideology of the American Revolution "introduced a nebulous concept of popular sovereignty, which somehow existed both at state and at national level." "Several of the new constitutions incorporated Congress's declaration of independence in whole or in part, thus illustrating how legitimate authority was based on popular sovereignty simultaneously expressed at national and local level." In Spanish America, it was unclear whether self-rule extended to a town's immediate vicinity or whether administrative centers could claim to govern vast areas. The assumption of sovereignty in Spanish America implied a return to nature. As Clément Thibaud has explained, that meant not a return to a Hobbesian world of lone individuals but *pueblos*, peoples in the sense of free communities. If indeed the *pueblo* was the repository of sovereignty, opinions differed on the *pueblo*'s identity, at least in New Granada. Was it the town, the province, or all of New Granada?[30] Federalists in many parts of the Atlantic world, often inspired by the United States and opposed to the horrors to which centralism had allegedly given rise in Jacobin Paris, usually found support outside traditional political centers. To legitimize the dispersion of political power, Dutch federalists used the climate argument – according to which each land had its own character and was therefore entitled to its own legislation – to plead for separate laws for each of the seven small provinces. Another argument was that the distance between the population and its rulers was much smaller on

---

[29] His name was Jean-Joseph Mounier. Nicolai von Eggers, "Popular Sovereignty, Republicanism, and the Political Logic of the Struggles of the French Revolution" (Ph.D. dissertation, University of Aarhus, 2016), 216.

[30] Clément Thibaud, "Des républiques en armes à la République armée. Guerre révolutionnaire, fédéralisme et centralisme au Venezuela et en Nouvelle-Grenade, 1808–1830," *Annales historiques de la Révolution française* no. 348 (2011), 57–86: 63; Isabel Restrepo Mejía, "La soberanía del 'pueblo' durante la época de la independencia, 1810–1815," *Historia Crítica* 29 (2005), 101–23: 102–5.

Introduction

a provincial level. Such democratic reasoning had its limits, though, because the federalists' emphasis on the preservation of provincial laws and customs was at odds with the new egalitarian spirit.[31]

Penetrating everywhere, that new spirit changed the nature of political debates, which were no longer confined to elite venues. **Javier Fernández Sebastián** points out in Volume III, Chapter 12 that the "increase in the pace of publication of newspapers and readers' insatiable demand for news rapidly accelerated the circulation of new concepts and multiplied the uses, often contradictory, of basic political terminology." To succeed in achieving political goals, the mobilization of public opinion became indispensable, as in the Dutch Republic, where Patriot newspapers were not just sold widely but also carried many readers' letters, showcasing public opinion.[32] Public opinion, which rebels constantly invoked, came to be seen as an enlightened court with universal authority.[33] In order to expose the French king to this new "court" and remove him from the royal court in Versailles, plebeians forced Louis XVI to settle in Paris, where he would be surrounded by "the people." In Venezuela, conversely, several representatives proposed to move the seat of Congress away from Caracas and avoid the crushing weight of the capital's public opinion. Their adversaries opined that at least in Caracas, some Enlightenment may be found. One of them argued: "Public opinion is not power, but the sum of all opinions that cannot be formed without knowledge. And could it be that they exist among shepherds, farmers or peasants, who don't even know the name of those who govern them? Public opinion, in matters of government, resides only in the big cities and not in the villages and shacks, especially in America, where the previous government has always kept under a black veil even the inhabitants of the capital city."[34] And even in the big cities, only a small group of men were zealots for liberty, Genevan native Étienne Dumont noted when he arrived in Paris on the eve

---

[31] Peter A. J. van den Berg, *Codificatie en staatsvorming: De politieke en politiek-theoretische achtergronden van de codificatie van het privaatrecht in Pruisen, de Donaumonarchie, Frankrijk en Nederland, 1450–1811* (Groningen: Wolters-Noordhoff, 1996), 306, 307, 314, 319.

[32] Nicolaas van Sas, "The Patriot Revolution: New Perspectives," in Margaret C. Jacob and Wijnand W. Mijnhardt, eds., *The Dutch Republic in the Eighteenth Century: Decline, Enlightenment, and Revolution* (Ithaca, NY: Cornell University Press, 1992), 91–120: 102–3.

[33] Keith Michael Baker, *Inventing the French Revolution: Essays on French Political Culture in the Eighteenth Century* (Cambridge: Cambridge University Press, 1990), 186, 193–6.

[34] Véronique Hébrard, "Opinion publique et représentation dans le Congrès Constituant Vénézuélien (1810–1812)," *Annales historiques de la Révolution française* no. 365 (2011), 153–75: 162 (quote), 167, 170–1.

of the revolution: "There are in the immense population of this metropolis about fifteen or twenty thousand persons, who consider the meeting of the Estates-General as a matter of the utmost importance, and who anxiously watch all the measures of the court; these men, being to be found everywhere, in coffee-houses, at the theatres, in private companies, and in public places, may be said to form the public opinion."[35] That most delegates at the Estates-General and National Assembly would have agreed with Dumont is suggested by the highly centralized polity they set up. **David Andress** argues in Volume II, Chapter 1 that the revolutionaries expected only obedience from locally elected leaders, did not introduce intermediary bodies outside Paris, and opted not to set up institutional checks on the legislature.

To focus single-mindedly on the politically active members of a society would obscure the politicization on a vast scale – inside and outside France – of ordinary people, who appropriated the official rhetoric that was expressed in official documents and proclamations, and employed it when they thought it useful.[36] A new democratic culture emerged in the countries neighboring France, characterized by newspapers, pamphlets, societies, republican catechisms, and civic feasts which featured freedom trees and Phrygian hats.[37] In Italy, writes **John A. Davis** (Volume II, Chapter 17), "freedom of the press, official and unofficial newspapers, pamphlets and broadsheets offered unprecedented platforms for public debate, while the newly created consultative and executive committees, public assemblies, the drafting of constitutions, the debates on the procedures and formalities of government, the organization of plebiscites and formalized civic and public ceremonies gave opportunities to experience active citizenship, as did the political clubs and societies."

Essential to the process of cultivating peoples bound together by horizontal ties of citizenship and shared visions of revolutionary transformation, writes Michael Kwass, was material culture "as legislators, producers, and

---

[35] Richard Whatmore, "Étienne Dumont, the British Constitution, and the French Revolution," *The Historical Journal* 50:1 (2007), 23–47: 32.

[36] Jean-Luc Chappey, "Révolution, régénération, civilisation. Enjeux culturels des dynamiques politiques," in Jean-Luc Chappey, Bernard Gainot, Guillaume Mazeau, Frédéric Régent, and Pierre Serna, eds., *Pour quoi faire la Révolution* (Marseille: Agone, 2012), 115–48; Maxime Kaci, *Dans le tourbillon de la Révolution: Mots d'ordre et engagements collectifs aux frontières septentrionales (1791–1793)* (Rennes: Presses universitaires de Rennes, 2016), 288; Eugenia Molina, "Politización y relaciones sociales en Mendoza (Argentina) durante la década revolucionaria (1810–1820). Conflictos y consensos en la configuración de un nuevo orden," *Boletín Americanista* 58 (2008), 251–71: 253.

[37] Annie Jourdan, *La Révolution, une exception française?* (Paris: Flammarion, 2004), 271–2.

consumers imbued everyday objects with revolutionary meaning. More than merely reflecting political ideas and aspirations, material objects mediated their very expression . . ."[38] In one rural part of the Dutch Republic in the 1780s, all sorts of everyday objects demonstrated one's allegiance on both sides of the political divide: crockery, pottery, drinking utensils, sugar-casters, cookie boards, scent bottles, and tobacco and snuff boxes.[39] Just as cultural objects were invested with a revolutionary meaning, cultural *practices* underwent a transformation. They served, argues **Nathan Perl-Rosenthal** (Volume I, Chapter 4), as vehicles for new political ideas and practices. These cultural practices, such as letter-writing, were not in themselves revolutionary, and could be used by the revolutions' opponents, but in the hands of revolutionaries they were given new forms.

Politicization was not by definition, or at least not exclusively, ideological. **Joris Oddens** contends in Volume II, Chapter 13 that "in some rural areas [of the Dutch Republic] passions ran high, but what was at stake seems to have been a long-running tribal conflict rather than an ideological divide dating to the revolutionary era itself: rival factions in a village sided with the Patriots or with the Orangists, but more particularly *against* each other, or the entire population of one village sympathized with one camp because the people of a neighboring town politically or economically dwarfing them supported the other." This phenomenon existed everywhere. Preexisting disputes or grievances often conditioned the choice for revolution or status quo. If a large town in Spanish America embraced revolution, nearby smaller towns seeking greater autonomy would remain faithful to the old regime. Similarly, the feuding Anglicans and Presbyterians ended up on opposing sides in the American Revolution in good part to avoid each other. Yet another example can be found in Africa. Shortly after Brazil declared its independence, the elite of Benguela (Angola) used the crisis of the Portuguese empire to try to break away from its subordination to Luanda, join Brazil, and become a province attached to Rio de Janeiro. **Roquinaldo Ferreira** reveals in Volume III, Chapter 22 that this was no surprise move. Benguela and Rio were linked through the transatlantic slave trade, the Benguela elite sent its sons to study in Brazil, and it had regularly imported foodstuffs from Brazil in time of need.

---

[38] Michael Kwass, *Consumer Revolution, 1650–1800* (Cambridge: Cambridge University Press, 2022), 198.

[39] Jouke Nijman, "Politieke cultuur en volkscultuur in de Patriottentijd," *Groniek* 30 (1997), 417–31: 425, 426.

Rhetoric was, of course, also largely strategic. No fewer than 227 towns in France petitioning the National Assembly to reassign lawcourts and other institutions to them adopted egalitarian language.[40] Similarly, in German cities, writes **Michael Rowe** (Volume II, Chapter 18), "demands that had previously been couched in the familiar language of historic rights and privileges now included references to the universal liberties triumphant in France." Elsewhere, old and new regime values mixed, as in the case of a free merchant of color from Guayaquil who petitioned the Cortes of Cádiz in 1820 for both citizenship and recognition as an *hidalgo*.[41] And in the hinterland of the Swiss canton of Zurich, the language of reform was combined with an insistence on inalienable rights. This pragmatic republicanism, writes **Marc H. Lerner** (Volume II, Chapter 11), was typical of Switzerland in the age of revolutions.

The defenders of the status quo responded to revolutionary activity in various ways, appealing to the public themselves in person or in writing, or simply muzzling the press, as the viceroy of New Spain did in Mexico City, an act he defended by alleging that press freedom had led to an "extraordinary number of seditious and insulting publications."[42] Nor were the revolutionaries, once in the saddle themselves, content with an alternative opinion being expressed. During the American Revolutionary War, Patriots bullied printers into retracting contentious statements. In other instances, they seized and destroyed the entire print run of pamphlets they considered dangerous. In addition to book burnings, there were monetary rewards for the capture of certain pamphleteers. Amid such escalating levels of violence, Loyalists found it increasingly hard to make their voices heard.[43]

Not everyone engaged in political contestation. Many peasants and urban workers were indifferent to the revolutions as long as they could maintain such a stance. Farmers in Chile were only gradually drawn into the political conflict as they were mobilized on either side of the divide through ties of clientage. Indifference could also give way to outright opposition to the state,

---

[40] Wim Klooster, *Revolutions in the Atlantic World: A Comparative History*, new edition (New York: New York University Press, 2018), 173–4; Ted W. Margadant, *Urban Rivalries in the French Revolution* (Princeton: Princeton University Press, 1992), 157.

[41] Federica Morelli, *Free People of Color in the Spanish Atlantic: Race and Citizenship, 1780–1850* (New York: Routledge, 2020), 127–8.

[42] Juan Ortiz Escamilla, *Calleja: Guerra, botín y fortuna* (Xalapa: Universidad Veracruzana; Zamora: El Colegio de Michoacán, 2017), 112.

[43] Holger Hoock, *Scars of Independence: America's Violent Birth* (New York: Crown Publishers, 2017), 38–9. See also Harry M. Ward, *The War for Independence and the Transformation of American Society* (London: Routledge, 1999), 59–65.

Introduction

as it did in the Dutch province of Friesland, where those who were largely interested in issues that were of their immediate concern such as food prices or high taxes ended up turning their back on the Batavian Republic when the electorate was forced to sign a declaration signaling their resistance to any form of rule by stadtholders, aristocrats, or autocrats.[44]

## Democracy

Most thinkers and activists conceived of freedom as the ability to live under laws that the inhabitants of a country made themselves.[45] The revolutionaries agreed that the regimes they built had to be supported by some form of popular control over the government. Only a political system that reflected the people's voice – which was often, but certainly not always, called democracy – could supplant aristocratic or monarchical rule. That voice was to be expressed through representation, which was inseparable from suffrage.[46]

Who constituted the people? At least a section of the adult population, and usually – in line with classical republicanism – those who had taken up arms to defend the revolution. The 1826 constitution of Bolivia said that Bolivians included "those who fought for liberty in Junín or Ayacucho," the sites of two battles that had doomed the Spanish empire in South America.[47] Similarly, the French constitution of 1795 singled out "veterans of one or more campaigns for the establishment of the Republic" as citizens who did not have to qualify financially in order to cast their vote.[48] The earlier French constitution of 1791, which was never implemented, had even granted suffrage to every adult male, a decision replicated only in

---

[44] Igor Goicovic Donoso, "De la indiferencia a la resistencia: Los sectores populares y la Guerra de Independencia en el norte de Chile (1817–1823)," *Revista de Indias* 74:260 (2014), 129–60: 136; Jacques Kuiper, *Een revolutie ontrafeld: Politiek in Friesland 1795–1798* (Franeker: Van Wijnen, 2002), 517.

[45] De Dijn, *Freedom*, 177–8.

[46] Minchul Kim, "Pierre-Antoine Antonelle and Representative Democracy in the French Revolution," *History of European Ideas* 44:3 (2018), 344–69: 351. Earlier forms of representation were now abandoned. Cf. Joaquim Albareda and Manuel Herrero Sánchez, eds., *Political Representation in the Ancien Régime* (London: Routledge, 2019).

[47] Constitution of Bolivia, 22 November 1826, in J. R. Gutiérrez, ed., *Las constituciones políticas que ha tenido la República Boliviana (1826–1868)* (Santiago: Imprenta de "El Independiente," 1869), 4–5.

[48] Andrew Jainchill, "The Constitution of the Year III and the Persistence of Classical Republicanism," *French Historical Studies* 26:3 (2003), 399–435: 418.

Paraguay (1813).[49] Some constitutions extended voting rights not to every male, but the vast majority of men. That of Cádiz (1812) enabled many inhabitants in the Spanish empire to cast their vote. In Mexico City, for example, 93 percent of the adult male population was enfranchised. Likewise, the Brazilian constitution of 1824 incorporated in the electorate vast numbers of small urban and rural proprietors as well as tenant farmers and sharecroppers, although it did not give the vote to journeymen and free men who lived from piecework or who were not regularly employed.[50] Formal exclusion did not necessarily mean the inability to take part in the election process. In both France and Spain, communities were represented by well-known individuals, who received the vote after days of deliberation, during which anybody could chime in. Commoners who could not vote were still believed to be *virtually* represented through their public demonstrations of support or rejection of elected candidates.[51] North American Patriots, of course, scoffed at the notion of virtual representation. During the crisis that preceded the American Revolution, Britain's insistence that Americans were represented in Parliament despite their inability to vote had alienated numerous Americans from the metropole.

In most parts of the Atlantic world, representative democracy was introduced sooner or later, but without citizens resigning themselves to the reduced role that would later become the norm, when their input became largely limited to the periodic casting of votes. Many North Americans left little leeway to the delegates, whom they saw as "mere agents or tools of the people" who could give binding directions "whenever they please to give them."[52] During the Cortes of Cádiz, Spanish newspapers as well as politicians invoked the demand that the people control their representatives very closely, reserving for themselves the last say in expressing the general will.[53]

---

[49] Richard Allan White, *Paraguay's Autonomous Revolution, 1810–1840* (Albuquerque: University of New Mexico Press, 1978), 56.

[50] Jaime E. Rodríguez O., *The Independence of Spanish America* (Cambridge: Cambridge University Press, 1998), 105; Cecília Helena de Salles Oliveira, "Contribuição ao estudo do Poder Moderador," in Cecília Helena de Salles Oliveira, Vera Lúcia Nagib Bittencourt, and Wilma Peres Costa, eds., *Soberania e conflito: Configurações do Estado Nacional no Brasil do século XIX* (São Paulo: Editora Hucitec, 2010), 185–235: 214.

[51] Jean-Clément Martin, *Nouvelle histoire de la Révolution française* (Paris: Perrin, 2012), 208; François-Xavier Guerra, "The Spanish-American Tradition of Representation and Its European Roots," *Journal of Latin American Studies* 26:1 (1994), 1–35: 7.

[52] Gordon S. Wood, *The Creation of the American Republic, 1776–1787* (Charlotte: The University of North Carolina Press, 1969), 371.

[53] Javier Fernández Sebastián, "Democracia," in Javier Fernández Sebastián and Juan Francisco Fuentes, eds., *Diccionario político y social del siglo XIX español* (Madrid: Alianza Editorial, 2002), 216–228: 218.

Militant Parisians known as Enragés, who were wrongly portrayed at the time as forming a movement, considered direct democracy the only option for their city. They agreed with Rousseau that sovereignty could not be delegated. The people should have the right to sanction the laws and if there were to be delegates, they must be revocable at will.[54] A form of direct democracy was actually established in one city 400 kilometers to the north. In 1796, voters in Amsterdam received the right to send proposals to the municipal government. If two-thirds of the electorate backed a proposal, it would be binding.[55]

The man who crucially intervened in the French Revolution on more than one occasion, the Abbé Sieyès, disagreed with the view that delegates should be kept on a leash by the voters. He summarized the legislative process as follows: "The members of a representative assembly ... gather in order to balance their opinions, to modify them, to purify some through others, and to extract finally from the *lumières* of all, a majority opinion, that is to say, the common will which makes the law. The mixing of individual wills, the kind of fermentation that they undergo in this operation, are necessary to produce the result that is desired. It is therefore essential that opinions should be able to concert, to yield, in a word to modify one another, for without this there is no longer a deliberative assembly but simply a *rendez-vous of couriers*, ready to depart after having delivered their dispatches."[56]

Sieyès did not simply favor representative democracy; he also introduced the distinction between active and passive citizens that was adopted in France. Fulfilling income or property requirements, the first group was allowed more extensive participation in political life. Sieyès' distinction was soon copied in other new regimes. By virtue of Brazil's 1824 constitution, for example, citizens were all males of age at least twenty-five years who lived on their own and did not work as domestic servants. They also had "a yearly net income above a hundred thousand reis derived from real estate property, industry, trade, or employment." These men could vote in the parochial assemblies, which chose the provincial electors. Electors, however, could

---

[54] Albert Soboul, "Audience des Lumières. Classes populaires et Rousseauisme sous la Révolution," *Annales historiques de la Révolution française* 34:170 (1962), 421–38: 425.

[55] Thomas Poell, "The Democratic Paradox: Dutch Revolutionary Struggles over Democratisation and Centralisation (1780–1813)" (Ph.D. dissertation, University of Utrecht, 2007), 91.

[56] Murray Forsyth, *Reason and Revolution: The Political Thought of the Abbé Sieyes* (Leicester: Leicester University Press; New York: Holmes & Meier Publishers, 1987), 134.

only be members of the active citizenry, made up of all men with an income of at least 200,000 reis, who had not been freed from slavery.[57]

Underlying this division was a difference between the people as conceptualized by Enlightenment thinkers and the actual population. The abstract people were a source of legitimacy, whereas the real people were deemed ignorant and superstitious by the elites.[58] The natural representatives of the people, d'Holbach and Diderot had taught, were those who were the best informed and educated.[59] Where revolutionaries succeeded in toppling a regime, they commonly began the process of enlightening the vast mass of the population. Delegates presented themselves as moral guides in a society that allegedly had become corrupt, which meant that it would take time for civilization to become rooted. The moral decay that he accused Spain of bringing to its colonies at the same time made Simón Bolívar oppose the establishment of a genuine democracy. The people, he maintained, were simply not ready yet for a political role. He was not alone. Six days before the storming of the Bastille, one deputy of the Third Estate wrote that the revolution – a term he presciently used – should be postponed by ten years, allowing the people to educate themselves.[60] To the Italian intellectual Vincenzio Russo, representative democracy was a temporary stage that should last as long as popular education was needed. Once that goal had been achieved, direct democracy could be introduced.[61]

Thomas Paine asserted, on the other hand, that the educational effect of representative democracy would be immediate. "[T]he case is," he wrote, "that the representative system diffuses such a body of knowledge throughout a nation, on the subject of government, as to explode ignorance and preclude imposition ... Those who are not in the representation, know as much of the nature of business as those who are. An affectation of

---

[57] Márcia Regina Berbel and Rafael de Bivar Marquese, "The Absence of Race: Slavery, Citizenship, and Pro-slavery Ideology in the Cortes of Lisbon and the Rio de Janeiro Constituent Assembly (1821–4)," *Social History* 32:4 (2007), 415–433: 416, 425.

[58] Valérie Sottocasa, *Les brigands et la Révolution: Violences politiques et criminalité dans le Midi (1789–1802)* (Ceyzérieu: Champ Vallon, 2016), 363.

[59] Jonathan Israel, *A Revolution of the Mind: Radical Enlightenment and the Intellectual Origins of Modern Democracy* (Princeton: Princeton University Press, 2010), 66.

[60] Adrien Duquesnoy, *Un révolutionnaire malgré lui: Journal mai–octobre 1789*, ed. Guillaume Mazeau (Paris: Mercure de France, 2016), 137. See for the changing meaning of the term "revolution" in those days: Keith Michael Baker, "Enlightenment Idioms, Old Regime Discourses, and Revolutionary Improvisation," in Thomas E. Kaiser and Dale K. Van Kley, eds., *From Deficit to Deluge: The Origins of the French Revolution* (Stanford: Stanford University Press, 2011), 165–97: 191–6.

[61] Luciano Guerci, *"Mente, cuore, coraggio, virtù repubblicane": Educare il popolo nell'Italia in rivoluzione (1796–1799)* (Turin: Tirrenia Stampatori, 1992), 112–13.

mysterious importance would there be scouted. Nations can have no secrets; and the secrets of courts, like those of individuals, are always their defects. In the representative system, the reason for everything must publicly appear. Every man is a proprietor in government and considers it a necessary part of his business to understand."[62] Although Jacobins embraced it, this conviction was not widely shared. While they may have hoped for a rapid enlightenment of the masses, most revolutionary regimes adopted constitutions that included a literacy requirement. This was necessary, explained French lawmaker Boissy d'Anglas, because a man "is only truly independent when he does not need anyone to enlighten him about his duties and to convey his ideas."[63] The leaders of the new Spanish American republics shared the Enlightenment ideal of popular education, many of them embracing the system of mutual education invented by the Englishman Joseph Lancaster. In that way, writes **Karen Racine** (Volume iii, Chapter 15), large numbers of people could become literate in a short amount of time. The goal of education, however, was to train not participatory citizens, but moral subjects who were economically useful.

Even so, urban crowds made up of literate and illiterate residents alike often performed an important legitimizing function for revolutionary elites. Leaders of Central American revolts, writes **Timothy Hawkins** (Volume iii, Chapter 6), "relied on the energy of subaltern groups, in particular the urban masses, to advance their causes. In not a few cases, these uprisings arose from popular demands for redress of traditional grievances, which suggests a disconnect between the priorities of the leadership and the protesters." Some of the watershed moments in the age of revolutions saw the intervention of vociferous crowds that had been invited to show up. One such occasion was the popular response in Bogotá to the refusal of the viceroy of New Granada to form a junta that would be the local government. The crowd's anti-Spanish demonstrations on 20 July 1810 forced the viceroy to change his mind. Agents working for the rebel elite had used various methods to urge the plebeians to make their way to certain downtown sites, where they energized them. These agents were scribes and other middle-rank local officials who mingled with working men and were known to the elite because of their positions.[64]

---

[62] Thomas Paine, *The Rights of Man for the Benefit of All Mankind* (Philadelphia: D. Webster, 1797), 31.

[63] Jainchill, "The Constitution of the Year III," 421.

[64] Manuel Pareja Ortiz, "El 'pueblo' bogotano en la revolución del 20 de julio de 1810," *Anuario de Estudios Americanos* 71:1 (2014), 281–311: 283–4, 287, 291.

When crowds were not manipulated but operated autonomously, they instilled fear in the elites. **Anthony McFarlane** writes in Volume I, Chapter 18 that elites in Quito and Arequipa (both in the viceroyalty of Peru) backed local revolts against Spanish policies until they "took fright at plebeian mobilization and rallied to defend the established order," terrified of a breakdown in social discipline.[65] John Adams feared that new claims would arise. "Women will demand a Vote. Lads from 12 to 21 will think their Rights not enough attended to, and every Man, who has not a Farthing, will demand an equal Voice with any other in all Acts of State. It tends to confound and destroy all Distinctions, and prostate all Ranks, to one common Levell."[66] Although such arguments were usually self-serving, they also expressed a sense of reality, as **Howard Brown** argues in Volume II, Chapter 7: "Actually implementing democratic ideals meant dismantling existing structures of authority and risked unleashing less appealing impulses across all social strata. Too often, notions of liberty, equality, reason, and progress acted as bellows on the glowing coals of resentment and jealousy."

Pursuing their own agendas, peasants and urban plebeians nonetheless achieved many of their loftier goals. In France, **Noelle Plack** (Volume II, Chapter 3) notes, "for four years the peasantry rose in waves of protest and insurrection which ultimately forced legislators in Paris to abolish once and for all the feudal regime. These actions should not be underestimated as it has been argued that without them, peasants in France would most likely have been responsible for feudal dues until at least the middle of the nineteenth century." She adds that "[t]ax revolt, in the form of petition, riot, resistance, and noncompliance was far more prevalent in the French Revolution than many historians realize. Popular refusal to pay taxes was as important an aspect to bringing down the *ancien régime* as subsistence riots and attacks on seigneurial chateaux." The balance sheet looked different in Brazil, where the struggles of the popular classes ended in defeat. A dozen years into the construction of the new independent polity, the goal of most legislators was to obtain more local autonomy and an increased federalization of the provinces instead of more social participation in politics. The social structure was consequently left largely untouched, which set off riots

---

[65] See, for Buenos Aires, Gabriel di Meglio, "Un nuevo actor para un nuevo escenario. La participación política de la plebe urbana de Buenos Aires en la década de la revolución (1810–1820)," *Boletín del Instituto Argentina y Americana "Dr. Emilio Ravignani,"* 3rd series, 24 (2001), 7–43: 32–3.

[66] Cited in Joan Hoff, *Law, Gender, and Injustice: A Legal History of U.S. Women* (New York: New York University Press, 1991), 62.

Introduction

and revolts of those whose demands did not find an expression on the parliamentary level.[67] Their defeat, however, writes **Hendrik Kraay** (Volume III, Chapter 20), does not mean "that these struggles were unimportant; rather, they were what made independence such an uncertain and contingent process and these years such a dynamic period in Brazilian history." **Gabriel Paquette** (Volume III, Chapter 16) adds that by contrast with preceding years, the decades after Brazilian independence "were characterized by tempestuous relations between the capital and the provinces, between urban and rural areas, between landed proprietors and their subalterns, between masters and slaves." At independence, "the destruction of the Old Regime was incomplete, perhaps not even yet under way."

## Women

Women's contributions to revolutions and counterrevolutions have often gone unheralded. In France and Spanish America, more than a few examples have been found of women who actually took part in the armed struggles, sometimes disguised as men.[68] More frequently, their role was that of noncombatants, as **Ami Pflugrad-Jakisch** mentions in Volume I, Chapter 14. During the American Revolution, thousands of poor women "followed both the British and the continental armies as cooks, washerwomen, seamstresses, nurses, scavengers, and sexual partners." American women were also active on the political front, engaged in boycotts of British goods or in spinning bees, producing cloth to substitute for British manufactures. In numerous ways, women shared the plight of men. Loyalist women in South Carolina, for instance, were "verbally abused, imprisoned, and threatened with bodily harm even when they had not taken an active role in opposing the rebel cause." Those women who did help the British armies

---

[67] Andréa Slemian, "Os canais de representação política nos primórdios do Império: Apontamentos para um estudo da relação entre Estado e sociedade no Brasil (c. 1822–1834)," *Locus: Revista de história* 13:1 (2007), 34–51: 49–51.

[68] Claude Guillon, "Pauline Léon, une républicaine révolutionnaire," *Annales historiques de la Révolution française* 344 (2008), 147–59: 150–1; Christine Peyrard, *Les Jacobins de l'Ouest: Sociabilité révolutionnaire et formes de politisation dans le Maine et la Basse-Normandie (1789–1799)* (Paris: Publications de la Sorbonne, 1996), 231; Evelyn Cherpak, "The Participation of Women in the Independence Movement in Gran Colombia, 1780–1830," in Asunción Lavrin, ed., *Latin American Women* (Westport, CN: Greenwood Press, 1978), 219–34: 221–2; Alberto Baena Zapatero, "Las mujeres ante la independencia de México," in Izaskun Álvarez Cuartero and Julio Sánchez Gómez, eds., *Visiones e revisiones de la Independencia Americana: Subalternidad e independencias* (Salamanca: Ediciones Universidad de Salamanca, 2012), 115–35: 121.

also suffered physical abuse.[69] When their husbands fled, Loyalist women often stayed behind and, as one historian has argued, "seized this moment to exert a new form of independence. War shook up the existing social order and provided women with a brief moment to act independently of existing gender restrictions."[70]

Shortly after the French commissioners put a de facto end to slavery in Saint-Domingue, women in the southern part of the colony who benefited from emancipation contested the new labor regime under which they had to toil. Along with their male counterparts, the women protested the regulations that the same commissioners introduced in an attempt to keep the plantation economy afloat. On more than a few occasions, only women expressed their displeasure by refusing to work or working less than was expected from them.[71]

The small group of revolutionaries who championed women's rights in Europe, writes **Jennifer Ngaire Heuer** in Volume II, Chapter 10, "were often politically marginal, or only intermittently engaged with the issue," adding that Olympe de Gouges and Mary Wollstonecraft are probably better known today than they were in their own time. Gerrit Paape, a rare male activist for women's rights, still remains virtually unknown to this day. This prolific Dutch writer sketched the outlines of a Batavian Republic 200 years in the future, in which women were educated and had the same rights as men. Their inborn intelligence and their ingenuity were no longer "smothered in kitchen smoke." As Batavian citizens, they helped build a better world.[72]

In France, the revolution did entail a number of new rights for women, which Heuer sums up as follows: "Women acquired a decree of legal autonomy, were able to sign contracts and enter in justice in their own names, marry without parental authorization once they reached the age of majority, divorce their husbands, and inherit equally with their brothers." Women actively campaigned for equal rights within the family, presenting equality in petitions as a natural right. But they also invoked a moral

---

[69] Jim Piecuch, *Three Peoples, One King: Loyalists, Indians, and Slaves in the American Revolutionary South, 1775–1782* (Columbia, SC: University of South Carolina Press, 2008), 61.

[70] Kimberly Nath, "Left Behind: Loyalist Women in Philadelphia during the American Revolution," in Barbara B. Oberg, *Women in the American Revolution: Gender, Politics, and the Domestic World* (Charlottesville: University of Virginia Press, 2019), 211–28: 223.

[71] Judith Kafka, "Action, Reaction and Interaction: Slave Women in Resistance in the South of Saint Domingue, 1793–94," *Slavery and Abolition* 18:2 (1997), 48–72.

[72] Gerrit Paape, *De Bataafsche Republiek, zo als zij behoord te zijn, en zo als zij weezen kan: Of revolutionaire droom in 1798: Wegens toekomstige gebeurtenissen tot 1998* (Nijmegen: Vantilt, 1998 [1798]), 77–9.

Introduction

language to question the traditional gender hierarchy in the family.[73] Bringing up changes in gender roles was still anathema around the Atlantic world. In the early American republic, both men and women saw women's discussion of their natural rights as dangerous because they feared that women would give up their domestic tasks.[74]

Politicians and intellectuals in the Iberian world took every effort to exclude women from public affairs. Those who thought otherwise were ignored. **Nuno Gonçalo Monteiro** (Volume III, Chapter 17) mentions that Portugal's parliament did not even vote on the proposal by one deputy to at least allow the mothers of six legitimate children to take part in elections. **Mónica Ricketts** contends in Volume III, Chapter 13 that in Spanish America "much like in France after the Revolution, women's participation in war and politics was seen as a sign of disorder and anarchy, for it was believed that their passions made them prone to corruption." If women were to remain aloof from politics, some politicians expressed their desire to see women educated. However, the goals of education did not differ from colonial days. Women were to be prepared for marriage, motherhood, and domestic skills.[75] One could argue that women in the Americas were not as a rule excluded from political rights due to sexual discrimination, but because, just like two other categories that were excluded – children and domestic servants – they belonged to the family as a political unit. As such, they were presumed to share the interests of the male members of their households.[76] In British North America, **Jessica Choppin Roney** explains (Volume I, Chapter 8), citizenship denoted the performance of duties for the benefit of the community, especially military protection. Since women were viewed as incapable of performing such duties, they could not be citizens and their "political personhood was subsumed under that of the male head of her household."

## Economic Equality

If inequality of birth was a major target for revolutionaries, that cannot be said for inequality of property. **Lloyd Kramer** (Volume I, Chapter 20) cites

---

[73] Suzanne Desan, "'War between Brothers and Sisters': Inheritance Law and Gender Politics in Revolutionary France," *French Historical Studies* 20:4 (1997), 597–634: 624–6.

[74] Rosemarie Zagarri, "The Rights of Man and Woman in Post-Revolutionary America," *The William and Mary Quarterly* 55:2 (1998), 203–30: 217.

[75] Cherpak, "Participation of Women," 230.

[76] Anne Verjus, *Le cens de la famille: Les femmes et le vote, 1789–1848* (Paris: Bellin, 2002), 19–22.

the French Marquis de Chastellux, who became concerned during his travels in the early American republic about the political consequences of unequal wealth. He "identified a socioeconomic threat that could soon weaken or even destroy the institutional structures of republican equality." Although economic considerations were conspicuously absent from most political debates and writings in the age of revolutions, there was no lack of thinkers who proposed considerable economic reforms. In his *Agrarian Justice*, Thomas Paine cried out: "The present state of civilization is as odious as it is unjust ... [I]t is necessary that a revolution should be made in it. The contrast of affluence and wretchedness continually meeting and offending the eye, is like dead and living bodies chained together."[77] Charity, which had been the traditional response to poverty, would no longer do. The French revolutionaries made a serious effort to provide poor relief, as shown by fifty-six decrees enacted within just a year by the Legislative Assembly that targeted this issue.[78] Besides, the Convention adopted a maximum limit on the prices of a wide array of staples.

In *Du contrat social*, Rousseau had already warned of the dangers of economic inequality. "As for wealth," he wrote, "no citizen should be so rich that he can buy another, and none so poor that he is compelled to sell himself." When that happens, those who are less advantaged may be forced to follow the will of someone else rather than their own. In other words, dependence will lead to a loss of freedom.[79] The idea that equality must extend to the economic realm was articulated by a special deputy to the French National Assembly from a town in Auvergne: "In the division of benefits, poverty alone has rights, and wealth must be repulsed; legislators must remove all the means that can produce extreme wealth and extreme poverty. Equality must be the goal of all their institutions and all their laws, because from equality alone is born happiness, which is the purpose of all societies."[80] Why was it, one French author asked, that one person received more land than his fellow men? Since their needs are the same, why would enjoyment be different? Such a law can only derive from force. Another one

---

[77] Thomas Paine, *The Complete Writings of Thomas Paine*, ed. Philip S. Foner (New York: Citadel Press, 1969), vol. 1, 617.

[78] Alan Forrest, *The French Revolution and the Poor* (New York: St. Martin's Press, 1981), 23.

[79] Frederick Neuhouser, "Rousseau's Critique of Economic Inequality," *Philosophy & Public Affairs* 41:3 (2013), 193–225: 197.

[80] Margadant, *Urban Rivalries*, 164–5.

Introduction

agreed. The common good had become a source of pillage.[81] Such sentiments were not limited to France. Around the same time, a schoolteacher in Delaware named Robert Coram stressed economic equality by arguing that God had given the earth in common to all and for the benefit of everybody. Each person was therefore born with the natural right to enough land to survive.[82]

The question was how to achieve such equality. The naïve idea, adhered to by some North American politicians, that equal opportunity was the panacea did not find support among small farmers and marginal artisans in the early American republic.[83] Was a leveling of property a good idea? Jacob Green, a Presbyterian minister and advocate of the American Revolution, welcomed an equality of estate and property, but believed it could not be expected. Georg Forster, the prominent German revolutionary, admired the American constitution, which, he wrote, allowed for only one aristocracy, namely that of wealth. That, however, could not be removed without implementing an impracticable Spartan community. The French militant politician Jacques-Nicolas Billaud-Varenne agreed that, especially in a large country, the "balance of fortunes" could not be just and immobile.[84] The French Jacobins nonetheless did consider imposing a limit on the accumulation of property in response to a demand by the *sans-culottes*, but failed to take that step when push came to shove.[85]

Some authors living in parts of Germany unaffected by revolutionary turmoil, where practical changes were out of the question, proposed radical solutions. Since every person had the same right to the earth's goods, private property had to be abolished, argued Carl Wilhelm Frölich. It militates

---

[81] Antoine de Cournand, *De la propriété, ou la cause du pauvre: Plaidée au tribunal de la raison, de la justice et de la vérité* (Paris, 1791), 5; Pierre Dolivier, *Essai sur la justice primitive, pour servir de principe générateur au seul ordre social qui peut assurer à l'homme tous ses droits et tous ses moyens de bonheur* (Paris, 1793), 15.

[82] Seth Cotlar, "Radical Conceptions of Property Rights and Economic Equality in the Early American Republic: The Trans-Atlantic Dimension," *Explorations in Early American Culture* 4 (2000), 191–219: 193.

[83] Ruth Bogin, "Petitioning and the New Moral Economy of Post-Revolutionary America," *The William and Mary Quarterly* 45:3 (1988), 391–425: 392.

[84] S. Scott Rohrer, *Jacob Green's Revolution: Radical Religion and Reform in a Revolutionary Age* (University Park: Pennsylvania State University Press, 2014), 203. Georg Forster to Therese Forster, Arras, 21 August 1793, in Klaus-Georg Popp, ed., *Georg Forsters Werke: Sämtliche Schriften, Tagebücher, Briefe: Briefe 1792 bis 1794 und Nachträge* (Berlin: Akademie-Verlag, 1989), 425. Citoyen Billaud-Varenne, *Les élémens du républicanisme: Première partie* (Paris, 1793), 57.

[85] Massimiliano Tomba, "1793: The Neglected Legacy of Insurgent Universality," *History of the Present: A Journal of Critical History* 5:2 (2015), 109–36: 120.

against the fulfillment of the needs of everyone. For his part, the philanthropist Heinrich Ziegenhagen proposed the organization of small-scale agricultural colonies based on communal property in which children of the poor and the rich would be raised together to become sociable beings.[86] These plans had in common with contemporary radical French proposals that they did not reflect the rapidly changing economies of western Europe. Far from taking into account the reality of industrialization, they revered subsistence agriculture and idealized peasant simplicity.[87] If these were lone voices, a popular belief in genuine economic equality did take root in Italy. Various authors took up their pens to address the population and convince them that their ideas were mistaken and that they had to content themselves with equality before the law. Economic differences were the logical consequence of differences in natural abilities.[88]

Nor were the rural dwellers insisting on economic change in New York and Virginia looking for equalization of property. Confronted with unfair taxes and economic constraints, they simply tried to end their status as tenants and become part of a reformed society based on landownership. Revolutionary elites did not meet such demands but they made land available in the western parts of their states, thereby easing tensions.[89] In the Río de la Plata, José Artigas organized an agrarian reform, as **Gabriel di Meglio** writes (Volume III, Chapter 9). He distributed vast rural properties from the enemies of the revolution among free blacks, free *zambos*, Indians, and poor creoles. The independence war in northern Spanish America had no comparable outcome. Simón Bolívar's land policy was more concerned with preserving the support of the *caudillos* – the warlords who controlled regional supplies and soldiers – than with offering hope to the rural poor. The caudillos could thus form a new landowning elite who benefited from confiscated property and public land.[90]

---

[86] Helmut Reinalter, *Die Französische Revolution und Mitteleuropa: Erscheinungsformen und Wirkungen des Jakobinismus. Seine Gesellschaftstheorien und politischen Vorstellungen* (Frankfurt am Main: Suhrkamp, 1988), 126–8.

[87] R. B. Rose, "The 'Red Scare' of the 1790s: The French Revolution and the 'Agrarian Law,'" *Past & Present* no. 103 (1984), 113–30: 125. Inside and outside France, these values retained their strength into the nineteenth century. Cf. Giorgio La Rosa, "La représentation dans la pensée politique d'un jacobin italien. Luigi Angeloni (1759–1842)," in *Le concept de représentation dans la pensée politique* (Aix-en-Provence: Presses universitaires d'Aix-Marseille, 2003), 313–20.

[88] Guerci, *Mente, cuore, coraggio, virtù repubblicane*, 131–9.

[89] Thomas J. Humphrey, "Conflicting Independence: Land Tenancy and the American Revolution," *Journal of the Early Republic* 28:2 (2008), 159–82: 174, 182.

[90] John Lynch, "Bolívar and the Caudillos," *Hispanic American Historical Review* 63:1 (1983), 3–35: 25.

Introduction

If equalizing property may have ultimately been unachievable anywhere, the French Revolution did accomplish a comprehensive transformation of property. In Volume II, Chapter 2, **Rafe Blaufarb** explains what the famous abolition of feudalism entailed. In 1789–1790, the French revolutionaries did away with the old system of property and replaced it with an entirely new one. "Feudalism," Blaufarb writes, was "not a special form of property-holding specific to the nobility, but rather *the system* of real estate itself, a system whose essence was to produce a hierarchy of multiple claims to single parcels of land." By blurring public power and private property, feudalism blocked the establishment of national sovereignty. Feudalism was replaced by the national domain, which became the repository of confiscated ecclesiastical properties and properties that had belonged to the royal domain. The sale of these *biens nationaux* was a long, drawn-out process that benefited numerous groups in French society, including, as **Philippe Bourdin** mentions in Volume II, Chapter 9, "the *petite bourgeoisie* (innkeepers, butchers, and merchants, whose numbers were increasing), the stockjobbers who sometimes acted as intermediaries for families of the old nobility, and the state creditors." However, a law of 1796 that forbade the sale of *biens nationaux* in small lots shut the door to the small and medium-sized peasantry, which had fervently hoped to acquire more land since the start of the revolution.[91]

## Violence

Revolutions are not straightforward affairs. The search for freedom never leads directly to emancipation, but brings about a crisis in which the revolutionaries are presented with different solutions.[92] The initial claims to autonomy in Spanish America following the king's resignation in Bayonne, writes **Stefan Rinke** (Volume III, Chapter 1), "were not hard revolutionary ruptures, but rather events in which the elites cautiously groped their way into unknown territory and gradually expanded their own ideas and demands." Independence was not yet on the horizon. Revolutions could gain momentum when many plebeians suddenly stopped resigning themselves to the old hierarchical civic order and became aware of the potential power of the joint

---

[91] Bernard Bodinier and Éric Teyssier, *L'événement le plus important de la Révolution: La vente des biens nationaux (1789–1867) en France et dans les territoires annexés* (Paris: Société des Études Robespierristes, 2000), 383–98.

[92] Federica Morelli, "Guerras, libertad y ciudadanía. Los afro-descendientes de Esmeraldas en la independencia," *Revista de Indias* 76 (2016), 83–108: 84.

efforts of like-minded people. That was a nightmare scenario for the champions of the status quo. When the Haitian revolution broke out, one planter believed his class might need to kill half of the enslaved workforce to stop the "epidemic" and replace those killed with new imports from Africa.[93]

While polarization was deadly in Saint-Domingue, the middle ground was also lost sooner or later in other revolutionary theaters. In Mexico, any reluctance to support one side was seen as a sign of sympathy for the other.[94] Similarly, Patriot authorities in North America summoned, secured, or confined anyone suspected of being "unfriendly to the rights of America."[95] After the end of the revolutionary war, John Jay explained to Peter Van Schaack that the latter had been mistaken to try to maintain his neutrality: "No man can serve two masters: either Britain was right and America was wrong; or America was right and Britain was wrong. They who thought Britain right were bound to support her; and America had a just claim to the services of those who approved her cause. Hence it became our duty to take one side or the other."[96] **Liam Riordan** (Volume I, Chapter 13) cites Massachusetts Governor Thomas Hutchinson, who wrote in 1776 that "under the present free government in America, no man may, by writing or speaking, contradict any part of this Declaration, without being deemed an enemy to his country, and exposed to the rage and fury of the populace."

One of the features of the revolutions was the amount of violence that accompanied them. In Ireland, **Thomas Bartlett** writes (Volume II, Chapter 16), "the extreme violence witnessed during the 1798 rebellion, and during the run-up to it, bears comparison to that perpetrated in the Vendée, and later in Spain during the Peninsular War. As in these theaters, irregular combatants were simply not recognized as legitimate fighters and therefore the normal ethical constraints on soldiers' conduct could be ignored." In Mexico, another historian has suggested, the rebellion created "a political space for the emergence of violent men of little principle and

---

[93] Philippe Girard, *Toussaint Louverture: A Revolutionary Life* (New York: Basic Books, 2016), 125.

[94] Timo Schaefer, "Soldiers and Civilians: The War of Independence in Oaxaca, 1814–1815," *Mexican Studies/Estudios Mexicanos*, 29:1 (2013), 149–74: 168. As exemplary punishment, at least in Oaxaca, both sides also tended to set fire to villages. Ibid., 172.

[95] Christopher F. Minty, "'Of One Hart and One Mind': Local Institutions and Allegiance during the American Revolution," *Early American Studies: An Interdisciplinary Journal* 15:1 (2017), 99–132: 115.

[96] T. H. Breen, *The Will of the People: The Revolutionary Birth of America* (Cambridge, MA: The Belknap Press of Harvard University Press, 2019), 146.

large ambition."[97] During Hidalgo's revolt and the following counterinsurgency, thousands of people were executed. **Juan Ortiz Escamilla** writes in Volume III, Chapter 5 that the military dictatorship set up by the royalists in Mexico, which lasted six years, "was a period characterized by assassinations, plundering, arbitrary executions, exemplary punishments, the burning of villages, and the raping of women." In other parts of Spanish America, the death toll was initially relatively small, but as **Ernesto Bassi** tells us (Volume III, Chapter 8), northern South America was where the low-intensity confrontation first mutated into violent warfare under the banner of "war to the death." Bassi adds that in the same region, the Spanish recapture of most of South America was launched and took its most violent form. Chile and Upper Peru also registered a large mortality. A census held in La Paz in 1824 after hostilities had ceased revealed a very small number of men between ages fifteen and twenty-five.[98] Even by then, the end to violence was not in sight in Spanish America. **Juan Luis Ossa Santa Cruz** argues in Volume III, Chapter 7 that "the following decades witnessed countless armed conflicts, transforming violence into a daily and legitimate political practice that, with ups and downs, lasted for the rest of the century."

Was the French Revolution notoriously violent or has the violence unleashed in France been exaggerated? **Marisa Linton** writes (Volume II, Chapter 8): "The received opinion is that the French Revolution was unique in its time in its recourse to political violence. Yet comparisons with the death toll in the English Civil Wars (that stretched throughout the British Isles) and 'revolutions' of the seventeenth century, with the American Revolution, and with the suppression of the revolt in Ireland in 1798, suggest that it would be more accurate to see revolutionary violence in the context of wider factors such as fear, repression, and the degree of retaliation, rather than as the consequence of a specific ideology unique to the French Revolution." Revolutionary Saint-Domingue offers another example of widespread violence, and certainly not only on the part of enslaved insurgents. White residents, as **Bernard Gainot** shows (Volume II, Chapter 24), engaged in lynching and mutiny. These so-called "patriots" were driven by a violent rejection of equal rights.

---

[97] Eric Van Young, *The Other Rebellion: Popular Violence, Ideology, and the Mexican Struggle for Independence, 1810–1821* (Stanford: Stanford University Press, 2001), 196.

[98] Karen Racine, "Death, Destiny, and the Daily Chores: Everyday Life in Spanish America during the Wars of Independence, 1808–1826," in Pedro Santoni, ed., *Civilians in Wartime Latin America: From the Wars of Independence to the Central American Civil Wars* (Westport, CN: Greenwood Press, 2008), 31–53: 36.

The American Revolution was indeed remarkably violent as well. The British Army left in its wake landscapes that were so affected that it seemed they had been hit by a tornado or earthquake. "Rape," writes one historian, "was endemic within the British Army."[99] Areas that could not be held by either side were pillaged relentlessly, such as, for example, Westchester County, just north of New York: "From 1775 through 1782, the county became a no man's land whose four thousand families enjoyed neither personal security nor freedom from plunder. Contending armies, militias, and partisan bands took farm surpluses and left families with too little to last through winter. They raided friend and foe alike to pilfer personal property, steal livestock, burn barns and houses, and cut trees and fences for firewood. Soldiers and criminal gangs looted what armies and militias left behind."[100] Violence was also of central importance on the Patriot side, studied by **Wayne Lee** in Volume I, Chapter 12. He notes that "the American revolution and the accompanying war included a wide set of categories of political violence, all of which occurred within the same overall clash of wills." And in most cases, those categories were also *stages*. Lee distinguishes between violence that was "intimidative and catalytic," "regular and logistical," and "retaliatory."

Violence was not the monopoly of warring armies. In revolutionary Pennsylvania, acts of violence were often committed by those frustrated about the lack of decisive action on the part of politicians whose rhetoric they shared. Such violence required the revolutionary elites to take the rebels' grievances seriously.[101] The peasant revolts across early revolutionary France were part of a similar dynamics with massive consequences, since they helped bring about the end of "feudalism." In France, violence away from the battlefield continued in the years to come. Howard Brown has explained that "the Revolution not only destroyed the institutional constraints on popular violence, it eroded many of the cultural ones as well. This included the diminished role of the clergy in community life, the decline in deference accorded social status, the disruption in patronage patterns, and the reduced primacy of the local community."[102] There was a transatlantic continuity in

---

[99] Hoock, *Scars of Independence: America's Violent Birth*, 131, 170 (quote).

[100] Allan Kulikoff, "Revolutionary Violence and the Origins of American Democracy," *The Journal of the Historical Society* II:2 (Spring 2002), 229–60: 236.

[101] Kenneth Owen, "Violence and the Limits of the Political Community in Revolutionary Pennsylvania," in Patrick Griffin, Robert G. Ingram, Peter S. Onuf, and Brian Schoen, eds., *Between Sovereignty and Anarchy* (Charlottesville: University of Virginia Press, 2015), 165–86: 180–1.

[102] Howard G. Brown, *Ending the French Revolution: Violence, Justice, and Repression from the Terror to Napoleon* (Charlottesville: University of Virginia Press, 2006), 50.

Introduction

French violence, as one historian has argued. It was no coincidence that the French campaign in Saint-Domingue of 1802–1803 resembled that in the Vendée in its goal to exterminate the enemy. Contemporaries already referred to the "colonial Vendée" as they laid (at least partial) blame for both on the British enemy. As if to confirm this connection, the Directory appointed as its agent in Saint-Domingue one of the generals who had "pacified" the Vendée.[103]

## Royalism

The Vendée's opposition to the revolution was symbolized from the start by white cockades worn in public, which gave expression to the rebels' adherence to royalism. Yet royalism did not necessarily denote a progressive or conservative ideology. Neither the revolutionaries in the Americas nor those in France started out as republicans. Only when King George did not live up to the expectation of orators and writers to reclaim the royal privileges that his predecessors had lost did a republican solution become a possibility in North America. It was at that juncture that Thomas Paine's *Common Sense* came out, condemning the "royal brute of Britain."[104] Monarchist members of the French Assembly favored the revolution, but more as a set of early achievements than as a seemingly endless movement. They hoped to entrust the king with sovereign powers, assisted by a bicameral parliament that would provide counsel. After this constitutional project was rejected, they tried to maintain a centrist position between revolution and counterrevolution.[105] **Caroline Winterer** (Volume I, Chapter 1) stresses that during their revolution, North Americans were impressed by Europe's enlightened despots, who mixed monarchical rule with Enlightenment. And **Matthew Rainbow Hale** (Volume II, Chapter 5) notes that there was an intimate relationship between monarchy and democracy that proved to be resilient. What exerted a particularly powerful force in the 1790s on both sides of the North Atlantic was the allure, derived from monarchies, of indivisible sovereignty.

---

[103] Malick Ghachem, "The Colonial Vendée," in David Patrick Geggus and Norman Fiering, eds., *The World of the Haitian Revolution* (Bloomington: Indiana University Press, 2009), 156–76.

[104] Eric Nelson, *The Royalist Revolution: Monarchy and the American Founding* (Cambridge, MA: The Belknap Press of Harvard University Press, 2014), 33, 57–8, 63.

[105] Pascal Simonetti, "Les monarchiens. La Révolution à contretemps," in Jean Tulard, ed., *La contre-révolution: Origines, histoire, postérité* (Paris: Perrin, 1990), 62–84.

Nor were the political elites of Spanish America who assumed sovereignty after the forced abdication of Fernando VII in Bayonne natural republicans. Their intention was not to repudiate the monarchy, but to redefine it in a constitutional framework that was dictated locally and not in Cádiz. Before they embarked on independentist projects, the elites aimed to consolidate governmental rule and maintain the basic laws in a Hispanic structure.[106] Individuals and groups across the Atlantic world, then, continued to display allegiance to their hereditary rulers, from whom they sought protection and the concession of privileges.[107] Slaves in New Granada often understood the republican fight for independence as an attempt of their owners to limit the authority of the king. At the same time, they tried to have their defense of the king's power expressed in the form of individual or collective advantages.[108] Many enslaved freedom fighters in Saint-Domingue also supported a distant European king, carrying royalist banners and proclaiming that they wanted to restore Louis XVI to his throne after they had heard about his arrest.[109] Other rebels sided with Spain, in part because, as **Robert D. Taber** writes in Volume II, Chapter 22, "Spain also offered a king, a potent symbol of good government." Monarchism survived the revolution in Saint-Domingue and was alive and well in independent Haiti. Dessalines was crowned Emperor Jean-Jacques I, while Henry Christophe later led the kingdom of Haiti as King Henry I. And even the republic that Alexandre Pétion established, in which universal male suffrage was introduced, was "an oligarchy with a democratic veneer," writes **Erin Zavitz** (Volume II, Chapter 26).

In Latin America, too, monarchism remained a viable option after independence. One reason, as **Gabriel di Meglio** contends in Volume III, Chapter 9, was the Congress of Vienna's condemnation of governments created by revolution. That influenced the debate in Buenos Aires about postrevolutionary rule, in which some fancied a constitutional king, who could maintain order and put an end to local turmoil. In Brazil, the outcome of the independence process was an imperial state. Besides, writes **Jurandir**

---

[106] José M. Portillo Valdés, *Crisis atlántica: Autonomía e independencia en la crisis de la monarquía hispana* (Madrid: Fundación Carolina, Marcial Pons, 2006), 147–53.

[107] Hannah Weiss Muller, "Bonds of Belonging: Subjecthood and the British Empire," *Journal of British Studies* 53:1 (2014), 29–58: 57–8.

[108] Marcela Echeverri, *Indian and Slave Royalists in the Age of Revolution: Reform, Revolution, and Royalism in the Northern Andes, 1780–1825* (New York: Cambridge University Press, 2017), 60.

[109] Jeremy D. Popkin, *You Are All Free: The Haitian Revolution and the Abolition of Slavery* (New York: Cambridge University Press, 2010), 94, 104, 129–30.

# Introduction

**Malerba** in Volume III, Chapter 18, regent prince Dom João, who had moved the Portuguese court to Rio de Janeiro, played an important role in the independence process: "willingly or not, by coopting the Brazilian upper classes through his patriarchal and enticing policy, the sovereign helped decisively define the profile of the new elite that was formed in Brazil during the thirteen years he spent in Rio de Janeiro." When the unpopular first emperor, Dom Pedro, suddenly abdicated in 1831, a fresh opportunity was presented to radical leaders of the liberal opposition, writes **Jeffrey Needell** in Volume III, Chapter 19. The parliamentary leadership, however, "interwoven with the families and interests of the elite," balked. Instead, they chose, again, to support the vision of a constitutional monarchy that they had been trying to force upon Dom Pedro since 1823. Faced with radical republicanism, with its associated, clear threat of socioeconomic and national destabilization, they chose, again, the hope of constitutional, balanced partnership with a "unifying, charismatic national leader." Dom Pedro II thus started his reign as the new emperor.

Monarchical leadership also marked the start of Mexican independence. Cultivating close ties with the local elites, Agustín de Iturbide worked out the Plan of Iguala, which declared "the absolute independence of this kingdom," but also extended an invitation to Fernando VII or one of his family members to govern New Spain.[110] After the Spanish government declined, Iturbide assumed command and, supported by the Mexican elite, was enthroned as Emperor Agustín I. José de San Martín also strongly favored organizing independent states as monarchies, while even the committed republican Simón Bolívar had begun to flirt with monarchism by 1825. A British diplomat quoted him as saying in a private conversation: "Of all Countries South America is perhaps the least fitted for Republican Governments. What does its population consist of but Indians and Negros who are more ignorant than the vile race of Spaniards we are just emancipated from. A country represented and governed by such people must go to ruin." It would, however, take a while, he believed, for the inhabitants of the former Spanish colonies to embrace the notion of a new king.[111] Bolívar was not the only one during his presidency of Colombia to advocate a constitutional monarchy. A French agent wrote that the clergy, the army, and the common

---

[110] Jaime E. Rodríguez O., *"We Are Now the True Spaniards": Sovereignty, Revolution, Independence, and the Emergence of the Federal Republic of Mexico, 1808–1824* (Stanford: Stanford University Press, 2012), 253–63.

[111] Harold Temperley, *The Foreign Policy of Canning 1822–1827: England, the Neo-Holy Alliance, and the New World*, 2nd edition (London: Frank Cass & Co., 1966), 557–8.

people all favored that option. Some wanted Bolívar himself to be crowned, while others debated his possible succession, if he died, by a foreign prince.[112]

On the whole, royalists belonged to the counterrevolutionary camp, those desirous to maintain the status quo or pursue their goals without overthrowing the government. In Central America, people across the social spectrum steadfastly clung to Spain during the 1810s, when in all other parts of Spanish America people began to aspire to independence. **Timothy Hawkins** (Volume III, Chapter 6) notes that this was "despite exposure to the widespread political ideas of this revolutionary age and the kind of persistent internal grievances that united to spark and fuel independence movements in other colonies. Combined with a colonial administration single-minded in its dedication to root out dissent, this broad consensus helped marginalize and suffocate the few substantive challenges to the colonial order that did arise during this decade." More generally, writes **Marcela Echeverri** in Volume III, Chapter 10, "even within a position of loyalty, all subjects in the Atlantic empires embraced and produced radical lasting change."

In British America, royalists did not automatically adopt certain views. The only matter on which Loyalists agreed was the need to defend royal rule.[113] Royalist disunion in Spain during that country's constitutional triennium (1820–1823) even led to confrontations between different royalist factions, as **Juan Luis Simal** tells us in Volume III, Chapter 4. The constitutional monarchy was challenged by ultraroyalists, who engaged in guerrilla activities with the support of a rural population that resented taxes, conscription, and recent socioeconomic changes.

Loyalists in North America included members of ethnic and religious minorities who perceived the Crown as "a buffer against the tyranny of the majority."[114] Likewise, Indians in Spanish and Portuguese America sought to uphold the time-honored colonial pact, on account of which they paid royal tribute, and thus contributed to Crown income, in exchange for assuring themselves of the possession of their lands and the preservation of their way

---

[112] C. Parra-Pérez, *La monarquía en la Gran Colombia* (Madrid: Ediciones Cultura Hispánica, 1957), 95, 105, 129, 323.

[113] Maya Jasanoff, *Liberty's Exiles: American Loyalists in the Revolutionary World* (New York: Vintage Books, 2012), 189.

[114] David J. Fowler, "'Loyalty Is Now Bleeding in New Jersey': Motivations and Mentalities of the Disaffected," in Joseph S. Tiedemann, Eugene R. Fingerhut, and Robert W. Venables, eds., *The Other Loyalists: Ordinary People, Royalism, and the Revolution in the Middle Colonies, 1763–1787* (Albany: State University of New York Press, 2009), 45–77: 50.

# Introduction

of organizing their community.[115] Indian tributaries in the Spanish colonies had different demands than their caciques, who were exempt from tribute payments, and enjoyed the privilege to ride horseback and use arms. One feature of Túpac Amaru's revolt in Peru was the rift in many communities between caciques, who remained loyal to the Spanish Crown, and their tributaries, who supported the uprising.[116] The end of the colonial pact could be devastating. In Argentina, **Gabriel di Meglio** explains in Volume III, Chapter 9, "the end of tribute and juridical inequality meant that those villages no longer had rights to their common land, which they had used to pay the tribute, nor to maintain their ethnic leaders, who were in charge of the tribute. Thus, many villages lost their lands, which were sold out." Even the term "Indian" was being erased. The liberal Mexican politician José María Luis Mora proposed to the Congress of his country to do away with that term, since "the Indians should not continue existing" as a social group subject to special legislation. Nonetheless, the term was used throughout the 1820s, although at times the indigenous population was labeled "the so-called Indians."[117]

To the degree that the age of revolutions challenged royal authority, contemporary movements in Africa have been described by some historians as parallel. John Thornton has advanced the argument that Kongo's political system contained an absolutist concept that bestowed all power on the king. In the eighteenth century, absolutism was challenged by a movement (mis-labeled "republican" by Thornton) that stressed the need for popular consent to royal rule.[118] Even more forcefully, Paul Lovejoy has made a case for the great significance of jihad in west Africa, especially in the central Bilād al-

---

[115] María Luisa Soux, "Rebelión, guerrilla y tributo: Los indios en Charcas durante el proceso de independencia," *Anuario de Estudios Americanos* 68:2 (2011), 455–82: 458; Mariana Albuquerque Dantas, "Os indios 'fanáticos realistas absolutos' e a figura do monarca português: Disputas políticas, recrutamento e defesa de terras na Confederação do Equador," *Clio* 33:2 (2015), 49–73: 50, 56.

[116] Alexandra Sevilla Naranjo, "'Al mejor servicio del rey.' Indígenas realistas en la contrarrevolución quiteña, 1809–1814," *Procesos. Revista ecuatoriana de historia* no. 43 (2016), 93–118: 111; David T. Garrett, "'His Majesty's Most Loyal Vassals': The Indian Nobility and Túpac Amaru," *Hispanic American Historical Review* 84:4 (2004), 575–617: 597. Caciques in New Spain did not collect tribute, nor did they enjoy the same social standing as their counterparts in the viceroyalty of Peru: Aaron Pollack, "Hacia una historia social del tributo de indios y castas en Hispanoamérica. Notas en torno a su creación, desarrollo y abolición," *Historia Mexicana* 66:1 (2016), 65–160: 71.

[117] Laura Ibarra García, "El concepto de igualdad en México (1810–1824)," *Relaciones* 145 (2016), 279–314: 306.

[118] John K. Thornton, "'I Am the Subject of the King of Congo': African Political Ideology and the Haitian Revolution," *Journal of World History* 4:2 (1993), 181–214: 187.

Sūdān (south of the Sahara) between 1804–1808 and 1817. In response to the despotic rule of warlords, Islamic governments "based on religious leadership and consensus among Muslim officials" were established. How revolutionary west African jihad actually was remains to be seen. What is clear is that the universalist strain of the revolutions in Europe and the Americas was absent. Debates about slavery focused on the illegitimacy of enslaving Muslims, while ending slavery for non-Muslims never came up.[119] In other words, Islamic west Africans had arrived at the point that Christian Europeans had reached in the late Middle Ages, when they ended slavery, but only among their own.

## Counterrevolution and Banditry

Ideologies that challenged the revolutions were not exhausted by royalism. Revolts that were directed against revolutions, such as that in the Vendée, had in common their communal character; rural dominance; the importance of religious sentiments; their spontaneous nature; and the opposition to the politics of progress defended by the state that jeopardized the beliefs, structures, and functioning of traditional rural societies.[120] Across Europe and even in Spanish America, the fear of French influence and its ability to dramatically change traditional societies was enormous. Typical is the judgment of the Spanish Inquisition in late 1789 when it forbade the printing of materials that referred to the events in France: these works were produced by a new race of philosophers, who were men with a corrupted spirit. By posing as defenders of liberty, they actually plotted against it and destroyed the political and social order.[121] Spain's Secretary of State, the count of Floridablanca, did all he could stop the flow of information arriving from France. In Volume III, Chapter 2, **Emily Berquist Soule** writes that he "placed more Spanish troops on the border with France in order to deter unsanctioned crossings of people and goods. He implemented a policy of strict censorship designed to keep out all news of the events in France;

---

[119] Paul E. Lovejoy, *Jihād in West Africa during the Age of Revolutions* (Athens, OH: Ohio University Press, 2016), 90, 245–6.

[120] Jean-Pierre Poussou, "'Les autres 'Vendées,' jalons pour une thématique des 'Vendées,'" in Yves-Marie Bercé, ed., *Les autres Vendées: Actes du colloque international sur les contre-révolutions paysannes au XIX^e siècle* (La Roche-sur-Yon: Éditions du Centre vendéen de recherches historiques, 2013), 299, 304.

[121] Gonzalo Añes Álvarez de Castrillón, "España y la Revolución francesa," in Almudena Cavestany, ed., *Revolución, contrarrevolución e Independencia: La Revolución francesa, España y América* (Madrid: Turner Publicaciones, 1989), 17–39: 20.

Introduction

forbidding French newspapers, and even employing Inquisition officials to inspect mail coming across the Pyrenees."

British American Loyalists, writes **Trevor Burnard** (Volume I, Chapter 9), "especially those of higher social status, feared that the wild ideas of liberty thrown about by revolutionaries would have a leveling tendency and by promoting lawless anarchy" were harming the empire. Anarchy was projected onto the new republican regimes because of their commitment to democracy. Revolutionaries tended to believe that only republics, ruled as they were by laws and not the royal will, could resist the tendency of men to pursue only their own, personal interest.[122] Counterrevolutionaries rejected the way in which these laws took effect. The large mass of people, asserted a priest from Guayaquil in the viceroyalty of Peru, cannot judge for themselves their own interests unless they put themselves in the hands of a single individual. A Dutch thinker who supported the antirevolutionary Orangists wrote in the same vein that the "people" was incapable of acting by itself. Since they were dependent on a few among them, democracy was in practice always a struggle between various groups of demagogues.[123] The quest of revolutionaries to erect a new society was chimerical in the eyes of their opponents, who rejected the fictitious state of nature. The natural, transcendent order established by God could not be changed.[124]

While prominent rebels and conservatives created the script for each revolution, the vast mass of people involved in the revolutions were motivated by their own individual or group goals, as the abovementioned motives of peasants, slaves, and Indians make clear. In northern South America, **Ernesto Bassi** argues in Volume III, Chapter 8, "support from the *pardos* [the light-skinned free people of color] was highly contingent and depended on the fact that they tended to see political independence or continued allegiance to Spain not as an end in itself but as a means to achieving a more

---

[122] Anthony Pagden, *Spanish Imperialism and the Political Imagination: Studies in European and Spanish-American Social and Political Theory 1513–1830* (New Haven: Yale University Press, 1990), 136.

[123] Victor Samuel Rivera, "José Ignacio Moreno. Un teólogo peruano. Entre Montesquieu y Joseph de Maistre," *Araucaria. Revista Iberoamericana de Filosofía, Política y Humanidades* 15:29 (2013), 223–41: 238. Wyger R. E. Velema, "Elie Luzac and Two Dutch Revolutions: The Evolution of Orangist Political Thought," in Margaret C. Jacob and Wijnand W. Mijnhardt, eds., *The Dutch Republic in the Eighteenth Century: Decline, Enlightenment, and Revolution* (Ithaca, NY: Cornell University Press, 1992), 123–46: 138.

[124] Serge Bianchi, *Des révoltes aux révolutions: Europe, Russie, Amérique (1770–1802). Essai d'interprétation* (Rennes: Presses universitaires de Rennes, 2004), 447.

important aim: legal equality. The same assertion is valid for slaves, although in their case the goal was to secure freedom."

Principle often combined with opportunism to persuade people to join or oppose the revolution. **Liam Riordan** writes in Volume 1, Chapter 13: "The complex web of circumstance and opportunity that informs allegiance in times of uncertain change and military mobilization is necessarily shaped by perceptions of self-interest." In Mexico, Hidalgo's rebellion "encouraged certain marginalized and semi-marginalized Mexicans to employ violence in order to adjust deeply held grievances against the regime, provincial administrators, and members of the propertied classes who had long enjoyed the benefits of power, and it presented to many others an opportunity to get rich-quick, or at least to stake out for themselves a place in any new society."[125] These men engaged in guerrilla warfare, as **Juan Ortiz Escamilla** explains. Violent raids on towns and habitual looting of haciendas were their trademarks. Their leaders, often locally born, saw to the distribution of booty and captured livestock among their supporters. Italy's bandits engaged in robbery and armed revolt as a form of revenge against a society that had marginalized them. They found common cause in attacking the privileged classes, fighting government bureaucracy, as well as the French invaders. Those invaders' insults of personal or family honor convinced many a peasant to take up arms.[126] Besides, peer pressure and a search for adventure must have played a role as well.[127]

The distinction between rebellion/counterrebellion and banditry was often blurred, either because ordinary bandits sided with the royalists or the patriots, or – particularly in countries in which Napoleon's armies lived off the land and introduced mass conscription – because banditry doubled as resistance, but also because guerrillas on both sides often engaged in crimes that had no political dimension. At the same time, authorities were eager to label counterrevolutionary attacks as brigandage since that served to discredit the enemy's political demands. In France, the term "brigand," which had initially both caused aversion and won admiration among the members of the National Assembly, was increasingly defined negatively in the course of the Revolution, especially after the start of the war in the Vendée. In their

---

[125] Christon I. Archer, "Banditry and Revolution in New Spain, 1790–1821," *Bibliotheca Americana* 1:2 (1982), 58–89: 59, 88.

[126] Massimo Viglione, *Le insorgenze: Rivoluzione & Controrivoluzione in Italia, 1792–1815* (Milan: Edizioni Ares, 1999), 96–7; Michael Broers, *Napoleon's Other War: Bandits, Rebels, and Their Pursuers in the Age of Revolutions* (Oxford: Peter Lang, 2010), 110.

[127] Van Young, *The Other Rebellion*, 105–6.

Introduction

subsequent fight against insurgents in countries occupied by France, lawyers and gendarmes ceased to distinguish between bandits and guerrilla fighters.[128]

Bandits – with or without a political agenda – used the breakdown of law and order that was the result of revolution. Chilean banditry, for example, was encouraged by the anarchy of the civil war between republicans and royalists, as many poor people were displaced or otherwise affected.[129] In northern South America, the disruption of the colonial state and colonial institutions opened the door to the caudillos, military leaders who drew to them the *llaneros*. These plainsmen lived by plunder and lacked any political objectives. They followed "the first caudillo who offers them booty taken from anyone with property. This is how Boves and other bandits of the same kind have been able to recruit hordes of these people, who live by vagrancy, robbery, and assassination."[130] Such bandits may have been able to fill the political vacuum left by the disappearance of the old government, but in turn they prevented a new civilian government from taking hold. The Thirteen Colonies in North America fell prey to banditry – which included the stealing of slaves – that was hardly political in nature. As historian Holger Hoock observes, by 1780, "large swaths of the American lower South presented a scary scene – a virtually permanent little war of raiding and plundering between Patriot and Loyalist militias, prisoner abuse, even outright murder. In addition, armed gangs unaffiliated with any real military units operated in the semi-lawless wasteland between the lines."[131] Many of the smaller bands "operated independently, though often in the guise of serving one side or the other."[132] Nor can the Maroons who refused to remain on their plantations during the Haitian Revolution and retreated into the interior be categorized as counterrevolutionaries. As **Philippe Girard** writes (Volume II, Chapter 25), the Maroons distrusted all elite actions vying for control of Saint-Domingue, opposing "whichever side was dominant to preserve their freedom and autonomy."

---

[128] Sottocasa, *Les brigands et la Révolution*, 60, 146, 289; Broers, *Napoleon's Other War*, 55, 102–3.

[129] Leonardo León, "Montoneras Populares durante la gestación de la República, Chile: 1810–1820," *Anuario de Estudios Americanos* 68:2 (2011), 483–510: 487–8, 492.

[130] John Lynch, "Bolívar and the Caudillos," *Hispanic American Historical Review* 63:1 (1983), 3–35: 5.

[131] Hoock, *Scars of Independence*, 309.

[132] Matthew P. Spooner, "Origins of the Old South: Revolution, Slavery, and Changes in Southern Society, 1776–1800" (Ph.D. dissertation, Columbia University, 2015), 62.

Ideology, then, was just one of many factors motivating individuals. On both sides of the American Revolution, desertion was rampant. One historian has written, "A steady stream of Loyalists deserted, as they were converted to the American cause, discouraged because of limitations placed on looting, disheartened by the ever-lengthening conflict, enticed by the colonial life-style, or simply out of boredom." Patriots also deserted, "many of them for the same reasons as the Loyalists, because of uncertainty of the rightness of their cause, because the changing seasons meant they were needed for work on their farms, or because the war was not the adventure or sure meal ticket they had thought it would be."[133] If many men changed their minds, others avoided choosing sides as long as possible. Their lack of affiliation did not mean indifference. Instead, their personal or group goals might or might not align with the two main adversaries. Tenants in the northern Hudson Valley whose goal was to own the land on which they worked put off a choice for either side in the war until they could no longer avoid it. For their part, indigenous groups in Upper Peru often withdrew to their communities and only did the absolute minimum to satisfy patriots and royalists, waiting to see which side was gaining the upper hand.[134]

Nor did enslaved men and women in the Thirteen Colonies automatically take side with one of the two main sides. **James Sidbury** contends (Volume 1, Chapter 15) that "the Revolutionary War offered Blacks in North America many potential opportunities, but none that were reliable, so it is unsurprising that different people living in different places pursued different strategies." Still, 20,000 of them actually ran to the British armies during the course of the war, attracted by vague promises of freedom; 8,000 to 10,000 of them survived and managed to leave the United States, as Sidbury writes, "to live the rest of their lives as free people."

## International Dimensions

Textbook accounts of revolutions tend to obscure their strong international dimension. The American Revolution, for example, cannot be understood without acknowledging the role of the French colonies of Martinique and

---

[133] Anne Pfaelzer de Ortiz, "German Redemptioners of the Lower Sort: Apolitical Soldiers in the American Revolution?," *Journal of American Studies* 33:2 (1999), 267–306: 290.

[134] Thomas J. Humphrey, *Land and Liberty: Hudson Valley Riots in the Age of Revolution* (DeKalb: Northern Illinois University Press, 2004), 93; Soux, "Rebelión, guerrilla y tributo," 458.

Saint-Domingue and the Dutch island of St. Eustatius, as **Wim Klooster** stresses in Volume I, Chapter 19. As for Spain's role, **Gonzalo M. Quintero Saravia** argues in Volume I, Chapter 10, that when its government joined the French war effort against Britain in 1778, it "not only tipped the balance of the conflict, giving France and Spain numerical superiority both at land and at sea, but also profoundly changed the general strategy of the war ... This clear superiority opened up new theaters in this now truly global war, spreading British resources thin. Britain would be forced to abandon a purely American perspective of the conflict and adopt a more global view of the war ..." France's support for the American Revolution was accompanied in the same years by its defeat, alongside Bern and Savoy, of Geneva, where an insurrection had taken place against the magistrates. Geneva was unfortunate, writes **Richard Whatmore** (Volume II, Chapter 12), that in 1782 the strength of France was at a peak unparalleled since the 1680s. French invasions of foreign countries may have stopped during the early stages of the French Revolution, but the fear of an international conspiracy aimed at defeating the revolution helped forge a parliamentary majority in Paris in favor of war in 1792. From then on, warfare was a permanent feature of French life until the Battle of Waterloo, conquest of neighboring territories doubling or masquerading as liberation.[135]

The Spanish American independence movements were even more borderless than those in Europe. Troops from Buenos Aires were deployed not only in battles against Spanish forces in Chile and Upper Peru, but also outside the viceroyalty of the Río de la Plata in Peru. Similarly, natives of New Granada were instrumental in ending the Spanish regime in Peru. In addition, the independence movement in Spanish America was entangled with that in Brazil, as **João Paulo Pimenta** shows in Volume III, Chapter 21. One element of this braided history was the repeated Portuguese and later Brazilian interventions in the Banda Oriental, starting in 1811, which were predicated on fear of the successive revolutionary governments in Buenos Aires. These military incursions ended only with the creation of Uruguay in 1828.

International connections were not just military in nature. What gave the revolutionary age coherence was the spread of ideas and ideals, inspiring both enthusiasm and aversion. Pimenta notes that through "newspapers, as well as diplomatic reports, official and private correspondence, and the

---

[135] T. C. W. Blanning, *The Origins of the French Revolutionary Wars* (London: Longman, 1986).

circulation of people, rumors, and news, Spanish America became increasingly familiar in Brazil, arousing interest, fears, and expectations, and provoking reactions." All around the Atlantic world, the North American Declaration of Independence and the constitutions spawned by the new nation and its component states became powerful documents in the hands of rebels in other locales.[136] The French Declaration of the Rights of Man and Citizen and the French constitutions of the first revolutionary years served the same purpose. In Hungary, **Orsolya Szakály** writes in Volume II, Chapter 19, the radical Society of Liberty and Equality "called for a democratic republic of equal citizens in Hungary with references to the French Revolution." Political awareness in several Spanish colonies was also stimulated by the French Revolution. In Volume II, Chapter 6, **Clément Thibaud** shows that members of Spanish American elites could derive inspiration from the French Declaration as much as slaves and free people of color, as they both did during the French revolutionary decade and the Spanish imperial crisis after 1808. No explicit reference could be made to the French example, but, writes Thibaud, "between 1811 and 1813, all constitutional projects in Spanish America included a section on the Rights of Man and of the Citizen." The French model did not arrive alone, mingling with that of the Haitian Revolution to form a potent mixture of revolutionary ideas, slogans, and practices. In the 1790s, **Cristina Soriano** writes (Volume II, Chapter 28), the new revolutionary language "that arrived on the coast of the Spanish Main challenged the already tense relations that existed among different sociracial groups. The majority of the white population interpreted this revolutionary narrative as a violent torrent that sought to destroy their political system and social order, while many free and enslaved people of African descent saw this as their opportunity to achieve social justice and emancipation from the system of slavery, or to at least renegotiate their labor conditions and political roles." One free man of color in Spanish Louisiana expressed his admiration for French rule in Saint-Domingue, where, he said, men like himself enjoyed civil equality. "We can speak openly, like any white person and hold the same rank as they." It is unjust that we don't enjoy equality in Louisiana. Anticipating a line from Martin Luther King's famous speech, he added: "Only their method of thinking – not color – should differentiate men."[137]

---

[136] George Athan Billias, *American Constitutionalism Heard Round the World, 1776–1789: A Global Perspective* (New York: New York University Press, 2009).

[137] Kimberly Hanger, "Conflicting Loyalties: The French Revolution and Free People of Color in Spanish New Orleans," *Louisiana History* 34:1 (1993), 5–33: 26.

Among German radicals, debates revolved around the French catalog of rights, which they saw as the foundation for social order. The French example still resonated internationally when, in France itself, Thermidor set in and principles of natural law were no longer considered the foundation of liberty but denounced as an arsenal for anarchists and levelers which had produced the Terror.[138] The international impact of the ideas spawned by both the French Revolution and the American Revolution, as well as those associated with the Enlightenment, has often been presented as ideological absorption. It was, however, not the force of these ideas themselves that enabled them to spread to certain locales. As one historian has argued, ideas can make history only when they successfully process reality and offer ways out of a social impasse. Crises make those seeking solutions look for appropriate intellectual and political instruments.[139] And once a revolutionary situation is unfolding, creative energies are unleashed that produce new ideas and ideals.[140]

As had happened under the influence of the Revolution in France, a surge of politicization also occurred under the influence of the constitution of Cádiz of 1812, at least in the Iberian world. **Jane Landers** writes in Volume III, Chapter 11 that this constitution "reversed long-promulgated racial prohibitions and decreed that 'Spaniards of African origin' should be helped to study sciences and have access to an ecclesiastical career." The new constitution, Landers continues, was read in plazas across the Atlantic, to enthusiastic crowds that included free and enslaved Blacks. After the constitution reached Cuba, a series of slave revolts swept through the island, as hope born of debates in the Cortes and British Parliament helped launch rumors about abolition decrees authored by authorities as diverse as the king of Spain, the Spanish Cortes, the king of England, the king of Haiti, and the king of Kongo. Those debates did not create such beliefs but activated the often deep-felt conviction of Black men and women of the illegality of their enslavement. News from afar was not necessary to trigger such ideas, as suggested by the impact of the constitution of Antioquia (New Granada), which was saturated with the metaphor of liberty, on a group of slaves who

---

[138] Yannick Bosc, *La terreur des droits de l'homme: Le républicanisme de Thomas Paine et le moment thermidorien* (Paris: Éditions Kimé, 2016); Günther Birtsch, "Naturrecht und Menschenrechte. Zur vernunftrechtlichen Argumentation deutscher Jakobiner," in Otto Dann and Diethelm Klippel, eds., *Naturrecht – Spätaufklärung – Revolution* (Hamburg: Felix Meiner Verlag, 1995), 111–20: 119–20.

[139] Peter Blickle, *Von der Leibeigenschaft zu den Menschenrechten: Eine Geschichte der Freiheit in Deutschland* (Munich: Verlag C. H. Beck, 2006), 15.

[140] Kristin Ross, *Communal Luxury: The Political Imaginary of the Paris Commune* (London: Verso, 2015), 6–7.

claimed to represent more than 10,000 fellow bondspeople. Convinced of the existence of a liberating decree, they approached the tribunal of justice in Medellín, only to be arrested.[141]

The movement to abolish slavery was one that transgressed boundaries. In Volume II, Chapter 4, **Erica Johnson Edwards** shows that the French Society of the Friends of the Blacks and its successor organization, the Society of the Friends of the Blacks and the Colonies, enjoyed membership from both sides of the Channel and both sides of the Atlantic. In another sense, abolitionism also extended across international borders. As **Seymour Drescher** details in Volume II, Chapter 15, Great Britain sent a large fleet to Algiers, which succeeded in liberating many enslaved Europeans, victims of the Barbary corsairs, took great pains to stimulate international condemnation of the transatlantic slave trade, and made recognition of the new Latin American countries dependent on a commitment to abolish the slave trade. News about the termination of slavery in foreign lands was not always a welcome boon for abolitionists. Abolition in Saint-Domingue in 1793, sanctioned by the French Convention the following year, made antislavery activists both in Great Britain and in the United States lose ground in their struggle. **Ashli White** demonstrates in Volume II, Chapter 29 that those bent on upholding slavery in the United States spread the fiction that Black people in Saint-Domingue were fighting a war of revenge against their former masters after they had been set free thanks to false philanthropists.

The Haitian Revolution also proved to be a major source of inspiration among those living in bondage in the New World's many slave societies, while the French Revolution found resonance among both whites and nonwhites. That was in part due to the initiatives of Victor Hugues, France's most senior representative in the years 1794–1798, whose revolutionary troops were composed largely of former slaves. This massive force, **Jessica Pierre-Louis** tells us in Volume II, Chapter 27, "forced the British to recruit and emancipate more enslaved conscripted soldiers to cope with the increase in French troops. Thus, general French freedom also generated, albeit to a lesser extent, emancipation in the British colonies."

Separating the reception of the closely intertwined French and Haitian revolutions is not easy. In Brazil, **Alejandro Gómez** asserts (Volume III, Chapter 14),

---

[141] María Eugenia Chaves, "Esclavos, libertades y república: Tesis sobre la polisemia de la libertad en la primera república antioqueña," *Estudios Interdisciplinarios de América Latina* 22:1 (2011), 81–104: 87–9. Cf. Wim Klooster, "Slave Revolts, Royal Justice, and a Ubiquitous Rumor in the Age of Revolutions," *The William and Mary Quarterly* 71:3 (2014), 401–24.

Introduction

both the revolution in Saint-Domingue and the support of revolutionary activity by the French colonial regime in Guadeloupe affected the city of Salvador, where conspirators in 1798 criticized the "monarchical yoke" and praised the "freedom, equality, and fraternity" of the French.[142] The impact of these two revolutions on the Americas was dissimilar, David Geggus has argued: "If the French Revolution proclaimed the ideals of liberty and equality, the Haitian Revolution demonstrated to colonized peoples that they could be won by force of arms. Plantation societies built on bondage, prejudice, and inequality were peculiarly vulnerable to the ideology of revolutionary France, but the dramatic example of self-liberation offered by Saint-Domingue's transformation into Haiti brought the message much closer to home."[143]

In Spanish America, writes **Clément Thibaud** (Volume II, Chapter 6), the legacy of the French or Haitian revolutions was not explicitly invoked, but hiding in plain sight. Revolutionaries had a thorough grasp of what the French assemblies had accomplished and adopted several institutions that had originated in France. It would also be impossible to imagine the revolutionaries' acceptance of racial equality without the shadow of the Haitian Revolution.[144] And then there was the Haitian republic, a vivid reminder of the successful revolution, which officially maintained its neutrality, but provided crucial support to rebels in Caribbean South America. **Ernesto Bassi** writes (Volume III, Chapter 8) that the obvious sympathies for the Spanish American revolutions of Alexandre Pétion (the president of one of Haiti's two polities at the time) led to the characterization of his republic by Spanish officials as "the receptacle of all the adventurers."

Like the Haitian Revolution, that of France was particularly influential in its own hemisphere. In nearby Switzerland, for example, both intellectuals and peasants who had suffered under the remnants of feudalism responded enthusiastically in the first months after the storming of the Bastille, while in rural areas in western Germany peasants refused to pay tithes or perform the *corvée*, the unpaid labor owed to their lords.[145] Usually, however, the

---

[142] See also Luiz Geraldo Silva, "El impacto de la revolución de Saint-Domingue y los afrodescendientes libres de Brasil. Esclavitud, libertad, configuración social y perspectiva atlántica (1780–1825)," *Historia* 49:1 (2016), 209–33.

[143] Geggus, "Slave Rebellion," 27–8.

[144] David Geggus, "The Sounds and Echoes of Freedom: The Impact of the Haitian Revolution on Latin America," in Darién J. Davis, ed., *Beyond Slavery: The Multilayered Legacy of Africans in Latin America and the Caribbean* (Lanham, MD: Rowman & Littlefield, 2007), 19–36: 25.

[145] Marc H. Lerner, *A Laboratory of Liberty: The Transformation of Political Culture in Republican Switzerland, 1750–1848* (Leiden: Brill, 2012), 79; T. C. W. Blanning,

revolution's supporters were small in number and to be found among radical city-dwellers, who often pinned all their hopes on a French invasion. Joseph Schlemmer, a German lawyer, wrote in 1792: "The happiness of half the world depends on the luck or misfortune of French arms. For if they win, the subject can hope for equity and justice, for better laws to protect him. If they lose, the most terrible slavery in monarchical states is inevitable."[146] The French, indeed, brought freedom, introducing various degrees of rural emancipation in Belgium, the Helvetic Republic, several parts of northern and western Germany, and the Grand Duchy of Warsaw. These French policies also led to preemptive emancipation in German states that were not invaded.[147]

Despite the changes wrought, bitterness and opposition eventually prevailed in the areas subdued by French arms. In Volume II, Chapter 21, **Annie Jourdan** writes: "In view of the political, economic, and social consequences, the so-called sister republics were a flagrant failure. Their alliance with the French republic brought them continuous disorder, increased taxation, military violence and depredations, and infinite abuses of power." Italian territories were particularly badly affected. In Milan, the French provoked outrage by billeting soldiers in private homes, establishing a National Guard for which all able-bodied men between sixteen and fifty-five were recruited, and eliminating religious festivals and sacred wall paintings on public buildings.[148] Apart from strong local cultural and religious traditions, the French invaders were confronted with deep-rooted judicial cultures which challenged their uniformist impulse.[149] Sooner or later, although not universally, the French presence descended into boundless military violence, which inspired counterviolence.[150] **John A. Davis** (Volume II, Chapter 17) nuances this picture. Even brutal features of the French presence, he writes,

---

*Reform and Revolution in Mainz 1743–1803* (Cambridge: Cambridge University Press, 1974), 306.

[146] Jörg Schweigard, *Aufklärung und Revolutionsbegeisterung: Die katholischen Universitäten in Mainz, Heidelberg und Würzburg im Zeitalter der Französischen Revolution (1789–1792/3–1803)* (Frankfurt am Main: Peter Lang, 2000), 155.

[147] John Markoff, "Violence, Emancipation, and Democracy: The Countryside and the French Revolution," *The American Historical Review* 100:2 (1995), 360–86: 383.

[148] Laura Gagliardi, "Il volto della Rivoluzione: Milano di fronte all'invasione francese (1796–1799)," in Cecilia Nubola and Andreas Würgler, eds., *Ballare con nemico? Reazioni all'espansione francese in Europa tra entusiasmo e resistenza (1792–1815)* (Bologna: Società editrice il Mulino; Berlin: Duncker & Humblot, 2010), 23–34.

[149] Luigi Lacchè, "L'Europe et la révolution du droit: Brèves réflexions," *Annales historiques de la Révolution française* no. 328 (2002), 153–69: 162.

[150] Jean-Clément Martin, *Violence et révolution: Essai sur la naissance d'un mythe national* (Paris: Éditions du Seuil, 2006), 289–91.

# Introduction

"were not sufficient to reduce the republican experiments of 1796–1799 to a mere narrative of military oppression. The attraction of the promised new republican order had been evident when in April 1796 Bonaparte was greeted enthusiastically in Milan as a liberator. Republican sympathizers and political exiles from Naples, Rome, and Piedmont flocked to the city where political clubs and associations were founded, and newspapers and journals were launched." The response was similar in other parts of the Italian peninsula. Besides, Davis argues, the popular anger that did erupt in 1799 – on a scale vaster than the insurrection in the Vendée – "was in many respects a continuation of insurrections and unrest that had been evident throughout the peninsula from much earlier, but existing discontents had been exacerbated by the impact of the revolution, the military occupation, and the new republics."

In some countries, the fear of a French invasion caused officials to stoke fear about the baneful presence of imaginary Frenchmen. In Saxony and Austria, French agents were accused of stirring up the population or preparing a coup d'état.[151] Nowhere, though, was the fear of French emissaries so great as in Spanish America in the first years after Fernando VII and Carlos IV surrendered to Napoleon in 1808. A tremendous amount of bureaucratic energy was spent on detecting unknown travelers and checking the countless reports about their alleged activities.[152] In reality, Napoleon did send some agents to Spanish American shores, but they remained harmless.

By the time Napoleon seized power, France rarely served as a beacon of hope anymore, at least in Europe.[153] In the eyes of numerous commentators, who now looked to Great Britain for inspiration, the French Revolution had failed, and its supporters were simply terrorists and anarchists.[154] If books by

---

[151] Jirko Krauß, *Ländlicher Alltag und Konflikt in der späten Frühen Neuzeit: Lebenswelt erzgebirgischer Rittergutsdörfer im Spiegel der kursächsischen Bauernunruhen 1790* (Frankfurt am Main: Peter Lang, 2012), 411; Helmut Reinalter, "Gegen die 'Tollwuth der Aufklärungsbarbarei': Leopold Alois Hoffmann und der frühe Konservatismus in Österreich," in Christoph Weiß, ed., *Von "Obscuranten" und "Eudämonisten": Gegenaufklärerische, konservative und antirevolutionäre Publizisten im späten 18. Jahrhundert* (St. Ingbert: Röhrig Universitätsverlag, 1997), 221–44: 227–8.

[152] Timothy Hawkins, *A Great Fear: Luís de Onís and the Shadow War against Napoleon in Spanish America, 1808–1812* (Tuscaloosa: The University of Alabama Press, 2019).

[153] By contrast, liberals and conservatives at the Cortes of Cádiz tried to learn lessons from the early stages of the French Revolution. José M. Portillo, "El poder constituyente en el primer constitucionalismo hispano," *Jahrbuch für Geschichte Lateinamerikas* 55 (2018), 1–26. In addition, as seen above, radicals in the Spanish colonies continued to be inspired by French revolutionary thought and practice.

[154] Richard Whatmore, *Terrorists, Anarchists, and Republicans: The Genevans and the Irish in Time of Revolution* (Princeton: Princeton University Press, 2019), 349–50.

Voltaire, Rousseau, and Raynal had always been banned in the Catholic world, publications associated with the revolution in France were seen by moral guardians of monarchical regimes as equally impious, seditious, or obscene. It was not even necessarily a book's content that was judged – authorship by a disreputable person sufficed for a work to be condemned. Censors in Brazil in the 1810s prohibited the sale of the innocent-sounding *Liberty of the Seas* because its author, the former Jacobin Bertrand Barère, had been "one of the most bloodthirsty associates of the monster Robespierre." And although the *philosophe* Gabriel Bonnot de Mably had died in 1785, his works were blacklisted because his doctrines of equality and liberty were found to have contributed much to the French Revolution.[155]

Whereas anti-French feelings abated, anti-Spanish sentiment in Spanish America grew after 1808, as the fight between patriots and royalists intensified. In Buenos Aires, a series of repressive measures against the *peninsulares* commenced with the May revolution of 1810, although persecution was limited to those who openly rejected the new regime. It became much more comprehensive after the discovery of an antigovernment conspiracy with Spanish ringleaders.[156] At the tail end of the independence process, there was also a reckoning for Spanish natives in both Peru and Mexico. Their massive expulsion caused so much ill-will on the part of the Spanish government that it embarked on an unsuccessful reconquest of Mexico in 1829–1830.[157] Like in other former colonies, Brazil also initiated measures against natives of the former metropole. **Hendrik Kraay** (Volume III, Chapter 20) asserts that these policies were not simply aimed at eliminating an enemy ethnicity. Anti-Portuguese rhetoric and violence were also about political choices and local power struggles. Besides, "expelling Portuguese-born office holders also conveniently opened up spaces in the civil and military bureaucracy for Brazilian patriots."

The French themselves, meanwhile, were not above excluding foreigners, who were seen by the Jacobins as treacherous enemies of the revolution. Months after the outbreak of war with Britain, all British nationals were arrested, and their property was confiscated. Englishmen soon stood accused

---

[155] Lúcia Maria B. P. das Neves and Tânia Maria T. B. da C. Ferreira, "O medo dos 'abomináveis princípios franceses': A censura dos livros nos inícios do século XIX no Brasil," *Acervo* 4:1 (1989), 113–19: 116.

[156] Mariana Alicia Pérez, "¡Viva España y Mueran los Patricios! La conspiración de Álzaga de 1812," *Americanía. Revista de Estudios Latinoamericanos* special issue (May 2015), 21–55.

[157] Harold Dana Sims, *The Expulsion of Mexico's Spaniards, 1821–1836* (Pittsburgh: University of Pittsburgh Press, 1990).

of "lese humanity." War to the death was consequently declared on them.[158] Such policies stood in stark contrast to the universalism the revolutionaries had professed in the first years of the revolution. As late as January 1793, *Le Moniteur Universel*, the government's official newspaper, had invoked "the bonds of universal fraternity which the French have extended to all peoples and on which they stake their lives."[159] Universalism did not disappear once France's armies began to cross the country's boundaries, although its adherents were now usually to be found elsewhere. In his *A Letter to the People of Ireland* (1796), Irishman Thomas Russell connected the plight of those countrymen of his who had been impressed by the Royal Navy not only to the oppression of Catholics in Ireland but also to that of enslaved Africans. Impressment, after all, enabled Britain to wage wars that aimed at continuing the Atlantic slave trade.[160] Russell thus tapped into the remarkable popular success of Britain's abolitionist movement. **Seymour Drescher** writes (Volume II, Chapter 15): "Unlike its counterparts in France and America it endured for half a century as a national social movement. Its participants were initially aroused by what they deemed violations of the 'principle of humanity.' Their intended beneficiaries were not their own fellow Britons nor even residents of their own colonies. They differed from the enslaved in race, color, religion, or culture."

If imperialism did not raise its head in France until a few years into the revolution, the American Revolution was more blatantly imperialist from the very start. In Volume I, Chapter 16, **Colin Calloway** contends that "the Revolution was also, quite simply, a war over Indian land. Speculators like George Washington had worked long and hard to get their hands on the best western lands; western settlers sought to rid lands of Indian neighbors, and Congress and the individual states needed land to fulfill the bounties and warrants they issued in lieu of pay during the war." Those Indian neighbors paid the price for westward expansion. Calloway relates that the Cherokees sued for peace after a genocidal campaign had been waged against them. At the peace treaties they signed, they lost more than 5 million acres. The indigenous plight throws into relief the apparent contradiction discerned by **Patrick Griffin**

---

[158] The rebels in the Vendée, who were officially excluded from the nation – not humanity – were treated the same way: Sophie Wahnich, *L'impossible citoyen: L'étranger dans le discours de la Révolution française* (Paris: Éditions Albin Michel, 2010), 11, 359.

[159] Rachel Rogers, "The Society of the Friends of the Rights of Man, 1792–94: British and Irish Radical Conjunctions in Republican Paris," *La Révolution française* (2016), 1–26: 6, http://lrf.revues.org/1629.

[160] Anthony Di Lorenzo and John Donoghue, "Abolition and Republicanism over the Transatlantic Long Term, 1640–1800," *La Révolution française* (2016), 14, 48–9, http://lrf.revues.org/1690.

(Volume I, Chapter 7). The creoles of British North America, he writes, were "a people of paradox: anti-imperial when it came to the metropole and imperial when it came to dominance at home." Westward expansion continued after the peace treaty with Britain was signed in 1783, but, as **Mark Peterson** notes (Volume I, Chapter 5), the Confederation Congress (the body that initially governed the new republic) was ill-equipped to manage claims on western lands. It was in part to solve this problem that a constitutional convention was convened that ended up creating a new form of national government.

## The Realm of Freedom

Some revolutionaries, even those who stood to benefit more than others, had always doubted the possibility of introducing a new order.[161] The German "Jacobin" Joseph Görres believed in a four-stage development that had begun with the transition from barbarism to society, which was followed by that from a despotic to a representative regime. Next, a pure democracy would arise that would eventually give way to the period of "anarchy," during which people no longer needed a government. This progression took time, however. To move from the second stage to the third, as the French revolutionaries had tried to accomplish by introducing the constitution of 1791, did not make sense. That constitution came thousands of years too early. A long process of popular education was first required.[162]

Still, the upheaval of the late eighteenth and early nineteenth centuries created new regimes that often bore no resemblance to the old ones. These regimes made a start, however incomplete and reversible, and more in some places than others, with the emancipation of the many men and women who previously had been voiceless. And yet the belief, generated by the revolutions around the Atlantic world, in an imminent entry into the realm of freedom was proven to be misplaced. In the course of the revolutions, goals that had been embraced in the early stages mutated into ideological phrases that lacked urgency.[163] What gained currency was, once again, the idea that change would come only gradually. For most residents of the Atlantic world, true liberty would have to wait until a distant future.

---

[161] Domenico Losurdo, "Vincenzo Cuoco, la révolution napolitaine de 1799 et l'étude comparée des révolutions," *Revue Historique* 281:1 (1989), 133–57: 151.

[162] Joseph Görres, "Mein Glaubensbekenntnis (Juni/Juli 1798)," in Axel Kuhn, ed., *Linksrheinische deutsche Jakobiner: Aufrufe, Reden, Protokolle. Briefe und Schriften 1794–1801* (Stuttgart: J. B. Metzler, 1978), 240–50: 242–3.

[163] Stefan Greif, "Das Diskontinuierliche als Kontinuum. Aufklärung und Aufklärungskritik im Werk Georg Forsters," *Georg-Forster-Studien* 15 (2010), 77–93: 87.

# PART I

★

# THE SPANISH EMPIRE

I

# The Spanish Empire: General Overview

STEFAN RINKE

Between 1760 and 1830, revolutionary processes unfolded in the Spanish colonial empire that led to its dissolution. In the end, a new world of states emerged, which essentially still exists today. In close connection with the French Revolution, the ideas of freedom and equality had spread and the foundations of legitimate rule had been redefined. America was the continent of the first successful anticolonial freedom movements. These processes were very different from each other and also in themselves, and yet formed a unity.

In fact, the various revolutions in Spanish America were drastic events, for they drowned a colonial empire that had lasted 300 years, encompassed vast areas and was considered to be extraordinarily rich and promising in economic potential. In the Spanish American states themselves, independence quickly became the founding myth of the nation. National monuments in the central public places and independence days that celebrate the heroes of that epoch are still today decisive points of reference for national memory throughout the subcontinent and bear eloquent witness to the power of this narrative. History lessons at schools which derived the history of the fatherland, the *historia patria*, from the idealized events of independence in order to serve the integration of the nation have reinforced this perspective.[1]

---

[1] Stefan H. Rinke, *Revolutionen in Lateinamerika: Wege in die Unabhängigkeit, 1760–1830* (Munich: C. H. Beck, 2010), 11–19; Spanish translation: Stefan H. Rinke, *Las revoluciones en América Latina: Las vías a la independencia, 1760–1830* (Mexico City: Colegio de México Colegio Internacional de Graduados Entre Espacios, 2011), 15–25; see also Nikita Harwich Vallenilla, "La historia patria," in Antonio Annino and François-Xavier Guerra, eds., *Inventando la nación: Iberoamérica siglo XIX* (Mexico City: Fondo de Cultura Económica, 2003), 533–49; Rafael Valls, ed., *Los procesos independentistas Iberoamericanos en los manuales de Historia* (Madrid: Fundación Mapfre Tavera, 2005).

STEFAN RINKE

## Interpretations

The hero myths have long stood in the way of a critical examination of this part of Spanish American history. Although there has been a change in the historical images over the past few decades, with a tendency toward demythification, even if it has varied from country to country, the hero myths have prevented a critical confrontation with this part of Hispanic American history. But even today this still triggers polemics. In Venezuela, the pendulum has even been reversed since Hugo Chávez's presidency, and a direct relationship is being constructed between daily politics and the national liberation struggle at the beginning of the nineteenth century.[2] In short, independence remains an emotionally charged issue of high political and ideological – i.e. national – significance.[3]

In historiography, too, a narrative remained dominant in large parts of Spanish America until the end of the 1950s that presented the history of independence as the birth of the nation, ignoring or downplaying the great social and ethnic heterogeneity and regional differences. The wars of independence were thus the substrate of a national history in which good, American-born, "creole" white heroes fought against evil Spanish royalists. The "people" assumed to be homogeneous played only a subordinate role in this interpretation. Only through the leadership of the creole liberators, the *libertadores*, could this people become a nation.[4]

Since the 1960s, the interpretation of independence by professional historians have changed considerably, depending on the political situation and with different national variants. Influenced by the revolutionary upheavals that shaped the subcontinent in this phase, a revisionist historiography has

[2] Andreas Boeckh and Patricia Graf, "El comandante en su laberinto: El ideario bolivariano de Hugo Chávez," in Günter Maihold, ed., *Venezuela en retrospectiva: Los pasos hacia el régimen chavista* (Madrid: Iberoamericana, 2007), 151–79.

[3] Manuel Chust Calero and José Antonio Serrano, "Un debate actual, una revisión necesaria," in Manuel Chust and José Antonio Serrano, eds., *Debates sobre las Independencias Iberoamericanas* (Frankfurt am Main and Madrid: Iberoamericana Vervuert, 2007), 9.

[4] For more on this see the excellent overview by Chust Calero and Serrano, "Un debate actual," 10–25. For a historiographical synthesis of each individual country see the same compilation. For Mexico see Antonio Annino, Rafael Rojas, and Francisco A. Eissa-Barroso, eds., *La Independencia: Los libros de la Patria* (Mexico City: Centro de Investigación y Docencia Económicas, Fondo de Cultura Económica, 2008); as well as the essays in Josefina Zoraida Vázquez, ed., *Interpretaciones sobre la Independencia de México* (Mexico City: Ediciones Patria, 1997); for Brazil see István Jancsó, *Independência: História e Historiografia* (São Paulo: Hucitec, 2005), 53–206; Jurandir Malerba, "Introdução: Esboço crítico da recente historiografia sobre a Independência do Brasil (c. 1980–2002)," in Jurandir Malerba, ed., *A Independência Brasileira: Novas dimençoes* (Rio de Janeiro: FGV, 2006), 19–52.

questioned the old certainties of people and nation. The formerly untouchable heroes, their goals and limits, came under scrutiny and were thus taken from their pedestals. In this historiography the individual leader stepped more and more into the background anyway, as social theories like Dependency Theory helped put the focus primarily on social groups and classes and their interests and struggles.[5]

Revisionist historiography highlighted regional diversity and the contrasts between the regions, which were often counterproductive and continued to have an effect in the new states. The idea of a unified national path to independence could no longer be maintained. Instead, the focus was on the heterogeneity of the process. This also applied to the participants and protagonists of the wars of independence and the state-building processes, which were characterized by great differences in motivation and goals. In addition to the independence fighters – the patriots and the royalists – those who strove for autonomy under the umbrella of the liberal Spanish Constitution of 1812 also came into view. Independence, it was now pointed out, was not the a priori fixed goal of the elites with European roots, but initially only of a small minority which, however, asserted itself in the medium term. The myth of the inevitability of independence was thus questioned.[6] In addition to the creole ruling classes, the new historiography was devoted to other social and ethnic groups, Indigenous peoples, slaves, and other nonwhite population groups.[7]

Up until the 1980s, questions about the major structures were the guiding questions, but since the 1990s, the wave of democratization in the region has led to a renewed shift toward fresh themes. Since then, the great structuralist theories have been critically questioned, and small-scale negotiations have become the focus of historiographical interest. Political history, and in particular the question of the significance of elections, representation and citizenship have become the focus of attention. The different options for political action in the phase of independence could thus be clarified.[8] In

---

[5] Luis Navarro García, "La Independencia de Hispanoamérica," in Valentín Vázquez de Prada et al., eds., *Balance de la historiografía sobre Iberoamérica* (Pamplona: EUNSA Ediciones Universidad de Navarra, 1989), 395–440.

[6] See a good synthesis of this discussion in Brian R. Hamnett, "Process and Pattern: A Re-examination of the Ibero-American Independence Movements, 1808–1826," *Journal of Latin American Studies* 29:2 (1997), 279–328.

[7] George Reid Andrews, "Spanish American Independence: A Structural Analysis," *Latin American Perspectives* 1:44 (1985), 105–32.

[8] For an overview of the innovations until the mid-1990s see Victor M. Uribe-Uran, "The Enigma of Latin American Independence: Analyses of the Last Ten Years," *Latin American Research Review* 32:1 (Spring 1997), 237–55.

addition, the preoccupation with the "others," the nonprivileged, gained in importance, whose specific motivations and interests were revealed in recent historiography, thus adding an important dimension to the notion of the heterogeneity of the independence processes.[9]

For the contemporary actors and the early historiography, there was no question that a revolution had taken place and that it had brought positive results.[10] In his posthumously published manifest of 1799 the Peruvian Juan Pablo Viscardo y Guzmán wrote: "Let us rediscover America for all our brothers all over the world . . . !"[11] About two decades later, in 1820, at the height of the wars of independence, the radical politician Bernardo de Monteagudo from Buenos Aires spoke of irreversible "general laws" that subjected the states of the world to revolution during his time. The emphasis on a new beginning was characteristic of the early interpretations of events. It was comprehensive and concerned human beings as such, who were now perceived as individuals detached from corporate constraints, the society in which they lived, and the rule to which they freely submitted.[12] From the point of view of this generation, the break that the independence fighters experienced had a worldwide claim to effectiveness and was regarded as a process determined and necessary, as it were, by Providence, with a clear orientation toward the foundation of the nation, which was about to enjoy an equally straightforward success.[13]

---

[9] In particular, Eric Van Young has sparked a debate in this regard with his book *The Other Rebellion: Popular Violence, Ideology, and the Mexican Struggle for Independence, 1810–1821* (Stanford: Stanford University Press, 2001); see also Luis Miguel Glave, "Las otras rebeliones: Cultura popular e independencias," *Anuario de Estudios Americanos* no. 62 (2005): 275–312. Recently, Cultural Studies have examined particularly women's and gender-related issues in this perspective, see Barbara Potthast-Jutkeit, *Von Müttern und Machos: Eine Geschichte der Frauen Lateinamerikas* (Wuppertal: Hammer, 2003), 185–200; Catherine Davies, Claire Brewster, and Hilary Owen, eds., *South American Independence: Gender, Politics, Text* (Liverpool: Liverpool University Press, 2006); Claire Brewster, "Women and the Spanish American Wars of Independence: An Overview," *Feminist Review* no. 79 (2005): 20–35.

[10] Graciela Soriano, "Tiempos y destiempos de la Revolución," in Teresa Calderón and Clément Thibaud, eds., *Las revoluciones en el mundo atlántico: Una perspectiva comparada* (Bogotá: Taurus, 2006), 145–53.

[11] "Descubramos otra vez de nuevo la América para todos nuestros hermanos, los habitantes de este globo," in Juan Pablo Viscardo y Guzmán, *Carta dirigida a los Españoles Americanos*, ed. David Anthony Brading (Mexico City: Fondo de Cultura Económica, 2005), 91.

[12] François-Xavier Guerra, *Modernidad e independencias: Ensayos sobre las revoluciones hispánicas* (Mexico City: Fondo de Cultura Económica, 1993), 12; Annick Lempérière, "Revolución y Estado en América Hispánica (1808–1825)," in Calderón and Thibaud, *Las revoluciones en el mundo atlántico*, 55.

[13] Fabio Wasserman, "Revolución," in Noemí Goldman, ed., *Lenguaje y revolución: Conceptos políticos clave en el Río de la Plata, 1780–1850* (Buenos Aires: Prometeo Libros, 2008), 159–74: 164.

The revisionist historiography, however, questioned the formerly central idea of a revolutionary new beginning. Instead, it pointed to the obvious social and economic continuities between colonies and republics, thus creating the notion of a development from colonialism to neocolonialism. According to this interpretation, apart from Haiti, no revolution had taken place at all in America in the early nineteenth century. Depending on political intentions, the conclusion could be drawn that this revolution was still to come. There were important reasons for abandoning the optimistic metaphor of revolution: the realization that the persevering forces of the old elites hardly permitted social change. From a political point of view, critics also denounced the lack of radicalism, which had distinguished the Directory from the first stages of the French Revolution. Spanish American independence fighters, on the other hand, had regarded the Jacobin phase in France as a deterrent example. In view of these facts, a question came to the fore that George Reid Andrews formulated in 1985:

> How was it that violence of such duration and magnitude, provoking significant popular mobilization and taking place in societies riven by powerful internal conflicts and tensions, did not have a greater impact on the social and economic structures of the region? In short, why did the independence struggles, so often labeled "revolutions," in fact fail to produce anything remotely approaching a genuine social revolution?[14]

If historians of Spanish America still spoke of revolution at all, they did so by using the compromise formula of the "unfinished revolution."[15]

The latest historiography, on the other hand, has raised the question of what then is a "genuine social revolution" or a "complete revolution," and asks which criteria must be fulfilled in order to deserve this designation. For example, it was objected at an early stage that references to the French Revolution as an idealized model are questionable, since deviations from it are quickly misunderstood as deficits.[16] Besides, European movements that were in many respects "incomplete" are nevertheless called revolutions.[17]

---

[14] Andrews, "Spanish American Independence," 105.

[15] Alejandro Poli Gonzalvo, *Mayo, la revolución inconclusa: Reinterpretando la historia argentina* (Buenos Aires: Emecé, 2008).

[16] Manfred Kossok, "Alternativen gesellschaftlicher Transformationen in Lateinamerika: Die Unabhängigkeitsrevolutionen von 1790 bis 1830," *Jahrbuch für Geschichte Lateinamerikas*, 28 (1991), 223–49: 226.

[17] François-Xavier Guerra, "De lo uno a lo múltiple: Dimensiones y lógicas de la Independencia," in Anthony McFarlane and Eduardo Posada-Carbó, eds., *Independence and Revolution in Spanish America: Perspectives and Problems* (London: Institute of Latin American Studies, University of London, 1999), 49.

Undoubtedly, independence in Spanish America meant a political new beginning, which raised new questions about the location and legitimation of power. The fundamental discontinuity was evident in the political system with the system change of new elites, the new arguments about legitimacy, and the failure of efforts to return to the status quo ante. The political ideas of freedom and equality, of human and civil rights, and the practices used by the independence fighters to achieve broad political participation were revolutionary. These elements make it possible to speak for Spanish America during this period of revolutions in the plural, because the heterogeneity of the processes is obvious. Forms of anticolonial resistance grew into revolutions because they sought a new order in the sense of a nation state. This was not predetermined, but the result of dynamic processes with setbacks and of varying duration.[18]

In the course of the latest historiographical discussions about global history approaches, the dimension of the entanglements of Latin American events with the revolutions in other parts of the world has returned into the focus of interest.[19] This follows on from observations made by contemporaries such as Thomas Jefferson, who in 1797 referred to the events in Saint-Domingue as a "revolutionary storm" that swept across the globe.[20] Already in the older structuralist historiography the connections to Europe played an important role. Some historians interpreted Spanish American independence as a by-product of the rise of English industrial capitalism.[21] This Atlantic dimension of the revolutions also interested historians early on for ideological reasons against the background of the Cold War.[22] The focus,

---

[18] For an excellent discussion of the concept of "revolution" from the perspective of Global History see Jürgen Osterhammel, *Die Verwandlung der Welt: Eine Geschichte des 19. Jahrhunderts* (Munich: C. H. Beck, 2009), 736–47.

[19] For this discussion in Global History, see Sebastian Conrad and Andreas Eckert, "Globalgeschichte, Globalisierung, multiple Modernen: Zur Geschichtsschreibung der modernen Welt," in Sebastian Conrad, Andreas Eckert, and Ulrike Freitag, eds., *Globalgeschichte: Theorien, Ansätze, Themen* (Frankfurt am Main: Campus Verlag, 2007), 7–52.

[20] Jefferson to St. George Tucker, 27 August 1797, quoted in Simon P. Newman, "American Political Culture and the French and Haitian Revolutions: Nathaniel Cutting and Jeffersonian Republicans," in David Patrick Geggus, ed., *The Impact of the Haitian Revolution in the Atlantic World* (Columbia, SC: University of South Carolina Press, 2001), 79.

[21] Richard Graham, *Independence in Latin America: A Comparative Approach*, 2nd edition (New York: McGraw-Hill, 1994); Emilia Viotti Costa, *The Brazilian Empire: Myths & Histories* (Chapel Hill: University of North Carolina Press, 2000), 1–23.

[22] Jacques Godechot, *France and the Atlantic Revolution of the Eighteenth Century: 1770–1799*, trans. Herbert Harvey Rowen (London: Collier-Macmillan, 1965). A focus on the North

The Spanish Empire: General Overview

however, was on the North Atlantic "community of destiny," while the South Atlantic was only marginally mentioned.

Recent historiography has extended the Atlantic perspective more to the south. In this context, the idea of a "transcontinental liberation process" in America lasting about fifty years for the period from 1774 to 1826 gained currency.[23] Many studies in recent years have concentrated, for example, on the interactions of the American revolutions with the revolutionary upheavals in the mother countries. Especially the role of Spain with its liberal constitutions and the Cortes has been examined many times in recent years. A chain of revolutionary upheavals led from the detachment of Britain's North American colonies to the French Revolution, the revolution in Saint-Domingue and Napoleonic expansion on the Iberian Peninsula to the independence revolutions in Spanish America and Brazil.[24]

The independence of the United States challenged both the seemingly natural order of relations between Europe and America and of the monarchy as such. With the French Revolution, ideals of freedom and equality became even more central. The successful slave revolution in Haiti brought the entire economic and social system of slavery under attack. Finally, with the independence revolutions in the Iberian empires, two other pillars of colonial rule in America collapsed. In fact, a circle was closed that represented the "last common American experience," for after that the Americas went their separate ways.[25] Of the once proud Iberian empires, only the Spanish colonies of Cuba and Puerto Rico remained and France had lost its richest possession. However, the numerous possessions of different European powers in the Caribbean region continued to bear witness to the colonial past and to cause entanglements in the coming decades.

---

Atlantic is also central to Hobsbawm's argument, although his analysis is quite different from that of Godechot and Palmer. See also Eric J. Hobsbawm, *The Age of Revolution: Europe 1789–1848*, 3rd edition (London: Weidenfeld & Nicolson, 1996); Robert R. Palmer, *The Age of Democratic Revolution: A Political History of Europe and America, 1760–1800*, 6th edition (Princeton, NJ: Princeton University Press, 1969).

[23] Anthony McFarlane, "Issues in the History of Spanish American Independence," in McFarlane and Posada, eds., *Independence and Revolution*, vol. 1; Anthony McFarlane, "Independências Americanas na era das revoluções: Conexões, contextos, comparações," in Malerba, ed., *A Independência brasileira*, 387–417.

[24] Stefan Rinke and Klaus Stüwe, "Politische Systeme Amerikas: Ein Vergleich," in Klaus Stüwe and Stefan Rinke, eds., *Die politischen Systeme in Nord- und Lateinamerika: Eine Einführung* (Wiesbaden: VS Verlag für Sozialwissenschaften, 2008), 9-58.

[25] Felipe Fernández-Armesto, *The Americas: A Hemispheric History* (New York: Modern Library, 2003), 95.

In his monumental study on the world history of the nineteenth century, Jürgen Osterhammel has identified five levels of Atlantic integration in this period: administrative imperial integration, migration, trade (which gave rise to a common consumer culture), cultural transfers, and integration through an emerging transatlantic public sphere.[26] In fact, the Atlantic region consisted of large regions that were intertwined in many ways. Communication intensified and accelerated during this period, with the Caribbean in particular serving as a hub. Networks of enlightened thinkers emerged, moving back and forth between the American and European borders of the Atlantic. The Masonic lodges gave institutional support to these entanglements. The biographies of independence fighters such as Francisco de Miranda and Simón Bolívar are telling examples of these processes. Not only the revolutionary elites, but also common people, especially sailors and even slaves, were involved in these communication networks.

The United States and French revolutions were important as points of reference for Spanish American developments.[27] They showed that revolutionary upheaval was possible. The Spanish Americans also propagated the ideas of freedom and equality, of self-determination and of human and civil rights, which have had a global impact since 1776 and 1789.[28] These ideas contributed to the emergence of an – albeit limited – Atlantic space of experience from which the expectation of further revolutions could be derived.[29]

## Periodizations

Different approaches have come into play in the chronological classification of this process. In Spanish America, the founding of government juntas and the declaration of independence as such were the starting dates for the contemporaries and their early historiography. The end of the epoch was

---

[26] Osterhammel, *Die Verwandlung der Welt*, 770–1.

[27] Eric Van Young, "'To Throw Off a Tyrannical Government': Atlantic Revolutionary Traditions and Popular Insurgency in Mexico, 1800–1821," in Michael M. Morrison and Melinda S. Zook, eds., *Revolutionary Currents: Nation Building in the Transatlantic World* (Lanham: Rowman and Littlefield, 2004), 127–72: 131.

[28] Osterhammel, *Die Verwandlung der Welt*, 761.

[29] For Brazil in this context see João Paulo G. Pimenta, *Brasil y las independencias de Hispanoamérica* (Castelló de la Plana: Universitat Jaume I, 2007), 29; Jacques Godechot, "Independência do Brasil e a Revolução do Ocidente," in Carlos Guilherme Mota, ed., *1822: Dimensões* (São Paulo: Editora Perspectiva, 1972), 27–37.

# The Spanish Empire: General Overview

Colonial Spanish America, c. 1800

Map 1.1 Spanish America in 1800. From Leslie Bethell, ed., *The Independence of Latin America* (Cambridge: Cambridge University Press, 1991), 4.

then the last victorious battle, so that in classical representations the years from 1810 to 1826 can be found as chronological markers.

After European historiography, following Reinhart Koselleck's concept of the *Sattelzeit* of modernity, defined 1750 to 1850 as the decisive transformative period, historians of the Spanish American independence revolutions adopted this idea.[30] Thus, both the late colonial roots of events in the second half of the eighteenth century and the problematic processes of state-building up to the integration into the world market around the middle of the nineteenth century come into view. Eric Van Young has criticized this type of periodization because of its inherent eurocentrism, as it implied a unilinear development from enlightened absolutism to the revolutions of the United States and France and finally to the European revolutions of 1848, which were connected with a quasi-universal, unstoppable nation-building process and with the rise of liberalism.[31]

Nevertheless, there is much to be said for looking at the phase between 1760 and 1830 in its entirety, because both the prehistory and the deeper roots of the independence revolutions, as well as the direct consequences in state formation, come into view. Within this framework, however, there are different processes of change, each following its own temporal logic. It is important to consider these variations and heterogeneities in order to represent the multitude of intertwined but also independent liberation movements with their different orientations.

## The Crisis of the Empire

The crisis of the Spanish Empire did not start in the eighteenth century, but it intensified massively especially when the French Revolution broke out. In the late eighteenth century, as the threat of social unrest and foreign powers increased against the backdrop of the Atlantic revolution, while the Crown's ability to counteract diminished, the state of permanent setbacks and

---

[30] Important overviews are Tulio Halperín Donghi, *Reforma y disolución de los imperios ibéricos 1750–1850* (Madrid: Alianza, 1985); Kenneth J. Andrien and Lyman L. Johnson, eds., *The Political Economy of Spanish America in the Age of Revolution, 1750–1850* (Albuquerque: University of New Mexico Press, 1994); Víctor Manuel Uribe-Urán, ed., *State and Society in Spanish America during the Age of Revolution* (Wilmington, DE: Scholarly Resources, 2001). For individual countries see Alberto Flores Galindo, ed., *Independencia y revolución, 1780–1840*, 2 vols. (Lima: Instituto Nacional de Cultura, 1987); Jaime E. Rodríguez O., ed., *Mexico in the Age of Democratic Revolutions, 1750–1850* (Boulder: Rienner, 1994).

[31] Eric Van Young, "Conclusion: Was There an Age of Revolution in Spanish America?," in Uribe-Urán, ed., *State and Society*, 219–46.

The Spanish Empire: General Overview

insecurities was difficult to endure. The crisis was not least an expression of the problems of the Bourbon dynasty after the death of Carlos III in December 1788. His successor Carlos IV (1788–1808) was confronted with a difficult situation from the beginning, which he could not cope with. The state ministers Floridablanca and Aranda were unable to develop a constructive attitude toward the events in neighboring France.[32] In 1792, the king appointed Manuel de Godoy, the queen's twenty-five-year-old favorite, as first minister. He was to determine the fate of the country until 1808. This measure caused much envy and rejection; Godoy was considered corrupt and incapable. In view of the increasing burdens and unresolved problems, the displeasure with Godoy grew in the following period, as did the implicit displeasure with the Crown.[33]

The British American struggle for independence had different consequences for Spain, for it contributed significantly to the ruin of French public finances, which in turn was a major cause of the French Revolution. Spain and its colonies were soon drawn into the maelstrom of global conflicts from 1792 to 1815, although the Crown had wanted to stay out of the conflicts.[34] After the execution of Louis XVI, Carlos IV fought on the side of the European coalition against the neighboring country from 1793 to 1795, not least for fear of an invasion. After the Peace of Basel (1795), which was detrimental to Spain and brought, among other things, the loss of the eastern part of Hispaniola to France, the change of sides took place and in 1796, in the Second Treaty of San Ildefonso, they joined the French Directorate in the fight against England.[35] Until 1808, there was an almost constant state of war against England. A direct consequence was the growing dependence on France. Spain had clearly become a pawn in Napoleon's power politics in Europe.

This became very clear a short time later in America, when English troops threatened the Río de la Plata. After the Battle of Trafalgar (1805),

---

[32] Christian Windler, "Spanien und die Französische Revolution," in Christian Simon, ed., *Basler Frieden 1795: Revolution und Krieg in Europa* (Basel: Merian, 1995), 140–50. See also the essays in Robert M. Maniquis, Oscar R. Martí, and Joseph Pérez, eds., *La revolución francesa y el mundo ibérico* (Madrid: Sociedad Estatal Quinto Centenario, 1989).

[33] Peer Schmidt, "Absolutismus und Aufklärung: Die Bourbonen im 18. Jh.," in Pedro A. Barceló and Peer Schmidt, eds., *Kleine Geschichte Spaniens* (Stuttgart: Reclam, 2002), 242–47.

[34] Stig Förster, "Der Weltkrieg 1792–1815: Bewaffnete Konflikte und Revolutionen in der Weltgesellschaft," in Jost Dülffer, ed., *Kriegsbereitschaft und Friedensordnung in Deutschland, 1800–1814* (Münster: Lit, 1995), 17–38.

[35] Jean-Joël Brégeon, *Napoléon et la guerre d'Espagne, 1808–1814* (Paris: Perrin, 2006), 55–67.

the English tried to undermine Spanish rule in the colonies. In June 1806, they occupied the rich port city of Buenos Aires.[36] Since the viceroy fled to the hinterland, the mayor, Martin de Alzaga, a merchant from Spain, and the French officer in Spanish service, Santiago Liniers, took over the defense. Liniers vowed "the defense of the homeland" as "one of the most sacred duties of man."[37] The mobilization efforts were successful and the urban militias, which were clearly outnumbered and poorly equipped, defeated the English twice in 1806 and 1807. This success caused great patriotic enthusiasm among the creoles of America, for it proved to the world that the people of America, often regarded as inferior, were better able to defy the British superpower than the Spaniards themselves.[38] At the same time, the inability of the Spanish Crown and its representatives to satisfy elementary needs became apparent before all eyes. In particular, the element of insecurity, externally because of the threat posed by the major European powers but also internally because of social instability, for example, in areas of limited statehood shaped by escaped slaves or Indigenous groups, played an important role. The permanent compulsion to self-defense and the associated costs put the willingness to remain loyal to the king to the test.

The power situation changed abruptly in 1808 with the outbreak of the Spanish war against France, and Spain suddenly became an ally of England. The motherland, England and France were bound in Europe. Thus there was temporarily no Great Power present that could have intervened decisively in America. The resulting vacuum offered the creoles unprecedented opportunities.[39] In addition, the balance of power had also shifted significantly in favor of the American elites from an economic point of view. The almost permanent war undermined the Spanish economy. This was particularly true for trade with the colonies, since the English had been playing out their

---

[36] About the English policy see William W. Kaufmann, *British Policy and the Independence of Latin America, 1804–1828*, 2nd edition (London: Cass, 1967), 11–52; Ian Fletcher, *The Waters of Oblivion: The British Invasion of the Rio de la Plata, 1806–1807* (Tunbridge Wells: Spellmount, 1991).

[37] Proclamation by Santiago de Liniers, 9 September 1806, in Stefan Rinke, Georg Fischer, and Frederik Schulze, eds., *Geschichte Lateinamerikas vom 19. bis zum 21. Jahrhundert: Quellenband* (Stuttgart: J. B. Metzler, 2009), 6–7.

[38] Klaus Gallo, *De la invasión al reconocimiento: Gran Bretaña y el Río de la Plata, 1806–1826* (Buenos Aires: A-Z, 1994), 47–122; José Luis Speroni, *La dimensión de una agresión: América del Sur ante la invasión inglesa de 1805–1807* (Buenos Aires: Edivern, 2004).

[39] Jeremy Adelman, *Sovereignty and Revolution in the Iberian Atlantic* (Princeton, NJ: Princeton University Press, 2006), 179–80.

The Spanish Empire: General Overview

supremacy at sea, blocking Spanish ports and thus paralyzing communication routes to America.[40] Approaches to remedy the situation by liberalizing colonial trade were carried out only half-heartedly and did not have the hoped for success.

The attempt to manage the financial crisis by selling Church property, the so-called *desamortización*, which had become necessary due to the high costs of warfare and the associated national debt, also caused irritation. Many creoles experienced the fiscal measures as a deep cut threatening their existence. The effect for Spain, however, was limited in view of the ongoing wars. In many places, the unpopular Godoy was blamed for the misguided developments and discontent increased.[41]

The Spanish crisis reached rock bottom when Napoleon finally annexed the Iberian Peninsula and eliminated the Spanish Bourbons by forcing King Carlos and his son Prince Fernando at a meeting in Bayonne to abdicate and cede their throne to his brother Joseph Bonaparte in June 1808.[42] However, Napoleon had reckoned without the Spanish people, who from the outset had rejected the French Revolution with its anticlerical excesses and violence. Everywhere in the country, local committees of dignitaries, so-called juntas, were formed to take over the political decision-making power in the name of Fernando VII and to organize the armed resistance. The Napoleonic armies defeated the regular Spanish army supported by an English contingent. However, the conflict was not over, and it led to a guerrilla war to preserve the legitimate rule.[43] In September 1808, a newly formed central junta (Junta Suprema Central) claimed to exercise governmental power until Fernando's return.[44]

---

[40] The old monopoly hold by the port of Cádiz was particularly cut off from the overseas traffic. Antonio García-Baquero González, *Comercio colonial y guerras revolucionarias: La decadencia económica de Cádiz a raíz de la Emancipación americana* (Seville: Escuela de Estudios Hispano-Americanos de Sevilla, 1972), 114.

[41] For the situation in Mexico see Gisela von Wobeser, "La consolidación de vales reales como factor determinante de la lucha de Independencia en México, 1804–1808," *Historia Mexicana* 56:2 (2006), 373–425; Brian R. Hamnett, *La política española en una época revolucionaria, 1790–1820* (Mexico City: Fondo de Cultura Económica, 1985), 47–58.

[42] Brégeon, *Napoléon et la guerre d'Espagne*, 82–94; Timothy E. Anna, *Spain and the Loss of America* (Lincoln: University of Nebraska Press, 1983), 9–28.

[43] José Manuel Cuenca Toribio, *La guerra de la Independencia: Un conflicto decisivo, 1808–1814* (Madrid: Encuentro, 2006); José Gregorio Cayuela Fernández, *La Guerra de la Independencia: Historia bélica, pueblo y nación en España, 1808–1814* (Salamanca: Universidad de Salamanca, 2008).

[44] For more about the competition between the juntas see José María Portillo Valdés, *Crisis Atlántica: Autonomía e Independencia en la crisis de la Monarquía hispana* (Madrid: Marcial Pons Historia, 2006), 53–9.

## Colonial Reactions

The events in Spain could not leave the American colonies untouched. The danger posed by the French invasion drove the central junta to involve the creoles more closely in order to increase their loyalty to the empire and their financial support for the war effort.[45] The announcements were intensively discussed in public and aroused high expectations. At the same time, there was uncertainty about who was to govern in the interim. Following the Spanish models, regionally influential creoles started to form their own juntas in the name of the king, claiming equal rights to representation as their peninsular counterparts.[46] In 1809, elections were staged in the colonies. But from the outset there had been criticism of an electoral system that divided the huge and populous colonies into only nine constituencies, each with one deputy, whereas Spain had thirty-six seats. Equal rights remained out of reach.[47] The *audiencias* of Quito and Upper Peru counted among the American regions that were not represented. In both cases the creole juntas radicalized their demands in the face of stubborn denial by the Spaniards and were eventually defeated militarily. The incidents revealed that the situation was very tense. The more the royal authorities and bureaucrats opposed the creoles' wishes for participation, the more they were willing to dare the uprising.

The radicalization of creole demands took place against the background of the increasing weakening of the central junta in Spain. In view of the state crisis, the members of this body had realized that they did not have the mandate to reorganize the political relations of Spain and the colonies. In return, the Spanish legal tradition provided for a general assembly, the Cortes. After long discussions, it was decided on 1 January 1810 to call

---

[45] Richard Hocquellet, "La publicidad de la Junta Central española, 1808–1810," in François-Xavier Guerra and Annick Lempérière, eds., *Los espacios públicos en Iberoamérica: Ambigüedades y problemas: Siglos XVIII–XIX* (Mexico City: Centro Francés de Estudios Mexicanos y Centroamericanos, 1998), 140–67.

[46] Eduardo Martiré, *1808: Ensayo Histórico-Jurídico sobre la clave de la emancipación Hispanoamericana* (Buenos Aires: Instituto de Investigaciones de Historia del Derecho, 2001), 242–9.

[47] About the electoral procedures see also Víctor Peralta Ruiz, "Elecciones, constitucionalismo y revolución en El Cusco, 1809–1815," *Revista de Indias* 56: 206 (1996): 100–9; Nettie Lee Benson, "The Elections of 1809: Transforming Political Culture in New Spain," *Mexican Studies*, no. 20 (2004): 1–20; Jordana Dym, *From Sovereign Villages to National States: City, State, and Federation in Central America, 1759–1839* (Albuquerque: University of New Mexico Press, 2006), 75–82; Valentín Paniagua Corazao, *Los orígenes del gobierno representativo en el Perú: Las elecciones, 1809–1826* (Lima: Fondo Editorial PUCP, 2003), 65–9.

elections to the Cortes in order to prevent the collapse of Spain. The assembly was to begin its work in September 1810. The elections, which now had to be held, took place under severe conditions, because in America autonomy movements gained momentum and civil wars broke out. This was also an expression of the creoles' dissatisfaction with the electoral process. Despite their significantly higher population, they were allowed far fewer representatives than the Spaniards.[48]

The Spanish invitation to the Americans to send representatives, which came about under the pressure of the intensifying state emergency and was actually intended to weld the parts of the empire closer together, was ultimately to have a counterproductive effect. One reason for this was the discrepancy between the rhetoric of equality and the narrow-mindedness and paternalism that the Americans had to experience time and again in their dealings with the motherland and its officials. Another reason was the creole self-confidence that had grown since the end of the eighteenth century. Creoles were no longer satisfied with the more or less generous offers of participation and integration from Spain, but they were increasingly self-reliant and would quickly go beyond the demand for more autonomy. In the eyes of the creoles, the central junta, the Regency Council and, finally, the Cortes did not have the degree of legitimacy that seemed necessary to rule in the name of the king. Thus, the political crisis of the motherland caused by the international context in the Atlantic World led to an unprecedented politicization and radicalization of the colonies. If equality with Spain was not possible, it had to be achieved without Spain.

The year 1810 was to see creoles in many parts of America take a decisive step toward a more offensive pursuit of their own interests. The reasons for the creole pursuit of autonomy can be traced back to the multitude of internal and external crises of Spanish colonial rule at the end of the eighteenth and early nineteenth centuries. For some time, the frustration of the creole elites had been accumulating, partly due to the imposition of Bourbon reforms. But an external shock was necessary to get the process going. The reason for the first phase of the independence movements in Spanish America was the Atlantic context, more precisely the reaction to the

---

[48] Portillo Valdés, *Crisis Atlántica*, 124–58; Roberto Breña, *El primer Liberalismo español y los procesos de Emancipación de América, 1808–1824: Una revisión historiográfica del Liberalismo hispánico* (Mexico City: El Colegio de México, 2006), 131–40; Manuel Chust Calero, *La cuestión nacional americana en las Cortes de Cádiz* (Valencia: Biblioteca Historia Social, 1999), 36–41.

French invasion and the resulting collapse of the dynasty in Spain.[49] These events posed the problem of the legitimacy of rule and thus automatically the question of the modes of governance for public officials, whose authority was ultimately fed by the person of a king who was now absent. In fact, the very different movements in the American regions were linked by the common reference to the loss of legitimacy of the motherland by the forced resignation of Fernando VII and by the escalating crisis that began in 1808.

This argument was used by political leaders everywhere in America to defend their claims to autonomy and eventually even their declarations of independence. These were not hard revolutionary ruptures, but rather events in which the elites cautiously groped their way into unknown territory and gradually expanded their own ideas and demands. They were driven by the dynamics of the processes that they had triggered with their originally conservatively conceived actions. The developments remained integrated into a dense network of transatlantic interactions. The convening of the Spanish Cortes, the elections, and American participation brought about political upheavals that culminated in the liberal Constitution of Cádiz in 1812. The ideas of popular sovereignty and political representation formulated there were taken up by the creoles in America, and thus ultimately led to the demand for self-government. The Cortes policy toward America was an attempt to persuade the breakaway colonies to turn back peacefully.[50]

There were great differences in the local processes, of course. It was not a uniform liberation movement, even if an older historiography or the view from outside often suggested this. On the other hand, the different processes that unfolded in the spaces already created in colonial times were also intertwined with each other and were to become increasingly entangled over the course of time. This applied, for example, to the northern Andean region or the Río de la Plata, where local juntas interlocked but also fought against each other.

The initiators belonged to the creole population whose political experience was limited. Within this stratum, the rich landowning oligarchy was generally more moderate in direction, while a more radical orientation could be found among younger, academically educated men from professions such as lawyers, pastors, and the military. They used city councils as a breeding

---

[49] John Lynch, "Spanish American Independence in Recent Historiography," in McFarlane and Posada, eds., *Independence and Revolution*, 17.

[50] See also Demetrio Ramos Pérez, *España en la independencia de América* (Madrid: Editorial MAPFRE, 1996), 325.

ground of local authority and used the tried and tested method of convening open city councils to emphasize their demands for regional autonomy and political change. Following, and with explicit reference to, the Spanish role models, they created governing juntas, which at first emphasized that they exercised governmental power in the name of the legitimate king. Only in the course of the following years did further steps emerge, when regional juntas finally declared independence.

## The First Phase of Independence (1810–1814)

The early phase of independence was not completely unsuccessful despite the setbacks for the creole patriots caused by the reconquest of large portions by a Spanish expedition corps. Creoles invoked the old idea, generally shared among the Spanish kingdoms, that sovereignty should revert to the people in the absence of the monarch. The ideas of the Enlightenment, which until 1808 circulated only in secret, now gained importance as arguments in daily politics, which were carried out in new forms of publicity. On this basis the creole leaders succeeded – albeit often only temporarily – in pushing through the change of the system of government from the dynastic principle of divine grace and absolutism to the principle of popular sovereignty and the idea of citizenship.[51] At the same time they tried to create identity by increasing reference to their own homeland region, the *patria*. The old motherland of Spain, on the other hand, became the stepmother, the other from whom one had to distinguish oneself. The creoles used different symbolic actions such as the construction of monuments and especially the reference to the Indigenous heritage. In this way they constructed a history of centuries of oppression and heroic resistance that could become foundational myths.

However, these constructions of identity did not carry far and so the independence movements were not able to assert themselves in this phase. It was therefore comparatively easy for the Spaniards to strike back in the motherland after the restoration and, with the exception of the Río de la Plata, to recapture all areas by 1816. One reason for this was Fernando's return and the repeal of the Constitution of 1812, as this seemed to clarify the question of legitimacy. The fact that the old viceroyalties were strongholds of the royalists also contributed to Spanish military success. This applied in

---

[51] For a critical study on the sovereignty of the people see Isabela Restrepo Mejía, "La soberanía del 'pueblo' durante la época de la Independencia, 1810–1815," *Historia Crítica*, no. 29 (2005): 101–23.

particular to Peru, and, after the suppression of the social revolutionary attempts under Hidalgo and Morelos, also to New Spain. For royal officers like the Peruvian viceroy Abascal even the regulations of Cádiz were excessive. They undermined them, true to the old motto "[o]ne obeys but does not execute," to stop the dissolution of the Old Regime. Elsewhere the royalists were by no means defeated either and they were not only European Spaniards and their troops, but there was support from various social and ethnic camps.

Regionalism had an even more counterproductive effect. On the one hand, it resulted from different and sometimes contradictory interests of individual regions, for example in the question of free trade or inland navigation. In addition, personal animosities within the creole upper classes between rival caudillos and clan disputes torpedoed the common efforts in this phase. There was also a political element. The American patriots spoke of the sovereignty of the people, but did not yet mean the people of the state in the modern sense, but the corporate representation of individual communities.[52] This meant that individual cities or provinces insisted on their independence and were prepared to fight for it. The smoldering contrast between the provinces and old centers of the colonial empire became tangible again.

This conflict was manifest in an increasing level of violence. What rose in many regions of Spanish America were not only anticolonial liberation movements, but also bloody civil wars for power. The militarization of society took on new dimensions through forced recruitment and war contributions that had to be paid by all social classes. The French ideal of the political soldier also played an important role. The new citizen (*ciudadano*) was the born soldier, and in many places joining the militia was a precondition for the right to vote. As a result, the deserter became a new enemy of the state, who was outside the order and had to be eradicated. The fact that the desertion figures nevertheless remained high in many places shows how little the mobilization efforts ultimately yielded.

This was not least due to the problematic treatment of the nonprivileged population by the creole upper classes. The use of the "Indios" as a symbol of oppression and the abolition of the Indigenous tributes did not mean that the precarious situation of the Indigenous population, which represented the majority in many places, had fundamentally changed. Indeed, in many cases

[52] Riekenberg has developed this idea regarding the Río de la Plata in Michael Riekenberg, *Kleine Geschichte Argentiniens* (Munich: Beck, 2009), 60–1.

their situation had been aggravated by the Crown's lax protection. Therefore, Indians also took up arms to defend the king as guarantor of the order. As a rule, however, they tried to stay out of the conflicts of the whites and secure the survival of their communities in uncertain times. In principle, this focus on one's own narrowly defined space resembled the attitude of most creoles, but there were also Indigenous groups engaged in wider political goals on either side.

It was undoubtedly the greatest weakness of the heterogeneous independence movements in this phase that large sections of the nonprivileged population remained excluded, and that leading patriots feared their participation after the events in France and Haiti. Francisco de Miranda had already summed this up in 1799, when he wrote to a friend: "We have two great examples in mind: the American Revolution and the French Revolution, let us carefully imitate the first; let us carefully avoid the fatal consequences of the second."[53] The sociorevolutionary potential of the uprisings was visible only exceptionally, as in the case of New Spain.

On the other hand, because of the growing importance of the public there was a willingness to appeal to the general population. In a flood of printed matter, sermons and political speeches, various interest groups turned to the lower classes and attempted to mobilize them for their purposes and instrumentalize them as power factors. Repeatedly, the urban masses intervened when juntas were to be founded and Spanish officials removed. However, the "broad masses" could not always be controlled in the desired sense, but pursued their own specific interests. Their protest developed a sometimes-threatening momentum of its own. This was due to the fact that equality was invoked in the appeals to the lower classes and the revolutionary rhetoric of freedom spread from the Atlantic context.

A certain political participation – even if only as claqueurs – was now actually possible for many for the first time. Men from the lower classes fought in the revolutionary armies to which they were lured with great promises. Later they were glorified and celebrated as heroes. This awakened expectations, which were usually not fulfilled, because the sociopolitical interests of most creoles were conservative. Hope, however, remained alive and could not simply be forgotten, even when the Spanish Crown set about turning back the wheel of history in 1814.

---

[53] Francisco de Miranda to Manuel Gual, London, 31 December 1799, quoted in Michael Zeuske, *Francisco de Miranda und die Entdeckung Europas: Eine Biographie* (Münster: Lit, 1995), 291.

## The Road to Independence

The years 1814 and 1815 were dark years for the cause of the independence movements in America. The return of the king, according to the public statements of most local actors, should have meant the end of the uprising, because the juntas had claimed to rule in Fernando's name and were afraid of the radical measure of the final rupture for a long time. A peaceful return to the status quo ante did not and could not happen due to two factors. Firstly, the events in America and the idea of self-government had already taken on too much of a life of their own. For the new generation of liberators like Simón Bolívar or José de San Martín there could be no turning back. On the other hand, the harsh restoration policy of Fernando VII went far beyond what even the moderate creoles, which had been oriented toward the Constitution of Cádiz, were inclined to tolerate. Conflicts were therefore inevitable from May 1814 and they were to take place on two fronts, the inner-Spanish and the American.

Instead of reforms, Fernando VII had the Inquisition reintroduced and took back freedom of the press. He also sent the strongest military contingent in Spanish colonial history under the command of General Pablo Morillo to South America to reestablish the absolutist regime and silence the last trouble spots. This strategy was successful at first sight, as almost all areas except the Río de la Plata were reconquered by 1815. But those were pyrrhic victories. In 1815, not only Bolívar but most contemporary observers knew that the chance for a consensus was lost. Thus Fernando VII missed the opportunity to reunite the empire under his leadership, given the original willingness of the creoles to negotiate and the broad loyalty of the lower classes to the king.[54]

Essential prerequisites for the comparative ease of the Spanish reconquest were the inner strife and regionalism of the independence movements. In addition, however, there was another central element, the existence of a royalist stronghold in the old Viceroyalty of Peru. From here, the troops that defeated the junta movement in Quito stopped the advancing army from Buenos Aires in High Peru and killed the *patria vieja* in Chile.[55] Peru was the royalist sting in the flesh of the republicans and the core to which the Spanish

---

[54] Michael P. Costeloe, *Response to Revolution: Imperial Spain and the Spanish American Revolutions, 1810–1840* (Cambridge: Cambridge University Press, 1986), 60–75.

[55] Julio M. Luqui-Lagleyze, *"Por El Rey, La Fe y La Patria": El Ejército Realista del Perú en la Independencia Sudamericana, 1810–1825* (Madrid: Ministerio de Defensa, Secretaría General Técnica, 2005), 322–9.

The Spanish Empire: General Overview

restoration could tie itself. In Peru, the upheavals that had rocked the neighboring regions since 1808 had passed almost without a trace. In view of the social structure of the viceroyalty, with its high Indigenous population and the experience of the great uprisings of the 1780s, the willingness to take revolutionary risks was particularly low in Peru.[56] Not even the Peruvian liberals, who had the *Mercurio Peruano* at their disposal at an early stage as a printing medium, dared to think beyond the boundaries of the colonial system.[57] A relatively large number of conservative aristocrats and European Spaniards wanted to secure the social status quo in these troubled times, anyway.[58] Accordingly, the reactions to the Spanish election calls in 1808–1809 in Peru were very moderate.

Lima, despite its control over the trade and credit system, was not to be equated with the entire viceroyalty, throughout which upheavals took place under the royalist surface. Even in the Capital in 1810 there had been individual conspiracies of liberal creoles, which had in vain suggested the founding of a junta. Larger revolts then took place mainly in the local provinces with the rebellion of Pumacahua in Cuzco in 1814–1815 as a climax.[59] Yet the royalists had the upper hand. The Viceroyalty of Peru remained a constant threat to the independence movements in neighboring regions.

Especially in the Río de la Plata, the danger emanating from the northern neighbor had already been felt painfully several times. The fight against the viceroy in Lima tied forces that were consequently lacking for the suppression of the resident inner provinces such as the opposing side of the river, the so-called "Banda Oriental" where the creoles rejected the claims to supremacy from the rival port city of Buenos Aires. Indeed, under governor – and later viceroy – Francisco Xavier Elío, Montevideo became a royalist stronghold, though causing the rise of a local resistance movement under José Gervasio Artigas. After all, the area including the United Provinces of South

---

[56] Flores Galindo, "Independencia y clases sociales," in Flores Galindo, ed., *Independencia y revolución, 1780–1840*, vol. 1, 121–43.

[57] Carmen McEvoy, "'Seríamos excelentes vasallos y nunca ciudadanos': Prensa republicana y cambio social en Lima, 1791–1822," in Iván Jaksić, ed., *The Political Power of the World: Press and Oratory in Nineteenth-Century Latin America* (London: Institute of Latin American Studies, 2002), 34–63.

[58] Hamnett, "Process and Pattern," 297–8.

[59] John R. Fisher, "The Royalist Regime in the Viceroyalty of Peru, 1820–1824," *Journal of Latin American Studies*, 32 (2000), 55–84: 59; Lizardo Seiner Lizárraga, "La rebelión de Tacna de 1811," in Scarlett O'Phelan Godoy, ed., *La Independencia en el Perú: De los Borbones a Bolívar* (Lima: Pontificia Universidad Católica del Perú, Instituto Riva-Agüero, 2001), 57–76.

America, and the Republic of Paraguay was a region in which the independence movements had been able to assert themselves. However, this was not so much due to their own strength, which was still small due to domestic instability, as to the isolation and lack of an energetic offensive on the part of the Spanish.[60]

From Buenos Aires, under the command of General José de San Martín, the liberation of Chile and – at least indirectly – of the Banda Oriental could be prepared. This was not just a success story. The provincialist contrasts soon appeared in the Río de la Plata with undiminished severity. There were separatist tendencies that prevented the formation of a state for a long time. It was to take decades before the state of Argentina was united.[61]

The Spanish reconquest concentrated on the north of South America, especially New Granada and Venezuela. General Pablo Morillo recaptured large areas by the end of 1816 and subjected them to his ruthless regime. However, he provoked resistance. Bolívar returned to Venezuela as early as 1816 from exile in Haiti. Although he had to struggle with setbacks and rival caudillos, he was able to proclaim the Third Republic in the provincial city of Angostura in 1817. Bolívar was now prepared to take radical measures to assert himself. Thus he promised liberation to the slaves who were willing to fight for his cause. In addition, he allied himself with the leader of the cavalry of the *llaneros*, José Antonio Páez. After struggles that were by no means free of setbacks, in February 1819, at a congress in Angostura, he was able to announce his ideas for the drafting of the new state of Greater Colombia, which would include Venezuela, New Granada, and Quito. A little later, Bolívar led the victorious campaign in New Granada. The Battle of Boyacá (7 August 1819) tipped the balance in his favor.[62]

The threat from the Spaniards remained despite the military success of Bolívar. They still controlled the important cities of Cartagena and Caracas and held strongholds in the old viceroyalties of New Spain and Peru. At the end of 1819 a new expeditionary corps was assembled in Cádiz, with whom

---

[60] Anna, *Spain and the Loss of America*, 158–88.

[61] David Bushnell, *Reform and Reaction in the Platine Provinces, 1810–1852* (Gainesville: University Press of Florida, 1983), 124–5; José Carlos Chiaramonte, "El federalismo argentino," in Marcello Carmagnani, ed., *Estado y sociedad en América Latina, 1850–1930* (Barcelona: Editorial Crítica, 1984), 94–5; Sergio Guerra Vilaboy, *El dilema de la Independencia: Las luchas sociales en la Emancipación Latinoamericana, 1790–1826*, 2nd edition (Bogotá: Fundación Universidad Central, 2000), 285–8.

[62] Rebecca Earle, *Spain and the Independence of Colombia, 1810–1825* (Exeter: University of Exeter Press, 2000), 75–90; John Lynch, *Simón Bolívar: A Life* (New Haven: Yale University Press, 2006), 99–102.

General Morillo planned the reconquest. However, it could not run out because a liberal revolt in Spain gave the developments a decisive turn. There again a government junta was formed, which had the Constitution reinstated. The struggles against the independence movement were temporarily suspended and elections were scheduled. But the regions that had already achieved independence, such as the Río de la Plata, Chile, and "Gran Colombia," were not prepared to participate in the elections. The lack of confidence in Spanish politics proved to be justified, as the "American question" quickly revealed the well-known discrepancies between the members of parliament from the colonies and the European Spaniards. From 1821, Spain sank into domestic chaos and many American delegates returned to their home regions before time. Now the step toward independence was not far off.[63]

New Spain, which had been a royalist center in America since the suppression of the social revolution in 1815, regained a revolutionary dynamic. The participants, who were now primarily recruited from the creole ruling classes, deliberately proceeded cautiously in order to avoid the negative experiences of the early phase. In 1821, the officer Agustín de Iturbide opted for the compromise by which he was able to mobilize a majority in the so-called "Plan of Iguala." According to this plan, New Spain was to become independent, but at the same time the Catholic religion was to be preserved as the state religion, a balance was to be struck between creoles and Spaniards, and the constitutional monarchy was to be introduced. This compromise formula, which united a wide range of interest groups from creole liberals to monarchists and even Spaniards, was unusual. As expected, Fernando VII rejected the crown offered to him by the Mexicans. Thereupon, Iturbide proclaimed himself emperor of a hereditary monarchy in May 1822. A year later the monarchical experiment came to an end. A republican constitution came into force in 1824.[64]

The revolutionary events in Spain and Mexico also brought movement into the political landscape of Central America. The liberals, who advocated independence, and the conservatives, who were satisfied with reforms within the colonial system, confronted each other. In addition, there were pronounced local rivalries. Ultimately, the solution came from New Spain.

---

[63] Hans-Joachim König, *Auf dem Wege zur Nation: Nationalismus im Prozess der Staats- und Nationbildung Neu-Granadas 1750 bis 1856* (Stuttgart: Steiner, 1988), 225–31.
[64] Breña, *El primer Liberalismo español*, 430–3; Timothy E. Anna, "Agustin de Iturbide and the Process of Consensus," in Christon I. Archer, ed., *The Birth of Modern Mexico, 1780–1824* (Wilmington, DE: Scholarly Resources, 2003), 187–204.

The successful Iturbide militarily enforced Central America's annexation to Mexico at the beginning of 1822. With Iturbide's fall, however, this alliance also ended very quickly. The United Provinces of Central America dissolved and founded a federation comprising five more-or-less independent states.[65]

In the north of the former colonial empire, independence was finally secured in 1821. Only in the Caribbean did the "always faithful island" of Cuba and Puerto Rico remain as the remains of the formerly proud empire. There, the creole upper classes had arranged themselves for the time being with the colonial system. These slaveholders profited from the sugar boom that the loss of production on neighboring islands such as Haiti promoted.

What remained was the still fiercely contested Andean region. The liberators Bolívar from the north and San Martín from the south forced independence here by means of a forceps-like attack. Militarily at eye level, the Venezuelan was the more successful politician. After a meeting of the two in Guayaquil in July 1822, San Martín, who had advocated a monarchical solution, voluntarily withdrew into European exile. Bolívar was unable to complete the military liberation of the Andean region until 1826. In Quito, Peru, and High Peru, the creole ruling classes greeted him with mixed feelings. In Quito, the invasion itself was already controversial, while in Lower and Upper Peru, Bolívar's troops were soon regarded more as occupiers than liberators.[66] The creoles of Peru feared social revolution and had therefore called a *protector* into the country in 1821. Although Upper Peru took the name Bolivia in honor of the "Liberator," here too opportunism led the elites in 1825 to join the cause of independence. The existing conditions for the establishment of the new republican order were therefore not necessarily good.[67]

In fact, the independence movement quickly disintegrated after the end of the Spanish threat. The maintenance of the liberation army cost a lot of money and soon there were xenophobic riots in Peru and Bolivia. Bolívar's project of a large Andean confederation was doomed to failure. Frustrated, Bolívar's confidant, General Antonio José de Sucre, left Bolivia in 1828. The

---

[65] Carlos Meléndez Chaverri, *La Independencia de Centroamérica* (Madrid: Editorial Mapfre, 1993), 192–8.

[66] Timothy E. Anna, "The Peruvian Declaration of Independence: Freedom by Coercion," *Journal of Latin American Studies* 7 (1975), 221–69; Paniagua Corazao, *Los orígenes del gobierno representativo*, 274–8; Demetrio Ramos Pérez, *Entre el Plata y Bogotá: Cuatro claves de la Emancipación Ecuatoriana* (Madrid: Ediciones Cultura Hispánica del Centro Iberoamericano de Cooperación, 1978), 341–50.

[67] Jorge Siles Salinas, *La Independencia de Bolivia* (Madrid: Editorial MAPFRE, 1992), 325–30.

The Spanish Empire: General Overview

Map 1.2 The Spanish empire in 1824

"Liberator" himself had had to return to Greater Colombia two years earlier to halt the disintegration process that was looming there. By means of a dictatorship he wanted to stabilize the situation again. But this attempt failed just like the large-scale Pan-American Congress that Bolívar had convened in Panama in 1826. Disintegration ruled the day. Venezuela and Ecuador separated in 1830 from Greater Colombia, which now called itself New Granada again. The end of the Spanish threat had made the cohesion of the different regions superfluous. Now the old regionalisms clashed again with undiminished severity and led to nation-building wars.[68]

In sum, in 1814, the relapse into reaction triggered resistance. Capital mistakes by a monarch and an anachronistic Spanish policy that stubbornly refused to face reality were decisive. The behavior of the Spanish military strengthened the fighting spirit even of those parts of the population that had fought for the king for a long time. It also deepened the ideological divide created by the unfulfilled promise of popular sovereignty and political representation. The royalist commanders did not fulfill the population's longing for peace anywhere after their successes in the mid-1810s, and they unwittingly brought about a change of mind among many Spanish Americans through the burdens of recruitment and war contributions. From 1820 onwards, when the liberal revolution in Spain revived, chances

[68] Marta Irurozqui Victoriano, "De cómo el vecino hizo al ciudadano en Charcas y de cómo el ciudadano conservó al vecino en Bolivia, 1809–1830," in Jaime E. Rodríguez O., ed., *Revolución, independencia y las nuevas naciones de América* (Madrid: Fundación Mapfre Tavera, 2005), 474–7.

of a compromise solution with autonomous kingdoms in America were frivolously squandered. This opened the door to the assertion of independence. The continuation of the fighting and the processes of disintegration immediately after the victory of the armies of independence showed, however, that the creole revolution leaders had not succeeded in taming the centrifugal forces within their own ranks.

## Unfulfilled Promises

The independence revolutions in Spanish America had a common starting point in the French Revolution, the subsequent Napoleonic expansion, and the power vacuum on the Iberian Peninsula that followed. Everywhere the same question of the refoundation of legitimacy arose and ideas were exchanged in interregional and transatlantic transfer. The individual experiences of revolution, however, were very different when one compares, for example, Mexico with the other regions, or Chile with the central Andean region. Despite all the differences, there are clear interdependencies between the experiences, not only at the level of the political elites, but also at the level of the nonprivileged strata. Not only people, goods and ideas were exchanged during these revolutionary years, but also information about current developments.

The price of freedom was high, and the freedom gained in 1830 was limited in many ways. The political revolutions brought an end to colonial status, but independence began with new dependencies. The whole of Latin America was far from enjoying internal stability. After decades of war, the newly emerging states were too weak to establish a true republican order. The sovereign, the "people," remained a nebulous point of reference. The prerequisites and the political will of the elites were lacking for the implementation of a national state in the sense of a lasting community of values in these ethnically highly heterogeneous entities. The ethnic dimension in particular, which overlapped with the social problem, was a unique feature of the Spanish American revolutions of independence. It contributed to boosting the ideas of freedom, equality, and self-determination circulating worldwide, which the Spanish American elites also used, with a special revolutionary explosive force, because politicization had encompassed the entire social spectrum. Until 1830 and long after, this explosive force could not yet unfold. What remained, however, was the promise of the revolution, and that was not little.

2

# The Spanish Empire on the Eve
# of American Independence

EMILY BERQUIST SOULE

By most accounts, the eighteenth century did not begin well for Spain. On 1 November 1700 the sickly and feeble King Carlos II died without an heir. In his last will and testament, he named Philippe duc d'Anjou of France to succeed him, thereby placing a foreigner on the throne of Spain. For the first years of his rule, King Felipe V, as he came to be known, and his ministers largely followed the policy directives of his grandfather, Louis XIV of France. Felipe's succession to the Spanish throne advanced not only Louis' goal of extending French rule to new territories; it also offered Versailles convenient access to Spanish American consumer markets – and the coveted silver that Spanish American consumers spent there. Early eighteenth-century trade policies between Spain and France reflected this agenda: France supplied a vast quantity of the manufactures shipped to Spain's territories in America; France enjoyed favorable tariffs; France prohibited Spain from trading with other nations; and the French Compagnie Royale de Guinée won the lucrative *asiento* monopoly contract to supply Spain's American territories with African slaves. Trade was key: Although popular conceptions of the War of the Spanish Succession often pinpoint France's assumption of the Spanish throne as the cause of the war that engulfed much of Europe and the Americas from 1701 to 1714, in fact, when Britain and the Dutch Republic declared war on Spain and France in May of 1702, they were overwhelmingly focused not on succession itself, but on the generous commercial concessions France had received. Tellingly, their first target was the southern city of Cádiz – Spain's most important port for the Indies trade.[1]

---

[1] On the War of Spanish Succession, see Aaron A. Olivas, "Globalizing the War of the Spanish Succession: Conflict, Trade, and Political Alliances in Early Bourbon Spanish America," in Matthias Pohlig and Michael Schaich, eds., *The War of the Spanish Succession* (Oxford: Oxford University Press, 2018), 411–30; J. H. Elliott, "The Road to Utrecht: War and Peace," in Trevor J. Dadson and J. H. Elliott, eds., *Britain, Spain, and the Treaty of Utrecht, 1713–2013* (London: Legenda, 2014), 3–8; Henry Kamen, *The War of Succession in Spain, 1700–1715* (London: Weidenfeld and Nicolson, 1969).

The War of the Spanish Succession quickly expanded into a broader conflict, with Spain and France fighting against Portugal, Britain, Austria, and the Dutch Republic. Theaters of engagement emerged not only in Spain but also in France, Italy, Central Europe, and North Africa; as well as in borderland regions in both North and South America. At home on the Iberian Peninsula, King Felipe's decisive victory at Almansa affirmed his succession to the Spanish throne by 1707, but the war's geopolitical outcomes were not decided until the Utrecht complex of treaties in 1713. Ultimately, Felipe and the Bourbons retained the Spanish throne, where their descendants still rule today. The lion's share of the Utrecht spoils, however, went to Britain, which took Gibraltar and Minorca from Spain; territories in North America and the Caribbean from France; and the *asiento* slave trading contract. In one fell swoop, the Utrecht treaties strengthened and emboldened Britain through granting it significant territorial and commercial advantages that it would strategically employ throughout the remainder of the century in order to maintain geopolitical advantage in the Americas whenever possible.

While Britain's territorial additions may seem at first to be the most important of the gains negotiated at Utrecht, it soon became apparent that, in fact, their newly acquired slave trade *asiento* contract was the most valuable. British representatives had succeeded in gaining a new concession as part of this agreement: the right to bring one 500-ton annual "permission ship" to each of the Spanish American trade fairs held yearly at Portobelo and Veracruz. While one ship may appear to be relatively inconsequential, the contract terms stated that the single ship could be restocked by trailing packet boats. Officially, the permission ship allowed the British to offer more and higher quality goods at lower prices than those the Spanish themselves imported. The *asiento* provided for other means of penetrating the Spanish monopoly over the Indies trade as well. It permitted small numbers of British slave traders and merchants to settle in American ports; allowed the British to appoint their own legal experts to oversee the slaving business; and granted British merchants the right to stock strategically placed warehouses with British manufactures that were ostensibly used in the slave trade but of course could be siphoned off into illegal consumer transactions. But perhaps most importantly, all of these stipulations allowed for British traders, merchants, ship captains, and officials to cultivate a robust business of contraband. In all, the *asiento* was an excellent opportunity to supply cash-rich and goods-poor Spanish American consumers with the manufactures, textiles, and other imports that Spain promised to provision the colonies with but rarely did.[2]

Though Madrid responded by trying to mitigate British participation in Spanish American consumer markets, on the ground this proved to be no easy task. Spanish American consumers responded with great enthusiasm to illicit British trade. They were quite experienced at it as well – Spanish and British subjects in the Americas had a long history of engaging in mutually beneficial trade, despite such commerce being expressly forbidden by imperial dictates on both sides. This underground economy proved convenient for the Spanish Americans, who had ample cash for purchasing but often found markets and stores empty. This was because Madrid and Crown administrators continued to insist on a closed monopoly of trade with Spanish America, centered around a controlled fleet system of shipping (the *carrera de Indias*), tightly regulated tariffs and duties, and restrictions at ports of entry and exit. Furthermore, the fleet's departures from Spain were rarely on schedule. The lack of manufacturing in Spain created other challenges. Spanish merchants typically purchased goods imported from elsewhere in Europe, and then marked them up again before offering them for sale in America at above market price. As a result, a significant portion of the profits went to the foreigners – again, usually British – who manufactured and exported these items to Spain in the first place.[3]

Crown advisers recognized early on that both the official *asiento* contract and the illegal trading it promoted were among the most serious

---

[2] Excellent recent work on the British *asiento* includes Rafael Donoso Anes, *El Asiento de esclavos con Inglaterra (1713–1750): Su contexto histórico y sus aspectos económicos y contables* (Seville: Universidad de Sevilla, 2010); Reyes Fernández Durán, *La Corona Española y el tráfico de negros: Del monopolio al libre comercio* (Madrid: Ecobook, 2011); Adrian Finucane, *The Temptations of Trade: Britain, Spain, and the Struggle for Empire* (Philadelphia: University of Pennsylvania, 2016); Gregory O'Malley, *Final Passages: The Intercolonial Slave Trade of British America, 1619–1807* (Chapel Hill: University of North Carolina Press, 2014); and Adrian J. Pearce, *British Trade with Spanish America, 1763–1808* (Liverpool: Liverpool University Press, 2014).

[3] For good general overviews of the Spanish Indies trade, see J. H. Elliott, *Imperial Spain, 1469–1716* (New York: Penguin, 1990); John R. Fisher, *The Economic Aspects of Spanish Imperialism in America, 1492–1810* (Liverpool: Liverpool University Press, 1997); Henry Kamen, *Spain, 1469–1714: A Society of Conflict* (London: Longman, 1999); Henry Kamen, *Empire: How Spain Became a World Power, 1492–1763* (New York: Harper Perennial, 2004); Alan J. Kuethe and Kenneth J. Andrien, *The Spanish Atlantic World in the Eighteenth Century: War and the Bourbon Reforms, 1713–1796* (New York: Cambridge University Press, 2014); John Lynch, *Bourbon Spain 1700–1808* (Oxford: Basil Blackwell, 1989); Adrian J. Pearce, *The Origins of Bourbon Reform in Spanish America, 1700–1763* (New York: Palgrave Macmillan, 2014); Stanley and Barbara Stein, *Silver, Trade, and War: Spain and America in the Making of Early Modern Europe* (Baltimore, MD: Johns Hopkins University Press, 2000).

impediments to the economic revitalization of the Spanish empire. One of the earliest written proposals for remedying these problems came from royal functionary Jerónimo de Uztáriz, whose *Theory and Practice of Commerce and Maritime Affairs* (1724), contended that in order to regain power on the global stage, Spain needed to promote commercial shipping and build a strong navy. The two initiatives went hand in hand, he argued, because a favorable balance of trade "cannot be attained without the support of a considerable fleet ... on the other hand [it is] impossible to keep up a great fleet, such as one as the condition of this monarchy requires ... without the constant succor of a very extensive and advantageous commerce."[4] José Patiño, Secretary of State for Marine and the Indies from 1726 to 1736, transformed Uztáriz's prescriptions into policy, enlarging the Spanish navy by building new shipyards in Spain and Havana, the latter of which produced no fewer than thirty-nine warships in nine years. He also expanded the royal *guardacostas* (coast guard) in order to protect Spanish trade ships in America from foreign (mostly British) interlopers.[5]

Operating mainly in the Caribbean basin where problems with smuggling were most acute, the *guardacostas* boarded foreign ships in search of unsanctioned merchandise (human or otherwise). If they found evidence of illegal trade, international law permitted them to seize the ship as a *presa* or prize, taking its captain hostage. The *guardacostas* did this so eagerly that the British estimated they incurred £95,000 in losses at their hands.[6] By 1739, the conflict was becoming increasingly acute. That same year, a British sea captain named Robert Jenkins attended a House of Commons session about British–Spanish trade disputes in America. He purportedly recounted how *guardacosta* sailors had boarded his ship in 1731, slicing off his ear during an altercation. As evidence, he offered his long-dead ear, dramatically pulling it from his pocket. While historians now surmise the story about the ear is likely apocryphal, the record is clear that on 19 October 1739, Britain declared against Spain in a conflict that would come to be known in English as the War of Jenkins' Ear, and perhaps more truthfully in Spanish

---

[4] Gerónymo de Uztáriz, *The Theory and Practice of Commerce and Maritime Affairs*, trans. John Kippax (London: John & James Ravington, 1751), 343.
[5] Kuethe and Andrien, *Spanish Atlantic World*, 115; Alan J. Kuethe and José Manuel Serrano, "El Astillero de la Habana y Trafalgar," *Revista de Indias* LXVII: 241 (2007), 763–76: 767.
[6] Ignacio Rivas Ibáñez, "The Spanish Use of Deception and the Defense of America during the War of Jenkins' Ear (1739–1740)," in Francisco A. Eissa-Barroso and Ainara Vázquez Varela, eds., *Early Bourbon Spanish America: Politics and Society in a Forgotten Era (1700–1759)* (Leiden: Brill, 2013), 166.

as the *Guerra del Asiento*, or War of the *Asiento*. This time, war lasted for nine years, and again, all official trade between Spain, Britain, and their subjects was forbidden.

In battle, the Spanish mounted a highly successful strategy of defense in America, including besting British troops during an attempted invasion of Cartagena in 1741. By October 1748 the war was over. The Peace of Aix-la-Chapelle returned Parma and Plasencia to Spain, though Spanish claims to Milan, Tuscany, Minorca, and Gibraltar were not satisfied. Nevertheless, Spain and Britain thereafter entered into a short period of peace from 1749 to 1756. The relative quiet was in many ways attributable to Spanish chief minister José Carvajal's conciliatory attitude toward the British, whom he viewed as Spain's best possible allies against French expansion in America. But on the ground in the Americas, the more pressing problem was the ongoing illegal trade between Spanish and British subjects. In retaliation for rampant British smuggling, Spanish forces continued to seize British vessels suspected of carrying contraband. Land-use disputes simmered in peripheral areas as well: The British contested Spain's longstanding rights to fish on the Newfoundland Banks, while Spain looked critically at Britain's logwood cutting in Honduras and Central America. Meanwhile, Britain engaged in a series of attacks against French territory in North America starting in 1755. By 1761, Spanish officials logically feared their American territories might be next.[7]

Seeking to solidify the Spanish–British alliance, King Carlos III of Spain (1759–1788) entered into the Third Family Compact with the French Bourbons on 15 August 1761. As they had done in 1733 and in 1743, both houses promised to remain aligned during war or peace. This alliance was essential for Spain, whose naval development was still minimal. The need for a strong ally was made more pressing by British offenses against France in America during the Seven Years' War (1756–1763). Though the Spanish planned to declare war on Britain, Great Britain preempted such action by declaring war on Spain on 4 January 1762. Just six months later, 200 warships and transports arrived off the shores of Havana, bringing with them an invading force of 14,000 men. Despite the best efforts of the Cuban and Spanish troops, on 31 July the British blasted open the wall of Havana's iconic Morro Castle, gaining the upper hand that would ensure their success in the battle several weeks later. Lord Albemarle and his redcoats occupied Havana until February

---

[7] Jean McLachlan, "The Seven Years' Peace, and the West Indian Policy of Carvajal and Wall," *The English Historical Review* 53:211 (July 1938), 457–77.

of the following year, when the Treaty of Paris ended the Seven Years' War in North America on 10 February 1763. The Spanish gave up Florida to the British, but secured the much more valuable Havana in return.[8]

Once Cuba's most important city was back under Spanish purview, Spanish ministers began to imagine the island as a testing ground for political economy reforms aiming to improve Spanish American finance and defense. This is why John Elliott has referred to the Spanish agenda after the Havana occupation as nothing less than "a radical overhaul of the whole system of defense for the Spanish Indies,"[9] one that would have lasting effect through the eighteenth century and well into Age of Revolutions. First, King Carlos III created a *Junta de Ministros*, seating on it Julián de Arriaga (Secretary of Marine and the Indies), the Marqués de Esquilache (Secretary of War) and the Marqués de Grimaldi (Minister of State). They were tasked with not only improving the military defenses of Spanish America, but also increasing revenues within the viceroyalties and from the Indies trade. The committee quickly proposed additional fortification measures at Spanish America's most important northern ports (Veracruz, Havana, Campeche, and Cartagena). They also recommended sending soldiers from Spain to serve in America, in stark contrast to the prior strategy of defending the viceroyalties through local militias. The Spanish troops were not only to serve in the army, they would also train and professionalize the Spanish American militia.[10]

While improving Spanish defenses in America was rather straightforward, curtailing the worrisome British infiltrations into Spanish commerce in the Indies was a more daunting undertaking. To make matters worse, in 1766 Britain declared the Free Ports Act, opening several ports in Jamaica and Dominica to all foreign trade for seven years.[11] With one half of the restrictions on Spanish–British trade in America removed, Spanish Americans eagerly traveled to the British West Indies to purchase the same goods they were accustomed to buying from British contrabandists at home. Unsurprisingly, a great deal of this commerce centered around one of the most coveted commodities in the Americas: enslaved people from Africa. Desperate to stop British slave traders from infiltrating their markets, the

---

[8] Elena A. Schneider, *The Occupation of Havana: War, Trade, and Slavery in the Atlantic World* (Chapel Hill: University of North Carolina Press, 2018), 6.

[9] J. H. Elliott, *Empires of the Atlantic World: Britain and Spain in America, 1492–1830* (New Haven: Yale University Press, 2006), 299.

[10] Ibid.

[11] Frances Armytage, *The Free Port System in the British West Indies: A Study in Commercial Policy, 1766–1822* (London: Longmans, Green & Co., 1953), 13.

Spanish tried to develop their own traffic in slaves independently of British suppliers by lifting import duties; founding their own joint-stock slave trading companies; and, for the first time, attempting to import significant numbers of captives directly from Africa.[12] But the contraband slave trade and the broader infiltration of Spanish American markets it engendered continued. How to mitigate the associated financial losses would be one of the most important goals of the Bourbon reform initiatives of the second half of the eighteenth century.

## The Bourbon Reforms in the Eighteenth-Century Spanish Empire

As it was elsewhere in the Atlantic, war promoted military, economic, social, and administrative reform in Spanish America. Ministers in Madrid imagined how to make agriculture more productive, how to develop industry in Spain, and how to transform Spanish Americans into consumers of Spanish goods and foodstuffs. While in the sixteenth and seventeenth centuries, Spain's American possessions had been considered "overseas territories" little different from Spain itself, under the Bourbons in the eighteenth century, the Spanish American viceroyalties were to be transformed into colonies serving the Iberian Peninsula. Scholars generally characterize the resulting political, economic, and social plans for improvement as the "Bourbon reforms." Most broadly, these were intended to streamline the process of government administration and to generate greater profits for Crown coffers. As we shall see, their success was far from uniform, but the reforms – or at least the problems they attempted to rectify and the methods they proposed for doing so – are essential to understanding royal agendas for the Spanish colonies in America in the late colonial period and beyond.

Unsurprisingly, maximizing profits from transatlantic trade was central to the Bourbon reform agenda. In keeping with the trend toward market liberalization throughout the Atlantic colonies, the Spanish Crown sought to stimulate American markets through loosening trade restrictions. The Crown experimented with the Caribbean first; opening select ports there to trade with a larger number of Spanish ports in 1765. This was expanded on

---

[12] For an overview of these initiatives, see Emily Berquist, "Early Anti-slavery Sentiment in the Spanish Atlantic World, 1765–1817," *Slavery & Abolition* 31:2 (June 2010), 181–205; Rolando Mellafe, *Negro Slavery in Latin America* (Berkeley: University of California Press, 1975).

a piecemeal basis over the next thirteen years, with ports in New Granada and South America being added later. But the true "free trade" decree is the Regulation of Free Trade of 12 October 1778. This built upon the earlier expansions, adding more cities to unrestricted trade and systematizing taxes. As Alan Kuethe and Kenneth Andrien have argued, it was essentially an attempt to "undercut contraband, broaden markets, and draw the colonial economies into a tighter commercial dependence on the metropolis."[13] These liberalization measures were able to better integrate the Spanish and Spanish American economies because "free trade" meant only free trade *within the Spanish Empire*. The Spanish would not give up their monopoly so easily. And in some important ways, free trade was a success. By the end of the century, for example, it had indeed promoted industrial growth in Spain, above all in Catalonia (though this had created an inverse decrease in industrialization in America – just as the reformers had intended).[14] The benefits of liberalized trade policies became clear when the value of imports from America to Spain rose from just under 112,000,000 *reales de vellón* in 1782 to over 1,201,000,000 by 1784.[15]

Throughout the second half of the eighteenth century, Madrid initiated a similar related set of reforms that were specific to the slave trade. These were essential because the slave trade to the Spanish Empire had been outsourced to foreign traders since the Treaties of Alcaçovas (1479) and Tordesillas (1494) declared any foothold in sub-Saharan Africa to be outside Spain's purview.[16] Since then, most legal exports of slaves to Spanish America were the business of foreigners, who traded through the large-scale *asiento* contracts licensed to foreign powers (held successively by the Genoese, Dutch, Portuguese, and French from 1662 through 1712); or through smaller *asientos* issued by viceregal officials in America. Of course, there was also a hearty trade in contraband or smuggled slaves, so large that recent scholarship has suggested its numbers matched – or possibly even exceeded – those of officially permitted slave imports.[17] Slave trade reforms of the Bourbon

---

[13] Kuethe and Andrien, *Spanish Atlantic World*, 292.
[14] Fisher, *Economic Aspects*, 147; Lynch, *Bourbon Spain*, 361.
[15] Kuethe and Andrien, *Spanish Atlantic World*, 293.
[16] See Emily Berquist Soule, "From Africa to the Ocean Sea: Atlantic Slavery in the Origins of the Spanish Empire," *Atlantic Studies: Global Currents* 15:1 (2018), 16–39.
[17] See Alex Borucki, David Eltis, and David Wheat, "Atlantic History and the Slave Trade to Spanish America," *The American Historical Review* 120:2 (April 2015), 433–61; Gregory O'Malley and Alex Borucki, "Patterns in the Intercolonial Slave Trade across the Americas before the Nineteenth Century," *Revista Tempo* 23:2 (May/August 2017), 315–38.

period therefore focused at first on promoting direct Spanish access to sources of enslaved people. (Attempts to counter contraband slave imports would be ongoing.)

Although historians have only recently begun to consider the slave trade as an object of eighteenth-century Spanish reform agendas, two of the most well-known reformers of the period did in fact speak directly about how to optimize the slave trade according to the most current economic trends. In *Restablecimiento de las fábricas y del comercio Español (Re-establishing Spanish Manufacturing and Trade* (1740)), Bernardo Ulloa argued that Spain should set up its own factories in Africa and use its own ships to carry captives to America.[18] In 1762 Pedro Campomanes' *Reflexiones sobre el comercio Español a Indias (Reflections about Spanish Trade to the Indies)* bemoaned the fact that without its own territories in Africa, Spain was reliant on foreign slave traders to supply captives. "This trade is of much importance to the [Spanish] state," he argued. "Without a great supply of slaves, especially for the mines, the islands, and for lumber in Campeche [and] Honduras, we will not be able to make our colonies flourish."[19] His proposed solution was to transform one of the Canary Islands into a slave entrepôt where captives would be brought from sub-Saharan Africa and held until transport ships were full and ready to depart for Spanish America.

As of yet, historians have found no evidence that this scheme was ever undertaken on the Canaries. Perhaps one of the reasons why is that in 1765 the Crown chartered a joint-stock company of four merchants, granting it an *asiento* monopoly contract to import captives to Cuba. Although the Cádiz Company, as it came to be known, brought 13,684 enslaved people to the island by 1779, that year its contract was revoked. This was when Crown officials began to focus their attention on the Gulf of Guinea, where Spain had recently acquired Fernando Pó and Annobón, two small but conveniently placed West African islands. From 1778 to 1781, the Spanish navy attempted to install a Spanish settlement and establish slave trade centers on the islands. But the expedition's troops and crew faced foreign belligerents, local resistance, epidemic disease, and even a mutiny of the Spanish sailors. As 1781 came to an end, the captain and surviving troops left the Gulf to return to America. The Fernando Pó mission had failed.

---

[18] Bernardo de Ulloa, *Restablecimiento de las fábricas y comercio: Parte segunda* (Madrid: Antonio Marin, 1740), 19–24.

[19] Pedro Rodríguez de Campomanes, *Reflexiones sobre el comercio Español a Indias* (1762) (Madrid: Alisal, 1988), 335–6.

In the meantime, broader Spanish economic policies continued to move toward greater liberalization. Logically, reformers decided to mirror that opening in the slave trade, and soon Spanish fiscal policy surrounding the purchase and sale of slaves would come to represent the vanguard of economic liberalization in the Spanish Empire. On 28 February 1789, King Carlos III allowed Spaniards throughout Mexico and the Caribbean to trade directly with foreign merchants for slaves. Within several years the decree was expanded to include direct import of captives to Cartagena, Río de la Plata, Lima, Guayaquil, and Panama. Between 1789 and 1817, approximately 92,464 enslaved people were brought to mainland Spanish American ports via official channels, while contraband and smuggling likely brought that many or more into the black market.[20]

Alongside these initiatives designed to recapture profits from transatlantic trade and increase the flow of captive laborers to the American colonies, Bourbon reformers also sought to increase imperial tax revenues. They raised the *alcabala* (sales tax) from 2, to 4, and then 6 percent. New items were incorporated into tax structures as well: *aguardiente* liquor and coca in Peru, for example. With the assistance of new census data collected in Spanish America, tax collection was enforced more regularly. Most of the new tax schedules were introduced by crown-appointed *visitadores* sent to inspect the viceroyalties and suggest ways to improve their profitability. Unsurprisingly, measures imposed by *visitadores* like José Gálvez (Mexico, 1765–1771), José Areche (Peru, 1777–1785) and Juan Gutiérrez (New Granada, 1777) were often met with distrust and resistance. Sometimes these policies incited all-out protests, such as in New Granada's *comunero* rebellion, when creoles and mestizos not only refused to pay the new taxes, but also attacked government properties and temporarily drove out Spanish authorities.[21] Nevertheless, tax receipts in most areas of Spanish America grew over the course of the century.[22]

Spanish American silver mining was another key source of treasury returns, and here, as well, reformers' efforts were broadly successful, particularly in Mexico.[23] Many of these reform initiatives were based on Francisco Xavier de Gamboa's 1761 *Commentaries on the Mining Ordinances*. Gamboa called for creating a miners' guild and a mining tribunal to raise the industry's profile, as well as ensuring that mercury (essential for the amalgamation process) was widely available and relatively affordable. He also

---

[20] Berquist, "Early Anti-slavery Sentiment," 188.  [21] Lynch, *Bourbon Spain*, 344–6.
[22] Ibid., 296.  [23] Fisher, *Economic Aspects*, 186–7.

proposed that the price of gunpowder used for blasting be slashed by a quarter. Finally, he suggested that miners attempting to modernize their mines should receive generous tax incentives.[24] Thanks to these and related initiatives, silver production in Mexico rose from 50 million pesos for the first decade of the eighteenth century to 200 million pesos in the first decade of the nineteenth, by which point the Mexican silver mines were more productive than at any time in the colonial period.[25] To stimulate the mining industry in Peru, officials in Madrid implemented a similar plan, and also arranged for taxes on mining output to be reduced to one-tenth (the *diezmo*) from the previous *quinta real* (royal fifth) the Crown had demanded.[26] Production upswings there were not so dramatic, but nonetheless significant.

While reforms to commerce, the slave trade, and mining were designed to best suit the interests of the Spanish Crown, the Bourbon reformers also recognized the need to capitalize on another essential resource in the Spanish colonies – people. Here, they were guided by José del Campillo y Cosio's *New System of Economic Government for America*, which was written in 1743 but circulated only in manuscript form until 1789.[27] Inspired by the financial successes of Britain's American colonies, Campillo argued that if Spain properly utilized its resources in Spanish America, it could enjoy the same financial benefits. He proposed that the Spanish American viceroyalties should no longer be seen as the "overseas territories," geographically separate from but otherwise the same as Spain itself. Instead, they should be reconceptualized as colonies that would provide raw materials to Spain and foster markets for Spanish manufactured goods. To engender this new colonial relationship, Campillo recommended freeing shipping from the long-outmoded system of sending annual (or as often happened, less than annual) fleets across the Atlantic, as well as drastically curtailing contraband trade in America.

But at the true center of Campillo's plan for America stood its Indigenous people – "the Indians," he wrote, "are the true Indies and the richest mine of the world."[28] He proposed integrating them into Spanish society by giving

---

[24] Ibid., 192. Also see Christopher Albi, *Gamboa's World: Justice, Silver Mining, and Imperial Reform in New Spain* (Albuquerque: University of New Mexico, 2021).

[25] John J. TePaske and Kendall W. Brown, *A New World of Gold and Silver* (Leiden: Brill, 2010), 81–2.

[26] Fisher, *Economic Aspects*, 187–90.

[27] Eduardo Arcila Farias, "Campillo y Cosio en el pensamiento económico español," in Joseph del Campillo y Cosio, *Nuevo sistema de gobierno económico para la América* (Merida: Universidad de los Andes, 1971), 10. Farias also explains here how, unfortunately for Campillo, his ideas also formed the basis of Bernardo Ward's *Proyecto Económico*, which was published and widely distributed in 1762.

[28] Campillo y Cosio, *Nuevo sistema*, 90.

them land to work, offering them jobs, encouraging them to dress like Spaniards, teaching them Spanish, and providing them with basic primary education. Thus acculturated, they would become, he reasoned, the laboring backbone of Spanish American agriculture and mining. Their integration into the market economy would not only provide them livelihood and sustenance, it would also give them cash income that would transform them into able consumers of Spanish imports and manufactures. He insisted that such improvements in their circumstances would have the added benefit of increasing their population, creating more workers and more consumers who could bring the Spanish colonies into the age of nascent capitalism.[29]

Since the Bourbon reformers intended to focus on industrial development for Spain as opposed to in America, the labor they most wished to promote in the colonies was agricultural. In his *Report on Agrarian Law* (1795), Gaspar Jovellanos declared agriculture to be the kingdom's "prime source of wealth, given that population and riches, the main supports of national power, depend more immediately upon it than on any of the other lucrative professions."[30] Without agriculture, he thought, there would be no industry and no commerce. He reasoned that greater availability of food promoted better health, which led to a larger population with longer life spans. Well-fed people would work more efficiently, earn more money, and enjoy greater purchasing power. José Campillo laid out a similar plan in his *New System of Economic Government.* He proposed that the Crown give Indigenous smallholders empty land, reasoning that if they worked cotton and flax fields that they themselves owned, they would exert greater effort and produce more. To guide them, he suggested experienced agriculturalists form a cadre of advisers. Simultaneously, provincial administrators were to gather the necessary data about the soil and climate of each region, so they could make official recommendations about the best crops to plant and where to plant them.[31] Campillo envisioned the agricultural renovation of America as a collaborative effort of the Crown, elites, bureaucrats, and plebeians. Working together to harness knowledge of best farming practices, they would foster a society of hardworking smallholders who could form a ready market for Spanish manufactures.

In order to promote, enact, and oversee such a broad program of reform in America, Madrid also needed an able and loyal class of administrators on

---

[29] Ibid.

[30] Gaspar Melchor de Jovellanos, *Memoria sobre espectáculos y diversiones públicas / Informe sobre la Ley Agraria*, ed. Guillermo Carnero (Madrid, 1998), 379.

[31] Joseph Campillo y Cosio, *Nuevo sistema de gobierno económico para la América* (Madrid: Benito Cano, 1789), 105–33.

the ground. The best way to ensure this, Carlos III and his ministers reasoned, was to update, improve, and streamline the system of colonial administration in America. First, formerly peripheral areas were more closely incorporated into Spanish imperial rule when the Viceroyalty of Río de la Plata was established in 1776, the Captaincy General of Venezuela in 1777, and the Captaincy General of Chile the following year. (These followed the Viceroyalty of New Granada, which failed as an administrative unit in its first incarnation from 1717 to 1723, but was successfully reestablished in 1739.) Perhaps the most significant change of all, however, was the widescale effort to replace creole bureaucrats (Spaniards born in America) with *peninsulares* – Spaniards born in Spain, whom royal functionaries generally believed were more loyal to the program of Bourbon reforms for America, because they lacked the personal, familial, and business interests that colored the commercial, social, and political actions of their creole counterparts. Accordingly, in 1750 the Crown outlawed the practice of selling bureaucratic offices in America, a manner by which many wealthy creoles had gained influence in American government. Then, Madrid replaced the old *corregidores* – local administrators who had often purchased their positions and sustained themselves by using them to forge lucrative business dealings with relatives and friends – with Crown-appointed intendants who were paid a salary and expressly forbidden from such financial entanglements. The first intendants were installed in Cuba in 1764, and, as planned, they were all *peninsulares*.[32] The same policy was extended to the *audiencia* high courts and to high-level financial administration as well.[33] Creoles were becoming increasingly alienated from positions of power they had long enjoyed. Simultaneously, Madrid began to demand more financial contributions from its Indigenous vassals in America, increasing their tribute payments and doubling down on forced labor drafts. "All sectors were under pressure," John Lynch contends, "the king from his enemies, the elites from the king, and the Indians from everyone."[34] Soon in Peru and the Andes, a series of violent uprisings would make clear just how much pressure Indigenous communities felt.

## The Age of Revolutions in Spanish America and Beyond

It was because of the Bourbon reforms that in 1777, José Antonio de Areche became the most hated man in all of Peru. As the crown-appointed *visitador*

---

[32] Lynch, *Bourbon Spain*, 339.     [33] Ibid., 341.     [34] Ibid., 336.

to the viceroyalty, he was charged with conducting a thorough investigation of the political, social, and economic situation there – and making recommendations to improve it. In keeping with the general goals of the Bourbon reforms, Areche's task was to increase the viceroyalty's profitability, and he acted accordingly. After his visit, he increased the *alcabala* sales tax from 4 to 6 percent; ordered new censuses to be sure that all vassals in America were assessed at their proper tax rates; and subsequently upped Indigenous tribute percentages. When Viceroy Manuel de Guiror dared to question these initiatives in public, he was summarily dismissed. Guiror, however, had not been the only one who took issue with the Bourbon program to squeeze more profit from Peruvians. Discontent with Areche's reforms was widespread, but it was the Indigenous people who suffered most acutely under the new census and tribute regulations. Soon, they would rebel in a series of uprisings known as the Túpac Amaru rebellions of 1780–1783. Though in the end these revolts had only limited success in addressing the natives' grievances, the rebellions – and colonial bureaucrats' responses to them – would prove pivotal in how the Age of Revolutions unfolded in Spanish America.

The first revolt of native peoples in the Andes began in Chayanta, Upper Peru (today Bolivia) in 1777 – the same year Areche's stringent economic policies went into effect. Aspects of the conflict predated his arrival: the Aymara Indigenous community there had long complained about the exploitation they faced from both their *corregidor* (Crown-appointed administrator of an Indigenous community) and cacique (Indigenous leader who served as a liaison to the Spanish). In particular, they decried the *reparto de comercio*, a colonial tax that forced native vassals to purchase goods that they often did not need or want, such as eyeglasses or silk stockings, at inflated prices. In search of redress, the Indigenous people of Chayanta, who identified as "Macha," selected elder Tomás Katari to bring their grievances to the nearest *audiencia* high court in Charcas (today Sucre). The argument he posed on behalf of his community was one that Indigenous people throughout Peru had used for centuries: his people had fulfilled their duties as vassals, paying their tribute regularly and purchasing the goods the *reparto* required them to buy. Even more importantly, they had willingly undertaken their *mita* service (periodic labor drafts in the silver mines at Potosí). Nevertheless, they received abuse and mistreatment at the hands of their local officials. Therefore, Katari argued, while the Macha had willingly executed their responsibilities as vassals of the Spanish Crown, their *corregidor* and cacique, who exploited them and treated them cruelly, did not.

The Charcas *audiencia* agreed with Katari's argument. The judges ordered the offending cacique relieved of his position and appointed Katari in his place. However, when Katari arrived back in Chayanta, this did not happen. Instead, the *corregidor* ordered him whipped for insubordination, and then declared the offending cacique would remain. Katari's next move revealed just how much he and his community believed in the traditional Spanish system of colonial rule through petition and redress. Instead of disavowing the system itself, he moved his request up the bureaucratic chain, this time undertaking a three-month journey on foot to Buenos Aires, where he would seek an audience with the viceroy. The latter concurred with the Charcas *audiencia*'s earlier decision, again ordering the corrupt cacique expelled and Katari instated in his place. Nevertheless, upon his return to Chayanta, Katari faced rebuke again. This time, he was imprisoned.

After this, the Macha realized that the traditional Spanish system of allowing colonial subjects, even relatively powerless ones, to petition and negotiate up the bureaucratic channels to find redress was failing them. By August of 1781, they had arrested and imprisoned the Spanish *corregidor*, installing Katari in his place. From his new office, Katari worked on reducing tribute rates, but he also began to attempt more radical reforms that had not been part of the original requests, including the complete abolition of both the *reparto* and the *mita*. At the same time, he instructed the Macha to remain loyal to the Spanish Crown, and to continue making tribute payments until the new rates were made official. This too would come to be a feature of two subsequent native rebellions and, later, the movements for independence in Spanish America: while seeking redress from the very system that oppressed them, many Spanish American people of color, and especially Indigenous ones, would claim that their loyalty to the Spanish Crown remained intact. They positioned their grievances as against corrupt local officials, not the entire system of Spanish colonial rule itself. Conditioned for centuries to view the Spanish king as their benefactor, they appear to have believed that if they fulfilled their duties as Spanish vassals, they could expect justice and fairness in return – even when they rebelled against corruption at the local level. Unsurprisingly, in this case, their calculation was somewhat off: An army regiment was sent from Buenos Aires to put down the rebellion and capture Katari. The prisoner was marched back to Buenos Aires to face justice for his actions of insubordination. Along the way, he was pushed off a cliff to his death. His brothers Dámaso and Nicolás took over the fight, but by 1781 the Spanish had defeated them as well.[35]

---

[35] For the Tomás Katari rebellion, see the work of Sergio Serulnikov, including *Revolution in the Andes: The Age of Túpac Amaru* (Durham, NC: Duke University Press, 2013) and

While the Katari rebellion was taking place in Chayanta, another Indigenous uprising began outside the southern Peruvian town of Tinta. Here as well the Indigenous people complained of exploitation at the hands of their *corregidor*, but this time the local cacique, an Indian named José Gabriel Condorcanqui, stood with the people instead of against them. Condorcanqui began what would come to be known as the Túpac Amaru rebellion when he kidnapped *corregidor* Antonio de Arriaga on 4 November 1780, claiming that the latter had unlawfully extracted income from the Indigenous people under his purview. With Arriaga imprisoned, Condorcanqui summoned local Indigenous leaders to the nearby town of Tungasuca. He told them he had received direct orders from King Carlos III to abolish the *alcabala* sales tax, end the Potosí *mita* labor draft, and execute Arriaga. He then declared himself a descendant of Túpac Amaru I, the last Inca leader executed by Viceroy Toledo in 1572, and accordingly, he took the name Túpac Amaru II. He also had *corregidor* Arriaga dressed in the shameful clothing of a penitent and hanged. Soon, Túpac Amaru II's movement became a rebellion with an army that at one time counted on as many as 50,000 Indigenous and mixed-race troops. The formidable force struck fear in Spaniards and creoles throughout the Andes. After a failed attack on the highland city of Cuzco, however, Túpac Amaru II was captured, tortured, and dismembered in a gruesome ceremony in Cuzco's main plaza. His various body parts were shipped to different corners of the empire in an attempt to intimidate any possible future rebels and "prevent the spread of various ideas that have been extended throughout the nation of Indians," as *visitador* Areche put it.[36]

Areche's warning to the other native towns would prove to be too late, however, because soon thereafter, the third of the Indigenous rebellions –

---

*Subverting Colonial Authority: Challenges to Spanish Rule in the Southern Andes* (Durham, NC: Duke University Press, 2003).

[36] José Antonio Areche, "All Must Die!," in Orin Starn, Carlos Iván Degregori, and Robin Kirk, eds., *The Peru Reader: History, Culture, Politics* (Durham, NC: Duke University Press, 2005), 169–73. On the Túpac Amaru rebellion and Spanish–Indigenous relations in late eighteenth-century Peru, see Emily Berquist Soule, *The Bishop's Utopia: Imagining Improvement in Colonial Peru* (Philadelphia: University of Pennsylvania Press, 2014); John R. Fisher, *Bourbon Peru, 1750–1824* (Liverpool: Liverpool University Press, 2003); Scarlett O'Phelan Godoy, *Rebellions and Revolts in Eighteenth-Century Peru and Upper Peru* (Cologne: Böhlau, 1985); Ward Stavig, *The World of Túpac Amaru: Conflict, Community, and Identity in Colonial Peru* (Lincoln: University of Nebraska Press, 1999); Charles F. Walker, *The Túpac Amaru Rebellion* (Cambridge, MA: Harvard University Press, 2014) and *Smoldering Ashes: Cuzco and the Creation of Republican Peru, 1780–1840* (Durham, NC: Duke University Press, 1999).

The Spanish Empire on the Eve of American Independence

collectively known as the Túpac Amaru rebellions – began in the Puno region near Lake Titicaca. It was led by an Aymara *campesino*, Julián Apasa, who, when the conflict began, took the name "Viceroy Julián Túpac Katari," in reference to the two earlier rebellions that inspired him, and his desire to become as powerful as the highest Spanish official in the region. Túpac Katari was reputedly fierce in battle and soon raised an army of followers, though he was also known as a drunk and a womanizer. He led an epic siege against the Spanish stronghold of the city of La Paz, but his troops were poorly organized and difficult to control. Soon, his Aymara followers began to quarrel with the Quechua Indigenous people who had joined them after the defeat of Túpac Amaru II in Cuzco. In the disarray, the Spanish began to make inroads by offering the rebels clemency in exchange for surrender. After Túpac Katari's second failed attempt to take La Paz, many of his troops decided to accept the Spanish offer. Then on 14 November 1781, Túpac Katari was lured into a trap and captured. The Spanish quartered his body. The Túpac Amaru rebellions were over. They had engendered significant loss of life on both sides – according to some estimates, 100,000 individuals died during the years of conflict.[37]

In the aftermath, Spanish administrators implemented a new round of reforms designed to ensure that Indigenous communities would remain loyal subjects of the Spanish Crown. The Spanish began with important concessions. They replaced the *corregidores* with a new professional class of bureaucrats called intendants in 1784. These would be Crown-appointed and salaried (and theoretically less exploitive). Madrid outlawed the *reparto de comercio* – although reports suggest the practice continued in many places. These were changes that the Indigenous themselves had asked for. The native Andeans had decidedly not, however, suggested any of the accompanying sociocultural ordinances that attempted to limit the expression of their group identity. These stipulated that Indigenous children were to attend primary schools where, alongside basic reading and writing, they would learn to speak Spanish fluently. While these proposals were benign enough, the Spanish also decreed that all cultural productions celebrating the Andeans' Inkaic heritage – including traditional clothing, jewelry, and artwork – were henceforth prohibited. In general, these secondary reforms

---

[37] On the Túpac Katari rebellion, see Nicholas A. Robins, *Genocide and Millennialism in Upper Peru: The Great Rebellion of 1780–1782* (Westport, CT: Praeger, 2002); Serulnikov, *Revolution in the Andes*; Sinclair Thomson, *We Alone Will Rule: Native Andean Politics in the Age of Insurgency* (Madison: University of Wisconsin, 2002).

promoted the idea that Peru's native peoples should be forced to live, dress, work, and behave more like Europeans, so they might become more integrated in and loyal to Hispanic society. The Spanish had experienced firsthand the disastrous outcome of what they now perceived to have been overly lenient policies toward Indigenous communities. As the Andes had been gripped with rebellion, *peninsulares* and creoles saw their worst fear – a race war that pitted white colonizers against subordinated people of color – become reality. This would have effects far beyond the Andes, and ultimately shape the Spanish response to the Age of Revolutions in the Atlantic World.

Meanwhile, as Areche and other bureaucrats in Peru and Spain were responding to the Indigenous rebellions in South America, they were also eyeing a possible threat from the north. The North American colonists' declaration of war against Britain put Spain in a precarious position. Over the course of the eighteenth century, the Spanish and British Americans had cultivated a fruitful trading relationship, one that was sometimes sanctioned by their Crowns, but more often than not was forced underground due to Spanish–British conflict. At the same time, war between Spain and Britain had become ubiquitous since 1701; indeed, Gabriel Paquette has argued that "war with England ... was the most constant factor in Spanish foreign affairs" in the eighteenth century.[38] The American colonists' rebellion offered Spain a unique opportunity to strike back at Britain through aiding the rebels, but such a strategy had serious possible consequences – what if Britain decided to attack Spanish America or Spain in return? Initially, Spain settled on a position of official neutrality. But at the same time, Spanish ministers surreptitiously funneled financial support to the rebels (more than 9.5 million *reales* over the course of the war) and cultivated a network of spies that could provide much-needed information about the conflict.[39] Then in 1778, France, still allied to Spain through the Bourbon Family Compact, declared war against Britain. The agreement between the French and Spanish Crowns left Madrid little choice of alliance, and on 21 June 1779, Spain declared war against Britain as well (although it made no overt statement regarding allegiance to the American rebels). Spain's reasons to enter the war against

---

[38] Gabriel B. Paquette, *Enlightenment, Governance, and Reform in Spain and Its Empire, 1759–1808* (Basingstoke: Palgrave Macmillan, 2008), 37. On the broader Spanish geopolitical and commercial strategy for entering the war, also see Emily Berquist Soule, "The Spanish Slave Trade during the American Revolutionary War," in Gabriel Paquette and Gonzalo M. Quintero, eds., *Spain and the American Revolution* (London: Routledge, 2020), 100–21.

[39] W. N. Hargreaves-Mawdsley, *Eighteenth-Century Spain 1700–1788: A Political, Diplomatic, and Institutional History* (Totowa, NJ: Rowman and Littlefield, 1979), 138.

Britain were most obviously geopolitical: Spain hoped to recover territories it had lost in the War of the Spanish Succession (Gibraltar and Minorca) and the Seven Years' War (Florida). As Gonzalo Quintero Saravia argues, Spain also entered the war because it seemed like the most pragmatic choice. "Confronted with the option of sharing North America with the British Empire or with a new and small republic with an extremely weak central government," he writes, "Spain chose the latter."[40]

Spain kicked off its anti-British offensives in the North American territory it had previously held and wished to regain from Britain: portions of the southeast that are today Mississippi, Florida, and Alabama. By 1780, Bernardo de Gálvez – nephew of the unapologetically nepotistic José de Gálvez – had taken Mobile, and by 1781 Pensacola. He also arranged campaigns to combat Britain's unsanctioned interloping in the Central American logwood business, despite it having been officially sanctioned in 1763.[41] By the time the Treaty of Paris ended the American Revolutionary War in Fall of 1783, Spain had retaken all of its former possessions in North America, and made gains in Europe too, recouping Minorca in the Mediterranean. Gibraltar, however, remained in British hands. Spain had not accomplished all of its goals in declaring war against Britain, but it had saved face and managed to restore some of its international reputation. Perhaps most importantly, the anticolonial stance of the North American rebels had not spread to Spain's territories in America.

However, the death of King Carlos III in 1788 would introduce a new era of internal and geopolitical instability for the Spanish Empire. The new monarch, Carlos IV, was not the leader his father had been. He brought with him to the throne only scant formal education and even less interest in governance. His wife, Queen María Luisa, would instead assume much of the command of royal affairs, particularly through her treasured favorite, Manuel de Godoy. Also instrumental in Carlos IV's administration was Spain's Secretary of State, Conde Moñino de Floridablanca. Finding himself wielding immense power with few constraints, Floridablanca was largely responsible for initiating Spain's response to the Fall of the Bastille that marked the start of the French Revolution in July 1789. Fearing anticlerical, antimonarchical ideas would introduce radical politics and revolution that

---

[40] Gonzalo Quintero Saravia, *Bernardo de Gálvez: Spanish Hero of the American Revolution* (Chapel Hill: University of North Carolina Press, 2018), 4.
[41] Donald Grunewald, "The Anglo-Guatemalan Dispute over British Honduras," *Caribbean Studies* 5:2 (July 1965), 23.

could destroy the Spanish monarchy, he obsessively attempted to stop the flow of all information from France into Spain. He placed more Spanish troops on the border with France in order to deter unsanctioned crossings of people and goods. He implemented a policy of strict censorship designed to keep out all news of the events in France; forbidding French newspapers, and even employing Inquisition officials to inspect mail coming across the Pyrenees. By 1792, Floridablanca was dismissed after the French pointed out that his deep distrust of their government violated the terms of mutual support laid out in the Bourbon Family Compact.[42]

Carlos IV appointed the Conde de Aranda as the next Secretary of State, ordering him to assume a more conciliatory stance toward France. However, once King Louis XVI of France was deposed and the royal family imprisoned in August of that year, a moderate position toward revolutionary France was no longer possible, and Aranda was relieved of his duties. Next in line to assume the most powerful diplomatic position in the Spanish Empire was none other than royal favorite Manuel de Godoy, who had no real experience in government but was widely known as Queen María Luisa's *cortejo* or consort.[43] As an administrator, Godoy largely maintained existing Spanish policy, attempting to moderate the situation in France. This proved impossible when the French Convention voted to execute Louis XVI. King Carlos IV petitioned to save his cousin's life, but to no avail, and on 21 January 1793 the former king met his death by guillotine. On 7 March 1793, France declared war on Spain. Spain's ill-prepared troops were largely ineffectual against French forces.

As Spain grappled with upheaval in France, another threat was growing in the Caribbean. In August 1791, enslaved people across Haiti ravaged plantations on the island, killing countless French colonists and burning 1,400 estates in just one month. The Spanish soon realized that though this rebellion had a different cast than the Túpac Amaru uprisings in Peru, race war had come to the Americas again, and this time right next door to the island of Spanish Cuba. Cuba was central to Spanish defense of the Caribbean and becoming increasingly important to Crown finances as well, due to the growth of slave-based plantation agriculture on the island. Cuban slaveholders were nothing short of apoplectic. Advocating on their behalf in Madrid when the rebellion broke out

---

[42] On the Spanish response to the French Revolution see Jean-René Aymes, "Spain and the French Revolution," *Mediterranean Historical Review* 6:1 (1991), 62–85; Lynch, *Bourbon Spain*, 375–421; Richard Herr, *The Eighteenth Century Revolution in Spain* (Princeton, NJ: Princeton University Press, 1958).

[43] Lynch, *Bourbon Spain*, 375–83.

was slaveholder and lobbyist Francisco de Arango. His first response was terror – not that the rebellion would spread to Cuba, but that the Spanish Crown would outlaw the slave trade as a way to mitigate possible slave rebellions in Spanish territory, thereby condemning Cuba's booming plantation slavery economy to a slow death. As Ada Ferrer details in *Freedom's Mirror*, within days of the first actions against French slaveholders in Saint-Domingue, Arango had penned an essay sustaining the slaves had been inspired to rebel by the bad example set by the revolutionaries in France. The Cubans, he argued, were content with their government, and they treated their slaves exceptionally well, so they faced no such threat. Instead, according to Arango's treatise, "the revolution in Saint-Domingue was above all else an opportunity to be seized" – a time when Cuban cultivators could purchase more slaves and increase sugar and tobacco production in order to capture the market share previously commanded by Saint-Domingue. Within days, King Carlos IV agreed to extend the liberalization of the slave trade to Cuba for six more years.[44]

In February of 1792, governor Joaquín García of Cuba received his official royal orders for how to deal with the rebellion in Saint-Domingue. He was instructed to maintain perfect neutrality. Soon, observers in Cuba would notice something that likely seemed familiar to them, particularly if they had knowledge of the rebellions that had taken place in the Andes in the 1780s: The rebels in Saint-Domingue declared loyalty to their king (and respect for the Spanish one). Despite their superior numbers, they had not made any attacks against Spanish interests in Santo Domingo, in the east of the island. As an informal, unsanctioned trading relationship developed between the Saint-Domingue rebels and Spanish civilians in Santo Domingo, leaders on both sides began cautiously to explore a relationship that they imagined might prove useful in the future.

By winter of 1793, Madrid directed Santo Domingo governor Joaquín García to seek alliance with the Saint-Domingue rebel leader Jean-François and his subordinates, offering them weapons, cash aid, the status of Spanish vassals, and freedom from slavery if they were to agree to serve the king of Spain. By mid-1793, Spain had found itself with as many as 10,000 exiles from Saint-Domingue – the vast majority of these former slaves – serving in its army in the Caribbean. The alliance, however, was uneasy, with Spanish officials questioning the Black officers' motivation for alliance with Spain. By

---

[44] Ada Ferrer, *Freedom's Mirror: Cuba and Haiti in the Age of Revolution* (New York: Cambridge University Press, 2014), 33–5.

April 1794, these suspicions would play out when Toussaint Louverture's troops turned on the Spanish, angered that Spanish planters had continued to purchase captives in Santo Domingo in order to disperse them throughout Spanish America.[45] To make matters worse, though, the Spanish had originally promised freedom to all enslaved people who joined them to fight against France in Saint-Domingue, they had simultaneously offered to protect the property and businesses of the French Caribbean slaveholders.[46] After Toussaint Louverture attacked the center of Spanish power at San Rafael, the shaky partnership was officially dead. Spain was at war with the rebelling slaves in Saint-Domingue.

The news was not all bad. In July of 1795, war between France and Spain was ended by the Treaty of Basel. The rebel slaves in Saint-Domingue held their ground, despite being confronted by French, Spanish, and British troops. But the larger danger of the conflict was not the fighting itself, rather the future of Saint-Domingue. Once again, Francisco Arango was one of the first to articulate Cuban slaveholders' interests when he pointed out that if Saint-Domingue were to fall to the formerly enslaved people, these might well impede the slave trade to Cuba, encourage rebellion among their Cuban counterparts, and thereby take down slavery on Cuba as well. As Ada Ferrer has so masterfully shown, while the Haitian revolutionaries did attempt to seize slave ships in the Caribbean, and their example inspired rebellions and revolts in Cuba (especially the Aponte rebellion of 1812, in which Cuban slaves directly referenced Toussaint Louverture and the Haitian rebels as a source of inspiration[47]), in the end, this was not enough to destroy, or even to impede, slavery on Cuba, which experienced unprecedented economic growth thanks to enslaved labor, and by 1870 was producing no less than 41 percent of the world's sugar.

Nevertheless, the formerly enslaved of Saint-Domingue had changed the course of the Age of Revolutions when they managed to free themselves from slavery and overthrow a colonial power in one fell swoop, simultaneously executing the Western world's only successful slave rebellion and establishing its first independent Black republic. The effects of their actions reverberated throughout the Americas, the Atlantic, and the world. Planters

---

[45] Ibid., 116–7.      [46] Ibid., 122.

[47] On Aponte, see Matt D. Childs, *The 1812 Aponte Rebellion in Cuba and the Struggle against Atlantic Slavery* (Chapel Hill: University of North Carolina Press, 2006); Aisha Finch and Fannie Rushing, eds., *Breaking the Chains, Forging the Nation: The Afro-Cuban Fight for Freedom and Equality, 1812–1912* (Baton Rouge: Louisiana State University Press, 2019).

and slaveowners clung more tightly to their rights to buy, sell, and exploit enslaved people. The enslaved celebrated the Haitians' success. For their part, the Spanish had seen race war at their doorstep yet again. When the Age of Revolutions landed at the feet of the Spanish Empire in the wake of Napoleon's invasion of Spain in 1808, powerful Spanish Americans feared the *gente de color* (people of color) might turn on them again. Many creoles therefore responded with great caution to revolutionary ideas, at least until unrelenting political chaos in Spain created a sense of betrayal so deep, they gave up on reimagining how they might remain part of the Spanish Empire. By the 1820s, all of the mainland Spanish American territories had broken from Spain. But Cuba and Puerto Rico stood firm in making the opposite choice, deciding that they valued Spain's cultivation of the slave trade and protection of their slave economies more than they valued the political liberties of the Age of Revolutions.

## 3

# The Cortes of Cádiz and the Spanish Liberal Revolution of 1810–1814: Atlantic and Spanish American Dimensions

ROBERTO BREÑA

## The Cortes of Cádiz from an Atlantic Perspective

The Cortes or parliament that met in the Spanish port of Cádiz from 1810 to 1814 signified a political revolution of the whole Spanish Empire. The main practical result of this revolution was the Cádiz Constitution, also known as the Constitution of 1812.[1] It should be remembered that at that time the Spanish Empire was the largest European empire in geographical terms. It comprised not only contemporary Spain and what today we understand as "Latin America" (with the exception of Brazil), but also the Philippine Islands.

The events that evolved into what today historians define as "the first Spanish liberalism" or "Spanish liberal revolution," epitomized by the Cortes of Cádiz, began with the invasion of the Iberian Peninsula by Napoleon's army in the autumn of 1807. In reality, this was not an "invasion," because the Spanish Crown had signed the Treaty of Fontainebleau in October of that year with the French government, permitting the entrance of French troops to Spanish territory on their way to invade Portugal. Relatively soon, however, the purported transit of the Napoleonic army became an "occupation" in the full sense of the word. The peninsular Spaniards put up with this anomalous situation until the people of Madrid revolted against the French garrison of the city on 2 May 1808. From that moment on, Spain and

---

[1] I reviewed this whole process in detail in my book *El primer liberalismo español y los procesos de emancipación de América, 1808–1824: Una revisión historiográfica del liberalismo hispánico* (Mexico City: El Colegio de México, 2006). For a general overview in English, see my chapter "The Cadiz Liberal Revolution (1810–14) and the Spanish American Independence Movements: The *mundo hispánico* in the Age of Revolution," in John Tutino, ed., *New Countries: Capitalism, Revolutions, and Nations in the Americas, 1750–1870* (Durham, NC: Duke University Press, 2016), 71–106.

eventually its whole empire went through a political revolution of such a magnitude that, as this chapter will show, the Spanish *ancien régime* was turned upside down.[2]

This political upheaval lasted only six years (from May 1808 to May 1814) and it ended up in the failure of the Spanish liberal experiment of the early nineteenth century, but this fact does not diminish its importance from a historical perspective or from the perspective of constitutional history, the history of political thought, and the history of ideas.[3] This political revolution was essentially liberal, but it took place in the context of a popular uprising – the protracted and bitter war against the French army. This context had a series of implications that will become evident as this chapter advances. It should suffice for the moment to say that, precisely due to its popular and nationalist character, traditional aspects were present throughout this whole period (1808–1814), determined more than anything else by the unrelenting and brutal fight of practically a whole nation against the most powerful army of its time. The war against the French was started by the Spanish people, which explains to a large extent the character of the liberal revolution in which Cádiz was the platform and echo chamber between 1810 and 1814. However, in May of the latter year, Fernando VII returned to power in Spain, and along with him came absolutism. As might have been expected, the king also tried to reinstate absolutism in Spanish America. Although at first, during the biennium 1815–1816, he was relatively close to being successful in his endeavor, he ended up losing the whole of continental Spanish America.[4]

---

[2] A good collection of texts on the Spanish American independence movements, along with chapters on Brazil and the Caribbean, is Clément Thibaud et al., *L'Atlantique révolutionnaire: Une perspective ibéro-américaine* (Rennes: Les Perséides, 2013). For an interesting comparative study of Spanish America and the Thirteen Colonies, see Lester D. Langley, *The Americas in the Age of Revolution 1750–1850* (New Haven: Yale University Press, 1996), that also includes the Haitian Revolution. From the perspective of political thought, there is a recent contribution from a comparative approach (which is seldom applied in this field): Joshua Simon, *The Ideology of Creole Revolution: Imperialism and Independence in American and Latin American Political Thought* (New York: Cambridge University Press, 2017).

[3] On the influence of the 1812 Constitution on the constitutionalism of Latin America, see Matthew C. Mirow, *Latin American Constitutions: The Constitution of Cádiz and Its Legacy in Spanish America* (New York: Cambridge University Press, 2015).

[4] One of the best overviews of the loss of the American territories by the Spanish Crown (including the same process in the case of the Portuguese Crown) is a recent book by Brian Hamnett, *The End of Iberian Rule on the American Continent, 1770–1830* (Cambridge: Cambridge University Press, 2017). Another very good work, that also covers the Portuguese empire, is Jeremy Adelman, *Sovereignty and Revolution in the Iberian Atlantic* (Princeton, NJ: Princeton University Press, 2006), which assigns much importance to

The most evident example of the persistence of traditional elements is not only the fact that since its very start the war against the French had a religious character – the French were considered atheists by the common Spaniard – but also that the Catholic religion was the only one to be permitted by Article 12 of the Cádiz Constitution. However, it is very important not to focus on this article. Significant as it was, it was only one of the 384 articles of the constitutional document. Taken as a whole, the Cádiz Constitution meant a reversal of the main principles, tenets, and understandings that sustained political and social life during the *Antiguo Régimen*. In other words, what happened in peninsular Spain between 1808 and 1814 was a political *revolution* that, as can be seen in detail in Chapter 4 in this book by Juan Luis Simal, can be considered to have continued in the period known as the *Trienio liberal* (1820–1823). During those three years, liberals, along with the Cádiz Constitution, came back to power in Spain. Again, however, the liberal Spanish experience was brief, for in 1823 Fernando VII, with the support the Holy Alliance, reinstated absolutism. Naturally, as will be detailed below, the Spanish liberal revolution of 1810–1814 had implications in the territories of the Spanish Empire in America. In addition, during the 1820s the Cádiz Constitution had a political impact in Portugal, some Italian territories, Norway, and even in Russia.[5]

## The Prelude

During the first two years of the war against Napoleon there was a popular insurrection accompanied by the efforts of a disorganized Spanish army, *guerrillas* that hindered the French army constantly, the support of the British and Portuguese armies, and, finally, itinerant political authorities that were desperately trying to keep the monarchy alive. Napoleon had taken the crown away from King Fernando VII, gave it back to his father, Carlos IV, and

---

commercial issues, which Hamnett does not highlight. However, Adelman's book almost completely leaves out the viceroyalty of New Spain from its purview.

[5] The best article on the subject is Ignacio Fernández Sarasola, "La proyección europea e iberoamericana de la Constitución de 1812," in his book *La Constitución de Cádiz: Origen, contenido y proyección internacional* (Madrid: CEPC, 2011), 271–336. On the Russian case, see Richard Stites, "Decembrists with a Spanish Accent," *Kritika: Explorations in Russian and Eurasian History* 12:1 (Winter 2011), 5–23. Stites is the author of an excellent book: *The Four Horsemen. Riding to Liberty in Post-Napoleonic Europe* (Oxford: Oxford University Press, 2014); the second chapter is devoted to Rafael de Riego, the lieutenant colonel responsible for the return of liberalism to Spain in 1820.

then, in July 1808, appointed his older brother, Joseph, as king of Spain and the Indies. Meanwhile, the French emperor kept Fernando VII as a pampered prisoner in central France at the castle of Valençay. The Junta Central, improvised in September 1808 to face the absence of the legitimate king and the installation of a foreign one, was replaced by a *Regencia* in January 1810. The regency was the institution that set up the meeting of the Cortes that had been decided *in extremis* by the Junta Central. The Cortes was an ancient parliament that enjoyed certain political relevance in some Spanish kingdoms during the Middle Ages, but had fallen into disuse for several centuries. While, as mentioned above, the war was at first fought predominantly to keep the Spanish monarchy alive, it also became an organized political revolution once the Cortes began to meet in September 1810. The group responsible for this revolution was the one that had the upper hand in the assembly. They soon became known as *liberales*.

In fact, the term "liberal" with a political connotation was not used for the first time in Philadelphia, Paris, or London, but in Cádiz, where the Cortes were gathered.[6] It was in this Andalusian port that at the end of 1810 the term "liberal" was used for the first time to identify a political group. The Spanish liberals tried to use the war against the French to carry out a major overhaul of the Spanish political system. In fact, the national character of the war, the fact that the survival of the whole monarchy was at stake, the disrepute in which the monarchical institution had fallen under Carlos IV, and, finally, the extraordinary conditions that the French invasion had unintentionally created in the city of Cádiz, created a very peculiar sociopolitical context that the Spanish *liberales* used in their favor to carry out a diverse array of profound political changes. Only a few years before, changes of the type they designed and pretended to apply to the Spanish and Spanish American societies would have been unthinkable. The fact that they were able to carry out a revolution in such a short amount of time says much about their political deftness. It should be added that their demise in 1814 at the hands of Fernando VII also underlines how extraordinary the conditions were that enabled them to draft a document like the Constitution of Cádiz.

However, this liberal revolution was preceded by the two years and four months that separated the popular insurrection in Madrid of May 1808 from the gathering of the Cortes in September 1810. These years are known by

---

[6] This port was chosen as the venue because of its very peculiar geographical situation, which permitted the British navy to protect it from the French army; by then, Napoleon's forces controlled almost the whole Iberian Peninsula.

contemporary historians as the *bienio crucial* (the critical biennium),[7] during which the *Grande Armée* achieved a long list of victories on Spanish and Portuguese soil – the famous Spanish victory at Bailén in July 1808 was a notable exception. These defeats deepened the political uncertainty in the monarchy. In January 1810, the Junta Central, overwhelmed by the military adversities, without economic resources, and facing a campaign that their political enemies orchestrated, dissolved itself. However, just before that it took what in retrospect was its most important decision: to organize the election of Cortes. The vast majority of the members of the new Cortes were to be elected by a considerable part of the monarchy's adult male population, something never before experienced to that extent in any other part of the world. The innovations of the 1810 Cortes were not only electoral in nature. They included the American territories in the new representative body that was going to be put in place and electoral processes were organized in practically all the important American cities. In the end, more than 260 deputies participated in the so-called "Extraordinary Cortes" that opened in Cádiz in September 1810, about sixty of whom were Spanish Americans (Figure 3.1). Their participation in the debates was significant in several respects; in fact, several of the topics discussed would not have been present or would have been debated in a very different way without the American representatives. But, as a minority, these representatives were defeated at every turn when it came to vote on some of the most important economic or political issues, such as those concerning free commerce or political autonomy for their territories. For mostly the same reason and contrary to what is often said by some historians, if we consider the final text of the Cádiz Constitution, the direct contributions of the Spanish American deputies were meager.

The gathering of the Cortes did not translate into a more stable political situation or lead to military victories. The final defeat of the French army would have to wait until 1814, as a result of a patient and wise strategy of the Duke of Wellington, who was the commander-in-chief of the three armies (British, Spanish, and Portuguese). In the political sphere, the Cortes would

---

[7] As far as I know, the author who used the expression for the first time was François-Xavier Guerra, the French historian of Spanish origin who revolutionized the study of this whole period from the 1980s. His anthology of articles *Modernidad e independencias: Ensayos sobre las revoluciones hispánicas* (Madrid: Mapfre, 1992) has become a must-read for anyone interested in these revolutions. A much more recent anthology of Guerra's articles (excluding those that appear in the book just mentioned) is *Figuras de la modernidad: Hispanomérica, siglos XIX–XX*, ed. Annick Lempérière and Georges Lomné (Bogotá: Universidad Externado/IFEA/Taurus, 2012).

# The Cortes of Cádiz and the Spanish Liberal Revolution

Figure 3.1 The swearing in of the deputies to the Cortes of Cádiz (1810). Getty Images.

not reduce uncertainty, mainly because almost the whole country was under French control, because the Spanish American territories were thousands of miles away, and because of political strife in the city of Cádiz between the liberals and their staunch conservative enemies, called *serviles*. The *serviles* represented the traditional Spanish political institutions: concentrated monarchical power, great power of the Church in the political and social domains, the persistence of the Inquisition, and a very solid alliance between the Throne and the Altar. This alliance would guarantee the continuity with the pre-1808 situation and would uphold what the *serviles* considered the core essential values of Spanish history and of the Spanish people.

It was in this context that a relatively small number of men, who called themselves *liberales* and were known as such by their political adversaries, undertook what can be considered a radical transformation of the Spanish political institutions, the Spanish political landscape, Spanish society, and of many of the values that had sustained it for centuries. As mentioned, this effort and some of its outcomes are what is known by historians of this period as the "first Spanish liberalism" or as the "Spanish liberal revolution." This revolution took place at the same time that the emancipation movements in Spanish America were starting their trajectories.[8] It is important to state that these movements did not begin as independence movements in 1810. In fact, all of the Spanish American territories declared their allegiance to Fernando VII when the *crisis hispánica* broke out in the spring of 1808.

Little by little, depending on the territory in question and the year considered, Spanish Americans realized that the situation in the Peninsula was too difficult for the metropolitan authorities to handle and that, therefore, they had to take political decisions by themselves and for themselves. Some took advantage of the situation and tried to convince their fellow countrymen to seize the opportunity and declare independence. Others resisted ideas of this type and held on to the monarchy for many years after the crisis first erupted. Some others gradually passed from autonomy as an objective to independence, but even when they embraced the latter, sometimes they were not clear what "independence" really meant or the status they would maintain vis-à-vis the ex-metropolis once "independence" was achieved.

## The Cortes of Cádiz

As mentioned, about 200 deputies from peninsular Spain and around 60 from Spanish America participated in the Extraordinary Cortes (i.e., those that were in session between 1810 and 1813 and drafted the Constitution).[9] At first, many deputies had not arrived to Cádiz (mostly Americans, but not only them) and certain sessions that for one reason or another were considered important had a much higher attendance than others. In what sense

---

[8] On the first phase of the *revoluciones hispánicas*, see José María Portillo, *Crisis atlántica: Autonomía e independencia en la crisis de la monarquía hispánica* (Madrid: Marcial Pons, 2006). On the political situation and the policy changes that the Spanish Crown tried to apply to its empire during the fifty years prior to the *crisis hispánica*, see Gabriel B. Paquette, *Enlightenment, Governance, and Reform in Spain and Its Empire, 1759–1808* (Basingstoke: Palgrave Macmillan, 2008). Paquette is the author of a very suggestive assessment of the Cádiz Constitution and its historical significance: "Cádiz y las fábulas de la historiografía occidental," in Roberto Breña, ed., *Cádiz a debate: Actualidad, contexto y legado* (Mexico City: El Colegio de México, 2014), 49–62.

[9] Although dated in several aspects, a good book on the Cortes of Cádiz from a constitutional perspective is Joaquín Varela Suanzes, *La teoría del Estado en los orígenes del constitucionalismo hispánico: Las Cortes de Cádiz* (Madrid: Centro de Estudios Constitucionales, 1983). A more recent, slightly modified version, is *La teoría del Estado en las Cortes de Cádiz* (Madrid: CEPC, 2011).

were the methods of election in the Peninsula different from the ones applied in the Spanish American territories? The deputies from Spain were elected through a combination of procedures: In each administrative entity, one deputy would be elected by every 50,000 inhabitants; secondly, one deputy would be elected by each one of the *Juntas Superiores de Defensa* that had been created in the war against the French; thirdly, each one of the cities with a vote in the Cortes when it had met the last time – in 1789 – had the right to choose an additional deputy; finally, there were some special instructions on how elections would take place in two specific regions.[10]

In the case of Spanish America, the elections were organized completely differently due to the war in the Peninsula, the practical impossibility to carry out elections at that moment in all of the Spanish American territories, and the need to send the American representatives to Cádiz as soon as possible. In those territories where elections took place, they were carried out by the members of the *ayuntamientos* or municipal entities. Thirty-six deputies were elected through this process from New Spain, Guatemala, Peru, Cuba, Puerto Rico, and some regions in Venezuela and New Granada. As expected, it was impossible for the elected deputies to reach the metropole in time, so the *Regencia* decided to choose substitute deputies from the Spanish American inhabitants of the city of Cádiz. This process took place in September of 1810 and twenty-nine deputies were elected. Supposedly, these deputies would gradually leave their seats in the Cortes as the proper representatives started to arrive in Cádiz. Since this substitution never occurred, as mentioned, more than sixty Spanish American deputies ended up participating in the assembly.

Two matters need to be considered regarding the elections. Although the population of peninsular Spain (around 11 million in 1810) was smaller than that of Spanish America (roughly, 13 million), the number of peninsular deputies was far larger. This explains why in practically all of the issues that were voted regarding the main political and economic interests of the Spanish Americans, they were defeated by the peninsular majority. It is also noteworthy that the elections of the substitute deputies were considered illegitimate by many of the inhabitants of Spanish America and especially by those members of the creole elites who were seeking independence. This

---

[10] On the election of the Extraordinary Cortes, see Quintí Casals Bergés, "Proceso electoral y prosopografía de los diputados de las Cortes extraordinarias de Cádiz (1810–1813)," *Historia Constitucional*, 13 (2012), www.historiaconstitucional.com/index.php/historiaconstitucional/article/viewFile/330/294.

was the case in Caracas, Santa Fe, and Buenos Aires, where there was an increasing disaffection vis-à-vis the metropolitan authorities. Both factors contributed to the distancing between the Cortes and the American political leaders who were looking for political options after the start of the *crisis hispánica*. During the first years, these options were mainly sought within the empire, but gradually the objective became what we now understand as "independence" (a term used in a very flexible way at the time, as conceptual historians have noted). In this regard, no models were followed. From the declaration of independence that took place in Caracas in July 1811 until the independence of the Viceroyalty of Peru in December 1824, different types of political arrangements were sought in Spanish America. The variety and inventiveness of Spanish American constitutionalism attest to this. How protracted the process of effective independence was in several territories is an aspect that was ignored by traditional historiographies of Latin America until the end of the twentieth century, mainly because they refused to recognize the simple fact that many Spanish Americans did not want to become independent from the metropole.

Before proceeding with some of the main characteristics of the Spanish American deputies, it should be emphasized that what took place in the port of Cádiz between 1810 and 1814 was out of the ordinary due to a series of circumstances: the absence of the king; the occupation of almost all Spanish territory by the French army; the popular turmoil provoked by the war against Napoleon; the economic and military support of Britain (Spain's traditional enemy); and, finally, the de facto freedom of the press that existed in the Peninsula since 1808.[11] Of all these elements, the liberty to publish political texts is paramount to explain the Spanish liberal revolution. It was in the context of the daily gathering of the Cortes in Cádiz that liberal leaders quickly established a direct link between the war against Napoleon and *nuestra revolución* ("our revolution"). This revolution was liberal, nationalist, and popular at the same time. With respect to the last element, and having in mind the origin of the crisis (the deposition of the legitimate king), there is an important factor to be considered that helps explain ulterior events: the apparently unlimited devotion of the Spanish people to the absent King Fernando (very soon known as *El Deseado*, "the Desired One"). This devotion seemed to increase with the prolongation of a war that was incredibly cruel

---

[11] On this last element, see Fernando Durán López, Marieta Cantos Casenave, and Alberto Romero Ferrer, eds., *La guerra de pluma*, 3 vols. (Cádiz: Publicaciones de la Universidad de Cádiz, 2001–2008).

and very costly in human terms for the common people. In this regard, Goya's engravings titled *Los desastres de la guerra* are an insuperable testimony.

Another element that helps explain what happened once Fernando was set free by Napoleon is the peculiar situation of the city of Cádiz: an open, international and dynamic port, where Spaniards who were looking for political change had gathered, and where for the first time in Spanish history, hundreds of elected deputies were debating and making decisions for the whole monarchy. These factors and the protection that the invincible British fleet gave to its inhabitants not only created a unique situation in the city, but also help explain why the fall of Spanish liberalism came so fast in the Spring of 1814. Cádiz did not represent the political and social pulse of the whole of Spain; it was truly exceptional.

It is debatable who were the main protagonists of the Spanish liberal revolution that took place in Cádiz between 1810 and 1814. At this point, I will mention only those that I consider to be the most important names. Among the peninsular Spaniards, these are Manuel José Quintana, Agustín de Argüelles, the count of Toreno, Diego Muñoz Torrero, and, with hindsight and from a geographical distance (for he left Spain for England in 1810), José María Blanco White. Among the Spanish Americans representatives at the Cortes, three names are unavoidable from a liberal perspective: José Mejía Lequerica, José Miguel Ramos Arizpe, and José Miguel Guridi y Alcocer. However, as we will see below, many other names contributed to the liberal and American causes (which were linked, but can be separated for analytical purposes). Except for Quintana and Blanco White, all of the above were deputies in the Cortes. Four were priests (Muñoz Torrero, Blanco White, Ramos Arizpe, and Guridi y Alcocer), three had studied law (Quintana, Argüelles, and Mejía Lequerica), and one was a nobleman (Toreno).[12] This type of listing, though revealing in certain respects (showing, for example, the weight of churchmen in the *revoluciones hispánicas*), is clearly insufficient because it ignores the dozens of other individuals in their immediate circles who enabled many of the achievements of the liberal cause.

---

[12] Toreno is the author of the best history of the "Guerra de la Independencia" written by a contemporary witness: *Historia del levantamiento, guerra y revolución de España*, published originally between 1835 and 1837. An excellent edition was published in 2008 by Urgoiti Editores (Pamplona, Spain), with a brilliant preliminary study by Richard Hocquellet. On the shortcomings of Toreno's perspective regarding Spanish America, see Roberto Breña, "La *Historia* de Toreno y la historia para Toreno: El pueblo, España y el sueño de un liberal," *Historia Constitucional* 13 (2012), www .historiaconstitucional.com/index.php/historiaconstitucional/article/view/350.

Considering that the term "liberal" was only beginning its historical trajectory, it is impossible to define what "liberalism" was at this point. The names mentioned in the preceding paragraph are those of the political leaders or thinkers who most clearly identified themselves with a series of principles that were at odds with the political and social practices that had defined the Spanish monarchy for centuries. In ideological and institutional terms, the revolution that was taking place at that very moment revolved around a series of pivotal notions: "national sovereignty," "political equality," "division of powers," "individual rights," and "elections." If the Napoleonic invasion of the Peninsula provoked a political crisis, led to an explosive social situation, and gave rise to a liberty of expression that was unprecedented in Spanish history, what in due time turned these elements into a political revolution was the way in which the peninsular and Spanish American liberals used that opportunity to create and develop a series of ideas that, in political terms, proved to be very successful under the circumstances, not only inside, but also outside the Cortes, as many documents of the period attest.

The first Spanish liberalism was a mixture of traditional and revolutionary elements. It would be more accurate to say that, in a very particular historic context, traditional elements were carefully selected and adjusted in historical terms by liberal thinkers and politicians, thereby acquiring revolutionary connotations and having revolutionary consequences. For the first time in Spanish history, individual liberty played a very important role in a political design of which the 1812 Constitution was the epitome.[13] It was this particular combination between the old (the retrieval of medieval Cortes as a historic guide and example) and the new (national sovereignty, an eminently individualistic conception of certain rights, and the establishment of a completely different relationship with the Spanish American part of the monarchy) that defines to a great extent the first Spanish liberalism and where, it can be argued, its main doctrinal and ideological originality lies.

From a constitutional perspective, the main aspects of the first Spanish liberalism are contained in the following articles: national sovereignty (Art. 3), protection of individual rights (Art. 4), the purpose of government ("the happiness of the Nation and the wellbeing of the individuals that compose it," Art. 13), division of powers (Arts. 15–17), national

---

[13] A very complete study on the Constitution is Miguel Artola and Rafael Flaquer Montequi, *La Constitución de 1812* (Madrid: Iustel, 2008).

representation (Art. 27), electoral system for the whole monarchy (Arts. 34–103), inviolability of individual liberty by the king (Art. 172, section 11), fair administration of criminal justice (Arts. 286–308), inviolability of each person's home (Art. 306), general taxation (Art. 339), national education (Arts. 366–70), and freedom of the press (Art. 371). Many of these aspects may not seem new from a Western perspective, as they contain elements of the English Bill of Rights, the Constitution of the United States, and the French Constitution of 1791. However, to gauge the depth of the changes in a certain society, it is that particular society and its particular history that should be considered. Besides, it should not be forgotten that in aspects as important as the number of citizens that could participate in elections or aboriginal populations considered as citizens, the Constitution of Cádiz has no precedents in history. In aspects like these, the *revoluciones hispánicas* may have constituted the last Atlantic revolution in chronological terms, but made contributions to the Age of Revolutions that were unique (and that have seldom been recognized).

Regarding the very important issue of the Church and its social role, the revolution that took place in Cádiz did not limit itself to the articles in the Constitution. The number and importance of the decrees issued by the Extraordinary Cortes that diminished the Church's power cannot be ignored. Among them, the abolition of the Inquisition was, from a Spanish historical perspective, a major accomplishment of the *liberales*. The same can be said of other decrees, in very diverse areas, that either preceded or followed the Constitution and that contributed enormously to the effort on their part to build a new political and social order.

A good example of how ambitious the Spanish liberal project was are the six articles of title IX of the Constitution (Arts. 366–71), listed above under "national education." With these articles, education at all levels became the responsibility of the government and a "General Direction of Studies" was created with the mandate of reviewing and controlling public education. Oversight of education was given to the Cortes, which would "legislate on everything that has to do with [this] important object" (Art. 370). The significance of Article 371 from a liberal perspective cannot be greater, for it was the one devoted to freedom of the press. All of these articles were very important in launching a secularization process that may only seem modest when we ignore the role that the Church had played in Spanish society for centuries. The Cádiz Constitution did consider Catholicism the sole religion, but it also tried to control what up to that moment was an almost exclusive role of the Church in public education, publishing, and public discourse. The relevance of this title of the Constitution can hardly be exaggerated.[14]

Which were the main intellectual sources of the first Spanish liberalism? The most important are the following: scholasticism; the modern school of natural law; French constitutional thought (especially the Constitution of 1791); the Spanish Enlightenment; and historic nationalism (*nacionalismo histórico*). The mere listing of these currents shows the eclecticism of first Spanish liberalism. It is impossible to detail each of them, but it is also impossible not to dwell, if only briefly, in the last one, not only because it was the most important in ideological terms, but also because it was the most original.

The notion of a "historic constitution" was one of the most debated issues in Cádiz. The concept had been discussed in Spanish intellectual circles since 1780, when Gaspar Melchor de Jovellanos, the most important of the Spanish *ilustrados*, presented his discourse of admission to the Royal Academy of History. It was titled *"On the need to join the study of our legislation to the study of our history."*[15] In a nutshell, Jovellanos argued that the political liberty that individuals had enjoyed in Spain's medieval kingdoms had been lost with the arrival of the Habsburg dynasty to the throne of Spain at the beginning of the sixteenth century. Liberty had been assured until that moment by the existence of the Cortes, which were able to keep the king's power within certain limits. The situation changed with the arrival of the Habsburgs to the throne, especially under the first two kings, Carlos I and Felipe II. From Jovellanos' perspective, civil liberty was progressively lost (hence the importance that the first Spanish liberalism attached to the notion of "liberty recovered"). In the end, Jovellanos was suggesting the need to put an end to almost 300 years of what could be considered royal despotism. It may be

---

[14] One of the authors that has insisted the most on the centrality of religion and on the confessional character of the Cádiz Constitution is José María Portillo Valdés; see his *La Nazione Cattolica. Cadice 1812: Una costituzione per la Spagna* (Manduria: Piero Lacaita Editore, 1998). This perspective tends to downplay the liberal content of the Cádiz Constitution as well as the importance of individuals in the document. For a contrasting view, see Ignacio Fernández Sarasola, "La portée des droits individuels dans la Constitution espagnole de 1812," in Jean-Phillipe Luis, ed., *La Guerre d'indépendance espagnole et le libéralisme au XIX<sup>e</sup> siècle* (Madrid: Casa de Velázquez, 2011).

[15] There are several editions of this text. One of them is Gaspar Melchor de Jovellanos, *Obras en prosa* (Madrid: Editorial Castalia, 1988), 71–102. The best modern anthology of Jovellanos' political writings is Gaspar Melchor de Jovellanos, *Obras completas (Escritos políticos)*, vol. XI, ed. Ignacio Fernández Sarasola (Oviedo: Ayuntamiento de Gijón/ Instituto Feijoo/KRK Ediciones, 2006). The discourse in question can be found on pp. 815–22.

added that Jovellanos' conception of Spanish history included exaggerations and distortions; still, his idea of liberty reclaimed or recovered was one of the most powerful ideological forces at Cádiz.

The same can be said of the vision of Spain's history presented by the second most important author representing "nationalist historicism": Francisco Martínez Marina, the author of *Teoría de las Cortes*, the most important text of this current of thought.[16] Martínez Marina's life and work reflect, in paradigmatic ways, the ambiguities and inconsistencies of the first Spanish liberalism, to the extent that it is very difficult to locate him in the ideological spectrum of his age. He first collaborated with the government of José I, the French usurper, but his political past did not prevent his ideas from being read and discussed in Cádiz, and did not prevent his election as deputy in the Madrid Cortes of 1820. In *Teoría de las Cortes*, Martínez Marina developed Jovellanos' thesis on the despotism of the Habsburg and Bourbon dynasties. In the aftermath of the 1808 crisis, this argument was recuperated, modified, and developed by the Cádiz *liberales*, who found in it Spanish precedents not only for popular sovereignty, but also for the rejection of monarchical absolutism and for the recovery of individual and municipal liberties.

The third key contribution to historic nationalism, along with Jovellanos' discourse and Martínez Marina's *Teoría de las Cortes*, is the "Preliminary Discourse" that accompanied the Cádiz Constitution.[17] Usually, this "Discourse" is attributed to Agustín de Argüelles, the liberal deputy considered by friends and foes alike as the leader of the liberal representatives at the Cádiz Cortes. Although he was responsible for most of its content, other liberal deputies contributed as members of the Constitutional Commission. In any case, this document is the most important synthesis, doctrinal achievement, and political program of the first Spanish liberalism.

Although in the first lines of the "Discourse," Argüelles asserted the direct link between the Constitution and the fundamental laws of the monarchy, he knew very well that precisely because the constitutional document went well beyond those laws, it was going to meet with much resistance from many quarters of Spanish society (as is explicitly stated in the last part of the "Discourse"). What happened only two years afterwards proved he was

---

[16] The most recent and complete edition is the one by José Antonio Escudero: *Teoría de las Cortes*, 3 vols. (Bilbao: Gestingraf, 2002).

[17] The discourse is frequently included in editions of the Constitution. An edition exclusively of the discourse that contains a useful preliminary study by Luis Sánchez Agesta is *Discurso preliminar a la Constitución de 1812* (Madrid: CEPC, 1989).

right: After Fernando VII was freed by Napoleon in December 1813 and made his way back to Spain, it became clear that what had happened in the small port of Cádiz since 1810 did not have a national dimension. In May 1814, Fernando VII was reinstated in his full power as king of Spain. With him, absolutism returned, and the repression of the most important liberal leaders started immediately. It is true that liberalism would be back in Spain six years after, but the *Trienio liberal* (1820–1823) would only be another interlude of political freedom, during which the Cádiz Constitution was once again applied. Put simply, Fernando VII could not accept a constitutional monarchy. With the help of the conservative forces of several European countries (the Holy Alliance) and the invasion of Spanish territory by a large French army that barely met resistance, the Spanish liberals were defeated once again. Fernando VII regained his throne with unlimited powers in the autumn of 1823 and maintained an absolutist regime in Spain until his death in 1833.

## The Spanish American Deputies

Although many of the peninsular Spanish deputies could not be considered liberals, the majority of them supported change, albeit moderate change, and that is why on many occasions the Spanish liberal leaders were able to tip the balance in their favor when it came to voting. Exactly the same can be said with respect to the Spanish American deputies.[18] The fact that many of them were substitutes elected from the Spanish American inhabitants of Cádiz, and had a progressive mentality, contributed to the support that many Spanish American representatives gave to the proposals of the peninsular liberals. However, it is also true that the peninsular liberal deputies never accepted the proposals of their Spanish American counterparts regarding what could be defined as political and economic "autonomy." This is not to say that everything stayed the same politically or economically for Spanish America (e.g., concerning citizenship, agriculture, certain aspects of trade, the administration of justice, local representative institutions, and the weakening of social hierarchies), but these elements did not fulfill the expectations and interests of many Spanish Americans. Not only that, the Cortes was unable to put in practice an appeasement plan for a subcontinent in which several

---

[18] By far the best book on the Spanish American deputies is Marie-Laure Rieu-Millán, *Los diputados americanos en las Cortes de Cádiz: Igualdad o independencia* (Madrid: CSIC, 1990).

regions were in a state of war. Instead, they supported the sending of a relatively small number of troops to fight the "rebels." In retrospect, this lack of a serious plan to put an end to the warlike situation that began to spread in the Spanish American territories in 1810 may be considered a big mistake of the Cádiz Cortes.

The unanimous support for the Spanish Crown that the Spanish Americans expressed during 1808 and part of 1809 began to give way to clear fissures in 1810 and came to an end when the creole elite of the city of Caracas declared independence in July 1811. Showing an ingenuity that would cost them dearly, several of the leaders of the liberal group in the Cortes were convinced that the Constitution by itself would placate the situation in America. Their belief ignored several factors, among them the fact that several territories (such as the Viceroyalty of the Río de la Plata and many cities in the Captaincy General of Venezuela and the Viceroyalty of New Granada) never agreed to send deputies to the Cortes and therefore could not and did not expect anything from them. Besides, their belief also ignored that the discontent in several territories had to do with a lack of certain political and economic forms of autonomy that the Cortes never redressed. "Technical" issues complicated things even more: the enormous distances that the ships had to travel; the relatively small number of American ports where the news from the metropole arrived with a certain regularity; the fragmentary nature of the news that reached the American territories; and, finally, the convulsive political juncture affecting almost all of Spanish America. All these factors help explain why the measures taken by the Cortes were frequently almost obsolete upon arrival on American soil.

By the time the Cortes gathered in the last week of September 1810, the juntas of Caracas, Santa Fe, and Buenos Aires had decided not to recognize the *Regencia* and its decisions and, consequently, the Cortes. Besides, in the most important and wealthiest of all the Spanish American territories, the Viceroyalty of New Spain, just a week before the Cortes met, an insurrection led by the priest Miguel Hidalgo erupted against the peninsular authorities.

The political attitude of the Cortes regarding America was not different from the authorities that preceded them (i.e., the Junta Central and the *Regencia*) and from the one that followed (i.e., Fernando VII as an absolute king). However, since it was a representative assembly in which American deputies were present and in which liberal principles played such an important role, some historians seem to have expected a different stance toward the needs and interests of Spanish America. In this regard, it should not be forgotten that the mercantile community of the port of Cádiz was adamant that no significant commercial advantages should be given to the Americans and that, therefore, the insurgents had to be subdued at all costs. This same community was responsible for the relatively few expeditions that the Cortes was able to send to America in order to pacify the region. Given its economic and political clout and its enormous influence on the peninsular Spanish deputies, to expect a different attitude on the part of many of them seems a bit disingenuous.

What about the social composition of the American representatives in the Cortes? Though figures vary, around 30 percent were priests, about 20 percent were lawyers, about 20 percent were civil servants, around 15 percent belonged to the military, and about 5 percent belonged to the liberal professions. Other categories made up the remaining 10 percent. It should be noted that the percentage of priests was much higher among Spanish Americans than peninsular Spaniards. There were many variations, however, in absolute and in percentage terms. For example, more than 65 percent of the deputies from New Spain were priests (fourteen out of twenty-one), while in the case of Cuba, only 25 percent belonged to the Church (one out of four). However, contrary to what could be expected, and as was already mentioned, some clergymen, peninsular and American, played a very important role in the liberal revolution that took place in Cádiz between 1810 and 1814.

What about the ideological tendencies among the Spanish American deputies? The most important groups that can be discerned were absolutists, conservatives, and liberals. The absolutists were relatively few (among them, Foncerrada, Pérez, and Ostolaza were the most important), but along with the conservatives (including Mendiola, Rus, and López Lisperguer) and depending on the issue under discussion, they could present a considerable opposition to the liberals, especially because sometimes the liberals did not vote unanimously. Among the liberals, there were some who could be considered "progressives" and other that could be considered "moderates." Three of the most important "progressives" were already mentioned (Lequerica, Ramos Arizpe and Guridi y Alcocer), but to that minimal list could be added Gutiérrez de Terán, Feliú, Puñonrostro, and Fernández de Leiva. Among the "moderates," some of the most active were Gordoa, Morales Duárez, Castillo, Larrazábal, and Power.

As with any other classification, this one should be approached with caution, because from the perspective of several peninsular deputies (either liberals or absolutists), the vast majority of them were in favor of reforms. In this regard, it should be kept in mind that the defense of American interests was considered "progressive" by many peninsular deputies. At the same time, that was also considered radical, in the sense that those interests were a menace for what they thought to be the essential interests of the empire as a unified entity. This is what explains the fact that the peninsular liberals and the Spanish American liberals were frequently on different sides when it came to political or economic matters that were significant from an American perspective.

The main point of dispute was the lack of recognition on the part of the Spanish deputies of the particularity of the Spanish American territories and, therefore, of the different treatment that their representatives expected to receive. The Cádiz Constitution aimed to be "unitary," that is, it centralized political power in the hands of new *jefes políticos* or *jefes superiores* in each Spanish American jurisdiction. These political chiefs, appointed by the king, were to rule over the two local entities created by the Constitution – the *diputaciones provinciales* ("Provincial Deputations") and the *ayuntamientos* (city and town councils), that were only given administrative prerogatives. However, in reality the *ayuntamientos* progressively acquired capacities that were not only administrative, but also political. In this respect, some of the most distinguished peninsular liberals were proven right in their fears that due to distance from the center of political power, allowing political autonomy to Spanish Americans would sooner rather than later lead to federalism and, in the long run, to the dissolution of the monarchy.

These fears proved to be a politically paralyzing force, mainly because they unconsciously directed decisions toward the use of force, not negotiation. In the end, they are key to explaining the final result: the loss of the whole of continental Spanish America.[19] In other words, liberal principles and liberal discourse were insufficient not only to convince the Spanish Americans to lay down their arms, but also to convince them that the Constitution of Cádiz was the proper vehicle or adequate instrument with which a new relationship could be established between the European and the American parts of the empire, for the benefit of both. Constitutional monarchy was an enormous step forward regarding political modernity, but given the conditions created by the *crisis hispánica*, and ulterior developments, it was not enough from the American point of view. As mentioned, in

---

[19] Although published forty years ago, one of the best books on the motives that explain this loss in four of the Spanish American territories is Jorge Domínguez, *Insurrection or Loyalty: The Breakdown of the Spanish Empire in America* (Cambridge, MA: Harvard University Press, 1980). Another good study, much broader – covering the mid-eighteenth to the mid-nineteenth century – and that includes the Portuguese empire, is Tulio Halperin Donghi, *Reforma y disolución de los imperios ibéricos, 1750–1850* (Madrid: Alianza Editorial, 1985).

this regard the peninsular deputies of the Cortes, either absolutists or liberals, expected too much from a written document. In practical terms, they disregarded what was taking place on the ground, as well as different circumstances in different continents; thereby ignoring the nature and scope of the *problema americano* (as it was called in those days).

## Application of the Constitution in America

The Cádiz Constitution was not applied to all of Spanish America. The territories where it was enforced were the Viceroyalty of New Spain, the Captaincy General of Guatemala, the Viceroyalty of Peru, and some cities in the Captaincy General of Venezuela and the Viceroyalty of New Granada.[20] In all of them, the influence of the first Spanish liberalism was direct and, to that extent, indisputable. However, when historians talk about *liberalismo hispánico* they are not only referring to peninsular liberalism and to the liberalism in those territories. The term also applies to the rest of Spanish America during the first quarter of the nineteenth century. Recent historiography has shown that the Cádiz Constitution in particular and the first Spanish liberalism in general exercised a considerable influence in some of the Spanish American territories where the Constitution was never applied. This influence manifested itself not only through the constitutional debates in Cádiz and the Constitution itself once it was promulgated in March 1812, but also in the incredible number of political texts of very different kinds published in Cádiz that arrived in America, and which were frequently read, reprinted, and discussed. All these aspects and the fact that peninsular Spain had been the metropole for almost 300 years help explain the extent to which Spanish American politicians, publicists, and journalists felt the need to respond to what was going on in the Peninsula. Even in the territories where the Constitution was not applied, like the Viceroyalty of the Río de la Plata, the historiography of recent years has shown the considerable presence and influence of what was happening in Cádiz, of what was published there, and of what the Cortes was debating.[21]

---

[20] On the case of the Viceroyalty of New Spain, see Manuel Ferrer Muñoz, *La Constitución de Cádiz y su aplicación en la Nueva España* (Mexico City: UNAM, 1993). For a more succinct and more recent perspective, see Roberto Breña, "La Constitución de Cádiz y la Nueva España: Cumplimientos e incumplimientos," *Historia Constitucional* 13 (2012), www .historiaconstitucional.com/index.php/historiaconstitucional/article/view/337/301.

[21] A very good example is Marcela Ternavasio, *Gobernar la revolución: Poderes en disputa en el Río de la Plata, 1810–1816* (Buenos Aires: Siglo XXI Editores, 2007).

However, in the territories where the Constitution was introduced, it was applied in a selective way, especially with respect to elections and freedom of the press. In some cases that were mainly due to the prevailing war situation and the political costs of a general application of the Constitution (as in New Spain); in some others, the "centrifugal" tendencies were too strong and the economic conditions too adverse to enable a general application (as was the case in the Captaincy General of Guatemala); and in yet other territories the political and military capabilities of the viceroy permitted him to accumulate so much power that, in certain ways, he was able to modify or differ the application of the Constitution almost at will (as was the case in Peru with Viceroy Abascal).[22] In any case, it should be remembered that several factors mitigated against the application of the Constitution: the uncertain political and military situation in peninsular Spain; the lack of a constant communication between the metropole and its American territories; and, first and foremost, the political volatility and lack of unanimity in several American cities and territories with respect to the position to be taken regarding the Constitution in particular and the Spanish Crown in general. In the end, the Constitution was applied only in some territories, in a selective way, and, in any case, for a very short period of time.

## Final Remarks

Notwithstanding the many obstacles for the application of the Constitution and all of its limitations when viewed from a Spanish American perspective, there are some aspects that should be underlined. First and foremost, many elections at different levels took place in Spanish America between 1809 (when the elections for the Junta Central were held) and the beginning of 1814. This point can hardly be exaggerated, not only because of what any election implies in social terms, but also considering that Spanish Americans were experiencing elections of this type for the first time ever. Another aspect that cannot be ignored was the de facto freedom of the press that Spanish Americans societies also experienced during this whole period. At first, not due to legal rulings but to the extraordinary circumstances provoked by the invasion of the Iberian Peninsula by Napoleon's troops. In this regard, the publication of the decree on freedom of the press by the Cortes in

---

[22] On the Peruvian case contrasted with the Peninsular situation, there is a recent and interesting work: Mónica Ricketts, *Who Should Rule? Men of Arms, the Republic of Letters, and the Fall of the Spanish Empire* (Oxford: Oxford University Press, 2017).

November 1810 (i.e., almost a year and a half before the Constitution was promulgated), was of great significance. Only by considering the level of secrecy that characterized the Spanish *ancien régime* is it possible to gauge how revolutionary press freedom was for peninsular Spain and its empire. In other words, any assessment of the import and limitations of the Cortes of Cádiz regarding the Spanish American territories has to consider what had existed in social and political terms in the *mundo hispánico* for hundreds of years.

That the Constitution of 1812 was not the solution to *el problema americano* is a truism. However, it is also evident that the Constitution represented a political revolution in itself. From being considered "colonies" by the enlightened peninsular politicians of the second half of the eighteenth century, in less than five years after 1808 the American territories of the Spanish Empire had elected representatives in the assembly that was to guide its destiny. In other words, political legitimacy no longer had anything to do with the divine right of kings, but with the sovereignty of the nation. In this sense, more than in any other, the Cortes of Cádiz turned the Spanish political world upside down. Besides, the aboriginal people of Spanish America were granted citizenship and the vast majority of free adult Spanish Americans were granted the right to elect their representatives. It should be added that the colored castes were excluded from citizenship, a measure with which the peninsular Spaniards assured themselves of a majority in the future Cortes. Relatedly, it is true that deputies from both continents brought up the issue of slavery and its gradual abolition in the Cortes, but in the end the Constitution left it untouched.[23]

The changes brought about by the Cádiz Constitution with respect to political legitimacy, individual liberty, political equality, the rule of law, and elections (at different levels) would have changed the metropole and the relationship with its former colonies beyond recognition. This is counterfactual thinking, but it is important to keep in mind that what happened in peninsular Spain between 1808 and 1810, in Cádiz between 1810 and 1814,

---

[23] In this regard, the arguments in favor of it presented by the Cuban deputies were the ones that apparently tipped the balance. It is true that countries such as Chile and Mexico abolished slavery very soon after obtaining their independence, but the majority of the new Spanish American countries took several decades to do it. It should be added that under exceptional circumstances, especially during the wars of independence, some slaves were granted freedom. On this topic, see Peter Blanchard, *Under the Flags of Freedom: Slave Soldiers and the Wars of Independence in Spanish South America* (Pittsburgh: University of Pittsburgh Press, 2008) and the chapter in the present book by Jane Landers.

and in Spanish America during the whole independence period was a political revolution that deserves an important place in the history of the Atlantic Revolutions and in the history of the Age of Revolutions. This place has been denied or at least minimized by many historians that purportedly were "experts" on the Age of Revolutions.[24] The fact that this *revolución hispánica* was not enough to keep the Spanish American territories as part of the empire should not lessen its significance in historical terms or from the perspective of the history of political thought and the history of ideas. In this regard, for example, the constitutional "explosion" that these territories experienced between 1810 and 1815 (very much influenced by the Cádiz experience and which has no equivalent in Western political history) has scarcely received attention outside Latin America historiography.[25]

From the perspective of Spanish America, the *revoluciones hispánicas* ended up with independence and the beginning of a new history of the countries that emerged from it. All of them, except Mexico for a very brief period, were born as republics, not as constitutional monarchies like the one the Cortes of Cádiz proposed.[26] One question remains: How much did these revolutions change Spanish American societies? This is still an open question, not only regarding *these* revolutions, but any other. What is clear is that for the most disadvantaged groups, not much has changed. Nonetheless, the historic import of the political transformation that took place in Spanish America between 1808 and 1824 is undeniable.

---

[24] Two examples may suffice. The much-celebrated two-volume work by R. R. Palmer, *The Age of the Democratic Revolution* (Princeton, NJ: Princeton University Press, 1959 and 1964), that can be considered one of the main sources of the burgeoning historiography on this revolutionary age, ended its chronological coverage in 1800. As for Jacques Godechot, the other "godfather" of Atlantic History, not one of his several books on different aspects of the Age of Revolutions deals with the Spanish American independence movements in anything but a tangential way.

[25] About this constitutional outburst, see José Antonio Aguilar Rivera, *En pos de la quimera: Reflexiones sobre el experimento constitucional atlántico* (Mexico City: FCE/ CIDE, 2000), 15–56.

[26] On this topic, an ambitious contribution was recently made by Hilda Sabato, *Republics of the New World: The Revolutionary Political Experiment in 19th-Century Latin America* (Princeton, NJ: Princeton University Press, 2018).

4

# The Constitutional Triennium in Spain, 1820–1823

### JUAN LUIS SIMAL

In 1815, after Napoleon was definitively defeated at Waterloo and the Congress of Vienna remodeled the European map, the reactionary and conservative statesmen that ruled the continent longed for an era of social and political order under the restored princes. Yet revolution returned to Europe in 1820 in Las Cabezas de San Juan, a small town in southern Spain. On the first day of the year, a *pronunciamiento* led by officers of the expeditionary army heading for South America to quell republican separatists managed to reinstall the liberal Constitution of Cádiz, sanctioned in 1812 in the midst of the patriotic struggle against the Napoleonic invasion. King Fernando VII, who had established a neoabsolutist monarchy after his restoration in 1814, was now compelled to become a constitutional monarch. For the next years, amidst intense political mobilization and activism, the liberals struggled to implement a modernization program. Yet their factionalism and the persistence of a strong local counterrevolutionary movement submersed the country in a tumultuous state. The European powers intervened in 1823 and a French army restored Fernando VII to his absolute power, forcing thousands of exiles to flee the country.

## Fernando VII's Restoration and the Liberal Opposition, 1814–1819

The successful 1820 *pronunciamiento* was the culmination of years of conspiracy and the last of several failed insurrections carried out by Spanish liberals since 1814. In May 1814, upon his return from France, Fernando VII had put an end to the constitutional experience. He considered that it had not been a patriotic effort that saved the nation from its enemies, as the liberals believed, but rather a democratic attack on the monarchy made by impious revolutionaries. With the support of sectors of the army and Church – and the acquiescence of the British army led by the Duke of

Wellington, who oversaw the Spanish political situation – he staged a *coup d'état*, abolished the constitution and reinstalled the structures of the Old Regime.[1] He immediately ordered the repression of the Cádiz liberals and the *afrancesados* (the Spanish Bonapartists who had supported the "usurper" Joseph Bonaparte). Dozens of liberals were imprisoned, many others went into exile. As many as 10,000 *afrancesados* took refuge in France.[2]

The state of the country after the most destructive war ever fought on the soil of the Spanish monarchy was dreadful. Furthermore, the rebellions in Spanish America had led to the collapse of the continent's production and trade, damaging overseas revenue, an essential source of income for the monarchy. The prospects of recovery were dim and many of the king's decisions worked against it. He halted the tax reform initiated by the liberals and partially returned fiscal privileges to the aristocracy and the Church. The expeditionary army sent to Venezuela in 1815, which was able momentarily to crush the separatists, exhausted the scarce resources available. Moreover, the government was marked by constant instability, with ministers being continuously replaced by the king's whimsical decisions. A swift economic recovery was impossible under these conditions.[3] Support for maintaining the status quo kept diminishing, although the repression and vigilance of the population under the Inquisition, used by Fernando VII as a political police, hampered the opposition.[4]

Nevertheless, many considered that deep reforms were necessary. Conspiracies that used Masonic methods of organization commenced and several *pronunciamientos* were carried out: Espoz y Mina acted in Navarra in 1814, Díaz Porlier in La Coruña in 1815, and Lacy in Barcelona in 1817.[5] Only Francisco Espoz y Mina escaped alive. Usually, in a *pronunciamiento* a prestigious member of the army, in collusion with civilians, proclaimed in front of his troops a political project and asked to be followed. Many of the leaders of these *pronunciamientos* were heroes from the Peninsular War who felt disregarded by the regime, but their actions cannot be interpreted as

---

[1] Emilio La Parra, *Fernando VII: Un rey deseado y detestado* (Barcelona: Tusquets, 2018), 224–76.

[2] Juan López Tabar, *Los famosos traidores: Los afrancesados durante la crisis del Antiguo Régimen (1808–1832)* (Madrid: Biblioteca Nueva, 2001); Juan Luis Simal, *Emigrados: España y el exilio internacional, 1814–1834* (Madrid: CEPC, 2012).

[3] Josep Fontana, *La quiebra de la monarquía absoluta, 1814–1820* (Barcelona: Ariel, 1974).

[4] Emilio La Parra and María Ángeles Casado, *La Inquisición en España: Agonía y abolición* (Madrid: Libros de la Catarata, 2013).

[5] Luis P. Martín, "La masonería y la conspiración liberal (1814–1834). Los límites de un mito histórico," *Trienio* 22 (1993), 73–90.

purely egotistic and career-driven. Most had a sincere political component. Other conspiracies were crushed by the authorities before they could be started, like Vidal's in Valencia and the "Conspiracy of the triangle," an attempt on the king's life.[6]

In this context, absolutism was not able to find the social backing it needed to resist the erratic but unremitting plots of those sections of the elites and the frustrated middle classes who sought a return to the constitutional system. Still, there was no unanimity among liberal plotters, and some of them favored a moderate revision of the Constitution of Cádiz. In 1819 an intrigue formed by high military officers, including General Count La Bisbal, failed to mobilize the army assembled in the Gulf of Cádiz.[7] Yet this conspiracy of El Palmar, thwarted after a participant betrayed it, was to be the general rehearsal of the successful 1820 *pronunciamiento*.

## The Revolution

On 1 January 1820, a group of young officers overlooked in the repression of the El Palmar conspiracy initiated yet another *pronunciamiento* for the 1812 constitution. This time it was successful, but not in the way the revolutionaries expected. Rafael del Riego and Antonio Quiroga, its main leaders, won over part of the soldiers who were suffering from a yellow fever epidemic and feared the prospect of crossing the Atlantic to fight a dangerous war in America. However, their success was relative. Although Riego was not detained, the military insurrection proved insufficient. For the next two months he led a frail expedition that crossed southern Spain trying to gain support for the constitution (Map 4.1).[8]

Riego found no strong popular support in the rural areas he visited; yet, the monarchy proved unable to stop him. The turning point was the extension of Riego's example to several cities throughout the country, starting with La Coruña on 21 February. In the next weeks, juntas that deposed the authorities and proclaimed the reinstallation of the Constitution appeared in many urban centers. In early March, La Bisbal, sent by the king to crush the revolutionaries, endorsed the Constitution. In a context of confusion and uncertainty, Fernando VII first tried to calm down

---

[6] Miguel Artola, *La España de Fernando VII* (Madrid: Espasa, 1999), 485–501.

[7] Claude Morange, *Una conspiración fallida y una constitución nonnata (1819)* (Madrid: CEPC, 2006).

[8] Richard Stites, *The Four Horsemen: Riding to Liberty in Post-Napoleonic Europe* (Oxford: Oxford University Press, 2014), 65–72.

Figure 4.1 Massacre of the population marching for the Constitution in Cádiz. Courtesy of the Biblioteca Nacional, Spain.

the discontents by calling for the Cortes in the Old Regime fashion, that is, organized by estates. Yet he had lost control of the situation and found no support in the army. Under pressure from liberals in Madrid, he had no option but to accept the same constitution that he had obliterated six years earlier. On 9 March, he swore it in. Immediately, the Inquisition was abolished and political prisoners were released. After the king's decision was reported in the provinces, the constitutional movement, for the most part peaceful, could not be contained. No major clashes occurred, except in Cádiz, where troops massacred the population who marched for the Constitution.[9]

The new juntas were dominated by conservative men and members of the middle classes who wanted to preserve social order. The transition to the

---

[9] Pedro Rújula and Manuel Chust, *El Trienio liberal en la monarquía hispánica: Revolución e independencia (1820–1823)* (Madrid: Catarata, 2020).

Map 4.1 Spain in 1820

constitutional institutions was swift. A provisional and moderate central junta, headed by Cardinal Borbón – a liberal churchman who was the king's uncle and had been regent during the Napoleonic Wars – directed the transition.[10] It soon reestablished freedom of the press and the legislation of the Cortes of Cádiz, and convened a new Cortes.[11]

Optimism and, in most cities, popular enthusiasm, presided over the first steps of the constitutional regime. Many of the men who had suffered repression since 1814 were reinstalled in their posts or joined the new local and provincial constitutional bodies. On 18 March the first government was formed, mockingly called by the king the "government of the prisoners," because it was formed by men who had spent years in prison, like Agustín de Argüelles, José Canga-Argüelles, and Evaristo Pérez de Castro.

---

[10] Carlos M. Rodríguez López-Brea, *Don Luis de Borbón: El cardenal de los liberales (1777–1823)* (Toledo: Junta de Comunidades de Castilla-La Mancha, 2002), 284.
[11] Blanca Buldain Jaca, *Régimen político y preparación de Cortes en 1820* (Madrid: Congreso de los Diputados, 1988); Antonio Moliner Prada, "Las Juntas durante el Trienio Liberal," *Hispania* 195 (1997), 147–81.

## The Liberal Program

In 1820, the constitution could be implemented as the fundamental law of the Spanish monarchy in a more favorable context than that of its first short-lived period (1812–1814). In those years the War of Independence created insurmountable obstacles that impeded its full realization. Now, in a context of peace and with the apparent acquiescence of Fernando VII – a constitutional king subjected to national sovereignty – the liberals hoped to achieve the conversion of the monarchy to a liberal state respectful of civil and political liberties in which all citizens were equal before the law. The king was head of the executive, but his powers were checked by the Cortes, which represented the nation and was elected by indirect universal male suffrage.[12]

After the elections, on 9 July the first Cortes convened. A majority of moderate deputies supported the government. Most came from the affluent sectors of society and the professional groups (lawyers, military officers, doctors), and there was also an important number of clergymen. Under the constitutional system the king was at liberty to choose his ministers yet had no option other than to trust men of prestige of moderate liberal leanings.

The government and the Cortes initiated an intense reformist agenda reinstalling and expanding the legislation passed in Cádiz in 1810–1814. The first decisions dealt with the removal of the privileges of the Church and the nobility. Although the Cortes' suppression of seigneurial rights was repeatedly blocked by the king, important measures were taken to dismantle the aristocracy's and the Catholic Church's power and social influence. The regular clergy was reformed and the monasteries of monastic orders were dissolved. Part of the Church's property, mostly in urban areas, was seized by the state and sold in order to redeem public debt and obtain funds for a treasury in need, but also to create a class of propertied citizens directly linked to the new regime. The liberals also promoted an economic program based on a fiscal reform that included the reduction of the tithe, the liberalization of economic activities, and the promotion of commercial relations in an integrated market. To encourage the development of the national industry, protective tariffs were established (although foreign textiles were frequently smuggled in), and a plan for the construction of roads and canals was approved. Several of these measures, especially the redefinition of

---

[12] Joaquín Varela Suanzes-Carpegna, *La monarquía doceañista (1819–1837): Avatares, encomios y denuestos de una extraña forma de gobierno* (Madrid: Marcial Pons, 2013), 71–157, 245–78.

property rights under an individualistic conception and the new monetary taxes, affected the traditional communal practices in rural areas and upset the peasantry. At the same time, many communities invoked the liberal reforms to end paying seigneurial rents and resist the appropriation of common lands by the lords.[13]

## The Many Faces of Liberalism:
### *Moderados* and *exaltados*

From its beginning, factionalism characterized the constitutional regime. Its plural political culture included a variety of divergent and polysemic understandings of the constitution, and two main groups crystallized: *moderados* and *exaltados*. A generational gap set both groups apart. Most moderates, like intellectual leaders Argüelles, Count Toreno, or Alberto Lista, were veterans from the Cortes of Cádiz, or ex-*afrancesados*. Some men who had held relevant posts during the absolutist years also joined the moderate bloc. Among the *exaltados* young men abounded. They were less politically experienced but had been the protagonists of the revolution. They included most of the army officers that led the *pronunciamiento* as well as influential civilians like Antonio Alcalá Galiano, Francisco J. Istúriz, and banker Juan Álvarez de Mendizábal. Of course, there was no strict generational divide. Among the *exaltados* there were seasoned men like Álvaro Flórez Estrada, who had been in exile in England since 1814.[14]

For most of the *Trienio*, the national government was controlled by the *moderados*, who also amassed most local and regional power. They favored a reformist agenda aimed at expanding the benefits of liberalism and obtaining the support of conservative sectors. Many *moderados* considered it necessary to reform the Constitution. The *afrancesados*, proponents of a strong executive power, agreed. Moderates considered the 1812 code too radical, especially for its unicameralism that evoked the assemblies of the French Revolution. Thus, they proposed the introduction of a high chamber that would check the democratic impulses of the Cortes.[15]

---

[13] Joaquín del Moral, *Hacienda y sociedad en el Trienio constitucional (1820–1823)* (Madrid: Instituto de Estudios Fiscales, 1975); Ramon Arnabat, *Visca la Pepa! Les reformes econòmiques del Trienni Liberal (1820–1823)* (Barcelona: Societat Catalana d'Estudis Històrics – Institut d'Estudis Catalans, 2002).

[14] Emilio La Parra, *Los Cien Mil Hijos de San Luis: El ocaso del primer impulso liberal en España* (Madrid: Síntesis, 2007), 184.

[15] Antonio Elorza, "La ideología moderada en el Trienio Liberal," *Cuadernos Hispanoamericanos* 288 (1974): 584–650; Clara Álvarez Alonso, "Las bases

The *exaltados*, for their part, considered that the reinstallation of the Constitution was just the first step on a long path of deep reforms and believed that the revolution needed to go forward in order to survive. The *exaltados* identified themselves with the sovereign people and considered the legislative power to be the true representative of the nation. Popular sovereignty was to inform and control the institutions. They virulently rejected the reform of the Constitution and accused proponents of that idea of being counterrevolutionaries in disguise.[16]

*Moderados* and *exaltados* clashed particularly over the question of the political role of the people in the constitutional regime. The *exaltados* promoted popular participation in politics and mobilized the urban popular classes, while the *moderados*, evoking the events of the French Revolution, distrusted the "mob" as agent of social disorder and political disruption. *Moderados* and *exaltados* did not form modern political parties. Like other political factions in the contemporary Atlantic World, they lacked inner organizational structures, candidates did not run for elections in a coordinated fashion, and their deputies did not vote in concert in the Cortes. Political parties (*partidos*) were mostly distrusted, since they were considered to promote selfish and private interests against the common good.[17]

## Popular Politics under the Constitutional Regime

Public liberties created the conditions for an outburst of political debate and activism, embodied in the publication of many journals, leaflets, and books, the opening of almost 200 political clubs known as "patriotic societies," and the formation of national militia units in most cities. Although the patriotic societies, the national militia, and the press were dominated by learned and well-off middle classes, they also gave an impulse to popular politics.[18]

Journals representing the whole political spectrum were published, as well as periodicals dealing with literature, arts, and sciences. Writers and journalists debated in the press about current events, history, philosophy,

---

constitucionales del moderantismo español: El Fuero Real de España," in Ignacio Fernández Sarasola, ed., *Constituciones en la sombra: Proyectos constitucionales españoles (1809–1823)* (Oviedo: In Itinere, 2014), 453–500.

[16] Jordi Roca Vernet, "L'impacte dels projectes radicals del Trienni en l'exegesi exaltada de la Constitució de 1812," *Recerques* 52–3 (2006): 161–85.

[17] Ignacio Fernández Sarasola, *Los partidos políticos en el pensamiento español: De la Ilustración a nuestros días* (Madrid: Marcial Pons, 2009), 56–8.

[18] Pedro Rújula and Ivana Frasquet, eds., *El Trienio Liberal (1820–1823): Una mirada política* (Granada: Comares, 2020).

and national and international politics. Some satirical publications became immensely popular.[19] Although illiteracy precluded direct contact with published materials for most of the population, public readings were common, especially in the patriotic societies, which promoted debate and the participation of all citizens in public life. There were societies in at least 155 cities and towns, in particular along the coast and Madrid. Their success and increasing influence turned them into one of the first elements of friction between *moderados* and *exaltados*. The moderates considered them the source of dangerous radicalism. The *exaltados*, however, deemed them a central element of a healthy society as diffusers of the liberal creed and educators teaching constitutional values.[20]

The national militia, whose ranks were filled by committed citizens, was meant to be the main mechanism to defend the Constitution. It was stronger in urban centers than rural areas and comprised around 30,000 members or 1 percent of the male population between sixteen and forty years. The moderates did not trust a militia that was mostly formed by officers close to radical positions. It would become an essential element for the defense of the regime once the counterrevolutionary forces initiated their violent campaign.[21]

As a novel constitutional culture spread among the population, citizenship was universalized. The prerequisites for citizenship established in the Constitution of Cádiz – and the differentiation between *citizens* (who enjoyed political and civil rights), and *Spaniards* (who only had civil rights) – were challenged by the active political participation of those sectors of society who adapted the mainstream liberal discourse to reclaim equal rights. The *exaltados* understood citizenship as a natural right, incorporated advanced notions

---

[19] Juan Francisco Fuentes, "Estructura de la prensa española en el Trienio Liberal: Difusión y tendencias," *Trienio*, 24 (1994), 165–96; Ángel Romera, ed., *El Zurriago (1821–1823): Un periódico revolucionario* (Cádiz: Fundación Municipal de Cultura, 2005); Beatriz Sánchez Hita, *José Joaquín de Clararrosa y su Diario Gaditano (1820–1822): Ilustración, periodismo y revolución en el Trienio Liberal* (Cádiz: Universidad de Cádiz, 2009); Claude Morange, *En los orígenes del moderantismo decimonónico. El Censor (1820–1822): Promotores, doctrina e índice* (Salamanca: Universidad de Salamanca, 2019); *El argonauta español* 17 (2020), special issue "El Trienio Liberal en la prensa contemporánea (1820–1823)."

[20] Alberto Gil Novales, *Las sociedades patrióticas: Las libertades de expresión y de reunión en el origen de los partidos políticos* (Madrid: Tecnos, 1975); Jordi Roca Vernet, *La Barcelona revolucionària i liberal: Exaltats, milicians i conspiradors* (Lleida: Pagès – Fundació Noguera, 2011).

[21] Juan Sisinio Pérez Garzón, *Milicia nacional y revolución burguesa: El prototipo madrileño, 1808–1874* (Madrid: CSIC, 1978), 95–342; Roberto Blanco Valdés, *Rey, Cortes y fuerza armada en los orígenes de la España liberal, 1808–1823* (Madrid: Siglo XXI, 1988).

of equality, and promoted an exigent understanding of civic virtue. For them, the permanent mobilization of the people was necessary to strengthen the constitutional regime. Some even promoted equal access to property as a way to produce economically autonomous, virtuous citizens.[22]

Some women reclaimed access to citizenship, arguing that the Constitution did not exclude them. Several even participated actively in politics by joining political clubs – some explicitly feminine, like the *Junta Patriótica de Señoras* – or the formation of female militias. The liberal mainstream, however, was unwilling to grant them full political capacities.[23]

## The Spanish Model in Southern Europe

The *moderado* government was concerned about the international impact of the revolution and instructed its diplomats to placate the mistrustful European governments by assuring them that the transition in Spain had been peaceful and that order and responsibility would guide its policies.[24] However, the Spanish regime would soon find itself in an awkward position when the revolutionary impulse was emulated in two neighboring countries: the Kingdom of the Two Sicilies and Portugal. Those Europeans who believed that a great conspiracy was behind all the revolutionary upheavals of the continent found their position vindicated. However, the simultaneity of these revolutionary movements was rather the outcome of analogous and interconnected political cultures present in southern and western Europe responding in similar fashion to local conditions.[25]

In the new Kingdom of the Two Sicilies the Bourbon restoration had not been as violent and traumatic as in Spain. Since 1806, Naples had been ruled by Napoleon's brother Joseph, who after becoming King of Spain in 1808 was replaced by his brother-in-law Joachim Murat. In 1815, the restored King Ferdinando I did not root out the revolutionary and Napoleonic legacies.

---

[22] Jordi Roca Vernet, "La cultura constitucional del Trienni i el discurs sobre el ciutadà liberal," *Cercles* 11 (2008), 60–76; Florencia Peyrou, "Discursos concurrentes de la ciudadanía: Del doceañismo al republicanismo (1808–1843)," *Historia Contemporánea* 28 (2004), 267–83.

[23] Juan Francisco Fuentes and Pilar Garí, *Amazonas de la libertad: Mujeres liberales contra Fernando VII* (Madrid: Marcial Pons, 2014), 61–99.

[24] Gonzalo Butrón Prida, "From Hope to Defensiveness: The Foreign Policy of a Beleaguered Liberal Spain, 1820–1823," *The English Historical Review* 562 (2018), 567–96.

[25] Juan Luis Simal, "Circulación internacional de modelos políticos en la era post-napoleónica: Cultura, debate y emulación constitucionales," *Revista de Estudios Políticos* 175 (2017), 269–98.

However, the economic crisis and the growing inequality and social tensions it promoted, together with the restriction of public liberties, mobilized the opposition of significant sections of the middle classes. Organized in secret societies like the *Carboneria*, they conspired with the goal of installing a constitutional government. They found in the Spanish Constitution of 1812 a model that fit the needs of the kingdom, and when they learned of the Spanish revolution, took action. On 2 July 1820, young officers initiated an insurrection in Nola, on the outskirts of the city of Naples. They replicated the Spanish example and demanded a constitution. In the following days the rebels mobilized wide popular support, enrolled veterans of Murat's army, and enlisted thousands of *carbonari*. General Guglielmo Pepe assumed the direction of the movement, which was able to compel the king to adopt the Spanish Constitution. Ferdinando I delegated his rule to his son, who on 7 July proclaimed the Constitution and accepted a provisional government formed by former Muratists. What had taken three months in Spain was thus achieved in Naples in a week. The revolutionary pace accelerated as it traveled across southern Europe.[26]

Soon, it reached Portugal.[27] Portuguese liberals had been conspiring for years to reverse the situation in which the European part of the empire found itself after the Portuguese court was relocated to Rio de Janeiro in 1807. They wanted to put an end to the de facto British administration that ruled the country and bring back the king from Brazil, so he could install a constitutional monarchy and start the country's "regeneration." After a failed attempt in 1817 – several conspirators were executed – the Portuguese were inspired by the Spanish success. Some *exaltados* wanted Portugal to follow the liberal path as it would reinforce constitutional Spain in the European political balance of power. Articles in the press stressed the fraternal bonds between both nations. Leaflets with the Spanish Constitution and pamphlets of the patriotic societies circulated in Portugal, while Spanish diplomats addressed Portuguese liberals. Once again, the model of the *pronunciamiento* was replicated. On 24 August 1820, constitutionalist officers initiated in Porto an insurrectionary movement that soon reached Lisbon. In January 1821, the Portuguese Cortes was formed following the system

---

[26] Juan Ferrando Badía, *La constitución española de 1812 en los comienzos del Risorgimento* (Rome and Madrid: CSIC, 1959); Jens Späth, *Revolution in Europa 1820–23: Verfassung und Verfassungskultur in den Königreichen Spanien, beider Sizilien und Sardinien-Piemont* (Cologne: SH Verlag, 2012); Pierre-Marie Delpu, "Fraternités libérales et insurrections nationales: Naples et l'Espagne, 1820–1821," *Revue d'histoire du XIX<sup>e</sup> siècle* 49 (2014), 195–213.

[27] See also Nuno Gonçalo Monteiro, Chapter 17 in this volume.

established in the Cádiz Constitution. After the revolution, Portuguese political clubs corresponded with Spanish patriotic societies. However, the relationships between the governments of liberal Spain and Portugal were far from being smooth. Actually, mutual distrust pervaded them. The strength of Portuguese liberalism forced King João VI, who distrusted the revolutionaries, to return from Brazil. In 1822, he accepted the constitution framed by the Cortes after the Spanish model. In this critical situation his son Pedro declared Brazilian independence.[28]

## Liberal Struggles and Reactionary Conspiracies

In Spain, the constitutional regime was soon confronted with many challenges. First, factionalism divided the liberals as tensions surfaced that led to a growing division between *moderados* and *exaltados*. In August 1820, the government dismissed the army commanded by Riego that had initiated the revolution. Officially, the grounds for the decision were economic, yet many considered that concerns about the military's support for a radical interpretation of the constitution were the real motive. As Riego became a symbol for those who resisted the moderate program, he raised the suspicions of the conservatives. Soon after, he was removed from his post as military commander of Galicia and Argüelles insinuated to the Cortes that he concealed Bonapartist or even republican aspirations. Rumors about his political ambition, which he consistently denied, kept growing louder.[29]

Although Riego was soon reinstated in a high military position, from that moment on divisions engulfed the liberals. After intense parliamentary and public debate, in October 1820 the Cortes passed a law that restricted the activities of the patriotic societies, considered fomenters of instability.

---

[28] Isabel Nobre Vargues, *A aprendizagem da cidadania em Portugal, 1820–1823* (Coimbra: Minerva, 1997); Antonio Eiras Roel, "La política hispano-portuguesa en el Trienio Constitucional," *Hispania* 91 (1963): 401–54; Daniela Major, "A Imprensa do Triénio liberal e a revolução portuguesa: Entre o iberismo e o internacionalismo liberal," *Revista de História das Ideias* 37:2 (2019), 109–31; Marcia Regina Berbel, "A Constituiçao espanhola no mundo luso-americano (1820–1823)," *Revista de Indias* 68: 242 (2008), 225–54; Gabriel Paquette, *Imperial Portugal in the Age of Atlantic Revolutions: The Luso-Brazilian World, c. 1770–1850* (Cambridge: Cambridge University Press, 2013); Ana Cristina Araujo, "Confluencias políticas en el Trienio Liberal: El proceso de la Revolución portuguesa de 1820 y el modelo constitucional gaditano," *Historia y Política* 45 (2021), 53–83.

[29] Víctor Sánchez Martín, "*Que nada importa que yo sufra*, o la servidumbre de Riego: Mito y lucha política entre moderados y exaltados durante el trienio constitucional," *Ayer* 127 (2022), 81–106.

Although they subsequently resumed their activities under different forms (mostly as *tertulias*, conversation societies), protests abounded. In this critical context, and given the lack of consolidated political structures, the different liberal factions organized themselves around secret societies. In 1821, two of these appeared: the *Comunería*, founded by *exaltados* who distrusted the *moderados'* influence over the Freemasonry, and the *Sociedad Constitucional* (also known as the Society of the Ring), formed by men close to the government. The *comuneros*, endowed with Spanish symbolism, became the most radical defenders of popular sovereignty and the expansion of political rights and public liberties.[30] Thus, mutual distrust between political groups grew. The confrontation between the liberal families in the Cortes and the streets and plazas of Spain did not only destabilize the regime from within, it also gave arguments to those in Europe who believed that the revolutionary turmoil could not be controlled.

Local counterrevolutionaries did not wait. Since 1820 the first reactionary guerrillas had been appearing throughout the country, after the model of the *Junta apostólica* of Galicia. The liberal ecclesiastical reforms and the measures aimed at limiting the social influence of the Church alienated many clergymen, who interpreted them as direct attacks on religion. In their sermons they denounced the conflict in religious terms, and some priests even formed their own armed units to fight in what they believed was a "crusade." However, there also existed a minority of clergymen and bishops who sided with the constitutional regime.[31]

Besides the defense of strict Catholicism, the insurgents' main impulse was to preserve the king's sovereignty, considered to be in captivity. Fernando VII, for his part, continued to destabilize the regime. Most liberals wanted to believe that he was a sincere constitutional king and discarded all his previous reactionary policies as a consequence of bad advice by evil counselors. Their trust in him was not justified, for he conspired against the constitutional regime from the beginning. In January 1821, the king's

---

[30] Iris M. Zavala, *Masones, comuneros y carbonarios* (Madrid: Siglo XXI, 1971); Marta Ruiz Jiménez, *El liberalismo exaltado: La confederación de comuneros españoles durante el Trienio Liberal* (Madrid: Fundamentos, 2007); Albert Dérozier, *L'histoire de la Sociedad del Anillo de Oro pendant le triennat constitutionnel, 1820–1823: La faillite du système libéral* (Paris: Les Belles Lettres, 1965); Juan Luis Simal, "Conspiración, revolución y contrarrevolución en España, 1814–1824," *Rivista Storica Italiana* 130:2 (2018), 526–56; Francisco J. Díez Morrás, "Masonería y revolución liberal en España: La Confederación de Comuneros," *REHMLAC+* 2:2 (2019–2020).

[31] Manuel Revuelta, *Política religiosa de los liberales en el siglo XIX: El Trienio Constitucional* (Madrid: CSIC, 1973); Manuel Teruel, *Obispos liberales: La utopía de un proyecto (1820–1823)* (Lleida: Milenio, 1996).

chaplain, Matías Vinuesa, was arrested in the possession of documents that proved that a *coup d'état* was being prepared. However, Vinuesa's soft sentence enraged protesters, who claimed that the authorities were not really willing to punish the counterrevolutionaries. He was assassinated in prison by men who were publicly linked to the *exaltados*. The case became a scandal that added to an already heated environment. After the plot's failure, Fernando VII commenced secret contacts with foreign courts, especially with Tsar Alexander I, whom he asked to be "rescued." Besides, he obstructed the functioning of the political system by refusing to sanction certain laws, appointing public authorities without consulting with the government, and failing to comply with several requirements of the Cortes.[32]

The conflict between the king and the liberals became manifest when the Cortes reopened on 1 March. In his opening speech, Fernando VII accused the government of failing to defend him from the attacks he was receiving. Having lost confidence in his ministers, he deposed them and appointed a new government headed by the moderate but less prestigious Eusebio Bardají.

In their second session, the Cortes resumed the reformist program, intervening over the currency, legislating over the army to establish its national, constitutional, and egalitarian character, and implementing a public educational system. The Cortes also passed a law that severely punished conspirators, although it did not stop counterrevolutionary activism from growing.[33] On 30 June, the Cortes was adjourned due to the critical situation: The country was on the verge of civil war and the situation in the Americas was deteriorating. The Extraordinary Cortes that opened in September confronted a hostile situation. Ultra-royalist guerrillas kept growing in number, and the regime faced a growing disaffection while inner divisions widened. In September 1821, Riego was accused of participating in a republican conspiracy and dismissed from his command as captain general of Aragon. The decision took thousands of protesters to the streets, who paraded Riego's portrait and clashed with the moderate authorities. The tensions harmed the government and strengthened the *comuneros*.

The disenchantment of popular liberalism with the government grew. In late 1821 and early 1822, as counterrevolutionary activities and the fear of reactionary conspiracies increased, insurrections occurred in cities like Cádiz

---

[32] La Parra, *Fernando VII*, 408–9.
[33] Blanco Valdés, *Rey, Cortes y fuerza armada*, 378–404; Juan Pro, *La construcción del Estado en España: Una historia del siglo XIX* (Madrid: Alianza, 2019), 581–2.

or Seville in protest against the moderate government's appointment of unpopular local authorities, but also criticizing the reluctance of the Cortes to fully implement the Constitution.[34] Nonetheless, the Cortes continued its efforts and approved relevant legislation, such as the division of the country into fifty-two provinces, the first Spanish penal code, and an advanced public welfare act.[35]

Even if the *exaltados* won many seats in the new elections, in February 1822 the king appointed the moderate Martínez de la Rosa to head the new government.[36] He probably wanted to confront a moderate government with a Cortes dominated by the *exaltados* and presided over by Riego. Although Riego, Argüelles, Canga-Argüelles, and other leaders made an effort to unite the liberal family, eventually tensions rose and the gap between the factions widened. The *exaltados* accused the government of repressing the true liberals while appeasing the ultra-royalist conspirators, the true enemies of the nation. The *moderados* became increasingly alarmed by the radicalism of the *exaltados* and the destabilization that threatened to ruin the constitutional regime. They accused them of hatching Jacobin plans, although the *exaltados* never formulated explicit republican proposals. Ultimately, collaboration between the legislative and the executive powers ceased, while Fernando VII contributed to the stalemate by vetoing many legislative initiatives of the Cortes. The need for constitutional reform became evident for many moderates, while several proposals for steering the revolution in a more democratic direction appeared among the *exaltados*.[37]

## The Civil War and the King's *Coup d'État*

The real threat to the constitutional regime, however, came from the ultra-royalists, who enlarged their web of conspiracies and expanded their guerrilla activities, immersing some regions of the country, especially in the north and the Mediterranean region, in a state of permanent agitation. The role of the Church was central. Ultra-royalist propaganda presented the supporters of

---

[34] José María García León, *Cádiz en el Trienio Liberal (1820–1823)* (Cádiz: Ayuntamiento de Cádiz, 1999).

[35] Pro, *La construcción del Estado*, 144, 210.

[36] Francisco Carantoña, "Las elecciones de 1821, primer ensayo de competición de 'partidos' en el constitucionalismo liberal español," *Historia Constitucional* 21 (2020), 63–105.

[37] Roca Vernet, "L'impacte dels projectes radicals."

the constitutional monarchy as revolutionary heirs of the French Jacobins who aspired to install a republic. Actually, many thought that the country had in practice already adopted that form since the king was said to have been "kidnapped" by the liberals.

Using the notion that God and king were under attack by impious liberals, the reactionary elites were able to mobilize popular antiliberalism, especially in rural areas, where antagonism toward the socioeconomic transformations brought about by the liberal capitalist system – monetarization of the economy, expansion of individual property, the demise of the commons – abounded, and the intrusion of the state through taxing and conscription was resisted. Drought and bad harvests increased the discontentment of thousands of peasants, who decided to join the ultra-royalist forces.[38] But antiliberalism was not only a rural phenomenon, it also had an urban face. Several towns and cities witnessed disturbances and riots caused by opponents of the Constitution. In Valencia, for instance, artillery men rose in May 1822 in the name of the king and attempted to liberate General Javier Elío, one of the most prominent ultras, who was in prison for his participation in the repression of the Constitution in 1814.

Absolutists could also rely on foreign assistance. The complicity of the French government made the porous border at the Pyrenees a refuge for reactionary fighters. Joseph de Villèle, the head of the French *ultra*-government, facilitated their reception. The struggle against Spanish liberalism was also a French affair.[39] Only a few weeks after the 1820 *pronunciamiento*, the nephew of King Louis XVIII, the duke of Berry, was assassinated. The incident was immediately linked to the events in Spain.[40] Moreover, the French *carbonari* increased their activism, with the support of prestigious personalities like the marquis of Lafayette. Plots were aborted in Saumur, Belfort, Toulon, and Nantes. In September 1822, the Four Sergeants of La Rochelle, found guilty of conspiring to overthrow the French monarchy, were guillotined and immediately became martyrs for the liberals and republicans. Fleeing repression, many French revolutionaries found refuge in Spain, which increased the anxiety of French authorities about the

---

[38] Jaume Torras Elias, *Liberalismo y rebeldía campesina, 1820–1823* (Barcelona: Ariel, 1976); Pedro Rújula, *Constitución o Muerte: El Trienio Liberal y los levantamientos realistas en Aragón (1820–1823)* (Zaragoza: Astral, 2000); Ramon Arnabat, *Visca el rei i la religió! La primera guerra civil de la Catalunya contemporània (1820–1823)* (Lleida: Pagès, 2006).

[39] Nere Basabe, "Francia y la Revolución española (1820–1823): ¿Un espejo en el que mirarse?," *Historia y Política* 45 (2021), 85–114.

[40] David Skuy, *Assassination, Politics, and Miracles: France and the Royalist Reaction of 1820* (Montreal: McGill-Queen's University Press, 2003).

existence of an international plot.[41] The Spanish revolutionary threat needed to be contained if the French monarchy was to survive. In the summer of 1821, the French government installed in the Pyrenees a "sanitary cordon" against the yellow fever epidemic that had broken out in Catalonia, although its true purpose was to avoid a different kind of contagion: that of revolutionary ideas.[42] However, Villèle refused to intervene directly in Spanish affairs and ignored the petitions of Fernando VII to "rescue" him. The French government did not trust that the Spanish king would accept the installation of a political system labeled after the French Charter of 1814. French help, in any case, became essential to the persistence of the efforts of Spanish counterrevolutionaries.

By the summer of 1822 the ultras had pushed the country to a state of civil war. In July they captured the Seo de Urgel, a bishop's residence in the Catalan Pyrenees, and installed a regency made up by aristocrats (the baron Eroles and the marquis Mataflorida) and the archbishop of Tarragona, which claimed to preserve the king's sovereignty. Fernando VII encouraged these operations and ultimately sanctioned a *coup d'état*. At the beginning of July, he endorsed a conspiracy that concluded with the uprising in Madrid of the Royal Guard. However, the plotters failed to gain popular support. With the ministers confined to the royal palace, on 7 July the Royal Guards were defeated in an urban skirmish by Madrid's National Militia and *exaltado* units of the army (Figure 4.2). Fernando VII's participation in the plot, or at least his acquiescence vis-à-vis the Royal Guards, was suspected by many, and articles accusing him of incompetence or even treason appeared in the radical press. No explicit calls for a republic were heard, although some proposed his dethronement.[43] In any case, Fernando VII's prestige was seriously harmed. With the king clearly plotting, constitutional Spain's descent into turmoil seemed inevitable.

The coup also increased the disaffection within the liberal bloc. Some *exaltados* considered the government's passivity during the days of July a confirmation of its complicity with the conspirators. Actually, Martínez de la Rosa did negotiate with the king about modifying the Constitution as a way

---

[41] Alan B. Spitzer, *Old Hatreds and Young Hopes: The French Carbonari against the Bourbon Restoration* (Cambridge, MA: Harvard University Press, 1971); Laurent Nagy, "L'émissaire de charbonnerie française au service du trienio liberal," *Historia Constitucional* 15 (2014), 223–54.

[42] La Parra, *Los Cien Mil Hijos de San Luis*, 71.

[43] Jordi Roca Vernet, "¿Hubo republicanos en el Trienio Liberal? Historia, moral y federalismo en el discurso republicano del primer liberalismo," *Revista de Estudios Políticos* 156 (2012), 85–123.

Figure 4.2 The failed *coup d'état* of July 1822. Courtesy of the Biblioteca Nacional, Spain.

to assure Fernando's allegiance to the regime and appease the European powers. Indeed, the French ambassador in Madrid favored the introduction in Spain of a code similar to the *Charte* that Louis XVIII had introduced in France in 1814.[44] Yet Fernando VII would not accept anything that could delay his return to absolute power. Under the pretext of responding to demands of the opposition, he took advantage of the crisis to further destabilize the regime. He dismissed Martínez de la Rosa and appointed a government formed by ministers with *exaltado* leanings (many thought to be Freemasons) led by Evaristo San Miguel.

The new government took the initiative that the *moderados* lacked in fighting the counterrevolution and sent an army to the north. Generals Francisco Espoz y Mina and José María Torrijos succeeded in their campaign

---

[44] Sophie Bustos, "Francia y la cuestión española: El golpe de estado del 7 de julio de 1822," *Ayer* 110 (2018), 179–202.

Figure 4.3 King Fernando VII swears to uphold the Constitution, 1820. Courtesy of the Biblioteca Nacional, Spain.

in the north against the counterrevolutionary guerrillas, especially in Catalonia, where the repression achieved gruesome characteristics. Although the Seo de Urgel was recovered and the regency fled to France, the victory was not complete, and guerrillas continued in arms.[45]

In any case, the crisis was far from over. San Miguel could not placate the *exaltados*' calls for drastic measures against the insurgents and the *moderados* persisted in their attempts to reform the Constitution. An Extraordinary Cortes was convened in October 1822, while the European powers discussed the Spanish question in the Congress of Verona. In December 1822, after an incident related to ecclesiastical matters, the *apostolic nuncio* in Madrid was expelled and diplomatic relations with Rome were severed.[46] Although the nuncio would return months later, Spain grew increasingly isolated from Europe.

---

[45] Arnabat, *Visca el rei i la religió!*, 303–71; José Luis Comellas, *Los realistas en el Trienio Constitucional (1820–1823)* (Pamplona: Estudio General de Navarra, 1958), 141–52, 178–83.

[46] Carlos M. Rodríguez López-Brea, "La Santa Sede y los movimientos revolucionarios europeos de 1820. Los casos napolitano y español," *Ayer* 45 (2002), 251–74.

## The American Question

In most Spanish American territories, the independence process culminated during the *Trienio*.[47] The emancipatory movement had begun a decade earlier in the context of the crisis of the monarchy caused by the Napoleonic invasion and, after years of civil war, the Spanish American societies were profoundly divided. By 1820, some regions (the Río de la Plata, Paraguay, and Chile) had achieved de facto independence, and in others (Colombia and Venezuela) republicans and royalists were still at war, although the separatists had gained the upper hand. Yet the great viceroyalties of New Spain and Peru were still under the control of authorities loyal to Spain. In 1820, the Constitution was sworn in by the authorities of New Spain, Peru, Central America, Cuba, and Puerto Rico, and also in hundreds of towns in Venezuela, Colombia, Upper Peru, and Quito.[48]

Thus, the 1820 revolution revived the possibility of establishing an inclusive transatlantic constitutional monarchy in which both European and American Spaniards could thrive in freedom and equality. However, the resentment after the war, the continuation of ideological commitments, and the acceleration of the process of creating national identities in the states born out of the dissolution of the empire – including Spain, where a liberal nationalism was also developing – impeded such a development.

There was little information on American events in Spain. The difficulty in getting reliable information due to the vast distances, the state of war, and the disruption of commerce and navigation hindered the decision-making process in Madrid. The public could not get much news related to the Americas from the official *Gaceta de Madrid*. Yet that does not mean there was no interest on the matter. In fact, the *exaltado* press accused the government of purposely concealing information about the American crisis. The lack of news probably made many Spaniards believe that an agreement beneficial for the preservation of the empire, or even a military victory, could still be achieved.[49]

---

[47] Manuel Chust, ed. *¡Mueran las cadenas! El Trienio Liberal en América (1820–1824)* (Granada: Comares, 2020); Ivana Frasquet, Josep Escrig, and Encarna García Monerris, eds., *El Trienio Liberal y el espacio atlántico: Diálogos entre dos mundos* (Madrid: Marcial Pons, 2022).

[48] Jaime E. Rodríguez O., *The Independence of Spanish America* (Cambridge: Cambridge University Press, 1998); for the constitution in the Philippines see Patricio Hidalgo, *Liberalismo e Insurgencia en las Islas Filipinas, 1809–1824* (Madrid: Ediciones de Universidad Autónoma de Madrid, 2019).

[49] Scott Eastman, "America Has Escaped from Our Hands: Rethinking Empire, Identity and Independence during the *Trienio Liberal* in Spain, 1820–1823," *European History Quarterly* 41:3 (2011), 428–43: 433.

In any case, the American question was debated in the Cortes, the patriotic societies, and the press. Different approaches were put forward. Most liberals adopted an uncompromising posture. Initially, the moderate government and most deputies believed that the American crisis would be averted simply by the installation of liberal institutions that would revive the empire within a constitutional framework. A general amnesty and commercial benefits would regain the support of Americans for the Spanish liberal project. This proved to be an overoptimistic misconception, as the violent context created by the wars impeded any attempts at "pacification."[50] In fact, when the agents sent by the government to negotiate arrived in Caracas and the Río de la Plata in late 1820, they found that the insurgents were only willing to negotiate the ways in which their independent republics would be recognized.[51]

The unwillingness to face the depth of the American crisis, together with the many urgent problems in the Peninsula, paralyzed the action of the government. The special commission created in the Cortes proved inoperative and the timid initiatives taken at the Overseas Ministry, like those proposed to the Cortes in January 1822, only considered an armistice, the revision of certain reforms, and the opening of commercial relationships with foreign countries.[52] Previously, the Council of State had recommended sending new troops to the Americas (although some members preferred conciliatory gestures).[53]

For their part, the American "dissidents" refused to consent to any settlement that did not include the full acknowledgment of independence. Twice, negotiations were opened but never completed. In October 1820, Francisco Antonio Zea, representative of the Republic of Colombia in London, proposed to the Spanish ambassador to Britain the formation of a "federal empire" that would recognize the independence of the new American states while maintaining the Hispanic "family" of nations united and allowing Spain to maintain influence over the region. The Spanish government refused to study the proposal. After an armistice was signed in November 1820, in early 1821 Bolívar sent two agents to Spain to negotiate

---

[50] Salvador Broseta, *Autonomismo, insurgencia, independencia: América en las Cortes del Trienio Liberal, 1820–1823* (Cádiz: Fundación Municipal de Cultura, 2012).

[51] Ascensión Martínez Riaza, "Para reintegrar la nación. El Perú en la política negociadora del Trienio Liberal con los disidentes americanos, 1820–1824," *Revista de Indias* 71: 253 (2011), 647–92.

[52] William S. Robertson, "The Policy of Spain towards Its Revolted Colonies, 1820–1823," *The Hispanic American Historical Review* 6:1–3 (1926), 21–46.

[53] Martínez Riaza, "Para reintegrar la nación," 663–4.

an agreement. They traveled with instructions to reject any proposal that included a federal organization or a monarchical alternative, even under a foreign dynasty. Only complete independence of the Republic of Colombia would be admitted.[54] Under these conditions, it was impossible to reach a compromise.

Those Americans who confided in the benefits of the constitutional government for terminating the insurgencies in exchange for autonomy and commercial liberties were disappointed when they encountered the limits of Spanish liberalism in relation to its promise of equality. Thus, although American deputies were present in Madrid, unequal representation in the Cortes became a source of major discontent for those Spanish Americans who acknowledged the constitutional regime.[55]

On 25 June 1821, the deputy from New Spain José Miguel Ramírez presented a project to the Cortes in the name of the American deputies, although not all of them signed it. It was a proposal for the establishment in America of three kingdoms, each with its own Cortes, government, Council of State, and Supreme Court. Spain would still rule over their international relations. It was a desperate attempt, for the representatives knew the proposal would most likely be rejected by most Spaniards (including the king) and that the American insurgents would almost certainly not accept it either. The next day Miguel Ramos Arizpe proposed a similar plan for New Spain. Yet the Cortes were adjourned before the plan could be discussed. In the next Extraordinary Cortes, a majority approved the expulsion of most American deputies, arguing that their mandate was illegitimate as they were only provisional substitutes of the provinces that could not send representatives because of their turbulent circumstances.[56]

Nevertheless, some pragmatic liberals argued for the negotiation of some form of independence under conditions that would preserve Spain's influence over the American continent. In mid-1821, the minister of state Bardají, after meeting with Bolívar's agents, considered a federal project that would maintain the connection between Spain and its former colonies, which would

---

[54] J. Alberto Navas Sierra, *Utopía y atopía de la Hispanidad: El proyecto de Confederación Hispánica de Francisco Antonio Zea* (Madrid: Encuentro, 2000), 20–36, 201–304.

[55] Broseta, *Autonomismo, insurgencia, independencia*; Ramon Arnabat, "El impacto europeo y americano de la proclamación de la Constitución de Cádiz en 1820," *Trocadero*, 24 (2012), 47–64: 58.

[56] Ivana Frasquet, "La cuestión nacional americana en las Cortes del Trienio Liberal, 1820–1821," in Jaime E. Rodríguez, ed., *Revolución, independencia y las nuevas naciones de América* (Madrid: Mapfre, 2005) 123–57; Ivana Frasquet, "Independencia o constitución: América en el Trienio Liberal," *Historia Constitucional*, 21 (2020), 170–99.

receive a semi-independent status. He knew, however, that the plan would be difficult to implement and that the king would surely oppose it.[57] The prominent liberal Alcalá Galiano argued in the Cortes for the acknowledgment of independence, provided the Americans signed beneficial commercial treaties in exchange, and a minority of deputies even supported the American insurgents out of political solidarity. Yet in a context in which Spanish liberal nationalism was rapidly developing, even the *exaltado* press blamed the *moderado* government for the loss of Mexico when the news of the Treaty of Córdoba (August 1821) reached Spain.[58] The Cortes immediately nullified the treaty, while in January 1822 the Spanish MP Fernández Golfín presented a plan inspired by a report written by Miguel Cabrera de Nevares and commissioned by Overseas Minister López Pelegrín that proposed the formation of a "great Spanish American Confederation" with Fernando VII as protector. Yet the Cortes rejected the plan.[59] As the debates lingered without offering a solution, the last remaining American deputies started to abandon the Cortes.

In November 1822, Vicente Basadre, a shrewd man with personal experience in the Americas, published a pamphlet arguing that it was impossible to maintain military dominion over the American territories, and that the best course of action was to search for an advantageous agreement in exchange for independence.[60] A growing number of people subscribed to this opinion. A last attempt was made in early 1823, when the Spanish constitutional regime was about to face a French intervention. New agents were sent to Mexico, Venezuela, Colombia, and the Río de la Plata to negotiate an armistice. They could only certify that independence was a fact, except in some areas of Peru. In August 1823, with a French army invading Spain, a desperate overseas commission conceded that the best solution would be to open negotiations with the separatists without ruling out independence, provided an advantageous agreement was reached.[61] The fall of Spain's constitutional regime in October and the restoration of Fernando's absolutist monarchy impeded any diplomatic resolution. Decades would pass until Spain finally acknowledged the independence of the numerous states that emerged out of its empire.

---

[57] Navas Sierra, *Utopía y atopía*, 308–12.  [58] Eastman, "America Has Escaped," 435.
[59] Frasquet, "La cuestión nacional americana en las Cortes."
[60] Vicente Basadre, *Memoria histórica-política-geográfica relativa a la independencia de la América Española* (La Coruña: Imprenta de Iguereta, 1822).
[61] Martínez Riaza, "Para reintegrar la nación," 681.

## Foreign Intervention and the Fall
## of the Constitutional Regime

Although prudence had marked the initial response of Congress Europe to the Spanish revolution, by mid-1822 the continental powers became convinced that Spain's liberal regime posed a revolutionary threat to the stability of the continent and that action was urgent. Fearing the consequences of an open challenge to the international order, the Spanish government had actually withheld any open support for other European liberals, although some Spanish diplomats, deputies, and journalists did argue that the constitutional regime should side with the Italians and Portuguese in order to assure its position in an international context dominated by the reactionary powers.[62]

In March 1821, an Austrian intervention in Naples had already put an end to its constitutional regime, although the liberals in power had tried to avoid radicalization and even attempted to reform the Constitution to make it acceptable for the European powers. Yet liberal Naples was a direct menace to Austria's rule over Lombardy and Veneto, and Chancellor Metternich sought to quell the development of an Italian patriotic movement that would menace Austrian influence over the Peninsula. If Metternich had had reservations about the convenience of intervening in Spain, he was convinced of the necessity of crushing the Italian revolutionaries. With the consent of the European powers, the Congress of Laibach in early 1821 decided on an Austrian intervention.

Days after the decisive Austrian victory over the Neapolitans at Rieti (7 March), new upheaval began in the Kingdom of Piedmont-Sardinia. A coalition of aristocratic revolutionaries and reformists with the support of members of the army compelled King Vittorio Emanuele I to grant a constitution. With the acquiescence of the prince of Carignano, Carlo Alberto, the conspirators wanted to liberalize the regime while assuring the power of the ascending elites. However, after the prince turned his back on the project, a military insurrection supported by the Spanish ambassador – acting without orders from Madrid – proclaimed the Spanish Constitution and spoke out in favor of Italian unity. After the king's abdication in favor of his absent brother Carlo Felice, Carlo Alberto became regent and accepted

---

[62] Butrón Prida, "From Hope to Defensiveness"; Francisco Carantoña, "1820, una revolución mediterránea. El impacto en España de los acontecimientos de Portugal, Italia y Grecia," *Spagna Contemporanea* 46:1 (2014), 21–40.

the Constitution. However, Carlo Felice rejected any compromise and asked for an Austrian intervention. On 8 April 1821, the constitutionalists were defeated in the Battle of Novara.[63]

The Austrian interventions in Italy brought Spain and Portugal together, and Iberian solidarity incentivized the preservation of both regimes from foreign intrusion. In April 1821, the Spanish government – with the support of the *exaltados* – offered Portugal to form a defensive alliance and, in a rather idealistic fashion, even considered the prospect of bringing both constitutional monarchies together under a confederation, a possibility that not only France and Britain strongly rejected, but that the majority of the Portuguese liberals rebuffed, in the opinion of the Spanish representative in Lisbon. One year later, and more pragmatically, Silvestre Pinheiro, the Portuguese foreign affairs minister, used the prospect of an alliance with Spain – even an Iberian Union – to induce Britain to offer support for an independent constitutional Portugal. In the end, no Iberian alliance came into existence.[64]

Until mid-1822, Fernando VII had restrained from demanding a foreign intervention in Spain because he feared it would imply the imposition of a moderate royalist system like that of France. But when it became evident that the liberals could resist the counterrevolutionary forces, no other solution seemed plausible. After the failed coup of July 1822, and with the Italian precedent in mind, Fernando VII explicitly asked Louis XVIII of France and Tsar Alexander I to act, arguing that his life was at risk. The European powers came to accept this scenario and threatened the liberal government that if any harm was done to the royal family, they would interfere in Spanish affairs. Finally, in October 1822, considering Spain accountable for expanding the revolution across the continent, the Congress of Verona assented to France's intervention in Spain. After Austria, Prussia, Russia, and France broke off diplomatic relations with Spain, Britain offered to mediate in the crisis if the Spanish government agreed to modify the Constitution and install a reformed version acceptable

---

[63] Gonzalo Butrón Prida, *Nuestra Sagrada Causa: El modelo gaditano en la revolución piamontesa de 1821* (Cádiz: Ayuntamiento de Cádiz, 2006); Mark Jarret, *The Congress of Vienna and Its Legacy: War and Great Power Diplomacy after Napoleon* (London: I. B. Tauris, 2013), 248–85; Pierangelo Gentile, "Do as the Spaniards Do. The 1821 Piedmont Insurrection and the Birth of Constitutionalism," *Historia y Política* 45 (2021), 23–51.

[64] Eiras Roel, "La política hispano-portuguesa"; Butrón Prida, "From Hope to Defensiveness." The British philosopher Jeremy Bentham, an enthusiast of Iberian liberalism, advocated the signing of an alliance; see Gregorio Alonso, "'A Great People Struggling for Their Liberties': Spain and the Mediterranean in the Eyes of the Benthamites," *History of European Ideas* 41:2 (2014), 194–204.

The Constitutional Triennium in Spain, 1820–1823

by Fernando VII and France. However, the British reservations vanished after France assured that the intervention would not reach Portugal or the Spanish colonies.[65] For their part, San Miguel's government and the Cortes vehemently rejected diplomatic interference. In any case, the king would not have accepted the constitutional modification now that he believed his "liberation" was imminent.[66] Thus, with liberal Spain diplomatically isolated, a French army entered the Iberian Peninsula in April 1823.[67]

Before the invasion, in February, the government and the Cortes had decided to look for a safer location in the south of Spain. However, the king rejected the idea and persisted in eroding the constitutional system by deposing San Miguel's government, a decision celebrated by those radical *comuneros* critical of the ministry's shyness. Soon, the factions within the *exaltados* clashed in the streets of Madrid. After violent demonstrations for the government, Fernando reinstalled San Miguel, yet that only sparked the protests of the *comuneros*, who asked for a regency. The situation only settled down when San Miguel resigned after having obtained the king's momentary approval to travel to Seville. On 28 February, Fernando VII, probably in a move to destabilize the regime even more, appointed a new government formed by *comuneros* and led by Flórez Estrada, who nevertheless was open to negotiations with the French about a modification of the Constitution. However, this government never took office because the former ministers maneuvered to stay in charge. The chaotic situation, with two parallel governments, hindered any effective resistance against the expected foreign intervention.[68]

Indeed, the French invasion headed by the king's nephew, the duc d'Angoulême, met an uneven resistance. Several generals of the constitutional army (Ballesteros, La Bisbal) remained inert, and some, like Morillo, defected to the enemy. The troops of Espoz y Mina and Torrijos fought courageously, yet they could not prevent the French from occupying Madrid in late May. If in 1808 the French invaders had been received by the population as republican heretics, now they appeared as monarchical Catholics. The French troops compensated the local population for their supplies, and in certain regions the population received them with the hope

[65] Norihito Yamada, "George Canning and the Spanish Question, September 1822 to March 1823," *The Historical Journal* 52:2 (2009), 343–62.

[66] Butrón Prida, "From Hope to Defensiveness."

[67] Ulrike Schmieder, *Prusia y el Congreso de Verona: Estudio acerca de la política de la Santa Alianza en la cuestión española* (Madrid: Ediciones del Orto, 1998); Rafael Sánchez Mantero, *Los Cien Mil Hijos de San Luis y las relaciones franco-españolas* (Seville: Universidad de Sevilla, 1981).

[68] La Parra, *Fernando VII*, 434–8.

that they would establish order against the looting activities of the ultra-royalist guerrillas. The French army marched together with the Spanish "Army of the Faith," whose ranks were filled by ultra-royalist volunteers, who unleashed a bloody repression against the liberals. On many occasions French officers opposed revengeful punishments and even protected some victims. In the face of indiscriminate violence, on 8 August Angoulême instructed that all detentions would be overseen by the French military command. The Spanish ultras were outraged.[69]

Fernando VII's refusal to leave Seville for Cádiz when he was about to be "liberated" by the French forced the liberals to take the most revolutionary of all their decisions: Based on Article 187 of the Constitution, on 11 June the Cortes declared Fernando VII in a state of temporary insanity – as he could not realize he was in danger of being captured by the enemy– and formed a provisional regency. The Cortes, the government, and the king left for Cádiz with the intention of replicating the resistance put up against Napoleon.[70]

Once in Cádiz, Fernando VII was reinstated. The situation was critical, and the liberals could only resist for a few months. Although there were more attempts to reach an agreement by which a limited constitutional regime would be installed – Angoulême was authorized to negotiate with moderate liberals – Fernando VII would not accept anything less than a complete restoration. He only conceded that once in power he would grant an amnesty – a promise he immediately broke. Finally, the government decided to capitulate, although some cities like Barcelona, Cartagena, or Alicante resisted until November. On 1 October, the Spanish royal family met with Angoulême and Fernando VII annulled all the legislation of the Cortes. In the next weeks thousands of liberals left for exile while Riego, the symbol of the revolution, was executed in Madrid, becoming an internationally famous martyr of liberalism.[71]

## Constitutional Spain: A Sanctuary for European Liberals

During the *Trienio*, Spain became a refuge for liberal and republican Europeans persecuted in their countries. On 28 September 1820, the

---

[69] Gonzalo Butrón Prida, *La ocupación francesa de España (1823–1828)* (Cádiz: Universidad de Cádiz, 1996).

[70] La Parra, *Fernando VII*, 451–9.

[71] Alberto Cañas de Pablos, "Riego después de Riego: La pervivencia póstuma de un mito heroico liberal en España, Reino Unido, Francia y Rusia (1823–1880)," *Historia y Política* 45 (2021), 143–73.

Cortes passed an Asylum Law that guaranteed a haven for those "persecuted by political opinions."[72] In the following years many of the Frenchmen who had risen up or conspired against the ultra-conservative Bourbon monarchy, as well as hundreds of Italians fleeing repression, including the Neapolitan leader Guglielmo Pepe, arrived in Spain. The Cortes passed legislation that awarded them an allowance as refugees, although the government was not completely comfortable with their presence.[73] Their exile in Spain – some, like the Lombard count Pecchio, or Pepe, also reached Portugal – contributed to the ongoing construction of an international fraternal network of European liberals, as well as to the development of a transnational pantheon of heroes and martyrs.[74]

Foreigners in Spain organized themselves in secret societies, especially linked to the *Carboneria*, and intervened in local political debates. Their political ideologies were heterogeneous, and tensions arose among them. They clashed around the causes of their exile and their conflicting political positions (monarchical/republican, federalist/centralist, and moderate/radical). Some brought with them democratic traditions mostly unknown to Spain, like those of the Italian sister republics of the late 1790s, which were well received by some *exaltados*. For instance, the Roman-Neapolitan Bartolomeo Fiorilli redacted the project of a democratic constitution, which he translated and published in Spanish and brought to the consideration of the Cortes.[75]

---

[72] *Colección de los decretos y órdenes generales de la primera legislatura de las Cortes ordinarias de 1820 y 1821, desde 6 de julio hasta 9 de noviembre de 1820* (Madrid: Imprenta Nacional, 1821), 152.

[73] Agostino Bistarelli, "Vivere il moto spagnolo. Gli esiliati italiani in Catalogna durante il Triennio Liberale," *Trienio* 32–3 (1998–1999), 5–14, 65–91; Manuel Morán Ortí, "La cuestión de los refugiados extranjeros. Política española en el Trienio Liberal", *Hispania* 173 (1989), 985–1016.

[74] Maurizio Isabella, *Risorgimento in Exile: Italian Émigrés and the Liberal International in the Post-Napoleonic Era* (Oxford: Oxford University Press, 2009); Juan Luis Simal, "Letters from Spain. The 1820 Revolution and the Liberal International," in Maurizio Isabella and Konstantina Zanou, eds., *Mediterranean Diasporas: Politics and Ideas in the Long Nineteenth Century* (London: Bloomsbury, 2016), 25–41; Grégoire Bron, "Learning Lessons from the Iberian Peninsula: Italian Exiles and the Making of a Risorgimento without People, 1820–48," in Isabella and Zanou, *Mediterranean Diasporas*, 59–76; Pierre-Marie Delpu, "Eroi e martiri. La circolazione delle figure celebri della rivoluzione napoletana nell'Europa liberale, 1820–1825," *Rivista Storica Italiana*, 130:2 (2018), 587–614.

[75] Jordi Roca Vernet, "Democracia y federalismo internacional. Del exilio liberal italiano a los exaltados españoles," in Ignacio Fernández Sarasola, ed., *Constituciones en la sombra: Proyectos constitucionales españoles (1809–1823)* (Oviedo: In Itinere, 2014), 97–210.

Many of these French and Italian exiles were military men who asked to be allowed to fight against the reactionary guerrillas and the French invading army. The Spanish government was hesitant about the possibility, although eventually different units were formed and a Foreign Liberal Legion within the Spanish constitutional army was created in April 1823.[76] A powerful solidarity movement with Spain also appeared in Britain, where a number of politicians and intellectuals firmly criticized the government's policy of nonintervention against the French aggression. Some of them even took action. Robert Wilson, radical MP and hero of the Napoleonic Wars, formed a unit of volunteers that arrived in northwestern Spain to fight the French.[77] In France, the liberal opposition firmly resisted the government's decision to invade Spain.[78]

The exiles also engaged in cultural activities, publishing pamphlets and editing journals in French and Italian. Significantly, the journal *El Europeo* appeared in Barcelona in 1823, edited by two Italian exiles, two liberal Spaniards, and an Englishman of German origins who had also arrived in Spain from Italy after the Austrian intervention.[79]

Spain consequently became the first location of a liberal diaspora that promoted the development of shared constitutional values and concepts, and commenced building an international solidarity movement that would continue developing in the next decades.[80] However, international mobility was not restricted to the liberals. During the *Trienio*, thousands of Spanish counterrevolutionaries found a refuge in southern France, where they could rest and regroup, sometimes with French assistance.[81] Thus, the experience of the *Trienio* became a key moment for the internationalization of the conflict between revolution and counterrevolution.

[76] Manuel Morán Ortí, "Los emigrados italianos de 1821 en la guerra realista de Cataluña," *Itálica*, 18 (1990), 329–63; Walter Bruyère-Ostells, *La Grande armée de la liberté* (Paris: Tallandier, 2009), 81–107.

[77] Nadiezdha Cosores, "England and the Spanish Revolution of 1820–1823," *Trienio*, 9 (1987), 39–131; Simal, *Emigrados*, 167–70.

[78] Emmanuel Larroche, *L'expédition d'Espagne. 1823: De la guerre selon la Charte* (Rennes: Presses Universitaires de Rennes, 2013), 29–88.

[79] Paula A. Sprague, *El Europeo (Barcelona, 1823–1824): Prensa, modernidad y universalismo* (Madrid and Frankfurt am Main: Iberoamericana/Vervuert, 2009).

[80] Florencia Peyrou and Juan Luis Simal, "Exile, Secret Societies, and the Emergence of an International Democratic Culture," in Joanna Innes and Mark Philp, eds., *Reimagining Democracy in the Mediterranean, 1780–1860* (Oxford: Oxford University Press, 2018), 205–30.

[81] Arnabat, *Visca el rei i la religió!*, 353–5; Comellas, *Los realistas en el Trienio*, 124–34, 155–67.

The Constitutional Triennium in Spain, 1820–1823

\* \* \*

The French intervention in Spain accelerated the fall of the Portuguese constitutional regime. On 27 May 1823, an uprising led by Prince Dom Miguel, head of the Portuguese ultras, succeeded in convincing King João VI to dissolve the Cortes. The fall of constitutional Spain followed in October. Thus ended the constitutional regimes installed after the revolutions of 1820–1821 in the Italian and Iberian peninsulas. Southern European constitutionalism was effaced by the combination of local counterrevolution and foreign intervention. However, it was not definitively beheaded. It survived in exile, where a liberal international movement in which Spanish, Italian, and Portuguese émigrés figured prominently was shaped in the next years.[82]

[82] Isabella, *Risorgimento in Exile*; Simal, *Emigrados*.

# 5

# Mexico: From Civil War to the War of Independence, 1808–1825

### JUAN ORTIZ ESCAMILLA

## The Political Crisis of 1808

The events that led to the civil war of 1810 in New Spain were the results of the weakening and the internal crisis of the Spanish Crown – caused by Carlos IV's power struggle with his son Fernando, and Minister Manuel de Godoy's affair with the queen – as well as its everlasting wars against the British Empire for the control of the Mediterranean Sea, the Americas, and the Philippines. Henceforth, the extraction of resources from its colonies – regardless of the means used for their exploitation – put New Spain in the most unfair of positions among the four viceroyalties.[1] What started out as donations and voluntary loans, soon turned into mandatory taxes, and in 1804, the royal consolidation decree (*Real Cédula de Consolidación*) – which ordered the alienation or expropriation of funds that belonged to the Church – aggravated New Spain's economic crisis. Mid-scale proprietors as well as welfare and religious institutions were especially affected by these measures. In Mexico City, the currency deposits of abbeys, convents, colleges, hospitals, charities, *cofradías*, *archicofradías*, Indigenous communities, selected individuals, and the cathedral were expropriated. This measure was not only grave because it was unusual, but because a major part of the funds was lent as credits for an indefinite term to miners, farmers, and ranchers, who were forced to sell a part of their property to pay for these debts. Up to 1808, a sum around 10,500,000 pesos had been charged in New Spain, yet, paradoxically, half of it ended in the hands of Napoleon's government in Paris.[2]

---

This chapter has been translated by Roberto Breña.

[1] Brian Hamnett, *Raíces de la insurgencia en México: Historia regional, 1750–1824* (Mexico City: Fondo de Cultura Económica, 2010), 103–33.

[2] Carlos Marichal, *La bancarrota del virreinato: Nueva España y las finanzas del imperio, 1780–1810* (Mexico City: El Colegio de México, Fondo de Cultura Económica,

The decree stirred up social unrest, which was soon followed by political discomfort. On 9 June 1808, the news that King Carlos IV had abdicated in favor of his son Fernando, who had in turn ceded the throne to Joseph Bonaparte, became public. The elite of the capital of the Viceroyalty of New Spain soon started to gather to express their opinions about this crisis and how to deal with this problem. Transferring sovereignty to a foreign government broke the pact of rule that had been established in the Viceroyalty at the end of the conquest in the sixteenth century. In the three following months, the capital – like the main cities in the Iberian Peninsula – was wrapped up in a vortex of ideas, proposals, and counterproposals regarding this political juncture. As the capital of the Viceroyalty, the district of Mexico named itself the representative of all the other *ayuntamientos* (town councils). However, this caused discontent among the de facto powers of the city and eventually led to a *coup d'état* against Viceroy José de Iturrigaray, as well as the imprisonment and the execution of other residents of the district.

The attempt to create a provisional junta in the absence of the monarch seemed natural in this context, for most of the peninsular kingdoms and American viceroyalties started to organize in the same manner. These juntas sought to revert the legitimacy of power to its origin: The districts intended to swear an oath of loyalty to the Spanish monarch Fernando VII – whom they considered the legitimate heir to the Spanish Crown – instead of the French usurper, Joseph I.[3] Opinions became polarized. The ministers of the *audiencia*, the inquisitors, the peninsular elite, and the archbishop viewed the district's proposal – which was backed by Viceroy José de Iturrigaray – as an act of subversion. As evidenced in the documents of the time, their concern was based upon the perceived resemblance of this political conundrum with those of France in 1789 and Saint-Domingue in 1791. Many subjects of the Spanish monarchy did not forget that a similar call to action had led to the destruction of the French monarchy, the execution of King Louis XVI, and, eventually, the establishment of Napoleon's empire.[4]

---

Fideicomiso Historia de las Américas, 1999), 241–2; Gisela von Wobeser, *La dominación colonial: La consolidación de vales reales, 1804–1812* (Mexico City: Universidad Nacional Autónoma de México, 2003), 195.

[3] *Memoria póstuma de don Francisco Primo de Verdad y Ramos, síndico del Ayuntamiento de México, 1808*, ed. Marcelo Ebrard Casaubon (Mexico City: Gobierno del Distrito Federal, 2008).

[4] Real Decreto de la Junta de Sevilla, 6 September 1808, cited in Genaro García, ed., *Documentos históricos mexicanos*, 7 vols. (Mexico City: Consejo Nacional de Fomento Educativo, 1985), vol. II, 81–3.

Juan Gabriel de Jabat and Manuel Francisco de Jáuregui, representatives of the Sevillian junta, soon joined the debates regarding the future of the empire in New Spain. They evidently intended for the viceroy to recognize the legitimacy of their junta and sought to get hold of all public funds. These Sevillian authorities were authorized by their government to supplant Viceroy José de Iturrigaray if he did not comply with their wishes. That was the case, and they soon overthrew the regent by joining forces with miners, wealthy farmers, the *audiencia*, and the *Consulado* (merchant guild).[5]

This *coup d'état*, like any other, was plagued by major irregularities and contradictions between discourse and actions on the ground. For instance, the Laws of the Indies clearly established that during the absence of a viceregal authority, the *Pliegos de providencia*, which contained the names of the likely successors, ought to be opened. This law was disregarded, and the coup's perpetrators gave themselves the right to name a ruler of their own choice. This happened to be the oldest military leader in the Viceroyalty, Field Marshal Pedro Garibay. They neglected the law by arguing that, although the viceroy's successor could have been an official from Campeche, Guatemala, or Havana, all the potential candidates were too far away from the capital. The new government established an alliance with Seville, and, as a proof of its loyalty, sent 9 million pesos to the Iberian Peninsula. With these resources, the junta of Seville was able to dominate the other juntas in Spain that were still not bothered by a French siege, and managed to impose itself upon them, dictating what became their common political objectives.

On his part, the new viceroy of New Spain, Garibay, could not keep the revolutionary effervescence at bay for long. Unable to limit the influence of the coup's perpetrators in governmental matters, he was eventually replaced by Archbishop Francisco Javier de Lizana y Beaumont. This man ruled knowing that the same people who had overthrown Iturrigaray could do the same to him. The archbishop, who at first thought of the coup's perpetrators as men of "good will," quickly changed his mind and labeled them as "dangerous individuals and enemies of the kingdom's peace and tranquility." Lizana became the third viceroy to be removed in less than two years. His position was shortly occupied by the *audiencia*'s regent, Tomás

---

[5] Doris Ladd, *La nobleza mexicana en la época de la Independencia, 1780–1826* (Mexico City: Fondo de Cultura Económica, 1984), 159; Roberto Breña, *El primer liberalismo español y los procesos de emancipación de América, 1808–1824: Una revisión historiográfica del liberalismo hispánico* (Mexico City: El Colegio de México, 2006), 85.

González Calderón, who maintained a close relation with the *Consulado* of Cádiz. The next viceroy, Francisco Javier Venegas, belonged to the same group, having served as governor of Cádiz before he was sent to New Spain.

The political, economic, and social instability split New Spain's society in a disturbing manner. On 30 May 1810 – only four months before Hidalgo's insurrection – the bishop-elect of Michoacán, Miguel Abad y Queipo, sent a delegation to the regency of Spain, with the intent of preventing it from starting a possible uprising. He assured that throughout the American continent, and especially in New Spain, an overall insurrection was sprouting. He thought the French Revolution had influenced the minds of the Spanish Americans by feeding them with a blazing desire for independence, and that this had worsened the divisions within Spanish American societies. Moreover, he asserted that "the American-born wish to rule themselves and to be the sole proprietors of their goods, which has aroused envy, rivalry, and division." While the high clergy intended to obstruct the spread of liberal ideas and the Bonapartist plans that could lead to insurrection in New Spain, the lower clergy and more than a handful of the viceroyalty's elite dedicated their efforts to the opposite task.[6]

## Civil War

The dismantling of Spanish dominion started on the evening of 16 September 1810. A regime that was built throughout the course of 300 years was mortally wounded by a popular uprising led by a priest, Miguel Hidalgo y Costilla, which started in the town of Dolores in the province of Guanajuato. While the regime crumbled, new political and military authorities were installed in the territories controlled by either the insurgents or the royalists. The former intended to destroy what they saw as an illegitimate government and hand the crown back to Fernando VII, while the latter also defended the monarch, but for less "noble" reasons, i.e. for personal gain and advantage. Faced with the force of arms, former authorities, corporations, intendants, subdelegates, districts, special juries, clergymen, *repúblicas de indios*, and the ministers of the *audiencias* slowly abandoned their posts, which were filled by

---

[6] Diego Abad y Queypo, "Representación a la primera Regencia, en que se describe compendiosamente el estado de fermentación que anunciaba un próximo rompimiento, y se proponían los medios con que tal vez se hubiera podido evitar," Valladolid, 30 May 1810, in Juan Hernández y Dávalos, *Colección de documentos para la historia de la guerra de independencia en México de 1810 a 1821*, 6 vols. (Mexico City: Instituto de Estudios Históricos de la Revolución Mexicana, 1985), vol. II, 891–6.

the new political actors. Both armies were fed with economic resources that were taken from each locality's population and soil. Both sides also regulated codes of conduct, promulgated new legislation, and, in some cases, established new constitutions to govern the territories that each of them controlled. The war also marked the beginning of the demise of social hierarchies based on privilege, corporation, and ethnicity. It permitted scenarios that would have been previously unthinkable, such as the mingling of men and women from different social classes in a quest for self-protection.

The insurgent groups used three different types of warfare: the popular revolution, with laborers and soldiers side by side; the organized insurgence, whose recruitment and training operated in a similar fashion to the royalist army; and, finally, radical guerrilla warfare by groups that never gave up arms and fought the war until their death or their group's demise. By contrast, the royalists put the colonial model for defense to use. Royal forces, which had considered the possibility that the Spanish Crown's American territories could face a threat, had discussed and restructured their plan of action several times. Firstly, the few remaining battalions and regiments of the regular army and the military forces from the provinces were mobilized. Since they were not sufficient to overcome the thousands of armed masses, self-defense organizations called "Companies of Patriot Defenders of Fernando VII" sprang up across cities, *villas*, and towns. In 1812, all of these armed groups were backed up by forces from the Iberian Peninsula, who had recently fought against the French in Spain, and were now deployed to the Americas.

The first insurgent uprising was planned as an insurrection by only a handful of provincial armies that were mostly comprised of creoles. The situation changed when the military ceded their leadership in favor of clergymen, who would now organize and coordinate both political and military movements. Hundreds of priests – who had no experience whatsoever in the use of weapons or warfare – led the frontlines of local rebellions against colonial rule and its representatives. As Félix María Calleja, the chief of counterinsurgent operations, asserted, the rebels acted with a "very similar devotion to that of religious wars" as they were guided by what he considered a "clergy in revolt."[7] During its first phase, from September 1810 to January 1811, the rebellion spread across the center of New Spain. Local

---

[7] Archivo General Militar de Segovia (AGMS), leg. C-532, Hoja de Servicio del teniente general Félix María Calleja, Madrid, 28 June 1818.

governments were established across cities, towns, and *villas*, principally in the bishoprics of Michoacán and Guadalajara, which were comprised of the intendancies of Valladolid, Guanajuato, San Luis Potosí, Nueva Galicia, Zacatecas, and the Internal Provinces. Political groups appeared in the province of Mexico. During these months, many governments that had previously been in the hands of *peninsulares* were replaced by those controlled by native Americans, mainly creoles.

Looking back years later, Spanish brigadier Félix María Calleja asserted that every inhabitant of New Spain was using all the means at their disposal to achieve independence: "the rich man, his wealth; the poor one, his strength; women, their traits; the wise man, his advice; the employee, the news; the clergy, its influence, and the Indian, his murderous arm."[8] The new creole authorities that began to control the situation in some parts of the Viceroyalty assured the inhabitants that the critical situation was caused by the imposition of taxes, restrictions on commerce, and the Spanish monopoly over high office positions. Even their adversaries agreed on this: "Nobody ignores that the lack of financial resources is caused by the Peninsula; that the scarcity and its effects on higher prices are a direct result of commercial speculations in which too many hands are involved, and that the wealth and riches that the colonies lack are squandered in the metropole."[9] Although this movement started as a popular insurrection against a government considered illegitimate, at first, it did not imply the formation of a legitimate power or the establishment of a unique, strong, leading group that could conduct real military action. Multiple insurgencies emerged across the country and their leaders moved around people and their property according to their will and needs. Due to this situation, most of the proprietors that had joined the rebellion at first stopped sympathizing with the movement and switched to the opposition. Many of them obtained a pardon from the authorities and joined the ranks of the counterinsurgency to fight their former companions.

The military reaction from the viceregal authorities was immediate. They formed the "Army of the Center," with Brigadier Félix María Calleja as chief of operations, alongside Colonel Manuel de Flón, count of La Cadena, as second in command. Because of the haste with which these troops were assembled, the insurrection expanded in every direction with little or no

---

[8] Ibid.

[9] Archivo General de la Nación, México, Operaciones de Guerra, (AGNM, OG), t. 176, ff. 142–3, Calleja to Viceroy Venegas, Guadalajara, 29 January 1811.

resistance whatsoever.[10] Since this army lacked men, the government recruited them without regard for their social and economic background, it forcefully gathered provisions and funds, and collected all sorts of metals in order to forge new weapons.

From October 1810 until May 1812, the Army of the Center participated in several military operations. During this time, it fought two different types of war: the first insurgency, headed by General Miguel Hidalgo, and the second one led by José María Morelos. The former was comprised of a reduced armed force and thousands of civilians, including elderly men, women, and children. The latter was more successful, largely because of its military expertise, its selective recruitment, and its apt organization. Its action radius covered the provinces of Puebla, Oaxaca, Mexico, Valladolid, and Veracruz.

On 2 October 1810, the Army of the Center started its march from San Luis Potosí to the town of Dolores. The "reconquest" began in exactly the same place where the insurrection had been initiated. Its main objectives were to eliminate the main forces of the movement and to reestablish order within these populations. The military developed a single policy for all of the towns that were won back in name of Fernando VII: Insurgent authorities as well as residents who had sympathized with the movement were replaced by persons loyal to the viceregal government. Terror was used as an effective weapon for intimidation: Many rebel leaders and members of the lowest strata of society – the so-called *pueblo bajo* – were executed. However, pardons were decreed for those who regretted joining the movement, leading them to become part of the companies for local defense known as the "Faithful Royalist Defenders of Fernando VII."

The first battle between the Army of the Center and the insurgents led by Miguel Hidalgo took place on 7 November 1810. A few days before, the rebels defeated an army of 800 men sent by the viceroy to detain their march toward Mexico City at Monte de las Cruces. While the Army of the Center advanced with the intention of protecting Mexico City, the insurgent army decided not to attack the capital and ended up, by accident, in the margins of the town of Aculco. During this first confrontation, Calleja showed his ability and prowess as a military strategist by applying the offensive plan that he used throughout the two years during which he led the Army of the Center. He divided his force in five columns: left, right, center, rearguard, and reserve. Before the attack, Calleja, with the help of his quartermaster, scouted the terrain and the enemy's

---

[10] AGN, OG, t. 169, Viceroy Francisco Javier Venegas to Félix María Calleja, Mexico City, 17 September 1810.

Figure 5.1 Indigenous people fighting in 1810. Real Biblioteca, Spain, GRAB/261.

position, a rectangular hill that was circled by a stream and a canyon. Another of the army's flanks was protected by a rather rough mountain. "Their formation was set for a battle in two lines, but there was an oblong figure made out of people between the two, all of which were posed over the top of the hill, while the artillery stood on its sides." On lower terrain, between the town and the hill, there was another unit of soldiers that was accompanied by a crowd of civilians. While Calleja, who had military expertise, coordinated the attack and was followed by both his officers and his troops, exactly the opposite happened within the insurgent ranks. Despite the weaknesses that the Battle of Aculco made evident, there was no dialogue or agreement between the main chiefs of the insurgent army, Hidalgo and Ignacio Allende. The latter complained about the presence of Indigenous people among his troops, for they were mostly civilians who had no experience at all on the battlefield (Figure 5.1).[11]

In less than an hour, the royalists defeated the insurgent army. Its leaders blamed each other for this disaster, which affected their unstable relationship and the possibility of reorganizing the army in a serious way. Hidalgo headed toward the cities of Valladolid and Guadalajara, along with a select group of

---

[11] AGMS, leg. C-532, hoja de servicio del teniente general Félix María Calleja, Madrid, 28 June 1818.

men, while Allende took control of the city of Guanajuato. The Army of the Center attacked this city and defeated the insurgents. Calleja's army stayed in Guanajuato for various days to mete out exemplary punishments, publish some pardons, restructure the government, and create a military force that could defend the city.

From Guanajuato, the Army of the Center marched toward Guadalajara, the main base of the insurgent government and where most of its chiefs had gathered. This territory witnessed a battle that exceeded in importance those that came before it. Both forces had faced each other previously, and each of them knew how many enemies they would have to face. General Allende and his chiefs of staff – the most experienced in warfare among the insurgents – suggested that the numerous forces should be divided into five or six units, in order to attack the royalists on various fronts. However, Hidalgo opted to have the whole army march together in a single block. By this time, the Army of the Center was formed by no less than 4,000 soldiers in the cavalry, 2,000 men in the infantry, and ten pieces of artillery. During the nightfall of 16 January 1811, Calleja and his chiefs of staff recognized the enemy's positions as well as their numbers. The royalists were at a disadvantage against the insurgents. If they pretended to retreat, the enemy would know that they exceeded the royal army in numbers, and they could easily send 12,000 men to persecute them on horseback. If they actually retreated, the army would not be able to find a place to make base; there was no safe place to march to. For the royalist commander, the future of the Viceroyalty, as well as his military prestige, depended upon the battle in which he was about to engage. Finally, Calleja decided to attack the insurgents at dawn on 17 January, "so that the armies would not recognize each other," and used the same five column formation described above. The Army of the Center won the battle thanks to Calleja's ability, the use of the surprise factor, and the fortune that during the battle a royalist grenade destroyed the insurgents' arsenal. The count of La Cadena died during the confrontation, which lasted around nine hours. The heads of the insurgents fled the scene once again and escaped chaotically, leaving behind their artillery, their baggage, and their wounded. Calleja was lauded because of this triumph at the Bridge of Calderón. Until his death, he considered this battle as the greatest feat of his life and he stated this repeatedly.[12] In the short span of six months, the

---

[12] AGN, OG, t. 171, Manuel Espinosa to Calleja, Guadalajara, 29 January 1811; AGMS, leg. C-532, hoja de servicio del teniente general don Félix María Calleja, Madrid, 28 June 1818.

royalists took back the main cities and *villas* that had been held by the insurgents, but not many of the Indigenous and *mestizo* towns. While fleeing toward the United States, Hidalgo and the main insurgent chiefs were apprehended in Acatita de Baján, in the province of Coahuila. Their group was made up of fifty-two civilians, eight clergymen, and five religious followers. On 30 July, they were all executed in the city of Chihuahua.

The fourth main confrontation between the Army of the Center and the insurgents, who had been reassembled under the command of General Ignacio Rayón, took place in the *villa* of Zitácuaro in the province of Michoacán. On 11 November, the royalists left the province of Guanajuato to face an army that was better prepared and had achieved several victories. Zitácuaro was protected with thirty-six cannons that were placed at its four entrances, and it was also defended by a moat that covered all of its exits. Besides, in the higher side of the *villa*, the insurgents had built a dam to flood the moat in order to impede the enemy from entering. The battle, which ended up favorably for the royalists, lasted three hours. For consenting to the establishment of the first sovereign American junta in August 1811, Zitácuaro suffered the greatest punishment that a population had faced in the whole course of the war. Besides the execution of nineteen men and the town's subdelegate, the army ordered to burn the *villa*, along with the *pueblos de indios* in the vicinity.[13]

On February 1812, the Army of the Center marched against an insurgent army that was posted in the *villa* of Cuautla, under the command of another priest, José María Morelos. The peninsular chief of operations was sure that he would take and control the *villa* very easily. Morelos was defending Cuautla with 12,000 men, 2,500 of whom were armed with guns and the rest were cavalry. Morelos had some military experience. Having worked in his youth as a servant on a hacienda in a region called "Tierra Caliente," he later became involved in commerce and learned to use conventional weapons to survive this inhospitable land, notorious for its overbearing heat, tropical diseases, and deadly fauna. The royalists soon noticed that it would be difficult to defeat the besieged insurgents if they did not manage to get artillery that could destroy the convents of Santo Domingo and San Diego, since their enemies were using these as citadels. Following the arrival of Calleja's army, although the insurgents suffered numerous attacks, they still caused major damage to the royalist forces by cutting their train of

---

[13] AGN, OG, t. 197, Calleja to Viceroy Venegas, Zitácuaro, 12 January 1812.

Figure 5.2 Insurgents under Morelos capture the fort of Acapulco, 1813. Real Biblioteca, Spain, GRAB/261.

communications and supplies, preventing them from obtaining fodder for their horses, and subjecting them to hit-and-run operations, night and day, which in turn gave them a reason for celebration. Calleja had miscalculated and underestimated an army that was mostly made up of black men and mulattoes from the Pacific coast, and thus very different from the one he had faced in Guanajuato (Figure 5.2).

The Army of the Center was facing a strong, organized enemy, rich in supplies and committed to die before leaving its post. After an uncertain beginning, the insurgents had taken the initiative. The idea that the safety of Mexico City depended on the outcome of the battle of Cuautla was common at the time. The Army of the Center had to defeat the insurgents, apprehend its leaders – most of all, Morelos – and pillage the *villa*. However, after a month of confrontations, its optimism diminished notably. Spirits grew weary when the heavy artillery that had been sent to the royalists from the fortress of Perote in Veracruz was taken by the insurgents. The frustration of being unable to defeat an inferior army cast doubts over the aura of Calleja as a military strategist and caused him several ailments during the siege. Finally, the royalists managed to put an end to the encounter with the help of the

Lobera and Asturias regiments, which had recently arrived from Spain. They started a war of resistance by blocking the *villa*'s supply of water and obstructing the access of the cavalry to victuals. The situation became increasingly miserable for the inhabitants of Cuautla, especially because other insurgent armies, such as those of Ignacio Rayón, Francisco Osorno, and Julián Villagrán, did not show up to reinforce Morelos' army. They simply did not understand the strategic importance of Cuautla.[14]

The outcome of the siege of Cuautla was the result of a political event. The insurgents made the most of the suspension of hostilities that the royalists were compelled to announce in response to the Spanish Cortes' offer of amnesty. When the royalists called for a ceasefire to offer some pardons, the insurgents took advantage of the situation. Morelos and his troops escaped at midnight while the royalists slept. It was a masterful escape plan: The besieged soldiers simulated an attack while they breached the wall that faced the river, and escaped in an orderly manner. The Army of the Center tried to react, but its effort was useless, since by the time it reacted the insurgents had escaped the site. By dawn, the army made its way into the *villa*. The soldiers saw scenes of horror and desolation: Most of the constructions were destroyed, and an unbearable stench – provoked by the rot of both human and animal corpses – came out of the rubble. Among the filth, one could hear the desperate screams of hungry and wounded people. The royalists recognized the population's valor and honorable behavior and stated that Cuautla had suffered because of a mixture of "passions with courage and mercy," and hence decided not to burn down the *villa* or kill its inhabitants, allowing them to escape the terrible fate that Calleja had originally decreed for them. On the contrary, the royalist troops showed their human side amidst the tragedy: They fed the hungry population who had not fled the town with *atole* and tortillas, reestablished the water supply, buried the dead, and took care of the wounded.[15]

No doubt, the siege of Cuautla was one of the most dramatic episodes in the war. Not only due to the thousands of men that both sides lost, but also

[14] AGN, OG, t. 198, f. 147, Calleja to Venegas, camp of Cuautlixco, 24 February 1812; t. 198, ff. 171–4, Calleja to Venegas, Cuautla, 4 May 1812.

[15] "Informe del coronel d. José María Echegaray, gobernador de Cuautla al general Calleja, sobre el estado en que encontró aquella población y medidas que tomó," Cuautla, 8 May 1812, in Lucas Alamán, *Historia de México desde los primeros movimientos que prepararon su independencia en el año de 1808 hasta la época presente*, 2 vols. (Mexico City: Fondo de Cultura Económica, Instituto Cultural Helénico, 1985), vol. II, Appendix 21.

because of the professionalism, the dignity, and the honor of most of the soldiers that fought in it. At the same time, a terrible epidemic struck a great part of New Spain during the siege. It was an outbreak of typhus, which led to the deaths of thousands of people of all ages and social classes. Apparently, more people died due to this epidemic than as a consequence of the siege.

Despite the fact that the Army of the Center took the *villa* of Cuautla, the royalists counted this as a fourth defeat, following the one in Monte de las Cruces and the two in Zitácuaro. Calleja's army did not succeed in vanquishing the main enemy force, since the insurgent leaders managed to escape. For the latter, Cuautla became a glorious event: In their view, Morelos had humiliated Calleja. After a siege of seventy-six days, the royalists had spent over 2 million pesos and lost more than 4,000 soldiers, including the Asturias battalion and a cavalry squad whose members were decapitated. Cuautla was Calleja's last battle in the war. He never fought again. Furthermore, the Army of the Center was dissolved by orders of Viceroy Francisco Xavier Venegas, which from that moment on gave the multiple insurgencies the possibility to control larger territories in the Viceroyalty for longer time spans.

Among the insurgent groups that spread across the territory of New Spain, the army of the strategic province of Veracruz stands out. Its large coast allowed the rebels to set up a supply chain, mostly of weaponry, to the United States. This geographic advantage gave them total control of the royal road – which was the main route for commercial communication between Europe, the Caribbean, New Spain, and the Philippines – as well as the possibility of disposing of tobacco shipments that were very important for the wartime insurgent needs and expenses. This army was a multiethnic force, comprised of *mestizo*, Indigenous, black, mulatto, and European men. In principle, they were all united under the liberal principles of equality, freedom, and a republican form of government. In fact, the so-called "Battalions of the Republic" made up the army.[16] Its main leader, whose insurgent name was Guadalupe Victoria, never asked for a royal pardon, nor would he swear allegiance to the Plan of Iguala that Agustín de Iturbide, an ex-royalist general, promoted in 1821 to finish the conflict. But in 1824, Victoria became the first president of Mexico.

---

[16] AGN, OG, t. 924, "Inspección del regimiento de infantería de la República," Huatusco, 19 January 1816.

## The Military Dictatorship

Martial law was imposed by the dynamic of the civil war, in which both insurgents and royalists fought for territorial control. All the leaders and chieftains arbitrarily managed the lives and properties of the civilian population. Both forces recruited young males to strengthen their files and imposed taxes over territories to finance their armed groups. Amidst the chaos, the promulgation of the Cádiz Constitution in 1812 put a temporary end to the abuses of the royalist military. As the pacification process spread, many cities, *villas*, and towns partook in swearing allegiance to the Constitution of the Spanish monarchy that had been sanctioned in Cádiz in March of the same year. Although the war had led to the formation of self-governments in the main cities and *villas*, led by commander-subdelegates, the Constitution propelled the formation of thousands of districts, as long as these had more than 1,000 inhabitants. Many of the insurgent groups took the royal pardon, joined the royalist forces, and collaborated in the creation of their respective districts. In several ways, the enactment of the Constitution imposed a pause on those military that were abusing the civilian population under the pretext of war. For Félix Calleja, who had meanwhile been appointed as viceroy, ruling in accordance with the Constitution of Cádiz became a very difficult task. He stated that he found himself in a situation that kept him "unstable and depressed," because he ended up battling both armed groups and "hidden traitors." When the constitutional regime was dissolved in 1814, the situation changed once again.[17] Now the government could do what it had wanted since the beginning of the war: impose martial law and militarize the whole Viceroyalty with the objective of exterminating the insurgents.

Viceroy Calleja had more than 8,000 expeditionary soldiers at hand to take control of the Viceroyalty without restrictions. These were experienced troops that had fought Napoleon's forces in Spain. They were distributed across the whole of New Spain with the purpose of maintaining peace and allowing the free transit of people as well as of convoys of trading goods, silver, and cattle, among other products. Military commanders controlled the money and supplies that they could extract from civilians with the excuse of maintaining peace. This military dictatorship lasted six years. It was a period

---

[17] Archivo General de Indias (AGI), México, 1485, Calleja to the Minister of Mercy and Justice, Mexico City, 30 July 1814; AGI, México, 1484, Calleja to Lardizábal, Mexico City, 31 December 1814.

characterized by assassinations, plundering, arbitrary executions, exemplary punishments, the burning of villages, and the raping of women (Table 5.1).[18]

Successive military defeats, moreover, forced the insurgent forces to be constantly on the run, hounded by the royalist army, which was strengthened by the arrival of fresh troops from Spain. After the siege of Cuautla, the colonial government concentrated on destroying General Morelos, its main enemy. On 5 November 1815, Morelos was made prisoner at the Battle of Temalaca in the central province of Mexico, and was taken from there to Mexico City, heavily guarded, where he was placed before not only a military, but also an ecclesiastical tribunal – he was, after all, a priest. He was sentenced to death and executed at 3 p.m. on 22 December. An hour later his body was buried in the cemetery of the parish of San Cristóbal Ecatepec. Consequently, toward the end of 1815, Viceroy Calleja was convinced that the insurgencies had been practically destroyed by his efforts and strategies. Following Morelos' execution, the people of New Spain stopped paying attention to the remaining insurgent leaders, turned their backs on the rebellion or the idea of forming a new government. The success of the counterinsurgent plan was due to the considerable number of regional insurgent chiefs who had accepted royal pardons and, in many cases, had joined the armed royalist forces to persecute their former brothers-in-arms. The viceroy stated that to "animate and inspire confidence in them, I have ordered the pardoned soldiers to form companies of no more than fifty men, and I have given the former chiefs the charge of officers with the title of *guarda-campos*, a distinction that most of them have been enthusiastic about."[19]

## The Plan of Iguala and the Start of the War of Independence

The reestablishment of the Constitution of Cádiz in 1820 once again mobilized the society of New Spain. While the Europeans were mostly divided between those who supported the Constitution, those who pretended to

---

[18] Archivo Histórico Militar of Madrid (AHMM), c. 97, Xavier Castaños to Miguel de Lardizábal, Madrid, 12 October 1814; Christon I. Archer, "La militarización de la política mexicana: El papel del ejército, 1815–1821," in Allan J. Kuethe and Juan Marchena Fernández, eds., *Soldados del rey: El ejército borbónico en América colonial y vísperas de la independencia* (Castelló de la Plana: Universitat Jaume I, 2005), 255–77: 257–8.

[19] AGI, México, 1322, Calleja to Marqués de Campo Sagrado, Mexico City, 6 September 1816.

Table 5.1 *Military units and territorial demarcation of the royalist army in New Spain and the internal provinces in 1816*

| Force | Territory | Commander-in-chief |
|---|---|---|
| Division of Mexico | The capital and the valley of Mexico (Coyoacán, Tacuba, Ecatepec, Chalco, and Cuautla) | Félix María Calleja |
| Division of Apam | Texcoco, Otumba, Zempoala, Pachuca, Tulancingo, and Mextitlan | Manuel de la Concha |
| Huejutla Section | La Huasteca | Alejandro Álvarez Guitán |
| Army of the South | Puebla and Oaxaca | Ciriaco de Llano |
| Division of Veracruz | The coast from Tampico to Coatzacoalcos | José Dávila |
| Troops of Tabasco | Province of Tabasco | Francisco Heredia y Vergara |
| Troops of Isla del Carmen | Isla del Carmen | Cosme Ramón de Urquiola |
| Division of the road to Acapulco | Cuernavaca, Zacatula, and Acapulco | José Gabriel de Armijo |
| Toluca Section | Toluca, Lerma, Tenancingo, and Temascaltepec | Nicolás Gutiérrez |
| Division of Ixtlahuaca | Ixtlahuaca, Maravatío, Zitácuaro, and Cóporo | Matías Martín de Aguirre |
| Division of Tula | Tula, Xilotepec, Huichapan, and Zimapán | Cristóbal Ordóñez |
| Division of Querétaro | Querétaro, San Juan del Río, Celaya, and part of the Sierra Gorda | Ignacio García Rebollo |
| Army of the North | Valladolid and Guanajuato | Agustín de Iturbide |
| Reserve army | New Kingdom of Galicia, Zacatecas, and San Blas | José de la Cruz |
| Division of San Luis Potosí | San Luis Potosí | Manuel María de Torres |
| Division of the east internal provinces | New Kingdom of León, Texas, Coahuila, and New Santander | Joaquín de Arredondo |
| Division of the west internal provinces | New Biscay, New Mexico, Sonora, and Sinaloa | Bernardo Bonavía |
| Old California | Loreto | José Argüello |
| New California | Monterrey, Santa Barbara, San Francisco, and San Diego | Pablo Vicente Sola |

*Source*: AGI, Mexico, 2345, Félix María Calleja, "Estado que manifiesta los destinos de Guarnición y campaña en que se halla repartida la fuerza veterana y provincial del Ejército de Nueva España," 30 September 1816.

reform it, and others who stood by absolutism, most of the American-born were in favor of independence and a new government, ruling either a central or a federal state. A small group defended the option of a constitutional monarchy. In this context, there was a call-to-arms by Agustín de Iturbide, who had successfully fought against the insurgents during the previous years. The Plan of Iguala of 24 February 1821 represented the interests of political groups not only of Mexico City, but also of several provinces, such as Veracruz, Puebla, and Guadalajara. This project, conceived by Iturbide, was supported by the capital's elite, which – due to the war – had lost most of its fortune, power, and influence. As a result of the formation of new districts in many provinces, the permanence of coin mints in miner towns, and the opening of new ports for international commerce, the regional oligarchies had been strengthened to the detriment of the de facto powers of Mexico City's political and economic elite.

The main objective of the Plan of Iguala was to ignore the authority of the liberal Cortes in the Viceroyalty and to reestablish the absolutist rule of King Fernando VII. Among other things, the plan guaranteed citizenship to all inhabitants of the proposed Mexican empire, without any restriction, and made all of them eligible for office. Agustín de Iturbide, the leader of the uprising, affirmed that this movement did not intend to dismantle the viceregal order; its only wish was to have "a pacific reform in a country which has been overwhelmed by all types of evil throughout several years." The plan recognized the Catholic religion as exclusive and ratified the clergy's rights and privileges. It did not recognize the independence of New Spain, but did recognize its autonomy, and it granted monarch Fernando VII the right to rule it or to send one member of his family to govern the territory.[20]

This military movement joined forces with the provincial militias and patriot companies, the insurgents of the south of Mexico City, bishops and lower clergymen, as well as the districts of towns and *villas*. The districts of all the capital cities opposed the movement, for they considered it counterrevolutionary, anticonstitutional, and because they believed it would annul the regional autonomy that the provinces had recently acquired. High-ranking Spanish officials refused to recognize the Plan of Iguala; they thought that a call-to-arms led by a creole who was a militia lieutenant colonel, and

---

[20] "Plan de Independencia de la América Septentrional," Iguala, 24 February 1821, in Guadalupe Jiménez Codinach, *Planes en la Nación Mexicana* (Mexico City: Senado de la República, El Colegio de México, 1987), vol. 1, 123–4.

did not even form a part of the peninsular army's system of hierarchy was absurd. However, among their files there was a clear division between those who supported the constitutional order and those who remained faithful to an absolute Spanish monarch. As a matter of fact, in Mexico City a group of absolutist officials, headed by Field Marshal Francisco Novella, staged a *coup d'état* against Viceroy Juan Ruiz de Apodaca. During this time, Juan de O'Donojú, who had been named Superior Political Chief and captain general of New Spain by the Spanish Cortes, arrived in Veracruz. In his own words, the perpetrators of the coup did not defend the European cause "since they will never fight to defend a Constitution that they do not love, for they have given unequivocal proofs that they do not adhere to this system."[21] Perhaps this was the reason why, once the armistice had been signed, the Peninsular troops did not reorganize to continue the battle to defend Spain's interests. Most of them simply fled. The schism between those officials who remained on Mexican soil took place as O'Donojú arrived and signed the Treaty of Córdoba of 24 August 1821, whereby he recognized the independence of the Mexican empire with its moderate constitutional monarchical government and offer of the throne to Fernando VII or a member of the royal family. After the surrender of the main military bases of the Viceroyalty and achieving the allegiance of the main districts of the provincial capitals to the Plan of Iguala, Iturbide made his triumphal entrance in Mexico City on 27 September 1821.

From the capital, he would try to govern a newly born Mexican empire. He never intended to personally fight the Spanish troops that remained undefeated at the port of Veracruz. As a matter of fact, Iturbide did not participate in any of the few combats that happened during the seven months in which he made his way toward the capital city. During his stay in the government palace, he devoted himself to strengthening the military structures of his former brothers-in-arms and limiting the presence of insurgents. Likewise, he formed the National Sovereign Governmental Junta (*Soberana Junta Nacional Gubernativa*) with those men he thought he could trust the most from the capital's elite. However, Iturbide did not foresee that the groups in power in the provinces would organize a strong opposition. These groups represented the interests of recently arrived international traders and the former insurgents of the province of Veracruz, who now started adopting republican values to oppose Iturbide's monarchical and even imperial

---

[21] Archivo Servicio Histórico Militar ASHM, c. 5375, Juan O'Donojú to the Minister of War, Veracruz, 13 August 1821.

intentions. Furthermore, he underestimated the Spanish troops that had taken the fortress of San Juan de Ulúa in Veracruz as a military base. An alliance was formed in this province that would eventually put an end to the Mexican empire of Agustín I.

## Veracruz, the Tip of the Scale

The last battles for the independence of Mexico happened in the port of Veracruz, the only city that had been destroyed by Spanish bombs during the fifteen years of war. From 1821 to 1825, this was the site where the different armed forces, be that the peninsular groups – split into absolutists and liberals –, Iturbide's army, or troops made up of former insurgents clashed most violently, causing major destruction. Moreover, economic interests from Mexican, Spanish, American, French, and British traders were at stake. The representatives of the new political institutions that the Cádiz Constitution put in place – such as the port's town council and provincial deputation – actively participated in the conflict. All of these entities communicated with each other, engaged in political negotiations, and intended to create alliances to reinforce their positions. The complexity of this situation led to an intricate chain of events that continued until November 1825, when the fort was finally taken by Mexican troops.

Due to the siege put in place by the so-called *jarochada* – a group comprised of mulatto, *pardo*, and black men from the Gulf of Mexico who had previously fought for the insurgents –, the Spanish troops abandoned the city of Veracruz and made a base at the fort/island of San Juan de Ulúa, as their own protocol instructed. This action let them keep control over trade with Spain and, as mentioned above, survive five more years on Mexican soil.

In 1821, Veracruz became the treasure of which three armies hoped to take possession: the *jarochada* led by General Santa Anna, which operated within the city; the Spanish, who controlled the seaways from San Juan de Ulúa and pointed their cannons toward the city, and Iturbide's troops, who were led by Spanish general José Antonio de Echávarri and whose purpose it was to protect the royal roads to Mexico City. Since none of the groups was strong enough to impose itself over the others, the only possible ways to end this entanglement were political intrigue and the creation of alliances. From San Juan de Ulúa, Governor Francisco Lemaur started parleys with Echávarri, who seemed to be ambivalent in his loyalty toward Mexico or Spain. The two men ultimately opted for a political resolution. Echávarri was willing to sign an armistice with Lemaur that "could lead to peace with Spain."[22] Although the plan was contrived by two Spaniards, it was difficult to put it into practice without the consent of other leaders and several corporations. As a matter of fact, during the plan's discussions the goals of the former insurgents, led by Guadalupe Victoria, had to be taken in consideration. It seems that there was nothing that Echávarri could do to save the emperor's head because nothing "disgusted" Victoria more than the imperial figure of Iturbide and everything he represented.[23] For Victoria, the republican system was the only acceptable form of government.

By 22 July 1823, the events took an unexpected turn for Lemaur and Echávarri, for they were defeated by the republican forces. At that moment, the Spanish decided to form a military junta in Puebla that would coordinate and organize the operations for a new plan that rejected the Plan of Casamata. For this purpose, Echávarri traveled to this city – which was the base of the captaincy general of the provinces of Puebla, Veracruz, and Oaxaca – to hand the leadership of the movement to General José Morán. In this way Echávarri tried to evade Iturbide's charge that he had conspired with Lemaur to destroy the Mexican empire.[24] This plan did not succeed and Echávarri was soon substituted from his political and military leadership by the republican General Manuel Gómez Pedraza.

Meanwhile in Veracruz, Guadalupe Victoria took a daring measure by closing the seaways and impeding both the entrance and the embarkation of Spanish people and goods. While the republicans arrived to power in Mexico, in late 1823 the liberal government in Spain was finally crushed by French troops sent by the Holy Alliance to restore the absolutist monarchy of Fernando VII. Due to these events, the possibility of an agreement between Mexico and Spain was eliminated and a total war ensued.

On 23 September 1823, the city of Veracruz was bombed from the fortress of San Juan de Ulúa. The civilian population abandoned its properties to take refuge on haciendas and nearby ranches, and the Mexican government closed the port, and, in turn, activated those of Alvarado, Antón Lizardo, Tuxpan,

---

[22] ASHM, c. 100, José Antonio de Echávarri to Francisco Lemaur, Xalapa, 10 December 1822.

[23] ASHM, c. 101, Francisco Lemaur to the Secretary of War, San Juan de Ulúa, 8 March 1823.

[24] ASHM, c. 101, Francisco Lemaur to the "Secretario del Despacho," San Juan de Ulúa, 8 March 1823; Alicia Tecuanhuey, "Tras las trincheras del federalismo. Intereses y fuerzas regionales en Puebla, 1823–1825," in Josefina Zoraida Vázquez, ed., El establecimiento del federalismo en México (1821–1827) (Mexico City: El Colegio de México, 2003), 475–504.

and Tampico.[25] The Spanish were no longer able to keep their ships next to the castle as they had done before and were forced to hide them out of the reach of the cannons posted at Isla de Sacrificios in front of San Juan de Ulúa. The Spaniards suffered the blockade for more than two years, having barely any reinforcements and victuals come from Spain or Havana. This situation increasingly affected the discipline of the troops. A scurvy epidemic and gastrointestinal diseases worsened the situation among officers and troops that were already divided politically between those supporting the Constitution and the defenders of absolutism.

Desertion increased considerably once the news of the return of absolutism in Spain became known; many soldiers threw themselves into the sea with the purpose of reaching the coast. As Lemaur affirmed, the 3,000 Mexican bombs that fell in Ulúa did not cause the Spanish troops' demise. It was rather the maladies which drained their strength. The reinforcements sent by Cuba had been limited because the island had been attacked by Colombian warships during this period. The situation of the soldiers within the fort of San Juan de Ulúa turned dire in June 1824, when British ships blocked the commercial activities of traders from the United States at the castle.

The Mexicans had bet on the blockade since the start of the conflict. By the year 1824 the besieged soldiers' main concern was not to attack the city of Veracruz, but to survive the nightmare they were living. The scarce reinforcements stopped arriving from Cuba, and in some cases the soldiers who had arrived from that island preferred to return there rather than joining the combat. This led the besieged finally to yield their arms. The situation was unbearable: For fear of contagion, the men who were still healthy refused to take care of the sick, wash their clothes, or clean their overpopulated rooms. "Holes were cut through the beds so that the diseased could defecate through them," and the hospital became "the stenchiest of dunghills, where nothing resonated but screams of pain and death." By 1 November 1825, only seventy soldiers remained active; 341 had died and the rest of them were on their deathbeds.[26]

---

[25] Archivo Histórico Secretaría de la Defensa Nacional México, exp. 210, "Noticia extraordinaria de las desgracias de Veracruz en los días 14, 15 y 16 del presente," Mexico City, October 1823; exp. 211, Guadalupe Victoria to the Minister of War, Veracruz, 8 November 1823.

[26] Rafael Quesada, *Defensa del señor brigadier don José Coppinger sobre la entrega que hizo por capitulación del castillo de San Juan de Ulúa, de su mando, a los disidentes de México, leída por su defensor el coronel Rafael Quezada, el día 14 de marzo de 1826, en el Consejo de Generales celebrado en esta capital, para purificar la conducta de aquél jefe* (Havana: Imprenta Fraternal de los Díaz de Castro, 1826).

Throughout this time, the Mexicans, who were not keen on losing men unnecessarily, simply waited until the Spanish decided to capitulate. Finally, talks started on 22 September, lasting until 18 November. During this period, the Mexicans refused to give any help to the diseased, until they had the absolute certainty that the fort would surrender. It was not until the agreements were signed that the fortress was supplied with fresh food and medicines. The Spanish terms for surrender were simple: they sought an honorable capitulation, with the Mexican army saluting the Spanish flag. The king, Fernando VII, condemned the surrender and never recognized Mexican independence. It was the queen regent, Maria Cristina, who finally recognized independence in 1836, fifteen years after Iturbide's triumphant entry into the viceroyalty's capital and the subsequent events that ushered in the short-lived Mexican empire and the establishment of the Republic of Mexico.

6

# Central America

TIMOTHY HAWKINS

Early in November 1811, a popular uprising in the city of San Salvador toppled the provincial intendant and installed a local governing junta, thereby forcing the Spanish authorities in the colonial Kingdom of Guatemala to confront a manifestation of the political unrest that had already shaken Spain and many of its American possessions. This first test of the established order in Central America occurred more than three years after Napoleon's overthrow of the Spanish Bourbon monarchy had precipitated an empire-wide crisis. Eighteen months had passed since the creole elite in Caracas challenged the legitimacy of the Spanish loyalist governments by replacing their own colonial administration with an autonomous governing junta, a tentative step toward independence that soon evolved into an overtly separatist congress. Meanwhile, in neighboring New Spain a massive social revolution had raged since September 1810, following the outbreak of the Hidalgo revolt. Against this backdrop of colonial fragmentation, the captain general of Guatemala, José de Bustamante, agreed to cooperate with the creole-dominated *ayuntamiento* (city council) of Guatemala City to seek a peaceful resolution to the Salvadoran disturbances before they could spread to other parts of the isthmus.

Sensitive to the broader imperial crisis, Guatemala's creole establishment encouraged the suppression of the revolt but stipulated that Spanish authorities allow the local elite to manage the process of reconciliation. The council proposed sending two of its most influential members, José de Aycinena and José María Peinado, to lead the negotiations with the rebellious junta. The response from Bustamante was unexpected. While he refrained from asserting his unilateral power to restore order, neither did the captain general wish to legitimize an open-ended dialogue between creoles. Instead, he decided to send both *regidores* (council members) to San Salvador with an offer of amnesty pending full restoration of Spanish rule. To lend the negotiators greater authority, Bustamante appointed Aycinena as the new provincial intendant. Two weeks later, pleased with "the perfect restoration of public tranquility," San Salvador welcomed the Guatemalan delegation as it entered the disturbed province and submitted to the new leadership.[1]

While this particular outcome failed to prevent subsequent unrest on the isthmus, it illuminates the defining feature of both popular and elite responses to the disruptive political and social currents of the 1810s. In the decade leading to independence in 1821, Central Americans across the social spectrum demonstrated consistent loyalty to Spain and acceptance of the colonial order, despite exposure to the widespread political ideas of this revolutionary age and the kind of persistent internal grievances that united to spark and fuel independence movements in other colonies. Combined with a colonial administration single-minded in its dedication to root out dissent, this broad consensus helped marginalize and suffocate the few substantive challenges to the colonial order that did arise during this decade.

Consequently, the history of Central America during the Age of Atlantic Revolutions poses a conundrum. During the thirteen years that separated the Bayonne coup from isthmian independence, the Kingdom of Guatemala appeared to deviate from many of the revolutionary patterns by then well established in the Atlantic World. Unlike neighboring New Spain, Central America avoided the outbreak of popular insurgencies. Unlike Venezuela, it failed to nurture even one great emancipator of regional, much less international, significance. Unlike Haiti, it escaped racially inspired violence or an outright slave revolt. Unlike New Granada, it evaded an invasion from royalist armies. In fact, for more than a decade Central America was unable or unwilling to generate any sustained, substantive, or widespread display of opposition to the colonial order that had been in place for 300 years. Even the process that led to the kingdom's independence suggested limited revolutionary imagination, as local elites achieved emancipation by accepting incorporation into the nascent Mexican empire of Agustín de Iturbide, an accommodation that sought to preserve deeply ingrained institutions. This apparent lack of engagement with the Atlantic revolutionary experience suggests that the Kingdom of Guatemala was an anomaly in an empire that otherwise displayed multiple examples of revolutionary sentiment.[2]

---

[1] Timothy Hawkins, *José de Bustamante and Central American Independence: Colonial Administration in an Age of Imperial Crisis* (Tuscaloosa: University of Alabama Press, 2004), 106.

[2] References for Spanish American independence include Jaime E. Rodríguez O., *The Independence of Spanish America* (Cambridge: Cambridge University Press, 1998); Leslie Bethell, ed., *The Independence of Latin America* (Cambridge: Cambridge University Press,

Figure 6.1 Cathedral in San Salvador. Alamy.

In fact, the circumstances of the 1811 Salvadoran uprising and its successor revolts in Honduras and Nicaragua bely these generalizations and suggest that the forces that had already precipitated revolution in South America and Mexico had made some inroads in Central America. The local creoles who deposed the colonial authorities not only in San Salvador but also León and Granada, and briefly established autonomous governing juntas had much in common with their counterparts in Caracas, Quito, Buenos Aires, Bogotá, and Santiago, whose actions by the end of 1811 provided potent examples of the potential of creole-led rebellion. Yet, by the middle of 1812 the nascent threat to the colonial order on the isthmus had utterly collapsed. Over the subsequent decade, only a stillborn conspiracy in Guatemala City in December 1813, and a second failed revolt in San Salvador two months later interrupted the restoration of the colonial-era political and social consensus (Figure 6.1).

While it may be tempting to downplay a Central American connection to the larger historical currents that shaped this period, the fact that the isthmus failed to become a stage for great emancipators embarking upon dramatic

1991. See also Izaskun Álvarez Cuartero and Julio Sánchez Gómez, eds., *Visiones y revisiones de la independencia americana* (Salamanca: Ediciones Universidad Salamanca, 2003).

anticolonial movements is not an indication that the colony was immune to the challenges and disruptions of a revolutionary age. Instead, it suggests that Spanish Americans reacted to the imperial crisis by embracing political solutions that included both independence and continued accommodation to Spanish rule. At the outset, the news from Bayonne produced widespread concern and confusion throughout the empire, followed almost immediately by heartfelt displays of loyalty to the deposed Fernando VII. The Spanish Crown remained popular in the Americas after 300 years. Many of the first revolutionaries, including Hidalgo, claimed legitimacy as loyal subjects of *el rey deseado*. Others, like Bolívar, who sought independence from the earliest days of the imperial crisis, first emerged from autonomist movements and had to overcome years of bitter opposition from American loyalists before achieving their ultimate success. The absence of patriot armies, slave revolts, peasant uprisings, or liberators in Central America is not necessarily evidence of a colony out of step with the larger historical trends. Incorporating the isthmian revolutionary experience into the larger historical context only requires an acknowledgment that the Age of Atlantic Revolutions includes multiple examples of thoughts and actions intended to save and reform the colonial order rather than subvert it.[3]

## Central America in an Age of Reform, 1750–1796

The Kingdom of Guatemala was a Spanish colony that encompassed the modern nations of Guatemala, El Salvador, Belize, Honduras, Nicaragua, and Costa Rica, as well as the Mexican state of Chiapas. For two centuries following its conquest in 1524, the region remained largely isolated by geography and a lack of exportable resources from the forces shaping the wider Atlantic World. Populating the temperate valleys of the mountain chain that stretched along the western side of the isthmus and separated from each other by the rugged terrain, these Spanish subjects lived in an archipelago of autonomous communities, a fragmented and insular existence that remained a defining feature of the Central American experience throughout the colonial period.[4]

---

[3] Jeremy Adelman, "Independence in Latin America," in José C. Moya, ed., *The Oxford Handbook of Latin American History* (Oxford: Oxford University Press, 2011), 153–80; Eric Van Young, "Conclusion – Was There an Age of Revolution in Spanish America?," in Victor M. Uribe-Uran, ed., *State and Society in Spanish America during the Age of Revolution* (New York: Rowman & Littlefield Publishers, 2001), 219–46.

[4] Murdo J. MacLeod, *Spanish Central America: A · Socioeconomic History, 1520–1720* (Berkeley: University of California Press, 1973); Miles Wortman, *Government and Society in Central America, 1680–1840* (New York: Columbia University Press, 1982);

Map 6.1 New Spain and New Granada on the eve of the independence period

By 1800, the colony held just over 1 million people, with the vast majority concentrated in the northwestern provinces. Some two-thirds were Indigenous, a largely rural, disenfranchised, and impoverished population that was historically segregated from the Spanish conquest communities. Another third were mixed-race mestizos known in the region as ladinos or *castas*. While some were rural farmers, most integrated themselves into

Jordana Dym, *From Sovereign Villages to National States: City, State, and Federation in Central America, 1759–1839* (Albuquerque: University of New Mexico Press, 2006), 3–32.

urban life, where they made up the majority of the working-class tradesmen, shopkeepers, and menial laborers of the colony. A few ladinos, usually with the benefit of education, attained even higher status as *letrados* and entered the middle-class professions as clerics, lawyers, clerks, and minor officials. The remainder of the population were the Spaniards, a small minority that comprised the Central American elite. Most were creoles, native-born Americans of Spanish ancestry. A much smaller fraction were Spanish-born *peninsulares* who arrived in the colony either as colonial officials claiming the highest positions of Church and state or as immigrants seeking to exploit their social prestige and family connections for economic gain. While competition over economic and political power led to some tension between creoles and *peninsulares* by the end of the eighteenth century, American-born members of the elite tended to coexist with their European cousins and tried to absorb newcomers as a way to reinforce their own status.[5]

Each of the major urban centers on the isthmus spawned its own elite families. However, the most powerful concentrated themselves in and around the colonial capital, Guatemala City. Wherever they happened to reside, the primary motivation of the creole establishment was the preservation of their status at the top of the social order. At a fundamental level, the approach was the same. Whether in Comayagua, San Salvador, León, Ciudad Real or Guatemala City, elites practiced endogamy as a way to reinforce caste identity and strengthen family networks. They monopolized local political power by seizing control over town councils. They dominated local markets through their ownership of the land, its products, capital, and trade connections. And they sought to coopt senior Spanish officials to further their particular interests.[6]

The greatest practitioner of this strategy arrived in Guatemala in 1754 and left a political, economic, and social legacy that would shape the entire isthmus for the next century. Shortly after settling in the capital, the Spanish immigrant Juan Fermín de Aycinena married into a wealthy and powerful creole family, which provided him with a sizeable dowry and

[5] Carolyn Hall and Héctor Pérez Brignoli, *Historical Atlas of Central America* (Norman: University of Oklahoma Press, 2003), 86–7, 92; Julio Pinto Soria, *Centroamérica, de la colonia al estado nacional, 1800–1840* (Guatemala: Editorial Universitaria de Guatemala, 1986); Juan Carlos Solórzano Fonseca, "Las comunidades indígenas en Guatemala, El Salvador, y Chiapas (siglo XVIII)," *Anuario de Estudios Centroamericanos* 20:2 (1985), 93–130.

[6] Michel Bertrand, "Guatemala City Social Elites on the Eve of Independence," in Jordana Dym and Christophe Belaubre, eds., *Politics, Economy and Society in Bourbon Central America, 1759–1821* (Boulder: University Press of Colorado, 2007), 239–63.

access to local political office. Riding the indigo boom that soon hit the region, Aycinena became the most successful and influential merchant in Central America in the late eighteenth century, and the Spanish Crown rewarded him for his contributions to the colony with a noble title. By the death of the new marquis in 1796, the House of Aycinena, a vast interrelated network of elite members, had become known simply as the Family. Exercising outsized influence over a variety of political and cultural institutions, from the Guatemala City *ayuntamiento* to the University of San Carlos, in addition to their control over the production and distribution of provincial resources, the many descendants and relations of Juan Fermín claimed an unprecedented place in colonial society as the nineteenth century began.[7]

While it is impossible to overstate the concentrated power of the Family at the end of the colonial period, the Central American elite was not homogenous. Preserving the colonial order united all elements of the establishment, but self-interest created group dynamics that highlighted more subtle points of discord. At times, this took the form of tension between creoles and *peninsulares*, as American-born elite members grew discouraged with Spanish monopolization of the highest offices of Church and state. However, frustration with the Family also produced fissures within the establishment. While the Aycinena oligarchy dominated Guatemala City, a few creole and peninsular elite persons operated independently and even used institutions such as the *Consulado de Comercio* (the merchant guild) to promote their interests. Similarly, provincial elites had cause to resent both the political power emanating from the colonial capital and the economic monopoly enforced by the House of Aycinena. By the end of the eighteenth century, little production or trade could occur on the isthmus without the financing provided by Guatemala City merchants, a cockeyed economic system that the Family sought to preserve and provincial producers hoped to disrupt.[8]

In this environment, competition between elites was as normal as cooperation. In an ever-shifting power dynamic, the groups that comprised the colonial establishment used every means at their disposal to gain an edge over their rivals. When necessary, creoles sought group cohesion against the Spanish by playing up their American identity. If possible, provincial elites invoked regional and local bonds to draw power away from Guatemalan

---

[7] Richmond F. Brown, *Juan Fermín de Aycinena: Central American Colonial Entrepreneur, 1729–1796* (Norman: University of Oklahoma Press, 1997).
[8] Bertrand, "Guatemala City Social Elites," 245–54.

creoles. Meanwhile, Spanish officials played creole groups against each other to preserve their primacy within the colony. By the beginning of the nineteenth century, the Crown even began to view subaltern *ladinos*, who were increasingly educated, wealthy, and upwardly mobile, as possible allies and a potential counterweight to the creole elites.[9]

If Central American creole elites remained fully invested in the colonial order at the start of the nineteenth century, it was because they had become some of the great beneficiaries of the progressive reforms of the Bourbon kings of Spain. Designed to spark an empire-wide revival by increasing the power of the Crown, the reforms drew on Enlightenment-inspired concepts of rational governance. At once idealistic in its goals and practical in its approach, the Bourbon monarchy prioritized administrative centralization, economic revitalization, and targeted social experimentation as it sought to raise the level of civilization and improve the standard of living across the empire. While an absolutist state carefully coordinated this Spanish Enlightenment and viewed it in part as a means to reclaim power from Spanish Americans, creole elites, who reserved the right to complain about specific policies that they considered detrimental to their interests, embraced many of the progressive reforms that emanated from Madrid.[10]

The *sine qua non* of the Bourbon reforms was economic revitalization, for the Crown required sufficient and sustained funds to accomplish its other priorities. For more than 200 years, Guatemala's Pacific orientation, fragmented geography, and lack of easily exploitable resources marginalized the colony and kept it an imperial backwater. The isthmian situation changed dramatically by the mid-1700s as an explosion in overseas demand for locally produced dyestuffs such as indigo and cochineal combined with the metropolitan decision to loosen trade restrictions (and increase investment in imperial defense) to give the colony a viable export economy for the first time. The consequences were profound, as Central America finally found itself an integral part of the burgeoning Atlantic economy. As mentioned

---

[9] Gustavo Palma Murga, "Núcleos de poder local y relaciones familiares en Guatemala a finales del siglo XVIII," *Mesoamérica* 12 (1986), 241–308. See also Jane Landers, *Atlantic Creoles in the Age of Revolutions* (Cambridge, MA: Harvard University Press, 2010); Tomás Pérez Vejo, *Elegía Criolla: Una reinterpretación de las guerras de independencia hispanoamericanas* (Mexico City: Tusquets, 2010).

[10] For an imperial overview, see John Lynch, *Bourbon Spain, 1700–1808* (New York: Basil Blackwell, 1989); David A. Brading, "La España de los Borbones y su imperio Americano," in Leslie Bethell, ed., *Historia de América Latina* (Barcelona: Editorial Crítica, 1990), vol. II, 85–126. For Central America, see Wortman, *Government and Society*; Dym and Belaubre, *Politics, Economy and Society*.

above, Guatemala City soon witnessed the rise of a merchant elite with control over the isthmian economy. This trend then replicated itself on a smaller scale in regional centers as provincial producers of indigo and other products gained wealth and status.[11]

The Bourbon reforms also transformed the Central American political landscape. Always a decentralized colony, the introduction of intendancies under Carlos III (1759–1788) was designed to centralize power by replacing a multitude of autonomous provincial authorities with a handful of more manageable regional jurisdictions. By 1790, a crown-appointed intendant now governed from Ciudad Real (Chiapas), Comayagua (Honduras), San Salvador (El Salvador), and León (Nicaragua). The political reorganization, however, had the unintended effect of exacerbating the regionalism inherent in the isthmus' largely self-contained political communities by appearing to give royal sanction to the aspiration of provincial elites to seek less oversight from Guatemala City. Bourbon interest in the civilizing power of urbanization also led the crown to increase the number of municipal governments on the isthmus, a reform that disrupted the traditional dominance of the original fifteen conquest cities but at the same time opened new venues for local governance and new political opportunities for local elites.[12]

Even the daunting obstacles raised by the geography of Central America could not insulate the colony from the intellectual ferment of the eighteenth-century Atlantic World. With the growing economy, overland communication with Mexico increased and seaborne networks in the Caribbean expanded, thereby ensuring that news from across the Atlantic World reached into every corner of the isthmus. Growing numbers of Spanish immigrants also became conduits of European ideas. By the end of the century, Bourbon education reforms had instilled an enlightened mentality among the faculty and students of the University of San Carlos, which

---

[11] Adolfo Bonilla Bonilla, *Ideas económicas en la Centroamérica ilustrada, 1793–1838* (San Salvador: FLACSO-El Salvador, 1999); Troy S. Floyd, "Bourbon Palliatives and the Central American Mining Industry, 1765–1800," *The Americas* 18 (October 1961), 103–25; Troy S. Floyd, "The Guatemalan Merchants, the Government, and the Provincianos, 1750–1800," *Hispanic American Historical Review* (henceforth *HAHR*) 41 (February 1961), 90–110; Miles Wortman, "Government Revenue and Economic Trends in Central America, 1787–1819," *HAHR* 55 (May 1975), 251–86; Robert W. Patch, *Indians and the Political Economy of Colonial Central America, 1670–1810* (Norman: University of Oklahoma Press, 2013).

[12] Dym, *From Sovereign Villages*, 33–61; Alma Margarita Carvalho, *La Ilustración del despotismo en Chiapas, 1774–1821* (Mexico City: CNCA, 1994); Jordana Dym and Sajid Herrera, eds., *Centroamérica durante las revoluciones atlánticas: El vocabulario político, 1750–1850* (San Salvador: Ieesford Editores, 2014).

Central America

catered to the creole elite, and had begun to penetrate primary schools that served the ladino and Indigenous communities. Newspapers such as the *Gaceta de Guatemala* ensured that important ideas of the Spanish and European Enlightenments circulated widely. One notable beneficiary of the intellectual ferment was the Guatemalan chapter of the Crown-sponsored Sociedad de Amigos del País, which became one of the most active in the empire.[13]

As a result, by the end of the century the sense of order and well-managed progress achieved by the Bourbon crown was something that many in Central America believed to stand in stark contrast to the instability and destruction set in motion by Anglo-American, French, and Haitian revolutionaries. An Atlantic economy demanding indigo had enriched the creole elite, Bourbon trade policies had opened new markets, political reorganization had positive consequences for creole governance, and enlightened absolutism had inculcated the value of progressive reform and experimentation across social classes. At least internally, little evidence suggested that Spanish rule on the isthmus would be threatened in the new century.

## Imperial Crisis, 1796–1811

The 1793 decision of the Spanish Crown to join the first coalition of European monarchies in their war with the French Republic proved fateful for Spain and its empire, however. Within two years, Carlos IV had surrendered to France and then agreed to ally himself with his revolutionary neighbor. This remarkable turn of events brought Spain into conflict with Great Britain, which proceeded to use its naval supremacy to strangle Spanish trade in the Atlantic. The impact on Central America was catastrophic. By the end of the decade, the indigo market had collapsed, driving the isthmian economy into a decade-long depression. For the first time, a visible split emerged among the colonial elite over how to respond. The

---

[13] José Santos Hernández Pérez, *La Gaceta de Guatemala: Un espacio para la difusión del conocimiento científico (1797–1804)* (Mexico City: Universidad Autónoma Metropolitana-Iztapalapa/Universidad Nacional, 2015); John Tate Lanning, *The Eighteenth-Century Enlightenment in the University of San Carlos de Guatemala* (Ithaca, NY: Cornell University Press, 1956); Christophe Belaubre, "Bourbon Reforms and Enlightenment in Chiapas, 1758–1808," in Aaron Pollack, ed., *Independence in Central American and Chiapas, 1770–1823* (Norman: University of Oklahoma Press, 2019), 103–30; Carlos Meléndez Chaverri, *La Ilustración en el antiguo reino de Guatemala*, 2nd edition (San José: Editorial Universitaria Centroamericana, 1974); Adolfo Bonilla Bonilla, "The Central American Enlightenment 1770–1838: An Interpretation of Political Ideas and Political History" (Ph.D. dissertation, University of Manchester, 1996).

Family, which chafed at any restrictions on its commercial activities, including contraband, aspired to free trade and encouraged the Crown to relax commercial restrictions with neutral powers. Peninsular merchants and non-Family elite men argued that the colony should double-down on protectionism. Meanwhile, provincial producers found this debate to be yet more evidence that the colonial export model, with its dependence on Guatemalan merchant capital, did not prioritize their interests.[14]

As the nineteenth century began, therefore, Central America found itself, like its neighbors, fully embroiled in the Spanish imperial crisis.[15] As elsewhere, its creole elites held the key to subsequent developments. During this initial decade, Spain continued to suffer as an ally of France. With the metropolis effectively cut off from its colonies, imperial finances collapsed, leaving the Crown little choice but to seek unprecedented sources of income. With the war and the economy spiraling out of control, Carlos IV made matters worse by delegating political power to an incompetent favorite, Manuel de Godoy. As the shadow of Napoleonic France spread across Europe, Spain found itself unable to challenge the emperor's growing interest in the Iberian Peninsula. By the spring of 1808, following a popular uprising against Godoy and the subsequent abdication of Carlos IV in favor of his son Prince Fernando, and with French troops occupying Madrid, Napoleon seized the opportunity to replace the Spanish Bourbons with a Bonapartist dynasty headed by his brother, Joseph. For the next five years Spain became a battlefield as a loyalist resistance movement fought to defeat the French and restore Fernando VII to the throne.[16]

This peninsular context set off a political crisis in Spanish America. Napoleon's coup shocked the empire and left its inhabitants with an unprecedented political question: Who was the legitimate authority during the

[14] Timothy Hawkins, *A Great Fear: Luís de Onís and the Shadow War against Napoleon in Spanish America, 1808–1812* (Tuscaloosa: University of Alabama Press, 2019), 17–40; Gustavo Palma Murga, "Between Fidelity and Pragmatism: Guatemala's Commercial Elite Responds to Bourbon Reforms on Trade and Contraband," in Jordana Dym and Christophe Belaubre, eds., *Politics, Economy, and Society in Bourbon Central America, 1759–1821* (Boulder: University Press of Colorado, 2007), 101–27.

[15] Bernabé Fernández Hernández, *El reino de Guatemala durante el gobierno de Antonio González Saravia, 1801–1811* (Guatemala City: Comisión Interuniversitaria Guatemalteca de Conmemoración del Quinto Centenario del Descubrimiento de América, 1993).

[16] Hawkins, *A Great Fear*, 60–7; Hawkins, *José de Bustamante*, 42–79. For a broader overview, see Barbara H. Stein and Stanley J. Stein, *Edge of Crisis: War and Trade in the Spanish Atlantic, 1789–1808* (Baltimore, MD: Johns Hopkins University Press, 2009); Alfredo Ávila and Pedro Pérez Herrero, eds., *Las experiencias de 1808 en Iberoamérica* (Madrid: Universidad de Alcalá, 2008).

absence of the king? Spanish loyalists proclaimed their support for Fernando VII and set up a Junta Central to run the empire in his absence. Francophile Spaniards made peace with the idea of King Joseph and believed that this close association with imperial France would be beneficial to Spain. In the Americas, most Spanish subjects, as well as colonial officials, embraced the loyalist cause, though others considered the viability of supporting the claim of Fernando's sister, Carlota, who lived in Rio de Janeiro as the wife of the prince regent of Portugal. Some colonists pushed for the establishment of their own governing juntas, claiming this right based on the recent Spanish precedent, which, they argued, did not preempt American equivalents. Others, seduced by revolutionary movements across the Atlantic World since 1775, imagined the possibility of independence.

In Central America between 1808 and 1810, the vast majority of creoles came out as strong loyalists, a position that appeared to have broad popular support. Despite Napoleon's best efforts to convince them otherwise, most Spanish subjects viewed the French emperor as a diabolically inspired, Machiavellian tyrant untethered to the norms of civilization. For the first two years following the Bayonne coup, the colony hunkered down hoping to withstand what had emerged as an existential threat. At the end of 1808, the creole establishment joined with Spanish officials in proclaiming the everlasting fidelity of Guatemala to Fernando VII. They then underscored a number of symbolic gestures of allegiance with the creation of a *donativo patriótico* (patriotic donation) to support the Junta Central that sent more than 1 million pesos to Spain in 1809.[17]

However, despite these many good-faith gestures, Spanish authorities began to question the true loyalty of their American-born subjects. Over the course of 1809, Captain General Antonio González learned that Napoleon was sending emissaries to the region to undermine Spanish rule by promoting local support for Joseph or encouraging independence. Rumors of French-inspired subversives led to a number of treason cases at the time. And, in an event that only increased the levels of anxiety in the colony, members of the *ayuntamiento* of Ciudad Real justified their unilateral removal of the Chiapas intendant, José Mariano Valero, by claiming that he was a French agent. By May 1810, the captain general decided that the colony

---

[17] Hawkins, *José de Bustamante*, 46–7. See also Robert M. Laughlin, *Beware the Great Horned Serpent: Chiapas under the Threat of Napoleon* (Albany, NY: University of Albany Press, 2003).

required a special Tribunal of Loyalty to prosecute the dozens of cases of subversion that now demanded immediate attention.[18]

In the minds of Spanish officials, it was impossible to separate these disconcerting developments from the early and to date unsuccessful efforts to create creole autonomist governments in New Spain, Upper Peru, Quito, and Buenos Aires.[19] With the colonial bureaucracy on the defensive, anything that deviated from blind loyalty to the Crown became a cause for concern. While Central Americans had not called for a governing junta in 1808, the Guatemala City *ayuntamiento* soon began to argue that it had the right to represent all isthmian municipalities before the colonial authorities. Thus, this creole-dominated institution became something of a de facto junta, and its members seized every opportunity to claim a more visible role in colonial governance. In early 1810, for example, the council appropriated for itself the question of isthmian security, demanding that the captain general purchase additional muskets, expand urban militias, and reinforce provincial units in response to a potential French invasion. Harking back to earlier priorities, council members associated with the Family even used the issue of arms purchases to reintroduce proposals for trade liberalization.[20]

The imperial crisis deepened as creoles were forced to come to terms with the fall of the Spanish Junta Central, in January 1810, following the French occupation of Andalusia.[21] While it was quickly replaced by a new Council of Regency, concerns about the legitimacy of this transfer of power seized Spanish America. When this news arrived in Caracas in April, the creole elite claimed that colonial authorities had lost their right to rule and deposed the captain general. A similar movement swept an autonomist government to power in Buenos Aires in May. Hoping to reinforce its precarious position, the regency called for the convocation of a Cortes, one open to both Spanish and American representatives that would write a constitution for the empire. The reaction in Central America was illustrative. Creole elites had unanimously supported the establishment of the Junta Central in 1808. Two years later, however, the Guatemala City *ayuntamiento* claimed the right to determine the legitimacy of the Council of Regency. While a majority of the

---

[18] Hawkins, *A Great Fear*, 124–36.

[19] An overview of these revolts can be found in Rodríguez, *The Independence of Spanish America*.

[20] Ralph Lee Woodward, "The Guatemalan Merchants and National Defense: 1810," *HAHR* 44 (August 1964), 452–62.

[21] Barbara H. Stein and Stanley J. Stein, *Crisis in an Atlantic Empire: Spain and New Spain, 1808–1810* (Baltimore, MD: Johns Hopkins University Press, 2014), 454–65.

council approved, four powerful creoles, including the marquis of Aycinena, voted to withhold recognition of the new Spanish government. With the Family now overtly asserting Guatemalan rights in the depths of the imperial crisis, Spanish authorities became alarmed.[22]

During the summer, the newly empowered creoles petitioned the captain general to shutter the Tribunal of Loyalty. In September, the Guatemala City *ayuntamiento* provoked a fight with Captain General González by refusing his demand to turn over information it had received from Cartagena de Indias regarding the recent establishment of an independent junta in that city. However, the most significant concern for elites at this time was the election of an isthmian representative to the Spanish Cortes. In a positive development for the Guatemalan oligarchy, the new deputy turned out to be Dr. Antonio de Larrazábal, a respected scholar and cleric as well as a relative of the Aycinenas. Since Larrazábal represented creole hopes for equal rights within the empire, the Guatemala City *ayuntamiento* decided to send him to Spain with a detailed set of instructions to use during constitutional deliberations. The three-person committee selected to write the draft included José María Peinado, Antonio de Juarros, and Aycinena, each of whom had earlier refused to endorse the regency. Peinado, who emerged as the primary author of the *Instrucciones*, quickly produced a document notable for its progressive political outlook and its impact across the isthmus.[23]

Unable to travel to Spain until the following year, Larrazábal missed most of the Cortes debates in Cádiz that led to the promulgation of the liberal Constitution of 1812. The Guatemala City *ayuntamiento*, however, ensured that town councils across the isthmus received copies of the final draft of its Instructions to the Central American delegate in late October 1810. A symbolic gesture designed to confirm the lead role played by the Guatemalan oligarchy in setting the political objectives for the isthmian population, the distribution of the *Instrucciones* laid down an unambiguous marker to colonial authorities regarding the mindset of the colony's creole elites.

Peinado began by declaring the council's fervent support for the concept of a constitutional monarchy and justified this position with a fluent summary of Enlightenment-based political philosophy and the republican experiments in the United States and France. The *Instrucciones* then made the case for progressive reforms that would address the imbalance of power between creoles and *peninsulares*. As if he were anticipating the forthcoming Cádiz

---

[22] Hawkins, *José de Bustamante*, 69.    [23] Ibid., 71–3.

Constitution, itself, Peinado sought a liberal political order that would secure protections for individual rights, local autonomy, equal access to imperial offices, and free trade. While ostensibly speaking on behalf of all Central Americans, Peinado advocated a reform program that best served the interests of the creole elites. Far from a declaration of support for revolution, the *Instrucciones* demonstrated that Guatemala's creole oligarchy sought to seize this unprecedented opportunity to improve their position within the colonial order.[24]

Two years into the imperial crisis, the colonial establishment in Central America had coalesced into two competing groups. Both sides shared a basic level of accommodation with Enlightenment thought, though the most progressive of the loyalists, which encompassed the powerful Guatemala City creole oligarchy, embraced the emergence of liberal constitutionalism in the empire and its promise of increased regional autonomy, looser trade restrictions, and greater respect for the rights of Spanish Americans. Most Crown officials and peninsular residents of the colony, however, extolled the virtues of enlightened absolutism and advocated minimal change to traditional Bourbon institutions.[25]

These groups represented a small percentage of the overall population of Central America, however, and their political differences at the time amounted to little more than strategic posturing so long as the fate of Spain remained uncertain. In fact, contemporary events in Spanish America gave the creole and peninsular elite reason to come together as 1810 ended. When news of the Hidalgo revolt reached the isthmus, both sides reacted with dismay and concern to the possibility of a mass-based insurrection. Now the colonial establishment had to sensitize itself to the political sentiments of the heretofore-marginalized majority. In this tense environment, provincial voices already demanded to be heard within a system that prioritized the interests and concerns of the Guatemalan oligarchy. Similarly, many urban *ladinos* had become politicized. And, while social and cultural segregation left most Indigenous peoples sidelined, even the most isolated of the rural population felt the impact of the imperial crisis on Church and state.[26]

---

[24] *Instrucciones para la constitución fundamental de la monarquía española y su gobierno* (Guatemala City: Editorial del Ministerio de Educación Pública, 1953). See also Xiomara Avendaño Rojas, *Centroamérica entre lo antiguo y lo moderno: Institucionalidad, ciudadanía y representación política, 1810–1838* (Castello de la Plana: Universitat Jaume I, 2009).

[25] Hawkins, *José de Bustamante*, 76.

[26] Sajid A. Herrera Mena, *El ejercicio de gobernar: Del cabildo borbónico al ayuntamiento liberal: El Salvador colonial, 1750–1821* (Castelló de la Plana: Universitat Jaume I, 2013);

The imperial crisis created unprecedented space for political expression within the multiple layers of isthmian society. Some individuals would use this opportunity to seek radical or revolutionary solutions to their problems. However, what distinguished Central America during this period was its overall stability, a fact attributable to the degree to which subaltern and elite groups embraced Spanish rule at a time of incredible political shifts and reversals. In particular, the concentration of political, economic, and social power in the hands of a small number of interrelated families who prioritized the preservation of their status and therefore refused to move beyond imperial reform allowed the colonial state to survive the turmoil of the 1810s. This, however, does not mean that the Guatemalan oligarchy or its provincial counterparts embraced without question Spanish authority. To the contrary, disputes between the creole elite and colonial officials continued, while the twists and turns of imperial and local politics ensured that there would be multiple opportunities for confrontation.

## Colonial Confrontations, 1811–1814

The divide between peninsular and creole elites in Guatemala City deepened in March 1811, with the arrival of a new captain general.[27] The incoming governor, Vice-Admiral José de Bustamante, was an imposing and aloof figure with extensive experience in colonial administration and defense. Disdainful of creole political pretensions and concerned about the broader implications of liberal constitutionalism for the empire, Bustamante remained a fierce advocate for enlightened absolutism throughout his tenure in office. The creole elite, notably members of the Aycinena family, found their new governor to be a troublesome and troubling obstacle blocking their pathway to increased autonomy and political relevance. As a result, the conflict between the oligarchy and Bustamante played a significant role in Central America's path toward independence.

Seeking a productive start to his administration, Bustamante immediately wrote to provincial *ayuntamientos* asking for municipal reports on local and regional conditions. He followed this outreach with a general proclamation to his subjects, an address most notable for its effort to paint a picture of an inclusive empire, one where patriotism and citizenship flowed from the

---

Timothy Hawkins, "Fighting Napoleon in Totonicapán," *The Latin Americanist* 61:4 (December 2017), 490–510.

[27] Hawkins, *José de Bustamante*, 80–1.

religious, political, cultural, and legal bonds that Spaniards shared regardless of their place of birth. This distinction between *patria* (fatherland) and *país* (country) was a critical one for a colonial official who sensed the implicit dangers resulting from the growth of creole consciousness and an American identity. Hoping to inspire a patriotic movement among isthmian residents, Bustamante challenged his subjects to defend the Crown during the imperial crisis, while calling out certain groups, notably contrabandists and political agitators, as public enemies. Prioritizing order and stability, he announced his intention to govern according to rational principles. Then, shortly after the release of the proclamation and despite increased warnings about French subversion, the captain general announced the dissolution of the Tribunal of Loyalty.[28]

Despite these early efforts to promote harmony and cooperation, Bustamante's policies faced immediate pushback from isthmian creoles. Led by the Guatemala City *ayuntamiento*, provincial municipalities coordinated their reports to the captain general to emphasize specific concerns and grievances. Charged with summarizing the capital's position, José de Aycinena prepared a thirty-six page report, which he printed and distributed across the colony at his own expense. Aycinena framed his thesis as a defense of constitutional government and equal rights, arguing that a heterogeneous empire could only survive if it recognized "provincial particularities." In the name of the council, he demanded two specific reforms: improved education for the masses and an abolition of the state monopoly on *aguardiente*. Aycinena then asserted the unquestionable loyalty of the council and promised that its members would defend their *patria* at all costs. In a notable assertion of its own political perspective, the *ayuntamiento* of Quezaltenango informed its Guatemala City counterparts that its members would only be satisfied with the election of a junta based in the capital. The Guatemalans responded that this was also their goal, underscoring the degree to which creoles in Central America had embraced the reform agenda coming out of Cádiz in 1811.[29]

The uprising in San Salvador that broke out in early November became the first test of the strength of creole loyalty to Spain. In October, the Guatemalan archbishop, Ramón Casaus, had launched a campaign to expose sedition in the Salvadoran bishopric, an operation that led to the targeting of three members of a prominent local family and the imprisonment of one,

---

[28] Ibid., 82–94.   [29] Ibid., 98–9.

Manuel Aguilar, on charges of *infidencia* (treason). This blunt assertion of Guatemalan authority over Salvadoran religious affairs provided local elites with a pretext to challenge the provincial political order. Over the course of three days, a number of prominent creoles, including José Matías Delgado and Manuel José Arce, directed popular protests that forced the resignation of the intendant, Antonio Gutiérrez Ulloa, and ushered in an autonomous governing junta.[30]

Despite their best efforts to win the support of other provincial towns, the Salvadoran rebels found themselves isolated within the intendancy. Although it proclaimed its loyalty to Fernando VII, the junta urged the overthrow of Spanish authorities on the isthmus, a goal that had ominous implications. In response, the Guatemala City *ayuntamiento* declared its desire to preserve "peace, unity, and fidelity" with the Crown, a position in favor of the colonial order echoed over the next few weeks by other municipalities. As noted above, Bustamante and the Guatemala City elite then sought a way out of the crisis. Ironically, José de Aycinena and José María Peinado, two of the leading advocates for creole rights in the colony, soon found themselves on the road to San Salvador to restore Spanish rule.[31]

If the peaceful resolution of the Salvadoran uprising offered a model for future collaboration between creole elites and peninsular authorities on the isthmus, events in Nicaragua and Honduras at the end of 1811 put an immediate strain on a relationship that suffered from mistrust on both sides. At the time, Bustamante called his strategy toward popular unrest "prudent reconciliation" (*conciliación prudente*) and expressed his preference for negotiation as a means to resolve disputes. However, in late November riots among the urban poor in Usulafter, Santa Ana, and Metapán, which targeted Spanish officials and sought redress for grievances over colonial taxes and monopolies, threatened to inflame the intendancy of San Salvador again. While these manifestations of popular frustration were small in scale, on 13 December the contagion spread to León, the provincial capital of

---

[30] Ibid., 102–3; Luis Ernesto Ayala Benítez, *La iglesia y la independencia política de Centroamérica: El caso del estado de El Salvador, 1808–1832* (San Salvador: Editorial Universitaria Don Bosco, 2011); Rodolfo Barón Castro, *José Matías Delgado y el movimiento insurgente de 1811: Ensayo histórico* (San Salvador: Ministerio de la Educación, 1961); Eugenia López Velásquez, "Noviembre de 1811: Revueltas populares en la provincia de San Salvador," *Cuadernos de Ciencias Sociales* 2:4 (2011), 7–27; Elizet Payne Iglesias, "¡No hay rey, no se pagan tributos! La protesta comunal en El Salvador, 1811," *Cuadernos Intercambio sobre Centroamérica y el Caribe* 4:5 (2007), 15–43.

[31] Hawkins, *José de Bustamante*, 104–6.

Nicaragua. There, opposition to colonial economic policies forced the removal of Intendant José Salvador. Again, in response to the political vacuum, local creoles organized a provincial governing junta led by Bishop Nicolás García Jerez, declared their loyalty to Fernando VII, and asserted significant political autonomy from colonial authorities in Guatemala City. As in San Salvador, the Leonese elite sought but failed to receive recognition for its actions from neighboring municipal bodies. And, as in San Salvador, Captain General Bustamante successfully navigated the unrest and marginalized local elite men by appointing Bishop García Jerez as interim intendant of Nicaragua at the start of 1812.[32]

Ten days after the outbreak of unrest in León, the neighboring Nicaraguan city of Granada overthrew its own colonial officials. In a provocative and disturbing display of extreme localism, the Granada elite refused to submit to the authority of the Leonese junta or Bishop-Intendant García Jerez. Instead, they took advantage of week long popular disturbances and established a new governing *ayuntamiento* comprised exclusively of creoles. Over the course of a month of challenges to the colonial order on the isthmus, the Granada revolt proved to be the most intractable. But it was not the last. In January 1812, lower-class *castas* in Tegucigalpa, Honduras, agitated for moderate municipal reforms that included representation on the town council and expansion of education to the lower classes. Here, too, the popular unrest created an opportunity for more radical creole participation as two members of the local elite, Julián Romero and José Antonio Rojas, urged the masses to fight for greater civil rights.[33]

Despite the multiple grassroots grievances that fueled these uprisings, Bustamante concluded by the end of 1811 that the political unrest on the isthmus was the product of external forces, either in the form of inspiration from neighboring colonies experiencing rebellion or instigation from foreign subversives. In response, the captain general began to seek military solutions to a potential breakdown of the colonial order. With few Spanish regulars at his disposal, Bustamante ordered the expansion of the colonial militia and

---

[32] Ibid., 105–13; Jordana Dym, "Soberanía transitiva y adhesión condicional: Lealtad e insurrección en el reino de Guatemala, 1808–1811," in Manuel Chust, ed., *1808: La eclosión juntera en el mundo hispano* (Mexico City: FCE/COLMEX, 2007); Xiomara Avendaño Rojas and Norma Hernández Sánchez, *¿Independencia o autogobierno? El Salvador y Nicaragua, 1786–1811* (Managua: Grupo Editorial Lea, 2014).

[33] For Granada, see Elizet Payne Iglesias, "Local Powers and Popular Resistance in Nicaragua, 1808–1813," in Pollack, *Independence in Central America and Chiapas*, 133–57; for Tegucigalpa, see Hawkins, *José de Bustamante*, 116–18.

hoped to keep it mobilized as a force for the prevention and punishment of unrest. He also proposed the creation of a new Superintendency of Police, a reform that the *audiencia* rejected.[34]

Over the course of 1812, growing reports of provincial disturbances combined with creole demands for increased autonomy began to test the willingness (and ability) of Spanish authorities to tolerate challenges to the colonial order. Bustamante resolved the unrest in Tegucigalpa with a combination of accommodation and coercion. While he ordered the occupation of the town, he decided against mass reprisals. Instead, the captain general made an appeal to local interests by raising the administrative status of the region and appointing a local priest as its governor. During this time, colonial officials also began to uncover evidence of an anti-Spanish conspiracy among a small group of Guatemalan and Salvadoran creoles. Then, in February, popular hysteria over rumors of a French invasion caused a series of disturbances in the province of Chiquimula. In the meantime, much of Nicaragua remained in disorder. While declaring his continued preference to seek a peaceful resolution to the simmering rebellion in Granada, which included an offer of a general amnesty, Bustamante ordered a large military force to march on the province. Arriving in mid-April, the royalist army besieged the city for two days before Granada capitulated.[35]

In stark contrast to earlier conflict resolutions, Bustamante demanded a thorough investigation of the uprising, including the imprisonment and prosecution of all its leaders. The symbolism of this decision was significant, for the colonial authorities now targeted the creole establishment of a major provincial city. While creole loyalists across the isthmus found it difficult to support the Granada rebellion, neither could they simply disavow their compatriots, especially when the Nicaraguans felt the full weight of Spanish justice. In the meantime, with his belief in creole loyalty waning and with indirect support from the viceregal authorities in New Spain, Bustamante became increasingly reliant on a strategy that emphasized coercion and counterinsurgency. Over the summer, his administration expanded the number of militia units in the capital and across the provinces. In a controversial move made to counter the presence of insurgent armies in southern Mexico, Bustamante transferred mulatto troops from the Caribbean to Guatemala City and finally to the Chiapas border. And to help pay for the

---

[34] Hawkins, *José de Bustamante*, 126–31.     [35] Ibid., 119–21, 123–5.

increased militarization of the isthmus, he called on the colonial elite to make additional patriotic donations to the colonial treasury.[36]

Much more provocative was Bustamante's decision at this time to seek an expanded role for military justice in cases of *infidencia*. Since the fall of 1811, colonial prisons had begun to fill with suspected conspirators or rebels. Many of these individuals were creoles, and all sought the traditional protections established in civil courts. By the summer of 1812, a number of such cases were awaiting adjudication, and Bustamante believed that he had the authority to prosecute them in military tribunals. While recent imperial decrees seemed to affirm this position, the Guatemalan *audiencia* opposed the move as a threat to its jurisdiction. Sensing an opportunity to assert its own political status in the midst of this squabble between colonial authorities, the Guatemala City *ayuntamiento* began to challenge what it now perceived as the growing impunity of the captain general.[37]

Multiple factors emboldened the creole elite at this time. In May, the colony learned that José de Aycinena had received an appointment to the imperial Council of State, an unprecedented honor for a Spanish American, and his presence in Spain promised the Guatemalan oligarchy unrivaled access to the highest levels of power. Then, in September, the *ayuntamiento* received its copy of the Cádiz Constitution and rejoiced at its provisions. Among the most significant were the relegation of the captain general, an office with military, administrative, and judicial authority, to the status of superior political chief (*jefe político superior*), the creation of a regional representative assembly (*diputación provincial*) for both Guatemala and Nicaragua, and the replacement of traditional town councils with elected constitutional *ayuntamientos*. The creole elite now expected to dominate colonial politics on the isthmus for the first time. And this newfound power, which did not require a large-scale rebellion or the targeted overthrow of Spanish bureaucrats to achieve, appeared to come with the metropolitan stamp of approval.[38]

Implementation of the Constitution on the isthmus, however, remained largely in the hands of Bustamante. Considering the pervasive and persistent

---

[36] Ibid., 126–8. For more on the Mexican example, see Hugh M. Hamill, "Royalist Counterinsurgency in the Mexican War for Independence: The Lessons of 1811," *HAHR* 53 (August 1973), 470–89.

[37] Hawkins, *José de Bustamante*, 137–8. A provincial perspective can be found in Sajid A. Herrera Mena, "Escenarios de lealtad e infidencia durante el regimen constitucional gaditano: San Salvador, 1811–1814," *Mesoamérica* 53 (2011), 200–10.

[38] Hawkins, *José de Bustamante*, 142.

instability across Spanish America in 1812, the new *jefe político superior* was wary about much of the political reform emanating from Cádiz. From his perspective, anything that empowered the creole elite at the expense of Spanish authority rested on the uncertain loyalty of American-born subjects and, thereby, threatened the integrity of the empire. With the fate of Spain still uncertain and the details of the new colonial legislation still unclear, Bustamante determined to use his position to delay or resist significant structural changes to established institutions. Meanwhile, the creole elite in Guatemala City embraced the promises inherent in the liberal Constitution and sought to weaponize the newly representative assemblies and *ayuntamientos*, along with the individual rights and freedoms embedded in the charter, to weaken peninsular interests. As a result, for the next two years the isthmus found itself locked in a titanic political struggle between its Spanish governor and the Guatemalan oligarchy over the viability of the constitutional reforms, a confrontation that played itself out on a number of fronts.[39]

Building upon its increased profile during the early years of the imperial crisis, the Guatemala City *ayuntamiento* assumed for itself the responsibility of advocating for constitutionalism and sought to seize an advantage from even the smallest political reform. In some cases, this position required it to demand various symbolic accommodations from Bustamante, including acknowledgment of its new ceremonial rank of excellency, which he simply ignored. Most challenges, however, were substantive. Over the next year, the two sides fought fiercely over a number of issues, including the timeline for elections of representatives to the Spanish Cortes and the provincial assemblies, freedom of the press, and the right of the *ayuntamiento* to oversee the treatment of prisoners tried for treason in the capital, notably those brought to Guatemalan prisons from Granada. Dismissing the *ayuntamiento's* multiple demands for acceptance as a political equal, Bustamante moved forward with his plans to establish a counterinsurgency state, seeking tighter controls over information and communication, limiting travel, and prosecuting subversives. On his own initiative and with little oversight, the captain general even sent military forces to attack

---

[39] Mario Rodríguez, *The Cádiz Experiment in Central America, 1808–1826* (Berkeley: University of California Press, 1978); Jordana Dym, "Central America and Cádiz: A Complex Relationship," in Scott Eastman and Natalia Sobrevilla Perea, eds., *The Rise of Constitutional Government in the Iberian Atlantic World: The Impact of the Cádiz Constitution of 1812* (Tuscaloosa: University of Alabama Press, 2015), 63–90.

the Mexican insurgent army under Mariano Matamoros in the first half of 1813.[40]

By the end of this year, the constitutional experiment in the Kingdom of Guatemala was floundering. The Guatemalan oligarchy remained committed to the new liberal order and increasingly relied on José de Aycinena to convey to Spanish authorities the *ayuntamiento*'s dissatisfaction with what it perceived as Bustamante's obstructionism. Some members of the Family even sought to have the captain general replaced with the marquis of Aycinena. Other creoles believed that the time had come to end Spanish rule altogether. In late 1813, such sentiment drew together about two dozen disillusioned soldiers, priests, and council members in Guatemala City in a planned coup against the colonial administration. Bustamante uncovered this Belén Conspiracy in December and quickly imprisoned those connected to it. Then, in January 1814, San Salvador erupted again following elections for municipal government that brought a number of candidates of dubious allegiance into office. This uprising, which sought the overthrow of provincial authorities, also collapsed after a week of fighting between supporters of the revolt and local militias. For Bustamante, the lesson of Belén and San Salvador was unequivocal: despite their frequent protestations of loyalty, Central Americans had abused the reforms granted under the Constitution in order to achieve independence.[41]

While an outright break with Spain might have appealed to a small minority of Central Americans in 1814, the confused goals and fatal disorganization of the Belén Conspiracy and the Salvadoran revolt underscore the lack of widespread support for such radical action at the time. Notably, neither event sparked sympathetic movements on the isthmus, despite (or perhaps because of) the contemporaneous rebellion led by José María Morelos in neighboring New Spain. Instead, the majority of the population remained faithful to Spain and accepted the colonial order as it stood, with the creole elite finding some unity in their shared antipathy for Bustamante. From their perspective, the only opportunity for substantive political reform in Central America depended on the arrival of a new captain general,

---

[40] Hawkins, *José de Bustamante*, 143–79.
[41] Ibid., 170, 174–5; Mario Rodríguez, *La conspiración de Belén en nueva perspectiva* (Guatemala City: Centro Editorial "José de Pineda Ibarra," 1965); Christophe Belaubre, "Al cruce de la historia social y política: Un acercamiento crítico a la 'conjuración de Belén,' Guatemala (1813)," in Sajid Herrera, ed., *Revoluciones, guerras y revoluciones políticas en la América hispano-portuguesa, 1808–1824* (San Salvador: Universidad Centroamericana, 2013), 9–29.

someone more amenable to the interests of the oligarchy. At the beginning of 1814, the Council of State appeared ready to make such a change. However, the return of Fernando VII to Spain in March upended these plans as the restored monarch declared his intention to revive the absolutist regime.

## Absolutism Restored: 1814–1818

By the time Fernando VII abolished the Constitution in the summer of 1814, Bustamante had effectively won his battle with the Guatemalan oligarchy. Multiple complaints to Spain about the heavy-handed, autocratic captain general had either fallen by the wayside in the midst of the Cádiz debates or been dismissed by imperial authorities who sympathized with the hardline actions of a colonial governor who had managed to preserve Spanish rule on the isthmus. The end of the constitutional experiment provoked no overt distress among Central Americans. Instead, most appeared satisfied with the restoration of the institutions and practices of Bourbon absolutism. As a result, confident in the full support of the Crown, Bustamante now seized the offensive in his long-running campaign against the creole elite.

Over the next two years, the captain general sought to break the political, economic, and social monopoly enjoyed by the Aycinena oligarchy. His first move was to send the king a heavily annotated copy of the *Instrucciones* that the Guatemala City *ayuntamiento* had prepared for Deputy Larrazábal in 1810. Bustamante's parenthetical notes explicitly blamed the revolutionary sentiments expressed in this document for the subsequent unrest on the isthmus, and he urged the removal of all its signatories from public office. The captain general then restored the political institutions of the colony to their pre-1808 status, an act that effectively muzzled the Guatemalan oligarchy. Hitting hard at the economic foundations of the Family, he targeted the Aycinena and Beltranena merchant houses for suspected links to contraband trade, sued them for payment of back taxes, and confiscated their shipments. Elsewhere, Bustamante saw no reason to scale back his counterinsurgency measures, claiming that the isthmus remained threatened by subversive forces despite royalist advances in neighboring colonies. In the short term, Madrid supported these actions and ignored pleas from the creole elite for relief.[42]

---

[42] Hawkins, *José de Bustamante*, 181–94.

However, by 1816 the relative stability of the empire gave the Crown greater incentive to accommodate the concerns of leading Central Americans. Since the 1814 restoration, the Aycinena oligarchy had besieged imperial officials with protestations of loyalty. Blacklisted council members collected documents attesting to the unfair treatment they had received at the hands of Bustamante and sent the material to the Council of the Indies, where José de Aycinena now served alongside Juan Gualberto González Bravo, a Spaniard whose earlier appointment to the Guatemalan *audiencia* made him intimate with the Family. By this time, other segments of the colonial establishment, including the *audiencia*, had also begun to oppose the prolonged state of emergency on the isthmus. Unwilling now to dismiss the complaints and risk alienating the creoles, the Council of the Indies agreed to launch an investigation of Bustamante's administration.[43]

The royal decrees that arrived in Guatemala City over the course of a few weeks during the fall of 1817 served as a dramatic rejection of the counterinsurgency state that had held sway on the isthmus for five years and as a public repudiation of the captain general. Most notably, the orders rehabilitated the disgraced council members, pardoned the remaining prisoners charged with treason, and recalled Bustamante to Spain. In sum, Spain gave the Guatemalan oligarchy everything it desired. By March 1818, the creole elite found itself back in power with a new captain general, Carlos de Urrutia, who took pains to incorporate members of the Family into his administration and made it clear that his trade policy would not threaten its interests.[44]

## Creole Autonomy: 1818–1821

The three years following the fall of Bustamante witnessed the emergence of many of the destabilizing factors that would define the early republican period in Central America: elite partisanship, regionalism, race and class grievances, and rural disenfranchisement. In particular, this period laid bare a sharp political divide within the creole establishment, one that first coalesced after April 1818. Members of the peninsular and creole elite who had served in the former administration found themselves out of favor in the capital, and the Aycinena oligarchy sought swift revenge against those informally branded as the members of the Bustamante Party. Such personal

---

[43] Ibid., 195–6.  [44] Ibid., 193–206.

animosities quickly inflamed arguments over more substantive issues. Determined to recover its control over isthmian commerce, the Family once again took up the cause of free trade against those elite members who persisted in promoting antimonopolist policies. The restoration of the Cádiz Constitution in 1820 and the subsequent unrest in Spain then reawakened decade-old ideological disagreements and revived the debate about political centralization. Taken together, these developments paved the way for the mid-1820s rise of the Liberal and Conservative parties that would compete with each other for power on the isthmus for the remainder of the century. For the moment, however, fully entrenched in colonial political institutions and benefiting from a weakened metropolis, the creole establishment in Central America saw no advantage to outright independence.[45]

The Guatemala City oligarchy was not the only segment of the population that felt liberated after 1818. Now, provincial elites could concentrate again on regional interests without fear of intervention from the central authorities. Newly freed from the censorship of the Bustamante era, the isthmian press helped raise new political voices and enable heretofore-disenfranchised groups to speak out. Among these were nonelite professionals such as Pedro Molina, who used the printed media to debate the liberal politics of the revolutionary era. While some floated revolutionary ideas, advocates of independence found few allies. Politically and socially fragmented, leaderless, with few resources to compete with the oligarchy, the provincial elites, professional middle classes, and urban masses remained largely committed to the Crown.[46]

While urban populations on the isthmus became more politicized, rural Central America remained undisturbed by political unrest – with one great exception. Building on a tradition of protest over economic anxieties and specific objections to the formal reestablishment of the tribute in 1816, as well as growing desire for political autonomy in the western highlands of Guatemala, an Indigenous rebellion led by Atanasio Tzul seized control of

[45] Louis Bumgartner, *José del Valle of Central America* (Durham, NC: Duke University Press, 1963), 85–135; Víctor Hugo Acuña Ortega, "El liberalismo en Centroamérica en tiempos de la independencia (1810–1850)," in Javier Fernández-Sebastián, ed., *La aurora de la libertad: Primeros liberalismos en el mundo iberoamericano* (Madrid: Parcial Pons Historia, 2012), 117–45; Ralph Lee Woodward, Jr., "Economic and Social Origins of the Guatemalan Political Parties (1773–1823)," *HAHR* 45:4 (1965), 544–66.

[46] Sources on marginalized and subaltern reactions to the independence period include Ruben Leyton Rodríguez, *Doctor Pedro Molina o Centro América y su prócer* (Guatemala City: Editorial Iberia, 1958); Izaskún Álvarez Cuartero and Julio Sánchez Gómez, *Visiones y revisiones de la independencia americana: Subalternidad e independencia* (Salamanca: Ediciones Universidad de Salamanca, 2012).

much of the province of Totonicapán in the summer of 1820. While the uprising did not survive the mobilization of militia forces in the affected areas and did not inspire similar protests elsewhere, it drew inspiration from the Cádiz reforms, suggesting that certain grievances, liberal solutions, and the right leadership could mobilize the countryside. However, in this case, as with the municipal coups that occurred the following year in other western towns, an explicit desire for political separation from Spain was not a motivating factor in the unrest.[47]

Within Central America, neither social nor political conflict played a role in precipitating independence. The colonial order, its institutions, traditions, and caste structure, held fast through the end of the 1810s. When independence arrived in 1821, it came with little warning and within the context of the restoration of the Cádiz Constitution. Fernando VII's decision in 1820 to accommodate liberal forces in Spain by reviving the charter destabilized imperial politics yet again, at once empowering regional interests, inspiring progressives, and worrying traditionalists. This compelled heretofore-royalist Mexican creoles to support a path to independence through the conservative Plan of Iguala, a decision that caught the attention of Central Americans and inspired some communities on the isthmus to prepare their own declarations. However, the Guatemalan elite, which feared the consequences of a Mexican invasion and insisted on managing any break with Spain, prioritized its own interests by uniting with the nascent empire of Agustín de Iturbide. Full independence would not come until 1823 with the creation of the Central American Federation, a republic that held together for fifteen years before collapsing under the extreme stress of partisan warfare and regionalism.[48]

---

[47] Aaron Pollack, "Totonicapán, 1820: One of the Tips of the Iceberg?" in Pollack, ed., *Independence in Central America and Chiapas* (Norman: University of Oklahoma Press, 2019), 158–86; Victoria R. Bricker, *El Cristo indígena, el rey nativo: El sustrato histórico de la mitología del ritual de los mayas* (Mexico City: FCE, 1989); Daniel J. Contreras R., *Una rebelión indígena en el partido de Totonicapán: El indio y la independencia* (Guatemala City: Imprenta Universitaria, 1951). For the tribute see Manuel Fernández Molina, *Los tributos en el reino de Guatemala: 1786–1821*, 2nd edition (Guatemala City: Universidad de San Carlos, 2000). See also Jorge H. González Alzate, *La experiencia colonial y transición a la independencia en el occidente de Guatemala. Quetzaltenango: De pueblo indígena a ciudad multiétnica, 1520–1825* (Mérida: Centro Peninsular en Humanidades y en Ciencias Sociales, 2015).

[48] See Pablo Augusto Rodríguez Solano, "The Costa Rican Concordia Compact, 1821–1823: A Constitutionalist Perspective on Independence," in Pollack, ed., *Independence in Central America and Chiapas*, 57–80; Jorge Mario García Laguardia, "La independencia de la Capitanía General de Guatemala: El dilema del Nuevo régimen: Monarquía Constitucional o República," in Patricia Galeana, ed., *Historia*

## Conclusion

Central Americans did not reject wholesale the political currents that sparked movements for independence in other parts of Spanish America during the Age of Atlantic Revolutions. On the contrary, the isthmian population reacted in diverse ways to this unprecedented and destabilizing period. Individual responses varied from the handful of revolutionaries who supported independence to the large majority of loyalists who resisted such an extreme step. While this latter group agreed on what it did not want, it represented competing interests that included autonomists, enlightened absolutists, and fervent traditionalists, each with their own distinct motivations.

Not surprisingly, attitudes toward independence closely followed socioeconomic divisions. The peninsular elite, which monopolized the highest levers of political, social, and economic power, remained overwhelmingly loyal to traditional institutions, though some members were convinced that the empire could benefit from enlightened reform. The creole elite also saw its interests best served by a continuation of the colonial order, but the Guatemalan oligarchy, in particular, saw the political realignment in favor of constitutionalism as an opportunity to increase its power. Whether this group sentiment resulted more from opportunism or sincere devotion to liberalism is debatable. Certainly, both motivations were at play in service to the larger goal of political autonomy – with the Guatemalan elite seeking distance from Madrid and provincial elites hoping to break their dependence on Guatemala City.

Those few who envisioned independence and a radical new political order tended to emerge from a more marginalized group of educated creoles and *ladinos*. Individuals like Mateo Antonio Marure and Juan de Dios Mayorga found inspiration in the Age of Revolutions but could not win over many adherents.[49] While leaders of isthmian revolts during this period often utilized political rhetoric that drew upon Enlightenment and revolutionary

---

*comparada de las Américas: Sus procesos Independentistas* (Mexico City: Siglo XXI Editores, 2010); Mario Vázquez Olivera, "El Plan de Iguala y la independencia de Guatemala," in Ana Carolina Ibarra, ed., *La independencia en el sur de México* (Mexico City: FFYL-UNAM, 2004), 395–430; Vázquez Olivera, "El Plan de Iguala y la independencia de San Salvador," in Galeana, ed., *Historia comparada de las Américas*, 399–467.

[49] See Alejandro Marure, *Bosquejo histórico de las revoluciones de Centróamerica desde 1811 hasta 1834*, 2 vols. (Mexico City: Libreria de la Viuda de Ch. Bouret, 1913); Ramón A. Sálazar, *Historia de veintiún años*, 2 vols. (Guatemala City: Editorial del Ministerio de Educación Pública, 1956).

ideas, they relied on the energy of subaltern groups, in particular the urban masses, to advance their causes. In not a few cases, these uprisings arose from popular demands for redress of traditional grievances, which suggests a disconnect between the priorities of the leadership and the protesters. Notably, in each case, challenges to the colonial order occurred at a time when political developments in Spain encouraged Central Americans to believe that their demands for change would receive attention from imperial authorities. This allowed each social group to remain loyal to the Spanish Crown throughout the 1810s, a consensus that only broke when the isthmian elite decided that Spain had lost its ability to address their concerns. Ultimately, the history of the national period suggests that political independence was one of the few significant departures from the colonial model that had provided political, social, and economic order in Central America for centuries.

7

# War and Revolution in the Southern Cone, 1808–1824

JUAN LUIS OSSA SANTA CRUZ

The aim of this chapter is to study the main political-military events of the struggle for independence in the Southern Cone, specifically in current Buenos Aires, Santiago, and Lima. These three cities experienced both a profound political revolution, as well as a bloody civil war in the period 1808–1824. The fact that this revolution was also a military conflict in which a significant number of South Americans participated on both sides of the battlefield (i.e. "patriots" and "royalists") suggests that, in spite of what most historians have claimed, independence was not a struggle for national liberation.[1] The reactions to the Bayonne abdications in the main capitals of the New World were very diverse and had very different results. However, one element was common to them all: The option for independence was the corollary, not the cause, of the revolution. A corollary that was hardly thinkable when the first news of the fall of the Spanish monarchy to Napoleon began to arrive in South America.

A first hypothesis developed here is, then, that the concepts of "revolution" and "independence" did not necessarily have the same meaning at that time and that, therefore, they must be analyzed on their own merit. Indeed, one can even appreciate revolutionary changes on the monarchical side, as shown by the case of Lima, the last bastion of the royalists in the region. A second hypothesis proposes that the processes of independence were consummated in the early 1820s, once the three fledgling countries declared their sovereignty not only in relation to Spain, but also to their neighbors.

---

[1] For historiographical accounts on the Spanish American independence, see John Lynch, "Spanish American Independence in Recent Historiography," in Anthony McFarlane and Eduardo Posada-Carbó, eds., *Independence and Revolution in Spanish America* (London: Institute of Latin American Studies, 1999), 87–101; Alfredo Ávila, "Las revoluciones hispanoamericanas vistas desde el siglo XXI," *Revista de Historia Iberoamericana*, online, 1 (2008); Gabriel Paquette, "The Dissolution of the Spanish Atlantic Monarchy," *The Historical Journal* 52:1 (2009), 175–212.

Those who once fought together against the Madrid authorities (more or less between 1814 and 1822) gradually distanced themselves from each other, which is why the "Americanist" projects (both of José de San Martín and Simón Bolívar) lost legitimacy as time went by. Understanding the loss of that legitimacy is key when analyzing the origins of the South American national states. Indeed, thinking about Argentina, Chile, and Peru requires getting rid of the nationalist and teleological blinders and not taking their existence for granted.

In order to test both hypotheses the chapter is divided into four sections and a conclusion. In the first section, I present a brief account of the South American reactions to the imperial crisis of 1808, emphasizing the different political options arising from the power vacuum and the crisis of legitimacy left by the king's absence. On the other hand, I dwell on some of the most important armed confrontations between 1810 and 1818, that is, the years in which the South American ruling groups mutated from a reformist stance to an openly pro-independence program. The third section reflects on San Martín's Americanist project and its influence in the Río de la Plata, Chile, and Peru, from both a political point of view and a military perspective. The fourth section summarizes the defeat of Americanism at the hands of local groups and the emergence of the national states we know today. The conclusion proposes a few general reflections on this period.

## South American Reactions to the Imperial Crisis of 1808

News of the Bayonne abdications (May 1808), by which Carlos IV and Fernando VII successively surrendered to Napoleon, began arriving in South America in mid-1808. The first city to acknowledge them, as was expected due to its strategic position in the Atlantic, was Buenos Aires, whose inhabitants had experienced a degree of politicization and militarization never seen before as a result of the British invasions of the immediately preceding years. Buenos Aires faced its own crisis when forced to defend its territory in 1806–1807 without the help of Madrid. The news from Bayonne, of course, caused as much consternation in Buenos Aires as in Lima or Santiago. However, given that Buenos Aires had a relatively autonomous administration (since becoming a viceregal capital in 1776, but especially after the British invasions) the fall of the Spanish monarchy was experienced in a different way. More concerned about the process of local militarization,

Buenos Aires residents concentrated, more than anything, on solving their internal differences.[2]

To a certain extent, nevertheless, the decisions of the Buenos Aires authorities were inspired, as in Spain, by the neoscholastic doctrines and the theory of natural rights. Once the head of the government disappeared, power was to be "recovered" by the "people."[3] This theory, however, did not necessarily have practical and immediate consequences, for behind the Spanish pactist idea there was a tricky but very central question: If the king disappeared, and the legitimacy of his rule along with him, what governmental body or individual should assume sovereignty? Should it be the *Real Audiencias*, the *cabildos,* or the merchants' guilds? The answer was not clear, although soon the different opinions were resolved when it was accepted, at least tacitly, that sovereignty should be exercised locally, that is, through the *cabildos* or town councils: They were the representatives of the "people." This occurred in Spain, where between 1808 and 1810 executive juntas were established in places like Oviedo, Seville, Jaén, Granada, Badajoz, Zaragoza, Tortosa, Valencia, Alicante, and Valladolid.[4] And so it also happened in Spanish America, the cases of Buenos Aires and Santiago being two of the most important.

Between May and September 1810 juntas were established in the two capitals with the aim of making the "people" the "depository of sovereignty."[5] The members of the Buenos Aires city council argued on 25 May that political sovereignty would rest on two types of actors: the "beloved Sovereign, Mr. Fernando VII and his legitimate successors," on the one hand, and a governing board or junta with executive powers, on the other.[6] Buenos Aires asserted itself as the sole depository of royal sovereignty in the dissolved Viceroyalty of the Río de la Plata, a decision that, despite following

---

[2] Tulio Halperin Donghi, *Revolución y guerra: Formación de una elite dirigente en la Argentina criolla* (Buenos Aires: Siglo Veintiuno Editores, 2002), 123–67; Klaus Gallo, *Great Britain and Argentina: From Invasion to Recognition (1806–1826)* (New York: Palgrave, 2001), 33–50; Gabriel Di Meglio, ¡*Viva el bajo pueblo! La plebe urbana de Buenos Aires y la política entre la Revolución de Mayo y el Rosismo (1810–1829)* (Buenos Aires: Editorial Prometeo, 2007), Chapter 2.

[3] Hilda Sabato, *Republics of the New World: The Revolutionary Political Experiment in 19th-Century Latin America* (Princeton, NJ: Princeton University Press, 2018), 26–9.

[4] Antonio Moliner, "El movimiento juntero en la España de 1808," in Manuel Chust, ed., *1808: La eclosión juntera en el mundo hispano* (Mexico City: Fondo de Cultura Económica, 2007), 51–83: 54.

[5] José María Portillo Valdés, *Crisis atlántica: Autonomía e independencia en la crisis de la monarquía hispana* (Madrid: Marcial Pons Historia, 2006), 53–60.

[6] www.argentinahistorica.com.ar.

the usual pattern, would be questioned by the provinces in the future.[7] This idea was also accepted by the Santiago *vecinos*: On 18 September 1810 a *cabildo abierto* met with the purpose of agreeing on "the Government most worthy of its trust and best fit to observe and conserve these domains to its rightful owner and unfortunate monarch, Mr. Fernando VII."[8] In addition, that same day it was determined that the "peoples" of the kingdom were to meet in a future congress.[9]

The autonomous resolution of the Buenos Aires and Santiago *cabildos* to face the *vacatio regis* and change the governmental structure of their respective territories shows the revolutionary character of the South American juntas. For the first time in centuries of colonial rule two cities of the Southern Cone[10] arrogated themselves the right to self-govern, thereby inaugurating a revolutionary process that, over time, would adopt separatist overtones. But in 1810, such a prospect was still unlikely: During that year, the few voices calling for a definitive break with Spain were silenced by a type of reformism that, at most, aspired to reinforce autonomy within, not without, the Spanish empire.[11] Radicals like Mariano Moreno, who among other things edited/translated the first South American edition of Rousseau's *Social Contract*,[12] must be seen as contributors to a revolutionary, but not yet pro-independence culture. In Chile, the number of separatists was even smaller; not even Juan Martínez de Rozas, who in the years to come would take a more radical position, aspired to declare Chilean independence. Revolution and independence, then, were not interchangeable terms in the South America of 1810.[13]

---

[7] José Carlos Chiaramonte, *Ciudades, provincias, Estados: Orígenes de la nación argentina (1800–1846)* (Buenos Aires: Emecé, 2007).

[8] www.historia.uchile.cl.

[9] Jaime Eyzaguirre, *Ideario y ruta de la emancipación chilena* (Santiago: Editorial Universitaria, 1957), 123; Alfredo Jocelyn-Holt, *La Independencia de Chile: Tradición, modernización y mito* (Madrid: Editorial Mapfre, 1992), Chapter 6; Simon Collier, *Ideas y política de la Independencia chilena, 1808–1833* (Santiago: Fondo de Cultura Económica, 2012), 49–51.

[10] The same can be said of New Granada and Venezuela. See Daniel Gutiérrez Ardila, *Un nuevo reino: Geografía política, pactismo y diplomacia durante el Interregno en Nueva Granada (1808–1816)* (Bogotá: Universidad Externado de Colombia, 2010), 198–207.

[11] Jeremy Adelman, "An Age of Imperial Revolutions," *American Historical Review* 113:2 (2008), 319–40: 320.

[12] Noemí Goldman, "¿Fue Moreno el traductor de Del Contrato Social? Nuevas consideraciones sobre su traducción y circulación en América," in Gabriel Entin, ed., *Rousseau en Iberoamérica: Lecturas e interpretaciones entre monarquía y revolución* (Buenos Aires: SB Editorial, 2018), 161–76.

[13] Juan Luis Ossa, "Independencia y revolución. Algunas (pocas) reflexiones sobre la historia política de Chile entre 1808 y 1826," in Rogelio Altez and Manuel Chust, eds.,

Those who opposed the juntas also experienced the revolution, although from the opposite side. That was the case of Viceroy José Fernando de Abascal, who not only managed to prevent the *juntista* fever from taking over Lima, but also transformed his city into the heart of the South American counterrevolution.[14] Abascal headed that outstanding group of *"fidelistas"* (i.e., those loyal to the king, but also to the metropolitan bodies that, like the Cortes of Cádiz, governed – or aspired to govern – the empire on behalf of Fernando VII) that fought to turn the clock back. Their goal was to preserve the monarchical regime unaltered, using ideological propaganda,[15] the resources of Lima's *Consulado* (merchant guild),[16] and the armies stationed in Upper Peru. It must be noted that in this search Viceroy Abascal adopted similar or identical strategies to those of the revolutionaries. To begin with, both sides employed the word "patriot" to refer to their respective armies: While Abascal spoke of the "Motherland," the latter advocated their localities (or *"patrias chicas"*) and, in some cases, the whole American continent.[17] In addition, just like the South American autonomists who were not seeking to break the ties to the metropolis, in these preliminary years of the revolution Abascal accepted that the Constitution of Cádiz had the force of law in its territory, even if imperfectly.[18] There, however, the similarities end: The viceroy ultimately could not accept that the autonomist juntas became completely separatist governments.

Thus, by 1810 there were governmental juntas in Buenos Aires and Santiago, and in both cases the ideological justification for their formation rested on the Spanish pactist tradition. In Peru, however, the viceroy

---

*Las revoluciones en el largo siglo XIX latinoamericano* (Madrid: AHILA-Iberoamericana-Vervuert, 2015), 131–51.

[14] Brian R. Hamnett, *Revolución y contrarrevolución en México y el Perú: Liberales, realistas y separatistas, 1800–1824* (Mexico City: Fondo de Cultura Económica, 2011), Chapter 3.

[15] Ascensión Martínez Riaza, *La prensa doctrinal en la Independencia de Perú* (Madrid: Ediciones Cultura Hispánica, Instituto de Cooperación Iberoamericana, 1985); Víctor Peralta, *En defensa de la autoridad: Política y cultura bajo el gobierno del Virrey Abascal. Perú, 1806–1816* (Madrid: Consejo Superior de Investigaciones Científicas, 2002); Víctor Peralta, *La independencia y la cultura política peruana (1808–1821)* (Lima: Instituto de Estudios Peruanos, 2010), second and third parts.

[16] Patricia Marks, *Deconstructing Legitimacy: Viceroys, Merchants and the Military in Late Colonial Peru* (University Park, PA: Pennsylvania State University Press, 2007).

[17] See Gabriel Di Meglio, "Patria," in Noemí Goldman, ed., *Lenguaje y revolución: Conceptos políticos clave en el Río de la Plata, 1780–1850* (Buenos Aires: Prometeo Libros, 2008), 115–30.

[18] One English-language work on the Cádiz Constitution is Scott Eastman and Natalia Sobrevilla Perea, eds., *The Rise of Constitutional Government in the Iberian Atlantic World: The Impact of the Cádiz Constitution of 1812* (Tuscaloosa: University of Alabama Press, 2015).

managed to stop the *juntista* attempts that could have surfaced had it not been for Abascal himself, who led the effort to keep the absolutist monarchy with all the political and economic power that his privileged position gave him. Between 1810 and 1815, Viceroy Abascal was by far the most successful defender of the Spanish empire as it had been conceived prior to 1808. And war was his main tool.

## Civil War in the Southern Cone

In the eyes of Abascal, the junta of Buenos Aires was more dangerous (because of its incendiary rhetoric inspired by Moreno's writings) than that of Santiago. To a certain extent, he was correct: More explicitly than the Chileans, the people of the Río de la Plata not only sought to safeguard the sovereignty of Fernando VII as "depositories," but also aspired to "represent it."[19] Not yet through a declaration of independence, but through acts that, for Abascal, constituted a new and direct threat against the authority of the monarchy in the Southern Cone.

For Lima's ruling groups, the creation of the Viceroyalty of the Río de la Plata had in many ways, but above all economically, been a total defeat.[20] In 1776 King Carlos III decreed that Buenos Aires, Paraguay, Tucumán, Potosí, Santa Cruz de la Sierra, and Charcas were now part of the newly created viceroyalty, "with absolute independence of my Viceroy of the *Reynos del Perú*."[21] That Potosí, with all its wealth and geographic potential, would become part of a different administration from Lima was a hard blow for its merchants and politicians. It should not be surprising, therefore, that Abascal saw in the imperial crisis of 1808 an opportunity to return Lima to its privileged position, for which he first had to halt the military incursions that the Buenos Aires junta would surely undertake in Upper Peru to retain the Potosí region within its territory. In this, the Peruvian viceroy acted alone, without Madrid's explicit consent.

Before describing the beginning and development of the war that struck the South American continent, it is important to say something about the formation of the armies. Without going into much detail, three fundamental

---

[19] Noemí Goldman, *Mariano Moreno: De reformista a insurgente* (Buenos Aires: Edhasa, 2016) 145.

[20] Brian Hamnett, "La política contrarrevolucionaria del virrey Abascal: Perú, 1806–1816," *Documento de Trabajo*, 112 (Lima: Instituto de Estudios Peruanos, 2000).

[21] Guillermo Lagos, *Historia de las fronteras de Chile: Los títulos históricos* (Santiago: Editorial Andrés Bello, 1985), 528.

points stand out: first, that most of the officers and soldiers who fought on the revolutionary and royalist (or *fidelista*) sides were born in Spanish America. Indeed, the colonial armies – especially those based in peripheral colonies – experienced a deep Americanization from the 1780s, when Spain stopped sending reinforcements due to the imperial wars taking place in Europe or in other American areas, such as the emerging United States.[22] Second, and precisely because of the above, the different armed conflicts (carried out by regular armies and by irregular forces such as guerrillas or *montoneras*) amounted to a violent civil war among Spanish Americans during the period 1810–1824. The documentation shows that there were as many Spanish Americans in the counterrevolutionary army of Abascal as among the revolutionary troops of Buenos Aires and Chile; forces that, either in defense of the king or of an autonomist ideal, disputed the legitimacy of government in South America.[23] Finally, as Alejandro Rabinovich has shown, it is important not to lose sight of the role of the provincial militias in the civil war. Many who fought did so in the name of an abstract idea or concept like "revolution," but many others did so to defend their immediate interests, linked to a commitment not so much to the central authorities as to their localities and militias.[24]

For the purpose of this chapter, I will concentrate on the first two points, so a certain degree of generalization will be inevitable. How are the origins of the war between Buenos Aires and Lima and, later, between Lima and Santiago and Concepción (the second most important city in Chile) to be explained?[25] As I have argued, Upper Peru – a large part of which constitutes today's Bolivia – was the epicenter of the first years of the civil war in South America. One of the first steps taken by Buenos Aires was to send military detachments to the provinces of the Río de la Plata to make them swear allegiance to the junta. "The expedition to the interior villages was not meant to be limited to finding the enemy army and beating it," says Rabinovich. "Emerging from a popular demand, its auxiliary function consisted in reality

---

[22] Juan Marchena, *Oficiales y soldados en el Ejército de América* (Seville: Escuela de Estudios Hispano-Americanos, 1983); Juan Marchena, *Ejército y milicias en el mundo colonial americano* (Madrid: Editorial Mapfre, 1992).

[23] Anthony McFarlane, *War and Independence in Spanish America* (New York: Routledge, 2014).

[24] Alejandro Rabinovich, "El fenómeno de la guerra en Sudamérica: Regiones, problemas y dinámicas. Primera mitad del siglo XIX" (unpublished ms.).

[25] For Concepción, see Armando Cartes Montory, *Concepción contra "Chile": Consensos y tensiones regionales en la Patria Vieja (1808–1811)* (Santiago: Centro de Estudios Bicentenario, 2010).

in expanding the Revolution to the rest of the viceroyalty. This involved identifying, capturing and executing the counterrevolutionary leaders, installing similar governments in the provinces, having deputies elected, mobilizing the peoples and transmitting, in a more general way, the principles of the new system."[26] Among these provinces, those of Upper Peru were the most relevant, especially at a time when opponents of the junta in Buenos Aires were beginning to organize and "threatened to cut off access to its very rich resources." The governor of Potosí, Francisco de Paula Sanz, and the president of the *Audiencia de Charcas*, Vicente Nieto, quickly declared their opposition to the revolutionaries and "requested protection from the viceroy of Peru, who responded with the annexation of all of Upper Peru to his Viceroyalty."[27] This led Abascal to assume the sovereignty of a region that, legally, belonged to another viceroyalty, with all the jurisdictional complications involved in that decision.

Between 1810 and 1812 the armies of Buenos Aires and Lima participated in a series of clashes of different intensity. While it is difficult to identify a winner, it was the royalists who came out better, at least in terms of strategic positioning. This became clearer at the end of 1812, when Abascal extended his military operations to Chile in order to keep the *porteños* (the men from Buenos Aires) from there and from Upper Peru. Until then, the viceroy had maintained a certain distance from Chilean politics, in the belief that, compared to the *porteños*, the Chilean revolutionaries were more moderate and less threatening. As Abascal put it in a letter: "The *Junta* of Chile, echoing that of Buenos Aires . . . continues like it making continuous mutations in her Government, albeit with some moderation; because until now it has not declared itself in favor of terrorism, nor has it cut off trade with this Kingdom [Peru], nor its correspondence."[28] The word "terrorism" refers to the radical groups who dominated, according to the viceroy, the Buenos Aires government; a government that had not only confronted Abascal's military attacks, but had cut off trade relations with Peru. This explains why the royalist army was stationed, almost exclusively, in Upper Peru, where the rich mines of Potosí were located.

But things began to change in 1812. That year, three key events occurred: (1) In June, the authorities of the city of Valdivia – located in the south of

---

[26] Alejandro Rabinovich, *Anatomía del pánico: La batalla de Huaqui, o la derrota de la revolución (1811)* (Buenos Aires: Editorial Sudamericana, 2017), 54.

[27] Ibid., 59.

[28] Archivo General de Indias, Diversos, 2. The document does not have an exact date, but it is likely to have been written in October 1811.

Chile and historically dependent on Lima's treasury to pay for its military expenses – came under the direct protection of Viceroy Abascal, thus ending any link that had previously existed with the revolutionary government in Santiago.[29] The relationship between Santiago and Valdivia was relatively fluid until the military officer José Miguel Carrera, who arrived from Spain in mid-1811, became supreme master of the capital. Carrera's case is one of the most interesting examples of the sort of military leaders who played an important political role during these years. Carrera "was not a replica of Bourbon general captains; he was a modern military" leader, one whose actions reflected "the image of French young revolutionary officers who domesticated the Revolution or simply the image of the governor soldier, that is: Napoleon."[30] (2) In October 1812, Carrera and his closest allies published a *Reglamento Constitucional* that asked Fernando VII to become the "King of Chile," which prevented the viceroy, and the imperial authorities gathered in the Cortes of Cádiz, from getting involved in Chilean politics. Although Abascal was never a convinced supporter of the Cádiz Constitution, as the highest Spanish authority in South America he had to ensure its implementation not only in Peru, but also in the surrounding jurisdictions. Hence, he vehemently rejected the publication of the *Reglamento;*[31] and (3) In November, the Carrera government criticized Abascal because of the hostile attitudes that, in its mind, the viceroy was imposing on Chilean commerce.[32] The viceroy answered these three questions by sending a first military reinforcement to the island of Chiloé, from where the officer Antonio Pareja had to set up an army to advance toward the north and face the Chilean revolutionaries. Thus began the civil war between the forces of Carrera and Bernardo O'Higgins, and the royalist troops recruited in southern Chile.[33]

In 1813 and 1814, revolutionaries and royalists met in various skirmishes and occasional battles. It is interesting to note the changes that the beginning of the war brought in terms of forced recruitment, desertions, and political

---

[29] Cristián Guerrero Lira, *La contrarrevolución de la Independencia en Chile* (Santiago: DIBAM, 2002), 71.

[30] Jocelyn-Holt, *La Independencia de Chile*, 158–9.

[31] Juan Luis Ossa, "De Cádiz a la América del Sur: El viaje de una ilusión constitucional," in Antonio de Francesco, Luigi Mascilli Migliorini, and Raffaelle Nocera, eds., *Entre Mediterráneo y Atlántico: Circulaciones, conexiones y miradas, 1756–1867* (Santiago: Fondo de Cultura Económica, 2014), 255–78: 271.

[32] Diego Barros Arana, *Historia General de Chile* (Santiago: Editorial Universitaria and DIBAM, 2002), vol. VIII, 438.

[33] Juan Luis Ossa, *Armies, Politics and Revolution: Chile, 1808–1826* (Liverpool: Liverpool University Press, 2014), Chapter 1.

polarization. Differences between revolutionaries, moderates, and royalists intensified to the point that by mid-1814 a peaceful solution seemed impossible. There is documentary evidence that as late as September, Carrera continued to hope that Chile would become a constitutional monarchy headed by Fernando VII, an idea not necessarily supported by O'Higgins, who by then had become Carrera's opponent.[34] In any case, the outcome of the Battle of Rancagua, in which the revolutionaries suffered the worst defeat of the civil war, inflamed the spirits even more. More than 700 revolutionaries were forced to flee to the other side of the Andes and seek refuge in the Río de la Plata. This happened at the same time that the royalist commander, Mariano Osorio, triumphantly entered Santiago on 5 October 1814. The fact that the local inhabitants applauded the triumph of Osorio's men in Rancagua demonstrates once again that the independence movement was still in its infancy among Chileans. Some may have planned to declare independence from the viceroy of Peru, but without breaking with the Spanish king.[35] It was not until José de San Martín's anti-Spanish ideas influenced the Chilean revolutionaries that independence from Spain became a real option.

Arriving from Spain in Buenos Aires at the beginning of 1812, San Martín quickly became an important actor in the revolution of the Río de la Plata.[36] His alliances were built on his militancy in the *Logia Lautaro*, a politico-military organization whose ultimate goal – at least for a large part – was Spanish American independence. The *Logia* was formed by *rioplatense* officers like Juan Martín de Pueyrredón, San Martín and Ignacio Álvarez Thomas and, soon afterwards, also by Chileans like Bernardo O'Higgins and Ramón Freire. San Martín was assigned the mission of creating a body of cavalry grenadiers, a force that had a resounding military success in the battle of San Lorenzo in February 1813. This triumph was not, however, enough to overcome the royalist forces in the northern regions of the Río de la Plata. The Army of the North, commanded by the revolutionary general Manuel Belgrano, suffered defeats in Vilcapugio (October 1813) and Ayohuma (November 1813). These defeats showed "not only the mistakes of an inexperienced general in the war, but also the limits imposed by an unknown

---

[34] *El Monitor Araucano*, Santiago, 20 September 1814, II-80 (the proclamation is, however, dated 15 September).

[35] Juan Luis Ossa, "1814 en Chile: De la desobediencia a Lima al quiebre con España," *Anuario de Estudios Americanos* 73:1 (2016), 231–60.

[36] Bartolomé Mitre, *Historia de San Martín y de la emancipación sudamericana* (Buenos Aires: Editorial El Ateneo, 2010), Chapter 3.

geography, . . . and the chronic shortage of resources to preserve the troops that fed the 'plague' of desertion."[37]

Aiming to help Belgrano, the Buenos Aires government appointed San Martín head of a new expedition to the north. In Tucumán, San Martín understood that the future of the revolution depended on a joint offensive between the different armies and factions that opposed Abascal's reconquest plans, both in Upper Peru and in Chile. His ideas seemed to have taken hold in the first half of 1814 among the ruling classes of Buenos Aires. They were the only ones who had not been directly attacked by the Peruvian viceroy and who, for that very reason, were better positioned to lead this offensive. San Martín thus received the support of the Buenos Aires government, which named him governor of the province of Cuyo in September 1814. That is, just before the Chilean revolutionaries suffered the severe defeat at Rancagua. From Cuyo, San Martín would launch his continental or Americanist campaign with the double objective of defeating the royalist forces and declaring the independence of the South America territories.

## The Americanist Strategy

More than 700 Chilean *émigrés* began to arrive in Mendoza, capital of the province of Cuyo, ten days after the Battle of Rancagua. The journey was painful in a double sense: On the one hand, it meant for many a dramatic change in their lives, as shown by the state of destitution in which they found themselves as a result of a forced and uncertain exile.[38] On the other hand, during the journey the antagonism grew between the supporters of O'Higgins and Carrera. Those who were upset with Carrera for not adequately helping O'Higgins with men and resources in Rancagua were at odds with those who believed that his decision had been correct and sensible. The first group accused Carrera of treason and cowardice, adding the imputation of using public funds from the revolutionary government of Santiago for the benefit of his faction. This situation forced San Martín to get involved in the dispute, and already on 15 October 1814 the governor of Mendoza ordered his men to search Carrera's baggage. No money was found, although some argued that the public funds had been effectively

---

[37] Beatriz Bragoni, *San Martín: De soldado del Rey a héroe de la nación* (Buenos Aires: Editorial Sudamericana, 2010), 51–2.

[38] Juan Luis Ossa Santa Cruz, "The Army of the Andes: Chilean and Rioplatense Politics in an Age of Military Organisation, 1814–1817," *Journal of Latin American Studies* 46:1 (2014), 29–58.

withdrawn from the capital after the Battle of Rancagua, but had been confiscated by the royalists a few days later.[39]

From his involvement in the affair of the Chilean treasury one can conclude that San Martín chose to support O'Higgins as early as October 1814.[40] Above all, San Martín objected to Carrera's claims of being "governor of Chile" in Mendoza. In his opinion, all inhabitants of the city were under the authority of the governor of the province of Cuyo; accepting Carrera's authority in Mendoza would be tantamount to accepting that San Martín's political faction was no longer supreme authority of the region. This view was shared by other military officers and politicians in Mendoza, especially by those who did not see José Miguel Carrera as the sole, legitimate authority of the "Chilean state."[41] O'Higgins' supporters insisted that Carrera had stolen the Chilean treasury and that he was responsible for the defeat of the revolutionaries in Rancagua. Both allegations convinced San Martín to expel Carrera and his relatives from Mendoza. Aware that San Martín's forces were much stronger than his own (San Martín led nearly 1,000 men, compared to the 400 who remained loyal to him), Carrera laid down his arms before the authorities. He and his allies left Mendoza on 3 November 1814, arriving in Buenos Aires at the end of that month.[42]

It was in this context of economic distress that the first plans to confront the Chilean royalists were developed. O'Higgins, who spent 1815 in Buenos Aires defending the interests of his political cause, presented the Supreme Director, Ignacio Álvarez Thomas, with a detailed military program to reconquer Chile. His aim was to assemble 6,000 men and then divide them into four divisions, each with the mission to cross into Chile from a specific region (the first three would go via Antuco, Río Claro, and Coquimbo, the last through the port of Arauco).[43] Carrera also prepared a plan to "restore the Chilean state." He believed that the revolutionaries should attack the royalists in the winter, regardless of the complications entailed by the crossing of the *Cordillera* during the season. In Carrera's words, "this invasion can be made across Coquimbo ... with only 500 Chilean soldiers and 1,000 muskets. It is known that Coquimbo's garrison has no more than 100 men

---

[39] Barros Arana, *Historia General de Chile*, vol. x, 103, 109.

[40] Jaime Eyzaguirre, *O'Higgins* (Santiago: Editorial Zig-Zag, 1946), 152. See also Patricia Pasquali, *San Martín: La fuerza de la misión y la soledad de la gloria* (Buenos Aires: Emecé, 2004), 210–4.

[41] Barros Arana, *Historia General de Chile*, vol. x, 104.

[42] Barros Arana, *Historia General de Chile*, vol. x, 113–7.

[43] Eyzaguirre, *O'Higgins*, 160–1.

and that they are willing to receive the assistance of the liberators."[44] In practical terms, Carrera's plan was the more unrealistic of the two, and when Álvarez Thomas asked the opinion of San Martín, the Cuyo governor answered that, in order to reconquer Chile, the army required "3,500 to 4,000 strong and disciplined men."[45] However, at that stage O'Higgins' plan was not practicable either. Álvarez Thomas needed concrete evidence that the efforts of Buenos Aires would not be in vain: San Martín had to persuade him that Chile was where the royalists should be attacked first.

Cuyo's governor was convinced that South American independence depended on taking the offensive to reconquer Chile and liberate Peru. But to achieve that it was key to have a disciplined army, trained and willing to cross the *Cordillera*. That was precisely the task to which San Martín committed himself from the middle of 1815. Called the "Army of the Andes," this force was raised in Mendoza, but had the support of Buenos Aires. As Minister of War, Tomás Guido stressed the importance of using the reconquest of Chile as a springboard toward other territorial conquests: "The occupation of Chile should be the government's principal aim. First, because it is the flank on which the enemy is weaker; second, because it is the shortest, easiest and safest way to free Upper Peru; and third, because the restoration of freedom in that country can consolidate the emancipation of America."[46] On the other hand, the situation in Upper Peru also played a part. Indeed, it was only after Belgrano was defeated by the Peruvian army led by Joaquín de la Pezuela and forced to undertake a defensive strategy in the region (May 1816), that San Martín was able to get the attention not only of Guido but also of other politicians in the Río de la Plata.

The *rioplatenses* changed their view regarding an invasion of Chile when they were gathered in a representative assembly at the Congress of Tucumán, which was installed in March 1816.[47] Two months later, Tucumán's congressmen appointed a widely respected military officer, Juan Martín de Pueyrredón, as Supreme Director of the Río de la Plata. San Martín made an astute move when he sent an emissary to convince the new chief executive of the importance of invading Chile. A couple of weeks later the general personally discussed his plan with Pueyrredón. It is unclear exactly what the two leaders talked about. What is known is that, more or

---

[44] Quoted in Barros Arana, *Historia General de Chile*, vol. x, 143.
[45] Barros Arana, *Historia General de Chile*, vol. x, 144.
[46] Quoted by Barros Arana, *Historia General de Chile*, vol. x, 263.
[47] Gabriel Di Meglio, *1816: La trama de la Independencia* (Buenos Aires: Editorial Planeta, 2016).

less at the same time that the Congress of Tucumán proclaimed the independence of the United Provinces of the Río de la Plata (9 July 1816), San Martín persuaded the Supreme Director both to attack royalist Chile and to expand the contingents of the army undergoing training in Cuyo. As San Martín told his friend Tomás Godoy Cruz, "in two days with their respective nights, we reached an agreement. There is nothing else we can do but act."[48]

Once back in Mendoza, San Martín resumed command of the organization of the Army of the Andes. Together with Bernardo O'Higgins, who arrived in Mendoza from Buenos Aires at the beginning of 1816, the governor implemented his plan to reconquer Chile. The recruitment of veterans intensified in the second half of 1816. In addition, new contingents of slaves were incorporated into the army, above all as infantrymen: "the best infantry soldiers we have," San Martín claimed in May 1816, "are the blacks and mulattos."[49] Yet the authorities took months to actually secure adequate funding. The help they received from the local inhabitants was invaluable, but never enough. Reports written between September and October 1815 by the army's newly appointed Commissioner of Food (*Comisario de Víveres*), Domingo Pérez, provide an idea of the army's needs: cattle, salt, chili pepper, biscuits, wine, garbanzos, alfalfa, brandy (*aguardiente*), candles, sugar, tobacco, paper, pots, funnels, weighing scales, blankets, ponchos, reins, saddle girths, stirrups, spikes, axes, etc.[50] The lack of clothing in "the middle of the winter," San Martín wrote on 2 May 1816, was especially worrisome, because "it exposes the soldier to sicknesses that are currently appearing, and compels him to desert from the army in order to find the shelter he does not find in military service."[51]

However, by the beginning of 1817 San Martín's preparations began to yield results. In his Instructions to San Martín, Pueyrredón ordered him to always bear in mind that the objective of the Army of the Andes was to assist the Chileans to reconquer their territory, but that any attempt to "keep possession of the aided country" had to be ruled out. In the second section of the Instructions, the neutrality of Buenos Aires in relation to Chilean politics was stated: "The division in two parties in which Chile found itself before the entrance of the king's troops being notorious ... we will procure to

---

[48] Quoted in John Lynch, *San Martín: Argentine Soldier, American Hero* (New Haven: Yale University Press, 2009), 267.
[49] Quoted in Lynch, *San Martín*, 86–7.
[50] Reports of September–October 1815, Archivo Histórico de Mendoza, box 500, doc. 1.
[51] San Martín to Secretary of War, 2 May 1816, Archivo General de la Nación Argentina (hereafter AGN), Room 10, 4–2–6.

extinguish the seed of disorder with impartial proclamations, without justifying either party and preventing the renewal of the causes of that fatal clash."[52] But despite this claim of impartiality, both Pueyrredón and San Martín were strongly and clearly in favor of O'Higgins once Chile's Central Valley (i.e. the area from Coquimbo to Concepción) was reconquered between 1817 and 1822.

The support given to O'Higgins was, of course, subject to some conditions, the main being that the future Chilean government would commit itself with men and resources to a more ambitious plan devised by San Martín. Such a plan considered the conquest of Peru as the last stage in his continental strategy of declaring and defending the independence of the Southern Cone. It was still too early to know the type of government to be implemented once political sovereignty had been gained on the battlefield. However, by 1817 very few doubted the legitimacy of the pro-independence project. Thus, when the Army of the Andes crossed the *Cordillera* at the beginning of February 1817, San Martín and the *Logia Lautaro* reaffirmed what for some time had seemed an undeniable reality: The reconquest of Chile was only the first step in a chain of military undertakings that should culminate in the invasion of Lima. If they could not take the Peruvian capital, San Martín thought, everything achieved in the last seven years would be compromised.

## From Americanism to the National States

The victory of the Army of the Andes in the Battle of Chacabuco (12 February 1817) put an end to a process begun in October 1814, when the first contingents of Chilean émigrés arrived in Mendoza. But Chacabuco did not finish the military confrontations between royalists and revolutionaries in Chilean territory, since San Martín only managed to reconquer the northern zone of the Central Valley, while the royalists, now led by José Ordóñez, regrouped in Talca and Concepción and spread from there throughout the south of the country.

It would not be correct, however, to lessen the military and political importance of what happened in Chacabuco and the days and months that

---

[52] The Instructions, which are dated 21 December 1816, are in José Juan Biedma, ed., *Documentos referentes a la guerra de la independencia y emancipación política de la República Argentina y de otras secciones de América a que cooperó desde 1810 a 1828 (Paso de los Andes y campaña libertadora de Chile)*, 2 vols. (Buenos Aires: Talleres gráficos del Instituto Geográfico Militar, 1917–1926), vol. 1, 284–7.

Figure 7.1 Battle of Maipú, 5 April 1818, at which San Martín defeated the royalist forces. Courtesy of Museo Histórico Nacional, Argentina.

followed. After entering Santiago, San Martín reached out to the dominant sectors of society. O'Higgins' appointment as Supreme Director on 16 February 1817 was the first step toward the consolidation of San Martín's plans in Chile. Once in charge, O'Higgins promoted the Americanist strategy, both in his communications with Pueyrredón and in his public acts during the first months of 1817. In his correspondence with Buenos Aires one can see O'Higgins' gratitude toward San Martín, but in his actions in Santiago we also appreciate his attempts to make Chileans understand the importance of Buenos Aires' role in the reconquest of his country (Figure 7.1).[53]

As already indicated, the alliance between the Chilean and *rioplatense* revolutionaries was strengthened after the Battle of Rancagua. This became clear in 1815, when O'Higgins was in Buenos Aires and became involved in the *Logia Lautaro*. The *Logia* did not act as a modern political party, but rather

[53] AGN, Room X, 4–2–8, 218, O'Higgins to the Supreme Director of the United Provinces, 4 March 1817; *Gaceta del Supremo Gobierno de Chile*, vol. 1, number 1, 26 February 1817.

as a "patriotic society" in which military activities went hand in hand with the introduction of a new political regime based on republicanism.[54] It is not surprising, therefore, that the main members of the *Logia* were military officers, nor that they would become key political figures in the 1820s. Some of the best-known Chilean officers involved with the *Logia* in Santiago were O'Higgins, Luis de la Cruz, and José Manuel Borgoño, to whom we must add a group of officers from the Río de la Plata such as San Martín, Hilarión de la Quintana, and Rudecindo Alvarado. All of them participated in the Liberating Army of Peru.

The organization of the Peruvian expedition began as soon as the O'Higgins government achieved some stability. A strong supporter of San Martín's Americanist plans, the Chilean Supreme Director hired the naval services of the British commander Thomas Cochrane, who arrived in Valparaiso on 28 November 1818.[55] The government appointed him commander-in-chief of the Chilean navy, while Manuel Blanco Encalada was named admiral and second in command. O'Higgins' appointment of Cochrane was reinforced by his decision to commit Chile's income to finance the expenses of the force that San Martín was forming with members of the Army of the Andes as well as the recently created local force called the Army of Chile. In August 1820, after the collapse of the Buenos Aires government prevented the *porteños* from helping to finance the invasion of Peru (obviating also the need for San Martín to help out the government of Buenos Aires with men and resources),[56] San Martín was appointed general-in-chief of the Liberating Army. The expedition departed on 20 August from Valparaiso, the "key point of America,"[57] for Peru. After taking the town of Pisco in September 1820, San Martín made use of one of his favorite tactics: the issuance of proclamations to explain to Peruvians the political goals of the Liberating Army. By the end of 1820, San Martín's strategy seemed to be working, both militarily and politically. On 5 November, Cochrane captured the Spanish frigate *Esmeralda*, while on 29 December the marquis of Torre

---

[54] Alejandro Rabinovich, "Las órdenes militares en tiempos revolucionarios. El republicanismo y la posibilidad de una aristocracia militar. Río de la Plata, Chile y Perú, 1810–1824," *Revista Universitaria de Historia Militar*, 5:9 (2016), 15–32.

[55] For a recent study on Cochrane and Chile, see Andrés Baeza, *Contacts, Collisions and Relationships: Britons and Chileans in the Independence Era, 1806–1831* (Liverpool: Liverpool University Press, 2019), Chapter 2.

[56] Marcela Ternavasio, *La revolución del voto: Política y elecciones en Buenos Aires, 1810–1852* (Buenos Aires: Siglo XXI Editores, 2002), Chapter 2. See also McFarlane, *War and Independence*, 357–8.

[57] *El Censor de la Revolución*, number 7, 10 July 1820.

Tagle, governor of Trujillo, proclaimed the independence of the northern province and swore allegiance to San Martín's army.[58]

At the same time that he negotiated with provincial leaders like Torre Tagle, San Martín held, from September 1820, talks outside of Lima with the royalist authorities, led by Abascal's successor, Viceroy Joaquín de la Pezuela. The fact that Pezuela acknowledged San Martín's envoys demonstrated a change in the relationship between the Spanish American revolutionaries and the royalist authorities. The "rebels" were suddenly summoned to negotiate, and officers like San Martín began to be seen by the viceroy as representatives of sovereign states. Pezuela's aim was to get the revolutionaries to send delegates to Spain to find a solution to the conflict, emphasizing, however, that he was not in a position to recognize the independence of Chile and/or the Río de la Plata. San Martín's envoys, meanwhile, proposed to create a constitutional monarchy in Peru, but only after Spain agreed to recognize Peruvian independence. With objectives as conflicting as these it is not surprising that the negotiations ceased on 1 October 1820. The revolutionary delegates returned to Pisco, while Pezuela went back to Lima.[59]

Upon returning to the Peruvian capital, the viceroy met with growing opposition from a group of Spanish officers who, led by José La Serna, claimed that the capital was lost and that it was more advisable to concentrate efforts on cities such as Cuzco. In the end, Pezuela resigned and La Serna assumed as viceroy; immediately thereafter, the royalists left Lima. San Martín entered the capital on 12 July 1821, and on 28 July he proclaimed the independence of Peru. The declaration was an important symbolic act, but it did not cause major changes within Peruvian society. Most of those who signed it did so simply because La Serna had left the city. San Martín's appointment as protector, as well as his indecision regarding the political regime to be implemented in Peru – whether a monarchy or a republic – did not help improve the relationship between him and the Peruvian ruling classes.[60]

Equally conflicting were the relations between the different forces that made up the Liberating Army. Even though the army supposedly represented South American interests as a whole, the respective declarations of independence (of the Río de la Plata, Chile, and now Peru) consolidated the

---

[58] *Colección documental de la Independencia del Perú*, tome VI, vol. 2, 219–21, 29 December 1820.

[59] Barros Arana, *Historia General de Chile*, vol. XIII, 58–9.

[60] Timothy Anna, *The Fall of the Royal Government in Peru* (Lincoln: University of Nebraska Press, 1979), 152–81.

origins of three politically and territorially sovereign states. San Martín himself made no greater effort to implement his Americanist plans. This can be seen in his determination to fill the highest positions of the Liberating Army and his Protectorate with people close to him and, in most cases, from the Río de la Plata. This determination generated unrest among Chilean officers, who resented being treated as a second-rate force. Without adjudicating the justice of the Chilean complaints, the fact that they existed shows that the separation of Spain did not end the conflicts on sovereignty. The prospect of the former revolutionary allies embarking on territorial disputes was increasingly feasible.[61]

In the case of Chile, differences with the Protectorate were strongly felt after 1822, both in Santiago and in Peru. The Chilean Senate defended O'Higgins' right to decide who to appoint general-in-chief of the Liberating Army to replace San Martín, who was too busy with government tasks. The tension between the Chilean state and the Protectorate increased during the following months. Shortly after the Senate expressed its opinion on the best method to choose San Martín's successor, O'Higgins sent Senator José María Rozas to Peru to ensure that at least some of the expenses incurred by Chile to prepare the expedition were paid by the Protectorate. In response, San Martín's Minister, Bernardo de Monteagudo, declared: "The Peruvian government will defray those expenditures when Chile pays Buenos Aires the money spent by that government to organize the 1817 expedition."[62] Monteagudo's answer could be seen as rude and impolitic. However, one might also argue that Monteagudo reacted as any politician would in trying to obtain the greatest benefit for *his* state (the Peruvian Protectorate on whose behalf he now spoke, even though he was a *rioplatense* by birth). Monteagudo, in fact, acted as representative both of a sovereign and of a newly created state. Peru, San Martín's allies believed, was reborn in 1821, and therefore any commitment made before that date was nullified, debts included.

Hence, by the end of 1821, both states understood that the rhetoric of the American project was no longer sufficient to politically sustain the revolution in Chile, Peru, the Río de la Plata, or any other South American territory. Since the royalists remained firmly in place in the southern Peruvian

---

[61] For an example of the Chilean officers' dissatisfaction, see Archivo Nacional Chile, Fondo Vicuña Mackenna, vol. XCII, 94–95v, Francisco Antonio Pinto to O'Higgins, 12 December 1822.

[62] Quoted in Barros Arana, *Historia general de Chile*, vol. XIII, 369.

provinces, a combination of forces between the Liberating Army, the Army of the Andes and the Chilean Army seemed to be the most reasonable decision. But such a combination was the result of the merger of three independent armies, which, in turn, represented three different states. On 12 February 1822, meanwhile, the Chilean Supreme Director appointed Luis de la Cruz as the first general-in-chief of the Chilean army in Peru. This action turned the existing de facto separation between the Chilean forces and the remaining revolutionary forces who fought against the viceroy finally into a de jure separation.

In mid-1822, the military and political situation in Peru also seemed unfavorable to San Martín. In addition to the problem created by the successor of the general-in-chief of the Liberating Army, two important factors must be considered: (1) 1822 was the year in which San Martín's defensive military strategy failed; and (2) the "Guayaquil Conference" held between San Martín and Simón Bolívar in July 1822 had the unexpected result of forcing the protector to leave his post.[63] When San Martín arrived back in Lima from Guayaquil, he found a restless city. In his absence, the Lima inhabitants had rebelled against Monteagudo, provoking a power vacuum in the capital. The protector was aware that he was partly responsible for the fall of his *protégé*, so he devoted the month of August 1822 to finding a solution.

In the end, San Martín and the Lima ruling groups established a congress in Lima, whose first session was held on 20 September 1822. This was followed by the resignation of San Martín, who left for Chile, where he was received by O'Higgins and the few friends he still had in the country. After fourteen months in office, San Martín had achieved little in political terms; while his military victories had been important but insufficient to consolidate the revolution. Although he had proclaimed the independence of Peru, won the support of the middle sectors and opened Peru's economy to the international market, he made policy moves that alienated his allies. Among these two stand out: First, he never managed to reconcile his passion for monarchism with the creation of the Peruvian republic; second, he ignored the Americanist rhetoric that he himself had designed since his arrival in Buenos Aires in 1812.

La Serna, for his part, concentrated his men in Cuzco and its surroundings. The war continued its course for a few years, although Bolívar's entry in Lima in

---

[63] John Lynch, *Simón Bolívar: A Life* (New Haven: Yale University Press, 2006), 171–5; Lynch, *San Martín*, 185–90.

September 1823 to take over the government San Martín had left a year earlier gave a new impetus to the revolutionaries.[64] Bolívar arrived accompanied by his army of "Colombians," which added a new divisive factor among the insurgent ranks. As had happened with the Peruvians, the Chileans, and the *rioplatenses*, the "Colombians" formed an independent army, which defended an increasingly national and less Americanist sovereign project. The end of the war against the royalists in the mid-1820s was the culmination of the multiregional collaboration that had originated in the Army of the Andes.

The revolutionaries won important battles in Junín and Ayacucho in late 1824, but they did not terminate military action in South America. On the contrary, new confrontations took place within the new countries, as well as between them. The implementation of republicanism and the creation of national states provoked profound differences concerning who should exercise political sovereignty and how, now that the legitimacy of the king had completely vanished. Wars between Colombia and Peru, between Argentina and Brazil, and, later, between Chile and the Peru–Bolivian Confederation were all events that, in one way or another, were connected to the independence struggle. The South American countries achieved their independence; an original mode of political rule, based on popular sovereignty, won more and more devotees; and new actors managed to ascend the military and social ladder. However, the following decades witnessed countless armed conflicts, transforming violence into a daily and legitimate political practice that, with ups and downs, lasted for the rest of the century.[65]

## Conclusion

In these pages I have presented a panoramic view of the revolutionary process that led to the independence of three countries of the Southern Cone: Argentina, Chile, and Peru. My approach followed a chronological narrative mainly featuring political and military issues. I could have taken a different path by emphasizing, for example, the ideological aspects behind the declarations of independence; the introduction of popular sovereignty as

---

[64] John Lynch, *Simón Bolívar*, 183–92.

[65] That violence became a central part of nineteenth-century Chilean political life (the rest could be said of most parts of Latin America) can be seen in various chapters of Iván Jaksic and Juan Luis Ossa, eds., *Historia política de Chile: Tomo prácticas políticas* (Santiago: Fondo de Cultura Económica, 2017). For a study of violence as an analytical category in the period 1810–1825, see Brian Hamnett, *The End of Iberian Rule on the American Continent, 1770–1830* (Cambridge: Cambridge University Press, 2017), Chapter 5.

the articulating axis of the republican system; the constitutionalist fever that affected Spanish Americans on both sides of the Atlantic as a consequence of the imperial crisis of 1808; or the role of the press in the construction of a modern public sphere. All these matters, of course, deserve to be studied on their own merit, as historians have done in the last decades. However, I argue that the revolutionary phenomenon had, above all, practical and material motivations that cannot be ignored and that, moreover, are at the basis of the ideological, economic, and social effects brought about by independence. These motivations, it seems to me, must be analyzed from the perspective of war, which I have seen here as a series of armed encounters in which flesh and blood characters struggled to change or maintain the monarchical legitimacy inherited from the colonial regime. Without war there was no revolution, and without revolution there was no independence.

Now, why should we use the concept of "revolution" to refer to this particular period? The answer is both historical and interpretive: historical, since the actors of the time used the word to refer to the changes that, for better or worse, were introduced in Spanish America beginning in 1810; interpretive, because despite the many continuities that one can appreciate in legal, social, and political matters between the old and the new regimes, the American continent was never again the same after the fall of Fernando VII. The idea of experiment, recently underlined by Hilda Sabato, shows how revolutionary this era was: there were governmental experiments, experiments in the way of waging war, and experiments in the implementation of geopolitical strategies never before rehearsed.[66] The years 1808–1824 bracket the maximum degree of experimentation within societies that, until then, had lived submerged in a more predictable type of politics that was no less political, but certainly more predictable.

The revolution of 1810 opened, precisely because of its experimental characteristics, many and very diverse alternatives to approach the imperial crisis. Independence was one of them, but by no means the most immediately desired or legitimate avenue. For this to happen, the revolution had to go a long way. The *juntista* revolution, as we saw, did not envision independence and, in fact, even those who opposed the insurgents experienced their own revolution. As it was not clear how monarchical sovereignty was to be resumed, it is not surprising that many different attempts were made to fill the power vacuum, including through an absolutist counterrevolution. This

---

[66] See Sabato, *Republics of the New World*, "Introduction."

was a counterrevolution that, at least in the case of Viceroy Abascal, tried to turn the clock back not only to 1808, but to the Bourbon reforms of the second half of the eighteenth century. In short, vacuum of power, crisis of legitimacy, and political sovereignty were three dimensions of the same problem, and of the same revolutionary context.

It is worth stressing once again that the "patriots'" triumph in 1824 did not put an end to these questions. Factionalism took hold of the countries under construction, all the more so as the legitimacy supposedly achieved by republicanism in place of monarchism did not reach the level expected by the ruling groups that became victorious in the 1820s. Thus, war continued its course in the following years, thereby prolonging what, before 1810, was believed to be alien to most of South America. The revolution had done its job.

8

# Caribbean South America: Free People of Color, Republican Experiments, Military Strategies, and the Caribbean Connection on the Path to Independence

ERNESTO BASSI

In May 1815, after failing to gain critical aid from the government of the independent Republic of Cartagena to fight royalist forces in neighboring Santa Marta, Simón Bolívar was forced to abandon New Granada and set sail to Jamaica. Shortly after his departure, a large contingent of Spanish troops under Pablo Morillo besieged and occupied Cartagena, putting an end to one of the earliest republican experiments of the wars of independence in Spanish America. The siege of Cartagena inaugurated a period known in Colombian history as the *Reconquista* and forced a large portion of Cartagena's inhabitants, many of whom were of African descent, to join Bolívar and other independence leaders in a Caribbean exile from which many never returned. Bolívar did return. After close to a year in Jamaica and Haiti, and thanks to the support of Haitian president Alexandre Pétion, Bolívar returned to Venezuela to relaunch the struggle for independence.

Bolívar's Caribbean exile and the fall of Cartagena's republic offer useful analytical windows to interpret the wars of independence as a Caribbean process, that is, as a historical development that responded to structures and dynamics associated with the fact that places like Cartagena, Santa Marta, Riohacha, Maracaibo, Coro, Puerto Cabello, and Caracas, among others, are coastal outposts in close proximity to Jamaica, Cuba, Puerto Rico, Haiti, and Trinidad (see Map 8.1). To emphasize the Caribbean structures and dynamics that influenced northern South America's path to independence, does not mean to deny the analytical validity of previous interpretations that highlight empire-wide dynamics or specific national frameworks. A focus on Caribbean South America should make a strong case for the analytical possibilities of considering multiple geographic units of analysis, as well as for taking seriously the multiplicity of potential outcomes that could have emerged from the process that resulted in the independence and ultimate establishment of the republics of Colombia and Venezuela. More specifically, the adoption of a Caribbean South America framework, given the particular demographic configuration of the Caribbean provinces of the Viceroyalty of New Granada and the Captaincy General of Venezuela, as well as the political and military developments unique to these provinces, makes it possible to present a narrative of the wars of independence in which other actors (people of African descent), political experiments (the small and short-lived republics of Cartagena and Caracas), military strategies (Bolívar's war to the death and the *Reconquista*), and connections (with Caribbean islands) take center stage. This reframing of geographic scale, thus, allows for both nuances that are lost in large-scale (Atlantic) interpretations, and comparisons and connections that tend to go unnoticed in analyses that work within smaller (local and national) geographical frameworks.

## Demographics: A *Pardo* Coast

It used to be standard for interpretations of the wars of independence in Spanish America to silence the role of slaves and free people of African descent in the military conflicts that resulted in the creation of more than a dozen independent republics in the Americas. The demographic configuration of many Spanish American regions, where Indigenous people, mestizos, and whites far outnumbered people of African descent, made this silencing possible. When present, slaves and free people of African descent tended to appear as cannon fodder strategically used by royalist and patriot elites to advance aims that had little or nothing to do with the lower classes. Alternatively, their actions tended to be depoliticized and presented as the result of their desire to obtain immediate benefits like cash and alcohol, instead of political goals and agendas associated with republicanism, patriotism, and citizenship. Black and mulatto agency, therefore, was historiographically unthinkable. Yet, on the Caribbean coast of South America, where people of African descent were the majority of the population, such a scene was not only possible but actually a reality. In Cartagena, for instance, "an angry mob of black and mulatto patriots" forcefully imposed their own political agenda when, on 11 November 1811, they "gave their petition for independence to the undecided members of the local revolutionary junta."[1]

[1] Marixa Lasso, *Myths of Harmony: Race and Republicanism during the Age of Revolution, Colombia, 1795–1831* (Pittsburgh: University of Pittsburgh Press, 2007), 1–2.

Map 8.1 Caribbean South America. Map made by Ernesto Bassi.

Their actions demonstrate that Blacks in Cartagena were not just a numerical force, but also one with the ability to turn the political tide in favor of specific political goals of their own making.

Unlike in central Mexico, the Andes, and central New Granada, where native populations had been able to recover after the demographic collapse that followed the arrival of Spaniards to the Americas, on South America's Caribbean coast Indigenous people, despite gradual recovery, remained a minority. The dramatic collapse of the Indigenous population throughout the Caribbean led to the importation of African slaves, who, during the first century after Spanish arrival to the Americas, acted as what David Wheat has called "surrogate colonists."[2] In this capacity, Africans initially brought as slaves slowly gained their freedom and their descendants gradually became the majority of the population throughout the Caribbean, including coastal South America.

By the late eighteenth century, the Caribbean provinces of New Granada and Venezuela were populated largely by people of African descent (see Tables 8.1 and 8.2). While slaves were a visible minority, most of the population of African descent in Caribbean South America was free. They

---

[2] David Wheat, *Atlantic Africa and the Spanish Caribbean, 1570–1640* (Chapel Hill: University of North Carolina Press, 2016), 14.

Caribbean South America

Table 8.1 *Population of late colonial Venezuela (1800)*

|  | Number | Percentage |
|---|---|---|
| Whites | 184,277 | 20.6 |
| Free people of African descent | 464,362 | 51.7 |
| Indians | 161,154 | 17.9 |
| Slaves | 87,800 | 9.8 |
| Total | 898,043 |  |

*Source*: Federico Brito Figueroa, *Historia económica y social de Venezuela: Una estructura para su estudio* (Caracas: Universidad Central de Venezuela, 1979), vol. 1, 160.

Table 8.2 *Population of late colonial Caribbean New Granada*

|  | Cartagena (1778) | Santa Marta (1793) | Riohacha (1778) | Caribbean New Granada |
|---|---|---|---|---|
| Whites | 13,850 (11.7%) | 5,183 (11.0%) | 333 (8.4%) | 19,366 (11.4%) |
| Free people of color | 75,490 (63.8%) | 29,050 (61.8%) | 2,513 (63.7%) | 107,053 (63.2%) |
| Indians | 19,416 (16.4%) | 8,636 (18.4%) | 633 (16.0%) | 28,685 (16.9%) |
| Slaves | 9,626 (8.1%) | 4,127 (8.8%) | 469 (11.9%) | 14,222 (8.4%) |
|  | 118,382 | 46,996 | 3,948 | 169,326 |

*Source*: Anthony McFarlane, *Colombia before Independence: Economy, Society, and Politics under Bourbon Rule* (Cambridge: Cambridge University Press, 1993), 353.

were usually called *pardos*. In urban areas, from the mouths of the Orinoco to Panama, *pardos* worked as artisans, masons, carpenters, barbers, and tailors. Free Blacks were also very active in the urban militias established in the 1770s, while women of color, who actually outnumbered men of color in coastal cities, worked as domestic servants and street and market vendors. Participation in economic activities and military service offered men and women of African descent opportunities to gain wealth and social status. In cities like Caracas and Cartagena, *pardos* constituted the largest portion of the workforce. Urban slaves, however, were also important to these cities' economic activity, with transportation, construction, domestic service, and market vending depending largely on slave labor. In the countryside *pardos* made up the absolute majority of the population. Their large presence, in conjunction with their tendency to withdraw from and challenge the norms of colonial society, constituted a major concern for authorities, who often complained that free people of color were smugglers, vagrants, squatters, and criminals. Rural slaves, particularly in Venezuela, toiled in plantations that produced export commodities such as cacao. Throughout this *pardo* coast, thus, people of African descent comprised the majority of the labor force. In a context characterized by revolutionary turmoil, they were also a major source of concern for colonial authorities.[3]

During the 1790s, with news of the French and Haitian Revolutions easily reaching South America's Caribbean coast, authorities in Venezuela and New Granada grew increasingly concerned about the possibility of revolutionary turmoil in their provinces. Fears turned into reality in 1795 and 1797, when slaves revolted in Coro and a mixed group of Spanish, creole, and *pardo* leaders planned a republican conspiracy in La Guaira. While both were quickly curtailed, they made tangible the dangers that mobilization of Blacks, enslaved and free, could pose to the security of New Granada and Venezuela's Caribbean provinces. They also revealed that slaves and *pardos* were political actors, willing and able to mobilize to advance aims of their own making.[4]

In 1808, when Napoleon's troops invaded Spain, urban Blacks along the *pardo* coast quickly gathered news of the events on the other side of the Atlantic and, alongside rural and urban slaves, became active participants in the political and military process that ensued. The initial reaction in Spanish America to news of Napoleon's invasion and Fernando VII's abdication can be characterized as a cautious, wait-and-see response. At first, expressions of loyalty to the captive king constituted the dominant reaction. As the Junta Central (established in Aranjuez in September 1808) that proclaimed to rule the Spanish world in the absence of the king transformed into a Council of Regency (established in February 1810), the political options for Americans began to expand. Under strong pressure from the French invaders, the Council was quickly forced to cease its functions. Before doing so, however, it called for the Cortes of Cádiz to draft a constitution for the Spanish monarchy.[5] By September 1810, when the Cortes opened its sessions, a

---

[3] Aline Helg, *Liberty and Equality in Caribbean Colombia, 1770–1835* (Chapel Hill: University of North Carolina Press, 2004), 42–120; Reuben Zahler, *Ambitious Rebels: Remaking Honor, Law, and Liberalism in Venezuela, 1780–1850* (Tucson: University of Arizona Press, 2013), 22–61.

[4] Lasso, *Myths of Harmony*, 29–33; Cristina Soriano, *Tides of Revolution: Information, Insurgencies, and the Crisis of Colonial Rule in Venezuela* (Albuquerque: University of New Mexico Press, 2018), 117–82. See also the chapters in this book by Clément Thibaud (Volume II, Chapter 6), Cristina Soriano (Volume II, Chapter 28), and Alejandro Gómez (Volume III, Chapter 14).

[5] See Breña, Chapter 3 in this volume.

number of American cities had already established governing juntas. While none of these juntas declared independence from the Spanish monarchy, several of them refused to recognize the authority of the Council or the Cortes. Juntas claiming to be temporary depositaries of sovereignty in the absence of the king, emerged in numerous cities. In many of these juntas, the initial support for the captive king quickly mutated into a call for increased autonomy within a transformed Spanish monarchy. By the end of 1811, while some cities had accepted the authority of the Cortes, others continued to claim they were only loyal to the captive king, and a minority had declared independence from Spain altogether. Grounded in longstanding economic rivalries, these divergent political choices evolved into the open conflict that characterized the first half of the 1810s.[6]

Along the *pardo* coast, the two largest cities, Caracas and Cartagena, took the most radical path of declaring independence, which put them at odds with their traditional rivals Maracaibo and Coro, and Santa Marta, respectively. *Pardos* and slaves featured prominently in the battles that confronted these rival cities. In both cities, *pardos* also played a pivotal role in the quick transition their governing juntas made from an autonomist position to the forceful declaration of total independence from Spain.

*Pardo* equality and rights to citizenship became a central issue in political debates in Caracas, Cartagena, and Cádiz. In 1811, representatives of the Caracas-based first Venezuelan constitutional congress agreed that *pardos* had the right to become citizens. In Cádiz, by contrast, the result of the debates on the *pardo* question, was to deny citizenship and, therefore, legal equality, to Americans of African descent. The combined effect of both decisions for well informed and already politically active urban *pardos* was to reinforce their commitment to independence and republicanism and to contribute to cement the commitment of elites in Caracas and Cartagena to independence. Outside the two main urban centers of Caracas and Cartagena, however, *pardos* tended to support royalist forces.[7]

In general, it can be asserted that support from the *pardos* was highly contingent and depended on the fact that they tended to see political independence or continued allegiance to Spain not as an end in itself but as a

---

[6] For examples see Jaime E. Rodriguez O., *The Independence of Spanish America* (Cambridge: Cambridge University Press, 1998); Anthony McFarlane, *War and Independence in Spanish America* (New York: Routledge, 2014); Brian Hamnett, *The End of Iberian Rule on the American Continent (1770–1830)* (Cambridge: Cambridge University Press, 2017).

[7] Lasso, *Myths of Harmony*, 36–49; Zahler, *Ambitious Rebels*, 42.

means to achieving a more important aim: legal equality. The same assertion is valid for slaves, although in their case the goal was to secure freedom. Since both royalists and those fighting for independence needed to secure recruits, it was natural for their leaders to offer freedom and citizenship to slaves and *pardos* who enlisted in their armies. In the particular context of Caribbean South America, given the preponderance of people of African descent in the population, the evolution of the fortunes of royalists and independentists, and the economic rivalries that pitted Caracas and Cartagena against smaller urban centers, three general observations tend to be valid. First, the large majority of fighters in both royalist and patriot armies were of African descent. Second, during the first half of the 1810s, outside of the republican enclaves of Caracas and Cartagena, slaves and *pardos* tended to be royalists. By the beginning of the 1820s, when the tide had definitely turned against royalist forces, soldiers of African descent fought overwhelmingly on the patriot side. In 1821, according to Venezuela's last captain general, insurgent forces were "in their totality . . . composed of descendants from Africa." Third, rivalries among cities and provinces played an important role in the allegiances of Blacks in Caribbean South America. Thus, while slaves and *pardos* in republican-dominated cities and provinces, such as Cartagena and Caracas, were overwhelmingly republican, the population of African descent in Santa Marta, Maracaibo, Coro, and Puerto Cabello tended to see more opportunities to achieve freedom and equality in siding with the royalist camp.[8]

A selected few soldiers of African descent, the most famous of whom are Manuel Piar and José Prudencio Padilla, even achieved fame and came close to glory. Piar, a mulatto from Curaçao who stood out as key leader of pro-independence troops in eastern Venezuela, climbed the military hierarchy thanks to his leadership in battles in the province of Guayana during the early 1810s. Padilla, a Riohacha-born *pardo* whose career included fighting against the British at Trafalgar before returning to New Granada to join Cartagena's insurgents, rose to the rank of general and became a national hero for his role in the defeat of Spanish troops in Maracaibo in 1823. In both cases, their ascendancy was closely followed by their demise. Perceived by Bolívar as potential challengers to his leadership and as evidence that *pardocracia* (rule

---

[8] Lasso, *Myths of Harmony*; Helg, *Liberty and Equality*; McFarlane, *War and Independence*; Peter Blanchard, *Under the Flags of Freedom: Slave Soldiers and the Wars of Independence in Spanish South America* (Pittsburgh: University of Pittsburgh Press, 2008), 79; Zahler, *Ambitious Rebels*.

of *pardos*) loomed as a threatening reality, both ended their lives facing the firing squad. Both Piar and Padilla are outstanding examples of the opportunities and risks that, even when fighting for the winning cause, the wars of independence offered to Americans of African descent.[9]

In their capacity as recruits in a war that they saw as a means toward aims that did not match those of the contending patriot and royalist sides, as political actors setting their own agendas, or even as key military leaders, individuals of African descent were highly visible in the landscape of war of Caribbean South America during the 1810s. Their participation in the wars largely determined some of the unique features of the conflict along the *pardo* coast.

## Political Experiments: An Ephemeral Republican Vanguard

Some historians have advanced the notion that the process that resulted in the creation of more than ten new republics in the Americas constituted a "political revolution" of Atlantic scale. The process, triggered by Napoleon's invasion of Spain, "sought to transform the Spanish Monarchy into a modern nation state with one of the most radical constitutions of the nineteenth century."[10] For some in the Americas, including politically active sectors of the population of Caracas and Cartagena, however, the intended transformations were not revolutionary enough. The reaction of their political elites and popular sectors set Caracas and Cartagena apart from the rest of Spanish America. It made them, according to Clément Thibaud, "exceptions," because they "declared their separation from Spain" not only earlier (in 1811) but also "in a much clearer and more radical way than the other American kingdoms."[11] While the independent republics of Caracas and Cartagena were ephemeral (by the end of 1815 both territories were back under Spanish control), their political experiments put them at the vanguard of Spanish America's republicanism.

According to Jaime Rodríguez, three elements were at the heart of the political revolution. First, the Junta Central established in Spain to rule over

---

[9] Helg, *Liberty and Equality*, 195–236; Lasso, *Myths of Harmony*, 115–28.
[10] Rodríguez, "The Hispanic Revolution: Spain and America, 1808–1826," *Ler Historia* 57 (2009), 73. See also Rodríguez O., *The Independence of Spanish America*.
[11] Clément Thibaud, *Repúblicas en armas: Los ejércitos bolivarianos en la Guerra de Independencia en Colombia y Venezuela* (Bogotá: Planeta, 2003), 43.

the Spanish Empire during Fernando VII's captivity "acknowledged the Americans' claims that their lands were not colonies but kingdoms"; second, "that they constituted integral parts of the Spanish Monarchy"; and, third, "that they possessed the right of representation in the national government."[12] How representation was to be determined, proved key to the quick transition from autonomism to total independence taken by Caracas and Cartagena.

Initially, representation was assigned according to administrative divisions. While the initial method, which assigned the Americas nine representatives (one for each of the four viceroyalties and one for each of the five captaincies general), was modified for one that granted representation based on population, the new formula to calculate representation did not fully satisfy a large portion of Americans. The root of the disaffection was the exclusion of people of African descent. By denying citizenship to individuals of African descent, the Cortes, which had convened in Cádiz on 24 September 1810, ensured that the representatives from the Iberian Peninsula outnumbered those of the Americas. In a system that claimed that now both Spanish and American territories were kingdoms and all free men should be treated as citizens, the exclusion of those who could not trace their origins to Spain or America was rightly perceived as unjust. In Caribbean South America, where news of the debates began arriving in early 1811, two key groups reacted adversely to the exclusion: the politically active urban *pardos*, who were directly affected by the exclusion, and the creole elites, who saw the measure as a way of limiting their territories' representation.

In Caracas and Cartagena, both of which had established autonomous juntas in 1810, the coincidence of interests of leading sectors of the creole elite and the large population of *pardos*, despite the racial tensions that also characterized the relations between the two groups, resulted in a quick transition from an autonomist position to declaring total independence from Spain. Caracas did it first, on 5 July 1811. Cartagena followed several months later, on 11 November 1811. Both the process leading to and the effects of the declaration were similar. In both cities, the transition from autonomism to independence was closely associated with events in Spain, in particular the debates on representation and the direct effect of their outcome on the representation of both Caracas and Cartagena. Also central to the quick transition was the presence of vast numbers of politically active urban *pardos*

---

[12] Rodríguez, "The Hispanic Revolution," 76.

and their ability to use their numbers to pressure creole elites leading the juntas to adopt the radical solution to declare independence.

In Caracas, the process of radicalization owed a lot to the establishment of the Sociedad Patriótica de Agricultura y de Economía (Patriotic Society of Agriculture and Economy), which offered a venue for revolutionaries, including a still unknown Bolívar, to voice their radical views, and to the arrival, in December 1810, of Francisco Miranda. Miranda, whose return to Venezuela responded at least partially to an invitation from Caracas' *pardos beneméritos* (wealthy *pardos*), quickly emerged as a leader capable of uniting the wealthy creole revolutionaries and the *pardo* masses.[13] Under his leadership, the *mantuanos* (Caracas' wealthy creole elite) and *pardos* pushed Caracas toward a political independence that enfranchised free individuals of African descent. While the Spanish Cortes denied citizenship to *pardos*, the Congress of Caracas, besides declaring total independence, turned legal equality for all males into law when it approved Venezuela's first constitution (21 December 1811).[14]

In Cartagena, *pardos* played an even larger role in the city's shift toward independence. Divided into two distinct camps, the *Piñeristas* or demagogues and the *Toledistas* or aristocrats, Cartagena's creole elite had been able to depose the Spanish governor and establish and sustain a junta thanks in large part to the active support of lower-class *pardos*. Throughout 1811, the junta, presided by José María García de Toledo (the leader of the *Toledistas*), grew wary of *pardos'* support and political pressure. In contrast to García de Toledo, Gabriel Gutiérrez de Piñeres (leader of the *Piñeristas*) based his political power on *pardos'* support. Thus, while *Piñeristas* supported *pardos'* push for immediate independence, *Toledistas* maintained a cautious approach in which independence should happen in an orderly fashion, avoiding the turmoil that, García de Toledo feared, could result from mass involvement of *pardos*. On 11 November 1811, right after it became clear that the junta was about to end its session without declaring independence, the *pardo* militia and a large group of *pardo* artisans forced the door of the city's armory, armed themselves "with spears, daggers, and guns, ... went to the government palace, ... requested that the junta approved their petition for

---

[13] Alejandro Gómez, "La revolución de Caracas desde abajo. Impensando la primera independencia de Venezuela ...," *Nuevo Mundos, Mundos Nuevos*, Debates (2008), https://journals.openedition.org/nuevomundo/32982#bodyftn48.

[14] Thibaud, *Repúblicas en armas*; McFarlane, *War and Independence*; Zahler, *Ambitious Rebels*.

independence," and, faced with García de Toledo's refusal, "invaded the session hall," forcing a reluctant but ultimately helpless junta to sign Cartagena's Independence Act.[15]

With their declaration of independence Cartagena and Caracas joined the United States and Haiti as the only republics in the Americas. Like Haiti (and unlike the United States), both Caracas and Cartagena adopted full legal equality for males. Their republican and liberal constitutions formally granted suffrage to any male head of household, "who lives off his rents or labor, without depending on another person [for a wage]."[16] Another common element resulting from their declarations of independence was the exacerbation of regional divisions. Preexisting rivalries over economic and political power, led secondary cities along the coast to stand in opposition to Caracas and Cartagena. Thus Maracaibo, Coro, Cumaná, and Valencia, in Venezuela, and Santa Marta, in New Granada, opposed Caracas and Cartagena, launching a period of "war between cities" that Clément Thibaud characterized as "a low-intensity confrontation" in which "small armies deploy(ed) a dilatory strategy aimed at putting pressure on the adversary without trying to destroy it." In this early stage of military conflict that preceded the more violent period that started in 1813, "battle is more feared than desired" and "everything possible is made to avoid [military confrontation]."[17]

The low-intensity confrontations started in Venezuela even before Caracas' declaration of independence, when the junta of Caracas sent troops to Coro with the aim of forcing the city into obedience. Coro's resistance resulted in a minor skirmish that forced Caracas' troops to retreat, which left the political future hanging in the balance. While Caracas moved toward declaring independence, Coro remained staunchly royalist. In July 1811, immediately after Caracas declared independence, a rebellion erupted in Valencia. First commanded by the Marqués del Toro and then by Francisco de Miranda, republican troops from Caracas managed to capture Valencia but were only able to hold it until November 1811. Royalist reinforcements from Cuba commanded by Domingo de Monteverde, in coordination with royalists from Coro, Maracaibo, and Guayana, made it impossible for Caracas' republican troops to secure territories beyond its

---

[15] Lasso, *Myths of Harmony*, 68–78; Helg, *Liberty and Equality*, 127–31.
[16] "Constitución del Estado de Cartagena de Indias," quoted in Helg, *Liberty and Equality*, 130.
[17] Thibaud, *Repúblicas en armas*, 75, 77.

jurisdiction. The stalemate lasted until mid-1812, when, following an earthquake (26 March) that devastated Caracas and spared Coro, Maracaibo, and other territories under royalist control, republican Caracas became unable to sustain the war effort. Thus, Monteverde forced Miranda to surrender and entered Caracas on 30 June 1812, putting an end to Venezuela's first republican experiment.[18]

In New Granada the rivalry between Cartagena and Santa Marta became an armed confrontation shortly after Cartagena's declaration of independence. In the preceding months Cartagena had levied a tax on all imports from Santa Marta and the authorities of both provinces had clashed (although not yet militarily) over control of the Magdalena River, which marked the border between the two provinces and was the main artery communicating them with the interior of New Granada. Throughout 1811 the interprovincial conflict took the form of a "war of words and opinions rather than of violence and death."[19] While both provinces deployed troops, especially along the Magdalena River, instances of military confrontations were few. After July 1812, however, the conflict escalated and military confrontations (still of low intensity) became more frequent.

The escalation of the conflict resulted largely from the arrival to Cartagena of many experienced republican officers expelled from Caracas, including a still unknown Bolívar. Reinforcements from Caracas allowed Cartagena to launch a successful attack on Santa Marta. Under Bolívar, Cartagena troops captured Tenerife, El Banco, and Tamalameque, key river towns in the province of Santa Marta. Closer to the coast, Pierre Labatut led the offensive against the city of Santa Marta. On 6 January 1813, when Labatut's forces entered Santa Marta, republicans achieved formal control of the province. Hundreds of royalists fled to Portobelo; others sought refuge in nearby rural areas. Pockets of resistance remained throughout the province. These became important several months later, when news of Labatut's abuses in Santa Marta mobilized royalists against republicans, forcing Labatut and his occupying force to retreat. By the middle of 1813, the war was at a standstill. Unlike in Caracas, where royalists managed to expel republicans, in Caribbean New Granada royalists lacked the manpower to defeat independent Cartagena.[20] The tense stalemate between Cartagena and

[18] Ibid., 72–9, 91–101; McFarlane, *War and Independence*, 90–6.
[19] Steinar Saether, *Identidades e independencia en Santa Marta y Riohacha, 1750–1850* (Bogotá: Instituto Colombiano de Antropología e Historia, 2005), 184.
[20] Ibid., 177–96.

Santa Marta lasted until 1815, when Spanish troops under Pablo Morillo besieged and captured Cartagena, ending its republican experiment.

Both the independent republic of Caracas and that of Cartagena were short lived. The first one lasted only a year, the second about four. Despite their ephemerality, putting them at the analytical center makes possible an interpretation of the Spanish American wars of independence that allows for republicanism to be considered a serious political option from the very beginning of the Spanish monarchical crisis. While the interpretation of the political revolution that emphasizes the process and problems of representation in a transformed Spanish monarchy certainly has much explanatory power, the early radicalization of creole elites and *pardos* in Caracas and Cartagena reveals a more complex political landscape in which the options went beyond autonomy or steadfast loyalism. The processes of Caracas and Cartagena demonstrate that total independence and the creation of republics, even in the early 1810s, were also part of the horizon of expectations of the politically active population of Spanish America.

## Military Strategies: War to the Death and *Reconquista*

If the early republican experiments of Cartagena and Caracas made Caribbean South America's road to independence somewhat exceptional, the intensity of warfare in the region and the casualties it produced further set it apart from other Spanish American territories. It was in northern South America where the low-intensity confrontation first mutated into violent warfare under the banner of "war to the death." It was also there where the Spanish recapture of most of South America was launched and took its most violent form. The military strategies of both republicans and royalists between 1813 and 1816 demonstrate the extent to which the process in Caribbean South America can be interpreted as unique.

The shift toward heightened violence and high casualties resulted from the actions of both royalists under Monteverde and pro-independence forces under Bolívar. While Bolívar's declaration of war to the death, in June 1813, offers a fitting opening for this phase of the war, the turn toward intense violence began earlier and quickly spread throughout the Caribbean coast of South America. Under Monteverde's command royalist forces in Venezuela followed their victory against Caracas' republicans by launching a repression campaign that quickly spread throughout the captaincy general. The reestablishment of royalist control in Cumaná, Barinas, Barcelona,

La Guaira, and Valencia was characterized by lootings and torture. By the end of 1812, violent repression had secured royalist control of Venezuela.[21]

In New Granada, the arrival of defeated republicans from Caracas took the low-intensity conflict between Cartagena and Santa Marta in a more violent direction. Under Bolívar's command, troops from Cartagena successfully attacked several towns along the Magdalena River, while troops under Pierre Labatut captured the city of Santa Marta, ensuring republicans the upper hand in the interprovincial conflict. By March 1813, while royalists had a firm grasp on Venezuela, republicans had established control over most of Caribbean New Granada.[22]

With New Granada under republican control, Bolívar marched toward Venezuela. There, he quickly adopted measures that resembled those of his royalist counterparts. Claiming that Monteverde, Antonio Azuola, Francisco Javier Cervériz, José Tomás Boves, and other royalist commanders were waging a war of extermination against insurgents, Bolívar embraced violence through the declaration of his famous "war to the death." The declaration, issued in Trujillo on 15 June 1813, concluded with one of Bolívar's most resounding statements: "Spaniards and Canarians, know that you will die, even if you are simply neutral ... Americans, you will be spared, even when you are guilty."[23]

From Trujillo, Bolívar's troops marched east toward Caracas. Launching a series of rapid attacks, the insurgents defeated royalist troops in the battles of Carache (18 June), Niquitao (2 July), and Taguanes (31 July). Victory in these battles allowed them to occupy Barinas, Barquisimeto, and Valencia, and left their path to Caracas open. On 6 August, Bolívar entered Caracas to cheers of "Viva el Libertador." As a last resort to avoid complete defeat, Monteverde had abandoned the city, fleeing to the royalist stronghold of Puerto Cabello. East of Caracas, the rule of Monteverde had suffered another devastating defeat. During the first half of 1813, insurgent troops loosely unified under Santiago Mariño captured Maturín, Cumaná, and Barcelona.[24]

Mariño's tactical approach, like Bolívar's and Monteverde's, called for matching violence with violence. Violence and cruelty were not limited to military confrontations. Throughout 1813, both royalist and insurgent forces terrorized civilians for aiding one side or the other. Denunciations against

---

[21] Thibaud, *Repúblicas en armas*, 101–3.
[22] Saether, *Identidades e independencia*, 189–96.
[23] Quoted in John Lynch, *Simón Bolívar: A Life* (New Haven: Yale University Press, 2006), 73.
[24] Ibid., 72–6.

royalist commanders Cervériz and Zuazola included that they offered monetary rewards to those who brought them ears of insurgents. Condemning Zuazola's cruelty, Bolívar declared that the royalist commander had "skinned [people] alive, and then thrown [them] into contaminated lakes or put to death by slow and painful methods." Moreover, Bolívar continued hyperbolically, Zuazola had "destroyed" unborn babies "in the wombs of expectant mothers by [using] bayonets or blows." Seeking to retaliate and terrorize, Bolívar responded by shooting those he deemed "criminal Europeans and Canarians," including 800 royalist prisoners whom he ordered executed in February 1814. Violence begot violence; cruelty was repaid with cruelty.[25]

By the beginning of 1814, thus, the political tide had shifted in favor of the insurgents. While royalists had retreated to Maracaibo, Puerto Cabello, and Guayana, republicans were in possession of Caracas, Valencia, Maturín, Cumaná, and Barcelona, and their surrounding territories. Republicans, however, were far from united. While Bolívar concentrated his authority on Caracas and western Venezuela, Mariño emerged as the caudillo of the east. Throughout the land, the confrontations of 1813 had left a trail of death and devastation.

Early 1814 also marked the beginning of a successful counterrevolution that brought even more violence, physical destruction, personal suffering, and ultimately the demise of Venezuela's so-called second republic. From Venezuela's interior plains, José Tomás Boves led the royalist resurgence. Leading large troops of Blacks and *pardos* drawn to war by the promise of economic rewards, Boves defeated republican troops at La Puerta on two occasions (February and June 1814). Despite minor republican victories at La Victoria (February 1814) and Carabobo (May 1814), by the end of July Boves and his troops had recaptured Valencia and forced Caracas to surrender. Executions of prisoners and killings of thousands of civilians accompanied Boves' march to Caracas.

From Caracas, Boves' troops marched east toward Barcelona and Cumaná. His second in command, Francisco Morales, dealt republicans a crushing blow by defeating them on the outskirts of Barcelona. In the Battle of Aragua de Barcelona (August 1814), more than 3,000 patriots and over 1,000 royalists died. In addition, following the pattern of terror that characterized confrontations during 1813 and 1814, Morales' troops, as recounted by an observer, "killed all civilians in Aragua." Victory in Aragua allowed Morales to proceed

---

[25] Ibid., 77–80 (for Bolívar quotes, see page 79).

to Barcelona, which he entered on 20 August. From there, Boves and Morales continued their march of terror toward Cumaná (where, in October 1814, they killed about 1,000 civilians) and Maturín (where, despite Boves' death, the royalists scored a sounding victory). The Battle of Maturín (December 1814), where patriots were slaughtered and the abuses perpetrated on civilians included raping hundreds of women, secured royalist control of Venezuela.[26]

By the beginning of 1815 the vast majority of South America's Caribbean coast from Portobelo, in the west, to Cumaná, in the east, was under royalist control. Of all the major urban centers along the *pardo* coast only Cartagena had escaped the royalist takeover. With the dispatch of about 10,000 Spanish soldiers from Cádiz, Cartagena's political situation was about to be upended. Commanded by Field Marshal Pablo Morillo, the expeditionary army arrived in Carúpano in March 1815. With Venezuela firmly under royalist control, Morillo did not spend much time in Venezuela, instead sailing toward New Granada as soon as possible. In July 1815, his army entered the royalist bastion of Santa Marta. From there, Morillo quickly moved to Cartagena, which his troops laid under siege from mid-August. By the time it ended, on 5 December 1815, the siege had reduced Cartagena to a deplorable state. The toll of 106 days of siege was catastrophic. According to Rebecca Earle, "[o]ver seven thousand people, more than a third of the city's population, had died of hunger and disease." Those who survived had been forced to eat boiled leather and many fell victim to the executions that Morillo ordered immediately after retaking the city. Royalist losses during the siege (Morillo's army lost more than 3,000 troops to disease and desertion) added to the number of casualties.[27]

The siege of Cartagena not only opened the door for Morillo's troops to reconquer New Granada. Cartagena's brutal siege, which historians have characterized as the military action with the highest number of losses in New Granada, also offered a powerful example that determined the character of the next stages of the *Reconquista*. For both royalist troops and pro-independence factions, avoiding the type of violence and destruction of the siege became a reasonable proposition. In hindsight, the siege of Cartagena effectively marked the end of the most violent phase of the wars of independence in South America. Thus, as Morillo's troops moved south from the

---

[26] Ibid., 81–7 (quote on page 86).
[27] Rebecca Earle, *Spain and the Independence of Colombia, 1810–1825* (Exeter: University of Exeter Press, 2000), 61–4 (quote from page 63); McFarlane, *War and Independence*, 138.

Caribbean to the Andean interior, they no longer needed to use the strategy of scorched earth and massive killings that both royalists and republicans had used during the 1813–1815 period. While not a "military parade" (as it was once described), once the military center of gravity shifted to New Granada's interior, the "military fury" of the early *Reconquista* was superseded by a "moderate pacification."[28]

A cursory look at some of the key battles mentioned in this section offers a clear sense of the violence with which the battles of the 1813–1815 period were fought. The combined strategies of Monteverde, Boves, and Bolívar produced a cycle in which battles (often with thousands of casualties in direct combat) were followed by punishment of civilians, execution of prisoners, and more battles. While estimates of the casualties are hard to come by, the calculations of Vicente Lecuna (which he characterized as "the most prudent") put the number of casualties in Venezuela during 1813 and 1814 at 225,000.[29] Since the brunt of the combat during this period took place in Venezuela's Caribbean provinces, it is reasonable to conclude that Caribbean Venezuela witnessed the most violent phase of the wars of independence in South America. Similarly, given the brutality of Morillo's siege and the powerful example it set for the population of New Granada, Caribbean Colombia, in particular the province of Cartagena, suffered the cruelest stage of the Spanish *Reconquista*.

For many survivors of the siege and some of the bloodiest battles along the *pardo* coast, fleeing became the only choice. Following well-trodden sea routes many sought refuge in Jamaica and Haiti. Throughout the 1810s, Jamaica, Haiti, Cuba, Trinidad, Curaçao, and other Caribbean islands served not only as refuge for royalists and republicans, but also as weapons' suppliers, pantries, key recruiting sites, crucial diplomatic battlegrounds, and, for hundreds of unlucky ones, graves.

## Caribbean Connections

The Caribbean fortunes of hundreds of exiles who escaped Cartagena before Morillo's troops entered the city varied widely. A quick overview of the fate of some of the most notorious exiles reveals that some of them were abused,

---

[28] McFarlane, *War and Independence*, 138–40, 301–3. For the transition from "military fury" to "moderate pacification," see Daniel Gutiérrez Ardila, *La restauración en la Nueva Granada (1815–1819)* (Bogotá: Universidad Externado de Colombia, 2016), 26.

[29] Vicente Lecuna, *Crónica razonada de las guerras de Bolívar* (New York: Colonial Press, 1950), vol. 1, 395.

robbed, and abandoned by the captains who helped them flee (e.g. Cartagena's governor, Juan de Dios Amador, and his family, who were robbed and abandoned on tiny Providence island); many were captured by Spanish authorities and quickly sent back to Cartagena, where some were swiftly executed (e.g. Miguel Diaz Granados and José María García de Toledo, both signatories of Cartagena's independence declaration); others were imprisoned (e.g. most members of the Pombo family, wealthy merchants who actively participated in the political debates that resulted in the establishment of independent Cartagena); a few were sent to prisons in Spain and northern Africa (e.g. Vicente Ucrós); some joined Bolívar and other exiles in Jamaica and Haiti and later returned to the *pardo* coast to continue fighting (e.g. José Prudencio Padilla, Carlos Soublette, Antonio José de Sucre, Luis Brion, Remigio Márquez, Mariano Montilla, and other leaders of Colombia and Venezuela during the 1820s); and a good number died in their Caribbean exile never being able to see their homelands again (e.g. Diego Laza and Pedro Romero, who died in Haiti, and Juan José de León Vigil, who perished in Jamaica).[30]

Cartagena's exiles were neither the only nor the first ones to seek refuge on Caribbean islands. In May 1815, about six months before Cartagena's exiles fled the city, Bolívar had entered Jamaica seeking aid from British authorities. Three years before that, in August 1812, Bolívar had fled to Curaçao to avoid capture after the defeat of Caracas' First Republic. The fall of this first republican experiment also forced Santiago Mariño and many other patriots to flee from eastern Venezuela to nearby Trinidad. The first half of the 1810s, according to Paul Verna, saw three waves of emigration from the *pardo* coast to the Caribbean islands: First, in July and August 1812, after the fall of the First Republic of Caracas; second, at the end of 1814 with the demise of Caracas' Second Republic; and, third, in December 1815, during the final days of the Siege of Cartagena. On the three occasions, hundreds of patriotic émigrés sought refuge in Curaçao, Trinidad, Saint Thomas, Jamaica, and Haiti.[31]

Patriotic émigrés were not the only ones seeking refuge in the Caribbean. Whenever the tide turned against royalist forces, hundreds of royalists, facing punishments and execution, saw no alternative but to leave their homelands.

---

[30] "Emigrantes de Cartagena en 1815," in Manuel Exequiel Corrales, ed., *Efemérides y anales del estado de Bolívar* (Bogotá: Casa Editorial J. J. Pérez, 1889), vol. II, 214–25.

[31] Paul Verna, *Bolívar y los emigrados patriotas en el Caribe* (Caracas: Instituto Nacional de Cooperación Educativa, 1983), 10–21.

During late 1812 and early 1813 more than 451 exiles from Santa Marta arrived in Portobelo, with many others fleeing Santa Marta to seek refuge in Cuba, Jamaica, and Riohacha.[32] While Portobelo, Cuba, and Riohacha remained firmly under royalist control (hence only offering refuge to royalists), Jamaica, in keeping with Britain's neutrality policy, was open to both royalists and republicans. Thus, Jamaica, along with Trinidad, Curaçao (under British control during the 1810s), and other neutral islands, particularly Danish Saint Thomas, became havens where exiled royalists and patriotic émigrés coexisted in high tension.

In Haiti, patriotic émigrés found a more generous, although unofficial supporter. While the Haitian republic, under Alexandre Pétion, also adhered to a policy of neutrality, Pétion's obvious sympathies for Spanish American rebels made his state a sanctuary for revolutionaries that Spanish authorities characterized as "the receptacle of all the adventurers."[33] There, patriotic émigrés, including Bolívar, who moved to Haiti from Jamaica in December 1815, converged in Les Cayes (on Haiti's southern coast) to organize military expeditions to different points along the *pardo* coast. From Pétion, Bolívar obtained weapons and other military supplies. He also recruited hundreds of volunteers, many of whom were exiles from Venezuela and New Granada but the majority of whom were anonymous Haitians. With the generous, though unofficial aid of Pétion, Bolívar organized two expeditions to Venezuela (in March and December 1816). Other pro-independence exiles, including the Venezuelan brothers Miguel and Fernando Carabaño and Scottish adventurer Gregor MacGregor, also used Haiti as a recruiting and logistical site to ready expeditions to the Atrato River in northwestern New Granada (1815), Portobelo (1818), and Riohacha (1819).[34]

The islands also served as weapons repositories and recruiting grounds to which both Cartagena and Santa Marta sent commissioners to purchase weapons and enlist combatants. Historian Daniel Gutiérrez Ardila has documented at least four such missions: two in 1810, one in 1812, and one in 1813.

---

[32] Saether, *Identidades e independencia*, 192.

[33] Ernesto Bassi, *An Aqueous Territory: Sailor Geographies and New Granada's Transimperial Greater Caribbean World* (Durham, NC: Duke University Press, 2016), 158–66.

[34] The Carabaño brothers sailed toward the Atrato in late 1815; MacGregor to Portobelo in 1818 and to Riohacha in 1819. In 1817, MacGregor used Haiti to launch an expedition to Amelia Island, off Florida's Atlantic coast. Francisco Xavier Mina, who sailed toward Mexico in 1815, and Louis Aury, who sailed toward Galveston in 1816, also used Haiti as an expeditionary base. Bassi, *An Aqueous Territory*, 159–60; Verna, *Bolívar y los emigrados*, 47–80; Paul Verna, *Petion y Bolívar: Cuarenta años (1790–1830) de relaciones haitiano-venezolanas y su aporte a la emancipación de Hispanoamérica* (Caracas, 1969).

For merchants in Jamaica and other Caribbean islands supplying weapons, ammunitions, and food to warring factions in the mainland made the 1810s the most profitable time.[35] When it came to recruiting soldiers, Cuba and Puerto Rico were for royalists what Haiti was for republicans. If Haiti made it possible for Bolívar to revive the independence cause in early 1817, Cuba and Puerto Rico had enabled royalists to counter earlier republican threats. Just in 1811, three expeditions (one from Cuba and two from Puerto Rico) came to succor royalists in Venezuela. The arrival of several hundred men, including Domingo Monteverde, who soon became Venezuela's captain general, was key to defeating Caracas' First Republic. While much smaller than Morillo's expeditionary army, these early expeditions forced Caracas' leaders to fight a war for which they were not prepared.[36] Moreover, under Monteverde's leadership royalists were able to contain Bolívar's 1813 offensive, laying the groundwork for Morillo to enter an already "pacified" Venezuela in mid-1815. The combined efforts of Monteverde and Boves, who came to Caribbean Venezuela from the south, allowed Morillo to sail as quickly as possible to New Granada, having exhausted few resources in Venezuela. Thus, the ability of Venezuelan royalists under Monteverde and Boves to keep Bolívar and other republicans at bay in Venezuela facilitated Morillo's *Reconquista* of New Granada.

The Caribbean islands also played a critical role as diplomatic battlegrounds. During the first half of the 1810s, both royalists and republicans in Caribbean New Granada and Venezuela saw British official support as crucial to tip the balance in their favor. For royalists, official British support would restrict insurgents' access to weapons and other supplies. For insurgents, British support could not only result in continued supply of weapons and food, but also offer the legitimacy in the international sphere that could turn their republics into permanent features of the Atlantic's political map. Given Jamaica's proximity to the *pardo* coast and the long history of commercial connections that tied it to South America's Caribbean coast, it comes as no surprise that both royalists and insurgents turned to Jamaica's authorities to obtain this vital support.

---

[35] Daniel Gutiérrez Ardila, *Un nuevo reino: Geografía política, pactismo y diplomacia durante el interregno en Nueva Granada (1808–1816)* (Bogotá: Universidad Externado de Colombia, 2010), 459–79; Frances Armytage, *The Free Port System in the British West Indies: A Study in Commercial Policy, 1766–1822* (London: Longmans, Green and Co., 1953), 127–30.

[36] McFarlane, *War and Independence*, 90.

The diplomatic battle in Jamaica began in 1812, when New Granada's viceroy Benito Pérez sent Pablo Arocemena to the island. Arocemena's aim was to convince Jamaican authorities to deny refuge to insurgents and to forbid any type of business with them. Shortly afterwards, in 1813, Cartagena's independent government sent Ignacio Cavero to ask vice-admiral Charles Stirling to mediate between Pérez and the authorities of Cartagena. Two years later, in 1815, Cavero, accompanied by John Robertson, returned to Jamaica as envoy of Cartagena, seeking to secure British aid against an imminent Spanish attack. That same year Bolívar also spent several months in Jamaica trying to secure Britain's support in the fight against Morillo and the royalists. Neither royalists nor republicans secured official support. For Jamaican authorities, who were following Britain's policy of supporting Spain in the war against Napoleon in Europe and adhering to a policy of neutrality in the war between Spain and its territories in the Americas, "observ(ing) the strictest neutrality and avoid(ing) all interference between the contending parties in the South American provinces" was an official position not worth breaching. As a result of these diplomatic efforts, republican and royalist envoys to Jamaica were only able to obtain Stirling's personal, yet unofficial mediation in peace negotiations (that ended up being unfruitful) between Viceroy Pérez and Cartagena's republican authorities. In addition, both royalist and republican envoys secured some important contracts to obtain weapons. Beyond these minor achievements, the missions were short of disastrous and left both sides complaining. While royalists decried the fact that Jamaican authorities were allowing insurgents to seek refuge and conduct business in Jamaica as an outright breach of Britain's neutrality policy, republicans complained that they were abandoned and denied the protection they so desperately needed.[37]

Republicans had better luck in Haiti. While there is little information about two early missions led by Pierre Antonine Leleux (in 1813) and Marco Marcantoni (in 1814), the critical support that Pétion and the governor of Les Cayes, Ignace Marion, offered to Bolívar in 1816 has been amply documented. In fact, Pétion's pro-insurgence diplomacy allowed Haiti to become an international revolutionary center actively spreading revolution throughout the Greater Caribbean. Pétion's aid, while significant, was still unofficial. Given his state's adherence to international commitments incorporated into its own constitution, Pétion was not legally endowed to turn his

---

[37] Gutiérrez, *Un nuevo reino*, 563–77; Bassi, *An Aqueous Territory*, 151–8.

revolutionary sympathies into official policy. For Bolívar and others, however, he did turn these sympathies into concrete aid in the form of ships, weapons, ammunitions, and men. While Pétion's support was clear and decisive, it remained critical for him to be able to maintain that Haiti was adhering to its neutrality policy. Since no less than Haiti's survival was at stake in keeping the veneer of neutrality, Pétion asked Bolívar to refrain from publicizing Haiti's aid. Any sort of official diplomatic recognition, therefore, was clearly out of the question.

Official or not, decisive or hardly significant, the contributions of Jamaica, Trinidad, Haiti, Cuba, Puerto Rico, and other islands to the war effort along the *pardo* coast may lead to conclude that the Caribbean was an area adjacent to the actual battleground, not a battleground in its own right. Such an interpretation, as Edgardo Pérez Morales recently argued, denies the "hemispheric and maritime aspects of Spanish American independence."[38] Pérez Morales' analysis of the corsairs of independent Cartagena makes a convincing case for Caribbean South America as a battleground that included both the many bloody battles along the *pardo* coast and hundreds of encounters at sea. For corsairs associated with the independent republics of Caracas and Cartagena, many of whom, just as the majority of the combatants on the *pardo* coast, were of African descent, the Caribbean was an actual battleground where some found glory and many others death.

Among those who found glory was a *pardo* from Riohacha whose naval talents first gained him recognition during his time serving for independent Cartagena. In 1823, when the independence of Colombia and Venezuela was already secured but not yet sealed, Padilla reached the peak of his naval career as the commanding officer of the republican troops at the Battle of Lake Maracaibo, the last battle of the wars in Caribbean South America. For Padilla, as for many other *pardos* along South America's Caribbean coasts and waters, independence was a maritime struggle fought and won at sea.[39]

## Conclusion: Shifting Perspectives and Recalibrating Scale

As historians of the Age of Revolutions continue to scrutinize the Spanish American wars of independence, the analytical roads continue to expand.

---

[38] Edgardo Pérez Morales, *No Limits to Their Sway: Cartagena's Privateers and the Masterless Caribbean in the Age of Revolutions* (Nashville: Vanderbilt University Press, 2018), 157.

[39] For Padilla's life, see Lasso, *Myths of Harmony*, 115–28; Helg, *Liberty and Equality*, 195–236; Bassi, *An Aqueous Territory*, 193–6.

Scholars no longer take for granted the interpretation of the process as a preordained transition from colony to nation, nor do they accept characterizations derived from patriotic narratives that equate patriotism with good and royalism with evil or that present popular groups as mere cannon fodder without desire or ability to advance political agendas. Shifting analytical perspectives and recalibrating geographical scales have allowed historians to ask (and answer) probing questions about the political cultures of Spanish subjects throughout the Atlantic.[40] Much more can be achieved and explained by continuing to explore alternative perspectives and geographical scales.

By focusing on Caribbean South America, a geographic space that does not neatly map onto past or present political geographies but that many at the time of the wars of independence experienced as a lived geography, this chapter has centered processes that often get lost in analyses that use national frameworks as units of analysis or that are perceived as uniquely local when using smaller regional lenses. Far from being an arbitrary exercise of developing alternative ways of approaching a historical process by forcing us out of entrenched habits of narration that pay excessive respect to political geographies, uncovering the *pardo* coast and its Caribbean waters as the cohesive and coherent geographical space that they were shines a light on peoples, ideas, and strategies that do not fit in conventional interpretational frameworks. Thus, *pardos*, who constituted the majority of the population of Caribbean South America but not of Spanish America as a whole, emerge as key actors who not only were a force with which independence and royalist leaders had to grapple, but, most important, appear as the central characters in a story that often relegates them to the background. Similarly, the recalibration of geographical scale proposed in this chapter requires taking seriously the possibility that political projects, such as the first and second republics of Caracas and independent Cartagena, that ended up being ephemeral could have endured as permanent features of the Americas' political map. Finally, without denying the richness of the political debates that characterized the wars of independence throughout Spanish America, centering Caribbean South America makes it impossible to

---

[40] For analyses of political cultures in the Spanish Atlantic during the revolutionary era see Jaime E. Rodriguez O., *"We Are Now the True Spaniards": Sovereignty, Revolution, Independence, and the Emergence of the Federal Republic of Mexico, 1808–1824* (Stanford: Stanford University Press, 2012); Marcela Echeverri, *Indian and Slave Royalists in the Age of Revolution* (New York: Cambridge University Press, 2016); Lasso, *Myths of Harmony*.

bypass the wars' violent and bloody nature. All these aspects that made the independence process in South America's Caribbean coast unique are incomprehensible by looking at this coast from an Andean vantage point. Interpreting the independence era from the *pardo* coast requires understanding that this portion of the South American mainland was not merely adjacent to the Caribbean but was as quintessentially Caribbean as the Caribbean islands themselves.

9

# The Southernmost Revolution: The Río de la Plata in the Early Nineteenth Century

GABRIEL DI MEGLIO

In the first quarter of the nineteenth century, as part of the collapse of the Spanish empire in continental America, the Viceroyalty of the Río de la Plata disappeared, and four new countries emerged in its place. This chapter explains this outcome by integrating into a single narrative a political history that is quite often accounted for separately by each national historiography. The chapter also stresses the revolutionary nature of this process. As in other parts of Spanish America, the creation of new independent states was only one of the novelties of the period, which witnessed major political, economic, and cultural transformations. This was also a social revolution. Although the elites led the process, the decisive involvement of many peasants, rural laborers, artisans, urban plebeians, enslaved people, and members of the Indigenous communities granted them an opportunity to pursue other goals. Even if many of these were not achieved, revolutions should not be analyzed by their results only, but consider the multiple actors and contradictory expectations at play.

The chapter is organized chronologically. After a brief description of the region in late colonial times, I analyze the imperial crisis in the beginning of the nineteenth century, the coming of revolution and the war that ensued, the emergence of rival revolutionary projects, the crooked way into independence, and the fall of the revolutionary regimes.

## A Young Viceroyalty

The Crown created the Viceroyalty of the Río de la Plata in 1776, as part of the broad plan of imperial reforms implemented after the Seven Years' War. The aim was to secure the area and prevent the Portuguese – who had been established on the northern shore of the Río de la Plata until they were ousted that very year – from taking hold of it. Buenos Aires was made capital city. The new jurisdiction had a diverse geography, from the Andean highlands in Upper Peru (present-day Bolivia) to the fertile plains of the Pampas. It was large, but looked even bigger on a map: Theoretically, the viceroyalty included Patagonia, part of the Pampas, and the vast area of the Chaco, all of which were in fact in the hands of many different Indigenous groups who had never been conquered by the Spaniards.[1]

The viceroy and the main imperial bureaucrats were appointed by Spain, and usually assimilated quickly into local elites of merchants, *hacendados* or mine owners. Every town had a city council, a *cabildo*, which was the only authority elected locally and represented these elites. The Church was organized along similar lines: bishops were selected in Spain, while local priests comprised ecclesiastical *cabildos*.[2]

There were two main economic poles. One was the rich mines of Potosí, which demanded cereals, mules, textiles, and other products that were supplied by the surrounding areas. The other pole were the Atlantic ports of Buenos Aires and Montevideo, which only started to grow late in the eighteenth century. Silver from Potosí was by far the main export, distantly followed by hides. The leading import were African slaves, followed by European manufactures.[3] The majority of the viceregal population – more than 1,100,000 people by 1778 – were peasants and wage laborers that lived in rural areas. The only city that was more populated than its outskirts was Buenos Aires – which, numbering over 60,000 inhabitants in 1810, was the

---

[1] For many topics of the chapter there is a vast bibliography, which I do not quote here. I just chose some key books and articles. For the creation of the viceroyalty see Zacarías Moutoukias, "Gobierno y sociedad en el Tucumán y Río de la Plata, 1550–1800," in Enrique Tandeter, ed., *Nueva Historia Argentina* (Buenos Aires: Sudamericana, 2000), vol. II, 355–411.

[2] John Lynch, *Spanish Colonial Administration 1782–1810: The Intendant System in the Viceroyalty of the Río de la Plata* (New York: Greenwood Press, 1969). For the elites in Buenos Aires see Susan Socolow, *The Merchants of Buenos Aires, 1778–1810: Family and Commerce* (Cambridge: Cambridge University Press, 1978), and *The Bureaucrats of Buenos Aires, 1769–1810: Amor al real servicio* (Durham, NC: Duke University Press, 1987). A general summary of the rest of the elites is given in Tulio Halperin Donghi, *Politics, Economics and Society in Argentina in the Revolutionary Period* (New York: Cambridge University Press, 1975).

[3] Jorge Gelman and María Inés Moraes, "Las reformas borbónicas y las economías rioplatenses: Cambio y continuidades," in Jorge Gelman, Enrique Llopis, and Carlos Marichal, eds., *Iberoamérica y España antes de las independencias, 1700–1820: Crecimiento, reformas y crisis* (Mexico City: Instituto de Investigaciones Dr. José María Luis Mora, 2014), 31–74.

second largest in Spanish South America. Trade, artisanry, construction, and food production were the central activities in cities.[4]

The viceroyalty was ethnically and juridically diverse. The Indigenous were the majority in Upper Peru – the most populated region – and Paraguay, but not in the rest of the territory, which was much more heterogeneous. Quechua, Aymara, and Guaraní were massively spoken languages in wide areas. Some regions had a strong presence of people of African origins. The slave trade peaked during the viceregal period: between 1778 and 1812, over 70,000 Africans were legally entered through the Río de la Plata. Those Afro-descendants who were not enslaved were still juridically inferior to the whites due to the prevailing caste system, which discriminated against free Blacks, *pardos* (offspring of whites and Blacks), mestizos (offspring of Indigenous and white people), and *zambos* (offspring of Black and Indigenous people). Even those considered whites were not treated equally: the New World natives – the creoles – had fewer rights than those born in Europe.[5]

Collective identities were thus marked by "color" and place of birth, which separated groups that shared a common Catholic identity. Regardless of the narratives that nationalist historiographies have put forward, national identities cannot be traced back to the colonial period. Before independence, people identified their *patria* (homeland) with the city or town where they were born. On a broader level, people considered themselves *americanos* – that is, not Spaniards – but no intermediate, "protonational" identities existed.[6]

The viceregal years were politically agitated. Except for a brief conflict in 1801, the constant wars with the Portuguese had been left behind, and, after decades of interethnic violence in Chaco and the Pampas, the authorities had managed to make peace with the independent Indigenous on the frontiers.

---

[4] Raúl Fradkin, "Población y sociedad," in Jorge Gelman, ed., *Argentina: Crisis imperial e independencia* (Madrid: Mapfre, 2011), 165–207: 194–5; Raquel Gil Montero, "Population and Economy in Present Day Bolivia – 18th Century," in Guy Brunet, ed., *Mariage et métissage dans les sociétés coloniales* (Bern: Peter Lang, 2015), 188–205. On Buenos Aires, see Lyman Johnson, *Workshop of Revolution: Plebeian Buenos Aires and the Atlantic World, 1776–1810* (Durham, NC: Duke University Press, 2011).

[5] Alex Borucki, *From Shipmates to Soldiers: Emerging Black Identities in the Río de la Plata* (Albuquerque: University of New Mexico Press, 2015). A general view of society is offered by Raúl Fradkin and Juan Carlos Garavaglia, *La Argentina colonial: El Río de la Plata entre los siglos XVI y XIX* (Buenos Aires: Siglo XXI, 2009).

[6] This was a contribution made by José Carlos Chiaramonte. For the four countries see José Carlos Chiaramonte, Carlos Marichal, and Aimer Granados, eds., *Crear la nación: Los nombres de los países de América Latina* (Buenos Aires: Editorial Sudamericana, 2008).

Yet major uprisings took place within the viceroyalty. The most explosive one was the "Great Rebellion" of 1780 in the Andes, started by Tupac Amaru in Cuzco, and followed by revolts in three other hubs in Upper Peru, including a massive and radically antiwhite movement led by Tupac Katari in La Paz. The rebellions, which had echoes in more distant areas, were violently suppressed. More Spanish troops sent to stabilize the region caused resentment among the local population in places from which the repression had been organized, such as the city of La Plata (now Sucre).[7]

Other areas in the viceroyalty were not shaken by big commotions but instead underwent more silent changes. Economic growth caused social tensions in different regions, like the valley around the city of Salta – where big and small mule breeders competed for land – and the Banda Oriental (present-day Uruguay) – where new legal owners claimed land that was occupied by poor peasants with no titles, which led to evictions and discontent. The latter area increasingly attracted Guaraní migrants from the former Jesuit missions, deepening a process of depopulation that had started before the expulsion of the Order in 1767.[8] Meanwhile artisans and laborers in Buenos Aires experienced new forms of collective action by contesting the framework of guilds. African organizations – "nations" and brotherhoods – were also growingly politicized, both in that city and Montevideo. News of the slave revolution in Saint-Domingue instilled fear among the elites, and in 1795 there was a rumor of French neighbors and their slaves planning to take over Buenos Aires. After the discovery of a leaflet which stated "long live freedom," the *cabildo* conducted an investigation against the supposed conspirators.[9]

In addition, the whole population of the viceroyalty was invited to build a new kind of relationship with the Crown after the latter, undergoing a fiscal crisis, asked its subjects to donate money for financing the war against revolutionary France, and after Spain changed sides, against Britain.[10]

---

[7] A very good summary of the Upper Peru uprisings is provided by Sergio Serulnikov, *Revolution in the Andes: The Age of Túpac Amaru* (Durham, NC: Duke University Press, 2013).

[8] Sara Mata, *Tierra y Poder en Salta: El Noroeste Argentino en vísperas de la Independencia* (Seville: Diputación de Sevilla, 2000); José Pedro Barrán and Benjamín Nahum, *Bases económicas de la revolución artiguista* (Montevideo: Ediciones de la Banda Oriental, 2007); Julia Sarreal, *The Guarani and Their Missions: A Socioeconomic History* (Stanford: Stanford University Press, 2014).

[9] Johnson, *Workshop of Revolution*; Borucki, *From Shipmates to Soldiers*.

[10] Viviana L. Grieco, *The Politics of Giving in the Viceroyalty of Rio de la Plata: Donors, Lenders, Subjects, and Citizens* (Albuquerque: University of New Mexico Press, 2014).

Thus, notwithstanding the traditional historiographical image of colonial immobility, the viceregal period was anything but quiet.

## British Invasions and Metropolitan Collapse

After losing the battle of Trafalgar in 1805, Spain lost contact with its colonies, and the imperial crisis that had begun in the 1790s worsened. This situation enabled a British attack on Buenos Aires, which was taken by a small force in 1806 (Figure 9.1). The city was recuperated after a month and prominent neighbors gathered in a *cabildo abierto*, a type of municipal meeting that took place in periods of crisis, while a crowd demonstrated outside. The assembly decided to forbid Viceroy Rafael de Sobremonte, who had escaped when the invaders arrived, to return to the capital. The meeting also appointed an officer who had organized the reconquest of the city, Santiago de Liniers, commander of the military forces. Simultaneously, a voluntary militia was created composed of most adult men from the city and its outskirts, and funded by the local *cabildo*. The following year, a second and much larger British expedition captured Montevideo; this time, a new *cabildo abierto* in Buenos Aires deposed Sobremonte. The invaders attacked Buenos Aires again and were defeated in an urban battle, after which they were compelled to leave the region. In the end, the Spanish monarchy had triumphed. But along with the victory had come important changes: Buenos Aires had removed a colonial authority and created a military force controlled by the city and not the imperial structure.[11]

Therefore, the Río de la Plata was already undergoing turbulent times when news arrived of Bonaparte's occupation of Spain, the captivity of Fernando VII, his replacement by Napoleon's brother Joseph as king, and the broad resistance against him.[12] As elsewhere in the Empire, there was an urgent need to discuss what to do.

Three options were considered. The first was promoted by Fernando's sister, Carlota, who lived in Rio de Janeiro with her husband, the Portuguese prince, Dom João, and wanted to become regent of the viceroyalty. A group

---

[11] Tulio Halperin Donghi, "Revolutionary Militarization in Buenos Aires, 1806–1815," *Past & Present*, 40:1 (1968), 84–107.

[12] Therefore, it is not possible to explain the independence movements by putting an excessive emphasis on the French invasion of 1808, as some authors have done. See mainly François-Xavier Guerra, *Modernidad e Independencias: Ensayos sobre las revoluciones hispánicas* (Mexico City: Fondo de Cultura Económica, 1993).

The Southernmost Revolution

Figure 9.1 The capture from British troops of Buenos Aires by Liniers's army in 1806. Getty Images.

of *porteños* – natives of the port of Buenos Aires – supported her project, but many others feared the Portuguese presence and the plan did not work out.[13]

A second possibility was to follow the lead of cities in Spain, which had organized urban councils (juntas) that ruled in the name of the rightful king. A junta formed in Montevideo in September 1808 decided to break away from Buenos Aires, but remained loyal to the authorities in Spain, who a few months later forced its dissolution. There was a similar attempt in Buenos Aires in January 1809, when a faction based in the *cabildo* accused the new viceroy Liniers – who had been born in France – of colluding with Bonaparte, and tried to replace him with a local junta. But most militia units backed Liniers and kept him in power. That same year, two other juntas were created in La Plata and La Paz in Upper Peru. These were more radical: they decided to become autonomous until the return of Fernando VII to the throne; they stopped obeying the viceroy and managed to get popular support. The colonial authorities violently repressed them with troops sent from Buenos Aires and Lima.[14]

---

[13] Marcela Ternavasio, *Candidata a la corona: La infanta Carlota Joaquina en el laberinto de las revoluciones hispanoamericanas* (Buenos Aires: Siglo XXI, 2015).

[14] Ana Frega, "La junta de Montevideo de 1808," in Manuel Chust, ed., *1808: La eclosión juntera en el mundo hispano* (Mexico City: Fondo de Cultura Económica-Colmex, 2007),

Thus, the third option prevailed: sticking to the status quo, accepting the temporary rule of the Junta Central that had replaced the monarch in Spain, and fighting a war against France. But it was not an easy situation. Liniers was replaced by a new viceroy, Baltasar de Cisneros, who decided to allow free trade with foreign countries as a way of resolving the financial problems.

In the beginning of 1810, almost the entire Iberian Peninsula fell in the hands of the French army. The Junta Central was dissolved. Like in other parts of Spanish America, news of the French victory caused turmoil when it reached Buenos Aires in 1810. A *cabildo abierto* was summoned, in which one group claimed that the viceroy no longer had power now that the metropole had been lost; others argued that Buenos Aires could not make such a decision without consulting the rest of the viceroyalty. Since the former group outvoted the latter, Cisneros was dismissed. He tried to resist and negotiate with the *cabildo*, but on 25 May, a small revolutionary group organized a demonstration. A crowd and some militia units imposed the names for a junta that did not include any colonial bureaucrats.[15]

This junta differed from its recent predecessors in that it was not only seeking autonomy for the city, but also tried to maintain it as capital of a new system. Thus, as its first measure, the junta invited the major cities of the viceroyalty to acknowledge the new government and send their representatives to be part of it. Most cities accepted the new situation, but some did not. Upper Peru remained in the hands of the Spanish authorities, even if the revolution had enthusiasts there. Three other cities opposed Buenos Aires and declared themselves loyal to a new Regency Council formed in Spain: Córdoba, Asunción, and Montevideo. The junta reacted by turning the militia created after the British invasions into a regular army, and sending it on an expedition to Upper Peru. On their way north, the revolutionary troops crashed into loyalist resistance in Córdoba, led by former viceroy Liniers. He was so popular in Buenos Aires that the government feared he could cause trouble by returning to the city, so they executed him. It was a turning point for the revolution.[16]

---

242–68; Johnson, *Workshop of Revolution*; José Luis Roca, *Ni con Lima ni con Buenos Aires: La formación de un Estado nacional en Charcas* (La Paz: Plural Editores-IFEA, 2007); Rossana Barragán, María Luisa Soux, Ana María Seoane, Pilar Mendieta, Ricardo Asebey, and Roger Mamani, *Reescrituras de la Independencia: Actores y territorios en tensión* (La Paz: Plural Editores, 2012).

[15] Noemí Goldman, "Buenos Aires, 1810: La 'revolución' y el dilema de la legitimidad y de las representaciones de la soberanía del pueblo," *Historia y Política* 24 (2010), 47–69.

[16] Halperin Donghi, *Politics, Economics and Society.*

Traditionally, the war that broke out in 1810 has been called the Independence War, yet in this initial phase it was actually a civil war, fought by the local population with local resources. While most Spanish Europeans took the loyalist side, the creoles were divided and many fought to preserve the old system.

## Revolution

The revolutionaries' main objective was self-government. The junta proclaimed that its aim was "to emancipate the colonies from the tyranny of the Mother Country, and to present them as a great and flourishing state for the legitimate representative of the Spanish Monarchy." It added that it had "at this moment no ulterior view of independence, a system which Spanish America would only adopt as an alternative to escape from the greatest of all evils, a return to the ancient order of things."[17] The revolutionaries wanted to end their submission to Spain, keep their own resources and elect their authorities, while remaining within a Spanish monarchy that would have to be transformed into a federal system. The Americas should have the same status as Spain's European territories, and not be colonies any longer. This autonomist project was defended by the moderate branch of the revolutionary leadership, gathered around Cornelio Saavedra, president of the junta.

At the same time there was a radical group, whose leading figure was the secretary of the junta, Mariano Moreno. They criticized social distinctions and many aspects of the colonial regime while pursuing total independence, although they did not speak of it openly. Moreno was the writer of the government's paper and made reading it out loud in church mandatory before the services. He also published a translation of Rousseau's *The Social Contract* for educational use. Moreno opposed the enlargement of the junta, and promoted instead the proposal to convene a congress, which would be able to assume sovereignty. But when the representatives of the other cities arrived in the capital, they agreed with Saavedra's positions and became members of the junta by the end of 1810. This meant Moreno's defeat, and he resigned, dying shortly afterwards.[18]

---

[17] Lord Strangford to the Marquis Wellesley, 20 June 1810, in *Mayo documental*, vol. XII (Buenos Aires: Universidad de Buenos Aires, Facultad de Filosofía y Letras. 1965), 32. On a "federal monarchy," see José María Portillo Valdés, *Crisis Atlántica: Autonomía e independencia en la crisis de la monarquía hispana* (Madrid, Marcial Pons, 2006).

[18] Noemí Goldman, *Mariano Moreno: De reformista a insurgente* (Buenos Aires: Edhasa, 2016).

However, the radicals maintained their opposition to the cautious policy of the junta, and the tension increased. The majority of the military corps in the city supported the moderates, but in order to preserve their legitimacy they preferred not to resort to force to solve the conflict. Therefore, they looked for another way out: street mobilization. On 5 April 1811, a crowd showed up in the major plaza demanding the removal of the radical deputies from the junta. The demonstrators were mostly plebeians and led by some moderate figures with influence in the suburbs. Since their success depended on finding a message capable of stirring plebeians into action, their campaign targeted Spaniards. The main demand of the demonstrators was the eviction of every Spaniard from Buenos Aires. Resentment of them was already extensive, given the better conditions they generally enjoyed when migrating to the city. These included communitarian aid, credit, a better position in the marriage market – marrying a Spaniard was more prestigious for a woman –, and different judicial treatment for the same offense. None of this caused the revolution, but when it started, the old grievances became politicized. The junta had rebelled against "tyranny" and colonial authorities. But the campaign stressed something new: Each and every Spaniard became an enemy. After the demonstration a Court of "Public Security" was established, and many Europeans were denounced. Besides, the demonstrators presented themselves as "the People of Buenos Aires." Distinguished inhabitants and not suburban plebeians had formed the "people" in the colonial period, but the concept had by now widened to include every man (and no women, although they were going to participate actively in the new political life, too).[19]

Factional struggle marked by plebeian mobilization became a steady feature of Buenos Aires' politics since then. Five months later, in September 1811, news of a military defeat of the revolutionary army in Upper Peru provoked a new movement that dissolved the junta and replaced it with a Triumvirate. It was the triumph of a new and different moderate faction, integrated only by *porteños*. The jurisdiction governed by the Triumvirate was smaller than the former viceroyalty as a result of war. The campaign of the revolutionary army was initially effective; it occupied all of Upper Peru by the end of 1810. Some Indigenous communities and the city of Cochabamba had risen against the colonial authorities before the expedition arrived. The colonial bureaucrats who had been responsible for

---

[19] Gabriel Di Meglio, *¡Viva el bajo pueblo! La plebe urbana de Buenos Aires y la política entre la Revolución de Mayo y el rosismo* (Buenos Aires: Prometeo Libros, 2006).

the repression of the juntas of La Paz and La Plata the previous year were executed. The political leader of the expedition was one of the radical *porteños*, Juan José Castelli, who tried to get the support of the Indigenous people. On the first anniversary of the revolution, 25 May 1811, some of the communities were summoned to the ancient ruins of Tiahuanaco, where Castelli proclaimed that "Indians are and should be considered for all positions, jobs, destiny, honors and distinctions with the same chance as the other national inhabitants, given the equal rights of citizens, with no other difference than that provided by merit and aptitude." He also declared ethnic chiefs could not be elected without the consent of their communities, a cause that had often driven them into action since the eighteenth century.[20]

The position of the revolutionaries seemed strong, but they were defeated by an army coming from Peru in June 1811, and the junta of Buenos Aires lost Upper Peru all of a sudden. Nevertheless, many Indigenous groups pursued the fight against the loyalist forces after what was left of the revolutionary army had abandoned the area. They even laid siege to loyalist La Paz, until they were defeated by the Peruvian army. The latter force was also partly comprised of Indigenous troops, and one of their commanders was chief Mateo Pumacahua, who had defeated Tupac Amaru thirty years before. After the victory, the Viceroyalty of Peru gained control of all of Upper Peru.[21]

The junta also failed to subordinate Asunción, which was aligned with the Regency Council. The Paraguayans, who refused to follow the *porteños*, defeated the junta's expedition in March 1811. However, the triumphant officers and part of the local elite decided to follow a similar path as Buenos Aires, ridding themselves in April of the Spanish governor and forming their own junta, which became autonomous from both Spain and Buenos Aires.

At the same time, a third front was opened in the Banda Oriental. In February 1811, a rural insurrection in favor of the junta of Buenos Aires challenged the control of the area by the loyalists of Montevideo – which had become the new viceregal capital. A local leader, José Gervasio Artigas, guided the insurgents to a victorious battle against Montevideo's troops

---

[20] Fabio Wasserman, *Juan José Castelli: De súbdito de la Corona a líder revolucionario* (Buenos Aires: Edhasa, 2011). The speech can be found in Noemí Goldman, *Historia y lenguaje. Los discursos de la Revolución de Mayo* (Buenos Aires: Centro Editor de América Latina, 1992), 128. The translation is mine, as are all other translations in this chapter.

[21] Alejandro Rabinovich, *Anatomía del pánico: La batalla de Huaqui o la derrota de la revolución* (Buenos Aires: Sudamericana, 2017); María Luisa Soux, "Rebelión, guerrilla y tributo: Los indios en Charcas durante el proceso de independencia," *Anuario de Estudios Americanos* 68:2 (2011), 455–82.

and laid siege to the walled city with support from Buenos Aires. Under the pretext of preserving the Spanish dominions for Fernando VII, the Portuguese seized the opportunity to send an army to the Banda Oriental. The proximity of the traditional enemy frightened both Buenos Aires and Montevideo, leading to an armistice in October, by which the former withdrew its troops and the latter its naval squadron, which was blockading the rivers. Artigas' forces were not consulted, and the new agreement left them under the rule of Montevideo. The Artiguists refused to accept that and organized a massive migration toward the insurgent territories of Entre Ríos and Corrientes, where Artigas would see his influence increase. The Portuguese offensive was finally stopped by a British diplomatic intervention in the name of the alliance against Bonaparte in which all three European powers took part.[22]

Meanwhile, in Buenos Aires, the Triumvirate remained moderate. For instance, when General Manuel Belgrano created an ensign for his revolutionary units in February 1812 – which is nowadays the Argentine flag – the government forbade him to use it, to avoid any suspicion of independentist aspirations. However, some important changes were introduced, like the abolition of the Indigenous tribute and the prohibition of the slave trade – any new slave who landed in what were now called United Provinces of the Río de la Plata would be freed. After this decision was made, the African population showed a stronger support for the revolution. This became clear when a slave named Ventura denounced a Spanish conspiracy against the Triumvirate in June 1812. As a result of this denunciation, the accused were imprisoned and executed in the central plaza. The executions, which took place every day throughout a month, were watched and celebrated by big crowds. In order to stop the public agitation in the city and restore order, the authorities had to ordain the eviction of hundreds of Spaniards. The unrest in Buenos Aires was connected to the fear created by an offensive of the counterrevolutionary army from Upper Peru. But in September 1812 the loyalists were defeated by Belgrano's troops in a crucial battle at Tucumán.[23]

Some important changes had taken place by then. One was the consolidation of an elite fully dedicated to politics. A good example among many

---

[22] About migration, see Inés Cuadro, "La migración o Redota en la revolución de independencia," in Ana Frega and José López Mazz, eds., *Los caminos de la Redota: Enfoque histórico arqueológico y georreferenciación* (Montevideo: Universidad de la República, 2013), 21–38.

[23] Mariana Pérez, "¡Viva España y mueran los patricios! La conspiración de Álzaga de 1812," *Americanía: Revista de Estudios Latinoamericanos*, (2015), 21–55.

others is Belgrano. The son of a wealthy merchant, he was a respected "enlightened" lawyer who in the previous decade had proposed economic and educational reforms. In 1810 he became a revolutionary and was a member of the junta. Soon after, he was designated general – although he lacked professional military training – and later, he would be a diplomat. This kind of trajectory was shared by Catholic priests, who also played a crucial role by using passages of the Bible, like the struggle against the Pharaoh, to justify the revolutionary project, or putting representations of the Virgin at the head of the armies.[24]

Another novelty was the free discussion of public affairs by women, who thereby rejected the subordinate role they had been assigned. An anonymous *porteño* showed his concern in a leaflet: "It is almost outrageous how freely a considerable number of young Patrician ladies express themselves regarding political affairs." The author suggested they should be punished.[25] A third change was the leveling effect brought by popular mobilization. For many members of the popular classes, men and women alike, being on the revolutionary side signified a symbolic social promotion. And enslaved people started to talk openly about the end of slavery. Politics subsumed social and racial tensions.[26]

## Rival Projects

The autonomist project was weakened by the revolutionaries' refusal to take part in the constitutional monarchy promoted by the Cortes of Cádiz. Although these territories kept their alleged loyalty to the imprisoned king, discussions around independence started in 1812. The radicals that had followed Moreno, now reorganized in the "Patriotic Society," promoted a declaration of independence. They were joined by a group of military officers, including Carlos de Alvear and José de San Martín (both originally from the area of the former Jesuit missions), who had fought against

---

[24] See Halperin Donghi, *Politics, Economics and Society*; Roberto Di Stefano, *El púlpito y la plaza: Clero, sociedad y política de la monarquía católica a la república rosista* (Buenos Aires: Siglo XXI, 2004); Pablo Ortemberg, "Las Vírgenes Generalas: Acción guerrera y práctica religiosa en las campañas del Alto Perú y el Río de la Plata (1810–1818)," *Boletín del Instituto de Historia Argentina y Americana "Dr. Emilio Ravignani,"* third series, no. 35–6 (2012), 11–41.

[25] Anonymous, "Memoria sobre la necesidad de contener la demasiada y perjudicial licencia de las mujeres en el hablar," 1813, John Carter Brown Library, Providence, RI, 68-334-181.

[26] Di Meglio, *¡Viva el bajo pueblo!*

Bonaparte as part of the Spanish army and had later left it to serve the revolution in their homeland. The two groups merged into a new one – the Masonic-styled, secret *Lautaro* Lodge. The Lodge had a clear set of goals: the declaration of independence, the establishment of a republican system, and winning the war. In October 1812 they seized power by mobilizing troops and some plebeian support. A new Triumvirate was formed. Its first measures were to launch a new campaign against Montevideo, which was put under siege, and to ask the cities to send deputies for a constituent assembly.[27]

Most of them accepted. There were even a couple of deputies from Upper Peruvian provinces, which were under loyalist rule. The only refusal came from Paraguay, which summoned a giant provincial congress of 1,000 deputies sent from many towns and villages to Asunción. They declined the invitation to participate in the assembly in Buenos Aires, and proclaimed Paraguay a republic, without declaring its formal independence.[28]

The Assembly, which began its meetings in Buenos Aires in January 1813, abolished the Inquisition and titles of nobility, adopted Belgrano's flag, coined a currency, forbade the personal service by Indians, and passed a Free Womb Act which would start a gradual abolition of slavery.

For the anniversary of the Revolution – which had become a crucial public celebration – the deputies and many others enthusiastically wore the Phrygian cap, a clear homage to the French Revolution – the very use of the term *assembly* instead of *congress* evidenced the weight of the French tradition at that point. The elites were not the only ones to reference the French tradition: In a failed mobilization organized by enemies of the Lodge in Buenos Aires, some plebeians asked for those who were not patriots to be "guillotined."[29]

Other references to the Age of Revolutions are also found around that time. For example, the Lodge's newspaper proclaimed the people's right to "radically alter forms of government that were contrary to their interests,"

---

[27] Pilar González Bernaldo, "La Revolución Francesa y la emergencia de nuevas prácticas de la política: La irrupción de la sociabilidad en el Río de la Plata revolucionario, 1810–1815," *Boletín del Instituto de Historia Argentina y Americana "Dr. Emilio Ravignani,"* third series, no. 3 (1991), 7–27.

[28] Herib Caballero, "Los congresos de 1811 y 1813: Representación política y ciudadanía," in Ignacio Telesca, Liliana Brezzo, and Herib Caballero, eds., *Paraguay 1813: La proclamación de la república* (Asunción: Taurus, 2013), 117–33.

[29] Archivo General de la Nación (Argentina), sala X, 29-9-8, Sumarios Militares, 83a, January 1813. The cap is mentioned in the diary of Juan Manuel Beruti, published as *Memorias Curiosas* (Buenos Aires: Emecé, 2001), 232–3.

and opposed "government for kings," following the arguments of the "wise Thomas Paine."[30] Meanwhile, in the city of Mendoza, one of the accused instigators of a slave conspiracy was denounced for saying that the enslaved should do as in Saint-Domingue and kill all whites. In addition, the first cannon cast in Buenos Aires was baptized Tupac Amaru, who was considered a forerunner in the war against Spain. When the constitutional debates began in the Assembly, the models discussed were the British "Bill of Rights" (1689), as well as the constitutions of the United States (1781 and 1787), France (various ones from the 1790s), Venezuela (1811), and Cádiz (1812).[31]

The initial optimism quickly vanished when a new conflict arose around the issue of centralism. Since 1810, every revolutionary government had kept the colonial centralized system. Buenos Aires appointed all local authorities and controlled the direction of the economy. The Assembly of 1813 gathered deputies from the different provinces – that is, the main cities and the rural areas around them, which were becoming crucial political spaces. Yet once the deputies took up their posts, they did not have to consult the provinces that had elected them to make decisions. In fact, the Lodge led the Assembly into an extremely centralist direction. In order to strengthen the central government, the Triumvirate was replaced by a Supreme Director.[32]

Nevertheless, resistance against centralism was growing, especially among the followers of Artigas. The Banda Oriental gave its deputies clear instructions, including the transformation of the union into a federation with its capital located outside Buenos Aires. This was unacceptable for the Lodge. The Assembly rejected the Oriental deputies under the pretext of a contested election. In response, the Artiguists ended their obedience to Buenos Aires (and left the Siege of Montevideo). Soon, other provinces followed Artigas, and in 1814 the Banda Oriental, Corrientes, the former Jesuit missions, and Entre Ríos formed a confederation of provinces, later joined by Santa Fe.

---

[30] *El Grito del Sud*, no. 26, Buenos Aires, 5 January 1813, 202–3.

[31] Beatriz Bragoni, "Esclavos, libertos y soldados: La cultura política plebeya en Cuyo durante la Revolución," in Raúl Fradkin, *¿Y el pueblo dónde está? Contribuciones para una historia popular de la revolución de independencia en el Río de la Plata* (Buenos Aires: Prometeo Libros, 2008), 107–50; Noemí Goldman, "Formas de gobierno y opinión pública, o la disputa por la acepción de las palabras, 1810–1827," in Hilda Sabato and Alberto Lettieri, eds., *La vida política en la argentina del siglo XIX: Armas, votos y voces* (Buenos Aires: Fondo de Cultura Económica, 2003), 45–56; Marcela Ternavasio, *Gobernar la revolución: Poderes en disputa en el Río de la Plata, 1810–1816* (Buenos Aires, Siglo XIX, 2007).

[32] José Carlos Chiaramonte, "El federalismo argentino en la primera mitad del siglo XIX," in Marcello Carmagnani, ed., *Federalismos latinoamericanos: México, Brasil, Argentina* (Mexico City: Fondo de Cultura Económica, 1993), 81–132.

Buenos Aires used military force to put an end to the confederation, but it was defeated. The revolutionaries thus split in two rival blocks: the confederation, under the "protection" of Artigas, and the United Provinces, ruled from Buenos Aires.

Artiguists were political radicals. They proclaimed the right of every village or small town to be sovereign and elect its own authorities. They also tried to introduce some social transformations. Many of Artigas' followers were peasants and laborers that came from areas that had witnessed intense social tensions during the viceregal period, particularly the Banda Oriental. They showed "a frenetic enthusiasm for freedom" and a remarkable animosity against Spaniards. At the same time, they struggled for land and access to natural resources, such as grass and water, which had been customary before landowners had started to evict people from their properties. In 1815, Artigas organized an agrarian reform in the Banda Oriental, distributing the large properties seized from the enemies of revolution among "the unhappiest ones," defined as "free blacks, *zambos* of this class, Indians, and poor creoles."[33] Numerous members of the elites felt menaced by this movement. One of them wrote: "The dogma of equality stirs up the crowd against any government, and has established a war between the poor and the rich, master and lord; who commands and who obeys. This is now a country bordering on Anarchy."[34]

Another Artiguist hub was the area around the Guaraní villages of the extinguished Jesuit jurisdiction. There, an Indigenous chief rebelled against the authorities appointed by Buenos Aires in 1813 and proclaimed: "Brothers, we know God endowed us with freedom when he created us, and we know we are equal before Him and before the Law." Such a declaration of equality by an Indian constituted an attack on the entire colonial system, which had relied on judicial inequality from the start. Many villages in this area began to demand Indigenous self-government and the reunification of the Jesuit Province – but without the Jesuits or the *porteños*, Paraguayans, and Portuguese. Their leader was Artigas' godson, Andresito Guacurarí.[35]

---

[33] Ana Frega, "El Reglamento de Tierras de 1815: Justicia revolucionaria y virtud republicana," in Gerardo Caetano and Ana Ribeiro, eds., *Tierras, reglamento y revolución: Reflexiones a doscientos años del reglamento artiguista de 1815* (Montevideo: Planeta, 2015), 487–533: 487.

[34] Nicolás Herrera to the Portuguese Minister of State, 19 July 1815, in *Archivo Artigas*, vol. xxx (Montevideo: Comisión Nacional Archivo Artigas, 1998), 10.

[35] Raúl Fradkin, "Los grupos sociales subalternos y la revolución en el litoral rioplatense," in Sara Ortelli, ed., *Las independencias desde abajo: Historias de subalternos, excluidos y olvidados en América a principios del siglo XIX* (Mexico City: Universidad Autónoma

The *Lautaro* Lodge had to deal not only with the rise of this rival block, but also with a sudden change of the situation in Europe after Bonaparte was defeated and the French empire collapsed. In this new context, the independentists decided to slow down and wait. By 1814, Fernando VII was king again. The Lodge sent diplomats for negotiations, presenting him with two options: the recognition of independence or autonomy. The monarch, who had abolished the Cádiz Constitution and wanted to rebuild the old system, naturally refused. Instead, he began organizing a powerful army to recover the Río de la Plata. Yet once this force left Spain in 1815, it changed its target and stormed Venezuela and New Granada. The reason for this strategic decision of the Spanish army was the capture by the Lodge of the loyalist base in the Río de la Plata, Montevideo, in June 1814 (although the *porteños* could not hold the city for long, and it was soon occupied by the Artiguists). It was one of the Lodge's few achievements.

Meanwhile, on the other front, Belgrano's army had managed to enter Upper Peru, but suffered a serious defeat in November 1813, and as a result the loyalists recovered the whole area. They then entered the revolutionary territories and captured Salta once again. However, they lacked local support, and their confiscation of livestock in the surrounding areas triggered a rural uprising that forced them to retreat to Upper Peru in August 1814.

Seizing cattle was not unusual at a time when the economy was seriously affected by the years of military conflict. Many resources had been consumed and trade routes had become obsolete; the governments could not afford the maintenance of the armies; and salaries were always delayed. Thus, armies, as well as militias and guerrillas, used exactions, cattle raiding, looting, and robbery, making war more violent and afflicting the civilian population. In several regions, the number of cattle decreased considerably.[36] Silver production also collapsed, mainly because some Indigenous communities which for centuries had been forced to provide labor for the mines – a tribute called *mita* – stopped sending their members once the revolution began. Others continued to do so, but many workers deserted.[37]

---

Metropolitana, 2020). See also Guillermo Wilde, *Religión y poder en las misiones de guaraníes* (Buenos Aires: SB, 2009); Jorge Machón and Oscar Cantero, *Andresito Artigas: El líder guaraní-misionero del artiguismo* (Montevideo: Tierradentro Ediciones, 2013).

[36] Raúl Fradkin, "Las formas de hacer la guerra en el litoral rioplatense," in Susana Bandieri, ed., *La historia económica y los procesos de independencia en la América hispana* (Buenos Aires: Prometeo, 2010), 167–213.

[37] Enrique Tandeter, *Coacción y mercado: La minería de la plata en el Potosí colonial, 1692–1826* (Buenos Aires: Sudamericana, 1992).

The military draft also gave the population reasons for discontent. The armies were formed by three types of combatants. First there were the volunteers, who found a steady job as soldiers. Then there were slaves requisitioned from the Spaniards or bought by the state from their owners; once in the army they became *libertos*, and this promise of freedom at the end of service made many slaves press their masters to allow them to join the ranks. Third, there were forced recruits, often poor men without protection. The Lodge was responsible for several levies and for exerting a strong pressure on the population, especially in Buenos Aires.[38]

Anger with the government increased all around. In the beginning of 1815, some provinces elected their own authorities without consulting the capital. Finally, a military revolt followed by street turmoil in Buenos Aires forced Supreme Director Alvear to resign in April. The Assembly was also dissolved. The project started in 1810 was now in critical condition.

By 1815, the combined effort of local loyalist forces and troops sent from Spain had recovered most insurgent territories in Spanish America. Only the Río de la Plata remained revolutionary, although divided into three parts: the United Provinces, the Artiguist Confederation, and Paraguay, where in 1814 a congress concentrated power in a Supreme Dictator, José Rodríguez de Francia, who continued an isolationist policy and opposed any cooperation with Buenos Aires or Artigas. If we add the defenders of the old system in Upper Peru, we can see that years of war had led to a division of the former viceroyalty into four jurisdictions.

## From Independence to Crisis

The crisis that began in 1815 would be a long one. After Alvear's fall, the new central government, fearing the Spanish expedition that was eventually detoured to Venezuela, tried to approach the Artiguists. But negotiations failed and no union was achieved. In Buenos Aires, turmoil persisted. In the following months, there were many *cabildos abiertos* – which were no longer by invitation, but open to any man who attended–, one failed attempt to transform Buenos Aires into a federal province, and three different Supreme Directors.[39]

---

[38] Peter Blanchard, *Under the Flags of Freedom: Slave Soldiers and the Wars of Independence in Spanish South America* (Pittsburgh: University of Pittsburgh Press, 2008); Fradkin, "Las formas de hacer la guerra"; Di Meglio, *¡Viva el bajo pueblo!*

[39] Fabián Herrero, *Federalistas de Buenos Aires 1810–1820* (Remedios de Escalada: Ediciones de la UNLa, 2009).

The provinces also witnessed increased unrest. Córdoba joined the Artiguist Confederation for a while in 1815, but soon exited.[40] Simultaneously, Salta, which had become the shifting border separating the revolutionaries from the loyalists, was the stage for another episode of popular radicalization. Led by Martín Miguel de Güemes, a member of the local elite, peasants, laborers, and deserters from the army formed guerrilla groups to fight the loyalists. Pressured by his men, Güemes gave them the possibility of being judged only by their officers for any offense they committed, such as taking cattle from big ranches. He also exempted them from paying rent to landowners for as long as they served. Their radicalization also had a racial side, some of them shouting against those who were "whitefaced." A few members of the elites feared the emergence of a new Artigas, but although Güemes became a powerful figure and was chosen governor of his province, he did not break off relations with the central administration.[41]

Revolutionary guerrillas were also active in Upper Peru. In November 1815, the United Provinces' army tried to occupy the area for the third time. But once again, as in 1811 and 1813, it was completely crushed. After the army's remnants retreated, eight local guerrilla groups continued the struggle. Their leaders included officers from the defeated army, a priest, an Indigenous chief, a former marquis turned insurgent, local creoles, and a mestizo "Amazon" woman called Juana Azurduy. Meanwhile, the loyalist commanders decided that before advancing into revolutionary territory they needed to secure Upper Peru. Therefore, during 1816 they focused on fighting the guerrillas, which despite fierce resistance were mostly suppressed. Upper Peru was thus consolidated as a loyalist stronghold.[42]

A few revolutionaries moved south to take part in a new congress summoned by the United Provinces, which opened its sessions in Tucumán in March 1816. The interior city was selected because some of the provinces refused to meet in Buenos Aires. Both the Artiguist provinces and Paraguay

---

[40] Geneviève Verdo, "En vísperas del congreso. La construcción de una identidad política en las Provincias Unidas del Río de la Plata en los años 1815 y 1816," *Anuario del IEHS*, no. 21 (2006), 37–52.

[41] Sara Mata, *Los gauchos de Güemes: Guerras de independencia y conflicto social* (Buenos Aires: Sudamericana, 2012); Gustavo Paz, "'El orden es el desorden.' Guerra y movilización campesina en la campaña de Jujuy, 1815–1821," in Raúl Fradkin and Jorge Gelman, eds., *Desafíos al orden: Política y sociedades rurales durante la Revolución de Independencia* (Rosario: Prohistoria, 2008), 83–101.

[42] Marie Danielle Demélas, *Nacimiento de la guerra de guerrilla: El diario de José Santos Vargas (1814–1825)* (Lima: IFEA-Plural, 2007); María Luisa Soux, "Rebelión, guerrilla y tributo: Los indios en Charcas durante el proceso de independencia," *Anuario de Estudios Americanos* 68:2 (2011), 455–82.

were invited but declined to attend. The new congress achieved three things. First, it smoothed the tension between the provinces and Buenos Aires, thereby enabling the election of a new Supreme Director respected by all, the *porteño* Juan Martín de Pueyrredón, in a unanimous vote. Secondly, it declared independence on 9 July 1816. Most deputies were politically moderate, and yet they took the step that previous radicals had not taken, arguing that this was the only possible option. The vagueness of the name chosen for the new state, the "United Provinces in South America," shows there was not a clear definition of the territories that would be included in the future.

The third achievement was a reorientation in the war strategy through the adoption of general San Martín's plan. San Martín – who had been a member of the Lodge but had broken with Alvear before his fall – was in Mendoza as governor, and his proposal was to attack Chile from there, defeat the loyalists, and continue to Peru, the king's power base in South America. Pueyrredón and many congressmen accepted the plan. They canceled the preparations for a new offensive to Upper Peru, forced the wealthy to provide loans, "rescued" many slaves for the army – 1,500 of 5,200 soldiers were African *libertos* – and included most of their resources in San Martín's campaign. In a complicated operation, this army was able to cross the Andes, defeat the loyalists, and enter Santiago in February 1817. One year later, its decisive victory over a loyalist counteroffensive in the Battle of Maipú opened access to Peru.[43]

Yet back in the United Provinces the situation was again difficult. The Congress had decreed "the end of Revolution and the start of Order," condemning any act of disobedience as a serious offense. In addition, the election of Pueyrredón, who would act as Supreme Director until 1819, meant the return of Buenos Aires to prominence and a reinforced centralism, buttressed by the move of Congress to the capital in 1817. This led to uprisings in some provinces. Belgrano's army, which abandoned the War of Independence for a new role as an internal police force on behalf of the central government, was in charge of repressing the upheaval. Meanwhile, the defense of the northern borders was left to Güemes' guerrillas, who proved their efficiency against a new loyalist offensive from Upper Peru in 1817.

Simultaneously, the Portuguese army attacked the Banda Oriental and the Missions. It soon managed to take Montevideo, where part of the elite

---

[43] Patricia Pasquali, *San Martín: La fuerza de la misión y la soledad de la gloria* (Buenos Aires: Emecé, 2004); Juan Luis Ossa, *Armies, Politics and Revolution: Chile, 1808–1826* (Liverpool: Liverpool University Press, 2014).

preferred the invaders to the social instability they identified with Artiguism. Pueyrredón offered to help if Artigas recognized his leadership, but there was no agreement. Artiguists kept resisting on their own in the rural areas. Later, Pueyrredón took advantage of the invasion: Leaving the Banda Oriental to the Portuguese, he attempted to recover the provinces of Entre Ríos and Santa Fe for the United Provinces, but all his attempts failed. Pueyrredón ordered San Martín to return and fight the Artiguists, but the general disobeyed and stayed in Chile organizing the expedition to Peru. By then, Buenos Aires' resources did not suffice for a new powerful force, and its authority over the United Provinces weakened. In the capital, Pueyrredón's administration had become authoritarian, sending many opponents into exile.[44]

Another unresolved issue after the declaration of independence was the adoption of a system of government. Although revolutionaries were republicans, some hesitated or changed their minds after the triumphant European monarchies condemned any government created by a revolution at the Congress of Vienna of 1815. Some argued for a constitutional king, hoping that monarchical legitimacy would put an end to local turbulences and guarantee order. In a secret session of the Congress of Tucumán, Belgrano had suggested to crown a descendant of the Incas, who would reign from Cuzco once the war was over. The project had a practical goal: to gain Indigenous support for the independence cause. It also showed an ideological shift of part of the elite, generated by the ongoing war with Spain. Many said they descended both from Spanish conquistadors and Indians, but they should emphasize the latter: "Our natural, essential and true law is that of our Indian ancestry." But republicans refused and attacked those willing to "establish a despot, who would tyrannize our rights and our freedom."[45] The question remained open for years. Monarchists abandoned the Inca plan but made some secret inquiries to find a European candidate. In 1819, the Congress sanctioned a constitution that established a centralist system which could be either monarchical or republican. But the central government was falling apart, and the constitution was never ratified.[46]

---

[44] Halperin Donghi, *Politics, Economics and Society*; Alejandro Morea, "El Ejército Auxiliar del Perú y la gobernabilidad del interior, 1816–1820," *Prohistoria* 18 (2012), 26–49.
[45] Respectively, *El Censor* no. 56, 19 September 1816, in *Biblioteca de Mayo* (Buenos Aires: Senado de la Nación, 1960), vol. VIII, 6872; *La Crónica Argentina* no. 19, 30 September 1816 in ibid., vol. VII, 6318.
[46] Rubén Darío Salas, *Lenguaje, Estado y poder en el Río de la Plata (1816–1827)* (Buenos Aires: Instituto de Investigaciones de Historia del Derecho, 1998).

## Many Endings

In January 1820, the troops that Fernando VII assembled to recover the Río de Plata mutinied just before going on board and started a liberal rebellion in Spain. By the time this good news arrived in revolutionary territory, both the United Provinces and the Artiguist Confederation had suddenly disappeared. Both blocks fell at the same time. That very January, Artigas suffered his last defeat to the Portuguese troops and was forced to abandon the Banda Oriental, while a couple of weeks later, the united forces of the Artiguist provinces Santa Fe and Entre Ríos decided to confront the central government. By entering Buenos Aires and forcing the Supreme Director and the Congress to resign, they put an end to the United Provinces. Then Entre Ríos' army turned against the "Protector" Artigas. After this final defeat, Artigas went into exile in Paraguay. This was the end of the Confederation.

Some months later, San Martín's army arrived in Peru and the last phase of the Independence War began. Yet the state that had sent him no longer existed. Only autonomous provinces remained, without any legal links to each other or authorities over them. The Banda Oriental was incorporated into the Portuguese monarchy and would later become a province of the new Brazilian empire.

Only Paraguay escaped the crisis of 1820. After discovering and disarming a conspiracy against him, Supreme Dictator Francia managed to maintain a strict centralist system and internal peace, keep external contacts to a minimum, and prevent the emergence of political factions. He also granted the state a strong role in the economy by accumulating public land – which was rented out to peasants at low prices – and protecting artisans. Francia remained in power until his death in 1840.[47]

While most territories stopped fighting the loyalists, guerrilla warfare continued on the Salta–Upper Peru border. Skirmishes persisted even after Güemes was killed in a loyalist incursion. The war was concluded by an offensive from the Colombian and Peruvian army coming from the north, led by generals Simón Bolívar and Antonio José de Sucre. Their victory was facilitated by a military conflict among loyalists, as General Pedro Olañeta had opposed the policies of the viceroy of Peru. After the victory of the independentists at Ayacucho in December 1824, Bolívar's troops entered

---

[47] Ignacio Telesca, "Tierra, nación y construcción del Estado en el Paraguay del siglo XIX," *História: Debates e Tendencias* 15:2 (2015), 321–34; John Hoyt Williams, *The Rise and Fall of the Paraguayan Republic, 1800–1870* (Austin: Institute of Latin American Studies, The University of Texas at Austin, 1979).

Upper Peru. The provinces in the region sent deputies to an assembly which refused to join Peru or the Río de la Plata. On 6 August 1825, the assembly declared the independence of a new republic, which would be named after the Liberator. And thus Bolivia was created, with the Venezuelan Sucre as its first president. The constitution, written by Bolívar, established a centralist system and a president for life.[48]

The Independence War was over, but an extension of this conflict was about to start. In 1824 the one-time United Provinces, including the former Artiguists, agreed to reunite in a congress in Buenos Aires. Their aim was to be recognized by Britain as an independent state and to sanction a constitution. By then, establishing a monarchy was no longer considered a possibility. It was at this congress that the name Argentine Republic was used for the first time. The meeting sparked a rebellion in the Banda Oriental. The combatants, who wanted to be incorporated in the United Provinces, successfully attacked Brazilian forces. When the Congress accepted the incorporation of the Banda Oriental, Brazil declared war. The imperial fleet blockaded the port of Buenos Aires, which was essential for the economy. Although the republican army – as it was baptized in opposition to the Brazilian monarchy – won many battles, it could not finish the war. In order to break this tie, Britain proposed the creation of an independent state in 1828, and a new country, later called Uruguay, was born.

In a separate conflict, Federalists and Centralists – now called Unitarians because of their conception of a unique national sovereignty – continued to battle inside the Argentine Republic. The combination of internal and external conflicts led to the collapse of the congress in 1827. Once again, only autonomous provinces remained, with nothing above them. A civil war ensued, and a Federalist triumph in 1831 led to the creation of a confederation with no unified constitution or central state, which would last for two decades.

## Aftermath

Years of revolution and war completely transformed the former viceroyalty. The most obvious change was the emergence of four new countries. From the beginning, all of the new states adopted a republican system. Even if they did not have a central state, the provinces that slowly started to be identified

---

[48] Roca, *Ni con Lima ni con Buenos Aires.*

as Argentina also became republican, and many sanctioned constitutions. The colonial *cabildos* were replaced by legislatures, whose members were elected by popular vote and which included deputies from the rural areas that had lacked representation in colonial times. In many provinces, all adult free men were given the right to vote. Suffrage was more restricted in the first Bolivian and Uruguayan constitutions, which excluded from active citizenship all men who depended on others.[49] The 1820s were a decade of republican celebration. A newspaper in Buenos Aires captured the mood by portraying the conservative Europe of the Holy Alliance as a symbol of barbarism, whereas the independent Americas were praised for their "civilized" republicanism.[50]

The elites tried to recreate a political and social order to replace the colonial one. It was not an easy task, given the politicization brought about by revolution. Factional struggle among the elites would favor the continuous presence of the popular classes in the political arena. Successful popular leaders, who could represent some of the lower-class interests, became crucial in the following decades. Some of them were labeled caudillos, although this is such a loaded term that perhaps it is better not to use it anymore.

The economy had declined significantly in most of the region in the first years of independence, given the general destruction of wealth and the collapse of economic ties to Potosí. The livestock of the big leather producers in colonial times – the Banda Oriental, Entre Ríos, and Santa Fe – was seriously diminished by the wars. But Buenos Aires was less affected by military destruction and increased its exportation of hides and, to a lesser extent, salted meat. With a new free trade system, local merchants suffered the competition of the British, who took over the transatlantic networks. Therefore, many merchants invested their capital in the countryside and received public land concessions from the provincial state. The outcome was the rise of a powerful landowner class in Buenos Aires, which thanks to commerce would be, by far, the richest Argentine province.[51]

---

[49] Marcela Ternavasio, *La revolución del voto: Política y elecciones en Buenos Aires, 1810–1852* (Buenos Aires: Siglo XXI, 2001); Ana Frega, "La vida política," in Ana Frega, ed., *Uruguay: Revolución, independencia y construcción del Estado, 1808–1880* (Montevideo: Planeta-Mapfre, 2016), 31–85; Rossana Barragán, Ana María Lema, and Pilar Mendieta, eds., *Bolivia, su historia: Los primeros cien años de la República, 1825–1925* (La Paz: Coordinadora de Historia, 2015).

[50] *El Argentino*, Buenos Aires, 14 May 1825.

[51] Jorge Gelman, "La Gran Divergencia. Las economías regionales en Argentina después de la Independencia," in Susana Bandieri, ed., *La historia económica y los procesos de independencia en la América hispana* (Buenos Aires: Prometeo, 2010), 105–29.

The collapse of the caste system was another crucial change, at least in Argentina and Uruguay. Juridical inequality was over after the revolutionary years. Racism would continue and skin "color" would still be important in daily life, but racial difference was no longer based on the law. That change had an impact on the Indigenous communities. In the Argentine provinces, the end of tribute and juridical inequality meant that those villages no longer had rights to their common land, which they had used to pay the tribute, nor to maintain their ethnic leaders, who were in charge of the tribute. Thus, many villages lost their lands, which were sold out. On the other hand, Bolivia reestablished tribute after its independence, since it was the only tax that could sustain the fragile new state. Many communities promoted that solution, which allowed them to maintain common lands and ethnic authorities. Indigenous communities remained in Paraguay, too.[52]

Among enslaved people, the prohibition of traffic in 1812 and the Free Womb Act of 1813 had created expectations of abolition. Many used the new legislation to attain their freedom. Others showed a remarkable interest in entering the army, which was impossible for women. In the 1820s, strong African organizations were created in Buenos Aires and Montevideo, which raised funds for buying others' freedom. But despite all the pressure, a weakened slavery continued, and it was not abolished until 1842–1846 in Uruguay, 1851 in Bolivia, 1853 in Argentina, and 1869 in Paraguay.[53]

Having kept their language, religion, and independence for centuries and controlling vast areas in present-day Argentina, Paraguay, and Bolivia, the Indigenous groups that had never been conquered by the Spaniards also suffered the effects of the revolutionary years. The pacts made by different groups with the colonial authorities to stop the frontier violence in the eighteenth century were dissolved when the system collapsed, and many

---

[52] Gabriela Sica, "Las sociedades indígenas del Tucumán colonial. Una breve historia en larga duración. Siglos XVI a XIX," in Susana Bandieri and Sandra Fernández, eds., *La historia nacional en perspectiva regional: Nuevas investigaciones para viejos problemas* (Buenos Aires: Teseo, 2017), 41–82; Raquel Gil Montero, *La construcción de Argentina y Bolivia en los Andes meridionales: Población, tierras y ambiente en el siglo XIX* (Buenos Aires: Prometeo, 2007); Tristan Platt, *Estado boliviano y ayllu andino: Tierra y tributo en el Norte de Potosí* (La Paz: Biblioteca del Bicentenario de Bolivia, 2016).

[53] George Reid Andrews, *Afro-Latin America, 1800–2000* (New York: Oxford University Press, 2004); Magdalena Candioti, "'El tiempo de los libertos': Conflictos y litigación en torno a la ley de vientre libre en el Río de la Plata (1813–1860)," *História* 38 (2019), online at http://dx.doi.org/10.1590/1980-4369e2019001; Paulina Alberto, "*Liberta* by Trade: Negotiating the Terms of Unfree Labor in Gradual Abolition Buenos Aires (1820s–30s)," *Journal of Social History* 52:3 (2019), 619–51; Oscar Chamosa, "To Honor the Ashes of Their Forebears. The Rise and Crisis of African Nations in the Post-Independence State of Buenos Aires, 1820–1860," *The Americas* 59:3 (2003), 347–78.

Indigenous people allied with revolutionaries or loyalists during the war. That conflict, and the pressure of some territories to expand their borders for economic reasons, led to new periods of interethnic violence in different areas.[54]

Finally, the metamorphoses of the times gave birth to a new literary genre, later known as *Gauchesca*. Some poets of the Banda Oriental and Buenos Aires began writing verses with political content, using words and tones of the rural population, the so-called *gauchos*. Some of these poems made strong statements about equality and republicanism, such as "Kings are not necessary to govern men." They also expressed the popular resentment for having given so much in the revolutionary years and obtaining so little.[55]

For all the changes, there was also much continuity, as in the case of gender relations (although more research is needed in that field). But it is clear that the dissolution of the Viceroyalty of the Río de la Plata was much more than a "political" revolution for self-government. It did not transform the social structure to promote the rule of new social class, as in some classic Marxist definitions, but it did cause social, economic, cultural, and political modifications. For contemporaries, there was no doubt: They experienced that period as a crucial turn, an acceleration of time, a moment of fear and hope that transformed their lives.

---

[54] Silvia Ratto, "Los indios y la revolución en el Río de la Plata. El proceso independentista de Pampa y Chaco," in Beatriz Bragoni and Sara Mata, eds., *Entre la colonia y la república: Insurgencias, rebeliones y cultura política en América el Sur* (Buenos Aires: Prometeo Libros, 2008), 143–68.

[55] Josefina Ludmer, *The Gaucho Genre: A Treatise on the Motherland* (Durham, NC: Duke University Press, 2002). The quote is from Bartolomé Hidalgo, *Cielitos y diálogos patrióticos* (Buenos Aires, Centro Editor de América Latina, 1967), 31.

# 10

# Royalists, Monarchy, and Political Transformation in the Spanish Atlantic World during the Age of Revolutions

MARCELA ECHEVERRI

Though historically loyalty and royalism have been classified within a conceptual binary that – particularly for this period – opposes revolution to monarchism, and associates the latter with conservatism or backwardness, this chapter argues that such a representation only reproduces the limited understanding of political options and processes embodied in the so-called revolutionary camp. In fact, the depth of structural transformations in the eighteenth and nineteenth centuries across the globe suggest that even within a position of loyalty, all subjects in the Atlantic empires embraced and produced radical lasting change. One of the reasons for this was that the monarchical institutions themselves changed and that, once revolutionary processes were unleashed, it was impossible to reverse them from any side.

A look at the complexity of political discourses, institutions, and positions in the revolutionary era reveals that the process of change taking place within the Spanish monarchy enabled all Spanish subjects to address the accelerated critical circumstances creatively, either from the "royalist" camp or from a "revolutionary" one. Understanding how both of these options could be inherently radical, and how together they produced deep transformations, is the objective of this chapter. This analytical perspective requires distancing ourselves from the most traditional accounts that painted the royalists as the enemies of revolution and their intrinsic position as rejecting change. It also implies accounting for the social, military, and political dimensions of royalism and framing it in the Atlantic, hemispheric, regional, and local contexts. This evinces how legal or military actions promoted from the position of royalism overlapped with those of the insurgent camp to shape the course of events during the revolutionary era.

The term "royalist" has mostly been defined and explored in relation to the crisis of the monarchy unleashed by the Napoleonic invasion of the

Peninsula in 1808.[1] This is because in Spanish America the crisis of the monarchy eventually led to a civil war and, in that context, royalists were core actors, most obviously as military agents and as representatives of Spanish power in the revolutionary Americas. More broadly speaking, in the period leading to and during the independence wars, societies all across the empire polarized between a faction that defended the king's sovereignty and another one that progressively consolidated around the project of independence. The alternatives – or poles – were never set in stone; rather, they were constantly shifting as the political process evolved.

This chapter traces the history of royalism in Spanish America during the Age of Revolutions beginning with the monarchical crisis sparked by the 1808 Napoleonic Invasion of the Iberian Peninsula, and then focuses on the independence wars, the monarchical restoration, the return of liberalism, and the final declaration of independence across Spanish America. Until recently, historians had treated these processes and themes mostly as national problems and investigated them within national frameworks.[2] The effort here is thus to think about the Atlantic and transregional dynamics that influenced each other. At the same time, while keeping the social dimension centered, the goal is to understand the institutional and discursive changes of royalism in a broader Spanish American perspective. As we will see, regional processes also determined royalism, and these are important because they reveal the highly local history of royalism (as opposed to one that is thought to be centered in Spain or responding to the interests of a colonial regime). In the past, national histories moreover flattened the political dimension of royalism by establishing a (mostly implicit) social framework that associated royalists either with the elites or Spaniards, overlooking the relevance of vertical alliances in the constitution of the royalist fronts during the years following 1808. Significantly, this chapter will show how and why royalists also were divided in their interests and outlook, and how their history was dynamic and evolving with the revolutionary age.

It is possible to identify the moment in which loyalty to the king began to emerge as a source of political identification, affiliation, and association. At first, the question of loyalty to Fernando VII unified (rather than fractured) the empire in his absence. After the crisis in 1808, all over the Hispanic

---

[1] In Spanish *lealtad* or *fidelidad*. Loyalists were called either *realistas* or *fidelistas*.

[2] Marcela Echeverri, "Monarchy, Empire, and Popular Politics in the Atlantic Age of Revolutions," *Varia Historia* 35:67 (2019), 15–35; Andrea Rodríguez Tapia, *Realistas contra insurgentes: La construcción de un consenso historiográfico en el México independiente (1810–1852)* (Bilbao: Editorial del País Vasco, 2019).

Royalists, Monarchy, and Political Transformation

territories people pledged loyalty to the king and committed to defending the empire from French ambitions to take control of the Spanish Americas. The critical events in the Peninsula included Napoleon's appointment of his brother Joseph as king of Spain. In this context, debates among the anti-French resistance in the Peninsula – about the form of government that could safeguard Spanish sovereignty in the absence of the monarch – heightened. Soon, many Spanish Americans manifested criticisms of the mechanisms devised by the representatives of the Spanish king in the Peninsula to rule the overseas territories: the regency, the Junta Central, and later the Cortes. In a slow and uneven process between 1808 and 1812, many cities and towns claimed the right to self-rule and declared autonomous governments, rejecting peninsular authority. At this time, individuals and communities that continued to profess loyalty to Spain both maintained links to the Spanish government and set out to repress dissidents who now contested the monarch's power in Spain's American territories. This process whereby royalism's meaning changed in the context of growing and fast polarization illustrates why and how, given the dynamic circumstances in these years of revolutionary change within the Spanish monarchy, royalism was, from the beginning, constantly in transformation.

As a result of the most radical institutional innovation during this period, the proclamation of the Spanish imperial Constitution in Cádiz in 1812, the meaning of monarchical rule and of belonging to the monarchy shifted even more radically. People of different classes, races, and ethnicities – men and women – redefined their relationship to the Crown, particularly around the question of rights. As a consequence, new forms of manifesting loyalty began to emerge. Yet, naturally, at this time of rapid change, not all Hispanic subjects professed the liberal principles being developed through the Constitution. Just as there were factions espousing different philosophical approaches to legal change, on the ground in the Americas, people in the royalist camp could take different positions within a broadly defined range between absolutism and liberalism.

The process was further entangled at the imperial level as other extreme shifts took place again in 1814 and 1820. In 1814 Fernando was restored to the throne and reversed the liberal processes undertaken under the Cádiz Constitution. The return to absolutism implied a destabilization of the monarchical regimes both in the Peninsula and the Americas. It generated new fissures within the royalist camp. One was linked to the preexisting range in positions within royalism between liberalism and absolutism, because, at the juncture of the restoration, people who identified with absolutism began to benefit. Other fissures were linked to the empowerment of military figures, since the restoration was put in practice by establishing military regimes.

When in 1820 the king was forced to reinstitute the Constitution, a similar process ensued, giving liberals the upper hand. In places under Spanish control where the Constitution was applied, the return of liberal discourses and laws again redefined the options available for all Spanish subjects to engage with the monarchy. However, this was also the juncture at which the most intense military confrontations of the independence wars were taking place in most of South America. The war, a process that had framed and incentivized local and regional antagonisms, determined political choices as well as fiscal priorities and decisions across Spanish America.

First and foremost, the monarchical crisis that hit the Spanish Empire in 1808 after the Napoleonic invasion was itself a process of revolutionary proportions, given that one of its consequences was the transformation of the absolutist monarchy into a constitutional one. It is in this measure that – aside from the shifts brought about by the war – royalism as an option was embedded in the radical dynamics of the reinvention of the imperial monarchy, in a process that allowed all Spanish subjects to engage creatively in political transformations. It was not the first time that Spanish subjects acted politically. Much the opposite, all Spanish subjects, as vassals, had a long history of political involvement with the monarchy through legal channels, violent protest, and participation in militias.[3] These experiences were the base or background for political action in the context of the monarchical crisis and the following decade of experimentation (in the Peninsula and in the Americas), when the radical stakes intrinsic to royalism only increased. The highly transformative process made clear that the terms and meanings of loyalty were conditional and modified within the changing imperial contexts.

While it is obvious that, as with any historical subject, partisanship was fluid and that in many cases political allegiances shifted due to opportunism or desperation, it is crucial to take seriously the question of the ideological and social grounds for loyalty and the formation of royalist alliances. One especially significant reason is that through the lens of royalism and royalists

---

[3] On the intersection between legal and direct action in the politics of indigenous people and people of African origin and descent in Spanish America, see Marcela Echeverri, *Indian and Slave Royalists in the Age of Revolution: Reform, Revolution, and Royalism in the Northern Andes, 1780–1825* (New York: Cambridge University Press, 2016); Sergio Serulnikov, *Subverting Colonial Authority: Challenges to Spanish Rule in Eighteenth-Century Southern Andes* (Durham, NC: Duke University Press, 2003).

we better understand the importance of empire and monarchy during the Age of Revolutions, coming to terms with their resilience and flexibility during that time. Similarly, through a focus on the social positions engaged with royalism, we account for the multiple possible political options available to all subjects across the Atlantic World in the turbulent decades that characterize the period.

Royalists are fundamental actors, and loyalty is a fundamental theme for understanding the Age of Revolutions across the Atlantic World. In Spanish America, where the revolutionary age encompassed both the period of imperial reform and revolution (the independence wars), political discourses, institutions, and social relations transformed deeply, giving way to multiple meanings of subjecthood and loyalty. At the same time, in societies that were structured around race, ethnicity, gender, class, and *calidad*, political identities were contingent on issues of rights that were shared by collectivities.[4] This chapter argues that the study of royalism in Spanish America requires taking these two dimensions into account: emphasizing the question of chronology and that of social specificity, separately and together, to reconstruct the social perspectives that gave meaning to royalism and explain how it was recast across space and time. In other words, royalism was constantly changing and its meaning was different according to the social position of its bearers. For this reason, context is crucial for understanding loyalty and its consequences.

There are two dimensions or scales that best frame the study of royalism in Spanish America. On one hand is the local or regional dimension that obviously shaped political and military dynamics both before and after the monarchical crisis broke out in 1808. On the other hand, the imperial or Atlantic dimension is also fundamental for making sense of the discursive and institutional transformations that constituted crucial opportunities for the emergence of alliances around royalism. These alliances involved colonial

---

[4] Works that engage with the topic of royalism and loyalty in Spanish America from a social perspective include Sarah C. Chambers and Lisa Norling, "Choosing to be a Subject: Loyalist Women in the Revolutionary Atlantic World," *Journal of Women's History* 20:1 (2008), 39–62; Echeverri, *Indian and Slave Royalists*; Jane Landers, *Atlantic Creoles in the Age of Revolutions* (Cambridge, MA: Harvard University Press, 2010); Cecilia Méndez, *The Plebeian Republic: The Huanta Rebellion and the Making of the Peruvian State, 1820–1850* (Durham, NC: Duke University Press, 2005); Steinar Saether, *Identidades e independencia en Santa Marta y Riohacha, 1750–1850* (Bogotá: Instituto Colombiano de Antropología e Historia, 2005); David Sartorius, *Ever Faithful: Race, Loyalty, and the Ends of Empire in Spanish Cuba* (Durham, NC: Duke University Press, 2013); Tomás Straka, *La voz de los vencidos: Ideas del partido realista de Caracas, 1810–1821* (Caracas: Universidad Central de Venezuela, 2000).

officials, the clergy, members of the army and militias, as well as people from different racial backgrounds such as Indians, slaves, and free people of African descent. In this sense, the social diversity of royalism requires a micro lens that disentangles the particular relationship that people from different social backgrounds had with the monarchy and that shows how their political identities, which were tied to legal structures, transformed in the context of the opportunities for change offered by the war.

## The Hispanic Revolution: The Spanish Nation and the Cádiz Constitution

One of the most important processes of institutional experimentation and innovation that took place in the Spanish monarchy during the Age of Revolutions was the creation and implementation of the Cádiz Constitution, which itself was devised as a way of safeguarding the Spanish monarch's sovereignty from French takeover. In this sense, liberalism emerged from the Hispanic response to the crisis of the monarchy and, therefore, in the Spanish world, liberalism was itself tied to monarchy – they were not opposed.

Under siege from French troops, representatives of the Spanish Cortes met in the city of Cádiz to debate about the form that the new Hispanic charter would have. This imperial parliament included men from Spanish America who were convoked to participate in representation of the American juris-dictions.[5] The unprecedented constitutional process and its result (the Constitution and the laws it promulgated) were a visible expression of the revolution of the Spanish monarchy in the years 1810–1815. In the absence of the monarch, the creation of a constitutional monarchy implied that new mechanisms of participation were developed at an imperial level. Simultaneously, the Spanish nation was conceived as a transatlantic commu-nity under the umbrella of monarchy.[6]

The constitutional process was also illustrative of the divergent forces that came together in the Cádiz Cortes. This was officially the arena in which Spanish sovereignty was upheld against the French invasion, yet the political interests of diverse sectors of the Spanish world collided in Cádiz. Some sectors sought a profound renovation of the monarchy while others were

---

[5] See Breña, Chapter 3 in this volume.
[6] José María Portillo, *Crisis atlántica: Autonomía e independencia en la crisis de la monarquía hispana* (Madrid: Marcial Pons, 2006).

interested in using the Constitution as a vehicle for maintaining hierarchies and privileges.[7] Regarding the overseas territories, the most important fissure that Cádiz revealed was linked to the place of Spanish America in the Spanish nation. Dissatisfied with the terms of representation set by their peninsular counterparts, and in rejection of the unequal position assigned to the Spanish American territories by Spanish liberals, the radical responses among Spanish Americans included defection from the monarchy and search for local sovereignty.[8]

Among the significant elements in the constitutional debates leading to the promulgation of the charter that generated heated confrontations were those related to the status of people of African and Indigenous descent across the empire. Both of these represented significant portions of the population in the Americas, and the institutions and relations that bound them socially to forms of unfree labor and categories of inferiority became the focus of critiques within the framework of the liberal thrust of the Cádiz Cortes.

The status of people of African descent, many of whom were free and numerous in the American territories, constituted a variable that mattered at the moment of deciding on the proportion of American representation in Cádiz. Moreover, it was a thorny theme when considering the question of citizenship and inclusion in the Spanish nation. Though the final decision was to exclude them from that category, the debate illustrated their controversial centrality to American realities – and, by extension, to the Spanish world.

Indigenous people, on the other hand, did get recognition as citizens. At the same time, in one of the measures that aimed to foster the Indians' legal transformation, the Cádiz Cortes abolished tribute. Though contested and hardly lineal, this radical change unleashed a mutation in the status of Indigenous people whose main fiscal duty for centuries had defined their connection to the monarchy and their organization as communities. The contentious character of this issue is clear when we consider the example of how two Peruvian ethnic elites participated in the process: while Dionisio

---

[7] A basic distinction between these two extremes could be made by labeling them "radicals" and "moderates." Federico Suárez Verdeguer, *Conservadores, innovadores y renovadores en las postrimerías del antiguo régimen* (Pamplona: Publicaciones del estudio general de Navarra, 1955); Federico Suárez Verdeguer, *El proceso de convocatoria a Cortes (1808–1810)* (Pamplona: Ediciones Universidad de Navarra, 1982).

[8] Marie Laure Rieu-Millán, *Los diputados americanos en las Cortes de Cádiz* (Madrid: Consejo Superior de Investigaciones Científicas, 1990); María Teresa Berruezo, *La participación americana en las Cortes de Cádiz, 1810–1814* (Madrid: Centro de Estudios Constitucionales, 1986).

Inca Yupanqui advocated this reform during the constitutional debates in Cádiz; in Cuzco, Mateo Pumacahua turned against the measure.[9]

The question of the abolition of slavery and citizenship for *casta* populations across Spanish America also became specifically tied to the interests of *pardos*, who promoted ideas of racial equality. Given that the deputies in the constitutional debates finally resolved not to include people of African descent in the category of citizens, it is particularly interesting to assess their widespread engagement with the royalist option during the different periods of the independence/revolutionary process. In this regard it seems clear that free Blacks had their own interpretation of the charter in places such as Venezuela, Popayán, Yucatán, and Cuba, where they actively supported the Crown and sought recognition for their loyalty as Spanish citizens.[10]

The rights of *pardos* and tribute abolition are only two of many illustrations of the conflicting interests and interpretations of the liberal constitution. And even in the places where the ruling authorities were royalists, the implementation of the Constitution across the Spanish monarchy was very uneven, given that by 1812 war had intensified across all of Spanish America. In that context, the Cádiz Constitution became one element defining of the royalist discourse and the institutional options that gave legitimacy to the notion of continued Spanish rule under the constitutional monarchy. A fundamental transformation was triggered, for example, through the process of elections that the new system put in motion at local and provincial levels. The other pole of the political energy that fed the opposition of royalists to the insurgents was the battlefield. Antagonisms grew as a result of military confrontation, and the identities of royalists, as defenders of the Crown and opponents of the insurgents, were in a large degree shaped by war itself.[11]

---

[9] Scarlett O'Phelan, "Dionisio Inca Yupanqui y Mateo Pumacahua: Dos indios nobles frente a las Cortes de Cádiz (1808–1814)," in Juan Luis Orrego Penagos et al., *Las independencias desde la perspectiva de los actores sociales* (Lima: Pontificia Universidad Católica del Perú, 2009), 93–104.

[10] Echeverri, *Indian and Slave Royalists*; Melchor Campos García, *Castas, feligresía y ciudadanía en Yucatán* (Mérida: Universidad Autónoma de Yucatán, 2005); Sartorius, *Ever Faithful*; Clément Thibaud, *Repúblicas en armas: Los ejércitos bolivarianos en la guerra de independencia en Colombia y Venezuela* (Bogotá: Planeta, Instituto Francés de Estudios Andinos, 2003).

[11] On elections see Antonio Annino, "Cádiz y la revolución territorial de los pueblos mexicanos," in *Historia de las elecciones en Iberoamérica, siglo XIX* (Buenos Aires: Fondo de Cultura Económica, 1995), 177–226; Jordana Dym, *From Sovereign Villages to National States: City, State, and Federation in Central America, 1759–1839* (Albuquerque: University of New Mexico Press, 2006); Jaime Rodríguez, "Las primeras elecciones constitucionales en el Reino de Quito, 1809–1814 y 1821–1822," *Revista Procesos* 14 (1999), 13–52.

## Scales of Loyalty: Local and Hemispheric Territorial Dynamics

The crisis in Spanish America began shortly after the arrival of news about the French invasion. The governments in cities and towns reacted by displaying widespread allegiance to the monarch. Local governments performed public oaths in support of the king's sovereignty. People pled for the monarch's well-being and safe return to the throne, also swearing to repeal French rule over the Americas.[12]

Yet this unity that was framed in Spanish Americans' defensive attitude did not last long. After 1809, political allegiances fragmented following a territorial logic whereby preexisting rivalries between cities and towns reemerged. This was a consequence of the breakdown of the chain of government in the absence of the monarch. Some examples of these widespread regional confrontations include the antagonism between Montevideo and Buenos Aires, Cartagena and Santa Marta, Quito and Cuenca, and Caracas and Maracaibo. The geography of loyalty was shaped by previous political and jurisdictional histories of regional competition. Montevideo, Santa Marta, Cuenca, and Maracaibo chose to remain loyal to Spain and confronted their opponents' turn toward autonomist forms of governments that challenged Spain's legitimacy to rule. The territories that tended to initially defect were those that had been affected jurisdictionally during the Bourbon reforms. In South America, the Bourbons had created two new viceroyalties during the eighteenth century – New Granada and Río de la Plata – separating Charcas and Quito from Lima. It was precisely in Charcas and in Quito where the first two autonomist juntas were formed, in 1809.

In New Spain and Peru, the core viceroyalties in the Indies, viceregal power dominated throughout the crisis, while the legitimacy of the newer viceroyalties of New Granada and Río de la Plata would, instead, be challenged and divided as local municipal and provincial forces pulled jurisdictions apart in the struggle for sovereignty. Wielding a comparative lens, we can look at New Spain and South America together, and examine the effects of the crisis – the rise of war and the changes to the colonial government – even if they were obviously different jurisdictional units. What makes this comparison possible and useful is that, despite the size of Spanish South America, political and military dynamics there tended to polarize around the figure of the viceroy of Peru, José de Abascal.

---

[12] Marco A. Landavazo, *La máscara de Fernando VII: Discurso e imaginario monárquico en una época de crisis. Nueva España 1808–1822* (Mexico City: Colegio de México, 2001), Chapter 3.

The war in South America was different from the one in New Spain because in Río de la Plata, Chile, Venezuela, and New Granada creole elites took control of the government, deposing the viceroys, and making municipal governments central to the effort of reform with support of the militias. In New Spain, the viceroy continued to be the supreme authority, playing a fundamental role in the counterinsurgent struggle by leading the armed forces to fight against the rebels.[13] New Spain, beginning with the Hidalgo uprising, was the scene of widespread insurgency with roots in the countryside and with participation of Indigenous people.[14] Yet central cities such as Querétaro, Mexico, Puebla, and Veracruz never fell into insurgent hands as the counterinsurgency measures developed by the viceroy and army leaders succeeded in keeping the Viceroyalty under Spanish control.[15]

After 1809, Peru became a royalist bulwark in Spanish South America, while to the north and south of Peru insurgencies proliferated. Additionally, the South American position of Abascal was unique, especially when compared with the situation of the viceroys in New Spain between 1810 and 1816. Abascal was literally competing for hegemony at the subcontinental scale while he did not have to wage a counterinsurgency war within his own territories until 1814.[16] For this reason, the theaters of war and institutional experimentation across South America (in Venezuela, New Granada, Chile, and Buenos Aires) were all strategically linked to the extent that their military struggle involved combating Spanish power in Peru. Conversely, Peru was fighting insurgencies at a subcontinental scale, north and south. This is the reason why it is important to look at those theaters of war together, from a broader South American angle.[17]

Furthermore, there were areas where loyalty was widespread allowing territories to remain relatively free of war, namely Central America and the Caribbean islands of Cuba and Puerto Rico. The Central American territories were kept under control of the government after it put down some uprisings,

---

[13] Brian Hamnett, "El virrey Abascal y sus cinco homólogos novohispanos, 1806–1816: Un estudio comparativo," in Scarlett O'Phelan Godoy and Georges Lomné, eds., *Abascal y la contra-independencia de América del Sur* (Lima: Instituto Francés de Estudios Andinos, Fondo Editorial de la Pontificia Universidad Católica del Perú, 2013), 19–52.

[14] José Semprún and Alonso Bullón de Mendoza, *El ejército realista en la independencia americana* (Madrid: Editorial MAPFRE, 1992), 65–7.

[15] See Juan Ortiz Escamilla, Chapter 5 in this volume.

[16] In 1814 a rebellion in Cuzco changed this pattern. On this subject, see Scarlett O'Phelan Godoy, *1814: La junta de gobierno del Cuzco y el sur andino* (Lima: Instituto Francés de Estudios Andinos, Fondo Editorial de la Pontificia Universidad Católica del Perú, Fundación M. J. Bustamante de la Fuente, 2016).

[17] O'Phelan Godoy and Lomné, *Abascal y la contra-independencia*.

yet this does not mean that the region remained unaffected by the deep changes taking place within the monarchy in the years 1808–1821.[18] The Spanish Caribbean, it is well known, was an area where loyalty to Spain prevailed. This region would in time clearly reveal its exceptional path during the period that led to the independence of every other American possession, which severed ties with Spain. Cuba, Puerto Rico, and Santo Domingo continued to be Spanish strongholds in the Americas, along with the Philippines. The islands were important military centers from where Spain directed military operations into the mainland at different times. Even after most territories had declared independence, Cuba and Puerto Rico were the centers of Spanish rule in the Atlantic, where great numbers of loyalists arrived to settle down. They also were crucial in the development of a plantation economy unparalleled in Spanish America, based on the expansion of African slavery, which sustained Spanish colonial rule. As exceptions, the Caribbean islands do not illustrate the military process whereby war was one important component of the royalists' identity. The region and its inhabitants were, however, shaped by the waves of Hispanic liberal reform. Like in other parts of the Spanish Empire, liberalism defined their identities in the context of the imperial crisis. At that juncture, like before, free people of African descent, for example, took advantage of the opportunities to join the military, one of the sources of loyalty among that population. This mechanism of inclusion could officially be seen as a tool of subordination. Yet, precisely that relationship between the Crown and people of African descent fostered through the military institution also makes clear that the cause for loyalty in the Spanish Caribbean was not exclusively the product of white racial fears of slave rebellion, as the main explanation goes, but rather also had important connections to the free black population's interests and involvement with monarchical institutions.[19]

## War and Constitutions in Spanish America

When in 1810 and 1811 the first juntas were created in places such as Caracas, Cartagena, Santiago de Chile, and Buenos Aires, their initial

[18] Dym, *From Sovereign Villages*; Timothy Hawkins, *José de Bustamante and Central American Independence: Colonial Administration in an Age of Imperial Crisis* (Tuscaloosa: University of Alabama Press, 2004).

[19] The classic interpretation can be found in John Lynch, *The Spanish American Revolutions, 1808–1826* (New York: W. W. Norton, 1986 [1973]). For the most recent assessment of this period and the question of loyalty in Cuba, see Sartorius, *Ever Faithful*.

proclamations referred to Fernando VII as the legitimate monarch. This fact led nationalist historians to produce one of the most significant historical myths around independence in Spanish America, known as "Fernando VII's Mask" (la máscara de Fernando VII). Assuming that Spanish Americans had to be in favor of breaking away from Spain, a historiography that had naturalized emancipation saw the Spanish American juntas' declarations in favor of Fernando's sovereignty as merely strategic and essentially shallow. However, recent studies have recast this notion and shown that there were important philosophical bases for doing this. The juntas' declarations were based on the scholastic principle that in the absence of the monarch sovereignty returned to the people. In that sense, these were not hypocritical gestures but, much the opposite, meaningful statements in the process of positioning the local governments on a solid ground to defend the Spanish American territories' right to self-rule in the context of the Spanish dynastic crisis.

Soon after, however, the tensions escalated due to diverse dynamics with both local and Atlantic roots. In some cases, the crisis was sparked by fear of a French takeover. In other cases, the break came as a rejection of the Spanish Junta Central that sought to govern the empire, and measures of the Cádiz Cortes, and in many of the juntas created across Spanish America arguments turned more radical toward separating from Spanish rule.[20]

Given that power – and sovereignty – was concentrated at the municipal level, the new governments were established on the principle of popular sovereignty and consequently drafted constitutions. Noteworthy are the cases of constitutions in New Granada. They are important to mention because they did emerge, initially, as statements of loyalty but soon they were also clear stepping stones for moving toward independent republican experiments. Some constitutions like the one in Cundinamarca said the king was the head of the republic.[21]

At the same time, these first republican constitutions are historically relevant to the question of royalism because the constitutional experiments in Spanish America influenced the Cádiz Constitution that was at that time being drafted in the Peninsula. In some aspects – such as the rights for Indigenous people and people of African descent – there was a conversation between both sides of the Atlantic regarding the new politics of Hispanic

---

[20] Manuel Chust, ed., *1808: La eclosión juntera en el mundo hispano* (Mexico City: Fondo de Cultura Económica, 2007).

[21] Antonio Annino and Marcela Ternavasio, eds., *El laboratorio constitucional iberoamericano: 1807/1808–1830* (Madrid: Iberoamericana/Vervuert, 2012).

liberalisms.[22] This means that the priorities and political interests that shaped Hispanic liberalism and Spanish American republicanism were themselves established in dialogue with the social and political realities across the Americas, in which people of Indigenous and African descent (as objects and subjects of rights as well as military actors) played a large part.

The dialectical relationship between the Cádiz Constitution and the Spanish American constitutions underlay the most radical processes of social transformation that characterized the Hispanic revolutions. As examples illustrative of the Spanish American constitutional experiments, the juntas in Caracas, Antioquia, and Cartagena abolished the slave trade as part of their rejection of Spanish institutions. Emissaries of the junta of Buenos Aires were swift to propose the abolition of tribute to Indians in Upper Peru to get their support for the new government. In this way, the legal process on both sides of the Atlantic had radical-liberal undertones and, in siding with the different factions, peoples of Indigenous or African descent negotiated the political terms of their participation, framed in precisely those dynamic legal changes. The inclusion of people of African and Native descent into these military projects moreover determined the engagement of these popular sectors in state formation and had lasting incidence in social debates across Spanish America in ensuing decades.

There is one episode that stands out in terms of this popular involvement in royalism, in which people of African descent and of mixed Indigenous and African descent (*zambos*) in the Venezuelan *llanos* or plains mobilized against the creoles after they declared Venezuela independent on 5 July 1811, denying the vote to *pardos* in the new republic.[23] The royalist forces in other parts of the captaincy swelled with slaves. The slaves' participation was a result of the royalist officials' strategy to free slaves who joined them.[24] Most importantly, this case shows that one of the reasons why some *pardos* in

---

[22] Cesáreo de Armellada, *La Causa Indígena Americana en las Cortes de Cádiz* (Caracas: Universidad Católica Andrés Bello, 1979); Marcela Echeverri, "Race, Citizenship, and the Cádiz Constitution in Popayán (New Granada)," in Scott Eastman and Natalia Sobrevilla Perea, eds., *The Rise of Constitutional Government in the Iberian Atlantic World: The Impact of the Cádiz Constitution of 1812* (Tuscaloosa: University of Alabama Press, 2015), 91–110. I use the term liberalisms in the plural intentionally, following Gabriel Paquette, "Introduction: Liberalism in the Early Nineteenth-Century Iberian World," *History of European Ideas* 41:2 (2015), who advocates for an understanding of European liberalism as plural. I build upon this idea by expanding the study of liberalism to include the New Granadan experiments in the study of Hispanic *liberalisms*.

[23] The Constitution abolished the slave trade but not slavery.

[24] Peter Blanchard, *Under the Flags of Freedom: Slave Soldiers and the Wars of Independence in Spanish South America* (Pittsburgh: University of Pittsburgh Press, 2008), 23.

Caracas opposed the junta and organized a conspiracy against it was the question of their rights in the republican project and the issue of slavery's abolition. In Cartagena, the insurgent junta took the opposite position and mobilized *pardos* in its favor, to a large extent based on a critique of Spain's policies regarding that population.[25]

## Royalism between Absolutism and Liberalism

To understand the complexities and diversity in royalism during the Age of Revolutions in the Spanish Atlantic, we have to consider its multiple meanings ranging between absolutism and liberalism. In the territories that remained under monarchical rule, governments would have been expected to swear an oath to the Constitution, and to apply it. And many did. Yet, for many colonial officials across the empire, the Constitution generated problems either ideologically or in terms of governability. In those cases, colonial officers chose to ignore some of its articles or simply to challenge it by principle. For example, Viceroy Abascal in Peru hindered the application of the abolition of tribute for Indians that was part of the liberal reforms decreed in Cádiz, given that tribute was one crucial way of financing the war at that particular juncture.

In a similar way, all over Spanish America royalists inhabited multiple and at times contradictory positions that were visible in public debates or in the ongoing institutional disputes that emerged, especially between civil and military officials of the Crown. Part of the conflict unfolded precisely around the interpretations that people gave of the liberal constitution in the volatile context of the war. Among elites, tensions between different royalist positions were numerous. Viceroys as well as clerics were more prone to aligning with absolutist principles, while some military figures were influenced by liberalism. Viceroys had no intention of altering their customary method of government, constitutional changes or not. For example, royalist authorities in Mexico City remained essentially absolutist and Peninsula-oriented.[26]

The clergy was another sector that refracted monarchical institutional and ideological changes. Though since the nineteenth-century nationalist histories generally emphasized royalists' religious fanaticism to explain why some

---

[25] Marixa Lasso, *Myths of Harmony: Race and Republicanism during the Age of Revolution, Colombia 1795–1831* (Pittsburgh: University of Pittsburgh Press, 2007).
[26] Hamnett, "El virrey Abascal."

people in Spanish America had remained tied to Spain during the independence process, in reality, in many instances, priests and other members of the Church were involved in the pro-independence faction. Considering the heterogeneity of the clergy, it is also possible to identify a variety of positions among royalist Church actors. If there was an absolutist tendency among some priests, there were also priests who militated in favor of liberalism and became active in familiarizing people, including Indigenous people, with the precepts of the Cádiz Charter. Following the promulgation of the Constitution in 1812 and 1820, popular catechisms presented dialogues between a teacher and a student that could be memorized. Since the Constitution itself established freedom of the press, these catechisms proliferated and reached people beyond the literate minority. In this process, priests always played an important part.[27]

More broadly speaking, among many Spanish vassals, the early years of Napoleonic rule and Fernando's captivity were interpreted in mystical terms and this gave the king himself an aura of martyrdom.[28] There was a sense among people in the Americas that the monarch's tragic destiny required that they pray for him and defend his throne (in other words, his sovereignty). The Constitution itself held symbolic power in the absence of the king; it retained the solemnity and majesty associated with the king and his power.[29]

Analogous to other groups and institutions among the royalists, diverse positions and interests could also be found among the popular sectors. These multiple interpretations of loyalty reveal the creativity that took place during these years of the monarchical crisis and the extent to which underlying interests and political positions became articulated to specific strands of royalist discourse among people of all classes, races, and ethnicities.

An example is the Indigenous communities in the southwestern region of New Granada, around the city of Pasto. There the caciques of the communities aligned with the absolutist visions of society and monarchism that upheld their position as ethnic authorities, while the commoners generally aligned with the liberal premises of the Cádiz Constitution. This was due to the fact that Indian commoners were more interested in the promises of

---

[27] Scott Eastman, *Preaching Spanish Nationalism across the Hispanic Atlantic, 1759–1823* (Baton Rouge: Louisiana University Press, 2012).

[28] Landavazo, *La máscara*, Chapter 2.

[29] Federica Morelli, "La publicación y el juramento de la constitución de Cádiz en Hispanoamérica: Imágenes y valores (1812–1813)," in Johannes-Michael Scholz and Tamar Herzog, eds., *Observation and Communication: The Construction of Realities in the Hispanic World* (Frankfurt am Main: Vittorio Klostermann, 1997), 135–49.

equality that the liberal constitution brought to Spanish America than were the caciques, whose authority and standing hinged on established hierarchies. The latter also were mobilized as soldiers during the war and had an interest in the abolition of tribute payment that the Cádiz Charter proposed as part of making Indians citizens of the Spanish nation.[30]

From the perspective of the structural changes taking place, even in the period of restoration to absolutism it is possible to see some significant transformations in the discourse and mechanisms of rule instrumentalized by the Crown to attempt taking control of public opinion. At that time, absolutist discourse had to actively compete with the insurgency's discourse of revolution and independence circulating across Spanish America. The restoration to absolutism did not mean simply going back to the Old Regime – even if this was the wish of the king – because the new circumstances required novel strategies and language to engage the population.[31]

## The Royalist Army in the Wars of Independence

When frictions grew around loyalty to Spain, violence in Spanish America tied the war that emerged in the context of the vacuum of power to the changing dynamics in the realm of politics. Cities (municipalities) and towns became crucial units in defense of the Crown's sovereignty. There were two broad phases in the war that began in 1809–1810 in Spanish America, both closely linked to the events in the Peninsula. Obviously, during the period of the Napoleonic occupation of Spain (1808–1814), most of the military resources were devoted to the War of Independence being waged there, against France. In these years, the royalist militias that existed in Spanish America were the first resource that viceroys and other colonial officials had at their disposal to confront the insurgency. At the same time, in places where the insurgents took over the Viceroyalty and formed local governments, they were able to make the militias their army with which to confront the royalist attacks. Very quickly, these military forces expanded on both sides with volunteers as well as conscripts and waged a civil war during the years up to the monarchical restoration. After Fernando returned to the throne in 1814, the armies in the Peninsula became available for combating

---

[30] Echeverri, *Indian and Slave Royalists*, esp. Chapter 4.
[31] Alexander Chaparro, "Las armas y las letras. La reinvención de la legitimidad del orden monárquico en la Tierra Firme durante el momento absolutista, 1814–1819" (M.A. Thesis, Universidad Nacional de Colombia, 2017).

the insurgency in Spanish America. At that time, however, most places across the continent were under control of the royalist government. The only place where insurgents had been able to maintain a successful government was in Buenos Aires.[32]

A focus on the military dimension of royalism reveals that the armed forces clustered under the royalist cause were very diverse in form, composition, and interests. There were, first of all, the members of the royalist militias that the Crown had formed during the eighteenth century and which became central to the defense of Spanish sovereignty during the independence wars.[33] Rarely, if ever, did royalist commanders have at their disposal sufficient troops to effectively control one territory. Other bodies that took shape in some places from among local populations to expand the royalists' military forces were less structured and functioned as guerrillas. The distinction between these was that, like the regular army, militias were regulated while the guerrillas were not. However, in fact, in the Americas (like in Spain) guerrillas held important military power and were decisive for sustaining Spanish rule, especially, at different times, in places like Venezuela, New Granada, and Chile.[34]

What happened in New Spain is an example of the central role of the militias in the counterinsurgency. In Mexico's Bajío, following the Hidalgo uprising, Viceroy Francisco Venegas mobilized a battalion of volunteers in October 1810 that drew mainly from urban elites and was called the "Distinguished Battalion of Fernando VII." In March 1813, Viceroy Félix María Calleja transferred the operational focus of the counterinsurgency from Mexico City to the regions. Calleja considered that to revive economic life every hacienda and town in Guanajuato required a military presence. With the support of Agustín de Iturbide, Calleja developed a policy of organizing local villages, towns, and estates to combat the insurgency. Aside from some physical adaptations of the terrain (the fortification of the village or rancho by the royalist troops), they also created urban companies

---

[32] Anthony McFarlane, *War and Independence in Spanish America* (New York: Routledge, 2014).

[33] Juan Marchena, "¿Obedientes al rey y desleales a sus ideas? Los liberales españoles ante la 'reconquista' de América durante el primer absolutismo de Fernando VII (1814–1820)," in Juan Marchena and Manuel Chust, eds., *Por la fuerza de las armas: Ejército e independencias en Iberoamérica* (Castellón: Universidad Jaume I, 2008).

[34] Semprún and Bullón, *El ejército realista*; McFarlane, *War and Independence*; Rodrigo Moreno, "Los realistas: Historiografía, semántica y milicia," *Historia Mexicana* 66:3 (2017), 1077–122.

financed by local notables. This was a self-defense force ancillary to the regular army and colonial militia.[35]

The guerrillas were military units that had a widespread impact on the war dynamics in Spanish America. They formed in contexts where local populations mobilized to support the royalist cause, specifically the royalist army. The fact that guerrillas were a prevalent type of military mobilization across royalist Spanish South America shows that the defense of Spanish sovereignty hinged upon the participation of the popular classes in the war as individuals and communities, and the control of rural areas and towns.

In Venezuela, the first and second republics were defeated by an army composed mainly of *pardos* (people of mixed race, or mulattoes or *zambos*, generally free) and Blacks. In New Granada, in the southern province of Popayán, towns of Indians and free Blacks, along with slaves living in mining camps in the Pacific lowlands, were all stark defenders of the Crown. Similarly, in Peru, Indigenous people were central to the military offensive led by Abascal against the Buenos Aires insurgent junta. In Chile, Indians at the margins of colonial rule also got involved in the independence wars to defend Spain. An important point of contrast to these developments is the case of New Spain, where there were no royalist guerrillas. This is possibly due to the structured nature of the royalist army there, and the fact that popular sectors in cities and rural areas became formally integrated in the army through the militias. Thus, it is crucial to consider the political geography composed of the villages and towns where many Indigenous people and people of African descent lived, as these became central to the establishment of royalist control over certain regions.[36]

One of the consequences of this massive mobilization of people of African descent, which also included slaves from many plantations and mines across Venezuela and New Granada, respectively, as well as Indians in these and other regions to the south in Peru and Chile, was that eventually insurgent leaders understood the importance of integrating these sectors into the movement for independence. At the same time, it was not without controversy that the royalists dealt with the massive mobilization of popular sectors in favor of the king.

---

[35] Brian Hamnett, "Royalist Counterinsurgency and the Continuity of Rebellion: Guanajuato and Michoacán, 1813–20," *Hispanic American Historical Review* 62:1 (1982), 19–48: 25. See also Juan Ortiz Escamilla, Chapter 5 in this volume.

[36] Echeverri, *Indian and Slave Royalists*; Pilar Herr, "The Nation-State According to Whom? Mapuches and the Chilean State in the Early Nineteenth Century," *Journal of Early American History* 4 (2014), 66–94; Thibaud, *Repúblicas en armas*.

## The Monarchical Restoration and Return to Absolutism: 1814–1820

Fernando certainly brought about a radical reversal of the governmental framework when he returned to his throne in 1814 and abolished the Cádiz Constitution. Considering that during the preceding years the Constitution had held the monarchy together, this was an act that once more tested the foundations of the transatlantic empire. In particular, it delegitimized the fragile official governments that ruled across the Hispanic world at that time in the name of the Spanish king, and, to eradicate liberalism, turned to repressive or policing measures that in many cases alienated even loyal Spanish Americans. Given that royalists had been awaiting the return of the king, it was natural that the king's forceful reimplementation of absolutism, in many cases through violence, disoriented those who sought recognition for their loyalty and did not expect to be reprimanded.

It was at this moment when the experiment of Hispanic liberalism was abruptly ended and repressed as a result of the king's decision. In other words, the Cádiz Constitution was defeated not by its rejection in the Americas but mostly by the king's will. And when, as we will see below, the king was forced to reinstitute the Constitution in 1820, he had lost all credibility regarding the authenticity of his embrace of liberalism, which undermined his capacity to use the Constitution as a tool for negotiation with the American territories and avoid the final loss of a large part of the Atlantic empire.[37]

Here it is again relevant to consider the geography of the restoration. There were many different experiences on the ground, from New Spain to the Río de la Plata, shaped by the preceding years of war. By 1814, the Mexican military strategy had maintained the rebels out of the central regions. In South America the situation was uneven. In the north, the insurgency in Venezuela had largely been defeated by the royalists, most of whom were from the popular classes and specifically people of African descent. In New Granada important pillars of the new government remained, especially in the Andean region (Antioquia, Tunja, and Santa Fe) but also in Cartagena on the Caribbean, where an insurgent junta was still ruling. Peru remained under the control of Abascal while in Buenos Aires the insurgents prevailed.

---

[37] Marchena, "¿Obedientes al rey y desleales a sus ideas?"; Rebecca Earle, *Spain and the Independence of Colombia, 1810–1825* (Exeter: University of Exeter Press, 2000).

When Fernando returned to the throne, a major strategy in support of his decision to pacify the rebel territories was to send an army of 10,500 men and a complete naval fleet to the Americas.[38] After some debate, the army – led by Pablo Morillo – sailed toward *Tierra Firme* (New Granada and Venezuela) in February 1815. There, military pacification (or reconquest) became a fundamental part of the history of restoration and royalism in the period after 1814. In the Peninsula, too, the strategy to deploy the army to the Americas was calculated to allow Fernando's restoration of absolutism to run smoothly and prevent local resistance. The army's transatlantic mission was to bring back under royal authority the insurgent provinces in New Granada and Venezuela. This major military intervention in *Tierra Firme* was followed by lesser expeditions of troops sent to New Spain and Peru during the period of Fernando's absolutist rule, up to 1820.[39]

The restoration also had an impact in New Spain, where it was mainly shaped by viceroys Félix María Calleja and Juan Ruiz de Apodaca. The restoration became the context for policies seeking to expand territorial control through military strategies. During the early years (1814–1815), like elsewhere in Spanish America, the insurgency in New Spain was visibly weakened. The abolition of the Cádiz Constitution was prioritized alongside the reinstitution of absolutist values and institutions. Yet it was also a particular process that once more suggests how the context in New Spain was unique. For instance, some regions like Oaxaca that had recently been recuperated from the insurgency, and where the Cádiz constitutional regime had just been instituted as part of that process, now had to go through a second restoration in a short period of time.[40] Between 1818 and 1820, royalist commanders finally defeated remaining pockets of insurgent resistance in and around the Bajío and achieved the aims of the territorial demarcation or fortification policy.[41]

In New Granada and Venezuela, the arrival of Morillo's expedition implied deep transformations linked to the particular histories of royalism

[38] McFarlane, *War and Independence*.

[39] Marchena, "¿Obedientes al rey y desleales a sus ideas?" On the consequences for Río de la Plata, see Gabriel Di Meglio and Alejandro Rabinovich, "La sombra de la Restauración. Amenazas militares y giros políticos durante la revolución en el Río de la Plata, 1814–1815," *Revista Universitaria de Historia Militar* 7:15 (2018), 59–78; Marcela Ternavasio, *Los juegos de la política: Las independencias hispanoamericanas frente a la contrarrevolución* (Buenos Aires: Siglo XXI, 2021).

[40] Rodrigo Moreno, "La Restauración en la Nueva España: Guerra, cambios de régimen y militarización entre 1814 y 1820," *Revista Universitaria de Historia Militar* 7:15 (2018), 101–25.

[41] Hamnett, "Royalist Counterinsurgency," 33, 37.

in each region. As we have seen, in Venezuela the strength of the royalist response to the revolution in 1809–1814 had pivoted around the participation of mostly *pardo* populations who mobilized militarily. Thus, when Morillo arrived, he had to contend with the local military power of *pardos* and slaves who, though officially in favor or monarchical rule, represented a threat to the view of government that the king wished to see restored. Part of what Morillo had to do was to bring the local royalists under his control. Following instructions from Spain, Morillo thus deported around 4,000 men considered dangerous and sent them to New Granada in the royalist army. Similarly, as viceroy of New Granada in Santa Marta, Francisco de Montalvo complained to authorities in Spain about the indiscretion of the representatives of the Crown in this region who had armed Indians and Blacks.

The greatest shift of this moment of monarchical restoration and military reconquest was that Morillo, carrying out his instructions, established a military government which allowed him to do something extremely radical such as the abolition of the *audiencia*. Other measures included establishing a *Junta de Secuestros* (or Confiscations Committee), a *Consejo de Guerra* that would judge all cases involved in the insurgency, as well as a police tribunal that embarked on a project of espionage.[42]

At the municipal level, Morillo's policy involved drafting men for the construction of roads, which was similar to a practice established in Mexico, where the viceroys had devised strategies to have local populations become responsible for their own defense vis-à-vis the insurgency. In both places, too, these measures (that included both militia service and extra levies to supply royalist garrisons) turned into a burden that populations resented. In New Granada, notably, the measures of this pacifying project drove many local populations away from the monarchy and eventually led them to support the possibility of seeking a way out of the empire.[43]

---

[42] Stephen Stoan, *Pablo Morillo and Venezuela, 1815–1820* (Columbus: Ohio State University Press, 1974), Chapter 3, esp. 75–87.

[43] Peter Guardino, *Peasants, Politics, and the Formation of Mexico's National State: Guerrero, 1800–1857* (Stanford: Stanford University Press, 1996), 74; Daniel Gutiérrez, *La restauración en la Nueva Granada (1815–1819)* (Bogotá: Universidad del Externado, 2016), 56. On Morillo's recruitment of Indians around Tunja, see Marcela Echeverri, "'Sovereignty Has Lost Its Rights': Liberal Experiments and Indigenous Citizenship in New Granada, 1810–1819," in Brian Owensby and Richard Ross, eds., *Justice in a New World: Negotiating Legal Intelligibility in British, Iberian, and Indigenous America* (New York: New York University Press, 2018), 238–69.

At the same time, important and interesting elements of the restoration project indicate that even in what seemed to be a counterrevolutionary process, profound changes were taking place that were anything but backward. The battle of information waged between royalists and insurgents during the monarchical restoration shows how the royalist government became officially invested in a politics of propaganda that sought to establish absolutist rule again in the territories of the Spanish Main or *Tierra Firme*. For example, the government created a newspaper, the *Gaceta Oficial*, as a crucial strategy devised to simultaneously counter the republican control of the public sphere and to rebuild monarchical sovereignty by shaping public opinion.[44]

## Constitutional Rule, Again: 1820–1823

Liberalism returned to Spain in 1820 after military uprisings spread across cities in January and February. Soldiers issued *pronunciamientos* (public statements and calls for action) in favor of the 1812 Constitution and juntas proclaimed the Charter. By March, the king gave in to these pressures and swore to uphold the Constitution himself. This change had deep consequences in the territories in Spanish America that continued to be under Spanish rule. It was a time of renovation in which people – liberals – who during the restoration had been repressed or exiled again reclaimed some public space. Yet one crucial difference at this time was that the leaders of the new liberal process were military officers. In Spain, the most visible military figure who became a hero was Field Marshal Rafael Riego.

In Peru, it was Viceroy Joaquín de la Pezuela who received the new challenge to embrace the liberal constitution again. He initially feared that making such a shift was full of the dangers, such as the consequences of reinstituting the Constitution for the popular sectors (*"castas"*) and the problems it would entail for collecting taxes for the war, particularly because of the abolition of tribute.[45] Yet he complied with the publication, oath, and institutionalization of the laws in the 1812 Charter in September 1820, after he received orders from Madrid to do so. Pezuela also saw this as an opportunity to reconcile with the insurgents and made some gestures toward negotiating with San Martín, the leader of the insurgency, considering the possible convergence between the insurgents'

---

[44] Chaparro, "Las armas y las letras"; Gutiérrez, *La restauración*, 114.

[45] Víctor Peralta Ruiz, "De absolutistas a constitucionales. Política y cultura en el gobierno del virrey Pezuela (Perú, 1816–1820)," in Jaime Rodríguez, ed., *Revolución, independencia y las nuevas naciones de América* (Madrid: Fundación Mapfre-Tavera, 2005), 485–510: 494.

project and that of the Constitution of the Spanish Monarchy. In spite of the rejection from the insurgents, Pezuela made sure that the Spanish Constitution circulated in all regions and that people swore to uphold it. He also had the Inquisition, which had been reinstated in Lima in 1815 after the restoration, suppressed in line with the liberal laws.[46]

In another crucial example, between May and September 1820, people across New Spain swore to uphold the Constitution. And as had happened in 1812–1814, those sectors that had interests in maintaining absolutism were again opposed to proclaiming it.[47] Most importantly, however, the restoration of the Constitution had consequences for the independence process in Mexico, too. In 1820 Agustín de Iturbide became the head of the royalist army. He had plans to defeat the insurgency and then declare independence with the possibility of keeping the new state linked to the Spanish dynasty. This was a major shift in strategy on behalf of the royalists, who had until then sought to eradicate the insurrection very aggressively, as we have seen. Yet significantly, in light of the impossibility of defeating the insurgents, Iturbide negotiated with the leaders of the most resilient areas, for example Vicente Guerrero.[48] It is also crucial to consider the contributions of the insurgency to the Plan de Iguala (the document that resulted from those negotiations). What is fascinating about this alliance is not only – as Mexican independence historiography has remarked – that a royalist commander became the head of the coalition that created the Mexican state. Equally remarkable is that Guerrero demanded to provide citizenship for mulattoes, which was granted. Mulattoes were themselves important in the insurgency in the territory and army led by Guerrero and they had rejected the introduction of the Cádiz Constitution in 1820, in part, for that reason. Thus, it is clear that the dialectic between the Cádiz Constitution and the independence processes continued in the 1820s, squaring the priorities of the national states with the political interests of people from the popular classes who mobilized militarily during the war.[49]

---

[46] Víctor Peralta's research revised the earlier interpretations of this period of Peruvian history by Timothy Anna and Brian Hamnett, who had argued that Spanish liberalism's return had not impacted Peru. See Peralta Ruiz, "De absolutistas a constitucionales," 499.

[47] Pedro Rújula and Manuel Chust, *El Trienio Liberal: Revolución e independencia (1820–1823)* (Madrid: Los libros de la Catarata, 2019).

[48] Guardino, *Peasants, Politics*, 77.

[49] Guardino, *Peasants, Politics*, forcefully argues that "[o]ne of the most durable misconceptions in Mexican history is that of 'conservative independence,'" and "The Plan of Iguala did not bring a 'conservative independence' in reaction to the liberal Spanish constitution," 74, 77.

## Independence, Insular Loyalty, and the Royalist Diaspora

When in 1821 Spanish Americans in South America finally defeated Spain at the Battle of Carabobo, and Mexico and Central America declared independence, there was still a long road ahead before Spain and its representatives in the Caribbean accepted this situation. Santo Domingo was an exception. Protected only by a thin force of local militias, creoles succeeded in declaring independence there in 1821, initially seeking to join Colombia to prevent a Haitian attack, yet the island ultimately unified under the Haitian government in 1822 (until 1844). By 1826, Spain's overseas empire only included the islands of Cuba, Puerto Rico, and the Philippines.

All across the mainland the new states embarked on a campaign for recognition that solidified their legitimacy in the international arena. Civil and military royalists fled to the Spanish islands that continued to be under Spanish rule. However, as long as Spain itself did not recognize the new countries' independence, new projects were devised in the Peninsula to regain control of the mainland territories by means of expeditions from the Caribbean. It was a tense coexistence on the ocean front, exacerbated by Spanish American privateers attacking Spanish vessels and sabotaging Spain's slave economy.

These later years of the conflict are relevant to the story of royalism in three ways: First, in the reconstitution of the loyalist diaspora to positions in the monarchical government once the mainland territories were lost. Second, small pockets of royalist rebellion by Indigenous people and people of African descent resisted independence in the mainland. Finally, the project of the Mexican empire and Bolívar's and San Martín's own exploration of kingship suggests that monarchy and empire continued to be part of the political imagination in Spanish America even after independence. Together, these themes reinforce the relevance of the phenomenon of monarchism over time. Additionally, like the Holy Alliance in Europe, they exemplify the broader Atlantic dialectics between monarchy and republicanism in the Atlantic World during the nineteenth century.

Waves of émigrés had arrived in the islands of Cuba and Puerto Rico during the different phases of warfare in the mainland, and by 1826 most Spanish officers had fled the mainland toward the Caribbean seeking asylum. In part, their previous experience was a guarantee that they could expect to be relocated and rewarded for their efforts. For men whose wealth had been destroyed by the war, new positions in the government were the guarantee for future recovery of status. Though the king was supportive of the émigrés, there were also widespread tensions around their presence on the islands, since they had to compete for employment and resources. Examples are Miguel Tacón, who had led the royalists in Popayán, later to become a major figure in Cuba's nineteenth century, and Miguel de la Torre, who went from fighting in Venezuela to taking over Puerto Rico's government. A less-known case is that of George D. Flinter, who had become naturalized as a Spanish subject and had to live through the Independence War in Venezuela. When he ended up in Puerto Rico, he was a major advocate of the expansion of slavery on the island. Flinter's case suggests that the experience that some of these émigrés had accumulated during the war in the mainland shaped not only life and government in the Caribbean colonies but also imperial designs regarding slavery.[50]

In fact, the idea that Spain could still recover the territories in South America also generated movements during the early republican period that continued to profess support for the monarchical regime. Two examples we have were in the Andes. One was in the Pacific region of Popayán, where the royalist alliance composed of Indians, slaves, and free Blacks that held on to the lowland region and the city of Pasto continued to resist the invasion of the Bolivarian forces up to 1825. They believed that Spanish forces would aid them in their offensive against Bolívar. Likewise, the Indigenous population in Huanta (Peru) rose up in a royalist rebellion between 1825 and 1828. There were rumors that royalist troops would land in Callao, Lima's port, which motivated the Indigenous people in Huanta to persist. Aside from the restorationist rumors that inspired the monarchists to attempt a defeat of the republic, it is clear that in Peru some skepticism and uncertainty prevailed among people of all classes with respect to the patriots' triumph. In fact, only recently had most of Peru's military, aristocrats, and intellectuals converted to independence.[51]

Finally, it is impossible to miss the significance of the fact that Mexican independence was consolidated within a monarchical framework, much like in Brazil, and that the figures of Bolívar and San Martín both contemplated a

---

[50] Semprún and Bullón, *El ejército realista*, 170; Sarah Chambers, "Rewarding Loyalty after the Wars of Independence in Spanish America: Displaced Bureaucrats in Cuba," in Alan Forrest et al., *War, Demobilization and Memory: The Legacy of War in the Era of Atlantic Revolutions* (London: Palgrave Macmillan, 2016), 238–53; Christopher Schmidt-Nowara, "Continental Origins of Insular Proslavery: George Dawson Flinter in Curaçao, Venezuela, Britain, and Puerto Rico, 1810s–1830s," *Almanack* 8 (2014), 55–67.

[51] Echeverri, *Indian and Slave Royalists*, Chapter 5; Méndez, *The Plebeian Republic*, Chapter 3.

monarchy in the process of establishing the states in the Andes. There, in particular, it is also interesting that the ideas of an Incaic emperor were relevant to the political imagination for building strong imperial states. If historians of independence and republicanism have considered these to be worrying and problematic steps in the history of Latin America it is because they have been trapped in the teleology of republicanism and in a de-historicized theory of nationalism.

In the range of options between the absolutist and liberal positions, which underwent a constant transformation during the decades between 1810 and 1830, all Spanish subjects found opportunities. There were two main axes around which the royalists engaged the monarchy and renewed their loyalty with expectation for benefits: the legal and the military realms. As we have seen, legal changes enveloped the Spanish Atlantic and allowed for redefinitions of the political identities of different social sectors. While this was a process that was anchored in the Peninsula, the American territories and their populations were central to the definition and ultimate implementation and interpretation of those changes. The military arena radically reshaped political relations, and the flexibility of the army in times of urgency allowed for the participation of multiple actors from different ethnicities who benefited in the process. There was a precedent for the incorporation of people of varied backgrounds in the military reforms of the eighteenth century, which had already begun altering ideas of power and authority.[52] During the independence wars, moreover, Indigenous people were rewarded with medals and titles, like the cacique Antonio Núñez of Mamatoco in Santa Marta. This was a highly symbolic gesture that sought not just to reward the cacique's actions in favor of the Crown but also secure future loyalty among the Indians. There were other collective gains in this process around strategic themes for Indigenous people such as tribute reduction.[53] Similarly, for people of African descent, this was a period of rapid change around the question of citizenship within the monarchy. As individuals and collectivities, slaves gained freedom and sought to legalize their status as Spanish vassals. While elites' positions varied, it is clear that their engagement with the monarchy either as royal officials, military figures or ecclesiastics, to mention a few possibilities, was all but backward or conservative. The transformations to the public sphere brought about by the liberal revolution were irreversible

---

[52] Mónica Ricketts, *Who Should Rule? Men of Arms, the Republic of Letters, and the Fall of the Spanish Empire* (New York: Oxford University Press, 2017), 77.

[53] Saether, *Identidades e independencia.*

even in the restoration to absolutism when the Crown embraced the challenge of reconquering public opinion. A view of the Age of Revolutions from the perspective of royalists shows the vitality of empire and monarchy not only in the interests of elites or the Crown and his advisers. All across class lines people in the Spanish world actively engaged the revolutionary process, making the monarchy a vehicle of transformation.

11

# Africans and Their Descendants in the Spanish Empire in the Age of Revolutions

JANE LANDERS

Africans and their descendants had enjoyed more than four centuries of freedom in multicultural and polyglot cities across southern Iberia and the Spanish Americas before the Age of Revolutions transformed the world. This long history of freedom helps explain why some Africans and their descendants in the Spanish empire chose royalism over revolution when the time came. Spanish law that considered slavery "against the laws of nature and reason," the Catholic Church that incorporated both free and enslaved Africans, and lenient attitudes toward manumission led to the early creation of a free Black class across the Spanish empire.[1]

Free and enslaved Africans helped Spain explore and establish its Atlantic empire in the fifteenth and sixteenth centuries. A specialized, if limited, pool of experienced Africans joined Spaniards on their earliest explorations, Indigenous slaving voyages, and full-blown wars of conquest. As Spanish conquerors and their African allies marched across the Caribbean and North and South America, they spread devastating diseases among virgin Indigenous populations. The catastrophic collapse of native populations across the Spanish Caribbean and Central America in the sixteenth century left Spain largely dependent upon Black military support and provided yet another corporate institution through which the enslaved could become free and rise in society. This was especially true in the circum-Caribbean, where slaves and former slaves helped Spain maintain a tenuous control over thinly populated and greatly dispersed colonies under almost constant foreign attack and encroachment. Much of Spain's imperial expanse was an under-manned frontier, and there every hand counted. The Crown recognized as

[1] William D. Phillips, Jr., *Slavery in Medieval and Early Modern Iberia* (Philadelphia: University of Pennsylvania Press, 2013).

304

much and encouraged Black military service to combat French, Dutch, and English challengers in the Caribbean.[2]

By 1600, Cuban officials had organized a militia that incorporated many "persons of color" and a free mulatto company that numbered 100 men.[3] Spanish Jamaica's governor also organized a company of free mulattoes to fight enemy pirates and by mid-century similar units operated in Peru, Chile, Guatemala, Nicaragua, Costa Rica, and Panama.[4] Recognizing that Spain could not respond quickly enough with metropolitan troops to escalating foreign threats in the circum-Caribbean, in 1663, the king ordered the viceroy of New Spain to evaluate the formation of more free Black companies. His order noted that the mulattoes and Blacks who defended his circum-Caribbean realms were "persons of valor" who fought with "vigor and reputation."[5] Spain's vulnerability meant that geopolitical, economic, and military capital accrued to at least some Black men in the Atlantic World of the seventeenth century, all of which apparently encouraged enlistments. A Central American roster from 1673 listed almost 2,000 *pardos* (usually meaning mulattoes, but sometimes referring to non-Europeans of mixed ancestry) serving in infantry units throughout the isthmus. Similar units of free Black or *moreno* men were organized in Hispaniola, Veracruz, Campeche, Puerto Rico, Panama, Caracas, Cartagena, and Florida.[6]

The death of the last Habsburg king, Carlos II (El Hechizado), in 1700, left the already weakened Spanish empire in chaos. At the conclusion of the War of Spanish Succession (1701–1713), Bourbon reformers assumed the Spanish Crown and, among other reforms, created formal Disciplined Militias across the Atlantic. Spain needed every hand it could get during the seemingly endless wars of the eighteenth century – the War of the Spanish Succession or Queen Anne's War (1701–1713), the War of Jenkins' Ear (1739–1743)

---

[2] David Wheat, *Atlantic Africa and the Spanish Caribbean, 1570–1640* (Chapel Hill: University of North Carolina Press, 2016).

[3] Jane Landers, "Transforming Bondsmen into Vassals: Arming the Slaves in Colonial Spanish America," in Philip Morgan and Christopher Brown, eds., *Arming Slaves in World History* (New Haven: Yale University Press, 2006), 120–45; Royal Order to the Viceroy of New Spain, 6 July 1663, México, 1070, Archivo General de Indias (henceforth AGI).

[4] Carey Robinson, *The Fighting Maroons of Jamaica* (Kingston: William Collins and Sangster, 1971), 14; Rina Cáceres, *Negros, mulatos, esclavos y libertos en la Costa Rica del siglo XVII* (Mexico City: Instituto Panamericano de Geografía e Historia, 2000).

[5] Royal order to the Viceroy of New Spain, 6 July 1663, México, 1070, AGI.

[6] Stephen Weber, "Las compañías de milicia y la defensa del istmo centroamericano en el siglo XVII: El alistamiento general de 1673," *Mesoamérica* 14 (1987), 511–28; Christine Rivas, "The Spanish Colonial Military: Santo Domingo, 1701–1779," *The Americas* 60:2 (2003), 249–72.

which became the War of the Austrian Succession (1739–1748), King George's War (1744–1748) and the Seven Years' War (1756–1763). Military men of African descent, who had already served Spain for more than two centuries served in all these wars. They now elected their own officers and designed their unit's uniforms. More importantly, they received the *fuero militar*, a corporate charter that exempted them from tribute and prosecution in civilian courts and granted them equal juridical status with white militiamen.[7] Formal membership in the military corporation also granted these men and their families higher status in a status-obsessed world. Men of African descent across Spain's Atlantic holdings clearly appreciated the juridical and social benefits of militia membership and they developed traditions of multi-generational service.[8] As had long been the case, the military service of free men of color also redounded to the benefit of their wives and children, who could inherit pensions and property, as well as a certain social status, from their husbands and fathers.[9]

In desperate need of their military services, Spain also rewarded and incorporated maroons across the empire, granting them land (that the maroons already controlled), and formally recognizing their self-governing towns. When Spain went to war with England in 1762, maroons who had been in the mountains for more than forty years rode into the town of Veracruz to offer Spain their military assistance. Organized as the Mounted Lancers of Jaliscoya, their reward was liberty and a new town of their own, Nuestra Señora de Guadalupe de Amapa. When Spanish ranchers tried to encroach upon their land, the residents of Amapa challenged them in court and the Crown protected their Black *vecinos'* claims.[10]

---

[7] The *fuero* also granted Black soldiers military, hospitalization, retirement, and death benefits. Lyle N. McAlister, *The "Fuero Militar" in New Spain, 1764–1800* (Gainesville: University of Florida Press, 1957); Joseph P. Sánchez, "African Freedmen and the Fuero Militar: A Historical Overview of Pardo and Moreno Militias in the Late Spanish Empire," *Colonial Latin American Historical Review* 3:2 (1994), 117–33; Ben Vinson III, *Bearing Arms for His Majesty: The Free Colored Militia in Colonial Mexico* (Stanford: Stanford University Press, 2001).

[8] María del Carmen Barcia Zequeira, *Los ilustres apellidos: Negros en la Habana colonial* (Havana: Ediciones Boloña, 2009); Jane Landers, *Black Society in Spanish Florida* (Urbana: University of Illinois Press, 1999); Kimberly S. Hanger, *Bounded Lives, Bounded Places: Free Black Society in Colonial New Orleans, 1769–1803* (Durham, NC: Duke University Press, 1997).

[9] Landers, *Black Society*, Chapter 6; Karen Y. Morrison, "Creating an Alternative Kinship: Slavery, Freedom, and Nineteenth-Century Afro-Cuban 'Hijos Naturales,'" *Journal of Social History* 41:1 (2007), 55–80.

[10] Jane Landers, "*Cimarrón* and Citizen: African Ethnicity, Corporate Identity and the Evolution of Free Black Towns in the Spanish Circum-Caribbean," in Jane G. Landers

When the British captured Havana the same year, Cuba's free Black militia units fought bravely to defend their homeland. The free Black barber Gabriel Dorotea Barba recruited and equipped a battalion of other free Blacks, for which service the Crown rewarded him with the rank of captain. Enslaved Blacks in Cuba also defended Spain's sovereignty. A group of twenty Cuban slaves, armed only with machetes, launched an offensive against a superior English force at Cuba's great Morro Castle, killing some of the English enemy and capturing seven more. The "ladies of Havana" described the slaves' heroism in a letter to the king, who freed them and awarded their leader, Andrés Gutiérrez, the military title of captain.[11] Another slave, Manuel Medina, was similarly rewarded for leading fifty of his fellow slaves to meet the British enemy in Guanabacoa. The British gave no quarter to those Black men they captured, and the compensation claims of owners document other slaves who died fighting the British.[12]

In 1769, Spain sent Cuba's Black militia to help establish Spanish control of New Orleans and these units returned to the region during the American Revolution. In that war, Lieutenant José Francisco Sánchez, of the *pardo* battalion, and the *moreno* Manuel Blanco followed Captain Barba's earlier example and raised and uniformed companies of 100 men each. These men, like Barba, won captaincies, the right to name their subordinate officers, and the *fuero militar* for all their men.[13] As Cuba's Black troops fought for the Spanish monarch to help liberate British colonials, they adopted the rhetoric of independence. The motto emblazoned on the flag of Cuba's *moreno* battalions, "Victory or Death," nicely mirrored the sentiment expressed by Patrick Henry. During the American Revolution, Captains Gabriel Dorotea Barba, José Antonio Aponte, Francisco Miranda, and other Cuban militiamen fought in the Florida campaigns and in the Bahamas against the British. These men participated in many of the important military contests of their day. They had access to a wide range of political information, both printed

---

and Barry M. Robinson, eds., *Slaves, Subjects and Subversives: Blacks in Colonial Latin America* (Albuquerque: University of New Mexico Press, 2006), 111–45.

[11] Jane Landers, *Atlantic Creoles in the Age of Revolution* (Cambridge, MA: Harvard University Press, 2010), Chapter 4; Elena A. Schneider, *The Occupation of Havana: War, Trade, and Slavery in the Atlantic World* (Chapel Hill: University of North Carolina Press, 2018).

[12] Landers, *Atlantic Creoles*, Chapter 4; Pedro Deschamps Chapeaux, *Los Batallones de Pardos y Morenos Libres* (Havana: Instituto Cubano del Libro, 1976), 29–30; Gloria García, *Conspiraciones y revueltas: La actividad política de los negros en Cuba (1790–1845)* (Santiago de Cuba: Editorial Oriente, 2003), 13.

[13] Alan J. Kuethe, *Cuba, 1753–1815: Crown, Military and Society* (Knoxville: University of Tennessee Press, 1986), 74.

and oral, and made reasoned and informed choices to advance their rights as free men. Some spent as many as twenty years posted abroad before returning to Cuba, forming families and relationships with the free Blacks with whom they served in these foreign stations.[14] They also served on Spanish corsairing expeditions throughout the Caribbean, all the while gaining "geopolitical literacy," that is, knowledge of the politics and socio-economic systems of places not their own.[15]

Over time, free people of color from all these diverse backgrounds formed a significant middle class of artisans, small property owners, and militiamen and some even became slave owners in Spanish port cities like Havana, Cartagena, Veracruz, and New Orleans.[16] The free Black militiaman Juan Bautista Collins was born in New Orleans, the son of a French father and African mother. Collins owned a store in St. Augustine, Florida and kept the books in French and Spanish. Among his debtors were some of the most important figures in St. Augustine. Collins carried on business in Pensacola and Havana, Cuba and managed St. Augustine's cattle trade with the Seminole Indians. Many other Africans and their descendants also rose in status through their good services to the Crown (primarily military), their Catholicism, and their extended networks of fictive or actual kinship, and patronage.

Literacy was another critical marker of status and a route to upward mobility in Spanish America. Literacy enabled many free Blacks to use Spanish law to advance themselves and their causes, as well as assist those who were not literate. A Catholic school established in St. Augustine, Florida, in 1786 educated free boys of all ethnicities and former slaves received the

[14] Deschamps Chapeaux, *Batallones*, 50; Sherry Johnson, *The Social Transformation of Eighteenth-Century Cuba* (Gainesville: University Press of Florida, 2001), 66–7; Herbert Klein, "The Colored Militia of Cuba: 1568–1836," *Caribbean Studies* 6:2 (1966), 17–27; Landers, *Black Society*, 198–200.

[15] Despacho de Sub/te de Vandera, 1 June 1802, Cuba 1667, AGI; Hanger, *Bounded Lives, Bounded Places*, 109–35; Landers, *Black Society*, 198–200; Vinson, *Bearing Arms for His Majesty*, 7–8.

[16] Kimberly S. Hanger, "Patronage, Property and Persistence: The Emergence of a Free Black Elite in Spanish New Orleans," in Jane G. Landers, *Against the Odds: Free Blacks in the Slave Societies of the Americas* (London: Frank Cass, 1996), 44–64; Landers, "Acquisition and Loss on a Spanish Frontier: The Free Black Homesteaders of Florida, 1784–1821," in Jane G. Landers, *Against the Odds: Free Blacks in the Slave Societies of the Americas* (London: Frank Cass, 1996), 85–101; Sherry Johnson, "La Guerra contra los habitantes de los arrabales: Changing Patterns of Land Use and Land Tenancy in and around Havana, 1763–1800," *Hispanic American Historical Review* 77:2 (1997), 181–209; Pedro Deschamps Chapeaux, *El negro en la economía habanera del siglo XIX* (Havana: Unión de Escritores y Artistas de Cuba, 1971).

same education as the sons of their former masters.[17] In the eighteenth century the Jesuit order admitted free Black boys with ability and connections into the Colegio de San José de la Habana, where they received an excellent classical education. In the same period, other free Black boys received higher education in Peru and Mexico.[18] Captain Gabriel Dorotea Barba established a school for children of color in Havana that operated for at least thirty years. Barba advertised his school in the *Diario de la Habana* and by 1833 it consisted of two school buildings: one for boys and another for girls. Even more unusual was that Barba held evening classes for slaves whose owners were too busy to teach them the Christian doctrine, as was supposedly required.[19] Several other members of the militia also established schools in Havana in the first decades of the nineteenth century, as did at least four women of color. Poor white children attended these schools although Cuban officials tried to prevent it on the basis that people of African descent should not exercise control over those of Spanish descent. These prohibitions, like so many others, went unheeded and even the elite Jesuit Fathers of Belen admitted students of all origins to their school.[20]

In the multiracial and multiethnic port cities of the Americas, such as Havana, New Orleans, St. Augustine, and Cumaná, racial mixing was inevitable and unions between Spaniards and Africans were common. Couples even entered into mixed-race marriages with little stigma.[21] As they had also in West Africa, many African women married men of other nationalities and races and managed property and businesses for them. The Senegalese woman, Ana Gallum, a.k.a. Nansi Wiggins, was freed by and married to the Englishman who bought her, and when he died, she managed his plantation and cattle herds and slaves for the benefit of their seven children. Although she was illiterate and her husband died intestate, community networks helped Anna retain control of her property in the Spanish courts.[22] Her contemporary and fellow Senegalese, Anna Madgigine Jai

---

[17] Landers, *Black Society*, 116–17.
[18] Memorial of Antonio Flores, 1759 and response of the Council of the Indies, 28 February 1760, Santo Domingo (SD) 1455, AGI.
[19] Deschamps Chapeaux, *El negro en la economía habanera*, 122–25.     [20] Ibid.
[21] Jane Landers, "Ana Gallum, Freed Slave and Property Owner," in Nora E. Jaffary and Jane E. Mangan, eds., *Women in Colonial Latin America: 1526 to 1806* (Indianapolis: Hackett Publishing Co., Inc., 2018), 224–39; Daniel L. Schafer, *Anna Madgigine Jai Kingsley: African Princess, Florida Slave, and Plantation Owner* (Gainesville: University Press of Florida, 2018); Hanger, *Bounded Lives*; Landers, *Black Society*, Chapter 5.
[22] Testamentary Proceedings of Jacob Wiggins and Declaration of Ana Gallum, 3 October 1799, Civil Proceedings, East Florida Papers (EFP), microfilm reel 160, P. K. Yonge Library of Florida History, University of Florida (PKY).

Kingsley, whose amazing life Daniel Schafer has chronicled, followed a similar trajectory and enjoyed even more prosperity.[23]

Race relations hardened, however, with the revolutionary movements that swept the Atlantic in the eighteenth century. These conflicts engulfed Africans and their descendants across the Spanish empire and forced them to choose sides. Designed to overthrow corrupt monarchical regimes and incorporate lower classes into new democratic states, most of these experiments actually offered little more than rhetorical advantages to people of color. While some Blacks took up the new political ideologies, others remained committed royalists. Many Blacks ardently supported, in word and deed, the monarchs who freed, rewarded, and honored them.

The former slaves who led the revolution in Saint-Domingue and made themselves and their followers free fought bravely for more than two hard years but, in 1793, low on supplies, the three main leaders of the revolt, Georges Biassou, Jean-François Papillon, and Toussaint Louverture accepted the Spanish offer of alliance, declaring in a rhetorical flourish that they would "rather be slaves of the Spaniards than free with the French."[24] In fact, they never intended to return to slavery under any regime and were determined to cut the best deal possible for themselves, their kin, and their troops. Centuries-old institutional precedents encouraged Spain to treat with and enlist former slaves into military service and to incorporate them into a Spanish polity, but none of Spain's previous military recruits had been leaders of the largest slave revolt in the hemisphere. For this reason, the alliance Spain struck with the Black revolutionaries was an uneasy one, marked by distrust on both sides.[25]

Spain designated its newly recruited armies of risen slaves the "Black Auxiliaries of Carlos IV," a much more formal title and affiliation than earlier or later Black militias ever received. To celebrate the new alliance, Captain General Joaquín García, Governor of Santo Domingo, ceremoniously decorated Jean-François Papillon, Georges Biassou, and Toussaint Louverture with gold medals bearing the likeness of the king, and presented them with documents expressing the gratitude and confidence of the Spanish

---

[23] Schafer, *Anna Madgigine Jai Kingsley.*
[24] Estado (henceforth ES) 13, AGI; Captain General Joaquín García to the Duque de la Alcudia, 18 February 1794, ES 14, doc. 86, AGI; Captain General Joaquín García to the Duque de Alcudia, 12 December 1795, in Emilio Rodríguez Demorizi, *Cesión de Santo Domingo a Francia: Correspondencia de Godoy, García, Roume, Hedouville, Louverture, Rigaud y otros, 1795–1802* (Ciudad Trujillo: Impresora Dominicana, 1958), 46–8.
[25] Landers, *Atlantic Creoles.*

government. Twelve other subchiefs also received silver medals and documents attesting to their meritorious service.[26] Jean-François Papillon later decorated himself with the Cross of Saint Louis, and Biassou titled himself the "Viceroy of the Conquered Territories," while the subsequently more famous Toussaint Louverture initially served only as aide and physician to Biassou's large army.[27] Toussaint Louverture later switched his allegiance to the French Republic, but Papillon and Biassou and large numbers of their troops remained committed to Spain.[28]

Their bloody years of fighting ended when the 1795 Treaty of Basel required Spain and its Black Auxiliaries to evacuate the island. Spanish officials in Santo Domingo were compelled to honor the king's promises of freedom, relocation, and financial support, but they also watched the former slaves with fear and suspicion and tried to isolate them and the dangerous ideas they represented, as did the Spanish officials who received the exiles in locales as diverse as Cádiz, Panama, Guatemala, and Florida.[29] Spain's Black allies were embittered by the graceless way some Spanish officials treated them and never anticipated the diaspora they would experience at the end of the war. Biassou and Papillon, however, lived out their lives as free men in the service of Spain.[30] Their former ally, Toussaint Louverture, on the other hand, died in prison, betrayed by the French. Scattered across the Atlantic World, Spain's Black Auxiliaries struggled to maintain contact with one another, and Jean-François Papillon imagined that they would reunite again in Central America.[31] Meanwhile, in their new homes they continued to use the types of petition they had learned, and asserted the obligations of the Crown. They also engaged in centuries-old forms of association and civic

---

[26] Ibid.; Julius S. Scott, *The Common Wind: Afro-American Currents in the Age of the Haitian Revolution* (London: Verso, 2018).

[27] David Patrick Geggus and Norman Fiering, eds., *The World of the Haitian Revolution* (Bloomington: Indiana University Press, 2009); Laurent Dubois, *Avengers of the New World: The Story of the Haitian Revolution* (Cambridge, MA: Harvard University Press, 2004).

[28] Landers, *Atlantic Creoles*, Chapter 2.

[29] Jorge Victoria Ojeda, *Las tropas auxiliares de Carlos IV: De Saint-Domingue al mundo hispano* (Castello de la Plena: Universitat Jaume I, 2011); Miriam Rebekah Martin, "The Black Auxiliary Troops of King Carlos IV: African Diaspora in the Spanish Atlantic World, 1791–1818" (Ph.D. dissertation, Vanderbilt University, 2015); Renée Soulodre-La France, "'Los esclavos de su Magestad': Slave Protest and Politics in Late Colonial New Granada," in Landers and Robinson, eds., *Slaves, Subjects, and Subversives*, 175–208.

[30] Landers, *Atlantic Creoles*, Chapter 2; Captain General Joaquín García to the Duque de Alcudia, 12 December 1795, cited in Demorizi, *Cesión de Santo Domingo*, 46–8.

[31] Martin, "The Black Auxiliary Troops."

engagement, and circulated among themselves emerging news on abolitionism and world events, despite increasing suspicion and repression by Spanish officials.[32]

The shockwaves from the successful slave rebellion in Saint-Domingue reverberated across the Atlantic World and had particular resonance in locales with significant Black populations, free, and enslaved.[33] David Geggus has documented the wave of revolts that swept across the Atlantic in 1795, many of them referencing Saint-Domingue. Rebels such as those who rose in Coro, Venezuela, used the rhetoric of the Age of Revolutions to demand an end to slavery and rights for the freed. Coro's free Black leaders, José Leonardo Chirino and José Caridad Gonzalez, cited the French Revolution and called for "the law of the French, the republic, the freedom of slaves and the suppression of the *alcabala* and other taxes." Two years later another revolt of *pardos* and poor whites led by Manuel Gual and José María España, called for "liberty and equality, the rights of man and republican government" in Venezuela. They also demanded freedom of trade, abolition of slavery and Indian tribute, and distribution, and abolition of taxes like the *alcabala*.[34] At the same time, enslaved compatriots elsewhere were defending Spanish territories and deploying the language of loyalty and vassalage.[35]

The slave revolt in Saint-Domingue triggered economic as well as political change in the Atlantic. Following the destruction of Saint-Domingue's sugar plantations, Cuban planters had invested heavily in that crop and in the African slave trade on which it depended. The rise of a so-called "second slavery" in Cuba (largely funded by American capital) resulted in the "Africanization" of Cuba. Neither the British embargo of 1807, nor the US embargo of 1808, deterred Cuba and American slave traders. Nor did the Mixed Commissions for the Suppression of the Slave Trade Britain

---

[32] Ojeda, *Las tropas auxiliaries*; Martin, "Black Auxiliary Troops"; Soulodre-La France, "Los esclavos."

[33] Scott, *Common Wind*; Matt D. Childs, *The 1812 Aponte Rebellion and the Struggle against Atlantic Slavery* (Chapel Hill: University of North Carolina Press, 2006).

[34] Laurent Dubois, *A Colony of Citizens: Revolution and Slave Emancipation in the French Caribbean 1787–1804* (Chapel Hill: University of North Carolina Press, 2004); Lyman L. Johnson, *Workshop of Revolution: Plebeian Buenos Aires and the Atlantic World, 1776–1810* (Durham, NC: Duke University Press, 2011); Cristina Soriano, *Tides of Revolution: Information, Insurgencies, and the Crisis of Colonial Rule in Venezuela* (Albuquerque: University of New Mexico Press, 2018); Edgardo Pérez Morales, *No Limits to Their Sway: Cartagena's Privateers and the Masterless Caribbean in the Age of Revolutions* (Nashville: Vanderbilt University Press, 2018).

[35] Marcela Echeverri, *Indian and Slave Royalists in the Age of Revolution: Reform, Revolution and Royalism in the Northern Andes, 1780–1825* (Cambridge: Cambridge University Press, 2016), Chapter 5.

established in Havana, Rio de Janeiro, Suriname, and Sierra Leone to decide whether captured ships were illegally slaving. Between 1790 and 1820, Cuban planters imported approximately 325,000 slaves, a threefold increase in slave imports in only thirty years.[36] This demographic pattern contrasted with most other Spanish colonies, such as Colombia, where many former slaves had already gained their liberty. In those locales, the fights for abolition and independence often overlapped.

Latin American leaders took up both causes when Napoleon Bonaparte invaded Portugal in 1807 and Spain in 1808, destabilizing Europe and the Americas. In the joint causes of independence and abolition, Simón Bolívar, "the Liberator" of Spanish America, freed some 800 of his own slaves, declaring, "[o]ur unfortunate brothers who suffer enslavement are from this moment free. The laws of nature and humanity, and the interest of the government proclaim their liberty. From now on there will be in Venezuela only one class of inhabitants: all will be citizens."[37] As Spain's liberal government on the run ruled in resistance from Cádiz, liberals across Latin America followed suit, creating juntas claiming to rule in the name of their absent king. The Cádiz junta authored the famed liberal constitution of 1812 that reversed long-promulgated racial prohibitions and decreed that "Spaniards of African origin" should be helped to study sciences and have access to an ecclesiastical career, "so as to be ever more useful to the state."[38]

The new constitution was read in plazas across the Atlantic, to enthusiastic crowds that included free and enslaved Blacks. A copy of the Constitution reached Cuba in July of 1812 and Cuban officials, almost all of whom were monarchists, must have been galled to have to swear allegiance to the new form of government.[39] But alarmed by the example of slave rebellion in Saint-Domingue and by the growing abolitionist sentiment that threatened their way of life, Cuba's powerful sugar planters made every effort to shore up slavery. Captain General Someruelos understood the danger of allowing Cuba's large Black population to have access to such "inflammatory" political rhetoric. The African slave trade to the island was growing and free people of color constituted slightly more than one-fourth of Havana's population in 1812, many of

---

[36] Jane Landers, "Slavery in the Spanish Caribbean and the Failure of Abolition," REVIEW, A Journal of the Fernand Braudel Center 31:3 (2008): 343–71.

[37] Simon Bolívar, 6 July 1816, Obras Completas (Havana: Editorial Lex, 1947), vol. II, 1094.

[38] Asuntos Politicos (henceforth AP), Legajo 214, Signatura 118, Archivo Nacional de Cuba (henceforth ANC).

[39] Roque E. Garrigo, Historia documentada de la conspiración de los Soles y rayos de Bolívar (Havana: Imprenta "El Siglo XX," 1929), 100.

them, as noted, were literate and engaged in enlightenment projects of education and social ascension.[40] Alarmed that "seductive *impresos* [printed materials] circulated in the hands of everyone," Someruelos suppressed publication of the sessions of the Cortes in which abolition was discussed but this censorship only fueled widespread rumors of emancipation.[41]

In 1812, a series of new slave revolts, reminiscent of those of 1795, swept through Cuba. Angry slaves in Bayamo, Holguín, Puerto Principe, and Havana circulated stories that claimed the king of Spain, the Spanish Cortes, the king of England, the king of Haiti (Henri Christophe had crowned himself emperor that year), or the king of Kongo had planned to free them but local authorities had suppressed their abolition decrees. Authorities reacted swiftly and brutally suppressed these uprisings, executing some of the rebels and sentencing others to hard labor or military service in contested areas of the Caribbean.[42] Some of the Puerto Principe rebels, like Tiburcio Recio, were deported to Florida, where, ironically, they fought for Spain against Georgian "Patriots" and US Marines.[43] Exiled free Blacks like Recio and the dispersed Black Auxiliaries of Carlos IV helped disseminate news of the latest revolts and abolitionist rhetoric across the Atlantic.

Cuba's authorities might have thought they had dealt with the threat, when on 15 March 1812 slaves and free Blacks launched a revolt on the outskirts of Havana alleged to have been led by the free Black militiaman, sculptor, and *cofradía* member, José Antonio Aponte. Authorities arrested, interrogated, and finally executed Aponte, but other rebels nailed a manifesto to the door of the captain general's house that read, "[a]t the sound of a drum and a trumpet you will find us ready and fearless to end this empire of tyranny, and in this manner we will vanquish the arrogance of our enemies."[44]

The gruesome public executions of Aponte and his followers failed to silence Cuba's free Black leaders, who continued to assert their legal rights via memorials sent to the Cortes in Spain. Captain Gabriel Dorotea Barba led

---

[40] Childs, *1812 Aponte Rebellion*, 69.

[41] Captain General Someruelos, 11 February, 20 February, and 5 March 1812, Santo Domingo 1284, AGI cited in Larry R. Jensen, *Children of Colonial Despotism: Press, Politics, and Culture in Cuba, 1790–1840* (Tampa: University Presses of Florida, 1988), 39.

[42] Childs, *1812 Aponte Rebellion*, 157–62.

[43] List of the Blacks in the Castillo del Morro to be sent to the Presidio of Saint Augustine, Florida, 16 September 1812. Cuba 1789, AGI. Eighteen men were sentenced to ten years of labor and forbidden to return to Cuba. Also see Arrival of Miguel y Perico Gonzalez in St. Augustine, 14 April 1812, EFP, microfilm reel 12, PKY; Landers, *Atlantic Creoles*, Chapter 4.

[44] José Luciano Franco, *La conspiración de Aponte: 1812* (Havana: Editorial Ciencias Sociales, 2006), 19; Childs, *1812 Aponte Rebellion*, 156; Landers, *Atlantic Creoles*, Chapter 4.

the legal campaign to preserve and advance the rights and privileges of the free Black militia, but many other officers also filed complaints. Barba related a series of insults free Black officers had suffered from Spanish Subintendant Inspector Antonio Seydel [sic] such as being required to march in the same ranks as ordinary soldiers or take off their hats in the presence of white officers. He cited violations of specific articles of the 1769 Reglamento that reorganized the Black militias. Captain Miguel Porro, who would later fight the Georgia Patriots in Florida alongside the exiled Tiburcio Recio, also cited that Reglamento when he refused to doff his hat to a white officer. Cuban officials arrested Porro and he spent eleven days in jail for his principles before being released.

Undaunted, Barba and his fellow officers continued to press for equal pay and the status they felt they were due. In one long memorial Barba recounted for the king all the long service, the many battles, and the loyalty of the Black militia. Using the florid language of the day, he reminded the monarch of his obligation to his vassals and asked that that the sons of Black militiamen be given preference in officer appointment over those of men who had not served. He added that they "never lack the honor, good education, and status that they should inherit from their fathers." Barba closed this request by appealing to "the well-known beneficent heart of Your Majesty," adding that the Black militia had no other protection or source of help but "Your Royal majesty whom we consider our only Father."[45] A royal decree of 24 July 1812 "conceded the honorific distinction of the Royal Effigy" to Captains Ysidro Moreno and Gabriel Dorotea Barba and, on 19 October 1812, both men received their medals in a public ceremony on the plaza where Aponte had been executed six months earlier.[46]

The constitutional gains free Blacks enjoyed in 1812 were, however, short lived. With British support, Spain freed itself from French rule and King Fernando returned to the Spanish throne. Determined to restore absolute

[45] Memorial of Nicolás Lane to Captain General Juan Ruiz de Apodaca, 25 April 1812; Troops of the Batallón de Morenos de la Habana going to St. Augustine, 13 May 1812, and Memorials of the Captains and Officials of the Batallón de Morenos, 28 May 1812; 18 June 1812; 13 August 1812; 14 September 1812; 22 October 1812; 17 December 1812, Cuba 1798, AGI. Miguel Porro complained regularly about the poor conditions and was imprisoned in the Castillo de San Marcos in St. Augustine. Miguel Porro to the Governor, 29 March 1813, to and from the Commander of the Negro Militia, 1812–1821, EFP, microfilm reel 75, PKY.

[46] Francisco Montalvo to Captain General Juan Ruiz de Apodaca, 19 October 1812, Cuba 1798, AGI.

monarchy, Fernando abolished the liberal constitution that restrained him, charging that it was modeled after the "revolutionary and democratic French constitution of 1791." Cuba's recently installed Captain General Juan Ruiz de Apodaca suppressed that news, fearful of the "populations of color" and the many British "sailors with democratic ideas, like all commoners" who were then in Havana. Not until the British ships sailed away from Cuba did Apodaca permit the *Diario de la Habana* to publish news of the restoration of Fernando on 21 July 1814.[47]

In February of 1815, Fernando sent a fleet of warships and more than 10,000 troops under the command of General Pablo Morillo y Morillo to suppress independence movements in *Tierra Firme* (northern South America). Morillo's royalist army quickly overwhelmed Simón Bolívar's rebel forces. Forced to flee, Bolívar appealed to Haiti's Alexandre Pétion for weapons and financial support to keep his faltering independence movement alive. In exchange, Bolívar promised to abolish slavery.[48] Former slaves and free Blacks battled on both sides of the terrible wars without quarter that engulfed New Granada, and Black populations paid the heaviest cost of all. However, whether they chose to believe the royalist or independence leaders' promises, it is clear that the Black enlistees saw some advantage to be had and that they made their decision based on rational geopolitical assessments.[49]

Between 1810 and 1825, all the Spanish colonies except Cuba, Puerto Rico, and the Philippines had gained their independence from the metropole. In 1822 Haiti assumed control of Santo Domingo and the Spanish portion of the island did not achieve independence until 1844. Cuba, however, never even established a provisional junta and prided itself on being the "ever-faithful isle."[50] Morillo's large royalist force passed through Havana on the way to

---

[47] Cuba's late eighteenth-century papers included the *Guía de Forasteros*, the *Gaceta de Havana*, and the *Papel Periódico de la Habana*, although the first two were short-lived. The *Aurora: Correo Político-económico de la Habana*, the *Mensajero Político Económico-literario de la Habana*, and the *Diario de la Habana* were Cuba's most important nineteenth-century newspapers. Jensen, *Children of Colonial Despotism*, 3–21, 47–9.

[48] Wim Klooster, *Revolutions in the Atlantic World: A Comparative History* (New York: New York University Press, 2018), 117–57.

[49] Landers, *Atlantic Creoles*; Klooster, *Revolutions*, 151–2; Seth Meisel, "'The Fruit of Freedom': Slaves and Citizens in Early Republican Argentina," in Landers and Robinson, eds., *Slaves, Subjects, and Subversives*, 273–305.

[50] Jay Kinsbruner, *Independence in Spanish America: Civil Wars, Revolutions, and Underdevelopment* (Albuquerque: University of New Mexico Press, 2000), 35–7.

the battlegrounds of Venezuela and New Granada (Colombia). Refugees from those war-torn areas, in turn, scattered throughout the Caribbean. From both groups, populations of color in Havana and elsewhere learned about the liberators and the nascent republics of Spanish America. By 1820, Spain's wars were so unpopular that troops bound for the Americas finally mutinied and refused to serve. The so-called Sergeants' Revolt forced Fernando to restore the Constitution of Cádiz.[51]

This brought new hope to free Blacks and public intellectuals in Cuba who struggled to liberalize Cuban society and uplift its large African-born population. On 28 March 1821, Francisco J. de Burgos launched a new periodical dedicated to that purpose. Its title was *El Negrito* (little Black man), a diminutive form that may have been intended to minimize backlash from white Cubans threatened by its content. Its front page depicted a Black man with outstretched hand standing below a banner reading "Constitution or Death." The editorial below was entitled "Merit and virtue will open the doors of citizenship to Spaniards born in Africa." The author noted that while some Cubans believed that enlightenment led to excess, he believed ignorance was more likely to do so. He argued that if the still enslaved knew their potential to become citizens through "merit and virtue" they would behave more honorably to achieve this prize. They would also be less likely to behave badly as free citizens, because only a former slave could really appreciate the loss of liberty. Article 24 of the restored constitution also provided a strong incentive for education because after 1830, any Spaniards (including those free people of African origin) who did not know how to read and write would be excluded from citizenship. In the same issue, the free Black militiaman Juan José de León described being stopped and fined by a deputy for not carrying a lantern at night. Although he reminded the deputy of his military *fuero* (exemption from penalties) León was nonetheless taken into custody and harassed for the three pesos fine. The author planned to discuss subsequent articles of the Constitution, but never had the chance. Cuban authorities found an excuse to shut down his paper and no subsequent issues appeared.[52]

Like *El Negrito*'s author, most of Latin America's independence leaders espoused Enlightenment ideas of racial equality and republican political ideals. When they finally achieved independence, however, their new

---

[51] Garrigo, *Historia documentada*, 102–3.
[52] *El Negrito*, vol. 1, no. 1, 28 March 1821, https://merrick.library.miami.edu/cdm/compoundobject/collection/chc9998/id/851/rec/2.

republican constitutions abolished the slave trade, but not slavery. They settled for free-womb laws rather than immediate emancipation, thus assuring at least some enslaved labor persisted into mid-century. Gran Colombia's Constitution of 1821, for example, called for "equality" but required literacy to vote. A subsequent law abolished the slave trade and said all children born of slave mothers would be free, but these children would be required to work for their mothers' masters until age eighteen, to pay for their upbringing.[53] These "tutelage" systems were rife with abuse and parents went to court to seek the return of their children from owners who were not, as required, properly feeding and clothing and educating their children.[54] Free-womb laws effectively postponed full emancipation for another generation.

As they stalled on full abolition, many of the new governments created manumission funds and devised elaborate rituals in which a few "worthy" and "honest" and "industrious" slaves would be publicly freed to remind those still enslaved it was possible. The numbers freed by these means were minimal. Still, the mechanisms that had for centuries permitted some to exit slavery, the emancipation of those who fought on both sides of the independence wars, the great loss of Black life during the wars, and the cessation of the legal slave trade all contributed to the dramatic decline in enslaved populations in Spanish America.[55] Slowly, the new republics adjusted economic patterns and found other ways to secure labor, such as debt peonage, and only then did they finally end slavery. Full abolition was finally declared in Chile in 1823, Central America (1825), Mexico (1829), Uruguay (1846), Colombia (1850), Argentina (1853), Peru and Venezuela (1854), and Paraguay (1870).

Meanwhile, for economic reasons, Cuba remained loyal to Spain and paid only lip-service to abolition of the slave trade. Following the destruction of Saint-Domingue's sugar economy, Cuba embarked upon a so-called "second slavery."[56] Following the destruction of Saint-Domingue's sugar economy, Cuba embarked upon a so-called "second slavery." As we have seen, slave

---

[53] Peter Blanchard, *Under the Flags of Freedom: Slave Soldiers and the Wars of Independence in Spanish South America* (Pittsburgh: University of Pittsburgh Press, 2008).

[54] Nicolette M. Wilhide, "Child and Citizen: The Tutelage of Minors, Slavery and Transition in Rio de Janeiro, Brazil, 1871–1900" (Ph.D. dissertation, Vanderbilt University, 2015); Klooster, *Revolutions*, 155.

[55] Meisel, "Fruits of Freedom."

[56] Dale Tomich, ed., *The Politics of the Second Slavery* (Albany, NY: State University of New York Press, 2016).

imports into Cuba increased massively after 1790.[57] The "Africanization" of Cuba continued apace in subsequent decades.[58] Under duress, in 1817 Spain signed a treaty with Great Britain that prohibited the slave trade north of the equator and abolished the slave trade completely after 1820. But the Cuban slave trade continued with the clear collusion of Cuban officials, most of whom were members of the sugar plantocracy, even after British naval forces began interdicting ships off the African coast in 1819. Dispatches from the US Consul posted in Matanzas after 1820 document the growing trade with cities in the United States and Europe, and the local newspaper, *La Aurora de Matanzas*, documented the steady stream of ships going in and out of the port.[59]

As in Havana, the heavy influx of enslaved Africans into Matanzas and the geopolitical literacy of Matanzas' free Black population led Spanish officials to view both with suspicion. In 1821, the local priest denounced José Manuel Blonde, a mulatto militiaman and barber who operated shops in Havana and Matanzas, for "spreading rumors of general and absolute liberty" in the local tavern. The priest alleged Blonde was a Methodist who had associations with persons who had lived in England, "where Wilberforce said the trade should end and slaves should be freed." Blonde had also announced that Havana was in chaos after having received the news of the Sergeants' Revolt in Spain and that a proclamation from Mexico had invited Cubans to join them in independence.[60]

Blonde was arrested but assigned a public defender, who admitted that Blonde had made such statements but that the news was false and Blonde was drunk when he made them. Once sober, Blonde petitioned for his own release signing his request with a flourish. During his trial, white accusers stuck by their version of the events, while several free Black artisans, including two Black carpenters born in Havana, gave favorable assessments of Blonde's character. The prosecutor warned, "from a small spark of this nature, an electric fire could light that could result in the total dissolution of the social pact and tumble even the most solid political edifice." He cited a

---

[57] Childs, *Aponte Rebellion*, 49.

[58] Laird W. Bergad, *Cuban Rural Society in the Nineteenth Century: The Social and Economic History of Matanzas* (Princeton, NJ: Princeton University Press, 1990).

[59] Dispatches from US Consuls in Matanzas, 1820–1899, vol. 1, US State Department General Reports, US National Archives, T 339, microfilm reel 1; *La Aurora de Matanzas*, 19 February 1838, included in TR 339, microfilm reel 1, Latin American Collection, University of Florida Libraries.

[60] Criminal charges against the *pardo* Manuel José Blonde, Escoto Collection, Conspiracies, BMS Span 502 (700), Causas políticas en Matanzas por subversión y sedición, 1821–1822, folder 3, Houghton Library, Harvard University.

law that made it a crime to "copy, read, or even hear read [his underline] seditious papers" and that required that those sentenced for this crime should be judged as enemies of the state. He claimed it was necessary for "the inexorable knife of the law to fall on such delinquents."[61]

Spanish authorities expected free black militiamen like Blonde to monitor their own communities and enforce the increasingly repressive laws Cuban officials began enacting in this period. In 1831, the First Sergeant of the *pardo* battalion of Matanzas, Tomás Vargas, reported a suspicious gathering of between twenty and thirty free Black men and women, who had gathered in a house on Contreras Street to toast Simón Bolívar, the Liberator of New Granada, who had recently died.[62] Any mention of the independence leader was enough to trigger inquiries. Vargas determined that the house was rented to a free mulatto carpenter, Bernardo Sevillán. Those arrested in this investigation included all the captains and lieutenants of the free *pardo* and *moreno* militia of Matanzas and assorted other free people of color, men and women. Some were artisans such as masons, shoemakers, and cigar makers and they came from Matanzas, Havana, and Gibacoa. They all claimed to be members of a subscription group practicing "some comedies for the Christmas season," that included dramas such as *The Triumph of Ana María*, *The Duque of Viseo*, and *Othello!*[63]

What worried authorities most, however, was the collection of reading materials collected from the homes of this group. Sevillán owned a volume entitled *Diccionario o nuevo vocabulario filosófico democrático, indispensable para todos los que desean entender la nueva lengua revolucionaria* (*Dictionary or New Philosophical Democratic Vocabulary, Indispensable for All Those Who Wish to Understand the New Revolutionary Language*). His fellow subscriber, Jorge López owned *Meditaciones sobre las ruinas* (*Meditations on the Ruins*), *El bosquejo de la revolución de Méjico* (*The Design of the Mexican Revolution*), *Guillermo Tell o la Suiza Libre* (*William Tell or Free Switzerland*), and the *Catecismo o Cantón constitucional para la educación de la juventud española* (*The Constitutional Catechism for the Education of Spanish Youth*). Authorities destroyed these incendiary materials and sentenced Sevillán and López to six months' labor on public works. López appealed his sentence on the grounds

---

[61] Ibid.; Landers, *Atlantic Creoles*, Chapter 6.

[62] Comisión Militar de Matanzas (henceforth CMM), Legajo 9, numero 24, Archivo Nacional de Cuba (ANC). Also see Comisión Militar Ejecutiva y Permanente, Legajo 9, numero 25, ANC, cited in García, *Conspiraciones y revueltas*, 93–4. Also see Landers, *Atlantic Creoles*, Chapter 6.

[63] CMM, Legajo, 9, numero 24, ANC.

that he was a veteran lieutenant of the Loyal Battalion of *Pardos* and thus entitled to a less degrading penalty. He won that appeal and spent the next six months in San Severino Castle rather than working shackled in public view, but even that sentence must have embittered the loyal militiaman.[64]

The arrest and investigation of the free mulatto tailor, Jorge Davison, in 1837 yielded even more evidence that, despite the authorities' best efforts at censorship, free persons of color in Matanzas were receiving a wide range of abolitionist literature. They were also forming close, and potentially subversive, associations through leisure activities such as subscription societies, dances, and musical and theater groups. Spanish authorities were probably watching Davison for some time before they finally had grounds to arrest him. His interrogation revealed that Davison was born free in St. Ann's, Jamaica, a port city with frequent commercial exchanges with Cuba.[65] Davison had lived for some time in New Orleans before moving to Matanzas in 1829, but after three years in Cuba, he moved again to New York. Davison returned to Matanzas in 1835, allegedly because he could not find employment as a tailor in the United States.[66] It would seem a strange time for a free Black man to return to Cuba, knowing, as he would have, of the growing racial repression there.

Jorge's brother, H. W. Davison, it turns out, was an employee of the Anti-Slavery Society in Philadelphia and had shipped Jorge an astounding array of newspapers, pamphlets, and other literature on the *Carolina*, in from New York. All of the materials carried some discussion of slavery and the abolition debates under way around the Atlantic World. Before Davison even had time to read what his brother sent him, he was arrested on suspicions of "disseminating doctrines pernicious and dangerous to the slavery of this island" and of having gatherings of people of color in his home. Among the materials the authorities confiscated from Davison were *The New York Mirror*, *The New York Weekly Messenger*, and *The Examiner* and *The Transcript*, also New York papers; *The Boston Post* and *The Daily Evening Transcript*, also of Boston; *The Daily Herald* of New Haven; *The Mourning Courier and General Advertiser* of Providence; the *Diario de la Habana*, *The Norfolk and Portsmouth Herald and General Advertiser*, *The Alexandria Gazette*, *The American and*

---

[64] Fourteen years later, López was executed during the repression of La Escalera with another person arrested at Sevillán's house, Antonio Bernoqui. García, *Conspiraciones y revueltas*, 94–6.

[65] Escaped slaves from St. Ann's also found religious sanctuary in Cuba. Scott, *Common Wind*.

[66] CMM, Legajo 17, numero 1, ANC. Landers, *Atlantic Creoles*, Chapter 6.

*Commercial Daily Advertiser* of Baltimore; *The Transcript* of Nassau; and *The Albion, Or, British Colonial and Foreign Weekly Gazette*. Davidson's shipment also included various issues of *The Plain Dealer* of New York. One of them carried the *St. Augustine Herald*'s story of the "Dade Massacre," in which escaped slaves fighting with the Seminoles wiped out a US Army force in Florida. Another issue of the same paper carried an article entitled "Mr. Webster's Abolitionism."[67]

Investigators also seized an extensive library of books from Davison's home including *The Tale of a New Yorker, Three Experiments of Living, Society in America* by Harriet Martineau, an attack on slavery, and even a volume of Phyllis Wheatley poems, which is now sewn into the bound proceedings of his trial held in the National Archive in Havana. Davison's library also held speeches in honor of George Thompson with an appendix containing a remonstrance on the subject of slavery by the Paisley Emancipation Society and a pamphlet entitled, *The War in Texas Instigated by Slave Holders, Land Speculators*. Davison may have been an avid reader, but it seems likely, as authorities suspected, that this extraordinary collection was also meant to be shared. Signing his complaint in a beautiful script, Davison challenged his arrest and the seizures of the materials, some of which he said belonged to his wife. He needed no translator and must have been at least bilingual as well as literate.[68]

Davison was an active member of an Atlantic network of abolitionists, which launched a campaign to alert the world to Davison's arrest and to exert pressure on the Cuban government to free him. *The Colored American* in New York carried a report from Matanzas filed by William A. Gibbs, who had spent five weeks in Matanzas covering Davison's case. Gibbs warned "all persons of color to beware the Island of Cuba." Gibbs also reported, erroneously, that "Mr. George Davis [sic]" had been arrested and sent without trial to Havana where Captain General Tacón had sentenced him to death. Gibbs reported that the execution was carried out on 10 September and closed his report saying

> I would say further for the benefit of the public, and the abolition cause, that those persons who have friends in this island should be very cautious how they write letters to them, for one work concerning abolitionism in Havana or Matanzas, will seal a man's doom forever. My business is not finished yet;

---

[67] Landers, *Atlantic Creoles*, Chapter 6.

[68] Ibid. Davison's defender argued that he was a "hard-working man, always occupied and never vagrant or attending parties."

Africans and Their Descendants in the Spanish Empire

but things here have arrived to such a pitch, that I find the country too hot to hold me.[69]

Gibbs' dramatic report of Davison's demise was premature. Davison actually spent ten months in jail in Matanzas and Havana, before his brother was finally able to get the British Consul in Cuba to intervene in the case and he was released. Davison's exultant brother reported that Davison was finally "free from the grasp of tyranny" and had returned to St. Ann's, Jamaica "where he may freely breathe his natal air." H. C. Davison compared his brother to William Lloyd Garrison, "the colored man's friend," who had also been jailed for espousing liberty and whose poem Davison quoted in a letter to Friend Cornish (the Reverend S. E. Cornish, one of the paper's editors).[70] Atlantic creoles such as Blonde, López, Sevillán, and Davison had enjoyed a certain privilege in Cuba prior to the Age of Revolutions. Ironically, their race, their cosmopolitanism, their acquaintance with the powerful revolutionary concepts of the age, and their military engagement in the actual revolutions that reshaped the Atlantic World made them threatening to absolutist monarchs and racist plantation regimes alike. They were, ironically, undone by their very virtues.

Even more repression followed in the next decade. In response to a series of slave revolts and to the alleged conspiracy of La Escalera, hundreds of enslaved and free Blacks were executed in Matanzas and free Blacks whose families had served Spain for generations were deported to Mexico, Brazil, and Africa, among other locales.[71] The US Consul T. M. Rodney in Matanzas reported home, "[i]t is generally supposed that the free mulattoes and blacks

---

[69] William A. Gibbs, Matanzas, 20 September 1837, "A Caution to Travelers in General," *The Colored American*, New York, 21 October 1837, www.accessible.com/accessible. Gibbs had been briefly detained by the Military Commission of Matanzas, which reported that he was a Black carpenter from New York without a passport to travel to Matanzas. Captain General Miguel Tacón to the Governor of Matanzas, 7 September 1837, Esclavos, Legajo 23, no, 23, Archivo Histórico Provincial de Matanzas (henceforth AHPM).

[70] Gibbs, *The Colored American*, 24 October 1840 and 24 April 1841. Once free, Jorge Davison acted as an informal correspondent for *The Colored American* in Jamaica, sending Cornish articles and copies of the *Jamaica Mourning Journal* and the *Colonial Reformer*, to be published in *The Colored American*.

[71] After 1839, foreign-born Blacks had to present themselves to the authorities and justify why they should not be deported. Jane Landers, "Catholic Conspirators? Religious Rebels in Nineteenth-Century Cuba," *Slavery & Abolition*, 36:3 (2015), 495–520; Manuel Barcia, *Seeds of Insurrection: Domination and Resistance on Western Cuba Plantations, 1808–1848* (Baton Rouge: Louisiana State University Press, 2008); Manuel Barcia, *The Great African Slave Revolt of 1825: Cuba and the Forgotten Fight for Freedom in Matanzas* (Baton Rouge: Louisiana State University Press, 2012); Aisha Finch, *Rethinking Slave Rebellion in Cuba: La Escalera and the Insurgencies of 1841–1844* (Chapel Hill: University of

engaged in this affair, and it seems they are all engaged without an exception, will either be executed or driven from the island, the slaves will be dealt with severely, but only the prominent leaders will be executed."[72]

Although Spain finally abolished the slave trade in 1866, the end of slavery in Cuba was still long in coming. Cuban slave interests stalled as long as they could. And it would take an aborted bid for independence in the Ten Years' War (1868–1878), the Moret Free Womb Law of 1870, and a gradual emancipation law in 1880, to "break the yoke" and finally achieve abolition in 1886.[73] If slavery and racial categories had finally been eliminated in Spanish America, class and racial discrimination had not. In only a few cases did Blacks, like General José Padilla in Colombia or Vicente Guerrero in Mexico, rise to important military and political positions in the republican governments they helped achieve.[74] One could well argue that race and class remain barriers to full political participation in much of Latin America to this day.

> North Carolina Press, 2015); Robert Paquette, *Sugar Is Made with Blood: The Conspiracy of La Escalera and the Conflict between Empires over Slavery in Cuba* (Middletown, CT: Wesleyan University Press, 1988); Michelle Reid-Vazquez, *The Year of the Lash: Free People of Color in Cuba in the Nineteenth-Century Atlantic World* (Athens, GA: University of Georgia Press, 2011).
>
> [72] Paquette, *Sugar Is Made with Blood*, 22.
> [73] Rebecca J. Scott, *Slave Emancipation in Cuba: The Transition to Free Labor, 1860–1899* (Princeton, NJ: Princeton University Press, 1985).
> [74] Aline Helg, "Simón Bolívar and the Spectre of Pardocracia: José Padilla in Post-Independence Cartagena," *Journal of Latin American Studies* 35:3 (2003), 447–71; Klooster, *Revolutions*, 152.

12

# Concepts on the Move: Constitution, Citizenship, Federalism, and Liberalism across Spain and Spanish Atlantic

JAVIER FERNÁNDEZ-SEBASTIÁN

## The Iberian Atlantic: A Conceptual Laboratory in the Age of Political Experiments

In an oft-quoted passage from one of his letters, the second president of the United States, John Adams, wrote in 1815 that "the last twenty-five years of the last century, and the first fifteen years of this, may be called the age of revolutions and constitutions." This was the name Adams used to encompass the American Revolution, the French Revolution, and the revolution that was in full swing in the Hispanic world. Adams could have added that the era to which he was alluding was also an age of intense political experimentation. In those years of war and civil unrest, revolutions and constitutions were seen by some of their protagonists as genuine experiments. Washington spoke at various key moments of his career of the need to successfully perform the republican *experiment* entrusted to the North American people; in 1796, Jefferson expressed his hope that a new "age of experiments in government" was beginning, and five years later he hoped to continue advancing in "an age of revolution and reformation."[1] Barely four decades later, the influential US journalist John O'Sullivan did not hesitate to stress that, from a political point of view, his continued to be "an age of experiments."[2] Using the same language of historical actors, North American historians in the twentieth century, from Carl Becker (*The United States: An*

---

This work was supported by the University of the Basque Country (Research Group GIU 18/215); and the Ministry of Science and Innovation, Government of Spain (plus ERDF, EU) (Research Project HAR2017–84032-P). Translated by Mark Hounsell.

[1] Thomas Jefferson, *The Jeffersonian Cyclopedia: A Comprehensive Collection of the Views of Thomas Jefferson*, ed. John P. Foley (New York: Funk and Wagnalls Co., 1900), 327, 386.

[2] *The United States Magazine and Democratic Review*, October 1837 to March 1838, 9.

*Experiment in Democracy*, 1920) to Arthur Schlesinger Jr. (*America: Experiment or Destiny?*, 1977), adopted the word *experiment* – often linked to the word democracy – to describe those initial stages of the political institutions of the United States, and even to refer to the country's entire historical trajectory.

The historiography of the first constitutional and republican experiences in Hispanic America has also made frequent use of the notion of experiment to refer to those early times.[3] Moreover, the growing interest in Atlantic history and the emphasis on the language of republicanism have contributed in recent years to unifying to a certain extent the interpretative framework used to shed light upon that historical period in both Americas, and to highlighting the nascent Hispanic American states' ideological debt to the texts and foundational figures of the United States. In fact, it is commonplace for a set of very diverse events and processes, including the American, French, Haitian, and Ibero-American revolutions, to be subsumed under the colligatory phrase "Atlantic Revolutions."

The objective of this chapter is to open a small panoramic window on the semantic changes undergone by four key concepts – citizenship, constitution, federalism, and liberalism – in the Spanish Atlantic during that period of imperial revolutions and constitutional experiments.[4] Given the immensity of the spaces included under the name "Spanish Atlantic" and their enormous diversity, what follows – an exercise in intellectual history based on part of the results of the collective research project known as *Iberconceptos* – can be no more than a piecemeal outline of salient features of these transformations.

The fondness of historians – and, to a lesser extent, contemporary actors – for a notion that belongs more to scientific language, as in the case of "experiment," serves to emphasize two characteristic features of that political period: On the one hand, the open, necessarily "experimental" nature of some unprecedented institutional arrangements, whose designers might have seen themselves as explorers in uncharted territory; on the other, the use of the particular vocabulary of experimentation suggests that in the

---

[3] Mario Rodríguez, *The Cádiz Experiment in Central America, 1808–1826* (Berkeley: University of California Press, 1978); José Antonio Aguilar, *En pos de la quimera: Reflexiones sobre el experimento constitucional atlántico* (Mexico City: FCE, 2000); Hilda Sabato, *Republics of the New World: The Revolutionary Political Experiment in Nineteenth-Century Latin America* (Princeton, NJ: Princeton University Press, 2018).

[4] Jeremy Adelman, "An Age of Imperial Revolutions," *American Historical Review* 113 (2008): 319–40; Javier Fernández-Sebastián, "Friends of Freedom. First Liberalisms in the Iberian World," in Michael Freeden, Javier Fernández-Sebastián and Jörn Leonhard, eds., *In Search of European Liberalisms: Concepts, Languages, Ideologies* (New York: Berghahn, 2019), 102–34.

minds of their promotors those political tests had no guarantee of success and could hold more than one surprise (without excluding the possibility of their promotors feeling disappointed with the results, as was often the case).

Moreover, recourse to the metaphor-framework of the experiment prepares readers to put themselves in the place of those who lived the revolutions and to experience their situation of uncertainty. This situation was characterized by the implementation of a series of political measures the outcome of which, in terms of success or failure, was anything but predictable. Yet on the other hand, those enlightened elites tended to believe that if a certain political experiment was successful, as in the case of the North American Constitution, it could be equally valid and viable in other societies.

Before proceeding briefly to examine the changes in the aforementioned concepts, I would like to make some initial remarks.

Firstly, the prevailing mentality among the enlightened elites of Europe and America during the Age of Revolutions tended to infuse certain political concepts with great expectations. The traditional cult of custom, the reverential respect for familiar experiences, was being replaced by a far more proactive political attitude. This new attitude involved a permanent invitation to experiment with the unknown, to undertake unprecedented projects and courses of action, even fictitiously to situate oneself in a future that was expected to be far more satisfactory than the present. As Reinhart Koselleck has observed, this shift from experience to expectation, from routine to innovation, from the prestige of the past to the fascination with the future, is a crucial feature of the age that is applied to the four concepts that I shall address.

Secondly, what was said in the previous paragraph means that concepts should not be seen as abstract ideas, separate from the practices associated with them. Language and action are indissociable. Conceptual changes, far from being interpreted as mere epiphenomena of ongoing political and social transformations, also act as levers of social and political change. Thus, there are no experiences – much less experiments – without concepts that guide them because, as Koselleck has also emphasized, concepts are both indicators and factors of historical change. The emergence or reformulation of a new fundamental concept – as occurs in this case with those of constitution, citizenship, liberalism, or federalism – not only indicates that something important was changing in the political landscape, but that the emerging concept itself was an essential catalyst of that change.

Thirdly, in the years of imperial revolutions and systemic crises that shook the Atlantic Worlds from the Seven Years' War onwards, parallel to the passage from empires to nations, the Republic of Letters underwent profound changes, giving way to a new sociopolitical concept-phenomenon: public opinion.[5] This brand-new notion, generally associated with each individual nation, was accompanied by a new intellectual figure. Unlike the lettered, enlightened intellectual (*letrado/ilustrado*), the new type of public writer – journalist, publicist (*periodista/publicista*) – who was an intermediary between the great thinkers and the general public, would have been inconceivable without the boom in political journalism (a journalism often exercised by foreigners with strong international connections). The increase in the pace of publication of newspapers and readers' insatiable demand for news rapidly accelerated the circulation of new concepts and multiplied the uses, often contradictory, of basic political terminology.

Fourthly, the diffusion on an Atlantic scale – in French, Spanish, English, Portuguese and other, less prominent, languages, and the continual jumping from one language to another by means of translations – of a series of polemic words (including the four under consideration here) which had previously been highbrow terms and rarely the subject of public debate, accelerated the transoceanic, transimperial and transnational convergence of the political lexicon. Without leaving the Iberian-speaking area, we know that some of the most celebrated newspapers and doctrinal articles on the Peninsula were systematically republished in various American cities. An essay published in Seville in 1809 on the concept of public opinion, for example, was reproduced on numerous occasions in the New World throughout the first half of the nineteenth century.[6] However, the fact that they were given the same or similar names did not mean that those concepts encompassed identical realities or raised the same expectations among speakers in each and every one of those territories. Our *Iberconceptos* research has revealed that the diffusion in both hemispheres of the same repertoire of terms – terms that I suggested some time ago should be given the name *Euroamericanisms* – by no means equates to a semantic homogenization. On the contrary, the internationalization of vocabularies – which made it possible for debates to be held in various countries focused on a limited number of key concepts, as if these concepts were the same in all languages and

---

[5] François-Xavier Guerra, Annick Lempérière et al., *Los espacios públicos en Iberoamérica: Ambigüedades y problemas. Siglos XVIII–XIX* (Mexico City: FCE, 1998); Javier Fernández-Sebastián and Joëlle Chassin, eds., *L'avènement de l'opinion publique: Europe et Amérique XVIII–XIX^e siècles* (Paris: L'Harmattan, 2004).

[6] Javier Fernández-Sebastián, ed., *Diccionario político y social del mundo iberoamericano* (henceforth *DPSMI*) – I (Madrid: Centro de Estudios Políticos y Constitucionales, 2009), 990.

societies – occurred parallel to the increasing diversification of the range of usual meanings in each of the societies resulting from the disintegration of empires. The different historical trajectories and the need to adapt the shared uses of these and other words to local circumstances and expectations explains why conceptual "nationalization" increased with the creation of new republics and independent states in the territories of the former Spanish monarchy.

## Constitution

If one concept in particular stands out among the four to which I have referred in order to characterize the era under consideration, it is probably *constitution*. Along with other abstract concepts like freedom or revolution, this was certainly one of the most frequently used political terms. It was no coincidence that during those early decades of the nineteenth century various voices declared that Europe and America were experiencing an "age of constitutions," in which all civilized societies tended to organize themselves according to some kind of constitutional model. An increasing number of politicians and intellectuals, on both sides of the Atlantic, believed that the best guarantee for perfecting their societies was a good constitution.

Since the end of the eighteenth century, even prior to the lexical inflation of the word constitution caused by the outbreak of the French Revolution, there had been a debate in Spain on the need to reform the constitution of the monarchy, a debate that partly began in the genre of political economy. Various peninsular intellectuals of the late Enlightenment participated in this debate – among others, Jovellanos, Foronda, Cabarrús, Aguirre, Arroyal, and Martínez Marina – but also some Americans, like the Charcas Provincial Court Prosecutor Victorián de Villava, who wrote some *Apuntes para una reforma de España sin trastorno del Gobierno Monárquico ni de la Religión* (1797), which circulated in manuscript form.[7] These constitutional proposals emerged in a context in which, after nearly two decades of Bourbon reforms in the Spanish empire, expressions of discontent with existing institutions were voiced with increasing audacity in the incipient public sphere.[8] Whatever the case, the need for constitutional change became even more

---

[7] José M. Portillo Valdés, *La vida atlántica de Victorián de Villava* (Madrid: Mapfre, 2009).
[8] Gabriel Paquette, "The Reform of the Spanish Empire in the Age of Enlightenment," in Jesús Astigarraga, ed., *The Spanish Enlightenment Revisited* (Oxford: Voltaire Foundation, 2015), 149–67.

pressing in the Iberian world with the outbreak of the monarchic crisis, followed by the Napoleonic intervention in the spring of 1808 and the subsequent patriotic uprising. From then onwards, and especially after 1811, the true era of written constitutions unfolded in the region. In fact, during the initial decades of the nineteenth century, the Hispanic world was the planet's principal manufacturer of constitutions as a result of the collapse of the monarchy and the consequent proliferation of declarations of independence in the Spanish and Portuguese Americas.[9] Until mid-century, over fifty constitutions of various types were enacted, starting with the Statute of Bayonne (1808) and followed by those of Cundinamarca, New Granada, Venezuela, Cádiz, Chile, Apatzingán, and many more. This overabundance of constitutional charters is revealing of the centrifugal dynamic and chronic instability of the region during the first half of the nineteenth century.[10]

The very concept of constitution, of course, was extremely controversial,[11] although the codes of the first batch implied that such a high ranking law constituted a "barrier against despotism" and a guarantee "of the inviolable rights of man and citizen" (Art. 1 of the Constitution of Cundinamarca, 1811). *Constitución* was an old Castilian word that used to refer to laws or statutes for the good government and management of a corporate body, but which could also refer to basic laws, and even to the physical-geographical characteristics of a territory or province. And *constituir* (to found) could mean establish, provide laws for a "kingdom, province or community," with a view to founding strong and lasting institutions. However, depending on whether the discourse in question was addressing a rationalist or historical, contractualist or consuetudinary constitution, the contrasting definitions show that the opinions with regard to what exactly comprised a constitution could vary considerably. While some used the word to refer to a sort of "natural order" of society, others imagined it as a voluntarist law of laws, a result of the irresistible *fiat* of an unconditioned constituent will. And while in peninsular Spain most publicists – led by Jovellanos – argued that Spain already had an old constitution, and it was simply a question of recovering it and putting it into place in a suitably rejuvenated form, others thought it necessary to draft

---

[9] David Armitage, *The Declaration of Independence: A Global History* (Cambridge, MA: Harvard University Press, 2007); Alfredo Ávila, Érika Pani, and Jordana Dym, eds., *Las declaraciones de independencia: Los textos fundamentales de las independencias americanas* (Mexico City: El Colegio de México – UNAM, 2013).

[10] Roberto Gargarella, *Latin American Constitutionalism, 1810–2010: The Engine Room of the Constitution* (Oxford: Oxford University Press, 2013), 1–19.

[11] Fernández-Sebastián, *DPSMI – I*, 305–422.

a new constitutional code, via recourse to the constituent power attributed to the sovereign nation. But, as would be seen in the Cortes of Cádiz, even the revolutionary liberals paid tribute to the *fueros* and "basic laws" of the monarchy's old kingdoms and presented the Cádiz Constitution – without doubt the most influential and prestigious code produced at the time anywhere in the Spanish-speaking world – as a mere reform or "recasting" of the allegedly libertarian, medieval legislation.[12] The new constitution was understood by its authors, then, as an update of the old historical constitution.

Among the American creoles there were also a few advocates – such as the friar Servando Teresa de Mier from New Spain – of recovering the old Laws of the Indies, understood as the historical constitution of America, although most leaders of American independence movements, especially in South America, clearly broke with the Hispanic constitutionalist tradition. Almost all agreed, as was proclaimed by the French National Assembly in Article 16 of its Declaration of the Rights of Man and Citizen – a text translated and disseminated by Antonio Nariño in New Granada in 1793 – that without separation of powers there could be no true constitution. And, as we read in one of the most widely read constitutional catechisms, constitution was generally understood as "an ordered collection of a nation's fundamental or political laws," in other words, "those that establish the form of government."[13] In the case of the new successor states of the former imperial monarchy, this establishment sought above all to consolidate their recently acquired independence.[14]

It is worth noting that the nascent Euro-American constitutional culture, in its Hispanic form, very soon penetrated the American Indigenous communities, including those subaltern groups that spoke languages other than Spanish. Thus, while the American insurrectionists distributed pamphlets in Quechua and Aymara in the Andean regions and among the Guaraní-speaking populations,[15] the 1812 Spanish Constitution was translated, often in abbreviated didactic versions, into several languages of northern, central, and

---

[12] Joaquín Varela, "La doctrina de la Constitución histórica: De Jovellanos a las Cortes de 1845," *Revista de Derecho Político* 39 (1994), 45–80; Jaime E. Rodríguez, ed., *The Divine Charter: Constitutionalism and Liberalism in Nineteenth-Century Mexico* (Lanham: Rowman & Littlefield, 2007); M. C. Mirow, *Latin America Constitutionalism: The Constitution of Cadiz and Its Legacy in Spanish America* (Cambridge: Cambridge University Press, 2015).

[13] José Caro Sureda, *Catecismo político arreglado a la Constitución de la Monarquía española* (Cádiz: Lema, 1812), 3.

[14] Roberto Gargarella, *Latin American Constitutionalism, 1810–2010: The Engine Room of the Constitution* (Oxford: Oxford University Press, 2013), 3.

[15] Capucine Boidin, César Itier, and Rossella Martin, *Ariadna histórica: Lenguajes, conceptos, metáforas*, Suplemento Especial 1: *La propaganda política en lenguas indígenas en las*

southern America. It should be borne in mind that this *magna carta*, more Hispanic than Spanish, was in force in large parts of the American continent, in some areas – such as the case of New Spain (Mexico) – longer than in peninsular Spain, and gave rise to the formation of numerous constitutional town councils, not only in cities, but also in many remote corners of rural America.[16] In Europe, there were a number of translations of this emblematic constitutional text and the catechisms through which it was disseminated into the continent's main languages, including French, English, German, Italian, and Russian, and also into minority languages in Spain, like Catalan and Basque. In this respect the Cádiz Constitution is a singular case, not only in the context of Spanish constitutionalism, but also on a global scale, as during the years following its enactment it was familiar and admired on both sides of the Atlantic and beyond, to the extent that many liberals of the 1820s called for it to be adopted in their countries. From Manila to Mexico and Peru, from Havana to St. Petersburg, via Oporto, Lisbon, and Madrid, the Canary Islands, Ceuta, Turin, Naples, and Sicily, but also in many rural settings and remote Indigenous villages, this constitution was translated, defended, celebrated, and proclaimed in one way or another and came into force, usually for short periods of time and with small variations, in very different latitudes and places on four continents.[17] The duality, at once parochial and universalist, traditional and cosmopolitan, of this code – which aspired to nothing less than the transformation of an imperial monarchy into a transcontinental nation – is certainly not unrelated to its Catholic-ecumenical and enlightened-revolutionary (even republican in the old sense of the word) double facet, characteristics that several critics and commentators considered to be contradictory and incompatible, but which need to be understood historically against the backdrop of a hybrid political culture at a moment of transit between systems.[18]

---

*guerras de independencia sudamericanas* (2016), 9–95, www.ehu.eus/ojs/index.php/Ariadna/issue/view/Suplemento%20Especial%20I.

[16] Antonio Annino, "Imperio, Constitución y diversidad en la América hispana," *Historia Mexicana,* 58:1 (July–September 2008), 179–227; Marta Irurozqui, "Huellas, testigos y testimonios constitucionales: De Charcas a Bolivia, 1810–1830," in Antonio Annino and Marcela Ternavasio, eds., *El laboratorio constitucional iberoamericano: 1807/1808–1830* (Madrid: Iberoamericana; Frankfurt am Main: Vervuert, 2012), 157–78.

[17] Dominique de Pradt, *L'Europe et l'Amérique en 1821* (Paris: Béchet aîné, 1822), 1; Scott Eastman, "'America Has Escaped from Our Hands': Rethinking Empire, Identity and Independence during the Trienio Liberal in Spain, 1820–1823," *European History Quarterly* 41:3 (2011), 428–43.

[18] Javier Fernández-Sebastián, "Entre el Espíritu Santo y el espíritu del siglo. Sobre la Constitución de las Cortes y el primer liberalismo hispano," *Anthropos* 236 (2013): 55–75.

Owing perhaps to this common cultural backdrop, and in spite of the fact that the Hispanic constitutions of those years were often very different from one another, all of them have a certain family resemblance. To begin with, one is struck by the relative earliness of those experiences, since, though it is true that those constitutional revolutions were preceded by the US, French, and Haitian experiences – the former generally extolled and taken as a source of inspiration, the last two usually repudiated as anti-models – it is no less true that the Hispanic countries had written constitutions before most European countries, and the Spanish American republics are older than almost all their counterparts in the Old World. Among those shared features that characterize Hispanic constitutional culture, I would firstly highlight the exaggerated confidence manifested a priori by many actors in a constitution's capacity to ensure the prosperity of its societies. Secondly, the confessionally Catholic nature of almost all those early constitutions shows that for the legislators, religious unity was a higher value that needed to be preserved, even at the expense of freedom of worship. Thirdly, generally speaking, Hispanic constitutionalism assumed a more democratic, open and participatory complexion than tended to be the case in the constitutions of other countries, including those regarded as politically more advanced. In fact, at the time of the restoration, the Cádiz Constitution – unicameral, based on national sovereignty and often described as democratic – was, along with the French *Charte* of 1814 – bicameral and inspired by the English constitution – one of the most influential constitutional models in Europe and South America. However, while the latter represented the conservative liberalism of Anglophile doctrinaires, the former – belonging to a generation of "revolutionary constitutions" dating from the late eighteenth century[19] – was until 1830 the reference model for democratic and revolutionary liberalism.

## Citizenship

The fundamental political concepts of that "era of constitutions" are interwoven in the sources, forming complex semantic and argumentative networks. The terms *revolución* and *constitución*, for instance, are closely interrelated in many kinds of discourse. What is not at all clear in the sources is whether a revolution began or rather finished when its instigators succeeded in enacting a constitution. Some openly defended the latter thesis,

---

[19] Markus J. Prutsch, *Making Sense of Constitutional Monarchism in Post-Napoleonic France and Germany* (New York: Palgrave, 2013), 70.

given that the objective of the revolution was, in their view, to establish a representative regime that would ensure that citizens enjoyed certain basic rights enshrined in a constitution.[20] Others, on the other hand, more demanding or more radical, maintained that the constitution was only the first step along a long road of revolutionary transformations with a view to guaranteeing a new era of public happiness. And in the ensuing years, in the new national societies that emerged following the disintegration of the monarchy, the problem would repeatedly arise of "how to end the revolution" by means of some kind of just balance between the principles, considered to be equally necessary, of freedom and order.[21]

What almost all the revolutionaries agreed upon was that, to be able to claim that they truly possessed a free country (*patria*), in the republican sense of the word, there had to exist a constitution that clearly defined citizens and their rights. So, as the Spanish economist and lawyer Álvaro Flórez Estrada wrote, without a constitution there would be neither freedom, nor *patria*, nor citizens.[22]

The ideal of citizenship was, judging by the proclamations of its ideologues, one of the motors of those revolutions. In a letter dated 29 May 1810, shortly before the Bogotá revolution, creole lawyer Camilo Torres sensed that "we are very close to ... that great day" when the New Granadans would shake off slavery and could declare themselves citizens.[23] There were countless other examples. However, since the beginning of the revolutions, metropolitan liberals and American creoles had a very different way of understanding citizenship. The latter, though they could accept being citizens of a vast constitutional monarchy on equal terms with the citizens of the Iberian Peninsula (provided they were granted a certain degree of home rule), were not prepared to be represented by fewer delegates in the Cortes than their proportional share on the basis of population. Less still, they refused to see themselves degraded to the subordinate status of inhabitants

---

[20] Javier Fernández-Sebastián and Gonzalo Capellán de Miguel, *"Revolución* en España. Avatares de un concepto en la 'edad de las revoluciones' (1808–1898)," in Fabio Wasserman, ed., *El mundo en movimiento: El concepto de revolución en Iberoamérica y el Atlántico Norte (siglos XVII–XIX)* (Buenos Aires: Miño y Dávila, 2019), 141.

[21] See, for example, for the Chilean case: Gabriel Cid, *Pensar la revolución: Historia intelectual de la independencia chilena* (Santiago de Chile: Universidad Diego Portales, 2019), 345 ff.

[22] Javier Fernández-Sebastián, "Patria, Nación y Constitución: La fuerza movilizadora de los mitos," in *España 1808–1814: La Nación en armas* (Madrid: Ministerio de Defensa-SECC, 2008), 185.

[23] Fernández-Sebastián, *DPSMI – I*, 235.

Concepts on the Move

of peripheral territories, understood as simple overseas possessions of the Spanish nation.[24]

In many of the texts, a mixed liberal-republican language predominates. Their authors are as quick to insist, in classic Ciceronian style, on the duties the *patria* requires of the citizen, as they are to underline the new rights associated with citizenship. It was no coincidence that upon the classic Latin sound of the word citizen had been superimposed the echoes of the French revolutionary experience, since while in Ciceronian language the Roman *cives* appeared above all as a virtuous *vir* aware of his duties to the *patria*,[25] the *citoyen* was also assigned a set of rights. As might be expected of such an era of wars and revolutions, the rhetoric of virtue and patriotism overwhelmingly dominated the discourse on interests and rights. We can see, moreover, that the favored sphere of the first, the republican language, is the nation as a whole, while the language of political economy is more present when issues related to the local sphere are being discussed. In any case, the traditional definition of citizen, in a society like Spain's, where a person's local roots and the legal category of *vecino* were the basis of political identity and of the acquisition of nationality,[26] was significantly altered during those years.

"The word citizen *can no longer be understood* in such a vague and indeterminate way as it has been to date. In spite of being an old term, *it has just acquired* through the Constitution *a meaning* ... that is precise and exact. It is new in legal nomenclature and *cannot be confused* henceforth with the word *vecino* (resident of a town) ...."[27] The cautionary tone and the illocutionary force of these and other similar phrases which fill the political discourse of the age seek to produce in the reader or the listener an immediate transemic effect. It is a question of distancing the speaker from the traditional meaning of certain words and urging them to embrace new meanings or alternative

---

[24] Xosé-Manoel Núñez, "Nation-Building and Regional Integration: The Case of the Spanish Empire, 1700–1914," in Stefan Berger and Alexei Miller, eds., *Nationalizing Empires* (Budapest and New York: NED-CEU Press, 2015), 195–246, 221; Josep María Fradera, *Gobernar colonias* (Barcelona: Península, 1999), 82–5.

[25] J. G. A. Pocock, "The Ideal of Citizenship since Classical Times," in Ronald Beiner, ed., *Theorizing Citizenship* (New York: SUNY Press, 1995), 29–53; Fernández-Sebastián, *DPSMI – I*, 249.

[26] Tamar Herzog, *Defining Nations: Immigrants and Citizens in Early Modern Spain and Spanish America* (New Haven, CT: Yale University Press, 2003); Fernández-Sebastián, *DPSMI – I*, 184.

[27] Deputy Agustín Argüelles' speech of 4 September 1811, *Diario de Sesiones de las Cortes Generales y Extraordinarias* (Cádiz: n.p., 1811), 1765 (emphasis added); Javier Fernández-Sebastián, *Historia conceptual en el Atlántico ibérico: Lenguajes, tiempos, revoluciones* (Mexico City: FCE, 2020), 277.

definitions, more in line with a new general vision of politics. We should bear in mind that, according to Spanish legal tradition, the resident was not the mere inhabitant or denizen, but the freeholder taxpayer with emotional links to their local community and with a desire to stay.

Thus, the citizen was redefined as a sort of *vecino nacional* ("national resident," a term proposed by various delegates in the Cortes of Cádiz as a way of distancing themselves from the French revolutionary *citoyen*).[28] In the constitutions of the Hispanic world, the notions of *ciudadanía* and *vecindad* (national and local citizenship, respectively) are usually associated with an intensity rarely seen in other constitutional cultures. Thus, the Constitution of Cundinamarca (1811) establishes in several of its articles not only that citizens, in order to be considered as such, must *dwell* in the territory, but also that, in order to be accepted as a candidate for national representation, president of the government, member of the Senate, of the judiciary, etc. it is necessary to have resided for several years in a locality of the country (preamble, Tit. IV, Art. 14, Tit. V, Art. 36, Tit. VII, Arts 29 and 51; the federal Constitution of Venezuela of the same year, in Arts 26, 28, 35, 36, 49 and 112, lays out similar conditions). According to these and other constitutions, apart from the usual prerequisites of the time (being male, of legal age, economically independent, and in many cases, literate), a *sine qua non* of being a citizen is the legal status of *vecino* – which implies being recognized as such by the local authorities, and a commitment to a long-term relationship with the locality where one is based. One might say that citizenship, although on a national level, was eminently local in its basic definition; to be a full citizen it was necessary to be registered on the electoral roll, and it was the mayors and parish priests who compiled the census.

Along with the citizens' civil and political rights, several of those early Spanish American constitutions also stipulated their duties, which usually included that of taking up arms to defend the *patria*. The figure of citizen-soldier or militiaman was particularly important during the wars of independence. The 1812 Cartagena Constitution, for example (Title I, Art. 34), states that those who refuse to serve the *patria* will be stripped of the rights of citizenship.[29] Old republican language, which extolled, often in a Rousseauian vein, citizens' self-sacrifice and dedication to the community of which they formed a part, was also very present in Spanish America. But,

---

[28] Fernández-Sebastián, *DPSMI – I*, 247 ff.
[29] Manuel Antonio Pombo and José Joaquín Guerra, eds., *Constituciones de Colombia*, 4 vols. (Bogotá: Prensas del Ministerio de Educación Nacional, 1951), vol. II, 103.

Concepts on the Move

above all, numerous texts of the era reveal that the condition of citizen was regarded by many as "the greatest distinction that may be conferred upon an individual."[30] The proclamation by a Catalan farmer, published in the *Periódico político y mercantil* of the town of Reus (No. 71, 1813), and immediately reproduced in numerous newspapers all over Spain under the title *El Labrador de Reus*, is one of the pamphlets that best reflects pride in the fact that the *patria*, thanks to the constitution, has finally covered her children "with the sacred mantle of Citizenship," a new status that, according to the author, by guaranteeing equal rights for all, eliminates privileges and renders all citizens equal before the law, so for Spaniards, the title of citizen should represent more of an honor than any noble title.[31]

Generally speaking, that first Hispanic constitutionalism was characterized by a broad franchise. In the case of the Cádiz Constitution – more American than Spanish – this right was conferred upon the vast majority of male adults, although the vote was normally exercised at three levels, and the distinction between active and passive citizens, based on the right of the former to vote and their capacity to occupy certain public offices, and the simple civil rights of the latter, reappears in one form or another in many of the constitutions. The Constitution of Cádiz, for instance, distinguishes between citizens and Spaniards or "individuals" of the nation. Ethnically and according to the wording of this text, creoles of European origin, Indigenous Americans, and mestizos were initially considered citizens. Not so the slaves, although the constitution had also provided for a mechanism (Art 22) for the extraordinary concession of citizen's rights to those free men of African descent "who distinguish themselves through their talent, application and conduct." We know, in any case, that the subaltern groups, including mestizos, Blacks, and mulattoes, sometimes even people subjected to slavery, participated in the elections and made intelligent use of the constitutional discourse to promote their interests and seek opportunities for emancipation.[32] And the versions of the concept of citizen in certain Amerindian languages – terms

---

[30] Fernández-Sebastián, *DPSMI – I*, 251.

[31] Javier Fernández-Sebastián, ed. *El "Correo de Vitoria" (1813–1814) y los orígenes del periodismo en Álava* (Vitoria: Ayuntamiento de Vitoria-Gasteiz, 1993), lxxx–lxxxiii.

[32] James Sanders, *Contentious Republicans: Popular Politics, Race, and Class in Nineteenth-Century Colombia* (Durham, NC: Duke University Press, 2004); Marixa Lasso, *Myths of Harmony: Race and Republicanism during the Age of Revolution. Colombia 1795–1831* (Pittsburgh: University of Pittsburgh Press, 2007); Karen D. Caplan, *Indigenous Citizens: Local Liberalism in Early National Oaxaca and Yucatan* (Stanford: Stanford University Press, 2009); Marcela Echeverri, *Indian and Slave Royalists in the Age of Revolution: Reform, Revolution, and Royalism in the Northern Andes, 1780–1825* (New York: Cambridge University Press, 2016).

such as the Quechuan *wiraqocha* or the Guaraní *karaí*, previously used to refer to Spaniards – appear to indicate that Indigenous communities conceived of citizenship as a form of dignification and social advancement.[33]

## Liberalism

Of the four concepts being briefly examined here, only *liberalism* is peculiar to the Hispanic revolutions. However much the French and American revolutions have been described on occasion by some historians and political theorists as *liberal*, this label is anachronistic, because until the second decade of the nineteenth century there were no liberals anywhere.

As far as we know, the first true liberals were a group of European and American delegates in the Cortes of Cádiz who took control of that Atlantic assembly and were christened thus by the members of the public that attended the parliamentary debates. Shortly afterwards, their traditionalist political rivals began to refer with disdain to the language and ideology of those reformists, attributing to them a sinister combination of purpose and action. Liberalism, they said, was a system of thinking invented by a handful of Cádiz parliamentarians and journalists, anxious to implement a radical reform of the constitution that was contrary to national traditions – the Catholic religion included – and largely inspired by foreign sources, above all by Montesquieu, Rousseau, and other luminaries of the Lumières, as well as the leaders of the French Revolution.[34] Other critics took liberalism less seriously. For a certain Cuban newspaper of antiliberal leanings, it was no more than a frivolous political fad to which many subscribed out of pure snobbery.[35]

The word liberalism and the term "liberal party" began to be employed in tentative fashion in 1811, though it was not until the following decades that both expressions became recognizable labels throughout Europe, in America

---

[33] Capucine Boidin, César Itier, Noemí Goldman, and Joëlle Chassin, "Las traducciones del decreto de liberación de la mita al quechua, aimara y guaraní de la Asamblea General Constituyente de las Provincias Unidas del Río de la Plata (1813)," in Noemí Goldman and Georges Lomné, eds., *Los lenguajes de la República: Historia conceptual y traducción en Iberoamérica (siglos XVIII y XIX)* (Madrid: Casa de Velázquez, 2023).

[34] Javier Fernández-Sebastián, "Liberalismo en España, 1810–1850. La construcción de un concepto y la forja de una identidad política," in Javier Fernández-Sebastián, ed., *La aurora de la libertad: Los primeros liberalismos en el mundo iberoamericano* (Madrid: Marcial Pons Historia 2012), 261–306: 261–2.

[35] *El Filósofo Verdadero*, Havana, 4 October 1813.

and beyond.[36] The use of the neologism increased gradually throughout the century. Although textual databases show that until 1830, the use of the word in Spanish was more frequent than in other European languages, its presence in the lexicon was relatively discreet until well into the century, when it began gradually to penetrate the lexicographical repertoires of the age.[37] The official dictionary of the Real Academia Española, parsimonious as ever, did not include the word liberalism until its 1869 edition. There it was defined, alternately, as "the order of ideas professed by the advocates of the liberal system" and as "the party or political communion that they form."

The descriptions of liberalism that we find in Hispanic sources from the first half of the nineteenth century are very diverse (so much so that present-day historiography prefers to speak of *liberalisms*, in plural), and tend to oscillate between the ideological and the organizational. Most agree that at the center of the liberal system is the idea of freedom (a polysemic word if ever there was one), but the procession of core, adjacent, peripheral, and opposite concepts varies considerably, depending on authors, ideological movements, places, moments, and circumstances.[38] These first self-descriptions of the liberals reveal a philanthropic and universalist bias. They very soon referred to themselves as "friends of humanity."[39] In their publications, they subscribe to a kind of internationalism consistent with the experience of so many Atlantic individuals who during those years traveled voluntarily or involuntarily and spent more or less long periods of time far from their countries of origin, many of them in cities like London, Paris, or Philadelphia.[40] This relationship with liberals from other countries, specifically, in the case of several Hispanic intellectuals, with Lord Holland House,

---

[36] *Liberalism* was, incidentally, the forerunner of the modern ideological–political *isms* – *socialism, nationalism, conservatism, communism* . . . – most of which were coined in the first half of the nineteenth century.

[37] Javier Fernández-Sebastián, "From Patriotism to Liberalism. Political Concepts in Revolution," in Javier Muñoz-Basols, Laura Lonsdale, and Manuel Delgado, eds., *The Routledge Companion to Iberian Studies* (London and New York: Routledge, 2017), 305–18: 314–5.

[38] Javier Fernández-Sebastián, ed., *DPSMI – II*, vol. v, *Libertad* (Madrid: Centro de Estudios Políticos y Constitucionales, 2014); Michael Freeden and Javier Fernández-Sebastián, "European Liberal Discourses. Conceptual Affinities and Disparities," in Freeden, Fernández-Sebastián, and Leonhard, eds., *In Search of European Liberalisms*, 1–35.

[39] *Abeja Española*, Cádiz, 16 December 1812.

[40] Javier Fernández-Sebastián, "Liberales sin fronteras. Cádiz y el primer constitucionalismo hispánico," in Fernando García Sanz et al., eds., *Cadice e oltre: Costituzione, nazione e libertà* (Rome: Istituto per la Storia del Risorgimento Italiano – Escuela Española de Historia y Arqueología, CSIC 2015), 465–90; Fernández-Sebastián, *DPSMI – I*, 713–15.

played a very important part in the ideological evolution of liberalism, especially in its shift toward more conservative positions.[41]

For its detractors in the era of the restoration, in both mainland Europe and Great Britain, *liberalism* was a misleading political term, little more than a lexical mask donned by European Jacobins to appear in public as respectable and generous politicians, courtesy of the positive connotations long associated with the moral virtue of *liberality*.[42] Some of the more elaborate characterizations and definitions of liberalism during those years are to be found in the Madrid press of the Liberal Triennium (1820–1823). As a (macro) concept of movement, liberalism was an idea focused on action, which looked above all to the future. Very soon, however, the champions of liberalism began to justify that call to action with a historicist rhetoric, that inserted the liberal movement of their time in a transgenerational dynamic of *longue durée*, be it on a national – which, in Spain's case, dated back to medieval freedoms and the revolt of the *comuneros*[43] – or transnational, Euro-American scale. In this latter vein, Sevillian priest Alberto Lista constructed a historical-philosophical narrative according to which freedom is the necessary product of the unstoppable progress of civilization, and in particular of the development of industry and commerce. "Liberalism," he wrote, "is linked to the essence of European societies" and "is the result of all ancient and modern history."[44]

A few days later, the same, moderately liberal-leaning Madrid newspaper in which Lista's article appeared, published a summary of the liberal vision, in which it is apparent that the concepts of liberalism, democracy, representative government, and republic overlap to a certain degree. Indeed, reflecting the opinions of French politician Antoine de Carrion-Nizas, the columnist states that it matters not whether a democracy is monarchic, like Spain's, or republican, like that of the United States. Both are equally acceptable, provided that freedoms and rights are guaranteed. This requires six principles to prevail in legislation, namely: individual

---

[41] Manuel Moreno Alonso, *La forja del liberalismo en España: Los amigos españoles de Lord Holland, 1793–1840* (Madrid: Congreso de los Diputados, 1997); Joaquín Varela, "El pensamiento constitucional español en el exilio: El abandono del modelo doceañista (1823–1833)," *Revista de Estudios Políticos* 88 (1995), 63–90.

[42] Jörn Leonhard, *Liberalismus: Zur historischen Semantik eines europäischen Deutungsmusters* (Munich: Oldenbourg, 2001).

[43] José Manuel Nieto Soria, *Medievo constitucional: Historia y mito político en los orígenes de la España contemporánea (ca. 1750–1814)* (Madrid: Akal, 2007).

[44] "Origen del liberalismo europeo", *El Censor*, 31 March 1821. This discourse, as occurred with many other journalistic and doctrinal articles, did not take long to cross the ocean: "Origen del liberalismo," *Amigo de la Constitución*, Havana, 28 February 1823.

## Concepts on the Move

freedom or security, property, freedom of opinion, equality before the law, fair distribution of taxes, and equal access to public functions on the basis of candidates' merits. "All representative government founded on these principles," concludes the author, "is liberal."[45]

There are also plenty of "negative definitions." In fact, the most common discursive uses of liberalism by its proponents merely contrast the lofty values associated with this concept-ideology with its vilified opponents: absolutism, despotism, arbitrariness. The great metaphor of slavery and its antidote, emancipation, frequently furnish the central argument, especially in America. Others interpret liberalism in a developmentalist sense, as improvement, advance, and progress. For many Hispanic liberals at the time, "true liberalism consists of the steady trend toward perfect government" in accordance with "the progress of human reason."[46] According to this philosophy, liberalism was, then, nothing other than time itself, marching onwards to leave behind archaic and obsolete institutions. "Liberalism is the representative of civilization," the goal of which is "social improvement."[47] Years later, a Spanish progressive leader declared that the *liberal party* was the one that fought for the "reform of abuses, intellectual progress, civil liberty, the progress of civilization in its different spheres," and added that "the champions of liberalism have declared themselves in every era to be advocates of the rights of humanity, promotors of equity and justice, defenders of civil equality, so akin to the dignity of mankind, and zealous supporters of the rule of law as all that prevents us from being slaves of one another."[48]

With regard to its intellectual roots, in the absence of a canon of authors recognized by all – a canon that would not be established until the twentieth century – the selection of the "fathers of liberalism" was the source of no little debate. While Bilbao's Juan de Olavarría – who argued in favor of a "great federation" of free nations that would promote the "language of universal liberalism" shared by European and American liberals[49] – includes in the list of "princes of universal liberalism" the names of Bentham, Mirabeau, Constant, De Pradt, Destutt de Tracy, Dunoyer, and Sismondi, for South American Vicente Rocafuerte, "the theories of liberalism [were]

---

[45] *El Censor*, 14 April 1821, 77–80.
[46] Juan de Olavarría, *"Reflexiones a las Cortes" y otros escritos políticos*, ed. Claude Morange (Bilbao: Universidad del País Vasco, 2007), 222–3: 314.
[47] *El Nivel*, Mexico City, 6 and 25 December 1825.
[48] Evaristo San Miguel, *De la guerra civil de España* (Madrid: Miguel de Burgos, 1836), 18.
[49] Claude Morange, *Una conspiración fallida y una Constitución nonnata, 1819* (Madrid: CEPC, 2006), 374–408.

discovered, explained and developed by Montesquieu, Mably, Filangieri, Benjamin Constant, Franklin, and Madison." The same author invited South Americans to imitate the "liberal spirit of the United States" and argued that the promised land of "true liberalism" must be the New World.[50] José M. Blanco White and Antonio Alcalá Galiano, in their essays on the origins of Hispanic liberalism, argued that, along with Mariana, Locke, Fénelon, the eighteenth-century *philosophes* and Burke, the great enlightened authors of the eighteenth century – Feijoó, Jovellanos, Aranda, Olavide, Campomanes – should appear in the select list of the fathers of liberalism.[51]

It is worth recalling, meanwhile, that the leaders of the North American revolution – some of them already known in Iberian America for two decades[52] – were cult figures for the Spanish American patriots. Glowing praise of Franklin, "the first American genius," the "immortal Washington" and the "illustrious Paine" filled page after page of newspapers and political literature during the initial phase of the Hispanic revolutions. The calls for Spanish America to follow the example set by the North Americans, and the discussions over whether or not it was advisable to adopt the institutions that had so quickly brought prosperity to their northern neighbors, beginning with the Philadelphia Constitution, were commonplace in debates during those years. Authors like Miranda and Rocafuerte agreed that it was a good idea to imitate the "liberal spirit of the United States" and eschew the unfortunate French example. And, as the years went by, individuals such as Bolívar, San Martín, and Iturbide were likened to the founding fathers of the North American republic, the former being described, for instance, as the "Washington of South America."[53]

Thanks largely to the Constitution of Cádiz, reintroduced in 1820 after the *pronunciamiento* of Riego, and the myth of a heroic Spain that spread across Europe in the wake of the Iberian resistance against Napoleon, Spanish liberalism – which succeeded in combining republican, moderate, and

---

[50] Olavarría, *"Reflexiones a las Cortes" y otros escritos políticos*, 214–9 (9 October 1820); Vicente Rocafuerte, *Bosquejo ligerísimo de la revolución de Méjico, desde el grito de Iguala hasta la proclamación imperial de Iturbide* (Filadelfia: Imprenta de Teracrouef y Naroajeg, 1822), vii.

[51] José María Blanco White, "Spain," *The Quarterly Review* 57 (April 1823), 240–76; Antonio Alcalá Galiano, "Orígenes del liberalismo español," [1864] in *Obras escogidas*, 2 vols. (Madrid: Atlas, 1955), vol. II, 440–5.

[52] Merle E. Simmons, *La revolución norteamericana en la independencia de Hispanoamérica* (Madrid: Mapfre, 1992), 42–3, 265 ff.

[53] Simmons, *La revolución norteamericana*, 298–9.

Catholic features – attained the apex of its prestige and overseas influence in the first half of the 1820s, when it acquired global dimensions.[54]

## Federalism

The *vacatio regis* resulting from the captivity of King Fernando VII and the Napoleonic usurpation of the Crown led first to the collapse and then the disintegration of the monarchy. In the face of that existential challenge, there was an attempt to fill the power vacuum in the Peninsula by means of improvised authorities at a provincial level (juntas), which converged a few months later in a Junta Central with a view to coordinating the uprising against *el intruso* (the Usurper) Joseph I. Some historians have described that process as a de facto "federalization" of the body of the monarchy (whose structure, let us not forget, was that of a "composite monarchy"). In fact, this composite, polycentric structure had also given rise in recent troubled times to imaginative proposals of various federated monarchies to safeguard the basic unity of the whole.[55]

The sudden retroversion of the sovereignty to the people – by virtue of the traditional Hispanic theory according to which, in the king's absence, the power conferred upon the monarch should return to the *pueblos* (towns) – resulted in the fragmentation of the body of the monarchy into a multitude of *corpora* on a territorial basis, each of which demanded its own supremacy. The Hispanic revolutions evidence the extreme difficulty involved in, firstly, reconstituting the lost unity of such a gigantic political body; and then, once it was clear that this reconstitution was impossible – even under the formula of reconverting it into a multicontinental constitutional nation – constructing viable nations upon the ruins of the imperial monarchy. After the failure of the first attempts to renew the mechanism of reunification on the basis of the autonomy of its components, the advocates of American independence succeeded in imposing their projects, albeit with great difficulty.[56] The

---

[54] John Davis, "The Spanish Constitution of 1812 and the Mediterranean Revolutions (1820–5)," *Bulletin for Spanish and Portuguese Historical Studies* 37:2 (2013), Article 7; Jorge Luengo and Pol Dalmau, "Writing Spanish History in the Global Age: Connections and Entanglements in the Nineteenth Century," *Journal of Global History* 13:3 (November 2018), 428–34.

[55] Manuel Lucena Giraldo, ed., *Premoniciones de la independencia de Iberoamérica: Las reflexiones de José de Ábalos y el conde de Aranda sobre la situación de la América española a finales del siglo XVIII* (Madrid: Mapfre Tavera, 2003).

[56] José M. Portillo Valdés, *Crisis atlántica: Autonomía e independencia en la crisis de la monarquía hispana* (Madrid: Marcial Pons, 2006).

decisive influence of local factors in the first Ibero-American pro-independence movements (town councils and juntas, clashes between cities and towns that demanded sovereignty, multiplication of constitutional municipalities, federalization of territories) is in fact one of the most characteristic features of that whole intricate revolutionary process, territorially and socially far more complex than previous experiences in the Thirteen Colonies, in France or in Haiti.

Far from the motherland, in the Western Hemisphere of the monarchy, projects of a federal nature resurfaced, inspired, usually, by the Philadelphia Constitution. Given that in the neighboring "Anglo-American" republic the federal *experiment* had proved to be a success, why not try the same formula in the new Hispano-American states? For Miguel de Pombo from New Granada, the answer was crystal-clear: "South America," he declared emphatically, "wishes to imitate North America."[57] Meanwhile, however much Spanish jurists had been reiterating for centuries that the government of the *pueblos* (towns) had to be exercised by the towns themselves,[58] the fact is that in the Cortes of Cádiz the majority of peninsular delegates warned against the dangers of provincialism and federalism. However, this did not prevent the Constitution of Cádiz (Title VI, Art. 309 and ff.) from recognizing the self-government of town councils and provinces. In fact, the implementation of the constitution applied the principle of representation at a municipal level and significantly reinforced the autonomy of local communities.[59]

In practice, federal language could serve very different purposes depending on the actors and subjects to be federated. While, as I have said, at the beginning of the crisis a few people resorted to that language in an attempt to reestablish unity upon new foundations, at a later stage the pro-independence insurgents applied it to the new national political bodies under construction. In light of the evidence that dispersion was irreversible (*ex unum pluribus*), the federal path was seen by many as an ideal solution with which to establish links between neighboring cities and provinces in order internally to organize the new nations (*e pluribus unum*).[60] Even beyond

---

[57] Miguel de Pombo, *Constitución de los Estados Unidos de América* ... (Santafé de Bogotá: Imprenta Patriótica de D. Nicolás Calvo, 1811), 119.

[58] Tomás Pérez Vejo, *Elegía criolla: Una reinterpretación de las guerras de independencia hispanoamericanas* (Mexico City: Tusquets, 2010), 249.

[59] Antonio Annino, "Imperio, Constitución y diversidad en la América hispana," *Historia Mexicana*, 58:1 (July–September 2008), 179–227.

[60] Clément Thibaud, "De l'Empire aux États. Le fédéralisme en Nouvelle Grenade (1780–1853)," *Anuario de Estudios Bolivarianos* 12:13 (2006), 135–75.

the political sphere, the federal link was sometimes presented as a "general law valid for the entire universe."[61]

In the consciousness of some ideologues of independence, for some time the desire persisted for an ascending scale of increasingly ambitious federative pacts with a view to constructing great political bodies, even of a continental scope. Various provincial constitutions kept open the possibility of joining other polities by means of (con-)federation. A handful of political experiments, from the Central American Federal Republic (1824–1839) to the Peruvian–Bolivian Confederation (1836–1839), show that the federal ideal survived the failure of the Panama Congress of 1826.[62] However, based on the principle that, as Arequipan Francisco Xavier Luna Pizarro declared in 1827, in every federal state its "component parts are independent, free and sovereign states with regard to their internal administration,"[63] the difficulty involved in clearly establishing the responsibilities of the federal nation and the federated states – at a time when the distinction between federation and confederation, if any, was extremely tenuous and the writings of Paine were much better known than *The Federalist* papers – manifested itself on several occasions.[64] A number of supposedly federal texts in the Hispanic world reveal, indeed, that the emphasis was not on union, but on the local power of the federated states.[65]

While it is true that the North American federal model, albeit only partially known, bewitched many Spanish American leaders, not all were convinced by the federal structure, and they certainly did not interpret federalism in the same way. The question of how central government and local government powers should be combined and harmonized was the object of endless discussion. And, in contrast to the proponents of the "federative system," some intellectuals, soldiers, and politicians, like

---

[61] The "federal link" (sometimes called "the federative pact") is, for some Spanish-speaking intellectuals, a sort of "universal system" (something akin to Newton's law in physics), a general principle underlying the whole world, based "in the immutable order and the eternal laws of nature." Miguel de Pombo, "Discurso preliminar sobre los principios y ventajas del sistema federativo," in *Constitución de los Estados Unidos de América según se propuso por la convención tenida en Filadelfia el 17 de septiembre de 1787 . . .* (Bogotá: Imprenta Patriótica de D. Nicolás Calvo, 1811), xiv–xv.

[62] Fernández-Sebastián, *DPSMI – I*, 487–8.

[63] Francisco Javier de Luna Pizarro, *Escritos políticos*, ed. Alberto Tauro (Lima: UNMSM, 1959), 191.

[64] Fernández-Sebastián, *DPSMI – II*, vol. IV, *Independencia*, 169.

[65] Juan José de Aycinena, *Otras reflexiones sobre reforma política en Centro-América* (Philadelphia: E. G. Dorsey, 1833), 17; see also José Cecilio del Valle, "La constitución federal," in Jorge del Valle Matheu, ed., *Obras* (Guatemala City: Tipografía Sánchez & de Guise, 1829–1830).

Venezuelan Simón Bolívar or Chilean Juan Egaña, maintained that, in the South American context, the concentration of power was preferable to its dispersion and that unitary governments were more efficient than their federal counterparts.[66]

In those decades of political essays, some federal proposals began to take the form of constitutional documents. In various parts of Spanish America we find early constitutions and federal projects – in Venezuela, New Granada, and the Río de la Plata – but also, in the 1820s and 1830s, unitary constitutions, like that of Cúcuta, which gave rise to the experiment of "Gran" Colombia, those of Chile, Peru, etc. Perhaps the most popular federal constitution of those years was the Mexican Constitution of 1824, which has often been interpreted as "framed almost entirely upon the basis of that of the United States."[67] Some authors, however, have identified in its content the imprint of the Constitution of Cádiz, which, as has been demonstrated ad nauseam by recent historiography "was not a Spanish document; it was a charter for the Spanish world."[68] Particularly involved in the drafting of both laws – the Hispanic one of 1812 and the Mexican text of 1824 – were New Spain's delegates José Miguel Guridi Alcocer and Miguel Ramos de Arizpe, and the decentralized, quasi-federal system of provincial councils introduced in Cádiz is one of the keys to understanding that first Mexican federalism.[69]

On occasion, abstract opinions were nuanced on grounds of pragmatism. Thus, Vicente Rocafuerte, while acknowledging that the federal system is the best that had been invented, had no qualms about admitting that, for Colombia's specific circumstances, the centralist system of the Constitution of Cúcuta was preferable.[70] In that same decade of the 1820s, marked by intense political experimentation, some disappointed publicists began to think that – as Bolívar recognized in his Angostura address – the specific conditions

---

[66] Juan Egaña, *Memorias políticas sobre las federaciones y legislaturas en general y con relación a Chile* (Santiago de Chile: Imprenta de la Independencia, 1825); Juan José Dauxion Lavaysse, *Del federalismo y de la anarquía* (Santiago de Chile: Imprenta Nacional, 1823); Roberto Gargarella, *Latin American Constitutionalism, 1810–2010: The Engine Room of the Constitution* (Oxford: Oxford University Press, 2013), 3.

[67] *Democratic Review*, March 1838, 486.

[68] Jaime E. Rodríguez, ed., *The Divine Charter: Constitutionalism and Liberalism in Nineteenth-Century Mexico* (Lanham: Rowman & Littlefield, 2007), 13.

[69] Nettie Lee Benson, *The Provincial Diputacion in Mexico: Harbinger of Provincial Autonomy, Independence, and Federalism* (Austin: University of Texas Press, 1992); Jaime E. Rodríguez, ed., *The Divine Charter: Constitutionalism and Liberalism in Nineteenth-Century Mexico* (Lanham: Rowman & Littlefield, 2007).

[70] Vicente Rocafuerte, *Ensayo político: El sistema colombiano, popular, electivo, y representativo, es el que mas conviene a la América independiente* (New York: A. Paul, 1823), 171–88.

of each society were important. Transplanting the laws of one society and mechanically applying them to another, they suggested, was not the best solution, since, as a Lima journalist wrote, "a political constitution is not a magic wand that alters nations with its spell."[71] In this respect, Venezuelan-Chilean Andrés Bello wisely warned his contemporaries against the error of thinking that "our constitutional definitions," conceived "for an abstract people" would be transformed as if by magic into stable institutions.[72]

## Final Remarks

In the preceding pages, I have described in broad terms the evolution of four fundamental concepts of Latin lineage that, along with others like people (*pueblo*), nation, sovereignty, freedom, independence, representation, and dozens more, articulated the new political practices and institutions that were tested during that era of revolutionary experiments. Two ancient terms, *cives* and *constitutio*, upon which various strata of meaning had accumulated over the centuries, were suddenly resemanticized in the light of the Atlantic revolutions and by the end of the eighteenth century had become two dazzling concepts, laden with expectation. As regards the neologisms liberalism and federalism, no less "futuristic" than citizen and constitution, suffice it to say that their coining during those years – forged from a diversity of materials in which one detects their distant roots, *foedus* and *liber*, but in which it is possible to discern far more recent, significant contributions – is very symptomatic of that decisive moment when the first political -isms introduced a new political period that some would call the "age of ideologies."

The four concepts appear in interconnected fashion in a discursive tangle that is difficult to unravel. While in a number of discourses the words *constitución* and *federación* are interwoven,[73] in numerous Spanish American texts from those early decades of the nineteenth century, *liberalismo* and *constitucionalismo* operated almost as synonyms (the first occurrences of the latter term, as tends to be the case, are to be found in pamphlets critical of constitutionalism almost a decade after the coining of the former).[74] As regards *citizenship*, it is clear, as is reiterated time and time again in the press

---

[71] *Mercurio Peruano* (Lima), 29 July 1828.
[72] Natalio R. Botana, "Las transformaciones del credo constitucional," in Antonio Annino and François-Xavier Guerra, eds., *Inventando la nación: Iberoamérica siglo XIX* (Mexico City: FCE, 2003), 654–82: 656.
[73] Fernández-Sebastián, *DPSMI – I*, 425 ff.
[74] Rafael de Vélez, *Apología del altar y el trono*, 2 vols. (Madrid: Imprenta de Cano, 1818).

and publications, that the status of citizen presupposed the existence of a liberal, constitutional state.

The 1820s, a period of feverish political experimentation followed by a decade of certain disenchantment, pragmatism, and emphasis on order,[75] unsurprisingly coincided with the most intense debates over the concepts addressed in this chapter. And, although the vocabularies of these debates were essentially the same in the Hispanic revolutions as in the other revolutions that preceded them in the North Atlantic, when things are analyzed more closely, it is possible to detect a distinctive family resemblance in the legal-political culture of the Iberian Atlantic. It was a Catholic and jurisdictional culture that linked Hispanic constitutionalism to other similar experiences, mainly those of southern Europe, characterized, unlike their counterparts from other latitudes, by confessionalism and by the prevalence of corporative-pluralist and community values over individualist-statist values. It should be stressed, however, that neither the fact that the basic notions were largely the same everywhere, nor the fact that the elites in the region sought inspiration in North American, French, and British models, prevented semantics from differing considerably at different times and in different places depending on the specific problems with which agents were confronted in each case. The vocabulary was global, the meanings largely local. In this sense, we could paraphrase Bernard Bailyn when, referring to eighteenth-century North America, he wrote that the vocabulary of politics "was metropolitan, transcultural, European if not universal," but the reality of the Americans' lives – and the same could be said of the Ibero-Americans – their "political and social context, was parochial."[76]

By way of conclusion, let me add a brief reflection in relation to a controversial point: I refer to the balance between both extremes of the misleading change / continuity polarity in the Hispanic revolutions. In one of her most quoted essays, Hannah Arendt famously observed that "revolutions are the only political events which confront us directly and inevitably with the problem of beginning."[77] Well, if we adopt this criterion to measure the degree of "revolutionism" of those processes, the express will of their protagonists could hardly be more disruptive. A number of writers and journalists in Spanish America seemed to be possessed by an Adamic

---

[75] Tulio Halperin Donghi, *Reforma y disolución de los imperios ibéricos 1750–1850* (Madrid: Alianza, 1985), 220–7.

[76] Bernard Bailyn, *To Begin the World Anew: The Genius and Ambiguities of the American Founders* (New York: Vintage Books, 2004), 7–8.

[77] Hannah Arendt, *On Revolution* (London: Penguin Books, 1990), 21.

"passion for new beginnings" similar to that of the most radical North American and French revolutionaries. When Peru declared its independence, the Lima press published various articles reflecting this *pathos* of absolute beginning. "We are at the beginning of time," exclaimed Manuel Pérez de Tudela before the Lima Patriotic Society. "Our society," he added, paraphrasing Thomas Paine, "is going to be formed as if the world had just left its Creator's hands."[78] Meanwhile, Honduran José Cecilio del Valle called on people to "create everything over again," and Ecuadorian Vicente Rocafuerte insisted that "everything should be new in this new world."[79]

Soon afterwards, the greatest leader of South American independence could not conceal his satisfaction with his latest constitutional creature. In awe of his own creative power, Bolívar confessed in a letter to General Santander that the Republic of Bolivia held a special attraction for him: the new constitution he had written for this country that bore his name and that a few days later he would present to the Bolivian citizens as "the most liberal constitution in the world," struck him as "a little wonder."[80] The "experimentalist mania" typical of those frantic years is clearly visible in many other political and constitutional experiments. However, sources reveal that, almost overnight, the boundless optimism of a self-satisfied demiurge could become the most hopeless defeatism. In such a fluid and changing world, political scenarios succeeded one another at a furious pace. Bolívar himself would move in a matter of months from the refined pleasure of experimenting with new constitutions in his Andean laboratory to the bitterest disenchantment, to such a degree that at the end of his days he looked back on his entire political career as a resounding failure.

And, though Bolívar's final pessimism may have been just as excessive as his early enthusiasm, it seems undeniable that the high hopes that some visionary leaders had pinned on emancipation – great expectations that the revolutionaries projected upon each and every one of the concepts briefly analyzed here – soon evaporated. In the second quarter of the nineteenth

---

[78] *El Sol del Perú*, Lima, 4 April 1822; Fernández-Sebastián, *DPSMI – I*, 1347.

[79] *El Amigo de la Patria,* Guatemala, 30 November 1821; Vicente Rocafuerte, *Ensayo político: El sistema colombiano, popular, electivo, y representativo, es el que mas conviene a la América independiente* (New York: A. Paul, 1823), 27.

[80] Bolívar to Santander, 12 December 1825. See Vicente Lecuna and Harold A. Bierck, eds., *Selected Writings of Bolívar,* 2 vols. (New York: Colonial Press, Banco de Venezuela, 1951), vol. 1, 439; Luis Barrón, "La tradición republicana y el nacimiento del liberalismo en Hispanoamérica después de la independencia. Bolívar, Lucas Alamán y el 'Poder Conservador,'" in José Antonio Aguilar and Rafael Rojas, eds., *El republicanismo en Hispanoamérica: Ensayos de historia cultural y política* (Mexico City: CIDE, 2002), 244–88: 271 ff.

century, the list of politicians disappointed by that painful discrepancy between past hopes and present achievements would be a long one, and would include many leaders of the emancipation movements and first rulers of the brand-new republics. And it was this very process of learning through disappointment that, following reflection upon what had occurred, led a group of authors to sharpen their historical consciousness.[81] It can be assumed that the failed experiments prompted a revision of expectations that in turn encouraged new endeavors and experiences, which inevitably affected the semantic content of the political concepts that encapsulated and projected these experiences and expectations.

The contrast between the results expected and the results obtained was even sharper when the country of reference that a sector of Hispanic leaders observed and hoped to emulate – i.e. the United States – continued on its upward path and appeared to overcome every difficulty that it encountered. The truth is, however, that apart from functioning as incentive, the North American example was employed selectively and pragmatically in Spanish America as a tool and a quarry of arguments and *exempla* when it came to addressing certain problems and taking certain decisions, much more so than as a genuine legal-doctrinal model.[82]

In any case, the extent of the historical rupture produced by the Spanish American revolutions cannot be measured solely according to the eagerness of the revolutionaries to break with the past, renouncing en masse the cultural legacy of their elders. Beyond some leaders' rejection of their own political tradition and their firm decision – vehemently endorsed two decades later by a group of young writers from the romantic generation – to change masters and turn to foreign mentors, it would be worthwhile evaluating the efficiency of cultural traditions in order to impose their own logic and counter with their inertia the break with the past by a handful of politicians and intellectuals intent on changing the course steered by their countries. And in that vein, everything suggests that some deep-rooted cultural trends in the Iberian Atlantic – limited conception of constituent power; municipally based citizenship, linked to residence; exclusivity of the Catholic religion, among others – prevailed for a long time, tempering to a degree the radicalism of the conceptual revolution undertaken during those crucial decades.

---

[81] Fernández-Sebastián, *Historia conceptual en el Atlántico ibérico*, 474–81.
[82] Isidro Vanegas, "La revolución angloamericana como herramienta. Nueva Granada 1808–1816," *Co-herencia* 15:25 (2016), 89–118.

13

# Patriarchy, Misogyny, and Politics
# in the Age of Revolutions

MÓNICA RICKETTS

The Age of Revolutions has always been a central topic in the historiography of Latin America. In looking for what changed and what did not, scholars have delved into the different kinds of imperialisms or neo-imperialisms that affected the region after independence, state formation, *caudillismo*, new concepts and practices of citizenship, and the roles public spaces and new ideas played in forming republican citizens. More recently, the bicentennials of the liberal era of Cádiz (2008–2012) and the first movements toward autonomy and independence in several countries of Spanish America (2010–2021) have produced a renewed effort to take some necessary distance and study these histories in new and multidimensional ways. While historians have long been interested in the radical shifts, we are now increasingly exploring continuity as well, and study the persistence of ideas and structures, such as inequality, patronage, monarchism, racism, and corruption.[1] And yet, despite all this progress and attempts at revisionism, one area remains seriously understudied for this period: gender.

What could explain such neglect? One of the reasons might lie in the reluctance historians of the colonial and early republican eras have shown to seriously connect gender and politics. Gender studies developed in the historiography of Latin America in the last decades of the twentieth century, when – as often happened – women historians took the lead. Facing the dismissal and snub of their peers, specialists of the colonial era looked for their own niches. Many followed pioneer scholar in this field, Asunción Lavrin,[2] who claimed that "[w]omen's history in the colonial period cannot be measured by events or developments of a political character – the marks

---

I thank Wim Klooster and Jennifer Heuer for their meticulous and constructive critique.
[1] See Matthew Brown and Gabriel Paquette, "The Persistence of Mutual Influence: Europe and Latin America in the 1820s," *European History Quarterly* 41:3 (2011), 387–96.
[2] Asunción Lavrin, "Women in Spanish American Colonial Society," in Leslie Bethell, ed., *The Cambridge History of Latin America* (Cambridge: Cambridge University Press, 1984), 321–56.

of distinction of a man-oriented world." Since women were not welcomed in the political world, she argued, women historians needed to look for other spaces in which women dominated or exercised decisive agency.[3] Thanks to her Herculean efforts and those of her followers, the historiography of colonial Latin America now counts on almost entire subfields dedicated to analyzing women's roles in convents, market places, and family legal disputes.[4] As a consequence, however, the field of political history was confirmed to be for more "traditional" historians, which left the analysis of the Age of Revolutions, a foundational moment in the reconfiguration of the patriarchal order, in the margins of the new gender history. The extensive and rich works of Sarah Chambers as well as those of Rebecca Earle and Matthew Brown are notable exceptions to this trend.[5] While historical research still remains limited, historians should be aware that literary scholars, following their interest in female writers and discourses, have made much more progress in this field and have shown us the importance of using literary sources when discussing politics.[6]

The years 1760–1830, which roughly encompass the long era of reform, rebellions, revolution, and independence, offer an ideal arena to reflect on the connection between gender and politics, as the changes brought about at this time forged a new politics and patriarchy. This new order demanded a different kind of man in politics, the brave and daring individual, and ousted women and homosexuals with a powerful misogynist discourse that has

---

[3] Lavrin, "Women," 321.

[4] Asunción Lavrin, *Brides of Christ: Conventual Life in Colonial Mexico* (Stanford: Stanford University Press, 2008); Kathryn Burns, *Colonial Habits: Convents and the Spiritual Economy of Cusco, Peru* (Durham, NC: Duke University Press, 1999); Jane Mangan, *Trading Roles: Gender, Ethnicity, and the Urban Economy in Colonial Potosí* (Durham, NC: Duke University Press, 2005).

[5] Sarah Chambers, "Masculine Virtues and Feminine Passions: Gender and Race in the Republicanism of Simón Bolívar," *Hispanic Research Journal* 7:1 (2006), 21–40, and "The Paternal Obligation to Provide: Political Familialism in Early Nineteenth-Century Chile," *American Historical Review* 117:4 (2012), 1123–48; Rebecca Earle, "Rape and the Anxious Republic: Revolutionary Colombia, 1810–1830," in Elizabeth Dore and Maxime Molyneaux, eds., *Hidden Histories of Gender and the State in Latin America* (Durham, NC: Duke University Press, 2000), 127–46; Matthew Brown, *Adventuring through Spanish Colonies: Simón Bolívar, Foreign Mercenaries and the Birth of New Nations* (Liverpool: Liverpool University Press, 2006).

[6] See Catherine Davies, Claire Brewster, and Hilary Owen, *South American Independence: Gender, Politics, Text* (Liverpool: Liverpool Scholarship Online, 2013); Catherine Davies, "The Gender Order of Postwar Politics: Comparing Spanish South America and Spain, 1810s–1850s," in Alan Forrest, Karen Hagemann, and Michael Rowe, eds., *War, Demobilization and Memory: The Legacy of War in the Era of Atlantic Revolutions* (Basingstoke: Palgrave Macmillan, 2016), 182–99.

forged gender inequalities and exclusionary practices Latin America endures to this day.

This chapter brings together three basic avenues of gender analysis usually seen in isolation with the aim of expanding our understanding of the Age of Revolutions and showing us the benefits of examining them in unison. The first section connects the rise of new political actors with the emergence of a new dominating masculine identity in the late eighteenth century. The analysis turns next to male homosexuality in the context of revolutions. After all, as Joan Scott so convincingly argued, gender history only makes sense if we think about the relation of different genders to one another and to power.[7] Unfortunately, I could not find enough scholarly works or sources to include female homosexuality in the discussion. Finally, the last section examines women and politics, paying particular attention to the discourses that excluded them from the new political order. The chapter will both review historiographic trends and offer insights from my own primary source research on the Viceroyalty of Peru in the context of the Spanish empire.

## The New Man

While the history of masculinities used to be a marginalized topic among scholars of Latin America, there is fascinating new scholarship on this subject. When it came to analyzing men, historians of the colonial era were concerned with the role that honor played in this society, a crucial element in a study on masculinities.[8] Only recently, scholars have addressed male sexual identities directly. For the early colonial era, Rebecca Earle has examined the bodies of conquistadors in relation to notions of science.[9] Taking on a longer span of time, Sonya Lipsett-Rivera has analyzed the coexistence of diverse ideas of masculinity in Mexico using court cases with the aim of understanding the interconnections between occupation and identity.[10] Notions of

---

[7] See Joan Scott, "Gender: A Useful Category of Historical Analysis," *American Historical Review* 91:5 (1986), 1053–75. For an illuminating analysis on gender and politics see her *The Politics of the Veil* (Princeton, NJ: Princeton University Press, 2007).

[8] James Lockhart, *The Men of Cajamarca: A Social and Biographical Study of the First Conquistadors of Peru* (Austin: University of Texas Press, 1972); Richard M. Morse, "Towards a Theory of Spanish American Government," *Journal of the History of Ideas* 15 (1954), 71–93.

[9] Rebecca Earle, *The Body of the Conquistador: Food, Race, and the Colonial Experience in Spanish America, 1492–1700* (Cambridge: Cambridge University Press, 2012).

[10] Sonya Lipsett-Rivera, *The Origins of Macho: Men and Masculinity in Colonial Mexico* (Albuquerque: University of New Mexico Press, 2019).

paternity and patriarchy have also been key areas of interest, leading historians to work on education and family relations.[11] Other themes of growing interest are domestic violence and the intersection of masculinity and race.[12] For the specific Age of Revolutions, the works of Sarah Chambers and Matthew Brown stand out. Chambers has worked on the symbiotic roles of caudillos and *pater familias*, and Brown on the personas of the new military adventurers to Gran Colombia.[13]

When thinking about masculinity and power, it is worth taking a long-term view to assess changes and continuities, which in this case means going back to the early Bourbon era of reform. After succeeding to the Spanish throne and War of Succession (1700–1714), the new Bourbon Crown tried adamantly to create a new trustworthy elite, who could transform the Spanish world into a first-rate monarchy. Per the Crown's rhetoric, the new court demanded new "men of merit and virtue." A new power elite came into being, made up of men with professional or semi-professional training, lawyers and military officers from the provincial elite, educated in the most progressive schools of the Spanish Peninsula or abroad. In a larger study, I have analyzed the social and professional profiles of the men the Crown brought to new positions of authority.[14] What I omitted was that the reconceptualization of power this reform entailed not only undermined traditional ideas of authority and the political foundation of the monarchy, but forged a new masculine identity that was directly connected with the new politics. Moreover, these changes happened at a time when the Enlightenment was putting the individual at center stage in the hope of forging a new man of reason and virtue. Slowly and in contrast to the past, men began to conceive of themselves – their honor and status – as largely a product of their own personas and achievements, their individual daring, and strength.

---

[11] See Pilar Gonzalbo Aizpuru, *Familia y orden colonial* (Mexico City: El Colegio de México, Centro de Estudios Históricos, 1998) and her *Historia de la educación en la época colonial: El mundo indígena* (Mexico City: El Colegio de México, Centro de Estudios Históricos, 1990); Asunción Lavrin, ed., *Sexuality and Marriage in Colonial Latin America* (Lincoln: University of Nebraska Press, 1989). See also Bianca Premo, *Children of the Father King: Youth, Authority, and Legal Minority in Colonial Lima* (Chapel Hill: University of North Carolina Press, 2005).

[12] See Víctor M. Uribe-Urán, *Fatal Love: Spousal Killers, Law, and Punishment in the Late Colonial Spanish Atlantic* (Stanford: Stanford University Press, 2016).

[13] Chambers, "Masculine Virtues"; Chambers, "The Paternal Obligation;" Brown, *Adventuring through Spanish Colonies*.

[14] Mónica Ricketts, *Who Should Rule? Men of Arms, the Republic of Letters, and the Fall of the Spanish Empire* (New York: Oxford University Press, 2017).

Patriarchy, Misogyny, and Politics

In pursuit of this major reform, Bourbon authorities waged aggressive campaigns in newspapers, pamphlets, churches, and schools advocating for the rise of men of merit to positions of power. These were not only reserved for men, but conceived of for a new kind of man, one with professional training, skill, bravery, audacity, and bravura, preferably a military man. Numerous texts and regulations explained meticulously what virtue and merit now meant and how the new man ought to behave.

In an era of intense international competition, the Bourbon ideology of reform remained inextricably tied to war. After the Seven Years' War and the British seizure of Havana in 1762, the Spanish monarchy hurried to put together a military reform. The new governors, viceroys, and local commanders would all be men with military training, ready to fight. Where it was implemented across the board, as in Cuba and the Viceroyalty of Peru, the military reform would have long-lasting political, social, and cultural effects. Its role in forging a "new man" still needs to be examined. In the years 1764–1769, the Crown produced an ambitious new set of military regulations to swiftly organize militia units along a regular army force. These long texts explained in detail what was expected of army men, professionally and personally. The new military man was to excel at being brave, daring, skillful, loyal, energetic, and ready for sacrifice.[15] Officers were to learn these new rules of conduct and communicate them to their men, thus "giving the soldier a martial demeanor."[16] According to the regulations, colonels also needed to make sure that soldiers were neat and clean in appearance and kept their uniforms tidy, avoiding in their fashion "those excesses that ridicule the youth, effeminate it, and shatters a solid mode of thinking."[17] Soldiers were to be disciplined, punctual, methodic, brave, and athletic.

Crimes and punishments were strictly regulated too. Listed among the worst offenses were blasphemy, attacks to the Church, and disobedience. Insults to superiors, sedition, lack of punctuality, abandonment of a post,

---

[15] See my "The Rise of the Bourbon Military in Peru, 1768–1820," *Colonial Latin American Review* 22:3 (2012), 413–39. See also *Ordenanzas de S.M. para el regimen, disciplina, subordinacion, y servicio de sus exercitos*, 4 vols. (Madrid: Oficina de Pedro Marin, Impresor de la Secretaría del Despacho Universal de la Guerra, 1768); *Reglamento para las milicias de infanteria, y caballeria de la Isla de Cuba* (Lima: Imprenta de la Real Casa de los Niños Expósitos, 1779).

[16] "Tratado segundo. De las obligaciones de los militares. Titulo segundo. Del cabo. Art. 6," *Ordenanzas de S.M.*, vol. 1, 96. The translation is mine, as with all other Spanish sources translated in this chapter.

[17] Art. 25 and Art. 5, Titulo xviii, "Forma y distincion con que han de ser los cadetes admitidos, y considerados," *Ordenanzas*, vol. 1, 245.

oversleeping, stealing arms, robberies, disorganization in marches, and forging coins followed. The last two serious crimes contemplated in the regulations were related to gender: violence against women and the nefarious sin (sodomy). In these cases, the regulations ordered that the military would relinquish its authority over the Inquisition if the latter took over the case. Yet the opposite happened when the military tribunals captured the offender first. Per the military norms, army men who forced an honest woman, married or maiden, would be executed. Yet if this crime was only intended but not committed, men could be exiled for ten years to a jail in Spain's African colonies or for six to an arsenal. Those who perpetrated the bestial or sodomitical crime (no specifications) would be hanged or burned, which meant that the offender would not only undergo a cruel death, but a humiliating one too.[18] The regulations had established that the king's soldiers who committed a crime ought to be judged by a court of peers and treated with respect and dignity. When it came to sodomy, however, a major offense to the king and God, shame was expected. The new military man was to stand as a model for others.

This militaristic ethos, so clearly outlined in the regulations, impregnated the world of letters too. The new Bourbon Crown demanded writers to design and implement an ambitious social and cultural reform; lawyers were to produce a whole new legislation that would transform the Spanish world into a great imperial power; writers were to fight old privileges. Men of letters responded accordingly and began to wage a war with their pens.

One of the leaders of the social reform, Pedro Rodríguez de Campomanes (1723–1802), campaigned for a new society composed of useful and industrious subjects who would help the Crown recover its lost standing role in the world. The leading members of this society would carry comparable duties to those of officers with their troops, he argued.[19] *Limeño* Pablo de Olavide (1725–1803), one of Campomanes' closest allies, shared this utilitarian and militaristic view. In 1768, he was commissioned to write a new program of studies for the University of Salamanca, Spain's oldest and most important university, to be applied in elite schools all over the Spanish world. Olavide

---

[18] See *Ordenanzas*, vol. III, Titulo X, 342. On how sodomy was conceived of and sanctioned prior to the eighteenth century see María Elena Martínez, "Sex and the Colonial Archive: The Case of 'Mariano' Aguilera," *Hispanic American Historical Review* 96:3 (2016), 421–43.

[19] Pedro Rodríguez de Campomanes, *Discurso sobre el fomento de la industria popular* (Madrid: Imprenta de Antonio Sancha, 1774), www.cervantesvirtual.com/obra-visor/ discurso-sobre-el-fomento-de-la-industria-popular–o/html/fee99972-82b1-11df-acc7-002185ce6064_2.html#I_4._.

presented Spain as a body without "vigor" or "energy" in need of regeneration. He criticized universities for having become frivolous institutions that educated men in useless subject matters, such as the scholastic method, forcing them to embody the Church's sectarian spirit in the use of ecclesiastical robes, which led them to hide their body shapes and sizes, to shame, and to bad hygiene, he claimed. As a remedy, Francophile Olavide proposed the use of modern black military uniforms, an attire in fashion that in his view would eradicate boast and vanity.[20]

The Bourbon ideology's stress on the Spanish need for new men of action willing to serve the monarchy spread in legislation, essays, newspapers, and literature all over the Spanish world. By the end of the eighteenth century, military men held most positions of power; men of letters, while struggling to find a clear space in a changing society, wrote in newspapers, taught, and organized new societies to spread useful knowledge and change the world that surrounded them. It is no coincidence that in his vicious satire of 1797, Spaniard Esteban Terralla y Landa had his main character, Simon Ayanque, advise a friend who was moving to Lima to dress like a soldier if he did not want to be seen as plebeian or confused for a Black man.[21]

In 1808, Napoleon invaded the Spanish Peninsula, lured the Spanish monarch Fernando VII and his father, former king Carlos IV to France, where he took them captive, and created an unprecedented vacuum of authority. A struggle for power unfolded, as it was not yet clear who should take the lead in the absence of the Spanish king: men of arms who were waging the war against Napoleon with arms, or men of letters who were using words to take the French invaders down and change Spanish society in the meantime. Their constant clashes changed the nature of politics and consolidated new ideas of power and rule that were inextricably tied to a new masculine identity. A man's worth was now measured in terms of his capacity and willingness to fight aggressively and to sacrifice for the country, with their sword or pen, according to the circumstances.

In the Viceroyalty of Peru, the expansion of the military and persistent unrest dominated the early nineteenth century. With its large forces, Peru became a bastion of royal power, curtailing insurgencies north and south. Expansion reached its peak during Viceroy Abascal's tenure (1808–1816), who took advantage of the wars to increase his prerogatives and govern as a

---

[20] Pablo de Olavide, "La Reforma Universitaria. Plan de Estudios Universitarios. Idea General," in Estuardo Nuñez, ed., *Obras Selectas* (Lima: Banco de Crédito, 1987), 544–5.

[21] *Lima por dentro y fuera* (Valladolid: Editorial Maxtor, 2012 [1798]), 158.

quasi-military dictator. Insurgencies proliferated in the 1810s in the southern regions of Peru, Cusco, Arequipa, and Tacna, which connected with the Río de la Plata and Charcas. These confrontations offered leeway for the newly empowered men. The chiefs of these conspiracies dreamed of creating a new order in which they could lead; royal army men expected that a victory would grant them new status and power. While their clashes undermined the foundations of royal power in Peru, they also consolidated their leading roles in the eyes of the people.

By the time the actual wars of independence began in Peru in 1820 with the invasion of José de San Martín's army of liberation, it was clear that politics was in the hands of new men of action. War intensified but reached a stalemate by 1822, which led San Martín to request Simón Bolívar's aid.[22] Bolívar concentrated his attention on winning the war to secure the continent's independence. Following a Napoleonic model of rule centered on his persona, Bolívar demanded full powers. Much like Bonaparte, he would embody the ambitions of many aspiring new men and become a model for them. The long-lasting era of the caudillos was under way.

Analyzing *caudillismo* became a central concern for Latin American historians and social scientists of the late twentieth century. There is an extensive scholarship trying to explain the nature of their power, social base, ideologies or lack thereof, and charisma.[23] Much of the historiography on *caudillismo* follows the powerful and biased portrait that novelist and politician Domingo Faustino Sarmiento laid out in his romantic novel of 1845, *Civilización y barbarie: La vida de Juan Facundo Quiroga*. Only recently have historians embraced gender analysis to examine caudillos as father figures of new patriarchal bourgeois orders. For the most part, this scholarship has been interested in explaining the rise of a "bourgeois masculinity." For example, Lipsett-Rivera has argued that caudillos were instrumental in reshaping the patriarchy, as they presented themselves as father figures of the new countries. Sarah Chambers and Magaly Alegre have also taken this path, analyzing the new symbiotic relationship between caudillos and fathers and their roles in forming a new patriarchy.[24] What we are still missing, however, is a study

---

[22] See Timothy Anna, *The Fall of the Royal Government* (Lincoln: University of Nebraska Press, 1979).

[23] See Domingo Faustino Sarmiento, *Facundo: Civilization and Barbarism* (Berkeley and Los Angeles: University of California Press, 2003). For a still influential historical analysis on caudillos that follows Sarmiento's framework see John Lynch, *Caudillos in Spanish America 1800–1850* (Oxford: Clarendon Press, 1992).

[24] See Lipsett-Rivera, *The Origins of Macho*; Magaly Alegre, "'Hombres de temperamento delicado.' Determinismo climático, moda masculina y cuidados maternos en la prensa

examining caudillos in relation to the new masculine identity that was tied to the new politics. We have plenty of sources to explore in this regard. For space constraints, I will focus here on portraits and manifestos.

Portraits gained renewed strength in the Spanish world of the eighteenth century. Authorities and the elite commissioned them to show off their status and power. Men appeared dignified and wealthy, as the main characters of their own stories, wearing for the most part military attires. By the nineteenth century, the genre included a new kind of man, the resistance leaders against French invaders who had come from lower origins but risen thanks to their actions in battlefields, such as Juan Martín, *El Empecinado*, painted by Goya in 1809. In Peru, José Gil de Castro represented a similar transition, from depicting viceroys and authorities to creating a visual image of the new political man, the heroes of independence. Gil de Castro was trained in the royal militias, where he learned to paint. He followed European conventions and Napoleonic models. Gil de Castro's military men appear solemn, athletic, virile, and clean. Most carried their swords, no longer used in battle but still a sign of traditional distinction, and decorated their uniforms with the new symbols of power: medals, awards, and badges.[25]

Caudillos not only used their bodies to show off their new power, they also commissioned manifestos and published speeches in which they were praised for their exemplary actions and sacrifices for the country. Former and new caudillos fought in the press to prove who had more merits and virtues to rule, who had sacrificed more and thus deserved more honor, rewards, and power. As political unrest took hold after independence and it was not clear who ought to rule the new republic, a war of words took off in the press.

General Andrés de Santa Cruz's (1792–1865) proclamations are good examples. A mestizo general, son of caciques, trained in the royal armies, Santa Cruz climbed to the highest military echelons when he switched to the insurgents in 1820 as General José de San Martín's army invaded Peru. He then joined and became a close ally of Simón Bolívar, who along with

---

ilustrada," in Claudia Rosas Lauro, ed., *Género y mujeres en la historia del Perú: Del hogar al espacio público* (Lima: Fondo Editorial, PUCP, 2019), 229–50 and "'It Is My Husband Who Has Such Weaknesses': A Mid-Nineteenth-Century Peruvian Divorce Case," in Sean Brady and Mark Seymour, eds., *From Sodomy Laws to Same-Sex Marriage: International Perspectives since 1789* (London: Bloomsbury Academic, 2019), 71–82; Chambers, "Masculine Virtues"; Chambers, "The Paternal Obligation."

[25] See Luis Eduardo Wuffarden, "Gil de Castro, el pintor de los libertadores," in Scarlett O'Phelan Godoy, ed., *La independencia del Perú: De los Borbones a Bolívar* (Lima: Instituto Riva-Agüero, Pontificia Universidad Católica del Perú, 2001), 455–77.

Napoleon became his role model. Santa Cruz served as temporary president of Peru in 1824 and president of Bolivia in 1829. In 1836 he led a campaign to rule over a Peruvian–Bolivian Confederation that brought war to both countries and neighboring Chile. Facing conspiracies and instability, Santa Cruz made sure to have writers sing his praises. In 1836, one of this *loas* (homages) presented him as "[t]he magnus General, the strong male / with the laurels of Pichincha[26] crowned / looking with attention at the fearsome death / in vanguard he goes across the terrain / to the formidable spot where fortune / awaits the enemy, while aligned / and from there he offers us a battle." While Santa Cruz fought bravely, the text stressed, his soldiers felt "the warlike wish for combat" while their "virile" chests beat strongly.[27]

## El señorito afeminado

The role male homosexuals played in this new political order is a crucial topic, as the campaigns to forge a new man led to the reconceptualization of masculinity and creation of "the effeminate man" in opposition: the fearful and lazy *señorito* (young master), useless to the state's needs, reflecting an enduring Latin American pejorative and discriminatory attitude. The history of homosexuality, neglected for so long and relegated to marginality, has been receiving a great deal of attention in the last few years in the field of colonial Latin America. Recent doctoral dissertations have engaged in queer history, thus showing us how much this topic matters to the younger generations of historians.[28] What is most fascinating about this subfield is the attention historians are paying to the use of sources and categories. Their debates are relevant and illuminating for any field.

Initially, scholars of the 1990s and 2000s traced Michel Foucault's steps and concentrated on understanding and reconstructing the repressive side of this history. Following also Joan Scott and the path outlined by Lavrin's history of sexuality, scholars have tried to explain how the social construction of queer

---

[26] Pichincha was the site of a victory of the Insurgents in 1822 that completed their control of Quito.

[27] *Batalla de Yanacocha: Canto heroyco al triunfo de las armas pacificadoras al excmo sr. Capitan Presidente de la República de Bolivia, Gran. Mariscal de la del Perú y Jeneral en Jefe del Ejército Unido, etc. etc, etc.* (Lima: Imprenta de Eusebio Aranda, 1836).

[28] Magaly Alegre Henderson, "Degenerate Heirs of Empire. Climatic Determinism and Effeminacy in the Mercurio Peruano," *Historia Crítica* 73 (2019), http://dx.doi.org/10.7440/histcrit73.2019.06 and "Androginopolis: Dissident Masculinities and the Creation of Republican Peru (Lima, 1790–1850)" (Ph.D. dissertation, State University of New York, Stony Brook, 2012).

identities actually happened.[29] For the most part, they have used Inquisition records. Since sodomy was considered a major sin against God, for this act defied His mandate to use sex to procreate, the tribunal exercised jurisdiction over those cases. Pete Sigal, for example, has pushed the historiography on sin and crime to explore the relations between desire and power. His studies on the conquest have made a strong case against the indiscriminate use of categories such as "sexuality" without considering them also as socially constructed.[30] Zeb Tortorici has brought the fields of science, sexuality, and medicine together to understand the ordering of nature, and the processing of certain ideas, such as the natural and unnatural in the sphere of sexuality.[31] In a fascinating (posthumous) article, María Elena Martínez explored how some male behaviors, such as *"sodomía,"* were criminalized in the archives.[32] More recently, queer history has turned to legal sources and to exploring the intersections between race and gender. For the Viceroyalty of Peru, Fernanda Molina has produced a rich history of subjectivities, identities, and intimacies for the early colonial era. By placing the discussion in the legal realm while connecting race and gender, she has shown how sodomy was sanctioned and regarded differently according to race and status.[33] For the Age of Revolutions, the central topic has been the relationship between honor, civic virtue, and masculinity. Historians working on homosexuality and the changes reconfiguring the patriarchal order in these years have mostly tried to explain how the new father figure created in a rising bourgeois order imposed the masculine idea of the *pater caudillo* and condemned dissenting masculine identities as effeminate.

What we still need to do is put politics at center stage. While other dissenting masculine identities were repudiated and socially marginalized in the era of reform and revolution, "the effeminate man" was also purposely excluded from a new politics that demanded men of bravery and action. Hence, to understand the new political makeshift that began in the eighteenth century and has persisted to this day, it is crucial to intersect

---

[29] Lavrin, *Sexuality and Marriage*; Asunción Lavrin, "Masculine and Feminine: The Construction of Gender Roles in the Regular Orders in Early Modern Mexico," *Explorations in Renaissance Culture* 34:1 (2008), 3–26.

[30] Pete Sigal, ed., *Infamous Desire: Male Homosexuality in Colonial Latin America* (Chicago and London: The University of Chicago Press, 2003).

[31] Zeb Tortorici, *Sins against Nature: Sex and Archives in Colonial New Spain* (Durham. NC: Duke University Press, 2018).

[32] See Martínez, "Sex and the Colonial Archive."

[33] Fernanda Molina, *Cuando amar era pecado: Sexualidad, poder e identidad entre los sodomitas coloniales (Virreinato del Perú, siglos XVI–XVII)* (Lima: IFEA, Plural, 2017).

gender and politics. Here I want to offer a few lines of inquiry from queering my own research on the educational and social reforms of the Bourbons and their political consequences. Bourbon efforts to transform the Spanish world and build a new society with active new men at its core led them to scrutinize men's habits and upbringing. Reformers tuned in with men of letters who, following the Enlightenment, also aspired to form a virtuous new man of reason.

As many authors have shown, a popular trope and concern among Bourbon reformers and enlightened-inspired writers became the *petrimetre*, the wasted and pampered elite boy or *"el señorito afeminado"* (the effeminate young master). Yet what did this identity mean in political terms? In the eyes of Bourbon reformers, the habits of the old Habsburg elite were associated with decadent practices, damaging and useless in a society in desperate need of armed and active citizens. Reformist writers made the courtier a target, presenting him as decadent, degraded, and, worse, effeminate, an association that endured and led to the condemnation of the "effeminate courtier" and its progressive exclusion from political arenas and leadership.

In 1760, Father Benito Jerónimo Feijoó (1676–1764), one of the most influential writers of the eighteenth century, published a brief essay on the philosophical proposition that there was a connection between spirit and materiality in all substances created. Resorting to pejoratives and animalistic comparisons, Feijoó concluded in the annex with a warning for *petrimetres*: "the soul of the voluptuous man would be placed in one of those beasts whose mutilation renders their service more useful; that of an arrogant man in a beetle or in another, even more despicable, insect; and that of the effeminate and presumptuous *petrimetre* (pejorative for little master) in a frog."[34]

Critiques of this type intensified as the Bourbons clashed with rooted elites who, unwilling to give up their habits and privileges, resisted change. For example, in 1787, playwright Tomás de Iriarte (1750–1790) published *El señorito mimado o La mala educación*, a moral comedy condemning old habits and advocating new ones, those of the "new man." In the story, Don Cristóbal, the main character's uncle and godfather, has come back from serving in a government position in America to discover that his late brother's household was a disaster. Superfluous spending had ruined the family's finances and left his nephew with a poor education. Instead of meeting a sensible young man,

---

[34] Benito Jerónimo Feijoó, "Apéndice a la Carta de arriba, en que se coteja el sistema de los Filósofos Materialistas con el de los Pitagóricos," *Cartas eruditas y curiosas*, vol. v, Carta II, www.filosofia.org/bjf/bjfc502.htm.

he found a *"caballero,"* who was turning twenty years old without even knowing how to make the sign of the holy cross, full of bad habits, and full "of a thousand concerns; / who is fearful, effeminate, / superficial, defiant, / enemy of labor; / incapable of committing/to follow by any means / a decent career."[35] His nephew was fearful, sassy, superficial, defiant, and effeminate. This was all his mother's fault, Don Cristóbal concluded.

Likewise, in emulation of Montesquieu's *Persian Letters,* José Cadalso (1741–1782) criticized Spanish society in his *Cartas Marruecas* by presenting its reprehensible habits as typical of Moroccan people, inferior in the eyes of many contemporary Spaniards. A highly educated man, who had traveled to France, joined the military by choice, and ended up stationed in Salamanca at the peak of the University's contentious reform, Cadalso wholeheartedly embraced the new ideas of the Enlightenment.

This epistolary novel consisted in the correspondence between two characters, the Moor Gazel Ben-Aly, who was a member of the Moroccan ambassador's delegation traveling to Spain, and his friend and mentor Ben-Beley. The novel also reproduced his conversations with his Spanish guide. Some of the letters came out posthumously in *El Correo de Madrid* in 1789 and the full version was printed in 1793. In the third letter, Ben-Aly claimed that the Arab conquest of Spain had been in part possible because of the *afeminación y flojedad* (feminization and laziness) in which the warrior nations of the north had fallen after invading Spain and surrendering to its benign climate. Cadalso condemned the excess in luxury and emphasized the need for a tough education for boys because, if the desire for luxury and indulgence prevailed, he anxiously added, nations would fall into a general state of depression, which would entrust the country to *los políticos afeminados* (effeminate politicians) and thus lead to its horrific destruction. Never shying away from extreme statements, Cadalso concluded via Ben-Beley:

> Those born in these eras tired themselves out in vain if they pretend to counter the force of such furious torrent. A people accustomed to delicate tables, soft beds, fine cloths, effeminate manners, affectionate conversations, frivolous entertainments, and to studies dedicated to refined pleasures and the remains of opulence, is not capable of listening to the voice of those who want to alert them of their upcoming ruin.[36]

---

[35] Tomás de Iriarte, "El señorito mimado o la mala educación," *Colección de obras en verso y prosa de D. Tomás de Iriarte* (Madrid: Imprenta Benito Cano, 1787), vol. IV.

[36] *Cartas marruecas del coronel D. Joseph Cadahalso* (Barcelona: Imprenta de Piferrer, 1796), 209.

As scholars have noted, this social and moral critique became particularly strong in Spanish America, where, in the eyes of eighteenth-century European writers, creole males embodied many of the condemned vices, a vision their Spanish American counterparts tried hard to refute.[37] Some, as Bianca Premo has argued for the Viceroyalty of Peru, produced a counternarrative that presented Indian men, instead of creoles, as effeminate and degenerate.[38]

The new press that emerged in Lima in the early 1790s carried these critiques forward. For example, the *Mercurio Peruano*, a newspaper published there with the support of the viceroy and the elite, targeted men's homosexuality directly. In 1791 the paper published a satirical text entitled *Carta sobre los Maricones* (*Letter on the Queer*), followed by a rebuttal. Both texts have been cited extensively by modern historians. The articles seem to have pursued two purposes: present an exaggerated satire of Lima's decadent tradition to justify urgent reform and save creoles from the European condemnation of degeneracy. After acknowledging that there were plenty of *maricones* in Lima, the *Carta*'s author, Filateles, proposed to offer a more "accurate" description than the previous one of what was actually happening. Having just arrived, he could not contain himself and expressed his shock to his host, who promised to take him out on an excursion to see things for himself. Per his account, they walked the streets of Lima at night to end in a crumbled house, where they found drag Blacks and "mulattoes" dressed like the highest Lima elite and talking as if they were royal authorities.

Three months later, the *Mercurio* published an anonymous rebuttal, actually written by the priest Tomás Méndez y Lachica. After condemning Filateles for attending those gatherings, the text discussed the roots of *afeminación*, "a monstrous disorder" of universal scope. The author claimed to have taken it upon himself to find the origins of this "disposition" in either an "anomaly" of nature, the climate's flaws, or the vices produced by inadequate education. The text continued to address several conundrums: How could nature have been so generous granting manly skills to Amazons but so mean with some men? One answer was the arrival of Blacks from Guinea "full of effeminate vices, true *maricones*. One must confess that these are so rare and extraordinary as monsters, dwarfs, and hermaphrodites, etc."

---

[37] On a gendered response, see Alegre Henderson, "Degenerate Heirs." On Creole efforts in correcting European views see Jorge Cañizares Esguerra, *How to Write the History of the World: Histories, Epistemologies, and Identities in Eighteenth-Century Atlantic World* (Stanford: Stanford University Press, 2002).

[38] Premo, *Children of the Father King*, Chapter 5.

## Patriarchy, Misogyny, and Politics

The roles of nature and climate did not strike the priest as decisive. Education and occupation were for him the keys. A woman, raised in open mountains and among peasants, could turn virile and rough while a vigorous young man, tied to his mother's loving lap, would turn effeminate, he argued. Hence, women preoccupied with a rough kind of work could develop a mannish complexion, while men occupied only with sensitive issues would inevitably become effeminate. The next piece to solve in the priest's puzzle was climate. Continuing with his rhetorical questions, the author asked if both effeminate and noneffeminate men could come out of the same climate. In answering this question, he pointed out to the readers the faults of the mother, the excess of delicacy, *regalo* (loving care), comfort, luxury, and attachment to her.[39] Hence, by ridiculing the queer and presenting their sexual preferences as associated with those of *castas* while blaming women for their conduct, reformers rescued creoles from the European condemnation of being predetermined to effeminacy, and urged education and social reform. The challenge to fully refute European critiques was, however, not easy. In 1797 Terralla y Landa's satire of Lima included lazy and broken nobles, people of different races constantly intermingling, pampered effeminate men, and *maricones*, a "plague of Lima's climate."[40]

This repressive and racist narrative persisted and shaped reformers, writers, and travelers of the nineteenth century. The political implications of the new morality spread in all these writings present us with new avenues of research yet to be explored, for it is time to turn their questions around to fit our current concerns and ask: After independence, when war dominated and the military prevailed, how did the overwhelming power of caudillos, the military, and the masculine ideals they embodied, affect other male identities in the public political arena? What was left for the soft-mannered men and advocators of peace and compromise? Where could those who did not want to wear a military uniform or act like a civilian in arms fit?

A scene from Flora Tristán's account of her stay in Peru in the years 1833–1834, where she counterpoints and judges two types of masculinity, serves as a good coda for this section. Of Peruvian parents but raised in

---

[39] "Carta sobre los Maricones," *Mercurio Peruano*, vol. III, no. 94 (27 November 1791), 230–2; "Carta Remitida a la Sociedad hacienda algunas reflexiones sobre la que se contiene en el Mercurio num. 94 en que se pinta á los Maricones," *Mercurio Peruano*, vol. IV, no. 118, (19 February 1792), 118–22.

[40] *Lima por dentro*, 73.

France, this self-described "daughter of the nineteenth century" was a proto-feminist but a social conformist when it came to masculinity.[41] Her unusual background, that of a foreigner, the highly educated but illegitimate daughter of an elite man, put her in a particular position to observe Peru critically. She liked to pause her narrative to describe in detail traditions and peoples, men in particular. On one occasion she recounted the day in Arequipa she had laughed the hardest when Swiss M. Violler had come to her concerned after meeting M. de Sartiges, a French viscount whose voice, skin, hair, and delicate complexion had made him wonder if he was a man or a woman. Only his delightful conversations had assured him that he was a man, a dangerous one for women, he stressed. Meeting the viscount also left Tristán puzzled, for he seemed to live only for "frivolous pleasures." Suspiciously, she stressed, he did not use a servant, but a former military officer, "strong, skilled, and smart." During de Sartiges' stay, Tristán was glad to see her cousin-in-law and friend Clement de Althaus, whom she presented as the better man. Tristán described Althaus as a German military engineer and officer, trained in the Napoleonic armies, who had switched sides to the allies and then joined José de San Martín's liberating armies of the south in the quest for new adventures. Flora reproduced their lively exchange on the unsettling encounter. Althaus argued that the viscount embodied France's decadence. Back in his day, he stressed, boys at that age had already earned prizes and fought a thousand battles. "Those were strong and robust men who could withstand the cold and heat, hunger and thirst, all kinds of fatigues," he exclaimed. What use could these men be to a country?, he asked Flora. She reproached him for only caring about physical strength and a military education, to which he responded: "Physical strength carries along moral strength. You will clearly not find a Caesar, Peter the Great, or a Napoleon in the fragile appearance of a *mujercilla* (little woman)." Flora acknowledged Althaus' harsh manners and severity, but considered them to be expected of a military man who had served a long time, underscoring: "one wishes that for the sake of civilization's progress, Peru would have men of Althaus' temper heading all its public affairs." He was "kind, magnanimous, a good father, hardworking, patient, intelligent, honest, funny, strong, and relentless. He was not loved, but feared."[42]

---

[41] Flora Tristán, *Peregrinaciones de una paria*, 2 vols. (Lima: Fondo Editorial UNMSM, Flora Tristán, Centro de la Mujer Peruana, 2006), vol. 1, 250.

[42] Tristán, *Peregrinaciones*, vol. 1, 292–9.

## The Useful Mother and Deceitful Woman

Women's fates were reshaped in this era of reform and revolution, too. In the hope of radically changing society, reformers considered it essential to change women's behaviors, so as to guarantee the proper upbringing of the new man and the stability of households. While no leading actors in the violent political struggles of these years, women became one of the main targets for Bourbon authorities and early republicans; their fates were discussed with an intensity akin to a true cultural war.

Scholars have produced important work on the history of women in this transitional period. Claudia Rosas and Margarita Zegarra have analyzed the roles reformers tried to assign to women during the Bourbon era in Peru. Based on rich primary source evidence, they have compellingly shown the constant preoccupation of writers with the *bello sexo*, the *petrimetras* (little female masters), and their roles as wet nurses, "enlightened mothers," and loyal wives.[43] These scholars have especially tried to understand how a new bourgeois patriarchal order was established. More recently, historians have intersected women's history and race to recover stories of the nonelite, deeper inequalities, and violence.[44] Scholars have paid attention to women embracing enlightened ideas, writing, and organizing salons.[45] They have also studied how they resisted Bourbon efforts to reform their behavior and how they organized, fought, and petitioned on behalf of their families during the wars. For the early republic, Sarah Chambers and Rebecca Earle have identified and examined the ways in which women took advantage of the unrest to carve out spaces for themselves and thus participate in the new public and political arenas.[46]

---

[43] Claudia Rosas, "Madre solo hay una. Ilustración, maternidad y medicina en el Perú del siglo XVIII," *Anuario de Estudios Americanos* 61:1 (2004), 103–38; Margarita Zegarra, "La construcción de la madre y de la familia sentimental. Una visión del tema a través del Mercurio Peruano," *Histórica* 25:1 (2001), 161–207.

[44] See Maribel Arrelucea, *Sobreviviendo a la esclavitud: Negociación y honor en las prácticas cotidianas de los africanus y afrodescendientes. Lima, 1750–1820* (Lima: Instituto de Estudios Peruanos, 2018).

[45] See Elizabeth Franklin Lewis, *Women Writers in the Spanish Enlightenment: The Pursuit of Happiness* (Burlington: Ashgate, 2004); Mónica Bolufer, *Eve's Enlightenment: Women's Experience in Spain and Spanish America, 1726–1839* (Baton Rouge: Louisiana State University Press, 2009). For a general gender history of Peru, see Mariaemma Mannarelli, *La domesticación de las mujeres: Patriarcado y género en la historia peruana* (Lima: La Siniestra Ensayos, 2018).

[46] Earle, "Rape and the Anxious Republic"; Sarah C. Chambers, *Families in War and Peace: Chile from Colony to Nation* (Durham, NC: Duke University Press, 2015).

And yet, when analyzing different genders in relation to one another, to power and politics in a broader perspective, women's achievements in these years of reform and revolution look more like pyrrhic victories. The new patriarchy that Bourbon and enlightened efforts forged and republicans embraced brought along a misogynistic discourse that blamed women for men's and society's destinies. This mean-spirited discourse took hold and shaped policies and institutions in powerful and enduring ways. Thus, while it is key to study women's agency, it is also essential to study their exclusion from the new politics or – as Mary Beard put it – the ways in which women were "shut up."[47] In these years of change and revolution, women were tested, judged, and sentenced in regulations and publications, but they were not allowed to take part in any of these decisions.

Here I will outline with a few examples some of the cornerstones on which this new patriarchal system and misogynistic discourse seems to have been built. For the sake of parallels, it is worth starting in 1726 with Father Feijoó's essay on the equality of the sexes that carried the misleading title *Defensa de las Mujeres* (*Defense of Women*). Here Feijoó criticized the easy condemnation of women, their constant blaming for bad outcomes, and the common assumption that they possessed a limited capacity for understanding. In a text that reads as a response to Sor Juana Inés de la Cruz's defense of women's right to knowledge,[48] in which he indeed cited Sor Juana, Feijoó compared women to men in all possible realms to conclude that they were as – or even more – virtuous, politically prudent, strong, hardworking, daring, talented in the arts, capable of secrecy, and understanding as men. If their talents had not yet become evident, he claimed, it had been for a lack of opportunities. Yet in concluding, Feijoó made sure to stress the need to exclude women from public affairs. With the original sin, he explained, God had dictated that women remain politically subjected to men. Having sinned first, women could not exercise a leading role in society. He warned men, however, to never take advantage of this situation, for women were too talented. They should be aware of the parity of the sexes, their equivalence in virtues and talents, and treat them well, with respect and kindness, so that women obeyed them happily and complied with their dictated submission. If loved, women would revere them, but if men abused them, they would find

---

[47] Mary Beard, "The Public Voice of Women," in Mary Beard, *Women & Power: A Manifesto* (New York: W. W. Norton & Company, 2017), 3–91.

[48] Sor Juana Inés de la Cruz, "Respuesta a Sor Filotea de la Cruz," (Mexico, 1692), www.marxists.org/espanol/tematica/mujer/autores/sorjuana/1692/marzo01.htm.

a lover and betray them. "Forget those wrong maxims and you will count on more faithful women," he advised in concluding.[49]

Numerous writings, regulations, poems, and plays of the late eighteenth and early nineteenth century shared this vision. Campomanes, for example, a student, admirer, and sponsor of Feijoó's works, discussed women's roles in his plans for a new society. Recognizing that a monarchy could not afford to have idle women wasting their talents, he envisioned women also as useful subjects, inspiring their children and husbands, and promoting industry in everything that is "compatible with the decorous of her sex and with her strengths." He advocated women taking on menial jobs so that men could take care of the toughest duties: field work, navigation, and militia duty. Commending industrious northern Spain, his region of origin, where women reputedly worked as shopkeepers, bakers, and fishermen, Campomanes criticized the rest of Spain, especially the south, where "Moors" and "Orientals" used to keep women shuttered in idleness. To eliminate the remains of those practices, he proposed to follow northern Europe, where the Asiatic and African "excrements" had not penetrated. His "defense" of women came alongside a racist condemnation of those who did not conform to his ideals of society.[50]

Women became a major target in the Viceroyalty of Peru, where the misogynistic discourse was disdainful. *Limeño* women, those of the elite in particular, would embody most of the reviled vices. They were presented as spoiled, lazy, luxury-dependent, vulgar, ignorant, deceitful, and dangerously beautiful. Newspapers dedicated lengthy articles to criticizing their behavior in the hope of reforming them; satires and plays made them a central and favorite topic. While enlightened European writings presented American men as examples of the degradation a mild climate and poor upbringing could cause, Spanish American writers seemed to have shifted the blame not only to *castas*, but also to American women.

The Enlightenment-inspired *Semanario Crítico* of 1791 used a vicious tone when discussing the reform of women, one of its preferred topics. Following Rousseau but without citing him, the editor engaged in lengthy discussions

---

[49] "Defensa de las mujeres," *Teatro Crítico Universal*, vol. 1, *Discurso XVI*, www.filosofia .org/bjf/bjft116.htm.

[50] Pedro Rodríguez de Campomanes, *Discurso sobre la educación popular de los artesanos y su fomento* (Madrid: Imprenta de Antonio Sancha, 1775), www.cervantesvirtual.com/ obra/discurso-sobre-la-educacion-popular-de-los-artesanos-y-su-fomento–0.

on breastfeeding, in which he condemned elite women for refusing to nurse their children and for surrendering them to "mercenary mothers" from the *castas* without any appropriate surveillance. Such behavior would never pass through the "widest confessionary bars that exist in the world; because God and the State are left poorly served."[51] This critique became more intense with the French Revolution. The government paper *La Gaceta de Lima* of 1794, as shown by Claudia Rosas, explicitly discussed how women did not possess the moral character needed to exercise the rights and duties of a citizen.[52] Much like in France after the Revolution, women's participation in war and politics was seen as a sign of disorder and anarchy, for it was believed that their passions made them prone to corruption. As several scholars have argued for France, the Enlightenment and Revolution not only excluded women, but constructed a myth against them.[53]

Terralla y Landa's satire targeted women from the start. In the prologue, he claimed to focus on *currutacos* (pejorative for vain men) and *madamitas de nuevo cuño* (ladies of the new fashion). While Terralla criticized *limeñas* of all colors, he paid more attention to elite women, who – in his view – tricked men by pretending to love them when in fact they only wanted their money.[54] They liked to wander around, all covered "behind curtains," he wrote referring to their fashion of wearing long scarfs covering their faces.[55] They barely ate, went to bed late, and cared only for love affairs. They were terrible mothers, teaching their daughters only gossip, lazy behavior, and the idea that money determined a man's worth. Their houses were a mess; their spending was extravagant. Terralla did not hesitate to express his indignation at seeing black women stroll freely and *"mulatas"* or *"zambas"* making use of titles and dresses such as the *tapada* that did not correspond with their status. Newly arrived Peninsular Spaniards used to get shocked when confronted

---

[51] "Concluye la materia del artículo Antecedente," *Semanario Crítico*, no. 9 (1791), 85. See also Margarita Zegarra, "Olavarrieta, la familia ilustrada y la lactancia maternal," in Scarlett O'Phelan and Carmen Salazar-Soler, eds., *Passeurs, mediadores culturales y agentes de la primera globalización en el Mundo Ibérico, siglos XVI–XIX* (Lima: PUCP, Instituto Riva Agüero and IFEA, 2005), 345–73. Confessionary bars were bars in a confession booth.

[52] Claudia Rosas Lauro, "Mujeres, hombres y género en el discurso modernizador de la Ilustración a fines del siglo XVIII," in Claudia Rosas Lauro, ed., *Género y mujeres en la historia del Perú: Del hogar al espacio público* (Lima: Pontificia Universidad Católica del Perú, Fondo Editorial, 2019), 203–28: 222.

[53] For a good summary of this matter, see Annette F. Timm and Joshua A. Sanborn, *Gender, Sex, and the Shaping of Modern Europe*, 2nd edition (London: Bloomsbury Academic, 2018), 23–8.

[54] *Lima por dentro*, 12–13: 25.     [55] Ibid., 20.

with the racial diversity of Lima, especially with the overwhelming presence of people of African descent in the city.[56] For example, it was common for wealthy women, and a way to show off their status, to dress up their female slaves and take them along to the theater and other public spaces, which scandalized foreigners.[57]

In Lima, women's habit of wearing long scarfs covering their whole face but one eye became a matter of major concern for authorities and reformers, for the *tapada* (the covered one) embodied the dangerously deceitful woman. Reformers considered this fashion an act of defiance and a tool women used to conceal their mischief and thus escape men's control. Hence, regulations were issued to ban *tapadas*; men of letters wrote against them, turning them into a symbol of intrigues and past decadent behavior. This critique lasted for decades until elite women gave up on this fashion by the mid-nineteenth century.[58]

Women also became a major target during the wars of independence. As in other liberating movements, the discourse on the war was gendered, for women would embody a nation in need of rescue. In Spain, the Constitution of Cádiz was colloquially known as *La Pepa* and took on the image of a popular woman, defiant of authorities, beloved by the masses. In Peru, writers and newspapers also presented the new nation and republic as a woman needing to be rescued. But women also took on active roles and acted as crucial fundraisers and organizers.[59] They sustained their families and engaged in politics by writing letters to viceroys and caudillos.[60] Their participation, however, brought much anxiety. In a world in turmoil like that of the Age of Revolutions it was crucial to set fixed gender roles and erase women's active participation from the public sphere and memory. For example, the case of Policarpa Salvatierra, examined by Rebecca Earle,

---

[56] Pilar Pérez Canto, "La población de Lima en el siglo XVIII," *Boletín Americanista* 32 (1982), 383–407.

[57] Robert Stevenson, "Memorias sobre las campañas de San Martín y Cochrane en el Perú," *Colección Documental para la Independencia del Perú*, vol. XXVII (Lima: Comisión Nacional del Sesquicentenario de la Independencia del Perú, Editorial Jurídica, 1971), 171.

[58] On *tapadas* see Laura R. Bass and Amanda Wunder, "The Veiled Ladies of the Early Modern Spanish World: Seduction and Scandal in Seville, Madrid, and Lima," *Hispanic Review* 77:1 (2009), 970–1044. For fascinating parallels see Scott, *The Politics of the Veil*.

[59] See Evelyn Cherpak, "The Participation of Women in the Independence Movement in Gran Colombia, 1780–1830," in Asunción Lavrin, ed., *Latin American Women: Historical Perspectives* (Westport, CT: Greenwood Press, 1978), 219–34.

[60] Earle, "Rape and the Anxious Republic." On family metaphors see Chambers, "The Paternal Obligation"; Earle, "Rape and the Anxious Republic."

served that purpose. The young seamstress from Bogotá planned a conspiracy against royalist forces in 1817 to end up brutally executed. Her death gave birth to a biased hagiographic literature that kept her memory alive to remind readers of the horrors of a war that brought women to fight. Women's struggles for independence were evoked, but mostly to condemn the violence of those years.

In the 1820s and 1830s, the theater of Lima used to offer *La Pola*, a play on "the beheading of a heroine from Bogotá for her liberal ideas," which became quite popular.[61] Manuela Sáenz's rise and fall is also revealing. After living openly with Bolívar as his lover and loyal adviser, achieving the highest military honors for her exemplary actions as liberator and her actual fighting in the Battle of Ayacucho, Sáenz spent the last years of her life in a convent in Paita, a small ghostly town in northern Peru. She met this fate not so much because of her Bolivarian connections (this faction dominated Peruvian politics for much of the 1830s and other Bolivarian male supporters did not meet this ending), but because she had been a dangerous public woman who had acted openly and without dissimulation in politics.[62] Sáenz kept an active correspondence on political matters with men until the end of her life, but she could never escape her exile of twenty-one years.[63]

Political instability and violence continued in Peru. While men spent decades struggling over who had more merits to rule the new republic, which translated into never-ending conspiracies and coups, the control of women remained a crucial task to be accomplished if the country were to climb the ladder of civilization. Literary critiques of women appeared as a vital part of this project and persisted. *Tapadas*, for example, continued to be targeted in the *costumbrista* genre, a literature interested in describing people's habits and traditions and filled with misbehaved women choosing bad marriages at first, intriguing and being tricked. As it commonly went, after deceit, a proper education or a good husband would rescue these

---

[61] Archivo General de la Nación (AGN), Lima, Perú, "Don Francisco Fresco se declare si debe ó no representarse la tragedia titulada la Pola. Mayo, 1827."

[62] On "dissimulation" see Lynn Hunt, "The Many Bodies of Marie Antoinette," *Eroticism and the Body Politic*, ed. Lynn Hunt (Baltimore and London: The Johns Hopkins University Press, 1991), 112–3. On Sáenz, see Pamela S. Murray, *For Glory and Bolívar: The Remarkable Life of Manuela Sáenz, 1797–1856* (Austin; University of Texas Press, 2008).

[63] Sarah C. Chambers, "Amistades republicanas. La correspondencia de Manuela Sáenz en el exilio (1835–1856)," in Scarlett O Godoy, Fanni Muñoz Cabrejo et al., eds., *Familia y vida cotidiana en América Latina, Siglos XVIII–XX* (Lima: Pontificia Universidad Católica del Perú, 2003), 315–54.

women, which would then restore order in the household and society at large.[64]

In conclusion, the Age of Revolutions brought about a new politics and a new patriarchy that shaped the old Spanish world in powerful enduring ways. The reconceptualization of the new politics as a purely "masculine" sphere, one for brave men of action ready to fight and sacrifice their lives, marginalized other kinds of masculinities, homosexuals, and women in a renewed way, depriving them of a public voice and presence in the new political spheres. While the old patriarchal order was reconfigured to fit the new individual man, women's identities, in contrast, remained collective, tied to their families and household. Additionally, these exclusionary policies brought along a misogynist discourse that justified the public use of physical and verbal violence.

Historians of Latin America have made enormous progress in the field of gender studies in the last decades and there are promising new works in the making. We need to carry on and, as the late María Elena Martínez put it, turn our interest into action by "returning to the archive and continuing to mine its sources for their limitations and possibilities."[65] The field of gender and politics in the Age of Revolutions is a large new mine yet to be explored.

---

[64] There is a large *costumbrista* genre dedicated to reform women for this purpose. See for example Felipe Pardo y Aliaga's play of 1830, *Frutos de la educación* (Lima: Sanmarti y Cía, 1962).

[65] Martínez, "Sex and the Colonial Archive," 443.

## 14

# Impact of the French Caribbean Revolutions in Continental Iberian America, 1791–1833

ALEJANDRO E. GÓMEZ

## Introduction

Probably more than anywhere else in the colonial world, the revolutions of France and the French Caribbean of the late eighteenth century had a tremendous impact in Iberian America. This can be noticed mainly, though not exclusively, in the Spanish Antilles and the Atlantic coasts of South America, which were more exposed to the period's revolutionary winds. That impact can be measured mostly by the study of political ideas. On the one hand, French constitutionalism and radical republicanism had an impact on white liberal politicians, and aroused political consciousness in certain individuals of African descent, both free and enslaved.[1] On the other hand, the same actors interpreted, either negatively or positively, certain events or processes such as the Reign of Terror, the Thermidorian Reaction, the revolution of Saint-Domingue, and the "confiscated revolution" of Guadeloupe – to use Alain Yacou's expression.[2] It is also worth mentioning the debate on the active citizenship of the so-called *gens de couleur* (i.e., mainly mixed-bloods and free Blacks) that led to the adoption by the Legislative Assembly of a law favorable to them in April 1792, and the

---

I would like to warmly thank Wim Klooster and Edward Blumenthal for their corrections and helpful comments. This work makes part of a larger research project, partly supported by: the Gilder Lehrman Center for the Study of Slavery, the Instituto de Historia at the Pontificia Universidad Católica de Chile, the Centro Franco-Argentino at the University of Buenos Aires, and the EU-funded project "ConnecCaribbean" (Marie Skłodowska-Curie grant agreement No. 823846).

[1] For an ideological approach of the impact of the French Revolution in Spanish America, see Clément Thibaud, Chapter 6 in Volume II of this book.

[2] Alain Yacou, "Una revolución confiscada: La isla de Guadalupe de 1789 a 1803," in J. A. Piqueras, ed., *Las Antillas en la era de las Luces y la Revolución* (Madrid: Siglo XXI, 2005), 43–66.

immediate abolition of slavery by the National Convention in February 1794, following a similar measure adopted earlier in Saint-Domingue.

This chapter seeks to identify and explain the different manifestations that denote the impact of the French Caribbean revolutions on continental Ibero-America. Considering the importance that social actors attached to the egalitarian proposals made during those revolutionary processes vis-à-vis the slaves and the *gens de couleur*, particular attention will be given to the perception they had (or lacked) of certain metropolitan political trends (mostly radical Jacobinism and popular sans-culottism), and the events that shattered France and its Antilles. As it has been argued by many historians and intellectuals (from Aimé Césaire onwards), the conflicts and political events that took place in these insular territories were so dialectically intertwined with the metropolitan revolution, that they cannot be considered as mere ramifications. Something similar could be argued for the political actors in Ibero-America, given how many of them were emotionally and ideologically affected by the ideas and events associated to the French Caribbean revolutions. Attention will also be given to the impact of gradual abolitionism as developed by British antislavery advocates, as this solution was also very much shaped by those revolutionary processes. Accordingly, the present work will start by following an analytical approach "from below," focusing on the emergence of manifestations of a new political consciousness among the slaves, free Blacks, and *pardos* (mixed-blood individuals, either free or slaves), inspired by the French Caribbean. Then I will move to a more elite perspective, which will be entwined with the former approach when necessary.

## "Common Winds"[3] in Continental Ibero-America

### Revolutionary Shocks in the Spanish Circum-Caribbean

After the outbreak of the first revolutionary conflicts in the French Antilles at the beginning of the 1790s, different written and oral forms of resistance inspired by the French Caribbean began to be noticed in neighboring Spanish colonies in the region, especially Cuba. Similar manifestations can be found shortly afterwards on the Spanish Main; thus, in early 1795, there was turmoil among the "people of color" in the city of Caracas due to the circulation of a "seditious paper" attributed to a certain "Archbishop of Paris." In May of that same year, a rebellion of more than 200 slaves and also several *zambos* (i.e., in

---

[3] Julius Scott, *The Common Wind: Afro-American Currents in the Age of the Haitian Revolution* (London: Verso, 2018).

Spanish America, the offspring of Blacks and Indians) and free Blacks broke out in the mountainous area of Coro in the Northwest of Venezuela. They rebelled seeking to eliminate the sales tax on tobacco (*alcabala*) that had been recently raised in the context of the Bourbon reforms, and to enforce some royal decrees in their favor that had presumably arrived from Spain. These decrees concerned the nonimplementation of new slave legislation (the so-called *Código Carolino*, which was suspended after being highly criticized by the creole elites) and the approval of a new legal mechanism of *Gracias al Sacar*, which allowed certain wealthy and well-reputed *pardos* and other nonwhites to be exempted from their lower socioracial status. The authorities also determined that the rebels in Coro had been encouraged by the example of what their counterparts had achieved in the French colonies, and that, once in power, they intended to apply an ambiguous "law of the French."[4]

The second half of the decade was a period in which the activities of French Republican privateers (especially from the island of Guadeloupe) increased considerably.[5] Their crews, largely composed of "new citizens" (former slaves and *gens de couleur*), greatly contributed spreading the *bonne parole* of the revolution throughout the Caribbean. Manifestations of resistance in the region became more numerous due to this military and propagandistic campaign, which can also be associated with a Jacobin-inspired conspiracy discovered at the coastal city of La Guaira in mid-1797. It was led by some Spanish prisoners (who had organized a similar plot in Madrid), two creoles, and two *pardos*. Among the latter, it is worth highlighting the role played by the militiaman Narciso Del Valle, who wrote some political documents and promoted the plot among the local "colored"[6] population. The inquiries showed that Del Valle had previously praised the French revolutionary process and had probably also come into contact with French "colored" officers. Furthermore, it seems that he had even organized clandestine political gatherings in the barbershop he owned at La Guaira since at least 1793. In these meetings (attended by other *pardos*, free Blacks, and even a Spanish officer) were discussed historical and juridical texts related to natural rights, Irish autonomy, the French Revolution, and the independence of the United States. By the time the project was discovered by the authorities, the Spaniards and the creoles had managed to escape, but Del Valle and the

---

[4] See Cristina Soriano, Chapter 28 in Volume II of this book.

[5] Anne Pérotin-Dumon, *La ville aux îles, la ville dans l'île: Basse-Terre et Pointe-à-Pitre, Guadeloupe, 1650–1820* (Paris: Karthala, 2000), 229.

[6] I use the notions "color" or "colored" to describe the nonwhite populations of African descent, both Black and mixed-blood.

Spanish officer were captured and executed. In the end, the authorities estimated that the conspiracy had the support of between 200 and 500 people, among both white and "colored" individuals.[7]

In the years that followed there were other events in the Spanish mainland that can be linked to the French Antilles, albeit none as fearsome from the perspective of the authorities. A failed attempt of insurrection in the city of Maracaibo in May 1799, planned by the crew of a French privateer and a local *pardo* militiaman, was dismissed by the authorities as an "act of piracy." Despite this, it is worth noting that among the referred crew were some members of André Rigaud's mulatto faction from Saint-Domingue, who had been defeated earlier that year by the forces of Toussaint Louverture. The rise of this Black chieftain as governor of that French colony and the invasion he attempted in Santo Domingo in 1801, were enthusiastically celebrated by many slaves in the Spanish American mainland. Some even composed a tune in his honor.[8]

Almost at the same time, in 1799, there was turmoil among some French slaves in Cartagena de Indias, which, although apparently innocuous from an ideological point of view, still alarmed the authorities because they associated it with Maracaibo's failed insurrection.[9] Later on, after the establishment of the Republic of Gran Colombia in 1821, we find in the same coastal region various references to Haiti attributed to *pardo* individuals. These occurred, firstly, in the declaration of Valentín Arcia, the *pardo* justice of the town of Majagual in May 1822, who criticized in a sedition trial against him the socioracial inequalities still prevailing under the republican regime, and claimed that the War of Independence would be followed by one against the whites, as had happened in Saint-Domingue. Then in April 1823, Haiti was mentioned in some placards in the city of Mompox, during the riots that followed the dismissal of the *pardo* general Remigio Márquez; and finally, in

---

[7] Ramón Aizpurua Aguirre, "Revolution and Politics in Venezuela and Curacao, 1795–1800," in Wim Klooster and Gert Oostindie, eds., *Curaçao in the Age of Revolutions, 1795–1800* (Leiden: KITLV Press, 2011), 97–122; Alejandro E. Gómez, "Entre résistance piraterie et républicanisme: Mouvements insurrectionnels d'inspiration révolutionnaire franco-antillaise sur la Côte de Caracas, 1794–1800," *Travaux et recherches de l'UMLV* 11 (2006), 91–120; Cristina Soriano, *Tides of Revolution: Information and Politics in Late-Colonial Venezuela* (Albuquerque: University of New Mexico Press, 2018), 162–3.

[8] Eleazar Córdova-Bello, *La Independencia de Haití y su influencia en Hispanoamérica* (Caracas: Instituto Panamericano de Geografía e Historia, 1967), 129; Gómez, "Entre résistance, piraterie et républicanisme."

[9] João José Reis and Flavio dos Santos Gomez, "Repercussions of the Haitian Revolution in Brazil," in David Patrick Geggus, ed., *The World of the Haitian Revolution* (Bloomington: Indiana University Press, 2001), 158–60.

ALEJANDRO E. GÓMEZ

March 1828 at Cartagena de Indias, Haiti was evoked by some "colored" soldiers for threatening the creole authorities over the nonpayment of salaries.[10]

A similar case can be found in Caracas in 1830, when a free Black (presumably upset at the raising of the age at which slaves would become free from eighteen to twenty-one) apparently evoked the example of Saint-Domingue seeking to "seduce the soldiery," aiming to kill all the whites.[11] Paradoxically, the reform of that legislation was advocated by the then-president José Antonio Páez himself, who used Haiti, not the revolution of Saint-Domingue, as a good example to claim that "the man of color is as capable as the Caucasian race to understand the benefits of democracy."[12]

### Isolated Cases in Southern Spanish America

Elsewhere in continental Spanish America, references to the revolutions in the French Caribbean made by nonwhite people were considerably fewer in number. The first case can be found in the port city of Buenos Aires, where the authorities unveiled an alleged rebellion that was to erupt on Good Friday 1795. The authorities believed that the movement was inspired by the freedom of the French and that several slaves implicated were calling for an alliance with the Indians and mulattoes. A Black man was even said to have praised the Tupac Amaru rebellion of 1781, which had had a significant emotional and ideological impact in the Andean region.[13] In the end, despite more than twenty arrests, only a sixty-two-year-old free Black or mestizo man was sentenced to ten years of imprisonment on the Malvinas Islands.[14]

Much more clearly inspired by the French Caribbean was a slave insurrection discovered in the Río de la Plata in 1812. By then, the autonomous governments that had emerged in Santiago de Chile and Buenos Aires had

[10] Marixa Lasso, "Haiti as an Image of Popular Republicanism in Caribbean Colombia," in David P. Geggus, ed., *The Impact of the Haitian Revolution in the Atlantic World* (Columbia: University of South Carolina Press, 2001), 176–90.

[11] Robert Kerr Porter, *Diario de un diplomático británico en Venezuela, 1825–1842* (Caracas: Fundación Polar, 1997), 441.

[12] Manumission law of 9 September 1830, in Germán Carrera Damas, ed., *Materiales para el estudio de la cuestion agraria en Venezuela*, 2 vols. (Caracas: UCV, 1964), vol. II, 21.

[13] See for example, Scarlett O'Phelan, "La construcción del miedo a la plebe en el siglo XVIII a través de las rebeliones sociales," in Claudia Rosas, ed., *El miedo en el Perú: Siglos XVI al XX* (Lima: Fondo Editorial PUCP, 2005), 123–38.

[14] In an unpublished work, Florencia Guzmán insists with newly discovered evidence on the version that the person arrested was not a free Black, but a mestizo. Lyman L. Johnson, *Workshop of Revolution: Plebeian Buenos Aires and the Atlantic World, 1776–1810* (Durham, NC: Duke University Press, 2011), 149 ff.

banned the slave trade and adopted the principle of free soil for any slave arriving in their territories. The Chilean assembly went even further in antislavery legislation by adopting a free-womb law, a measure that would soon also be adopted by the governments of Buenos Aires and Antioquia. It was in this context that the authorities in the Province of Mendoza were informed about the outbreak of a slave insurrection in May 1812. The inquiries discovered a proclamation that praised the autonomous assembly of Buenos Aires and the "kind of freedom" that had been established. This document was allegedly written by a free Black named Joaquin Freites, a former slave who had been symbolically freed by his former master, who incidentally was a revolutionary priest from Concepción, one of the most radical enclaves of revolutionary Chile. Freites had apparently assured other Blacks that they were free or would be freed and that in Chile and Buenos Aires slavery had been banned. Other slaves who were implicated justified the insurrection by erroneously believing that the Buenos Aires government had abolished slavery, but the local judges refused to comply with that measure. Another leader of the movement was a slave named Bernardo Aragón, who was allegedly in charge of military logistics and of recruiting fellow slaves. He had commented on one occasion "that it was necessary to do in this city what the blacks did at the Santo Domingo islands [sic], kill all the whites to free themselves." After a long trial, the authorities freed the slaves instead of applying the usual cruel punishments and carried out exemplary executions, a decision clearly in harmony with the revolutionary spirit of the time. Moreover, they were then ordered to join the freedmen regiments formed in Buenos Aires, which later on fought on different fronts in South America as part of the Andean army raised by José de San Martín.[15]

### French Caribbean Echoes in Rio de Janeiro and Bahia

Echoes and evocations of the events in the French Caribbean were more numerous in Brazil than in southern Spanish America. The first case was probably a conspiracy that aimed at the establishment of a republic, discovered in Salvador da Bahia in August 1798. Clearly inspired by French radical republicanism, the so-called Revolt of the Tailors was led by some young local white elite men, but several individuals of "color" also participated. In posters placed in various parts of the city on the morning of

---

[15] Beatriz Bragoni and Orlando Gabriel Morales, "Libertad civil y patriotismo en el Río de la Plata revolucionario. La experiencia de los esclavos negros en la provincia de Cuyo, 1812–1820," *Historia y Sociedad* 30 (January 2016), 131–67.

12 August, the conspirators criticized the "monarchical yoke" and praised the "freedom, equality and fraternity" of the French. The placards also called for a "memorable revolution," for whose execution they invited the support of *pardos* and free Black militiamen, who by participating would become soldier-citizens as in France. Once the authorities had thwarted the conspiracy, they confirmed the implication of numerous *pardos*, four of whom were executed three months later. Among them was the militia corporal João de Deus Nascimento, who was alleged to have said that "it was in everyone's interest to become French, so that they could all live in equality and abundance." With this objective in mind, the revolution intended to ban the statutory distinctions between whites, Blacks and *pardos*, as well as the socioracial restrictions to filling important public offices.[16]

Then in 1805, after the arrival of the news of Haitian independence, some *cabras* (i.e. in Brazil, the offspring of mulattoes and Indians) and free Blacks in Rio de Janeiro began to wear amulets with the image of Dessalines. Nearly a decade later, in 1814, after the outbreak of a slave rebellion in Salvador da Bahia, it was reported that some shouted on the streets of the city "Freedom! Long live to the blacks and their king!" and also "Death to the whites and mulattos."

### Northeastern Pardos in the Mirror of the "Mulatto Affaire"[17]

It was especially in Pernambuco, during the revolutions of 1817 and 1824, that references to the French Caribbean revolutions abounded. These evocations were also more complex and modern from an ideological point of view than the previous ones. The first of those uprisings, the so-called Pernambucan Revolution, which aimed at the establishment of a republic in the region, generated great enthusiasm in the population of "color," particularly among the *pardos*. After the first revolution was crushed in May 1817, the Portuguese authorities discovered that *pardos* had made the banner of the revolution, the flags of the new military regiments, and even

---

[16] This paragraph and the following ones are indebted to Luiz Geraldo Silva, "El impacto de la revolución de Saint-Domingue y los afrodescendientes libres de Brasil: Esclavitud, libertad, configuración social y perspectiva atlántica (1780–1825)," *Historia [Santiago]* 49:1 (June 2016), 209–33; Washington Santos Nascimento, "'São Domingos, o grande São Domingos': Repercussões e representações da Revolução Haitiana no Brasil escravista (1791–1840)," *Dimensões*, no. 21 (December 2008); Reis and Santos Gomez, "Repercussions of the Haitian Revolution in Brazil."

[17] The expression was coined by Yves Bénot to describe the debates on the political status of the mixed-blood individuals of African descent during the French Revolution. Yves Bénot, *La Révolution Française et la fin des colonies: Essai, textes à l'appui* (Paris: La Découverte, 1988).

the clothes of the future ambassadors of the Republic of Pernambuco. Among the detained was the *pardo* militia captain José do Ó Barbosa, who was accused of antimonarchism. Ó Barbosa and his son-in-law, Joaquim dos Santos, were singled out by a spy for having expressed their "desire to see Brazil as Santo Domingo." In January 1818, the spy sent a letter to the government of Rio de Janeiro in which he asserted that both men enjoyed "a great influence on the people," and that they were interested in the "way of life of the rebels of Santo Domingo."[18]

In 1824, another revolution broke out in Pernambuco, this time directed against the monarchical and centralist claims of Emperor Pedro I, and giving birth to the Confederação do Equador. Once again, many Pernambucan *pardos* expressed their enthusiasm and support for this new anti-absolutist and republican political movement. Among them was the *pardo* militiaman Emiliano Felipe Benício Mundurucú, who commanded a new battalion formed during the revolution called "Bravos da Patria." Mundurucú himself praised the people of Haiti and requested the composition of a quatrain in which the figure of the Black monarch, Henri Christophe, was exalted. The quatrain was then printed and distributed among the soldiers. After the defeat of the confederation, Mundurucú was arrested, but was able to escape first to the United States, then to Haiti, and finally to Caracas, where he joined the Venezuelan army of José Antonio Páez.

Around the same time, in Sergipe (a border province to the south of Pernambuco) the mulatto lawyer and secretary of the local government, Antonio Pereira Rebouças, was blamed for having put posters on the doors of many houses that read: "Death to the Portuguese and the whites." He was also known to own at least two books on the history of Saint-Domingue, and he had attended an anti-Portuguese meeting in which speeches were made praising the "King of Haiti" and the "Great Santo Domingo." In his defense, Pereira Rebouças argued that he had been slandered by the whites, who could not stand that a mulatto occupied such an important public office. Then, in August 1832, the same Rebouças again referred to the Haitian and Franco-Antillean revolutionary examples. By then, he was a member of the Brazilian parliament, and spoke in a debate in which he criticized a bill about the scope of active citizenship, which from his perspective, would deny that status to freedmen and, consequently, prevent them from becoming officers in the recently created

---

[18] Luiz Geraldo Silva, "El impacto de la revolución de Saint-Domingue y los afrodescendientes libres de Brasil: Esclavitud, libertad, configuración social y perspectiva atlántica (1780–1825)," *Historia* [Santiago] 49:1 (2016), 209–33: 229.

National Guard. In this debate he praised Toussaint Louverture, claiming that he was more of a French citizen than Napoleon himself. He also referred to the Code Noir of 1685, claiming that if the emancipated slaves had been granted the status of French subjects as indicated in that body of laws, the "horror scenes" that shattered the French colonies would have been avoided.[19]

## Radical and Moderate Antislavery Positions in Continental Spanish America

### *"New Citizens" as in Guadeloupe*

In the second half of the eighteenth century a series of conspiracies (or alleged conspiracies) took place in Spanish South America, mostly directed against the so-called Bourbon reforms. Three of these movements attacked slavery, namely the insurrection led by a mestizo in the Peruvian city of Huarochirí in 1750, the conspiracy planned by a French mathematics teacher in the Captaincy General of Chile in 1780, and finally the well-known Andean revolt led by the mestizo José Gabriel Condorcanqui, who called himself Tupac Amaru, in 1781. Of these cases, only the first one proposed banning slavery, while the other two only offered freedom to some slaves. None of them made these proposals for philanthropic reasons or enlightened ideals, but rather to attain certain practical strategic objectives: these were, respectively, to avoid any opposition by the slaves, to strengthen the rebel forces, and to weaken the economy of the enemy.[20]

The only conspiracy of the period that proposed to abolish slavery immediately was the abovementioned one discovered in the Venezuelan city of La Guaira in 1797. This plot was strongly inspired by the republican model of socioracial harmony established in France and on the island of Guadaloupe. Its main ideologue was the Majorcan Juan Bautista Picornell, who in the statutes of the movement (a document entitled *Ordenanzas*) included articles that established socioracial equality among Blacks, Indians, *pardos* and whites, and also the abolition of slavery "as contrary to humanity." In this same document, harsh penalties were established for those "new citizens" who did not join the republican army and refused to remain in their

---

[19] For further historical and historiographical details about the impact of the Haitian Revolution in Brazil, see Kraay, Chapter 20 in this volume.

[20] Scarlett O'Phelan Godoy, *Un siglo de rebeliones anticoloniales Perú y Bolivia, 1700–1783* (Lima: Institut français d'études andines, 2015); Miguel Luis Amunátegui and Gregorio Victor Amunátegui, *Una conspiración en 1780* (Santiago de Chile: Imprenta del Progreso, 1853).

former agricultural jobs. These penalties may have echoed a similar coercive mechanism introduced shortly before in Guadeloupe.[21]

### Thermidorian Gradualism in Spanish South America

While this transpired on the coast of Venezuela, elsewhere in the Americas enthusiasm for radical republicanism had begun to dissipate. This was mainly due to the state of anarchy and violence unleashed during the Reign of Terror in France and the conflicts that ravaged Saint-Domingue, which were seen as logical outcomes of Jacobin ideas and variations of sans-culottism.[22] Some had even been personally affected, like the Venezuelan Francisco de Miranda, who, like his friend Thomas Paine, was imprisoned during the Terror and witnessed the execution of many of his comrades of the Gironde party. Hence the sympathy both men expressed for Thermidor's "happy revolution" that ended the Reign of Terror in July 1794, and the support they gave to the formation of the Directory the following year.[23]

Miranda distanced himself from Jacobin ideals, which he described as a "plague," and proposed a doctrine of "rational freedoms" to avoid a state of anarchy such as had been unleashed in France and Saint-Domingue. This idea was shared by other revolutionaries, such as Manuel Gual (one of the creoles implicated in the conspiracy of 1797) and Francisco Isnardi (printer and secretary of first Venezuelan congress of 1811), who seemed to agree with his proposal for a more cautious revolution. Isnardi was also the editor of the revolutionary journal *El Mercurio Venezolano*, in which he criticized those who accused Miranda and his followers of being radical revolutionaries. Those critics, he argued, had a distorted view of the causes that generated "Jacobinism . . ., Robespierre's guillotine, Bonaparte's military despotism, [and] the black horrors of Guarico [Saint-Domingue]."[24]

Thereafter, many Spanish American revolutionaries preferred to adopt more gradual abolitionist mechanisms, namely the abolition of the slave

---

[21] Laurent Dubois, *A Colony of Citizens: Revolution and Slave Emancipation in the French Caribbean, 1787–1804* (Chapel Hill: University of North Carolina Press, 2004), 3.

[22] In Spanish America, some radical revolutionaries used "sansculottes," "descamisados" or "sin-camisas" to describe themselves or to accuse other politicians of being radical revolutionaries.

[23] Karen Racine, *Francisco de Miranda: A Transatlantic Life in the Age of Revolution* (Wilmington, DE: Scholarly Resources, 2003), 336; Bernard Vincent, *The Transatlantic Republican* (Amsterdam: Rodopi, 2005).

[24] "Mercurio Venezolano," Doc. No. 3 [1811], in Francisco Isnardi, *Proceso Político* (Caracas: Academia Nacional de la Historia, 1960), 171.

trade, the approval of free-womb laws, the conscription of slaves for military purposes, and symbolic emancipations during republican festivities. In some of them can be recognized the influence of British gradual abolitionism, as in the case of the same Miranda, who became acquainted with William Wilberforce and to whom he wrote a letter exalting the fact the autonomous assembly of Caracas had abolished the slave trade in 1810. There is also the case of José María Fagoaga, who spent some time in London before joining the slavery commission formed by Mexico's provisional government that had been formed in 1821 after the Plan of Iguala had been issued. The resulting report proposed a free-womb law and compensation for the masters. Although this text did not explicitly mention the French abolition of 1794, it commended the British initiative to abolish the slave trade, describing it as a victory in the name of reason, philosophy, and the rights of man.[25] There were, however, other Mexicans who did mention France in their political reflections, such as the liberal ideologue José María Luis Mora. In the 1820s, he published a series of articles and texts in which, following Benjamin Constant, he warned against the "horrible outrages" of the French Revolution, but without making – as far as we know – any reference to the abolition of slavery or the French Antilles.[26]

Notwithstanding the loss of faith in radical republicanism, in places where the impact of the French Caribbean revolutions was less important there was room for the adoption of immediate abolition of slavery, as did the independent governments of Chile in 1823, Guatemala in 1824, and Mexico in 1829. The case of Chile is particularly important for two reasons: that country was the first to pass a free-womb law, which – as Magdalena Candioti and Daniel Gutiérrez have shown – influenced the adoption of similar measures in Antioquia and Buenos Aires; and it was also the first to abolish slavery without granting compensation to the masters.[27]

---

[25] Juan Francisco Azcárate et al., *Dictamen de la comisión de esclavos* (Mexico City: Imprenta Imperial de D. Alejandro Valdés, 1821).

[26] Charles A. Hale, "The Revival of Political History and the French Revolution in Mexico," in Joseph Klaits and Michael H. Haltzel, eds., *The Global Ramifications of the French Revolution* (Washington, DC: Woodrow Wilson Center Press, 1994), 158–76.

[27] Magdalena Candioti, "Regulando el fin de la esclavitud: Diálogos, innovaciones y disputas jurídicas en las nuevas repúblicas sudamericanas 1810–1830," *Jahrbuch für Geschichte Lateinamerikas* 52 (December 2015), 149–72; Daniel Gutiérrez Ardila, "La politique abolitionniste dans l'État d'Antioquia, Colombie (1812–1816)," *Le Mouvement Social*, no. 252 (October 2015), 55–70.

## References in the Revolutionary Press

In the city of Santiago, in 1812 and 1813, the radical revolutionary newspaper *La Aurora de Chile* published various materials on the French Caribbean and the antislavery debate held at the Cortes of Cádiz. In the discussions regarding some antislavery proposals tabled by liberal representatives from both sides of the Atlantic, the "catastrophe" of Saint-Domingue was evoked – as frequently happened in other similar debates in the Atlantic World[28] – aiming to show it as the worst consequence of the immediate abolition of slavery as implemented by the French Convention in 1794. Among the interventions, it is worth mentioning that of the Asturian representative Agustín Argüelles, who during a session in March 1811 made a motion, in collusion with the British government,[29] for the suppression of the slave trade. On this occasion, he demanded that any subject related to the manumission of slaves in the Americas should be treated with the greatest "circumspection," bearing in mind "the painful example of Santo Domingo." Argüelles' intervention was published the following month in the aforementioned Chilean newspaper, but without the reference to Saint-Domingue;[30] this self-censorship was probably intended not to affect the approval of the antislavery measures that were under discussion by that time in the autonomous assembly. A few months later, in February 1812, that same newspaper mentioned Saint-Domingue in a story taken from *The Times* of London about the coronation of King Henri Christophe of Haiti. It included an explanatory note highlighting the importance of the Haitian revolutionary example in showing how Blacks could prevail due to their natural equality and indefatigable desire for freedom.[31]

In 1812, in a radical revolutionary context similar to that of Caracas and Santiago, the *Gaceta de Buenos Aires* printed a speech published in Philadelphia the previous year entitled *El amigo de los hombres a todos los que habitan las islas, y el vasto continente de la América Española*. The author was the Cuban José Álvarez de Toledo, who had been an alternate representative for Santo Domingo at the Cortes of Cádiz, but, accused of conspiring in favor of

---

[28] I have analyzed elsewhere the debates in the British parliament and the Spanish Cortes. Alejandro Gomez, *Le spectre de la révolution noire: L'impact de la révolution haïtienne dans le monde atlantique, 1790–1886* (Rennes: Presses universitaires de Rennes, 2013).

[29] Jesús Sanjurjo, "Comerciar con la sangre de nuestros hermanos: Early Abolitionist Discourses in Spain's Empire," *Bulletin of Latin American Research* 36 (December 2017), 8.

[30] "Discurso del Sr. Argüelles," *La Aurora de Chile*, No. 11 (23 April 1812), 4.

[31] "Coronación del rey de Haití," *La Aurora de Chile*, No. 1 (13 February 1812), 3–4.

the independence of Spanish America, had fled to the United States. The speech was a response to the arguments that appeared in the newspaper *El Español*, published in London by the Spanish liberal and antislavery advocate José María Blanco White, who claimed that the independence of Spanish America was unattainable considering, among other arguments, what had happened in similar circumstances in Saint-Domingue. Álvarez de Toledo refuted this claim by alleging that in the Spanish colonies, including Cuba, Blacks and mulattoes were not as numerous as they had been in the French colony. In addition, he argued that the "frightful disasters" of Saint-Domingue were the product – in line probably with British antislavery thinking (I will return to this in the conclusion) – of the sudden freedom granted to the slaves by the French, and that the "catastrophe" in that unfortunate colony could have been easily avoided by making the "men of all classes and states" happy and following the Roman example of granting slaves "civil liberty." He also acknowledged that "there is indeed opposition between blacks and pardos in the regions where they are numerous" in some French and Spanish colonies; but according to him, this dilemma could be resolved if the latter were assimilated to the whites, which would nullify the influence of the former.[32]

## Free-Womb Laws in Gran Colombia

Further north in 1812, in the former Viceroyalty of New Granada, a new constitution was enacted for the new Estado Libre de Antioquia, followed by a universal declaration of the rights of man. These events motivated a group of 200 slaves who, on behalf of "ten thousand and seven hundred slaves of Medellín and its surroundings," petitioned the city's municipal council. To organize the petition, the slaves had raised funds for the collection of signatures and for paying the author of the text.[33] In the petition, the slaves claimed their freedom and asked for an end to the breakup of slave families when their members were sold. Apparently, a rumor had previously reached

---

[32] El Amigo de los Hombres, "El amigo de los hombres a todos los que habitan las islas y el vasto continente de la América española" [Washington, 12 October 1810], *Gazeta Ministerial del Gobierno de Buenos Ayres*, 19 June 1812, 45–6; Nicolás Kanellos, "José Alvarez de Toledo y Dubois and the Origins of Hispanic Publishing in the Early American Republic," *Early American Literature* 43:1 (2008), 83–100.

[33] Unlike a similar request of 1781, on this occasion there were no mulattoes involved in the movement, which might denote the development of a modern corporate identity among the Antioquian slaves, or simply a refusal to support them by whitened mixed-bloods. Regarding the request of 1781, see John Leddy Phelan, *The People and the King: The Communero Revolution in Colombia, 1781* (Madison: University of Wisconsin Press, 1978), 110–1.

the slaves indicating that they had been freed. This petition raised the concern of the white creole revolutionary leaders, who feared that independence might foster slave rebellions, increase the Africanization of the territory, and even trigger – as asserted by the president-dictator Juan del Corral himself – a destructive revolution similar to that of Haiti. Hence some of the enslaved petitioners were tried and sentenced to hard labor, and the freedmen who had supported them were exiled.[34]

Nevertheless, according to María Eugenia Chaves, the concerns expressed by the slaves were a key factor behind the formulation of a free-womb law in Antioquia, inspired by that of Chile, proposed by deputy José Félix Restrepo, and adopted by the government in 1814. This law that was intended as the first step toward a complete abolition of slavery, also fulfilled the demand of the slaves to stop the separation of enslaved family members. An analogous bill was presented by the same Restrepo to the Congress of Cúcuta, which adopted it for all of Gran Colombia in 1821. The bill had the decisive support of Simón Bolívar, who had previously intervened at the congresses of Angostura in 1818 and Cúcuta in 1821 to request the abolition of slavery. On those occasions, he referred to the Haitian example, along with other historical references, to warn legislators that it was impossible to keep slaves in bondage indefinitely without risk.[35]

Despite his support for the abolition of slavery, Bolívar feared that it might trigger an anarchic revolution, as did many other Spanish American revolutionaries. However, his concerns differed from that of his fellow rebels in that he did not fear the slaves, but the *pardos*, who made up the majority of the population in Venezuela, and were also very numerous in New Granada. Moreover, since the beginning of the wars of independence many *pardos* had taken up arms for the royalist cause, while others had risen to high military ranks in the insurgents' army. Some of them, such as Admiral Padilla and General Piar, were accused, among other things, of inciting "race wars" against the creoles, for which they were tried and executed. The racial war of extermination waged by a royalist army in the Spanish Main in 1814[36] deepened Bolívar's negative view of *pardos*. For him, it would be a

---

[34] Ardila, "Politique abolitionniste."

[35] Maria Eugenia Chaves, "Esclavos, libertades y república: Tesis sobre la polisemia de la libertad en la primera república antioqueña," *Estudios Interdisciplinarios de América Latina y El Caribe* 22:1 (2013), 81–104; Maria Eugenia Chaves, "El oxímoron de la libertad: La esclavitud de los vientres libres y la crítica a la esclavización africana en tres discursos revolucionarios," *Fronteras de la Historia* 19:1 (June 2014), 174–200.

[36] Juan Uslar Pietri, *Historia de la rebelión popular de 1814: Contribución al estudio de la historia de Venezuela* (Caracas: Edime, 1968).

catastrophe if "pardocracy" as he called it, a Haiti-like regime led by people of African descent, were to be established in Gran Colombia. He also expressed this concern after the mixed-blood general Vicente Guerrero, whom Bolívar called the "new Desalines [sic]" became president of Mexico in a *coup d'état* in 1829.[37]

### Unfriendly Diplomacy and Pétion's Constitutional Model

Bolívar's fear of "pardocracy" may also have been behind Gran Colombia's refusal to recognize the independence of the Haitian Republic, and also of its exclusion from the anticolonialist congress held in Panama in 1826. What may explain this recalcitrant diplomatic attitude were the rumors of attempts by Haitian agents to destabilize the Spanish Main, and Haiti's occupation of Santo Domingo in February 1822. This former Spanish colony had declared its independence three months earlier, and its new government sought to join Greater Colombia, with Bolívar's consent. The Spanish-Dominican separatist leader, José Núñez de Cáceres, who migrated to Caracas following the Haitian invasion, described the Haitians as "white-eaters" and blamed them for having destroyed the ambitious project of incorporating the Estado Independendiente de Haiti Español into Gran Colombia.[38]

The attitude of Gran Colombia's government did not go unnoticed by Haiti's mulatto president Jean-Pierre Boyer, who privately manifested in 1829 his disappointment with the fact that Bolívar had not respected his promise to establish relations with his country. Bolívar, who genuinely felt great gratitude toward Haiti (mainly because of the support that the former Haitian president, also of mulatto origin, Alexandre Pétion, had given him in the campaigns he led to invade Venezuela in 1816), responded to Boyer's allegations defensively, asserting that he would be "unable to refuse to negotiate with the Haitian government because I owe it too much for that."[39]

Despite Bolívar's negative perception of Haiti and the *pardos*, he took Pétion's constitution of 1816 as a model for newly independent Bolivia. When he presented the new Bolivian constitution in 1826, he recognized Haiti's constitutional influence by claiming that he had chosen the executive power model of "the most democratic republic in the world," which established

---

[37] "Una mirada sobre la América Española" (Quito, 1829), in Simón Bolívar, *Obras completas*, 3 vols. (Havana: Editorial Lex, 1950), vol. III, 844.

[38] Emilio Rodríguez Demorizi, *Santo Domingo y la Gran Colombia: Bolívar y Núñez de Cáceres* (Santo Domingo: Editora del Caribe, 1971), 26–7.

[39] Bolívar to Francisco Fernández, Guayaquil, 16 August 1829, in Bolívar, *Obras completas*, vol. III, 742.

a president for life who had the power to elect his successor. Following Clément Thibaud, Bolívar made this paradoxical choice in times when the fear of anarchy was still very vivid, convinced as he was that that constitutional model would contribute to keeping the situation under control in the same way it had calmed down the state of "permanent insurrection" in which Haiti had found itself since its independence. Curiously enough, the model of a lifetime presidency on which Bolívar had placed his hopes would be widely rejected by the political classes in Bolivia, Peru, and Gran Colombia, eventually forcing Bolívar and his acolytes to yield power under accusations of tyranny.[40]

## Pro-slavery and Elite Arguments

### Robespierre in Brazil

As happened elsewhere in the Atlantic World, the French Caribbean revolutions fed pro-slavery thought in continental Ibero-America, especially in Brazil. The first reference can be found very early in the work of the enlightened bishop J. J. Cunha Azeredo Coutinho.[41] In his work *Mémoria on o preço do açúcar*, published in Portugal after the slave rebellion that shattered Saint-Domingue in 1791, this clergyman proposed to take advantage of the "unfortunate revolution of the French colonies" to increase sugar production in the Portuguese colonies. In another work entitled *Análise sobre a Justiça do Comercio do Resgate Two Escravos da Costa da África*, published in 1808, Azeredo Coutinho warned his countrymen about the existence of a certain "philosophical sect" in Brazil whose nefarious principles he associated with Jacques-Pierre Brissot and Maximilien Robespierre. Based on the writings of the Baron de Pradt and Dubu de Longchamp,[42] he described

---

[40] Clément Thibaud, "'Coupé têtes, brulé cazes': Peurs et désirs d'Haïti dans l'Amérique de Bolívar," *Annales. Histoire, Sciences Sociales* 58:2 (2003), 305–31: 330.

[41] E. Bradford Burns, "The Role of Azeredo Coutinho in the Enlightenment of Brazil," *The Hispanic American Historical Review* 44:2 (1964), 145–60; Maria do Rosário Pimentel, "O Bispo de Elvas D. José Joaquim da Cunha de Azeredo Coutinho e a defesa da escravatura," in Jorge Fonseca and Teresa Fonseca, eds., *O Alentejo entre o Antigo Regime e a regeneração: Mudanças e permanências* (Évora: Publicações do Cidehus, 2019), 193–208.

[42] De Pradt's work is a pamphlet published in 1791, in which he accused Jacques-Pierre Brissot of being an antiwhite traitor in English pay, and proposed the restoration of the slave trade once the slave rebellion had been controlled. Dubu de Longchamp's text is a two-volume set published in 1824, in which he recounts the history of the revolution to defend the right to indemnification for the former *colons* of Saint-Domingue. Dominique Dufour Pradt, *La France, l'émigration, et les colons*, vol. II (Paris: Béchet Ainé, 1824); Jean-François Dubu de Longchamp, *Mémoire et accusation contre M. Brissot de Warville* (Paris: 1791).

these men as true "monsters with a human figure," whose maxim "[p]erish the colonies, rather than one principle be abandoned!" (a well-known parliamentary slogan attributed to Robespierre) was the doctrine that led to the end of the social order in France and the destruction of Saint-Domingue.[43]

That maxim was also used as an argument in the debate about the scope of citizenship and the status of foreigners held at the Constituent Assembly in Rio de Janeiro in September 1823. In this assembly, deputy José da Silva Lisboa, who was in favor of extending the citizenship to freedmen, dismissed the allegations (supposedly based, in part, on testimony by Madame de Staël) that it was dangerous to discuss these matters in the light of what had allegedly happened to the French colonies in similar circumstances.[44] At the same time, he pointed at the "architects of ruins," the "fury of Robespierre," his despotic government and his "anarchist" colleagues who suddenly abolished slavery, as responsible for the destruction of Saint-Domingue. That is why he recommended his fellow deputies use "political prudence," and encouraged them to adopt a measure which ensured "slow emancipation." Although the abolition of the slave trade was not under discussion, the same deputy evoked the biblical arguments used by the "famous Wilberforce" to indicate that God is the same for all mankind.[45]

Another deputy, João Maciel da Costa, went even further in the same vein as he proposed to gradually end that human trafficking, to treat all slaves well, and above all, taking up the proposal of another deputy, to offer citizenship to the freed slaves born in Brazilian territory. "Political security," alleged da Costa, "and not philanthropy" is what should guide the representatives of the Constituent Assembly; since after all it was philanthropy and the "rights of man" that, according to him, had produced the "horrors" that ended the "flourishing French colonies."[46] This was an argument he had already used in a text published in 1821 in which he attacked the slave trade. There, he had claimed that the destruction of those colonies was the result of the way the French filled the heads of Africans with "contagious ideas of

---

[43] José Joaquim da Cunha de Azeredo Coutinho, *Analyse sobre a justiça do commercio do resgate dos escravos da costa da Africa* (Lisbon: Na nova officina de João Rodrigues Neves, 1808); Nascimento, "São Domingos, o grande São Domingos," 130–1.

[44] Madame de Staël was a noble woman of letters and abolitionist as well as an admirer of Wilberforce. "Sessão de 30 de setembro," in *Diário da Assambléia Geral, Constituinte, e Legislativa do Imperio do Brasil – 1823*, 3 vols. (Brasilia: Senado Federal, 2003), vol. III, 133–5.

[45] Ibid., 123, 135–40; Jeremy Adelman, *Sovereignty and Revolution in the Iberian Atlantic* (Oxford and Princeton, NJ: Princeton University Press, 2006), 98–9.

[46] "Sessão de 30 de setembro," in *Diário da Assambléia Geral*, vol. III, 138.

## Impact of the French Caribbean Revolutions

freedom and chimerical [ideas] of equality."[47] In the same vein, Silva Lisboa argued that a refusal to grant citizenship to freedmen would guarantee their perpetual hatred of the political system, which would aggravate the risks of introducing to Brazil the evils that destroyed the French colonies. Granting citizenship to Brazilian freedmen was the criterion that would be eventually chosen to avoid that fatality, as can be seen in Article No. 6 of the Constitution of the Brazilian Empire sanctioned in March 1824.[48]

### Alarming Views in Continental Spanish America

In the Viceroyalty of New Spain, where Indians, mestizos, and other *castas* or mixed-blood men and women made up the majority of the population, not many references were made to the French Caribbean revolutions. The only exception is the publication in 1805 of a Spanish translation of a devastating biography of Jean-Jacques Dessalines, authored by the Bonapartist writer Louis Dubroca. It was published in Mexico City by the editor of the *Gaceta de México*, Juan López Cancelada, who added some crude engravings to visually enhance the description of atrocities committed by the Haitian Blacks. In the introduction, the editor underlined the need to learn from the horrors experienced by the whites of Saint-Domingue, whose disunity and the introduction of "extravagant ideas" (particularly those of the French Revolution) caused their downfall. Behind these allegations could also be hidden an attack on modern political ideas, and a warning against striving for independence on the part of certain individuals imbued with the revolutionary spirit of the time.[49]

The clearest use of a pro-slavery argument that referred to the French Caribbean revolutions can be found in Peru. Almost immediately after this country achieved its independence in the mid-1820s, the landowner elite began pressuring for the restoration of Indian tribute and the African slave trade in order for the country's economy to recover. One of its members, José María de Pando, published an influential work entitled *Reclamación de los*

---

[47] João Severiano Maciel da Costa, *Memoria sobre a necessidade de abolir a introdução dos escravos africanos no Brasil* (Coimbra: Imprensa da Universidade, 1821), 23.

[48] "Sessão de 30 de setembro," 139; Márcia Berbel, Rafael Marquese, and Tâmis Parron, eds., *Escravidão e política: Brasil e Cuba, c. 1790–1850* (São Paulo: Hucitec & FAPESP, 2010), 168–71.

[49] Kelly Donahue-Wallace, "Ilustrando el terror de rebelión: Los grabados de la vida de J. J. Dessalines," in Fernando Guzmán Schiappacasse, Gloria Cortés Aliaga, and Juan Manuel Martínez Silva, eds., *Arte y crisis en Iberoamérica: Segundas Jornadas de Historia del Arte* (Santiago de Chile: RIL Editores, 2004), 86.

*vulnerados derechos de los hacendados de las provincias litorales del departamento de Lima* (1833). This text uses some of the classic arguments to support slavery and criticize immediate abolitionism, including the interpretation of the "catastrophe" of Saint-Domingue as a consequence of the abolition of slavery by France in 1794. But Pando's arguments with regard to the French Caribbean revolutions went further. He also criticized the granting of equality to the *gens de couleur*, the atrocities committed during the revolutionary period, and the restoration of servitude by Toussaint Louverture and Henri Christophe, which, according to Pando, was crueler than slavery itself. The pressure of the Peruvian landowners paid off, as in 1835 and again in 1846 the trans-American slave trade was legalized for short periods.[50]

## Grégoire's Ties with Ibero-Americans

Another avenue worth exploring is the contacts some Ibero-Americans established with one of the most active antislavery advocates in the North Atlantic: the Abbé Henri Grégoire. They were mostly priests and friars who discussed with him, or wished to discuss with him, a large variety of subjects. One of the first to get in contact with the prominent abbé was a Portuguese monsignor living in Brazil, Pedro Machado Miranda, who met Grégoire in person in Paris at some point in the beginning of the nineteenth century. According to historian Marco Morel, both religious men agreed on an enlightened vision of the Catholic Church in spite of their ideological differences. In 1821, Grégoire sent him some of his works, and also requested information on Black and mulatto writers in Brazil. His interest in this South American colony was also reflected in his work *De la littérature des Nègres* (Paris, Maradin, 1808), in which he strongly criticizes the pro-slavery ideas of the aforementioned bishop J. J. Cunha Azeredo Coutinho, whose work *Análise sobre a Justiça* had been translated to French and published in London in 1798.[51] A copy of that work probably reached the hands of

[50] José María de Pando et al., eds., *Reclamacion de los vulnerados Derechos de los hacendados de las provincias litorales del departamento de Lima* (Lima: J. M. Concha, 1833); Marcel Velázquez Castro, "José María de Pando y la consolidación del sujeto esclavista en el Perú del siglo XIX," *Boletín del Instituto Riva-Agüero*, no. 23 (1996), 303–25; Peter Blanchard, *Slavery & Abolition in Early Republican Peru* (Wilmington, DE: SR Books, 1992), 53–7, 181–2.

[51] Pimentel, "O Bispo de Elvas"; Marco Morel, "O abade Grégoire, o Haiti e o Brasil: Repercussões no raiar do século XIX," *Almanack Braziliense*, no. 2 (November 2005), 76–90; Marco Morel, "A Revolução do Haiti e o Império do Brasil: Intermediações e rumores," *Anuario de Estudios Bolivarianos* 11:12 (2005), 189–212: 206–7.

Wilberforce in 1810 through Francisco de Miranda, who became acquainted with Grégoire during the French Revolution.[52]

At the beginning of the nineteenth century, Grégoire also met Servando Teresa de Mier, the revolutionary and friar from New Spain. For Mier, the French revolutionary ideals were an anticlerical farce that had generated disasters wherever they were applied, as seen in Venezuela.[53] Despite this, during his two years of exile in France in 1802–1803, he formed a friendship with the French abbé with whom he shared an admiration for the figure of Bartolomé de las Casas. In a letter from 1825, Grégoire wrote to Mier about Haiti, explaining the amazing exceptionality of "a republic organized by the children of Africa" who had "shown so much boldness in conquering their freedom," overcoming the planters' calumnies and outrages. In the same letter, he expressed the necessity to invite Haiti to the congress of independent American nations that Simón Bolívar was organizing in Panama, and encouraged Mier to defend Haiti in that assembly and before the Mexican government.[54]

## Conclusion

The various manifestations of the impact of the French Caribbean revolutions in continental Ibero-America show, above all, the great diversity of ways through which political actors appropriated, both "from below" and "from above," the ideas and events associated with those processes. Their interpretations and political uses depended to a great extent on their political culture, the moments in which these different actors became politically active, the objectives they intended to achieve, and their condition or socioracial profile.[55]

This last aspect is crucial to understand the reactions (or lack of response) of "colored" individuals, whose different statuses and sociracial identities would shape their political attitudes and viewpoints. This population group

[52] Miranda to Wilberforce, London, 10 January 1810, in Francisco de Miranda, *Archivo del General Miranda*, vol. 1 (Caracas: Parra León Hermanos, 1929), 269.

[53] José Servando Teresa de Mier, *Considérations sur l'Amérique espagnole ou Appel à la verité, sur les causes, l'esprit et le but de sa révolution* (Paris: Rodriguez, 1817), 16.

[54] Grégoire to Mier [Paris, 30/09/1925], in José Servando Teresa de Mier Noriega y Guerra, *Escritos inéditos de fray Servando Teresa de Mier* (Mexico City: El Colegio de México, Centro de Estudios Históricos, 1944), 511.

[55] In his work on the different "popular republicanisms" that emerged in the Colombian Cauca region in the nineteenth century, James Sanders has shown the importance of differentiating the profiles of lower-class groups for the study of their political ideas. James E. Sanders, *Contentious Republicans: Popular Politics, Race, and Class in Nineteenth-Century Colombia* (Durham, NC: Duke University Press, 2004).

was particularly numerous on the coast of Brazil, New Granada, and Venezuela, which, as mentioned above, were more exposed to Atlantic revolutionary winds. Given the similar socioracial profile of the rebels in the French Antilles and the particular nature of the measures taken in Paris regarding the colonies, it is reasonable to think that people of African descent were more susceptible than other racialized groups to feel sympathy for the revolutions in question, not only in Ibero-America but elsewhere in the colonial world. This sympathy contrasts with the total absence of interest among the Indigenous peoples, to whom the French Caribbean revolutionary processes had no appeal whatsoever. Instead, because of their socioracial conditions and the particular "spaces of experience" – to use Reinhard Koselleck's theoretical formulation[56] – in which they lived, they were more willing to join the guerrilla units of independent provinces or *republiquetas* (as happened in Upper Peru) or to follow rebellious caciques invoking an ideology of "Inca nationalism" they could comprehend, and even to embrace the monarchist cause as many did during the wars of independence.[57]

The political imaginary of slaves as well as colored individuals of low socioracial status was limited by their illiteracy, brutalization, and lower degree of assimilation compared to other nonwhites. They were therefore less aware of the political principles and the legal scope of the egalitarian measures adopted in France, and later by local revolutionary governments in Spanish America. Nonetheless, they seem to have had a clearer idea, though still very blurred, of what happened in the French colonies, especially in Saint-Domingue. Hence, it is often hard to establish the difference between the manifestations of traditional resistance, and those responding to conceptual changes that denote the formation of new popular political ideologies either of Franco-Caribbean, Spanish liberal or Hispanic-republican inspiration. This can be seen in the way rumors affected the rebellions of Coro and Mendoza of 1795 and 1812 respectively, as in both cases the slaves and the freedmen misunderstood alleged emancipatory measures in their favor and wrongly believed that their masters or the local authorities refused to honor those measures. These mistaken perceptions can be explained from a *longue durée* perspective by what Michael Craton has defined as the "rumor

---

[56] Reinhart Koselleck, *Futures Past: On the Semantics of Historical Time*, trans. Keith Tribe (New York: Columbia University Press, 1985).

[57] John H. Rowe, "El movimiento nacional inca en el siglo XVIII," *Revista Universitaria* 43 (1954), 17–47; Marcela Echeverri, "Popular Royalists, Empire, and Politics in Southwestern New Granada, 1809–1819," *Hispanic American Historical Review* 91:2 (2011), 237–69. See also Echeverri, Chapter 10 in this volume.

Impact of the French Caribbean Revolutions

syndrome,"[58] which – as shown by Wim Klooster – had significantly increased during the revolutionary period given the antislavery agitation and political turmoil.[59] On the other hand, the cases of Coro and Mendoza contrast with the petition of the nearly 200 slaves from Medellín in 1812, whose determination to exhort the authorities, despite reflecting a "rumor syndrome," revealed a stronger political awareness "from below." Nevertheless, though this case was undoubtedly the most modern manifestation of slave agency of the period, it did not show any French Caribbean influence other than the fear of a Haiti-style uprising it caused among creoles.

Much more modern were the ideas expressed by mixed-blood individuals, many of whom had attained a higher intellectual level and, in spite of prevailing socioracial discrimination, were better assimilated to the colonial societies. This may explain why so many of them showed sympathy for the republican model, and for the system of socioracial harmony they thought had been implanted in France and some of the French Antilles. An important aspect of their mentality was the exclusion of slaves from their political agenda, which could be explained by their partially European ancestry, and by the fact that many of them were slave owners themselves. This exclusionary attitude, as Luiz Geraldo Silva pointed out for the case of Pereira Rebouças, is very similar to the attitudes shown by the quadroons of Saint-Domingue when they struggled exclusively for their rights as active citizens during the French Revolution.[60]

It is curious, however – as noted by two historians[61] – that some *pardos* such as Mundurucú and the same Pereira Rebouças exalted Haitian Black leaders such as Christophe and Louverture, and not mixed-blood chieftains of their own socioracial status like Rigaud, Pétion, or Boyer. These attitudes could be associated with the support they began to give for the granting of citizenship to freedmen, which might be explained either by the fact that they shared the whites' fears, or as evidence of the development of a new awareness against colonialism as seen around the same time among similar mixed-blood people in places like Jamaica and Martinique.[62] Narciso Del

[58] Michael Craton, *Testing the Chains: Resistance to Slavery in the British West Indies* (Ithaca, NY: Cornell University Press, 1982).
[59] Wim Klooster, "Slave Revolts, Royal Justice, and a Ubiquitous Rumor in the Age of Revolutions," *The William and Mary Quarterly* 71:3 (2014), 401–24.
[60] Silva, "Impacto de la revolución de Saint-Domingue," 231.
[61] Reis and Santos Gomez, "Repercussions of the Haitian Revolution," 292.
[62] Alejandro E. Gómez, "Apenas una parte de negro. Valores socio-raciales y accionar político de las élites de 'color Quebrado' en Jamaica, Venezuela, y las Antillas francesas (siglos XVIII y XIX)," *Revista de Indias* 75:263 (2015), 65–92.

Valle is a case apart; his enthusiastic involvement in the conspiracy of La Guaira of 1797, that sought the establishment of an egalitarian republic and the abolition of slavery, surely responded to the positive image he and his fellow plotters developed regarding the model of socioracial harmony that they thought had been established in Guadeloupe.

All these manifestations of political awareness among people of African descent, though often hiding economic claims and socioracial frustrations, are evidence – as Lyman Johnson has suggested for the case of the supposed conspiracy in Buenos Aires in 1795[63] – of the presence of the French Caribbean revolutionary imaginary among certain subaltern groups of African descent. The reference to Tupac Amaru and not Toussaint Louverture or other Black or mulatto "heroes" of the revolution in Saint-Domingue, may indicate the existence of a broader political imagination that linked the Andes with the Atlantic.

The most widespread consequence of the French Caribbean revolutions for Ibero-American creoles and other whites – as elsewhere in the Americas – was undoubtedly the paranoia they developed as a result of the "horrors" of Saint-Domingue. This phenomenon was particularly intense in the Caribbean regions of northern South America as well as in Brazil, where Haiti – as Rafael Marquese and Tâmis Parron have argued – was referred to more frequently by the authorities than the slaves themselves.[64] This was due to a large extent to the menace that the large nonwhite enslaved population presented to the whites, which caused, as in the case of Cuba and probably also of Antioquia,[65] a true "fear of Africanization," or *Haitianismo*, as Brazilian historians call it. Elsewhere in continental Iberian America, the fear of the masses was related to local events and Indigenous populations, as in the Andes after the rebellion of Tupac Amaru, and in New Spain, where a fear of *"casta* wars" emerged from the massive popular participation during the wars of independence in New Spain.[66]

Another important aspect of the impact "from above" of the French Caribbean revolutions was the rejection of Jacobinism and sans-culottism,

---

[63] Johnson, *Workshop of Revolution*.

[64] Rafael de Bivar Marquese and Tâmis Peixoto Parron, "Slave Revolts and the Political Foundations of Brazil and Cuba, 1790–1825," in Clément Thibaud et al., *L'atlantique révolutionnaire: Une perspective ibéro-américaine* (Bécherel: Les Perséides, 2013), 462.

[65] Although Antioquia was not a plantation colony, along with the nearby provinces of Cauca and Choco it comprised around 20,000 slaves, enough to "scare" the local white creole revolutionaries.

[66] Peter F Guardino, *Peasants, Politics, and the Formation of Mexico's National State: Guerrero, 1800–1857* (Stanford: Stanford University Press, 1996), 168.

as a consequence of the conviction these ideological trends were responsible for the Reign of Terror and the "catastrophe" of Saint-Domingue. This in turn led many Spanish American revolutionaries to remove radical elements from their political ideology, as can be clearly seen in the cases of Miranda and Bolívar; the latter's ideas and sensibilities, however, were also affected by the traumatic experience of the "popular rebellion" of 1814, as well as by the military rise of many men of African descent within patriotic ranks, and perhaps also by his own racial prejudices as a white aristocrat. In the words of Aline Helg, although Bolívar was ahead of many of his contemporaries when he opposed slavery, his prejudices vis-à-vis the *pardos* "showed his inability to transform the racial equalization required by the war against Spain into full republican equality."[67]

Despite that ideological turn, some Latin American revolutionaries continued to develop various forms of radical republicanism, although always seeking to avoid being labeled as *jacobinos*, as they did in Caracas and Buenos Aires. Some of the new governments assumed very radical positions in terms of the measures they took to improve the conditions of the subaltern masses (especially Indians and *pardos*), mainly by granting them citizenship.[68] White creole legislators were less "generous" vis-à-vis the slave population. Indeed, despite the fact that many autonomous and independent regimes abolished the slave trade and introduced free-womb laws, only Chile, Mexico, and Central America decided to abolish slavery in the 1820s. They did so, insofar as I have been able to determine, with little or no direct influence from the French Caribbean revolutions.

The influence of British antislavery is also crucial to understanding the impact of the French Caribbean revolutions in Ibero-America, since the consolidation of the gradual abolitionist paradigm in the United Kingdom owes much to those processes. Indeed, the revolutionary conflicts, the wars in the West Indies (especially in Saint-Domingue and Guadeloupe), and above all, France's loss of Saint-Domingue strongly contributed to convincing the British antislavery legislators that slaves were not ready to be set free.[69] This conviction remained active throughout the period of the Spanish

---

[67] Aline Helg, "Simón Bolívar and the Spectre of Pardocracia: Jose Padilla in Post-Independence Cartagena," *Journal of Latin American Studies* 35 (2003), 447–71: 471.

[68] See Bassi, Chapter 8 in this volume.

[69] I have studied this subject elsewhere: Alejandro E. Gómez, "Un argument très convaincant. Saint-Domingue dans le débat abolitionniste britannique (1791–1833)," in Marcel Dorigny et al., eds., *Couleurs, esclavages, libérations aux Amériques, 1804–1860* (Rennes: Les Perséides, 2013), 92–106.

American revolutions in the first three decades of the nineteenth century, which might help explain, along with the lack of impact of the French Caribbean revolutions, why there were so few proposals aiming at the immediate abolition of slavery. Evidence of the sympathy that British anti-slavery's cautious and gradualist views generated in continental Latin America can clearly be seen in the ideas of revolutionaries such as Miranda and Fagoaga. They can also be observed, although in a distorted way, among certain pro-slavery advocates in spaces where the servile institution was still very important for the local economies, as in Peru and Brazil. Accordingly, authors such as Pando, Coutinho, and Silva Lisboa underlined the evils of French immediate abolitionism, and contrasted it with the wiser example of British antislavery gradualism, as a means for preserving slavery as long as possible.

Another important source of influence was the international circulation of many Latin Americans and the contacts they established with figures related to the French Caribbean revolutions. Especially important in this regard was Abbé Grégoire, who not only represented the most radical faction of French abolitionism after the Thermidorian Reaction of 1794, but also the most important advocate in the Atlantic World at that time for the improvement of the image of Haiti and of "colored" people of African descent in general. Finally, the circulation and access to printed materials related to the revolutions in question was also crucial, as seen in the texts discussed at the meetings in Del Valle's barbershop, in Miranda's "gift" to Wilberforce, in Rebouças' personal library, and the references made during the debates held at the Constituent Assembly in Brazil in 1823.

## 15

# Deferred but not Avoided: Great Britain and Latin American Independence

### KAREN RACINE

In *Utopia*, written in 1516 and set in a fictional island in the New World, Sir Thomas More observed that "[w]hat is deferred is not avoided." The same words could have been said 300 years later by William Pitt, Lord Castlereagh, or George Canning as they struggled to reconcile Great Britain's interests with those of the Spanish American and Portuguese dominions in rapidly shifting conditions of war and sovereignty. Latin American independence might indeed have been deferred, but it could not be avoided. The government and people of Great Britain played a visible and significant role in those events but the admiration was mutual. British politicians, industrialists, and abolitionists looked toward Iberian America as a place of opportunity and fortune, and as somewhere far enough away to carry out experiments with reformist ideas. In return, Latin American patriots looked toward Great Britain for the naval protection it could provide, to its armaments and woolen factories for material goods, and to its banks for development loans. People on both sides of the Atlantic assessed their public and private interests and sought results on their own terms. But it also was more than a military, diplomatic, and commercial relationship. There were equally significant cultural exchanges in the form of scientific knowledge, legal structures, pedagogical theories, Masonic practices, incentives to abolish slavery, and the beginning of an active book trade. On an individual, human level, there were also hundreds of longstanding, fond personal friendships and family connections that spanned both language and geographical space.

## Background and Early Emancipation Schemes

There was nothing deferred or avoided about imperial competition in the early years of European exploration and settlement in the Americas. Notorious British pirate William Hawkins had stopped in Bahia and reported on the potential for the hardwood trade as early as the 1530s and 1540s. Between 1550 and 1646, English and Irish settlements existed in the Amazon Basin from Pará to Guiana, and in Mosquitía where the competition for hardwoods and protected harbors was intense. In the 1640s, a rascally Irish Catholic figure named William Lamport tried to foment a multiracial, cross-class uprising against the Spanish Crown in Mexico City with the goal of establishing an independent country and himself as king; it failed and Lamport was executed under an Inquisition decree in 1659. Yet contacts continued. After 1642, English merchants were given the right to engage in certain kinds of trade with Brazil, something reaffirmed in Anglo-Portuguese treaties of 1654, 1661, and 1703. Perhaps the most notorious early settlement scheme was the failed Scottish colony at Darién, which was undertaken by a company intending to triangulate trade to Africa and the Indies through a settlement at the Isthmus of Panama. Of the more than 1,200 settler-soldiers sent out, only a handful survived to abandon the attempt by 1700, the rest having succumbed to disease, exhaustion, malnutrition, or Spanish swords.

In 1711, Daniel Defoe, author of *Robinson Crusoe*, wrote a letter to the Earl of Oxford in which he enclosed "[a] proposal for seizing, possessing, and forming an English colony on the Kingdom of Chili in the south part of America."[1] In his view, Chile would be the ideal location for a British colony and commerce for the quality of the land, its suitability for settlement and its location far from Spanish settlements. In 1781, a Scottish fellow named Richard Oswald proposed a plan to coordinate with Russia to carry out a double-pronged attack in California and along the Pacific coast, on the assumption that Spain could not withstand such a joint force. The idea must have had currency because rumors that blonde-haired, blue-eyed Englishmen from the Royal Navy were acting as aides and confidantes to Tupac Amaru circulated in the Andes at the same time.[2] Six years later, Colonel William Fullarton proposed a similar surprise attack using troops raised on the Indian subcontinent. Very shortly afterward, however, in something known as the Nootka Sound crisis, Britain and Spain nearly went to war over access to the Alaskan fur trade and the right to settle in that territory, temporarily resolving their differences in a series of conventions between 1790–1794. In 1803,

---

[1] Defoe to the Earl of Oxford, 23 July 1711, reprinted in Historical Manuscripts Commission, *Calendar of the Manuscripts of the Marquis of Bath, preserved at Longleat, Wiltshire* (London: His Majesty's Stationery Office, 1904), vol. III, 58–61.

[2] Malcolm Deas, "Patrias viejas, patrias bobas, patrias nuevas. Reflexiones sobre los principios de la Independencia de los Andes," in Germán Carrera Damas, ed., *Historia de América Andina* (Quito: Universidad Andina, 2002), vol. IV, 69–195: 181.

Sir Home Riggs Popham submitted a plan to the British government that included plans to establish a naval station and a commercial trading post. It mirrored Francisco de Miranda's plans for a similar outpost in Venezuela and both were backed by a prominent Scottish military contractor named Alexander Davison. Both men continued to meet with William Pitt and various high-level Cabinet members and provided detailed memoranda through 1805.

Most of these plans, however, were envisioned merely as old-style inter-imperial transfers of overseas territory. Schemes to support Latin American emancipation were neither deferred nor avoided, but rather were not contemplated at all. The pattern changed when the British Navy's South Atlantic Fleet landed at the Río de la Plata delta and briefly occupied Buenos Aires and Montevideo on two occasions in 1806 and 1807. Then, in November 1807, the British Navy intervened again by transporting the Portuguese royal family and court to Brazil to escape Napoleon's advancing army. In both instances, the motivations and outcomes were complicated.

On 10 June 1806, Sir Home Riggs Popham and William Carr Beresford arrived off the coast of Buenos Aires with six frigates, three corvettes, five transport ships and more than 1,600 troops that they had diverted from a South Atlantic mission to Cape Town in South Africa. Viceroy Marqués de Sobremonte immediately abandoned the city and fled to the interior royalist stronghold at Córdoba, taking the treasury's coffers with him.[3] Nationalist accounts have tended to condemn the Viceroy as a coward and a rogue, but at least one historian has rightly pointed out that there was little alternative.[4] Buenos Aires only had 40,000 people at the time and its energetic merchant class was keen to expand their trade opportunities, but Popham and Beresford miscalculated and engaged in a violent and aggressive occupation which alienated potential allies and provoked a patriotic counteraction. It was an untenable situation all around. The British invasion of the Río de la Plata was a semi-rogue operation that was clearly informed by the longstanding desire of His Majesty's government to gain access to the strategic military and commercial possibilities of Cape Horn, South America, and the South Seas. Beresford himself had done some advance work making contact with

[3] Thomas Grenville, "Sir Home Popham's Naval Force at Rio de la Plata, 1806," Huntington Library, Mss STG, box 150 (30).
[4] Lyman L. Johnson, "The Military as Catalyst of Change in Late Colonial Buenos Aires," in Mark D. Szuchman and Jonathan C. Brown, eds., *Revolution and Restoration: The Rearrangement of Power in Argentina, 1776–1860* (Lincoln: University of Nebraska Press, 1986), 38.

amenable creoles like brothers Nicolás and Saturnino Rodríguez Peña, Juan José Castelli, and Englishman James (Diego) Paroissien. At the time, though, Britain's paramount concern was the European theater and it could not afford potentially expensive engagements around the world that might come at a high diplomatic cost. In the Río de la Plata, the British invasions created an opportunity for creole (and royalist) patriots alike to form militias, undertake their own autonomous self-defense, and, as Juan Luis Ossa puts it, "indulge their fantasies in the art of war."[5]

British forces consolidated their control over Buenos Aires and managed to hold it for six weeks. Parish priests tunneled from their Church of San Francisco and placed thirty-six barrels of powder under the British barracks, which they blew up in spectacular fashion.[6] Beresford attempted to create some support by abolishing trade restrictions and reducing customs duties (12.5 percent for British goods, 17.5 percent for all other nations). Popham sent "wagon loads of silver" and self-serving reports back to London to relay the good news to merchant communities and to the government to paper over their unsanctioned act.[7] On 20 July, Popham wrote to his friend Francisco de Miranda that they were "in possession of Buenos Ayres, the finest Country in the World . . . I am so preoccupied that I scarce know what to do first. I wish you were here. I like the South Americans prodigiously."[8] The tides turned quickly, however. Less than three weeks later, the Argentines forced him out of the city to the safety of his ship and captured Beresford and his land forces to hold for ransom. The British occupiers raised the white flag of surrender on 12 August and were permitted to slink out of the port. Ironically, because of the slowness with which news traveled, at the very same moment, *The Times* was announcing to its readers the glorious news that "BUENOS AYRES AT THIS MOMENT FORMS A PART OF THE BRITISH EMPIRE."[9]

---

[5] Juan Luis Ossa Santa Cruz, "La actividad política de Francisco Antonio Pinto. 1823–1828. Notas para una revisión biográfica," *Historia* 40:1 (2007), 91–128: 92.

[6] Alexander Gillespie, *Gleanings and Remarks: Collected during a Residence of Many Months at Buenos Ayres and within the Upper Country* (Leeds: Printed by B. DeWhirst for the Author, 1818), 89–90.

[7] Judith B. Williams, "The Establishment of British Commerce in Argentina," *Hispanic American Historical Review* 15:1 (1935), 43–64: 46–47; R. A. Humphreys, "British Merchants and South American Independence," *Proceedings of the British Academy* 51 (1965), 151–74: 157.

[8] Popham to Miranda, Buenos Aires, 20 July 1806, in *Archivo del General Miranda* (Havana: Editorial Lex, 1952), vol. XVIII, 245.

[9] "Capture of Buenos Ayres," *The Times* no. 6841 (13 September 1806), 2.

Popham and Beresford returned to London and were immediately sent to court martial. Popham's trial was a public spectacle, with the defense trying to make the episode as much about the country's honor during wartime rather than a judgment on the actions of a single man.[10] Nevertheless, William Windham, Secretary for War and the Colonies, actively continued to explore the potential for another expeditionary force to the Río de la Plata and Chile that could secure commercial trade routes and protect regular access to the Pacific. Back in Buenos Aires, the Rodríguez Peña brothers and Paroissien also sat before tribunals facing charges of treason for their collaboration with the British invaders; Juan José Castelli wrote their impassioned defense.[11]

Early in 1807, a second expeditionary force under Lieutenant General John Whitelocke was sent out to redeem the British Navy's reputation. Windham's official instructions to Whitelocke indicate the tricky line the British government was attempting to walk. He was explicitly ordered to end the Spanish imperial government's control over the territory, but he should take care not to provoke an insurrectionary movement. He should encourage the independence party, but under no conditions should he guarantee that they could count on a British military backstop for any autonomous government. Whitelocke was also supposed to create a British-style commercial depot while guaranteeing the former rights, privileges, and established uses of local residents.[12] It was the sort of optimistic plan that probably seemed reasonable when devised in the back rooms of power halfway around the globe but did not bear much resemblance to conditions on the ground. Whitelocke landed on 4 July and immediately faced a stronger, better-organized, and more practiced patriotic defense than had existed just a year earlier.

The British invasions of the Río de la Plata had obvious and immediate implications for the people and politics of that region. The viceregal and colonial authorities were hopelessly discredited and those local constituencies, both autonomy-minded and loyalist alike, were emboldened to assert their demands with more confidence. Repercussions were felt across the

---

[10] *A Full and Correct Report of the Trial of Sir Home Popham* ... 2nd edition (London: J. and J. Richardson and C. Chapple, 1807), v–vi; William Grenville, "Notes and Remarks on Popham's Courtmartial, November 1807," Huntington Library, Mss STG Box 150 (58).

[11] R. A. Humphrey, *Liberation in South America, 1806–1827: The Career of James Paroissien* (London: University of London, 1952).

[12] William Windham, "Draft Instructions to Lieutenant John Whitelocke," British Library, Add MS 37886, f. 145.

continent as well. The Spanish government had demanded a forced loan of 1.5 million pesos from Lima's Tribunal to improve their Pacific Coast defense.[13] In Charcas (today Sucre, Bolivia), Archbishop Benito María Moxó de Francoli regularly used his sermons to berate the foreign Protestant devils who threatened his parishioners and called upon the Virgin of Guadalupe to protect them in this time of great mortal danger. As he said, "England is a nation with neither God nor laws."[14] Residents of Santiago de Chile and Buenos Aires both experienced a significant militarization of their urban space and daily life as troops practiced regularly in city streets and curfews and watchwords regulated all public movement.[15] Throughout Spanish America, colonial administrators clamped down on dissent, issuing decrees that, among other things, made it illegal to read foreign works or to speak privately with foreigners. They extracted huge "voluntary contributions" for the royalist war effort; one scholar estimates more than 500,000 pesos in Buenos Aires alone.[16] Perhaps the most significant result of the British invasions, however, was the creation of a confident, experienced new generation of leaders that emerged out of the patriotic defense.

## The Napoleonic Era, 1808–1814

Geopolitical strategy continued to inform British government's interactions with the Iberian Crowns and their overseas dominions. As Napoleon Bonaparte's forces rapidly swept across the peninsula in 1808 subverting the Spanish monarchy and installing his brother Joseph on its throne, the Portuguese royal family rushed to make plans for their evacuation to Brazil. Oddly, it was an idea that had been floated as early as the 1580s and again during the period of Dutch occupation in the 1640s. By late 1807, the threat was real enough that the Braganzas, their court, and approximately 10,000–15,000 panicked people boarded British warships and fled across the

[13] Cristina A. Mazzeo, "Lima en la agonía del régimen colonial y la guerra de independencia, 1820–1826. El Tribunal del Consulado y la financiación de la Guerra," in Carmen Mc Evoy, Mauricio Novoa, and Elías Palti, eds., *El nudo del imperio independencia y democracia en el Perú* (Lima: IFEA-IEP, 2012), 271–93: 273.

[14] Pablo Ortemberg, "Las Vírgenes Generalas: Acción guerrera y práctica religiosa en las campañas del Alto Perú y el Río de la Plata (1810–1818)," *Boletín del Instituto de Historia Argentina y Americana "Dr. Emilio Ravignani"* 35–6 (2011–2012), 11–41: 24–5.

[15] Jaime Valenzuela Márquez, "La militarización de las celebraciones públicas en el Chile de los Borbones y la Independencia," *Revista Complutense de Historia de América* 37 (2011), 173–98: 186.

[16] Johnson, "Military as Catalyst," 27.

ocean to safety, taking as many of their possessions as they could hurl aboard. It was a grim voyage. King João VI forbade any discussion of politics or evacuation itself; the weather and the sea were the only safe, neutral topics permitted.[17] Nevertheless, João was quick to reward his British allies. In January 1808, even before arriving at their destination, he issued a *Carta Régia*, or official proclamation, that opened Brazil to the trade of all friendly nations, with His British Majesty's merchants receiving preferential status. Portuguese goods, merchandise intended for the Portuguese Crown, or cargo brought over on Portuguese ships were exempted from tariffs, but realistically these clauses functioned mainly as a salve to wounded national pride; the declaration of free trade enormously benefited British manufacturers at the expense of almost everyone else.

The fleet stopped briefly at Salvador de Bahia before landing at Rio de Janeiro on 7 March. The city of 50,000–60,000 people soon buckled under the strain of approximately 24,000 new Portuguese arrivals who flooded into the city over the course of the next decade. That number, of course, was dwarfed by the approximately 18,000–20,000 enslaved Africans who were unloaded and sold into the interior at the Valongo slave market each year. A flurry of activity took place as residents of Rio de Janeiro prepared to receive royalty to live among them. They pushed slave laborers to work punishing hours painting buildings, planting gardens, building shade covers for carriages, constructing new housing, and repairing roads.[18] The city had no functioning sewer system and received its water from a small number of decrepit public fountains. The newly arrived aristocracy expropriated the nicest houses around the Palace Square for themselves, forcing local elites to relocate to shabbier homes at some distance. Although Brazil was now the seat of empire, with all the pomp and growing demand that status brought with it, there were drawbacks as well. The Court quickly created the Intendência Geral do Policía, which enforced more rigorous discipline on residents, particularly slaves and freed Blacks, and issued a barrage of regulations to control everything from housing standards to cleanliness to manners and protocol. Similarly, many of the local artisans found themselves out of work as their own textiles or goods could not compete with British and French imports. And, the constant parades and illuminations and rituals of obeisance

---

[17] Kirsten Schulz, *Tropical Versailles: Empire, Monarchy, and the Portuguese Royal Court in Rio de Janeiro, 1808–1821* (New York: Routledge, 2001), 16, 69.

[18] Diane Brand, "Sets and Extras: Ephemeral Architecture and Urban Ceremony in Rio de Janeiro, 1808–1821," *Journal of Latin American Cultural Studies* 15:3 (2006), 263–79: 263.

that included kneeling and hand-kissing rankled local governors who had been accustomed to the autonomy that comes with distance from the center.[19]

Along with the newly granted preferential trade status, the British navy consolidated its station at Rio de Janeiro and young British servicemen offered their military knowledge to the Prince Regent in a variety of ways. British diplomatic interests were guided by the firm hand and clear leadership of Percy Clinton Sydney Smythe, the 6th Viscount Strangford, who remained at his post for several years, facilitating contacts between the Spanish American creoles and the British government and deftly funneling them much-needed support. British citizens resident in Brazil helped to found the Bank of Brazil, established maritime shipping companies, opened warehouses and granaries, engaged in mapping and biological expeditions, facilitated vaccine programs, and built colleges and schools. John Mawe undertook a survey of the mining and agriculture in a book he dedicated to the Prince Regent of Brazil saying "I have taken the liberty to summarize some improvements, which in my humble opinion, would tend to increase the revenue of Your Royal Highness, and multiply the resources of the country."[20] In fact, the British even imported ice skates to the country, which elicited much curiosity before being melted down and used to make tools instead.[21] Of course, the one other arena in which the British government exerted its influence was in its insistence on measures intended to lead to the abolition of the African slave trade. Ironically, as the European-descended population expanded, so did the demand for enslaved labor; the number of Africans disembarked and sold in Rio de Janeiro in 1807 was 9,689 and just four years later the figure was 23,230 souls.[22] By the 1820s, opposition to the slave trade would be the hallmark of British foreign and commercial policy toward the by-then-independent Brazilian Empire.

The nature of the contact changed dramatically during the summer of 1810 when the so-called Grafton Street Symposium took place.[23] In a separate but similar process, the creole juntas in Caracas and Buenos Aires sent representatives to London to consult with the British government, to

[19] Brand, "Sets and Extras," 269.
[20] John Mawe, *Travels in the Interior of Brazil* (London: Longman, Hurst, Rees, Orme and Brown, 1812), iii.
[21] Anyda Marchant, *Viscount Mauá and the Empire of Brazil* (Berkeley and Los Angeles: University of California Press, 1965), 24–5.
[22] Laurentino Gomes, *1808: The Flight of the Emperor* (New York: Lyons Press, 2013), 172.
[23] José Luis Salcedo Bastardo, *Crucible of Americanism: Miranda's London House* (Caracas: Lagoven, 1981), 19.

Great Britain and Latin American Independence

seek its aid and protection, and to initiate their existence as autonomous diplomatic entities. On Friday, 8 June 1810, the *Gazeta de Caracas* announced that Simón Bolívar, Luis López Méndez, and Andrés Bello were leaving on board *HMS General Wellington* with a special mission to deliver messages to the British government. Foreign Secretary Richard Colley Wellesley would only agree to meet them in a private capacity at his personal residence, Apsley House, in order to prevent any chance that the contact could be construed as official. The group had five meetings and exchanged several sets of notes and comments but, given the circumstances in which Britain was Spain's wartime ally against Napoleon, any action had to be deferred.[24] Matías de Yrigoyen arrived from the Río de la Plata on 8 August with a similar mission, held several similar meetings with Wellesley, and reported back that although a future envoy may meet with better luck, the "perplexity of the moment" meant that realistically nothing could be done.[25]

Although the diplomatic meetings had limited success, the Caracas and Río de la Plata delegations befriended other Spanish Americans in London: Venezuelan José Tovar Ponte, Ecuadorean José María de Antepara, the Mexican Marqués del Apartado, and an unnamed Peruvian. Miranda introduced them to his British society friends and took them on tours of sights like the gardens at Richmond and Hampton Court, the Greenwich Royal Observatory, and the ever-active Docklands. They dined with abolitionist William Wilberforce and utilitarian philosopher Jeremy Bentham, and toured Joseph Lancaster's model monitorial school on Borough Road. Daniel Florencio O'Leary later reported that while in London, Bolívar "dedicated and applied himself diligently and assiduously to the study of the British Constitution, and so great was his admiration that he resolved, if he ever had sufficient influence in his homeland, to transplant these institutions there."[26] Bolívar returned to Caracas in September 1810, Miranda followed in December, and Yrigoyen departed for Buenos Aires in January 1811. The Grafton Street Symposium was over. British politicians had successfully deferred the Spanish Americans' requests for recognition and thus avoided a breakdown in their own wartime alliance with Spain.

One of the most perennially interesting and controversial subjects of Britain's relationship with Latin America during the independence period has

---

[24] National Archives of Great Britain, Foreign Office, FO 72/106.

[25] Matías Yrigoyen to Sr. Don Manuel Belgrano, London, 10 September 1810, Argentina, Archivo General de la Nación, Sala X 1-1-2, ff. 17–20

[26] Daniel Florencio O'Leary, *Bolívar and the War of Independence: Memorias del General Daniel Florencia O'Leary* (Austin: University of Texas Press, 1975), 77.

been the debate over the existence and nature of a Masonic connection. Most scholars agree that Francisco de Miranda was at the center of a conspiratorial group based in London and affiliated with a branch in Cádiz, the collectivity of which is called variously the Gran Reunión Americana, the Gran Oriente Americana, or the Sociedad de Caballeros Racionales.[27] Although few records remain, it is clear that a fraternal association with the motto "Union, Firmness, Valor" was founded in Miranda's home where the Caracas deputies stayed. Members included Argentines José de San Martín, Carlos María de Alvear, José Matías Zapiola and his brother Carlos, the Chilavert brothers, Ramón Eduardo Anchoriz, Mexicans Wenceslao Villaurrutia, the Marqués del Apartado, Servando Teresa de Mier, and Venezuelans Luis López Méndez, and Andrés Bello.[28] In late 1811, Alvear wrote a letter to his "most esteemed brother" Rafael Mérida in Caracas informing him of London lodge news, including the establishment of a corresponding lodge in Philadelphia, and the imprisonment of "our brother Román de la Luz" for his role in a foiled Masonic conspiracy in Havana, and railing against "the Despotic Spanish Government."[29] Membership lists show that the Masonic network diffused outward from London and included a transcontinental American Lodge No. 2, and Lodge No. 3 centered in the Caribbean basin (Cuba, Mexico, Guatemala, Caracas, Santa Fé de Bogotá). The famous Lautaro Lodge to which most active patriots in Chile belonged had a definite connection to the London lodge via Bernardo O'Higgins and José de San Martín, and there is some indication that Los Guadalupes, a Masonic-inflected conspiratorial group active in New Spain in the 1810s did too.

The most dedicated and prominent Latin American Freemason in the independence era was the Brazilian expatriate Hipólito José da Costa who was a long-time London resident and editor of a monthly journal called *Correio Brasiliense* (1810–1821). Da Costa had come to London in 1802 to affiliate four Portuguese lodges with the London Grand Orient. While there, he became close friends with Master Mason, the Duke of Sussex, sixth son of King George III, for whom he eventually named his son Augustus Frederick. In 1813, da Costa was initiated as Grand Master Mason for the English

---

[27] María Teresa Berruezo León, "La propagandista de la logia mirandina en Londres," in José Antonio Ferrer Benimeli, ed., *Masonería española y americana* (Zaragoza: Centro de Estudios Históricos de la Masonería Española, 1991), vol. 1, 95–113: 105.

[28] Carlos María de Alvear to the Vice Presidente de la Logia No. 4, London, 21 October 1811, Mexico, Archivo General de la Nación, Indiferente de Guerra, vol. 22, ff. 29–30. Copy.

[29] Alvear to Mérida, London, 28 October 1811, Mexico, AGN, Indiferente de Guerra, vol. 22, ff. 27–9.

county of Rutlandshire and three years later was appointed the President of the Board of Finance of the United Grand Lodge of England and held the position until his death in 1823.[30] Da Costa was perhaps the outlier among notable independence era figures in the sense that Freemasonry provided a central organizing principle of his life. For most Latin American men who joined a group with a Masonic character in the independence era, the affiliation operated as a political fraternity, one that introduced a secret set of oaths, signs, and signals that could foster trust and confirm reliability across distances. It also granted them access to private information and material resources and signaled their attachment to a global vision of fraternity, equality, religious tolerance, and rational science that was neither French nor Jacobin in origin. Membership also facilitated personal connections between Latin American Masons and the British resident merchant and diplomatic communities.

## Road to Recognition, 1814–1824

Since Britain was the military ally of both Spain and Portugal during the Peninsular War, its politicians could not openly support any of the many autonomous juntas that sprung up in the early years of the 1810s, although they offered the patriots crucial naval protection under the guise of defending them against French incursions. Between the years of 1808 and 1812, Lord Castlereagh used all his considerable diplomatic skill to try to mediate some sort of new commonwealth arrangement between Spain and its colonies which would grant them significant autonomy – particularly in terms of commercial relations – while remaining subject to the Crown. Discussions with Spanish prime minister Eusebio Bardaxi y Azara proceeded relatively well, but eventually broke down over a secret clause which required Britain to break off all communication with America in the event that the juntas rejected the plan.[31] Not surprisingly, none of the representatives who came to London from New Granada (José María del Real, Manuel Palacio Fajardo), or Chile (Antonio José de Irisarri), or Buenos Aires (Manuel de Sarratea) were interested in reconciliation; the only notable exception was the mission of Bernardino Rivadavia and Manuel Belgrano, who came to Europe in

---

[30] J. M. Hamill, "Hyppolito Joseph da Costa 1774–1823. Masonic Biographical Notes," Freemasonry Museum and Archives, London, Hipólito José da Costa file.

[31] Henry Wellesley to Sr D. Eusebio de Bardaxi y Azara, Cádiz, 30 January 1812, Transl. Copy, Archivo General de Simancas, Estado 8.285, f. 40.

1815 to explore the possibility of establishing an American monarchy, perhaps inspired by the example of the Portuguese monarch's ongoing residence at Rio de Janeiro long after Napoleon's threat to Lisbon had dissipated. Fernando VII was incensed at the mere mention of the idea, and nothing ever came of it.

One of the most obvious and well-studied components of British involvement in Latin American independence is the participation of its citizens in the military and naval campaigns as officers and enlisted men. From the earliest days, and for many reasons, English, Irish, and Scottish men joined their lives to the cause of Latin American independence and actively fought and died for it. In 1808, British medical doctor James "Diego" Paroissien, who joined the conspiratorial circle around Saturnino Rodríguez Peña in Buenos Aires and found himself arrested and tried for treason against the Spanish Crown, was released and spent the next twenty years serving the Spanish American patriot cause, including roles with José de San Martín's Army of the Andes and later as a diplomatic envoy for Peru. Spanish guerrilla Francisco Xavier Mina fled to asylum in London in 1815, received a government pension and support from prominent politicians like Lord Holland and Sir Robert Peel, and outfitted an expedition that left Liverpool in April 1816 with the goal of liberating Mexico. Mariano Renovales followed the same route with the same intent a year later.

Latin Americans had come to London in search of men and material aid for their battles against the Spanish royalists since the days of the Grafton Street Symposium in 1810. After the Napoleonic Wars ended in 1815, Spanish American envoys in London seized on the chance to recruit its veterans to continue their fight against tyranny by joining patriotic armies abroad. Luis López Méndez and José María del Real set up offices in London, Edinburgh, and Dublin and advertised widely in the best newspapers in order to attract recruits with promises of good and regularly paid, salaries, promotions, and glorious service to the great cause of liberty. Méndez's house was sometimes called the colonel factory because it was so common to grant a promotion of one full rank to each officer who signed up.[32] Their efforts were certainly not secret. The newspapers were filled with advertisements for uniforms, saddles, buttons, swords, tents, and all the other accoutrements of war. Colonel Campbell and his marching band used the park in Chelsea for their daily rehearsals, and there was no way to hide the

---

[32] James Hackett, *Narrative of an Expedition Which Sailed from London in 1817 to Join the Spanish American Patriots* (London: John Murray, 1817), v–vi.

ships outfitting in ports. The Spanish ambassador, the Duke of San Carlos, lodged protests with Lord Castlereagh at the Foreign Office, most of which were met merely with tepid assurances of concern and promises of action. Matthew Brown estimates that approximately 6,000–7,000 foreign adventurers enlisted in the Colombian army, and perhaps 1,000 more in its navy. This is a figure that coincides roughly with Colombian historian José Manuel Restrepo, who calculated 5,800 British and Irish soldiers and hundreds of sailors, and who considers their participation to have been decisive.[33] Of these, the vast majority came over with the British or Irish Legions.

Great Britain's formal political recognition of Latin American independence was deferred but could not be avoided and, in the end, came about relatively quickly. The three major British statesmen of the era – William Pitt the Younger, Lord Castlereagh, and George Canning – all favored the change, and even gave it significant moral and material support within the constraints of their particular strategic moment. The Prince Regent (later George IV), however, was openly hostile to the idea and threw up as many obstacles as his position would allow. But by then, the government and merchants (and even some Latin Americans themselves), realized that they were in competition with the United States to establish formal, bilateral relations and to protect commercial access. In a special message to Congress in March 1822, President James Monroe had recommended recognition of South American independence, and the revanchist powers of the Holy Alliance had their own schemes to undermine British influence abroad. Accordingly, then, in September 1822, Earl Bathurst summed up the commonly held sentiment when he wrote in a letter to the Duke of Wellington that political recognition "may be regarded as a matter of time than of principle." And yet that was not entirely true. That very same month, Secretary of State for Foreign Affairs Canning told the Duke that "no State in the New World will be recognized by Great Britain which has not frankly and completely abolished the trade in Slaves."[34] When President Monroe

---

[33] Matthew Brown, *Adventuring through the Spanish Colonies: Simón Bolívar, Foreign Mercenaries and the Birth of New Nations* (Liverpool: University of Liverpool Press, 2006), 39; Matthew Brown, "Esclavitud, castas, y extrangeros en las guerras de la Independencia de Colombia," *Historia y Sociedad* 10 (2004), 109–26: 111; José Manuel Restrepo, *Historia de la Revolución de la República de Colombia* (Besanzon: Imprenta de José Jacquin, 1858), vol. III, 84.

[34] Earl Bathurst to Duke of Wellington, Downing Street, 14 September 1822, in Charles Kingsley Webster, ed., *Britain and the Independence of Latin America 1812–1830: Select Documents from the Foreign Office Archives* (London: Oxford University Press, 1938), vol. II, 71–2; George Canning to Duke of Wellington (27 September 1822) in Webster, *Britain and Latin American Independence*, vol. II, 73–4.

issued his famous policy statement that came to bear his name – the Monroe Doctrine – on 2 December 1823, the additional public pressure meant British politicians could no longer defer or avoid the matter.

By early 1824, merchants from London, Liverpool, Manchester, Birmingham, Glasgow, Edinburgh and endless smaller towns sent petitions to Parliament almost daily demanding their government recognize Latin American independence. Dozens of high-level Cabinet meetings were held that year, including one in July in which ministers tried to tread carefully around many potential destabilizing choices. They wanted to recognize Spanish American independence but still uphold existing treaty obligations with Spain and Portugal, to guarantee access to commercial markets and end the slave trade, all while remaining quite aware that Britain had its own colonies in the Western Hemisphere which it did not particularly care to lose.[35] When the long-awaited decision finally came, on 7 February 1825, King George IV refused to make the announcement, claiming that he had lost his false teeth and that gout prevented him from attending Parliament. Instead, Lord Eldon, in his capacity as Lord High Chancellor and despite his own vehement personal objections, rose in Parliament to announce the recognition of Mexico, Buenos Aires (now Argentina), and Colombia as independent states and the government's intention to invite envoys to negotiate treaties of peace, friendship, and commerce, and to send out its own consuls to the Americas.[36] Although there were exchanges of consuls and lower-level agreements, the British government deferred taking formal steps to recognize Chile, Peru, and Guatemala until 1831, claiming they needed proof that those countries were stable.[37]

Although there had already been extensive public and private exchanges between Great Britain and Latin America, once formal recognition had been exchanged and ratified, it meant a whole range of new relationships could be created without the lingering need to provide plausible deniability or engage

---

[35] Cabinet Minute (Foreign Office, 23 July 1824), West Yorkshire Archive Service, George Canning Manuscripts, bundle 131.

[36] Mariano Schlez, ed., *The Woodbine Parish Report on the Revolutions in South America (1822): The Foreign Office and Early British Intelligence on Latin America* (Liverpool: Liverpool University Press, 2022); Kaufman, *British Policy and the Independence of Latin America*, 179. Marco Antonio Landavazo, "La reconquista, el príncipe y la isla: Gran Bretaña y el reconocimiento español de la independencia de México," in Will Fowler and Marcela Terrazas y Basante, eds., *Diplomacia, negocios y política: Ensayos sobre la relación entre México y el Reino Unido en el siglo XIX* (Mexico: UNAM, Instituto de Investigaciones Históricas, 2018), 45–78.

[37] Andrés Baeza Ruz, *Contacts, Collisions and Relationships: Britons and Chileans in the Independence Era, 1806–1831* (Liverpool: Liverpool University Press, 2019), 217.

in subterfuge to placate Spain and Portugal. As Canning himself said in November 1825: "And so, behold! The New World is established and if we do not throw it away, it is ours."[38] One of the first joint actions was an effort to crack down on privateering vessels that had preyed upon ships of all nations carrying human and other cargo, which is a clear indication that the strengthening commercial ties and ending the slave trade were among the most urgent priorities. In 1826, Simón Bolívar decided to call a meeting of all the new states to discuss issues of hemispheric security, mutual defense, and cultural union, something later known as Pan-Americanism. The so-called Panama Amphyction, or Panama Congress, involved representatives from Gran Colombia, Peru, Central America, and Mexico. Great Britain sent Edward Dawkins with observer status. The United States and Brazil did not attend, and Haiti was not invited.

In 1826, Mexican Carlos María de Bustamante dedicated his edition of an earlier Jesuit history of Nezahualcoyotl and the grand city-state of Texcoco to "the Very Honorable George Canning . . . a minister who in our times used his good offices in Europe to consolidate our hard-fought independence for which we had long waited with bated breath. . . I offer my worthy gratitude to your Excellence for all that you have contributed to our happiness."[39] Thousands of miles away, in Buenos Aires, the Argentines took up a collection and raised a statue of George Canning. The newly elevated Colombian Minister to the Court of St. James, Manuel José Hurtado, also presented Canning with a special medal that the Congress had struck and which Bolívar sent over in his honor.[40] It was in this context that Canning made a rare display of hubris in his famous comment to Parliament: "I called the New World into existence, to redress the balance of the Old."[41]

Since the late eighteenth century, British Quakers and reformists had been lobbying for an end to the slave trade, an "odious commerce" that turned men into merchandise. In 1806 and 1807, Parliament passed a series of Abolition Acts that first banned British participation in the foreign slave trade, and then extended the ban to British dominions as well. From that

---

[38] Canning, quoted in Leslie Bethell, *George Canning and Latin American Independence* (London: Canning House, 1970), 12.

[39] [Lorenzo Boturini Benaducci], *Texcoco en los últimos tiempos de sus antiguos reyes* (Mexico: Imprenta de Mariano Galván Rivera, 1826), dedication page.

[40] British Library, George Canning Papers, Add MS 89143/2/22/7.

[41] George Canning, "Address on the King's Message, Respecting Portugal," in Great Britain, *Hansard's Parliamentary Debates*, House of Commons, 12 December 1826, vol. 16, 397.

point onward, and increasingly after the end of the Napoleonic Wars, one of the central aims of British foreign policy was "the international abolition of the transatlantic trade in African slaves."[42] The association of Great Britain with abolition circulated widely and clearly filtered down to farms and barracks; in April 1816, for example, slaves in Barbados expressed an awareness that abolitionist William Wilberforce existed and somehow promised to be their savior.[43] Throughout Spanish America, patriot legislators discussed the British legislation in their own debates. In Mexico, for example, a special study group within the Junta Provisional Gubernativa crafted a decree that outlawed African slavery, acknowledging the influence of the British juridical approach that reflected both humanitarian and pragmatic concerns.[44] The Congress of Angostura formally ended the slave trade in New Granada in 1819, intending to recruit the freedmen into patriot armed forces. Two years later, the Congress at Cúcuta emancipated all children born to enslaved women once they reached the age of eighteen.[45] Chile's Constitution of 1823 definitively abolished slavery throughout the country. In 1824, the Central American Congress passed its own abolition act.

William Wilberforce and Thomas Clarkson took a particular interest in the fate of Haiti and its Emperor Henry Christophe. Both men were long-time leaders of the abolitionist movement in Parliament and in the press, and both engaged in an extended correspondence with Christophe in which they offered him advice on governing strategy and international relations. They also facilitated introductions for activists, educators, investors, and writers to gain the Emperor's trust. Clarkson, in particular, acted as a sort of proxy agent for Christophe at the meeting of European powers at Aix-la-Chapelle in 1818, passing messages to Russian Tsar Alexander and surveying other powers' attitudes toward any potential French demands to reclaim Saint-Domingue and reinstate slavery on the island.[46] As I have noted elsewhere:

---

[42] Leslie Bethell, "The Independence of Brazil and the Abolition of the Brazilian Slave Trade: Anglo-Brazilian Relations, 1822–1826," *Journal of Latin American Studies* 1:2 (November 1969), 116.

[43] Manuel Barcia, "A Not-so-Common Wind: Slave Revolts in the Age of Revolutions in Cuba and Brazil," *Review: The Journal of the Fernand Braudel Center* 31:2 (2008), 169–93: 175–6.

[44] Mexico, Junta Provisional Gubernativa, *Dictamen de la comisión de esclavos* (Mexico City: Imprenta Imperial de D. Alejandro Valdes, 1821).

[45] Robin Blackburn, "Haiti, Slavery, and the Age of Democratic Revolution," *The William and Mary Quarterly* 63:4 (2006), 643–74: 648.

[46] Thomas Clarkson to King Henry Christophe I, London, 26 August 1818, British Library, Thomas Clarkson Papers, Add MS 41266, ff. 37–40.

Christophe wished to turn his citizenry into an outpost of Englishness, an unprecedented cultural experiment which included the introduction of the English language and the Anglican religion along with the Lancasterian school system. During Christophe's short reign, British teachers, pedagogical methods, and classroom materials were imported to support the King's social agenda. Imported Englishness characterized the complicated cultural agenda of the first post-colonial French Caribbean nation.[47]

Brazil and Cuba were the Latin American countries that were most directly affected by the British government's diplomatic, commercial, and naval pressure intended to end the slave trade. Both countries experienced a dramatic expansion of the use of slaves during the nineteenth century, during which time their leaders both courted British capital and markets while at the same time subverting the Foreign Office's attempts to link abolition of the slave trade to that same access. A major Spanish–British treaty on the Abolition of the Slave Trade was signed in 1817 which codified the rights of the British navy to intercept and seize cargoes of enslaved Africans. They were never very successful, though. Ten years later, in 1827, the *Bristol Mercury* reported "[t]his abominable traffic, we regret to find, is still prosecuted with energy from the island of Cuba. By an arrival at Charleston, we learn that a schooner from the coast of Africa, with 250 negroes, came to anchor about four leagues off Trinidad de Cuba on the 29th of June. She landed the negroes at night and entered on the 31st under Dutch colours . . . This is her third trip within a short time."[48] The Foreign Office tried to assert the same pressure in Brazil dating from the time when the Navy transported the Royal Family to Rio de Janeiro. In 1823, as part of the process of establishing relations with the new Brazilian Empire and mediating an agreement with Portugal, Canning expressed his understanding that both negotiating partners had agreed in principle to the "speedy abolition of the Slave Trade by the Brazilian Government."[49] Obviously that did not happen because slavery was not ended until 1888, but the British government regularly entered into agreements with the Brazilians to ameliorate or abolish aspects of the trade, including the creation of a Court of Mixed

---

[47] Karen Racine, "Imported Englishness: Henry Christophe's Educational Program in Haiti, 1811–1820," in Marcelo Caruso and Eugenia Roldán Vera, eds., *Learning from Abroad: The Reception of Liberalism in Education, Religion and Morality in Post-colonial Latin America* (London: Peter Lang, 2007), 205–30: 206.

[48] "Slave Trade," *Bristol Mercury* no. 1949 (20 August 1827).

[49] George Canning to Henry Chamberlain, Foreign Office, 5 August 1823, National Archives of Great Britain, FO 128/1, ff. 82–5.

Commission that would expand the definition of a *liberto* (liberated African), make arrangements to relocate some to the British West Indies, and extend domestic protections to others who remained.[50] Certainly in the case of both Cuba and Brazil, the abolition of slavery and the slave trade was deferred until the later decades of the nineteenth century, but it was never avoided as a topic of treaty-making (and treaty-breaking).

## Miners, Merchants, and Money in the 1820s

Alongside the military, political, and diplomatic influence of Great Britain in Latin American independence ran the constant effort to find and establish new commercial markets, secure access to raw materials (especially mines), and to gain profit and influence through loans made to the fledgling new republics. These strategies and structures, which persisted into the twentieth century, have been called informal empire. The British government established or retained formal colonies on important Caribbean islands and at British Honduras, but for the most part, preferred to exert its considerable influence through its merchant houses, local resident communities, mining partnerships, and bankers. To confuse matters – or perhaps rather to clarify them – in the early decades of the nineteenth century, the same person often exercised the offices of diplomatic consul and broker for the local expatriate commercial community. British economic influence came earliest in Brazil, the Río de la Plata region, and Chile, and was directly related to several phenomena: the presence of the British naval station in the South Atlantic; the invasions of Buenos Aires in 1806–1807; the dependence of the Portuguese court upon Great Britain during its Brazilian exile; and a growing rivalry with American merchants for access to the whaling grounds along the Pacific coast northward to California.

In 1818, David Barry arrived in Chile to seek out the rich coal deposits along the Bío-Bío River in the south. By 1821, he had sketched out and publicized a plan to transplant the English mining method known as "the Longwall system" and to recruit English, Cornish, and Welsh miners to do the work, and three years later, British-extracted Chilean coal was being used as energy sources aboard ships.[51] Much more significant, however, was the

---

[50] Beatriz G. Mamigonian, "In the Name of Freedom: Slave Trade Abolition, the Law and the Brazilian Branch of the African Emigration Scheme (Brazil–British West Indies, 1830s–1850s)," *Slavery & Abolition* 30:1 (2009), 41–66: 41.

[51] William Edmundson, *History of British Presence in Chile* (New York: Palgrave Macmillan, 2009), 148; Charles Centner, "Great Britain and Chilean Mining, 1830–1914," *Economic History Review* 12:1–2 (1942), 76–82: 76–7.

intense interest of British investors in the potential to realize windfalls in the silver and copper mines of the northern and Chaco regions. To give a sense of the flurry of speculation, four major joint English and Chilean mining companies raised capital in London during the first six months of 1825 alone: the Chilean Mining Association (January 1825, £1,000,000), the Anglo-Chilian Mining Association (January 1825, £1,500,000), the Chilean & Peruvian Mining Association (March 1825, £1,000,000) and the United Chilian Mining Association (June 1825, £500,000).[52] Antonio José de Irisarri, a close ally of Bernardo O'Higgins, came to London in 1819 and initiated a campaign that eventually resulted in a loan contract with Hullett Brothers for £1,000,000 in 1822, claiming in its prospectus that Chile's internal revenues alone were more than fourteen times the amount required to service the loan.[53] Once news reached Chile, the government quickly sent back its repudiation, but the bonds were already circulating in the market and suffered great losses when the debt bubble popped in 1825. Nevertheless, these London funds provided a good portion of the funds needed to equip the expedition against Spanish royalists in Chiloé. These mining and loan ventures were, without exception, failures and all ceased to exist by 1830.

The British merchant community established in Valparaiso was more successful and had a significant long-term impact on the demographics of the country's elite. When the Chilean government threw open the country to free trade with all nations in 1811, John and Joseph Crosbie quickly put together the first legal shipment and sent a cargo ship full of hardware, tools, wool, cotton, and linen to the country. By 1817, British exports to Chile had reached £28,888 and just five years later topped £443,580.[54] The British community grew just as rapidly and, because foreigners were not permitted to engage in retail sales or coastal trade, its members formed business partnerships and marital relationships with prominent local families. For this reason, some of the most prominent surnames in Chile have British origins: Mackenna, Blest, Edwards, MacAllister, Green, O'Brien, Gibbs, Fox, Andrews, Bunster, and many others. Resident María Graham described Valparaiso in 1821 as follows: "English tailors, shoe-makers, and innkeepers

---

[52] John Mayo, "The Development of British Interests in Chile's Norte Chico in the Early Nineteenth Century," *The Americas* 57:3 (2001), 363–94: 372.

[53] "Préstamo hecho a Chile de un millón pesos," Yale University, Stirling Library, Latin American MSS 307J, Box R, folder 195.

[54] Benjamín Vicuña Mackenna, *The First Britons in Valparaíso* (Valparaíso: Gordon Henderson & Cía, 1884), 19; Jay Kinsbruner, "The Political Influence of the British Merchants Resident in Chile during the O'Higgins Administration, 1817–1823," *The Americas* 27:1 (1970), 26–39: 27.

Figure 15.1 The British Arch in Valparaíso, Chile, a modern-day memorial.

hang out their signs in every street, and the preponderance of the English language over every other spoken in the chief streets would make one fancy Valparaiso a coast town in England" (Figure 15.1).[55]

A similar pattern could be observed in the Río de la Plata and its successor republics Argentina and Uruguay. Despite the ill-will that the invasions of 1806–1807 initially generated toward Great Britain, attitudes changed rapidly. The *porteño* (port-based, or Buenos Aires) middle classes and merchants provided the leadership for the May Revolution of 1810, and one of their most cherished projects was the establishment of free trade. Like its Chilean counterpart, the Argentine government authorized funds to be raised in London, in their case from a respected financial house called Baring Brothers, which subsequently offered shares of a £1,000,000 loan to the British public. Only about half of the money actually arrived in government coffers, most of which they applied to infrastructure projects like a harbor

---

[55] María Graham, Lady Callcott, *Journal of a Residence in Chile in the Year 1822* (London: Longman, Hurst, Rees, Orme, Brown, and Green, 1824), 131.

and waterworks (directed by Scottish engineer James Bevan), the construction of frontier defense, and to capitalize the newly founded Banco Nacional.[56] The Barings loan has remained a controversial subject for historians of the Argentine economy, in part because the financiers retained £280,000 for themselves as commission and advance payment of future interest. In 1828, the loan went into default and it was not until 1857 that the government returned to the outstanding debt and repaid with interest. Interest from mining companies was less pronounced here, but there were some British-Argentine companies founded with the intent of exploiting some of the silver in La Rioja province and related agricultural support industries. President Bernardino Rivadavia and the brothers William and John Parish Robertson founded the Río de la Plata Mining Company (and its successor, the Famatina Mining Company) in London in 1824; the company Barker Beaumont operated the Río de la Plata Agricultural Association (which also sought contracts for settlement colonies); and the Robertson brothers dominated economic activity in the littoral with the Colonia Monte Grande among several other ventures.[57]

British miners, merchants, and bankers took great interest in Mexico in the 1820s. After independence, Iturbide found himself at the head of a new state with an empty treasury and an exhausted populace. His friend and ersatz agent in London, Francisco de Borja Migoni, contracted a £3.2 million loan from the Goldschmidt & Company in 1824, which was more than twice the amount that Congress had authorized for the immediate needs of state.[58] Migoni engaged in further negotiations and contracted a second Mexican loan for the same amount with the merchant banking firm of Barclay, Herring, Richardson, but while the contracts were crossing the ocean for consideration and ratification, the Mexican Congress ousted Iturbide and sent its own Minister Plenipotentiary, José Mariano Michelena, to London to take charge of affairs. As the two men openly feuded about who was the legitimate Mexican representative, the financial sector, investing public, and

---

[56] H. S. Ferns, "Beginning of British Investment in Argentina," *Economic History Review* 4:3 (1952), 341–52: 347; D. C. M. Platt, "Foreign Finance in Argentina for the First Half-Century of Independence," *Journal of Latin American Studies* 15:1 (1983), 23–47: 27.

[57] Alina Silveira, "Nuevos actores entren en escena: Los británicos en el Río de la Plata, 1800–1850," in Mónica Alabert, María Alejandra Fernández, and Mariana A. Pérez, eds., *Buenos Aires, una sociedad que se transforma* (Buenos Aires: Prometeo Libros, 2011), 27–57: 30n.

[58] Barbara Tenenbaum, "Taxation and Tyranny: Public Finance during the Iturbide Regime, 1821–1823," in Jaime E. Rodriguez O., ed., *The Independence of Mexico and the Creation of the New Nation* (Los Angeles: UCLA Latin American Studies, 1989), 201–13: 206.

jittery public began to lose faith in the stability of the country, and its reputation suffered.[59]

The mining companies were not far behind. The Real del Monte Mining Company operated in Pachuca and Michoacán, the Bolaños Company in Jalisco and Zacatecas, the Tlalpujahua Company in Mexico and Michoacán, the Anglo-Mexican Mining Company in Guanajuato, Querétaro, and San Luis Potosí, the United Mexican Mining Company in Guanajuato, Jalisco, Zacatecas, Mexico, Chihuahua, and Oaxaca, and the Mexican Mining Company in Veracruz, Zacatecas, and Oaxaca. As with the mines in Argentina, there was a close collaboration between government officials and foreign entrepreneurs which led to charges of corruption, favoritism, and labor displacement. Lucas Alamán, statesman and foreign minister for much of the 1820s, was a director of the United Mexican Mining Company which worked the rich Rayas mines, who regularly took to the pages of *El Sol* to make the public case for foreign investment to rebuild Mexico's devastated infrastructure. Locals remained unconvinced. In April 1826, poor townsfolk shouted abuse and hurled rocks at Cornish workers who had just arrived and were on their way to work mines at Vetagrande; the Mexican government was obliged to provide an armed escort and posted guards at the company residences.[60]

## Education and Culture

There can be no doubt at all that the independence era's leaders were acutely sensitive about their perceived status as an intellectual backwater and were anxious to participate more fully as equals both in international scientific collaboration and in literary exchanges. Ever pragmatic, they also recognized the economic value that a literate population represented, and the vast potential of the printed word for nation-building purposes. As Guatemalan statesman José Cecilio del Valle bluntly put it: "Chinautla is poor because it is ignorant; London is powerful because it is enlightened."[61] Education and education reform was never far from the hearts of Spanish American patriot

---

[59] Richard Salvucci, *Politics, Markets and Mexico's "London's Debt,"* 1823–1887 (Cambridge: Cambridge University Press, 2009), 48.

[60] Hira de Gortari Rabiela, "La minería durante la guerra de independencia y los primeros años del México independiente, 1810–1824," in Rodríguez O., ed., *The Independence of Mexico*, 129–61: 159; Torcuato S. Di Tella, "The Dangerous Classes in Early Nineteenth Century Mexico," *Journal of Latin American Studies* 5:1 (1973), 79–105: 86.

[61] José Cecilio del Valle, "Ilustración," in *Sistema político y otros escritos* (Tegucigalpa: Secretaría de Cultura y Turismo, 1980), 53.

leaders, who revealed their own personal predilections by sending their children to school in England: José de San Martín, Bernardino Rivadavia, Agustín de Iturbide, Vicente Rocafuerte, Chile's prominent Toro family, and Guatemala's Aycinena and García Granados families are among those who sent their youngest members to be trained in English or Scottish schools in the 1820s. Others, like Simón Bolívar, Francisco de Paula Santander, Bernardo O'Higgins, and Lucas Alamán became convinced that Joseph Lancaster's system of mutual education, known as the monitorial method, offered Spanish America a cost-efficient, effective way to educate large numbers to basic literacy in a short amount of time. They contracted with the British and Foreign School Society to send out teachers instructed in the Lancasterian method to aid them in their national projects (Figure 15.2).

In 1810, Simón Bolívar made a point of touring Lancaster's London Borough Road school during his brief summertime visit, and promised to send over two Venezuelan youths to learn the monitorial system from the master himself. Their association lasted for nearly twenty years; in 1824, Bolívar invited Lancaster and his family to come to Caracas to superintend a school for Colombian youth, and the Liberator himself even made a grand speech at Lancaster's wedding to Maria Robinson in February 1827. Their professional relationship, however, soon soured over unpaid wages, poor facilities, and a fundamental incompatibility between two outsized personalities.[62] Nevertheless, the Lancasterian model, as it was later propagated by the British and Foreign School Society (BFSS) – itself working through the British and Foreign Bible Society (BFBS) – exerted a tremendous degree of influence over the entire generation of Latin American independence leaders. The BFSS Register of Students indicates eight Spanish American names, and its register of teachers who were sent out shows two British teachers being commissioned and trained for service in Buenos Aires and Chile in 1818 and 1820 respectively, and its *Annual Report* for 1825 mentions that one school-mistress was being trained for a Lancasterian girls' school in "South America."[63] Future president of Ecuador Vicente Rocafuerte and Colombian diplomat José María Vergara both were active voting members of the BFSS during their time in London in the 1820s. Bernardino Rivadavia, Bernardo O'Higgins, and Lucas Alamán all were active proponents of

---

[62] The text of the wedding toast, dated 2 February 1827, can be found at the American Antiquarian Society, Lancaster Papers, box 13, folder 7.

[63] West London Institute of Higher Education, Brunel University, British and Foreign School Society Archives; *British and Foreign School Society Annual Report* (May 1825), 38. The school almost certainly was the Lancasterian Girls School of Buenos Aires.

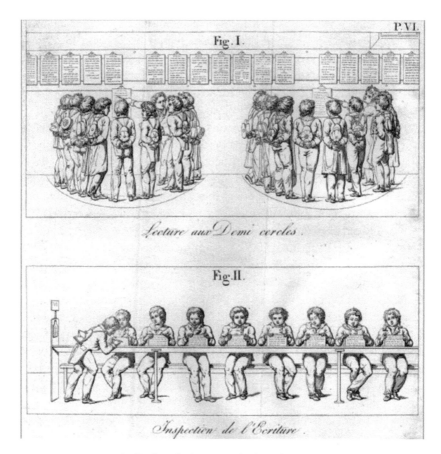

Figure 15.2 Monitorial school method. Top, each class of students is arranged in a semi-circle around its monitor, who indicates the words to be read on the reading board attached to the wall. Bottom, the monitor checks the writing exercises prepared by each of his classmates on a slate. From Joseph Hamel, *The Monitorial system, or the History of the Introduction and Spread of This Method through the Efforts of Doctor Bell and J. Lancaster and Others* (Paris: Colas, 1818).

Lancasterian schools in their new nations and openly supported James Thomson, the agent of both the BFSS and BFBS, who toured Spanish America setting up schools and selling translated New Testaments as texts.

The relationship between the new Spanish America patriot governments and British agent-evangelist-entrepreneur James Thomson was a complicated one, partly because of the man's idiosyncratic and messianic personality, but also because the newly active state intervention in the field of public education threatened one of the Catholic Church's traditional roles in society. Indeed, many of the most sensitive postindependence issues related to the role of religion in the newly independent states (secular education, burial of non-Catholic British residents in cemeteries, freedom of the press) arose from the patriot leaders' desire to accommodate British merchants and settlers and emulate its model of governance. It was the British aristocratic model adapted to a Spanish American environment: idealistic, educated, cosmopolitan elites desiring controlled social uplift through charitable works and their own benevolent acts. The educational goal was to create economically useful, moral subjects, not participatory citizens.[64]

In 1819, immediately after being elected President by the Congress of Angostura, Bolívar initiated a recruitment program and started to set up schools of mutual education throughout the territory under his control.[65] Francis Hall noted that there was a functioning Lancasterian school for sixty poor boys not only in the large Colombian municipalities of Boyacá and Bogotá but also in several other principal towns. In July 1822, San Martín and his aide Bernardo Monteagudo announced the dawn of a new order with the words "without education, there is no society" and then immediately proceeded to decree the establishment of a national school system, based on Lancasterian *escuelas normales*, which was to be placed under the superintendancy of James Thomson.[66] In 1823, Carlos Bello, the brother of Andrés Bello, opened a Lancasterian school in Caracas. On 21 January 1825, Bolívar introduced his pet scheme in Peru, issued a decree stating that "the Lancasterian system is the only method for the rapid and efficient method of public education," and therefore each department would establish a normal school according to its principles, and that poor youth of talent would be subsidized according to the founder's vision.[67] Lucas Alamán, Mexico's Secretary of State, who had twice traveled to London, actively sponsored the establishment of schools of mutual education and promoted

---

[64] Karen Racine, "Commercial Christianity: The British and Foreign Bible Society's Interest in Spanish America, 1805–1830," in Matthew Brown, ed., *Informal Empire in Latin America: Culture, Commerce and Capital* (Oxford: Blackwell, 2008), 78–98.

[65] Dario Guevara, "Bolívar y Lancaster," *Boletín de la Academia Nacional de la Historia* 51: 201 (1968), 81–90: 81.

[66] José de San Martín, "Decreto," Lima, 6 July 1822, printed as an appendix to *Peruvian Pamphlet, being an exposition of the administrative labors of the Peruvian Government* (London: Applegate, 1823), 86–7.

[67] Bolívar, "Decreto #17," Palacio Dictatorial, Lima, 31 January 1825, 4th Year of the Republic, Indiana University, Lilly Library, Latin American Manuscripts, Peru, box 12.

them in the various regional presses.[68] By 1828, the British and Foreign School Society was pleased to receive reports that Vice-Governor of the State of Veracruz Antonio López de Santa Anna had taken a personal interest in education, appointed a Lancasterian committee, and endowed their work with 30,000 pesos per year; indeed, it seemed that everywhere the schools had been established, they had been "hailed with joy, and the utmost zeal shewn in supporting them."[69]

Argentines were similarly affected by the practicality and promise of the Lancasterian system. In 1814, the Buenos Aires Assembly voted 40,000 pesos be given to Manuel Belgrano as a show of gratitude for the victory of Salta, and he asked them instead to use it to establish four primary schools of mutual education for the nation.[70] The author remembered that "a long time ago I read two small books written in England for use in these primary schools, and I admired them very much for their simplicity, wisdom, and the profound learning displayed by their author."[71] In November 1818, *El Censor* ran a series of articles advocating the monitorial system, which included transcripts from the meetings of the BFSS in London, which, they took care to emphasize, was supported by members of the aristocracy such as the Duke of Sussex, and important reformists like abolitionist William Wilberforce.[72] Joseph Lancaster's work was translated and published as *Origen y progresos del nuevo sistema de enseñanza mútua del Señor Lancaster*, making sure to stress that his system had spread rapidly throughout England because wealthy, patriotic citizens had sponsored its growth, to their great and disinterested credit; within three years, a subscription list for the Lancasterian Society of Buenos Aires contained 166 names, each of whom paid six pesos per year as a membership fee and often made a lump sum donation as well.[73] Bernardino Rivadavia took a personal interest in the school system and placed some of his own children in Lancasterian institutions. His secretary Ignacio Benito Núñez personally delivered papers from

[68] Lucas Alamán, "Instrucción para el establecimiento de escuelas, según los principios de enseñanza mutua," *La Sabatina Universal* 1 (28 September and 5 and 12 October 1822), 266–74, 279–99.

[69] *British and Foreign School Society Annual Report* (May 1827), 26 and (May 1828), 14. Santa Anna's decree no. 100 dated (Veracruz, 20 March 1828) in Indiana University, Lilly Library, F1227 Agency 385, broadsides.

[70] Margaret Hayne Harrison, *Captain of the Andes: The Life of Don José de San Martín, Liberator of Argentina, Chile and Peru* (New York: Smith, 1943), 61.

[71] "Educación de Lancaster y Bell," *El Censor* no. 7 (15 May 1817), 6–7.

[72] *El Censor*, no. 116 (21 November 1818) and no. 117 (28 November 1818).

[73] *Subscriptores y reglamento de la Sociedad Lancasteriana* (Buenos Aires: Imprenta de Hallet, 1823).

the BFSS to government officials in Buenos Aires when he returned home from London in 1825, telling its director that he was proud his native land was sharing in the light emanating from London to the rest of the world.[74] By the end of the decade, Lancasterian girls' schools were thriving in Buenos Aires, Mendoza, Montevideo, Santiago, and Lima.[75]

The greatest influence of the Lancasterian school system was probably found in Chile and the Río de la Plata, where Camilo Henríquez, Bernardino Rivadavia, and Bernardo O'Higgins all sought closer relations with Great Britain. In 1819, the Chilean Senate accepted Bernardo O'Higgins' request to establish a national school system using the monitorial method. The Chilean government clearly viewed its adoption of the British system as a form of participation in cosmopolitan modernity; Juan de Dios Vial enthused "in the greatest part of Europe, and in much of Asia, Africa and America, they have adopted the Lancasterian method with admiration and utility, which happily has now been planted in Chile."[76] Important figures in the early years of the republic like Miguel Zañartu, Manuel de Salas, Casimiro Albano, Francisco Ruiz Tagle, Francisco de Borja Fontecilla, José Ignacio Cienfuegos, Joaquín Echeverría, and Francisco Antonio Pinto all participated in the mutual education school project.[77]

The formal relationship between the British government and the emerging states during Latin American independence may have been deferred and avoided, but it was also dynamic and accommodating. On all levels of exchange – diplomatic, commercial, material, military, and personal – the connection was strong. For Latin Americans, it made sense to seek British support. The British navy was the world's strongest seagoing power and offered the best hope to block the reinforcement of Iberian power. Its reputation as a place where liberty was tempered by tradition, where elites could initiate social reforms while managing to maintain their privileged positions, held great appeal for them. British and Latin Americans shared an interest in many of the great issues of the day: abolition of the slave

---

[74] Núñez to Mr. Miller, Buenos Aires, 5 May 1825, BFSS Society Archives.

[75] *British and Foreign School Society Annual Report* (May 1825), 42.

[76] Antony Eaton to James Miller (Santiago de Chile, 16 June 1820), BFBS Archives, File Central America/South America. Eaton's contract with Irisarri can be found at Chile, Archivo Nacional, Archivo Fernández Larraín, vol. 42, pieza 22; Domingo Amunátegui, *El sistema de Lancaster en Chile* (Santiago de Chile: 1985), 13–14, 76, 100, 111–112; *Aviso: A los padres que tienen hijos en las nuevas escuelas de Lancaster* (Santiago: [n.p.], 1827), John Carter Brown Library, broadsides, bB827.A958a.

[77] Francisco Antonio Pinto, "Decreto," Santiago: 18 April 1828, Chile, Archivo Nacional, Fondo Varios, vol. 697, f. 281.

trade, religious toleration, libel laws and freedom of speech, the expansion of publicly supported popular education, vaccination campaigns, and industrial production using technological innovations. The exchanges went both ways. Latin Americans from across the continent traveled to London for refuge or resources, and English, Irish, and Scottish folk crossed the ocean as emigrants, entrepreneurs, agents, and adventurers. It was a complicated relationship, often imbalanced but never one-sided. Although a full and open political recognition might have been deferred, the meaningful exchange of people, ideas, and capital was never avoided.

PART II

★

BRAZIL, PORTUGAL,
AND AFRICA

# 16

# Overview: The Independence Era in the Luso-Brazilian World

GABRIEL PAQUETTE

The Portuguese Atlantic World largely avoided being swept up in the maelstrom of the Age of Revolutions until 1807.[1] In fact, the Luso-Brazilian empire was distinguished by, first, the relative paucity of vocalized discontent with Brazil's subordinate status and, second, the absence of resistance to Portugal's rule in Brazil. The political, economic, and social structures of the Old Regime went relatively unchallenged in the Old World and the New. In the period after 1790, this relative docility is chiefly attributable to the notable cohesiveness of Brazil's ruling elite, conscious of the perils inherent to their slave society – in 1800, two-thirds of Brazil's population was comprised of enslaved people, free persons of African ancestry, or those of mixed racial background – and fearful of a Saint-Domingue-like insurrection.[2]

Yet the comparative tranquility can also be explained by the weakness of Portuguese authority in the New World. With the notable exception of the 1750–1780 period, dominated by the iron-fisted first minister, the marquis of Pombal, there had been few efforts to centralize authority, leaving local elites with ample autonomy, leeway to conduct their own affairs, and few reasons

---

[1] For important recent comparative overviews, see Brian Hamnett, *The End of Iberian Rule on the American Continent, 1770–1830* (Cambridge: Cambridge University Press, 2017); David Armitage and Sanjay Subrahmanyan, eds., *The Age of Revolutions in Global Context, c. 1760–1840* (Basingstoke: Palgrave Macmillan, 2010); Wim Klooster, *Revolutions in the Atlantic World: A Comparative History* (New York: New York University Press, 2009); Jeremy Adelman, "An Age of Imperial Revolutions," *American Historical Review* 113:2 (2008), 319–40.

[2] The historiography of Brazilian independence is rich. Important contributions to the literature include Leslie Bethell, "The Independence of Brazil," in Leslie Bethell, ed., *The Cambridge History of Latin America*, vol. v: Part III, *From Independence to c. 1870* (Cambridge: Cambridge University Press, 1985), 157–96; István Jancsó, ed., *Independência: História e Historiografia* (São Paulo: Hucitec, 2005); Jurandir Malerba, ed., *A Independência Brasileira: Novas dimensões* (Rio de Janeiro: FGV Editora, 2006). On the imperial transitions of this period from the perspective of Portuguese historiography, see Valentim Alexandre, *Os sentidos do Império: Questão nacional e questão colonial na crise do Antigo Regime português* (Porto: Afrontamento, 1993).

to resent metropolitan meddling. The Portuguese viceroy stationed in Brazil, for example, wielded considerably less authority than his Spanish counterpart in New Spain. Far from the result of a sagacious policy, the absence of interference resulted from state weakness, an inability to impose authority across vast physical distances. Exacerbated by uncooperative topography, unfavorable prevailing winds, and sparse infrastructure, local autonomy was inevitable.

There also were conscious efforts, particularly in the final third of the eighteenth century, to forge a transatlantic governing elite. Unlike in Spanish America, where American-born creoles were systematically excluded from the plum official appointments, preeminent Brazilian families routinely sent their sons to study at the University of Coimbra, where they were groomed for positions in the imperial bureaucracy, from Goa to Angola to São Paulo.[3] Discontent was not altogether absent, then, but the combination of geography, fear of slave revolts, and the Crown's consciously conciliatory policy defused tensions and generated few conflicts that threatened to explode into a massive conflagration.

Nevertheless, the political ideas that inflamed the rest of the Atlantic World eventually reached Brazil's shores and permeated its political culture. The most famous conspiracy, which was nipped in the bud, transpired in the province of Minas Gerais in the late 1780s. This *Inconfidência Mineira* was animated by republican ideas. More alarming was the 1798 Tailors' Revolt in Bahia. There mulatto soldiers and artisans plotted based on the principles of the Haitian and French revolutions. They called for independence, the declaration of a republic based on electoral democracy, the abolition of slavery, and full equality between Blacks and whites.[4]

While there were long-term preconditions and medium-term precipitants of the Portuguese world's belated entry into the tumultuous Age of Revolutions, the short-term trigger was undoubtedly the invasion and occupation of Portugal by Napoleonic forces, with the treacherous complicity of the Spanish Crown. Napoleon had cut a deal to permit French troops to traverse Spain in order to invade Portugal, conquering it, dividing it into separate parts, with a view toward eventually controlling Portugal's

---

[3] Kenneth R. Maxwell, "The Idea of the Luso-Brazilian Empire," in Kenneth R. Maxwell, *Naked Tropics: Essays on Empire and Other Rogues* (New York and London: Routledge, 2003), 109–44.

[4] Kenneth R. Maxwell, *Conflicts and Conspiracies: Brazil and Portugal, 1750–1808* (Cambridge: Cambridge University Press, 1973); Roderick J. Barman, *Brazil: The Forging of a Nation, 1798–1852* (Stanford: Stanford University Press, 1988).

ultramarine empire. The capture of Lisbon and the surrender of the royal family (and their removal), it was believed, would make all of these designs possible.

The Braganzas relented to British pressure and evacuated the Peninsula. Britain, a longstanding ally, affirmed its commitment to the territorial and political integrity of the Portuguese Empire, guaranteeing the preeminence of the Braganza dynasty within it. Armed with such promises, though cognizant of their ally's reputation for perfidy, the Portuguese court, nobility, courtiers of all ranks, and servants of all stations of life prepared to evacuate Lisbon. As French troops raced unhindered toward Lisbon, the royal family and its entourage (together with state papers, much of the royal library, precious jewels, and other forms of movable wealth) removed themselves, abandoning Europe and sailing for Brazil. They transformed a former colonial capital, Rio de Janeiro, into the center of a global empire, an empire to be governed from the New World.

Such momentous decisions and unprecedented course of action, though pursued under duress and amidst the chaos triggered by foreign invasion, were something more than an improvisation. From the mid-eighteenth century, Crown strategists insisted that the eventual relocation of the capital of the empire was inevitable. They pointed to Brazil's burgeoning wealth and population, which soon outstripped Portugal itself. Whether judged in terms of the minerals extracted from mines, the export of tropical products such as sugar, or demographic change, it was self-evident that the balance had shifted decisively in Brazil's favor, making a recalibration necessary. Some commentators argued that increased security would be enjoyed if the seat of monarchy was moved to the New World. With a hostile Spain at its border, boasting a numerically superior army and myriad other advantages, a Luso-Brazilian monarchy based in Europe would remain vulnerable.

Though such arguments percolated in the eighteenth century, no concrete plans came of them. It was presumed that a European state such as Portugal would never consent to becoming a colony of a colony, governed from the New World, regardless of the logical and material basis for such a reconfiguration. But the calculus changed when France and Spain allied against Portugal in 1807 and the position of the Braganza dynasty became precarious. The transfer of the seat of the monarchy to Brazil, previously an imagined, fantasy scenario entertained by a handful of statesmen, became, at a stroke, an urgent necessity.

Under the British navy's protection, the royal family embarked and sailed across the Atlantic for an uncertain fate in Brazil. The ships first made landfall

431

in the northeastern port of Salvador da Bahia, formerly the jewel of the Portuguese imperial crown, with its gilded baroque churches, prosperous planter and mercantile class, and majority population of slaves and free people of color. The ships and their beleaguered passengers sailed south along the Brazilian coast to the city of Rio de Janeiro, since 1763 the seat of the Viceroyalty of Brazil, a distinction previously held by Salvador. When the royal family disembarked in Rio de Janeiro, they did not envision a lengthy residence. It would be a temporary capital, at least until the French could be repulsed from Portuguese territory. But it would have been impossible to contemplate such a return as they gazed across Guanabara Bay and beheld breathlessly the protruding, jungle-covered mountains ringing it. The verdant splendor, if undercut somewhat by the tropical humidity, must have awed and allured them. The city itself had progressed from its humble origins as a relative backwater just a hundred years earlier to a metropolis of almost 50,000. It had benefited handsomely from its strategic location, particularly its proximity to Minas Gerais, which had experienced a mining-led boom during the first half of the eighteenth century. But its rise to preeminence and economic prosperity was attributable primarily to its pivotal position in the transoceanic networks lubricated and powered by the traffic in enslaved Africans. Rio had emerged as a major hub for Africans destined both for Minas Gerais and Rio's own expanding hinterlands.

Taken as a whole, Brazil was a colonial society in the throes of transformation. The extraction of precious metals and diamonds, which had buoyed the economy in the first half of the eighteenth century, was giving way to a slave-dependent, plantation economy, based on the cultivation and export of commodities, particularly sugar, tobacco, and cotton. The number of sugar mills in Bahia doubled between 1760 and 1800. As revolution enveloped Saint-Domingue in the 1790s, Brazilian planters rushed to fill the void and meet global demand. This meant increasing production, benefiting from high prices, and importing an average of 23,500 enslaved Africans per year between 1790 and 1810.

The costs and consequences of the royal family's hasty departure from the Old World should be noted. British assistance was gained at an extraordinarily high price: the impairment of sovereignty. The terms of the treaties guaranteeing Britain's support for the Braganzas, signed in 1808 and 1810, entailed the opening up of Brazil to British merchants. They would henceforth pay the same duties as Portuguese merchants, which in effect gave them a significant competitive advantage given the superiority of their goods and the lower prices at which they were offered. Not only was the empire

The Independence Era in the Luso-Brazilian World

opened up legally to such economic penetration, but Britain also forced Portugal to pledge to end the slave trade. Parliament had decreed the end of the abominable traffic within the confines of the British Empire in 1807. Now Britain would pressure other powers to follow suit within their overseas dominions.[5] Sovereignty was further circumscribed when Dom João was effectively compelled to surrender control of Portugal's army to British commanders.

While the royal family and courtiers could marvel at the natural wonders encountered in Rio and revel in the adulation of subjects stunned by the presence of the royal family, the price they paid for political survival was steep. Less regulated trade angered Peninsular merchants long accustomed to (and reliant on) special privileges and the legal exclusion of foreign merchants. The removal of such restrictions threatened to attenuate the economic bonds which bound the European and American sides of the Luso-Atlantic World to each other. Yet the pledge to end the slave trade could never be honored except in the breach. The dependence of the Portuguese Atlantic system on slave labor made unrealistic the prospect of abolishing forced migration.

With Portugal occupied by French troops, the Braganzas' only chance of recovering their European territory was through the force of British arms. Their utter dependence on a foreign power was starkly revealed in 1808–1810, exposing their frailty and diminishing their legitimacy in the eyes of many subjects. Yet Brazil also offered fresh opportunities to bolster the dynasty's fortunes. Unloading the ships, they set about establishing a "Tropical Versailles." The French occupation of Lisbon necessitated the recreation in Rio of all of the institutions of government, such as law courts and ministries, needed to administer an empire and befitting its capital city. A massive public buildings and works program was undertaken, which soon endowed Rio with the requisite infrastructure: law courts, palaces, plazas, theaters, promenades, and improved roads.[6]

Brazilian subjects reacted to the arrival of the Court in divergent ways. Some were gratified, while others were perturbed by its presence. Those radicals who wished an end to slavery and monarchy were surely chagrined and disheartened. Much of the merchant and planter elite welcomed the

---

[5] Leslie Bethell, *The Abolition of the Brazilian Slave Trade: Britain, Brazil and the Slave Trade Question, 1807–1869* (Cambridge: Cambridge University Press, 1970).

[6] Manuel de Oliveira Lima, *Dom João VI no Brasil*, 3rd edition (Rio de Janeiro: Topbooks, 1996); Kirsten Schultz, *Tropical Versailles: Empire, Monarchy, and the Portuguese Royal Court in Rio de Janeiro, 1808–1821* (New York: Routledge, 2001).

Braganzas to Brazil with open arms, though they did so for a variety of sometimes conflicting reasons. The transfer of the court created enormous patronage opportunities. Thousands of laborers, skilled and unskilled, were needed to design, erect, and maintain the new edifices. New institutions required personnel to run them; government posts proliferated and brought the transplanted regime new adherents and dependents. Appointments and sinecures previously beyond the wildest dreams of even well-placed colonial subjects suddenly were within reach. Furthermore, the Crown's need to ingratiate itself prompted the creation of new titles of nobility for particularly deserving Brazilian subjects. The formation of a New World nobility, who enjoyed all of the trappings of social prestige which previously were the exclusive domain of their Old World counterparts, tightened the bond between the Brazilian elite and the monarchy, making the former deeply invested in the latter's survival and efflorescence.

It is important to recall that the transfer of the Court occurred in the midst of one of the most turbulent phases of the Age of Revolutions. Monarchies were crumbling or being toppled; slave systems in the Americas were being overthrown; republican and anticolonial, nationalist doctrines were spreading rapidly across the Atlantic World, transported by sailors, soldiers, and slaves. If such ideas took root in Brazil, the social order would be threatened. In a dangerously revolutionary world, the presence of the royal family in the New World, far from a burden, came to be viewed as a powerful buttress to the existing social, economic, and political order, a prophylactic against the chaos enveloping their Spanish American neighbors. Political stability was the indispensable precondition of economic prosperity. Brazil exploited the dislocation caused by civil strife elsewhere, including in neighboring Spanish America after 1809, where republican movements against Spanish rule gave way to internecine civil wars lasting two decades.[7] The presence of the royal family, then, promised to shore up the foundations of Brazil's social and economic hierarchy. The transfer of the capital from the Old to New World promised to remove the complaint of being ruled as a colony from afar. There was now de facto home rule. The elites and the Crown thus were natural allies in the defense of a system premised on top-down authority and forced labor. To survive, each needed to prop up the other.[8]

---

[7] João Paulo Pimenta, *A independência do Brasil e a experiência hispano-americana (1808–1822)* (São Paulo: Hucitec/Fapesp, 2015).

[8] Jurandir Malerba, *A corte no exílio: Civilização e poder no Brasil ás vésperas da independência (1808 a 1820)* (São Paulo: Companhia das Letras, 2000); Andrea Slemian, *Vida política em tempo de crise: Rio de Janeiro (1808–1824)* (São Paulo: Hucitec, 2006).

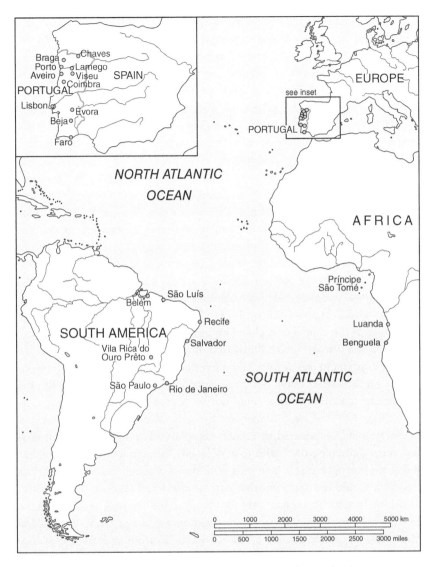

Map 16.1 The Portuguese Atlantic World, 1800. Map taken from Gabriel Paquette, *Imperial Portugal in the Age of Atlantic Revolutions: The Luso-Brazilian World, c. 1770–1850* (Cambridge: Cambridge University Press, 2013), xiv.

By some measure, the first years of the Braganzas' residence in Rio were an unequivocal success. Unlike in Spanish America, where the "captivity" of Spanish king Fernando VII and the "usurpation" of the throne by Napoleon's brother Joseph provoked declarations of self-rule which subsequently morphed into full-fledged independence movements, the presence of the royal family forestalled agitation of that sort in Portuguese America and provided an unmatched degree of stability. Furthermore, Portugal rode Britain's coattails as Napoleonic France was driven from the Iberian Peninsula and eventually vanquished.

In all of his public pronouncements since 1808, Dom João had repeated that the transfer of the monarchy to Brazil was a temporary measure and that the Court would return to Europe with the coming of a general peace. That claim, however, failed to reassure many in Portugal, who feared that the transfer of the Court would be made permanent. After all, they acknowledged, the definitive relocation of the monarch would reflect Brazil's superior wealth, population, and dynamism. But such a decision would also be a repudiation of tradition and history, inverting the metropole-colony relationship. It would deprive Portugal of all of the institutions and prestige belonging to the capital of a global empire, reducing it to a petty province. Tradition and history, which buttressed monarchy and justified its existence in an age when old truths were being rejected and longstanding assumptions turned on their head, could not be discarded. The decision to make Rio the permanent capital, therefore, could not be taken lightly.

In 1815, with the establishment of the general peace, Portugal was in a desperate state.[9] Plundered by French occupiers and ravaged by war, it now found itself straining under the yoke of its ally, Britain, which maintained its forces on Portuguese soil. The return of the royal family to Portugal, it was believed, would end this execrable state of affairs and regenerate the forlorn kingdom. In spite of poignant calls for the return of the royal family to rescue Portugal, Dom João showed no inclination to budge from his tropical Versailles. In fact, counseled by his advisers, he acted to further ensconce the Braganzas in Brazil and to delay their return to Portugal. He raised Brazil to the status of a kingdom, thus creating a "united kingdom" (*reino unido*, in Portuguese) of Brazil and Portugal. What this meant in practice was vague. The details would have to be filled in at a later date. But the significance of

---

[9] Jorge Pedreira and Nuno G. Monteiro, *O colapso do Império e a Revolução Liberal 1808–1834* (Madrid: Mapfre/Objectiva, 2013).

this action was unambiguous. Brazil was no longer a subordinate and Portugal was no longer the formal center of the empire. To a degree, this action gratified Brazilians, some of whom had become fearful of the relocation of the seat of the monarchy to the Old World: What would become of their new positions, prestige, and authority? The declaration of the *reino unido* was therefore a comforting reassurance. In this way, it flattered and justified the self-perception of Brazilian elites, undercutting a major cause of potential dissent and making the prospect of remaining within the empire, under monarchical government, palatable.

But not all Brazilians were pleased by Dom João's declaration. Recall that this period of prosperity and optimism in Brazil coincided with (and benefited directly from) revolutionary turbulence sweeping the rest of South America and the Caribbean. Throughout Spanish America, radicals armed with new-fangled political doctrines had sprung up. Many such movements sought a definitive separation from Spain and the creation of independent states. Such sentiments could be found in Brazil. The creation of the *reino unido* irritated those who desired the elimination, not entrenchment, of monarchy and who feared that the Crown's continuing presence would block revolution.

Yet another cause of discontent was that it confirmed the primacy of Rio de Janeiro at the expense of other cities of Brazil. During the sixteenth and seventeenth centuries, Salvador, in Bahia, and Recife, in Pernambuco, had been the richest and most populous parts of the empire, though they were in relative decline by the mid-eighteenth century, as previously discussed. The creation of the *reino unido*, with Rio at its center, irritated those who felt they were now relegated to second tier status and subservience to Rio. They worried that an increasingly centralized monarchy would funnel resources to Rio and deprive their provinces of the autonomy they had enjoyed prior to 1808. Anti-monarchical sentiment, republican political ideas, and provincial patriotism came together in 1817 in Pernambuco, particularly Recife, where a conspiracy was hatched to overthrow monarchy and establish an independent republic, not unlike what was transpiring throughout Spanish America at precisely the same moment.

In Portugal, the *reino unido* was met, predictably, with great resentment. Abandoned by their royal family, the Portuguese had waged (even if under British tutelage) war against the French occupiers, expelling them and repulsing successive invasions. This military valor had been exerted in the name of, and out of loyalty to, the royal family, subsequently reaffirmed by myriad oaths, proclamations, and celebrations. There was little criticism of the royal family for having fled the Iberian Peninsula and hastily installed a quasi-regency, *Governadores do Reino*, to administer affairs in their absence. But the failure to return to Europe in a timely fashion excited great antipathy, as did the creation of parallel political and judicial institutions in Rio de Janeiro. The scope and extent of their activities in Brazil increasingly appeared to amount to something greater than a temporary, ad hoc arrangement. Added to this caldron of Lusitanian anxiety were the aforementioned free-trade decrees and asymmetrical commercial treaties with Britain, which undercut the primacy of peninsular merchants, and seemed to deprive Portugal of the means necessary to recover from the severe economic dislocation caused by war.

When the *reino unido* was declared, then, the indignities suffered by Portugal were shown in a harsh, unflattering light. Would the Portuguese consent to becoming a colony of their former colony or, without hyperbole, a peripheral (even if historically important) component of a transatlantic empire whose center lay south of the equator? At least at first, the novelty, ingenuity, and great possibility of the new political arrangement was lost on Portuguese observers, who perceived only the insult latent in it and the dashed hopes it represented. Their indignant reception prevented them from grasping the potential benefits of an imperial federation for themselves. Instead of understanding the alternatives as either membership in an imperial federation or reduction to a minor state, shorn of its empire, on the periphery of Europe, surrounded by rapacious rivals, they believed that they could be restored to their former preeminence. After all that had been lost, after innumerable sacrifices and collective suffering, the *reino unido* could only be interpreted as cruel, and inadequate, recompense. Such widespread sentiments fed their delusion of recaptured grandeur.

There were further troublesome features of the new political arrangement, particularly those that went unmentioned in its establishment. In 1815–1816, Portugal was no longer at war, but it remained occupied, for all intents and purposes, by an allied army. After expending much blood and treasure in the Peninsular War, a large British force stayed on in Portugal after the cessation of hostilities. This suited, to some degree, British interests, but the force remained at the behest of Dom João. There were obvious advantages: A foreign army would suppress dissent, squash mutinies and conspiracies, and generally maintain order during the royal family's absence. There were disadvantages, too, of course, not least the resentment of the Portuguese populace, the substantial cost incurred in maintaining the troops, and the perception that the British were in charge.

There were good reasons to fear dissent. Even before the fateful year of 1808, Crown administrators had installed an effective, tenacious police system to root out dissidents, Freemasons and other threatening types. The events of 1808–1810 revealed that many seemingly docile subjects secretly harbored illicit political ideas and aspirations. Unsurprisingly, the army was a hotbed of radicalism and dissent. Freemasonry had spread through its ranks in the latter decades of the eighteenth century, laying the groundwork for the soldiers' attraction to, and cooperation with, the invading French armies. Some Portuguese commanders and rank-and-file troops had been absorbed into the French armies. The dual affront to national pride caused by the Court's seemingly permanent relocation to Brazil and the British presence was too much for many soldiers. In 1817, a conspiracy was hatched which rallied around General Gomes Freire (though the unfortunate general may have known little about the plot coalescing around his name). The conspirators sought to expel the British, force the king to accept a constitution (and hence govern as a constitutional monarch, not an absolutist ruler), and to insist on the return of the royal family (and hence the seat of the monarchy) to Lisbon. The eponymous conspiracy was uncovered and squashed without mercy. In the aftermath, official efforts to suppress dissent and maintain order went into hyperdrive.

The Portuguese monarchy thus dodged two bullets in 1817. From republicans in the northeast of Brazil to disgruntled soldiers in the barracks of Lisbon, it was clear that the status quo was unsustainable. Countless advisers and collaborators wrote to Dom João, urging bold action to address the underlying causes of discontent, a program to rescue Peninsular Portugal from the poverty and misery afflicting it. The replies to their plaintive pleas were distinctly unsatisfactory. If disinterest and intentional neglect are ruled out as explanations for Dom João's unresponsiveness, it could be argued that there were cogent arguments in favor of the status quo. A revolution in Portugal appeared to be a remote possibility, however dismayed the populace may have been. Anti-monarchical sentiment in both the Old World and the New seemed unlikely to amount to much.

Much of the Crown's confidence in the security of their position derived from the state of international affairs after 1815. The end of the French revolutionary era gave way to an age of restoration. Thrones were shored up, traditions were revivified (and sometimes invented), and the old sources of authority – monarchy, nobility, and Church – regained their sway. The Bourbon dynasty was restored in France and in Spain. In Spanish America, it appeared that the rebels had been driven back and that royalists were firmly in control. In Europe, the Great Powers that had defeated Napoleon, led by Austria and Russia, formed what they christened a Holy Alliance, whose principal purposes were to crush revolution, stabilize teetering thrones, prop up the religious institutions, and generate the tranquility necessary for the recovery of Europe. Dom João and his counselors believed that this new consensus, the reascendance of monarchical principles and "legitimacy," offered near immunity to the revolutionary contagion.

If dissent had been snuffed out within the borders of the Portuguese Empire, it spouted forth from the pens of journalists pushed into exile by the regime in previous decades. Many of these Luso-Brazilian exiles sought refuge in Britain and, after 1815, in France, where they enjoyed freedom from repressive censorship and published newspapers, pamphlets, and journals. These commented on the situation in the Portuguese Atlantic Monarchy, often critically. The writings of the exiles were often smuggled into Portugal and Brazil, where they enjoyed a wide circulation, introducing new ideas and generating great debate. These publications lambasted the *reino unido* and maligned the Braganzas' neglect of Peninsular Portugal. But perhaps the most trenchant criticism contained in these émigré publications concerned the political system governing the Portuguese monarchy. The absence of both a written constitution and an elected, representative body checking monarchical power soon became the main cause of complaint against the regime.

The origins of this criticism were not mysterious. The North American and then the French Revolution had fomented a mania for written constitutions across Europe and the Atlantic World.[10] Even while rejecting the French invaders, Spaniards, Portuguese, and Spanish Americans had embraced the idea of a written constitution in their dominions. While many of the constitutions devised in Spanish America were republican in nature, and thus rejected the idea of a monarch altogether, the most influential constitution in the Spanish and Portuguese World was the one framed, after intense debate, in the Andalusian port city of Cádiz in 1812. This constitution called for a mixed monarchy, with the king and an elected unicameral legislature working together to legislate for and govern Spain and Spanish America. The Cádiz Constitution also enshrined certain protections and rights in law and went some distance toward destroying the structure of politics of Old Regime Spain. Perhaps most importantly, subjects were

---

[10] Linda Colley, *The Gun, the Ship, and the Pen: Warfare, Constitutions, and the Making of the Modern World* (London: Liverlight, 2021).

turned into citizens while American colonists and Peninsular Spaniards were governed by the same laws, with some notable exceptions. The distinctions between colonist and peninsular were to be eliminated and universal jurisdiction was to replace the legal mosaic that characterized the composite monarchy.

The Cádiz Constitution never was given the chance to come fully into effect. In Spanish America, revolutionary movements animated by more radical political ideas (e.g., independence, the destruction of monarchy, the abolition of slavery) precluded its acceptance and implementation. In Spain itself, by the time the French armies were expelled from the Peninsula, the restoration of the arch-absolutist Fernando VII led not only to the suspension of the Cádiz Constitution, but to the repudiation of its tenets, the prosecution of its advocates and adherents, and the dismantlement of the first efforts to construct a liberal Spain. Such actions were consistent with the doctrines of the Holy Alliance, even if the actions of the vengeful Fernando were an extreme manifestation of this broader trend. This context makes it possible to appreciate the odd situation the Portuguese Atlantic empire found itself in between 1815 and 1820: an Old World monarchy, with all its trappings, on New World soil, surrounded by neighboring Spanish America territories veering toward republicanism, while revolutionary intrigue against the permanent relocation of the seat of government simmered in the diminutive, and much diminished, European fragment of this Atlantic empire, itself surrounded by restored monarchies in the wake of the Napoleonic Wars.

In 1820, resistance against the status quo began in the northern city of Porto, demanding the king's return to Europe and insisting that he rule as a constitutional monarch. The rebels wanted Peninsular Portugal to enjoy primacy once again within the empire, which would have entailed the reimposition of now-eviscerated trade restrictions and the elimination of the parallel administration – law courts, magistrates, tax collecting apparatus – established in Brazil from 1808. The Porto Revolution, which quickly spread to Lisbon and to the provinces, was part of that remarkable wave of southern European revolutions – in Naples, Lombardy, Spain, and Portugal – which began in 1820 and which took the 1812 Spanish Constitution as their standard and the basis for their national constitution-making projects (Figure 16.1).[11]

---

[11] Richard Stites, *The Four Horsemen: Riding to Liberty in Post-Napoleonic Europe* (Oxford: Oxford University Press, 2014).

Figure 16.1 Adoption in Rio de Janeiro in 1821 of the Constitution of Lisbon. Courtesy of the John Carter Brown Library.

The Brazilian response to the Portuguese upheaval paved the way for imperial collapse. Though Dom João was compelled to return to Europe, he left his son and heir, Dom Pedro, behind in Rio de Janeiro to serve as a counterweight to any political conspiracies that might be hatched in his absence. When the liberal Cortes in Lisbon demanded the prince's return as well, he refused and, following a complicated series of events, declared Brazil independent, an action that probably enjoyed his father's tacit blessing. In some senses, Dom Pedro's declaration merely formalized the de facto situation. Though his actions were fueled by his disdain for what he considered to be the insolent demands of the Portuguese liberals, they were prompted by fear of revolution from below. It was also a shrewd move. As Jeffrey Needell notes, Dom Pedro "successfully strengthened the appeal of his charismatic, dynastic role by identifying it with an independence movement."[12] Brazilian elites rallied around the monarchy, making their declaration of independence a rather peculiar one, at variance with the rest of the struggles for decolonization in the Americas. By opting for monarchy, retaining the same European dynasty on the throne and calling their new polity an empire, they guaranteed that Brazil's future would diverge sharply

---

[12] See Needell, Chapter 19 in this volume; on the broader political culture in this crucial period, see Lúcia Maria Bastos Pereira das Neves, *Corcundas e Constitucionais – A cultura política da Independência (1820–1822)* (Rio de Janeiro: Faperj/Revan, 2003).

The Independence Era in the Luso-Brazilian World

from that of its neighbors. As Jurandir Malerba observes, "the dynamic between the colonial upper classes and the Portuguese crown [was] a crucial factor in the conservative bias of Brazilian independence."[13]

An immediate problem was that not all regions were satisfied with Dom Pedro's solution. Throughout the colonial period, the northern provinces of Maranhão and Pará had maintained closer relations with Lisbon than with the rest of Brazil, due to proximity, Atlantic currents, and their large Portuguese-born merchant communities. Moreover, in northeastern provinces like Pernambuco and Bahia, whose economic halcyon days were long over, the political ascendancy of Rio de Janeiro, with its centralizing pretensions, and the economic efflorescence of the southeastern provinces in general, caused consternation. There were half-hearted attempts to resist a union with Rio and instead retain a link with Portugal. But the derelict former metropole was in no position to pursue such a course of action with conviction, and military (naval) efforts to reassert control were belated and feeble.

Yet even those Brazilians who welcomed independence were unenthused by its high price: the survival of monarchy and the retention of the Braganza dynasty proved distasteful to those for whom the recent precedent of the republican revolutions, from Boston to Buenos Aires, was the preferred model of political change. The stage was set, then, for a showdown between Dom Pedro and the provincial elites of the north and northeast. The suspicions of both republicans and proponents of regional autonomy were confirmed when Dom Pedro dissolved the Constituent Assembly he had convened to draft a new constitution, promising to promulgate a charter that would be "twice as liberal." The resulting 1824 Constitution was explicitly antifederalist and ensured the central government's oversight over provincial affairs.

It is customary at this point for historians of the Age of Revolutions, and scholars of Brazilian and Portuguese history, to lose interest in transatlantic relations. But that is precisely the moment at which the efforts of historians who seek to reframe and alter the dominant narrative must redouble their efforts to trace connections. Brazilian independence led directly to the overthrow of the constitutional regime in Portugal in 1823 and the restoration of Dom João as absolute monarch, ruling without a written constitution and unrestrained by any representative body. In Brazil, at exactly the

[13] See Malerba, Chapter 18 in this volume.

same moment, Dom Pedro's similar actions provoked major resistance, especially in the northeast. To many historians, such phenomena have seemed to be parallel, though bearing surprising resemblances to each other. But these are more than just coincidences and resemblances; rather, they are interwoven histories. This 1823 moment was crucial: the fate of the Luso-Atlantic World hung in the balance and the likelihood of reconciliation between Portugal and Brazil was great. Ultimately, both sides failed in their efforts to reach some mutually acceptable compromise.

Portuguese and Brazilian constitutional history in 1824–1826 transpired in the shadow of those failed efforts. The writing of new constitutions might appear to signal divergent historical trajectories, but the unresolved nature of the Portugal–Brazil relationship infused the process of constitution-making and influenced its outcome. Looking at the entwined constitutional cultures in Portugal and Brazil is a good way to grasp how "independence" masked the persistence of connections within the Luso-Atlantic and the potential for its reconstitution.[14] Portugal's 1825 recognition of Brazilian independence was a prelude to Dom Pedro's promulgation of a *Carta Constitucional* for Portugal in 1826. It was drawn up in Rio de Janeiro in late April 1826, immediately following the death of Dom João VI, which left Dom Pedro undisputed heir to the Portuguese throne. His *Carta*, and the associated plan to install his Brazilian-born daughter, Dona Maria, on the Portuguese throne, met with great resistance in Portugal, precipitating the Civil War (1828–1834). Imposing this constitution on Portugal, Dom Pedro clearly foresaw the eventual reunification of Brazil and Portugal, the revival of the Portuguese Atlantic empire.[15]

The 1826 Portuguese Constitution remained in force, except for brief periods (1828–1834, 1836–1842) and with only slight modification through revisions and "additional acts" (1852, 1865, 1896, 1907), until the fall of the monarchy. The *Carta* embodied the spirit of an antipopular, revivified monarchy. It was designed largely to mollify the Holy Alliance and appease Brazilians wary of their emperor's continued connection to the ex-metropole (Portugal). In Europe, however, it came to be viewed both as a threat to

---

[14] Matthew Brown and Gabriel Paquette, eds., *Connections after Colonialism: Europe and Latin America in the 1820s* (Tuscaloosa: University of Alabama Press, 2013).

[15] Gabriel Paquette, "The Brazilian Origins of the 1826 Portuguese Constitution," *European History Quarterly* 41:3 (2011), 444–71; on Dom Pedro, more generally, see Isabel Lustosa, *Dom Pedro I: Um herói sem nenhum caráter* (São Paulo: Companhia das Letras, 2006); Neil Macaulay, *Dom Pedro: The Struggle for Liberty in Brazil and Portugal, 1798–1834* (Durham, NC: Duke University Press, 1986).

royal legitimacy and the rallying cry of Portuguese liberals and their sympathizers abroad. In Portugal, the *Carta* emblemized the assumptions, aspirations, and fears of those who had not fully absorbed, or accepted, the break represented by Brazilian independence. With its strong resemblance to Brazil's 1824 Constitution, the *Carta* portended an eventual, if distant, reunion of the crowns. While Dom Pedro was motivated primarily by desire to ensure his dynasty's survival, his efforts were embraced by many in Portugal who believed that the ex-metropole's independence was imperiled without robust political and economic ties to Brazil. Contemporaries on both sides of the Atlantic understood Dom Pedro's unsubtle design in the same way: If both states had more or less the same constitution, then their legal integration at some point should be fairly straightforward. Of course, Dom Pedro could not effectively rule both states simultaneously without exciting all sorts of nativist resentment in Brazil (fear of European recolonization efforts remained their hobbyhorse for more than a decade following independence), so he abdicated the Portuguese throne in favor of his seven-year-old daughter, Dona Maria.

What is important to recognize here is that the breakdown of empire was not definitive. The ambiguous, incomplete nature of Brazil's independence left many threads untied and these unresolved aspects profoundly influenced the trajectory of postimperial Portugal. In this case, Portuguese constitutionalism throughout the nineteenth century was indelibly marked by the transatlantic empire's strange death (after a period of unprecedented prosperity) and Dom Pedro's unrealized ambition to reunite the two crowns. In this sense, the political history of nineteenth-century Portugal unfolded in the long shadow of imperial breakdown. The political ideas animating the exiled Portuguese "liberal" opposition coalesced around a regency established on the Azorean island of Terceira in the early 1830s and eventually prevailed in the civil war against the arch-conservative regime headed by the pretender Dom Miguel. The Civil War should be understood as an outgrowth of Portugal's unstable postimperial condition, with each faction espousing a distinct vision of Portugal's future, but it must also be situated in a broader international context, including Great Power rivalry, the advent of the July Monarchy in France, and the shifting terrain of Brazilian politics.

Constitutionalism was not the only way that Brazil's history continued to influence that of Portugal or the way that the histories of the two states remained connected well after independence. Recall that by the late eighteenth century, more than 20,000 Africans were sold into bondage each year in the port of Rio de Janeiro alone. In the 1820s, as Britain sought to coerce and coax various states into abolishing the slave trade and slavery itself, the number of slaves entering Brazil rose to almost 40,000 per year, numbers that would remain steady throughout the 1830s. Most of these enslaved Africans were taken from Portuguese controlled enclaves, chiefly those in modern Angola, Mozambique, and Guinea-Bissau. The breakdown of the Portuguese Empire profoundly affected the transatlantic slave pipeline and yet, paradoxically, made Portugal and Brazil even more dependent on each other than ever before.[16]

Already in the eighteenth century, Portuguese policymakers believed that Portugal's very existence as an independent state would be imperiled without colonies. With few exports, it imported most of its grain, including some from southern Brazil in the final decades of the eighteenth century, and ran a trade deficit, to say nothing of its meager population. Without colonial products to re-export and markets to open to larger powers, it had little leverage in negotiations. With Brazil's independence, many in Portugal feared that it was a matter of time before Spain swallowed up its smaller neighbor. In the late 1820s and 1830s, then, many in Portugal urged lavishing attention on Portugal's remaining derelict and neglected colonies, chiefly Mozambique and Angola, with some hoping to convert them into colonies of (free) white settlement, producing tropical commodities formerly obtained in Brazil.[17]

The practical (to say nothing of the moral) problem with this vision was that those colonies had been little more than depots for convict labor and entrepôts for the slave trade, the latter of which was controlled almost entirely by Brazilian slave traders with Brazilian capital. At the heart of Portuguese schemes for national survival and regeneration after 1825, then, lay a new imperial vision, one which was impeded by utter reliance on the former colony. Whatever economic vitality Portuguese claimed African territories enjoyed rested upon the Brazilian slave trade. And many feared that Angola and Mozambique would break with Portugal and join Brazil in a type of South Atlantic confederation. This never came to pass, but Portuguese colonial policy, until the final abolition – under intense British

---

[16] On the importance of the slave trade to the creation of the Luso-Atlantic world, see L. F. de Alencastro, *O trato dos viventes: Formação do Brasil no Atlântico Sul, séculos XVI e XVII* (São Paulo: Companhia das Letras, 2000); Roquinaldo Ferreira, *Cross-Cultural Exchange in the Atlantic World: Angola and Brazil in the Era of the Slave Trade* (Cambridge: Cambridge University Press, 2012).

[17] Gabriel Paquette, "After Brazil: Portuguese Debates on Empire, c. 1820–1850," *Journal of Colonialism and Colonial History* 11:2 (2010), online.

pressure – of the slave trade in 1850, hinged on Brazilian policy and agriculture. In this respect, Portuguese imperial schemes, and national regeneration efforts more generally, in the 1830s and 1840s occurred as much in the shadow of Brazilian decolonization as in that of the French Revolutionary Wars. Though in many respects Brazil's relevance to Portuguese politics faded in the largely forgotten decades of the 1830s and 1840s, the persistence of the slave trade – both Brazil's dependence on it and Portuguese Africa's economic orientation toward it – meant that the histories of Portugal and Brazil would remain entwined until nearly mid-century. Abolition, then, much more than independence, was the act that severed the fortunes of Brazil and Portugal from each other.

With regard to Brazil, the years between 1824 and 1840 were ones in which the political settlement of Brazilian independence was continuously challenged. That settlement was marked by the apparent (though tenuous) triumph of monarchism over republicanism, of territorial integrity and a centralized administration over dispersed power and provincial autonomy, and of the expansion of a slave-reliant economy over free (or at least less coercive) labor regimes. If the decades preceding independence had been notable by the relative paucity of challenges to the established order, the succeeding decades were characterized by tempestuous relations between the capital and the provinces, between urban and rural areas, between landed proprietors and their subalterns, between masters and slaves. When Brazilian independence was declared, the destruction of the Old Regime was incomplete, perhaps not even yet under way. Independence became decoupled from the wholesale dismemberment of the Old Regime. In fact, independence, with its illusion of change, neutralized such efforts, depriving Brazil of the opportunity to convert the transition from colony to nation into a revolutionary overhaul of politics, society, and economy.

The first reaction against Dom Pedro's high-handed tactics came from the north and northeast. Pernambuco, the hub of the 1817 conspiracy, rose again, this time against what revolutionaries considered to be the swap of one master in Lisbon for another in Rio de Janeiro, against becoming a mere colony so soon after throwing off the colonial yoke. These discontents coalesced to form what they called the Confederation of the Equator. Often depicted as a secessionist movement, seeking to establish an independent republic, the aims of the Confederation were at once more moderate and more radical than that. The president of the Confederation, Manuel de Carvalho, called for the obliteration of the oligarchical institutions of old Europe and for the creation of a federal Brazil, one in which the provinces retained some control over their own affairs. They wanted local control over local taxation, education, and public works. In short, they wanted devolution in the context of a genuine Brazil-wide revolution. Decentralized constitutional government was their goal. There were several radical streaks, including Carvalho's expressed desire to stop the importation of slaves into Pernambuco, though not the abolition of slavery, nor the manumission of existing slaves. This failure to come out in favor of abolition was a common thread linking the rebellions of the period 1824–1840.

Dom Pedro's imperial system escaped relatively unscathed from the Confederation's direct challenge to his authority, but the remainder of his reign was beset by difficulties. Discontent with Brazil's passage from colony to empire, instead of republic, simmered just beneath the surface of everyday political life. But Dom Pedro's problems went deeper than republican discontents and spasmodic bursts of lusophobia. His armies were bogged down in an ultimately futile and bloody war over the Banda Oriental with Argentina, a struggle that culminated in the creation of an independent Uruguay. The financial strain of this war was serious: It exhausted the treasury and forced the nascent imperial government to assume sizeable external debt.

Matters came to a head in 1831, forcing Dom Pedro to abdicate in favor of his five-year-old son, also named Pedro, and embark for exile in Europe. The child emperor was not ready, of course, to assume the reins of state. The remaining senators and government ministers filled the power vacuum by creating a three-man regency to govern on an interim basis until young Dom Pedro II reached majority. This regency's executive power, however, was severely diminished, as the legislature took advantage of the situation to appropriate power for itself. The first regency was elected by the Senate and House of Deputies, though future regents were elected by popular vote. There were many reasons why Brazil remained a monarchy in 1831 in spite of open disapproval of the monarch, but perhaps the most important factor was the fear that a slave-based society could not survive without a unifying institution of sufficient stature.[18]

---

[18] The political dynamics of the middle decades of the nineteenth century are masterfully analyzed in Jeffrey D. Needell, *The Party of Order: The Conservatives, the State, and Slavery in the Brazilian Monarchy, 1831–1871* (Stanford: Stanford University Press, 2006); on Pernambuco in the same period, see Jeffrey Mosher, *Political Struggle, Ideology, and State Building: Pernambuco and the Construction of Brazil, 1817–1850* (Lincoln: University of Nebraska Press, 2008).

The Independence Era in the Luso-Brazilian World

Although the gulf separating Portugal from Brazil widened throughout the nineteenth century, historians should reassess the boundaries separating colonial from national history and appreciate the legacies which colonialism left not only in the successor states, but in the metropole and in European states. In general terms, concepts such as "independence," "decolonization," and "Age of Revolutions" can obscure as much as they illuminate in the study of that first great age of eighteenth- and nineteenth-century imperial breakdown. Paying attention to connections after colonialism is a worthwhile enterprise for scholars of both prerevolutionary as well as revolutionary Europe and the Atlantic World. By bringing the persistence of connections after the end of empire into play, and by departing from the familiar teleology of anticolonial revolution, the late colonial period in the Luso-Brazilian Atlantic looks less like an impending cataclysm and more of a case of successful "policy learning" and counteremulation to avoid catastrophe. The existence of broad structural forces prodding breakdown notwithstanding, inevitability (in its various guises, and extreme and moderate versions) gives way to contingency, the play of individual decision-making, motivation, and personality, and the pressures of international diplomacy, and many other processes whose outcomes hung in the balance throughout the Age of Revolutions.

17

# Portugal's Social and Political Change from the *Ancien Régime* to Liberalism

NUNO GONÇALO MONTEIRO

## The Intercontinental Monarchy and the Reforms

The cycle of Atlantic revolutions reached the intercontinental Portuguese monarchy according to a specific chronology. Initially, the independence of the United States seems to have had an indirect impact by contributing to the commercial prosperity of the Portuguese Atlantic empire during the last decades of the eighteenth century. The population of Brazil in the areas under the administration of the Portuguese Crown had multiplied tenfold throughout that century, from around 300,000 to approximately 3 million at the beginning of the nineteenth century, reaching a similar level as that of the population of the European kingdom. These numbers are largely explained by the slave trade, as most slaves came from the domain of the Portuguese Crown in Africa, but also by an intense period of Portuguese emigration. Despite the onset of the conspiracy known as the *Inconfidência Mineira* (Minas Conspiracy) (1789) and other minor conspiracies, there was no widespread perception that the empire was undergoing a crisis. Moreover, Brazil, which served as a financial base for the monarchy, was always at the center of diplomatic options, and even helped cement the alliance with Great Britain. Thus, the projects of imperial reform were never very systematic. It was only within the context of the European wars with revolutionary France that more concrete alternatives began to develop, including in the early years of the new century the renewed idea of transferring the royal family and the headquarters of the monarchy to Rio de Janeiro.[1]

---

[1] Cf. Valentim Alexandre, *Os sentidos do Império: Questão nacional e questão colonial na crise do Antigo Regime português* (Oporto: Afrontamento, 1993); João Fragoso and Nuno Gonçalo Monteiro, "Apresentação," in João Fragoso and Nuno Gonçalo Monteiro, eds., *Um reino e suas repúblicas no Atlântico: Comunicações políticas entre Portugal, Brasil e Angola nos séculos XVII e XVIII* (Rio de Janeiro: Civilização Brasileira, 2017), 13–45; José Luís Cardoso, ed., *A economia política e os dilemas do império luso-brasileiro (1790–1822)*

## Portugal's Social and Political Change

Ideas about social and economic change in the Kingdom of Portugal were more debated than imperial reform projects during the last two decades of the eighteenth century and resumed successively in subsequent decades. As the French historian Albert Silbert has explained: "there was a vivid contrast between the vitality of the Enlightenment ... and the weak political consequences of that same Enlightenment." In fact, economic proposals were, as a rule, made by ministers and prominent figures of the monarchy, but its political model was never called into question. Notwithstanding the foundation of a Royal Academy of Sciences, there was a tight censorship and there were major limitations on the press.[2]

As a single kingdom in the European continent, Portugal did not incorporate any preexisting political units. Hence, it had not experienced tensions of a regional nature. The parliamentary general assembly had not met since 1697–1698, but the concerns of the moment did not translate into calls for it to be summoned. Although the Crown was very dependent on the proceeds from customs and commercial monopolies, agriculture and the meager revenue the royal finances drew from the interior of the kingdom would become the focus of concerns regarding internal order. Diplomat and future minister D. Rodrigo de Sousa Coutinho, whose thought was inspired by the ideal of a liberal political economy, raised the issue with great clarity in 1786: direct taxes were "very light," representing a revenue that was much lower than that of ecclesiastical tithes and local seigneurial rights charters (so-called *foral* charters)[3] paid by land tenants and donated by the Crown to aristocratic and ecclesiastical lords. And, he added, "[n]either the tithe nor the *jugadas* and *quartos* [seigneurial rights of *foral* charters] are currently part of

---

(Lisbon: CNCDP, 2001); Jorge Pedreira and Fernando Dores Costa, *D. João VI, O Clemente* (Lisbon: Círculo de Leitores, 2006); José Tengarrinha, *Imprensa e opinião pública em Portugal* (Coimbra: Minerva, 2006); Jorge Pedreira and Nuno G. Monteiro, *O colapso do Império e a Revolução Liberal 1808–1834* (Madrid: Mapfre/Objectiva, 2013); Gabriel Paquette, *Imperial Portugal in the Age of Atlantic Revolutions: The Luso-Brazilian World, c. 1770–1850* (Cambridge: Cambridge Univesity Press, 2013); Rui Ramos and Nuno G. Monteiro, "Liberalism in Portugal in the Nineteenth Century," in Michael Freeden, Javier Fernández-Sebastián, and Jörn Leonhard, eds., *In Search of European Liberalisms: Concepts, Languages, Ideologies* (New York: Berghahn, 2019), 135–60.

[2] Albert Silbert, *Do Portugal do Antigo Regime ao Portugal oitocentista* (Lisbon: Livros Horizonte, 1972), 48; Ana Cristina Araújo, *A cultura das Luzes em Portugal: Temas e problemas* (Lisbon: Livros Horizonte, 2003).

[3] Settlement letters granted by the Portuguese Crown since the end of the fifteenth century to most of the towns in the kingdom that contained the landlords' rights, which, since the previous centuries, were paid to the Crown and to the lords.

the royal income, and so there are two onerous land tributes ... which weigh upon agriculture without any profit to the state."[4] Actually, they were mainly paid to the aristocracy (the tithes through the commandaries (*comendas*) of the military orders) and clergy. D. Rodrigo therefore proposed the extinction of tithes and seigneurial rights and their replacement by a single tax. In later writings, when he was minister and responsible for finance, he questioned other aspects of the agrarian institutional structures of the *ancien régime*.[5] He advocated abolishing the *morgados* and *capelas* (entailed estates), emphyteusis (perpetual lease), and the disentailment of all goods belonging to religious orders, which would receive public debt securities in exchange. He also advocated abolishing all tax exemptions and jurisdictional privileges for the clergy and nobility. Except indirectly, he did not level any criticism at the high aristocracy but identified the foundations for what would be the subsequent internal reforms.

These proposals were only introduced to a very small degree, even though new taxes were imposed with renewed vigor on the high nobility and clergy, and, albeit sparingly, certain assets of the commandaries of military orders were sold off. Following the departure of the royal family to Brazil and the opening of ports of the former colony, the legal charter of 7 March 1810, signed in Rio de Janeiro by D. Rodrigo, proclaimed the goal of creating a committee that would deal with "the means that may fix the tithes ..., alleviate or change the system of *jugadas*, *quartos* and *terços*[6] ..., make the *foros* (emphyteusis land rents) redeemable ... and reduce or suppress the charters rights (*forais*)."[7] Yet little was done beyond these proclamations. Nonetheless, the liberalism of the 1820s would revive this heritage, combining it with a criticism of the aristocracy and regular clergy, and place it at the center of its projects regarding social order.

---

[4] Cf. D. Rodrigo de Sousa Coutinho, *Reflexões sobre a fiscalidade e finanças de Portugal* (*Reflections on the Taxation and Finances of Portugal*) (1786), in Pedro Cardim and Nuno Gonçalo Monteiro, eds., *Political Thought in Portugal and Its Empire, 1500–1800* (Cambridge: Cambridge University Press, 2021); Andrée Mansuy-Diniz Silva, *Portrait d'un homme d'État: D. Rodrigo de Sousa Coutinho*, 2 vols. (Lisbon: FCG, 2002–2006).

[5] António Manuel Hespanha, "O jurista e o legislador na construção da propriedade burguesa-liberal em Portugal," in *O século XIX em Portugal* (Lisbon: Análise Social, 1980).

[6] A quarter and a third of gross agricultural production, which constituted the most contested charter rights.

[7] Alberto Carlos de Menezes, *Plano de reforma dos foraes* (Lisbon: Impressão Régia, 1825), 332–5.

## The *Ancien Régime*

The implications of these reforms for Portugal's social order were, at the outset, more drastic than in most of the Spanish territories. This was, on the one hand, because lifelong and/or hereditary land concession, which was widespread, was very different from contemporary liberal notions of full ownership. The chief Portuguese institutions of the *ancien régime*, namely the Church, the court aristocracy, and the houses of the royal family were not predominantly large property owners in the sense that they had "absolute dominion" over the lands from which they derived. They did possess extensive properties, entailed estates (*morgados*) in the case of the aristocracy, mainly located near Lisbon and in the south (Alentejo), but the main part of their income came from agrarian charter rights (*forais*), ecclesiastical tithes, and emphyteusis land rents (*foros*) arising from the *dominium directum* of goods whose *dominium utile* had been transferred for lifetime or perpetual land tenants.[8] Tithes, seigneurial rights, and emphyteutic land rents (*foros enfitêuticos*) represented approximately 54 percent of the revenue from male convents, 52 percent from female convents, and 56 percent from the great houses of the Portuguese aristocracy.[9]

Indeed, in the Portuguese case, it makes no sense to speak of a nobility, but of several nobiliarchic groups. At the base, there was a large number of noblemen, who had acquired their status tacitly by their way of life. They included university graduates, army officers, and even businessmen, that is, groups that elsewhere would be called "bourgeois" or "middle class," which had no exact equivalent in eighteenth-century Portugal. While the top of the nobiliarchic pyramid was one of the most restricted in Europe, the base was open and imprecise, placing Portugal in the group of countries where the nobility was large in number. This top was constituted by a select group of the highest-born of the court nobility, which was headed by counts, marquises, dukes, and other great nobles who held titles. The aristocratic elite of the Braganza dynasty had been constituted, to a certain extent, during Portugal's process of separation from the Hispanic monarchy in 1640 and

---

[8] Rafe Blaufarb recently defined these concepts with regard to France: *dominium directum* "was an abstract right that allowed its holder to demand certain dues and to exercise certain prerogatives over the subordinate property upon which it rested"; *dominium utile* "represented the actual possession and right to use a physical property, albeit subject to the *seigneurie directe*." Rafe Blaufarb, *The Great Demarcation: The French Revolution and the Invention of Modern Property* (New York: Oxford University Press, 2016), 226.

[9] Fernando de Sousa, "O rendimento das ordens religiosas nos finais do Antigo Regime," *Revista de História Económica e Social* 7 (1981), 1–27.

the subsequent war, remaining essentially stable afterwards. Composed of about fifty houses that held titles with grandeeship (*grandeza*) and a few dozen others who aspired to receive them, they all lived in Lisbon. These noble titles could not be sold.

The identification between high nobility, royal court, and Lisbon was absolute. This elite, marked by strict rules of indivisibility in the transmission of patrimony, almost exclusively married among itself, relegating many daughters and second-born sons to ecclesiastical celibacy. The social exclusiveness of the high nobility and the strategies developed to perpetuate it were inseparable from the underlying monopoly of the main offices in the monarchy (viceroys, law court presidents, governors of military districts, chief colonial governors, etc.) and the corresponding remuneration of services to the Crown in royal donations, which resulted also from the activity of celibate second-born sons (bishops and cardinals, among others). From the mid-eighteenth century and the period of the Marquis de Pombal's governance, the court aristocracy lost power and influence that had been exercised through a body such as the Council of State. From then on, the secretaries of state (ministers) began to have more decision-making power than the high nobility, although the latter maintained a relevant role by occupying the main positions in the monarchy. Moreover, it was the services rendered that allowed the high nobility to accumulate royal donations of seigneurial rights, commanderies (*comendas*) and royal pensions (*tenças*), in other words, the range of benefits subject to royal confirmation, which amounted to more than 55 percent of the overall revenue of those aristocratic houses. In addition, they benefited from systematic protection against creditors, which limited the amount of tax executions on their houses.[10]

## The French Invasions

As in almost all other Iberian and Latin American territories, it was the wars of the French Revolution,[11] and especially the cycle of Napoleonic Wars, culminating in the French invasion of 1807 and the departure of the royal family and the Portuguese court to Brazil, that triggered a wave of changes.

---

[10] Nuno Gonçalo Monteiro, "Nobility and Aristocracy in Ancien Régime Portugal (Seventeenth to Nineteenth Centuries)," in Hamish Scott, ed., *European Nobilities in the Seventeenth and Eighteenth Centuries*, revised and expanded edition, 2 vols. (London: Palgrave Macmillan, 2007), vol. 1, 256–85.

[11] A first Spanish assault, with French support and known as the War of the Oranges, took place in 1801.

After the intervention of British troops in Portugal, the military confrontation would continue with successive French invasions until 1811. The British presence, however, would remain after peace was restored in 1814. As in Spain, the rebellion against the French gave rise to the formation of councils (juntas) and a sudden boom in newspapers that enjoyed no censorship for some time, but unlike the neighboring territories, no Cortes (parliamentary general assembly) was convened. As Silbert has stressed, the genesis of Portuguese liberalism differed greatly from the Spanish. While Spanish liberalism "was constituted at the time of the French invasion, that of Portugal does not seem to have acquired its own form until afterwards." A rare exception was a petition that circulated in 1808, asking Napoleon for "a constitution ... bearing the likeness of the one given to Warsaw." The author requested, among other things, for equality before the law – which implicitly meant that he asked for the Napoleonic Code of 1804 to be enacted – press freedom, the division of powers, the reform of public administration, disentailment, and a progressive tax system. This was the clearest ideological expression of the Portuguese Francophiles (*afrancesados*).[12] The attempts to promote reforms during the fight against the French were trivial. Some military in Oporto termed as liberal a local uprising and some other isolated incidents that had been severely repressed. The councils (juntas) formed against the French were dominated by an anti-Napoleonic culture with a traditional slant.[13]

In fact, the intense and sometimes violent popular mobilization unleashed against the French (and supposedly the Francophiles) occurred in the name of the Throne and the Holy Religion. It is true that in the anti-Napoleonic discourse references to the nation, in the sense of the Portuguese people opposed to the invading peoples, appeared more and more often. But its symbols, which then spread, were the flag of the Portuguese royal House and its armory. The nation was not yet disentangled from the people's loyalty to the Braganza dynasty, which had taken refuge in Brazil. In subsequent years, however, in the liberal camp the nation's affirmation would emerge in opposition to the British presence and later as an alternative principle of legitimacy to royal sovereignty. In the opposite camp, the

---

[12] These were small groups of supporters of the French occupation who expected it to produce reforms; Silbert, *Do Portugal do Antigo Regime ao Portugal oitocentista*; Ana Cristina Araújo, "Revoltas e ideologias em conflito durante as invasões francesas," *Revista de História das Ideias* 7 (1985), 7–90.

[13] Vasco Pulido Valente, *Ir Pró Maneta: A revolta contra os Franceses (1808)* (Lisbon: Alêtheia Editores, 2007).

royalists would invoke the Portuguese nation to oppose it to the liberals, considered a handful of denaturalized people, devoted to foreign ideas and Freemasonry.

The years following the French invasions (1814–1820) witnessed an explosion of the Portuguese press thanks to political exiles. Printed in London and Paris, the newspapers published could evade all prohibitions and circulate in Portugal and Brazil. These publications regularly invoked the theme of the "ancient constitution." Journalist Freire de Carvalho later asserted that he had done so "because he did not want to frighten the government ... and because he knew quite well that the old Cortes carried in its womb the new Cortes."[14] One of the legacies from those years was indeed the argument that the Cortes should assemble because this was in line with the monarchy's ancient (unwritten) constitution. It was, nonetheless, during the same years that a liberal current was formed in Portugal, which was strongly influenced by the Spanish Constitution of 1812.

## 1820

Between the first French invasion (1807) and the ultimate triumph of liberalism (1834), the fate of the Portuguese kingdom – officially called the Kingdom of Portugal, Brazil, and the Algarve between 1815 and 1822 – hung in the balance as it was tied in large part to Brazil and to Portuguese interactions with the Spanish monarchy. The departure of the royal family and the opening of the ports of Brazil in 1808 triggered a crisis in Portuguese external trade, and the abovementioned promise of 1810 to reform the agrarian structures was presented as a compensation for the loss of Brazil's trade. It was in this context that a conspiracy was organized in Oporto, mainly by jurists and the military, who would constitute the basis to promote the liberal military pronouncement of 1820. It aspired to return the king to Lisbon and adopting the Spanish Constitution of 1812 as the basis for a future Portuguese constitution.

This movement was responsible for drawing up the first Portuguese written constitution, which was crafted by a parliament with representatives from the entire monarchy, including Brazil. The proclamation of Brazil's independence in 1822 (analyzed in other chapters of this book) contributed to the overthrow of the Portuguese liberal triennium, which coincided with that

[14] Quoted in Nuno G. Monteiro, "Mouzinho da Silveira and the Political Culture of Portuguese Liberalism, 1820–1832," *History of European Ideas* 41:2 (2015), 185–93: 186.

Portugal's Social and Political Change

of Spain, but did not involve a French military presence. Infante D. Miguel, the youngest son of the king, placed himself at the head of the counter-revolutionary movement, with the support of his mother, the queen. After the death of King João VI in March 1826, the emperor and rightful successor to the Portuguese crown, D. Pedro, sent a Constitutional Charter (*Carta Constitucional*) from Brazil, which was inspired by the Brazilian Constitution of 1824. On his behalf and that of his daughter, to whom he yielded his rights, an undeclared civil war began in 1826 in which he and his constitution were fought tooth and nail. The war was only settled in 1828, under the ultra-royalist government of D. Miguel. The Portuguese liberals in the Azores resisted and, finally, led by D. Pedro and in the adamant belief that the loss of Brazil required great internal changes, they fought and ultimately triumphed, with international support, in the declared civil war of 1832–1834.

In his memoirs, the 7th marquis of Fronteira related that in 1820 "ideas of revolution were everywhere"; "those who knew the advantages of a representative government, wanted that government," but "everyone wanted the royal court in Lisbon, because they hated the idea of being the colony of a colony."[15] José Xavier Mouzinho da Silveira, a lawyer with a long-service career in public administration, including a stint in government, stated more precisely:

> In 1820, the example of Spain, the absence of the king, the allowances [*mesadas*] he demanded in Rio de Janeiro, and the English influence were what caused the uprising in Oporto, which galvanized all; and the so-called royalists cannot say that they did not esteem or applaud it; because I have never heard from those ... with whom I spoke during that period anything but applause and congratulations.[16]

The new political protagonists came from two backgrounds. On the one hand, they were jurists trained in modern natural law in Coimbra, who participated in the intense political socialization of the postwar years; and, on the other hand, they came from the military (Figure 17.1). These men formed a conspiratorial organization in Oporto, clearly inspired by Freemasonry, known as the Sinédrio. There were several disputes between

---

[15] *Memórias do Marquês de Fronteira e d'Alorna*, ed. E. C. Andrade, vols. I and II (1802 to 1824) (Coimbra: Imprensa da Universidade, 1926), vol. I, 194–5.
[16] José Xavier Mouzinho da Silveira, *Obras de Mouzinho da Silveira*, ed. Miriam Halpern Pereira, Valentim Alexandre, and Magda Pinheiro (Lisbon, 1989), vol. I, 620.

Figure 17.1 Meeting of the provisional Portuguese government, 1 October 1820. Courtesy of the John Carter Brown Library.

the two groups, with the military party advocating the proclamation of the Constitution of Cádiz, albeit with "appropriate modifications," although not "less liberal." Even though the military faction ended up being removed, the type of regime had been defined. The deputies were elected in December 1820 and voted in February and March 1821 on the "Bases of the Constitution," which in essence laid the groundwork for the future constitutional text. The first Portuguese written constitution determined that "sovereignty" resided "in the Nation," as it did in the Constitution of Cádiz; only the king was granted a suspensive veto on the decisions of the Cortes, which formed the legislative power; and a unicameral model was adopted, after a large majority rejected a second Chamber. One key passage stressed that the "Portuguese Nation is the union of the Portuguese from both hemispheres ... Its religion is the Roman Catholic Apostolic one," in other words, the nation encompassed the overseas Portuguese territories and it had an official religion. The Bases included, at the beginning, a declaration of rights that consecrated the principle of equality before the law and the freedom of thought.

In March 1821, the liberals unanimously extinguished the Inquisition, which would not be restored. They also abolished judicial privileges.

Figure 17.2 Triumphant entry of King João VI and his son D. Miguel in Lisbon, 27 May 1823. Courtesy of Museu de Lisboa.

However, while most deputies mistrusted the usefulness of the regular clergy, they recognized the essential social role of the parish clergy. Reinforcing an existing tendency – the number of monks and nuns was already in decline –, they therefore restricted admissions to monasteries even further, aiming at their gradual extinction. By contrast, the fundamental role that they wanted parish priests to play led the authorities to use them frequently as an instrument of diffusion of their own political objectives. In response to a major petition initiative by parish priests, they even planned to increase their salaries (*côngrua*). In any case, the objectives of *vintismo* (the Portuguese liberal movement from 1820 through 1823) were not achieved until the triumph of liberalism in 1834 (Figure 17.2).[17]

---

[17] José Horta Correia, *Liberalismo e catolicismo: O problema congregacionista (1820–1823)* (Coimbra: Universidade de Coimbra, 1974).

## Social Categories and Political Discourse

During the first liberal triennium (1820–1823), the number of petitioners expanded dramatically. By means of cultural and political intermediaries, many popular groups gained a new voice. Petitions that had previously been sent to various institutions of the central government were now transmitted to the "Sovereign Congress," having multiplied in number and diversity and having acquired a more assertive tone. Numerous petitions were authored by women, including those working in the streets in Lisbon such as roaming *adelas* (dealers in the business of second-hand objects), "poor and persecuted women," who targeted the police officers that beat them for selling cotton cloths. Petitions were also sent by washerwomen and the poorest from Campo Grande,[18] who fought the authorities, which forbade them to hang clothes based on the argument that it "disrupted what has been called the promenade of Campo Grande."[19] But there were also petitions from male artisans, servants, and a wide variety of other groups, and individuals.

The first Portuguese constituents of 1821–1822 considerably expanded the right to vote, refusing to introduce census limitations. The only men barred were those under the age of twenty-five (with some exceptions), dependent children, regular ecclesiastics (not secular ones), and, at a future date, the illiterate. To be eligible to become a deputy, one was required to draw an income from one's own property or from one's economic pursuit or employment. However, and contrary to the Spanish Constitution of Cádiz (1812), which had served as its inspiration, the constituents granted Portuguese citizenship to "slaves who obtained a letter of liberation (*carta de alforria*)." This was the result of a broad debate in which several elected deputies from the territories of Brazil took part. Slaves had almost disappeared from mainland Portugal after eighteenth-century legislation had set it apart from the rest of the monarchy. The concession of the right to vote to freedmen born in the United Kingdom of Portugal, Brazil, and the Algarve, was unquestionably an innovative dimension of the Constitution of 1822, just as the direct elections which would not be included in subsequent constitutional texts. Instead, the Constitutional Charter (*Carta Constitucional*) of 1826, bestowed by D. Pedro IV and based on the Brazilian Constitution of 1824, made a distinction between passive and active citizens, restraining the

---

[18] A parish in Lisbon.
[19] *Arquivo Histórico Parlamentar da Assembleia da República (Lisboa, Portugal)*, caixa no. 10, nn. 131, 107, and 174.

right to vote in indirect elections to those who met certain census criteria (in particular an annual income that was only attained by about one-fifth of the heads of households who could vote at the parish level). The income requirements to become an elector of a province or to become eligible for deputy were even higher.

Despite the participation of women in some of the spaces of political sociability during this time, the family laws advocated by liberals, and largely inspired by the French Code of 1804, confined women to their domestic role and stressed the inviolability of the "home of every Portuguese" (Const. 1822, title 1, Chapter 1, Art. 5). In the course of the parliamentary debates in April 1822, Domingos Borges de Barros, deputy for Bahia, owner of a sugar mill, graduate by the University of Coimbra, and future viscount, defended women's right to vote, advocating "that at least the mothers of six legitimate children have this right . . . ."[20] The Cortes did not even allow a vote on this proposal. As deputy and jurist Manuel Borges Carneiro put it shortly before, "a woman in Portugal can become Queen, but she cannot vote for deputies in the Cortes."[21] Although many women were involved in politics during those years at all levels and in all fields, liberalism and antiliberalism were affairs of men.

However, in its core, the discourse of *vintismo* implied a condemnation, although not an emphatic one, of the aristocracy and the "privileged classes." In June 1822, for instance, when the introduction of a second Chamber was discussed, deputy José Joaquim Ferreira de Moura declared his opposition to this proposal: "Who among us would make up that conservative body? Who of the grandees (high nobility), the high clergy or the high judiciary? These classes are the privileged classes; they are the ones who oppose and will forever oppose useful reforms."[22] At around the same time, during a debate about Brazil, he mentioned a "conspiracy of the aristocracy of São Paulo," using "aristocracy" in a derogatory sense. In August of the same year, deputy Borges Carneiro explicitly referred to the "factions that peace-loving people, proprietors and merchants, whether they are Europeans or Brazilians, detest, with on the one hand a gang of ambitious people and aristocrats who want to impose the yoke of the aristocracy or absolute monarchy; and on the other, a reckless and frantic bunch that want to rush us into a democratic and

---

[20] *Diário das Cortes Constituintes e Extraordinárias*, 22 April 1822, n. 63, 908 (http://debates .parlamento.pt/catalogo/mc/c1821/01/01/01/063/1822-04-22).

[21] *Diário das Cortes Constituintes e Extraordinárias*, 16 April 1822, n. 58, 566.

[22] *Diário das Cortes Constituintes e Extraordinária*, 26 June 1822, n. 41, 566.

demagogic government."[23] This was the language of the middle ground, and it also conveyed a tendency that would be fundamental in the liberal discourse to extol merchants and proprietors.

In fact, there was no doubt that "proprietors, merchants, and manufacturers" were a mainstay of the regime. At least for many deputies, it was evident what Mouzinho da Silveira would argue in 1830: "The commercial class was at the end of 1822 the only class that supported the liberals; but this excessively ignorant class encouraged liberalism with the intention to recover the monopoly of [trade with] the colonies . . . ."[24]

But even if liberalism, a term that only began to spread at that time, was politically a "representative system," it also resulted in "civil equality." In this respect, it was the French Revolution of 1789 that served as a great inspiration and provided the vocabulary employed. As deputy M. G. Miranda declared: "What are the assets that France possesses? Which prosperity does it enjoy? All this prosperity derives from the tempestuous discussion of 4 August (1789) which abolished the rights, privileges, and everything that oppressed that nation."[25] On this basis, repeated criticism was leveled at the "privileged classes" and the "aristocracy," with the latter often treated more as partisans of a political model – in the Aristotelian sense of a form of government – than as a social group. However, its counterpoint tended to be a broad and unifying concept of the people. The privileged classes were said to oppose the people or nation (rarely the "Third Estate"), not only because of the influence of this French reference, but also because the nation had previously rejected the census vote, and consequently the possibility of establishing a clear hierarchy among the people. As Bento Pereira do Carmo explained, "the privileges . . . are not in harmony with *civil* equality, which forms the basis of the representative system, in which the law must be equal for all."[26]

In spite of this, the political notion of middle class made a late appearance, in consonance with what happened in the French political culture in the 1820s, as well as in that of England of an earlier date. In April 1822, the deputy José Vitorino Barreto Feio gave one of the first speeches that invoked the concept:

---

[23] *Diário das Cortes Constituintes e Extraordinárias*, 30 August 1822, n. 24, 290.
[24] Mouzinho da Silveira, *Obras*, vol. 1, 622.
[25] *Diário das Cortes Constituintes e Extraordinárias*, 16 March 1822, n. 38, 522.
[26] *Diário das Cortes Constituintes e Extraordinárias*, 16 August 1822, n. 13, 159 (emphasis in the original).

The Portuguese nation, just as all those who have passed from slavery to freedom, believes it is divided into three classes: the noble, the people, and the vagabond. If we, with just cause, have excluded the vagabond because they have no interest in society, and for that reason don't have a steady income; all the more reason we should exclude the class of nobles from voting in the elections because they have opposing interests from the people, and aspire to enslave them, and we should only admit the middle class, because it is in the middle where virtue lies.[27]

It was a topic with a future.

The pamphlet *Revolução Anti-constitucional em 1823* (*The Anticonstitutional Revolution in 1823*), published in London in 1825, after the regime of the Constitution of 1822 had been overthrown, and whose authorship some have attributed to a minister of justice during the triennium, constitutes one of the earliest writings that insists on the opposition between the "privileged classes" identified as the high nobility, the high clergy and the high judiciary, and the middle class. That pamphlet describes these classes as adversaries of the "constitutional cause," and of the "Middle Class of Merchants and Proprietors who up to a certain time formed a strong opinion in favor of the constitutional system."[28] Nonetheless, it should be stressed that this vocabulary was occasionally applied as well by those representing the counterrevolution. In a text written in 1823, with a clear French inspiration and aimed at criticizing liberalism, the lord of Pancas stated that the deputies of the triennium,

unhappy with the antipolitical, erroneous, and extremely unjust exclusion of representation (of the nobility) in the Cortes, either as a class or as a separate Chamber, had the vileness of ranting for a system with the most atrocious slander and sarcasm in many sessions of the Cortes against the high clergy, the grandees (titled nobility) in particular, and the nobility of the kingdom in general.

And he added:

The Machiavellian inventiveness to present the nobility as ignorant is therefore so slanderous and false, that … I dare to prove that in the class of the nobility there is much more science and less ignorance than in what is commonly called the *middle* class, which the Liberal Party considered to be the nursery of deputies, diplomats, and constitutional civil servants.[29]

---

[27] *Diário das Cortes Constituintes e Extraordinárias*, 19 April 1822, 879–80.
[28] *Revolução anti-constitucional em 1823, suas verdadeiras causas e efeitos* (London: L. Thompson, Officina Portugueza, 1825), 11.
[29] José Sebastião de Saldanha Oliveira Daun, *Diorama de Portugal nos 33 mezes constitucionaes ou golpe de vista sobre a revolução de 1820 a constituição de 1822 a restauração de 1823 e*

Moreover, the royalist antiliberal discourse in subsequent years, which was much more radical and aggressive, assumed at times an openly anti-mercantile character in its criticism of liberalism: "The millionaire merchant, the presumptuous magnate, the celibate second son, the liberal philosopher, are not afraid to risk their power ... by becoming partners and even leaders of Jacobin Revolutions."[30]

Meanwhile, there was also a specific liberal discourse about the rural world, largely linked to the question of the local charters (*forais*) during *vintismo*, i.e., the agrarian seigneurial rights donated by the Crown to landowners. For many, such as deputy Miranda,

> the day that all local charters (*forais*) are extinguished will be the most beautiful day for Portugal ..., because agriculture will flourish, trade will flourish, the inhabitants will find themselves more comfortable, and may thus contribute more comfortably, while the nation and each individual benefiting from the resulting general prosperity.[31]

These assumptions were clear. As the mathematician and member of the parliament Francisco Soares Franco put it in an account of 1821, if "individual interest is the real source that leads men to undertake the greatest works and risks," "the interest for farmers, to be truly rational, must correspond to the regular interest rate [5 percent], after deducting the expenditures," but that was hindered by the excessive burden of the local charters (*forais*).[32]

Despite all the political advantages that were offered, the fear of antagon-izing the "privileged classes" imposed a moderate character on *vintista* legislation. Notwithstanding the numerous petitions on the matter, and a proposal by the Azorean deputy Medeiros Mântua, the Cortes refused to abolish entailed estates (*morgados*). On 5 May 1821, a decree was passed that transformed landed property donated by the Crown to individuals into national property. There were no immediate consequences, except theoret-ically, because these assets would only revert to the state in the case of noblemen who had received donations from the Portuguese Crown and commanders of military orders passed away, which did not affect ecclesi-astical landowners. Either way, the new political order required various oaths

---

*acontecimentos posteriores até ao fim de outubro do mesmo ano* (Lisbon: Na Impressão Régia, 1823), 56–7 (emphasis added).

[30] José Agostinho de Macedo (1828), quoted in Maria Alexandre Lousada, *O Miguelismo (1828–1834): O discurso político e o apoio da nobreza titulada* (Lisbon: FLL, 1987), 35.

[31] *Diário das Cortes Constituintes e Extraordinárias*, 11 November 1821, n. 228, 2123.

[32] *Diário das Cortes Constituintes e Extraordinárias*, 4 June 1821, n. 96, 1112.

from the titled nobility and the commanders, who incidentally were also compelled to pay new taxes. On 7 April of that same year, a law had passed abolishing the *banalités*, a term taken from French that meant rights and personal services, some of which, except in specific matters (such as seigneurial monopolies and the remnants of *geiras* or *corvée*), the deputies did not quite know what they were. Finally, at the end of a drawn-out debate, the agrarian seigneurial rights contained in the municipal charters were reduced by one-half, and the rest could be redeemed for payment.

There are no doubts about the political investment in the legislation regarding *foral* charters. For the liberals, the question was equivalent to the abolition of feudal rights in France on 4 August 1789.[33] They believed that it would have a huge impact by determining that the decree should be read during four consecutive Sundays in all of the country's town councils, both in towns whose population had requested the reforms through insistence and petitions, and in those that did not even have a charter (*foral*). The impact of the legislation was significant only in some large but somewhat confined areas of the kingdom. These were areas (mainly in the central parts of the country) where heavy duties were paid, which in most cases were proportional to the harvests, and made up about one-fifth of Portugal's territory. When in July 1824 almost the entire liberal legislation was revoked, in particular the law of charter rights (*a lei dos forais*), the reaction in the affected areas was obviously more emphatic. The most notorious case occurred in the district (*comarca*) of the Monastery of Alcobaça, where the farmers resisted the reinstatement of full payment of seigneurial dues and tithes to the monastery in that year of 1824. As the Crown magistrate of the district stated at the end of that month of July, "this is the insubordination and anarchic spirit that reigns in the plurality of the villages of these coutos (areas belonging to the clergy) ... which is not possible to remedy without the presence of the armed forces." The *coutos* of Alcobaça were therefore occupied by the army for six months with the aim of restoring the seigneurial order. As in other areas, the receptivity to liberal legislation was mainly reflected in the refusal by a large extent of farmers to pay duties, which was not necessarily a political act, and only turned violent when the compulsory collection of duties provoked resistance from farmers.[34] However, this

---

[33] See Rafe Blaufarb, Chapter 2 in Volume II of this book.
[34] Nuno Gonçalo Monteiro, "Lavradores, frades e forais: Revolução liberal e regime senhorial na comarca de Alcobaça," in *Elites e poder: Entre o Antigo Regime e o Liberalismo*, 3rd edition (Lisbon: Imprensa das Ciências Sociais, 2012), 215–99.

pattern of behavior by the population was only found in specific areas, which were also less receptive to counterrevolutionary mobilization.

In 1826, King João VI died, and D. Pedro granted the Constitutional Charter in Brazil at the same time that he renounced the crown of Portugal in favor of his daughter. This concession was regarded as an attempt at conciliation between the parties concerned, even though the royalists did not perceive it as such. The Charter contained what came to be called the "moderating power of the monarch," granting him absolute veto on the decisions taken in the national parliament, even though it possessed legislative power. The Charter consecrated a bicameral system, which included, in addition to a Chamber of elected deputies, a Chamber of hereditary peers appointed by royal nomination, for which all seventy-two secular grandees of the kingdom (dukes, marquises, and counts, and also viscounts with grandeeship) as well as the bishops were soon appointed. The Charter also sanctioned the distinction between active and passive citizens, curbing the right to vote in indirect elections to those who met certain census criteria in the parish assemblies, and introducing more restrictive income requirements to become the elector of a province or to be eligible for the position of deputy. The word "sovereignty" never appears in an explicit manner in the referred text; Article 12 of the Constitutional Charter of 1826 states that "[t]he Representatives of the Portuguese Nation are the King and the Cortes," which is generally interpreted as an affirmation of dual sovereignty, that of the king and the nation. The proclamation of the Constitutional Charter of 1826 did not result in its effective application, as it was immediately followed by successive rebellions led by royalists. Although the governments changed, partisans of D. Miguel would integrate the chief ministers with moderate liberals.

Another pattern of mobilization from the rural world differed from the antiseigneurial movement described above. Taking place during the ultraroyalist movements, in particular, between 1826 and 1828, this mobilization was more significant in the Douro region, in the areas of Minho and Beira Alta as well as the Algarve, in the south. Instigated on behalf of king and religion, these movements relied on the very active role of the officers of the *ordenanças* (local militia reserves) and a portion of the secular clergy, who frequently mobilized rural areas against the urban provincial centers where significant groups of liberals lived. The most notorious exception to this pattern was the Douro region, which was divided between liberal and royalist villages, where warfare continued up to the beginning of D. Miguel's government (1828). During these years, the persecution of liberal villages in Vila Real produced almost 1,000 political prisoners. Outside of the Douro region, however, the liberals were mainly urban, in other words, employees, military personnel, merchants, liberal professionals, and artisans, as well as members of the secular clergy. By contrast, the much more numerous royalist movement, which at times turned very violent, for example by looting the homes of alleged constitutionalists and frequently fomenting guerrilla operations, gained its support predominantly from younger and less skilled people from the rural and, in some cases, the urban population. It is not surprising that the liberals incited the use of a pejorative vocabulary shared by counterrevolutionary publicists and inspired by categories from the classical world and, more recently, the French Revolution. The *Miquelists* were described as "plebs," "ragged," "scoundrels," "rebels," "anarchists," and even "Jacobins." On the other side, the popular *Miquelists* used old discriminating labels such as "Negroes" or "Jews" to describe the liberals.[35]

The invocation of the nation took on a new tone in this context. The antiliberal movement embraced references and even symbols (such as the red ribbon) like the ones that had been used in the war against the French. Supported by a majority, those violent movements shared the assertion that the liberals were foreigners and that the royalists represented the nation. The liberals, who had changed national symbols (namely adopting the blue ribbon), were "a faction that hating the glory and honor of the nation, changed the Flag, the Portuguese Pavilion, with which we shook Africa, Asia, and America; it is an anti-national faction," one newspaper wrote in 1832.[36] It can thus be stated that there was a counterrevolutionary nationalism, which was grounded on extensive mobilization but rooted in local corporate institutions. In contrast, the significant liberal minority, which sometimes defended itself with weapons, could not assert itself as an expression of the nation's will, just only of the enlightened part of its members. The adoption by liberals, with clear inspiration from elsewhere, of the discourse of "class struggle" went along with the acknowledgment of what was termed the "middle class." The latter was considered the only class with legitimacy and independence to express the nation's will politically. The "active citizens," those who could vote, represented the nation.

---

[35] Nuno Gonçalo Monteiro, "Societat rural i actituds polítiques a Portugal (1820–1834)," in Josep Maria Fradera, Jesús Millán, and Ramón Garrabou, eds., *Carlisme i moviments absolutistes* (Girona: Editorial Eumo, 1990), 127–50; António Monteiro Cardoso, *A Revolução liberal em Trás-os-Montes (1820–1834)* (Porto: Afrontamento, 2007).

[36] *Gazeta de Lisboa*, n. 142, 16 June 1832, quoted in Lousada, *O Miguelismo*, 143.

A paradigmatic example of the liberal discourse in this period is that of J. J. Silva Maia (1777–1832), a Luso-Brazilian merchant, editor of the newspaper *Imparcial*, published in Oporto between 1826 and 1828, and who was the author of a posthumous memoir on the liberal revolt of 1828, in which the liberal Portuguese sought to oppose the coup by D. Miguel. In his writings, based on the events as well as in his subsequent memoirs, he maintained that the partisans of the "representative system" were recruited from the "middle class," "where the enlightenment, the riches and the arts have been rediscovered; it is the aristocracy of competence." The partisans of absolutism, on the other hand, were directly recruited from the "aristocracy of birth," which would be able to mobilize the "third class," "the plebeians, that is, the large mass of uneducated people, that only feel, and almost do not think," the same class that had already caused the havoc and damage that "Oporto had previously ... experienced in 1808," and that could have been steered in another direction and practiced the same acts "as it did in France in the disastrous year of 1793."[37] In much of the other liberal press during those years, one can find a similar rejection of absolutism and democracy, concepts which are explicitly juxtaposed in many speeches.

In fact, in 1826, references to the aristocracy and the middle class (in the extremely broad liberal sense of the term, ranging from large merchants to farmers and independent artisans) appeared periodically in the press. But the immense political divide experienced in the kingdom during those years adds another dimension to the matter. The intense royalist mobilizations, on the one hand, and the considerable adhesion to liberalism, on the other, which was reflected in the large number of people taken prisoner or persecuted, highlighted the dramatic nature of the rift. The utmost political repression in Portuguese history was carried out in 1828. There is no certainty, but what is known suffices to conclude that the number of victims was high. Silva Maia mentioned "8,000 citizens of the second class [the middle] who are clogging the prisons of Portugal; so many others are outlaws or in hiding so that they are not arrested."[38] The count of Lavradio estimated that the number of prisoners exceeded 30,000. More than 13,000 individuals whose names are known were defendants and/or were arrested during the government of D. Miguel, particularly in the later months of 1828. If we add to this number all the other emigrants and outlaws (some remained in hiding for five years), it is safe to assume that the number of

---

[37] Joaquim José da Silva Maia, *Memorias historicas, politicas e filosoficas da revolução do Porto em maio de 1828* (Rio de Janeiro: Typographia de Laemmert, 1841), 229, 237–9.

[38] Maia, *Memorias historicas*, 236.

Portugal's Social and Political Change

prisoners and escapees was more than 20,000, in a population of three million inhabitants. We know the professional identity of slightly less than 4,000: the largest group was composed of military personnel (24 percent), followed by employees and civil servants (14 percent), merchants, secular clergy, members of the liberal professions (approximately 13 percent each one), and artisans (11 percent). Most liberals were, therefore, urban and educated, and coincided with the "middle-class" self-image that they delineated for themselves.[39]

In fact, the political orientation of the antiliberal rebellion in 1826 and 1827 was determined by the nobility in the provinces, not the grandees (*Grandeza*) that pontificated in the Chamber of Peers. But their action was decisive in the seizure of power by D. Miguel in 1828. Most titleholders with grandeeship, who had a seat in the Chamber of Peers in 1826–1828, formally endorsed the kingship of D. Miguel, as did the majority (59 percent) of titleholders. There was a large minority of the titled nobility (24 percent) that unequivocally supported the cause of D. Pedro.[40]

The considerable number of liberals who had emigrated to England and France tended to condemn the Portuguese aristocracy. The topics they discussed came from the past, but received a new impetus. In essence, those topics were already contained in the pamphlet *A Revolução Anticonstitucional* from 1825, which stated that any reform in Portugal would be against the interests of the Portuguese nobility. Silva Maia should also be mentioned, when he synthesized the most frequent recriminations, written in his Brazilian memoirs of exile around 1830: "The first class, not numerous ... is nevertheless largely ignorant because in the absolute system it is only the quality of birth that grants access to exercising the highest jobs ... haughty and proud, considering themselves of another race, they see plebeians as despicable beings who were born to obey them." He endorsed a common critique of the aristocratic houses and their administration: "they pay their creditors when they want and how they want; some are in debt, other houses are in receivership; the largest number sustain themselves with the rents from Crown donations and military orders, and there are few who have their own assets and without debts."[41] These arguments were all discussed by Mouzinho da Silveira, from the very beginning of his writings in exile in France around 1830, and then during the liberal revolution in Portugal in 1832.

[39] Rui Cascão, "A revolução do Porto de 1828," *Revista de História das Ideias* 7 (1985), 111–53.
[40] Maria Alexandre Lousada, "D. Pedro ou D. Miguel? As opções políticas da nobreza titulada portuguesa," *Penélope. Fazer e desfazer a História* 4 (1990), 81–110.
[41] *Revolução anti-constitucional em 1823*, 25; Maia, *Memorias historicas*, 230.

469

## War and Change

Among the Portuguese political emigration in France, there were supporters of the liberal cause, such as Silvestre Pinheiro Ferreira and Filipe Ferreira, who considered it inappropriate to deprive the nobility "of their interests and honor." This had happened in France, but "through a combination of circumstances that cannot be found in any other country."[42] By contrast, "in Portugal, Spain, England and the German states, the question was infinitely more serious since in all of these countries the privileged classes, namely the secular and regular clergy, the nobility, and the judiciary make up a large part of the nation." There were more people among the emigrated liberals with a similar judgment. Incidentally, prominent figures of the exiled liberal aristocracy such as the count of Lavradio and the marquises of Palmela and Fronteira were surprised and displeased with the legislation of 1832.

However, Mouzinho da Silveira and mostly the so-called "friends of D. Pedro," did not share these thoughts. These former *vintistas* were now uncompromising advocates of connecting the implementation of the Constitutional Charter with major reforms with a clear French inspiration. Not only because, as Mouzinho would later write, they believed this was a way to "make propaganda for liberalism and obtain thousands of supporters," in a country that was yet to be conquered, but also because they considered that only when new laws were published would the Constitutional Charter be feasible, since they thought that the Charter was incompatible with an aristocracy dependent on royal gifts. To quote Mouzinho again, "the privileged people who lived on other people's sweat, estimated that the Kings would possess the goods of the People, because, in fact, they possessed such goods in their favor . . . ." He therefore considered it crucial to "take advantage of the knowledge of civilized Europe, and wrest the fruit of the work of the People from the hands of the enemies . . . ."[43] Nonetheless, as he stated several times, his main desire was to release property from limiting restrictions in order to increase wealth. In this matter, Mouzinho was embracing a Smithian optimism, by increasing wealth and thereby the amounts of wealth that could be taxed.[44]

---

[42] *Parecer sobre os Meios de se Restaurar o Governo Representativo em Portugal, seguido de Novas Observações que se Publicaram em Londres sem Aquele Parecer* (Paris: de Casimir, 1832).

[43] Reproduced in Miriam Halpern Pereira, *Revolução, finanças, dependência externa* (Lisbon: Sá da Costa, 1979), 163.

[44] Reproduced in Pereira, *Revolução*, 203.

In 1832, when Mouzinho was the Minister for Finances, he signed the decrees that abolished tithes, along with "the tithes-based commanderies of all military orders," town charter rights (*forais*), as well as Crown donations and the law that regulated primogeniture and the indivisibility of royal donations to aristocrats. As a matter of fact, as Mouzinho had previously written, "the clergymen possess the tithes which are shared with the aristocrats . . . and all of that far surpasses the state revenues."[45] The separation between public and private spheres, which those laws were meant to achieve, did not allow for the private sector to receive taxes: "The contributions and taxes paid by the people, being essentially intended for public expenditure, might not become the patrimony of any corporation or individual regardless of hierarchy."[46] Taxes should be shared among all the inhabitants of the Monarchy, according to the general laws. In all cases, compensation for the abolition of rights would only be paid if the grantees and commanders had not supported the government of the "usurper," D. Miguel. Furthermore, only the small entailed estates (*morgados*) were abolished, in sharp contrast with what happened in Spain. The intention was to extinguish the aristocracy's dependence on the Crown, guaranteeing, at the same time, the conditions to perpetuate an independent aristocracy, according to the Constitutional Charter that provided for the existence of a Chamber of perpetual and hereditary peers. The last entailed estates (*morgados*) would only be extinguished in 1863.

Mouzinho's legislation on administrative reform intended to produce a differentiation between the administrative and the judicial power at all levels of government by placing elected local councils under a government-appointed ombudsman. This aspect of the reforms is generally regarded as having produced a strong centralizing effect and having left a longlasting mark. Subsequent legislation, enacted after Mouzinho retired, allowed the liberal government to encompass almost all areas until 1834–1835. This government extinguished the regular religious orders and nationalized their possessions for subsequent sale; established that, after the abolition of tithes, the secular clergy would be paid a regular salary (*côngruas*); extinguished all superior courts; eliminated the crafts guilds; put an end to militias and *ordenanças* (local militia reserves); eradicated the rank of army cadets; and abolished most of the municipal councils.

The old aristocratic houses were heavily affected by the impact of the liberal legislation. The extinction of the commanderies (*comendas*) and of the

---

[45] Mouzinho da Silveira, *Obras*, vol. i, 509.    [46] Reproduced in Pereira, *Revolução*, 167.

Crown donations, which drastically reduced their revenues, took place without the overwhelming majority of the aristocrats receiving any kind of compensation. Many representatives of the titled aristocracy fled Lisbon when liberal forces entered the city on 24 July 1833. The consequences for their patrimony were so serious that in most cases their assets suffered huge debts that gave way to quick judicial executions after 1834. Many palaces in Lisbon changed hands in the course of the nineteenth century. The political decline of the *ancien régime*'s aristocracy was notorious, as it was reflected in the governments of the constitutional monarchy. In fact, in the first decades of liberalism, there were still members of the titled nobility (*grandees*) of the *ancien régime* among those heading the government, who were generally those who had aligned with the liberals during the civil war and who subsequently almost vanished. The last government presided over by an individual born into the court aristocracy dates to 1870; and the last one headed by someone with a title was that of 1878. The same applied to government ministers, among whom few members of the old aristocratic houses were found, their number in decline throughout the entire parliamentary monarchy. The decrease of the political influence of the old nobility spread to the Chamber of Peers that had originally been aristocratic. Never again would the old nobility, which predominantly supported D. Miguel, outnumber the other members.

The overall impact of the legislation on Portuguese society cannot be analyzed in the same straightforward way. It seems evident that the first decades of Portuguese liberalism were marked by substantial social mobility, with wider implications for the elites at the center. The parliamentary and political elites experienced a new and broader basis of recruitment. Unlike before, the municipal governments of Lisbon and Oporto became close allies of leading merchants, who started to occupy prominent positions as councilors. In the rest of the country, the social backgrounds of local government officials changed significantly, but varied from place to place. Finally, the vast redistribution of agricultural products resulting from the abolition of taxes and the transfer of ownership prompted by the confiscation of Church property and subsequent selling of national assets had a profound outcome on elites and middle groups, but its global economic and social consequences have not yet been thoroughly analyzed.[47]

In spite of the copious legislation produced by the liberals, it was the law abolishing the town charters and the donations by the Crown which

---

[47] Cf. Monteiro, *Elites e poder*, 139–75.

symbolized the changes wrought by a new social and political order. Indeed, many of the protagonists agreed on that, and so did the nineteenth-century historian and publicist Alexandre Herculano, whose work provided the main historical legitimation of liberalism.[48] That law was, however, just one element among numerous transformations and continuities during a period that revolved around the attempt to change the order of things.

[48] Alexandre Herculano, *Opúsculos*, ed. Jorge Custódio and José Manuel Garcia (Lisbon: Presença, 1982–1983), vols. i and ii.

18

# Conservative Tracks toward Independence: Transfer of the Court to Rio de Janeiro, the Porto Revolution, and Brazilian Autonomy

JURANDIR MALERBA

## Introduction

Considering moments as complex as the end of Iberian rule in America and the so-called "crisis of the old colonial system," this chapter aims to highlight the core features of the Brazilian political emancipation vis-à-vis the wars of independence in Spanish America. The complexity of such a subject lies in its scope, as it covers both the dissolution of the *ancien régime* in Europe and the emergence of new nation states in the former colonial territories of America.[1] The conservative features of Brazilian political emancipation owe much of their explanation to the transfer of the Portuguese Crown and head of state to Rio de Janeiro and to the way in which the rapprochement between the newcomers and local resident elites occurred during the years prior to the proclamation of independence.[2]

---

[1] J. H. Elliott, *Empires of the Atlantic World: Britain and Spain in America, 1492–1830* (New Haven: Yale University Press, 2006); David Armitage and Sanjay Subrahmanyam, eds., *The Age of Revolutions in Global Context, c. 1760–1840* (London: Palgrave Macmillan, 2010); David Armitage, *The Declaration of Independence: A Global History* (Cambridge, MA: Harvard University Press, 2007).

[2] Among the few studies that offer global, Atlantic, entangled, *croisée*, comparative approaches to the Latin American independence processes, Jeremy Adelman's *Sovereignty and Revolution* provides a rich joint approach to Brazil and Spanish America, despite not considering New Spain. Arguing that internal conflicts within the metropole explain imperial breakdown, Brian Hamnett considers developments on both sides of the Atlantic. Jeremy Adelman, *Sovereignty and Revolution in the Iberian Atlantic* (Princeton, NJ: Princeton University Press, 2006); Brian Hamnett, *The End of Iberian Rule on the American Continent, 1770–1830* (Cambridge: Cambridge University Press, 2017); Bernard Bailyn, *Atlantic History: Concepts and Contours* (Cambridge, MA: Harvard University Press, 2005), 3–56.

The separation of the American colonies from their respective metropoles during the so-called "Age of Revolutions"[3] was due both to the belligerence between rival European powers and to internal conflicts within the colonies. The crisis broke out at the center of the system. The French occupation of the Iberian Peninsula in 1807–1808 required answers from the main heads of administration of monarchical states, on both sides of the Atlantic. Dilemmas related to the origin and the exercise of sovereignty sparked common reactions to the Iberian absolutist regimes.[4]

The specifics of Brazilian political emancipation cannot be fully grasped without due consideration of the fact that the period in question is a crossroads of two temporalities in conflict: on the one hand, an *ancien régime* in accelerated disintegration, during which all statesmen and intellectuals formed their moral and political values and principles; on the other, the new liberal agenda, based on the philosophy of Enlightenment, science, and the new political economy. All the heavy investment in reforming the colonial administration since the rule of the marquis of Pombal (1755–1777), continued by the so-called "generation of the 1790s" was guided by the paradox that reform was needed in order to avoid revolution.[5]

If Portuguese enlightened reformism was essentially conservative, this conservatism gained momentum with the 1808 transfer of the Portuguese court to its American colony, definitively marking the character of Brazilian independence. That is the analytical perspective of this chapter. From the flight of the prince regent and the royal entourage and the Atlantic crossing in 1807–1808 onwards, emphasis will be given here to the establishment of

---

[3] On the concept of an "age of revolutions," see Robert R. Palmer, *The Age of the Democratic Revolution: A Political History of Europe and America, 1760–1800* (Princeton, NJ: Princeton University Press, 2014 [1959]), 5–21; Eric J. Hobsbawm, *A era das revoluções* (Rio de Janeiro: Paz e Terra, 1982 [1962]), 17–20. Criticism of this concept and its restriction to the North Atlantic has been offered by Wim Klooster, *Revolutions in the Atlantic World: A Comparative History* (New York: New York University Press, 2009), 1–10; Gabriel Paquette, *Imperial Portugal in the Age of Atlantic Revolutions: The Luso-Brazilian World, c. 1770–1850* (Cambridge: Cambridge University Press, 2013).

[4] Philip D. Morgan and Jack P. Greene "Introduction: The Present State of Atlantic History," in Philip D. Morgan and Jack P. Greene, eds., *Atlantic History: A Critical Appraisal* (Oxford: Oxford University Press, 2009), 3–33; Peter A. Coclanis, "Atlantic World or Atlantic/World?," *The William and Mary Quarterly* 63:4 (2006), 725–42; Peter A. Coclanis, "Beyond Atlantic History," in Morgan and Greene, eds., *Atlantic History*, 337–56.

[5] Kenneth Maxwell, "The Generation of the 1790s and the Idea of Luso-Brazilian Empire," in Dauril Alden, ed., *The Colonial Roots of Modern Brazil* (Berkeley: University of California Press, 1973), 107–44.

the Portuguese court in Rio de Janeiro and the dynamics between the colonial upper classes and the Portuguese Crown, a crucial factor in the conservative bias of Brazilian independence and the unfolding of Brazilian state formation and nation building throughout the nineteenth century.

## The Franco-British War and the Escape of the Royal Family

From the mid-eighteenth century onwards, Portuguese administrators were fully aware of the strategic role that Brazilian products and commerce played in the kingdom's economy as the main source of state revenue. Except for the slave trade, Portuguese domains in Africa and Asia were economically insignificant.[6] To maximize colonial income, the imperial administration implemented a complex tax system that affected production, consumption, internal circulation, and imports and exports. The loss of supremacy in Asia and Africa to rival empires imposed on Portuguese leaders the pressing task of restructuring the strategies of governance. They set about doing this following the guidelines developed in the restored University of Coimbra and the Lisbon Academy of Sciences, which functioned as Portugal's think tanks, where policy solutions were devised.[7]

Growing geopolitical tensions about colonial territories, especially between France and Great Britain began to directly involve and threaten the survival of smaller powers, such as the Iberian ones. The war for conquest and expansion of zones of influence unfolded in new forms of competition beyond military ones, notably as competition for new markets. The succession of treaties that mark the diplomatic history of the period, from Utrecht (1713), Madrid (1750), El Pardo (1761) to Santo Ildefonso (1777), London (1793), and Badajoz (1801) reflect this era of contention.[8]

Due to the strategic geographic situation of the metropole and the economic vigor of its American colony, Portugal was constantly threatened

---

[6] Alberto da Costa e Silva, "O Império de Dom João," *Rio de Janeiro, Revista Brasileira,* 14:54, (2008), 15–22.

[7] See, for synopses of these oceanic historiographic debates, António Manuel Hespanha, "Depois do Leviathan," *Almanack Braziliense* 5 (2007), 55–66; Iara Lis Schiavinatto, "Entre trajetórias e impérios: Apontamentos de cultura política e historiografia," *Tempo* (Niterói), 14:27 (2009), 23–35.

[8] Jorge Borges de Macedo, *História diplomática portuguesa: Constantes e linhas de força. Estudo de geopolítica* (Lisbon: Instituto de Defesa Nacional, s.d.), 303; Nívia Pombo, *Dom Rodrigo de Sousa Coutinho: Pensamento e ação político-administrativa no Império português (1788–1812)* (São Paulo: Hucitec, 2015), 58.

Conservative Tracks toward Independence

by the warring powers of France and Britain, delaying (until 1807) as much as it could a French invasion by means of diplomatic intelligence and massive bribes.[9] The way in which the militarily weakest countries achieved "neutrality" in the conflict is well known. A letter dated 25 June 1797 from Minister Antônio de Araújo e Azevedo (1754–1817), first count of Barca, allows us to glimpse how the "peace negotiations" that guaranteed temporary "neutrality" of the vulnerable nations in the conflict were carried out. In this missive, Azevedo openly mentioned that negotiations took place by means of copious bribes to public officials. He showed how, in order to buy off members of the Directory and other senior French politicians, and in order to prevent conflicts with Spain and advance negotiations, he had made extralegal payments. "In Paris", he wrote, "no step is made without money, and it is necessary to allocate three or four million pounds to buy off the directors." The secretary of the Directory, the minister of foreign affairs, and even the Directory's powerful executive, Paul Barras, were all corruptible.[10]

By these means, Portugal delayed adopting the position of "neutrality" as long as possible, signing "peace treaties" with both France and Great Britain, for which the state coffers were emptied. But the conduct of the war did affect the Lusitanian statesmen. The French threat became real after 1795, when France definitively got Spain on its side. The following year, when Britain declared war on Spain, Portugal faced a dilemma that could determine its survival. If it aligned itself with the French, Britain threatened to seize its overseas dominions; by joining the British, France could be expected to invade Lisbon. Under the rule of Rodrigo de Sousa Coutinho, Secretary of State for the Navy and Overseas Territories, the Crown expected that embracing peace with France would result in the worst of all losses – that of Brazil. That enlightened Portuguese minister believed that the act of closing ports to the British would lead, in retaliation, to the definitive loss of colonial domains, "sought by the English to compensate themselves for the lack of trade with Portugal, and to appropriate the interesting productions from overseas domains."[11] According to historian Valentim Alexandre, "all Portuguese foreign policy until 1807 would be an exercise in navigating

---

[9] Manuel de Oliveira Lima, *Dom João VI no Brasil*, 3rd edition (Rio de Janeiro: Topbooks, 1996); Valentim Alexandre, *Os sentidos do império: Questão nacional e questão colonial na crise do Antigo Regime português* (Porto: Edições Afrontamento, 1993), 93–166.

[10] Raul Brandão, *El-rei Junot* (Lisbon: Monteiro & Cia, 1919), 42.

[11] Arquivo Nacional do Rio de Janeiro (henceforth ANRJ), "Carta dirigida por Dom Rodrigo de Sousa Coutinho ao príncipe Dom joão, de 5 de janeiro de 1798," *Coleção Negócios de Portugal*, Caixa 716, pacote 02.

between these pitfalls, dropping ballast on one side or the other depending on the circumstances."[12] This dilemma lasted for ten years, until the removal of the Court to Rio de Janeiro in 1808.

## The Royal Family on the Run

Regent Prince Dom João postponed the decision to take refuge in Brazil as long as he could. Whether by pusillanimity or by a strategy of the sovereign – who, after all, proved effective in conserving his crown – the final signal for the squadron with the royal family to set sail from the Tagus was Napoleon's message in *Le Moniteur Universel*,[13] a copy of which Sir Lord Strangford, ambassador of Great Britain in Lisbon, handed over to the Portuguese prince, that the Braganza family no longer reigned in Europe.[14] The memory of these events has since produced different narratives, as the sympathies of chroniclers and historians vary. In *Histoire de Jean VI*, an anonymous libretto published in Paris after the death of D. João, it is said that the embarkation at the port of Belém occurred in the midst of great confusion, a spectacle at the same time sad and grotesque: pages and footmen stood side by side with ladies of the nobility and soldiers, precious objects were embarked along with coarser and useless objects. Dom João arrived at the pier of Belém with his nephew and *protégé*, Don Pedro Carlos of Spain, without the proper proclamations and customary reception. Owing to the hard rain of the previous day, the prince had to be carried on the shoulders by policemen, on boards lying in the mud. A stunned crowd followed the action.[15]

In one way or another, high ranking members of the imperial administration and the Court left with the king, taking with them the money that remained in the treasury after the numerous peace agreements. This generated discontent among members of the nobility who were unable or unwilling to accompany the royal family.[16] For those who ventured with their prince on the oceanic adventure, praising the glory of their guide's

---

[12] Alexandre, *Os sentidos do império*, 102.

[13] At the time, *Le Moniteur* was the official newspaper of the French government.

[14] *HISTOIRE de Jean VI roi de Portugal depuis sa naissance jusqu'a sa mort, en 1826* [...] (Paris: Ponthieu et Compagnie, 1827), 44.

[15] Also see Luís Norton, *A corte de Portugal no Brasil*, 2nd edition (São Paulo: Companhia Editora Nacional, 1979), 13; José de Souza Azevedo Pizarro e Araújo, *Memórias históricas do Rio de Janeiro*, 10 vols. (Rio de Janeiro: Imprensa Nacional, 1945); Manuel de Oliveira Lima, *D. João VI no Brasil (1808–1821)*, 2nd edition, 3 vols. (Rio de Janeiro: José Olímpio, 1945).

[16] Simão José da Luz Soriano, *História de El-Rei Dom João VI, Primeiro Rei Constitucional de Portugal e do Brasil* (Lisbon: Typographia Universal, 1866); Kirsten Schultz, *Tropical*

providential measure was a moral duty. They produced countless sapphic and pindaric odes and staged numerous *Te Deum Laudamus*, in which Dom João's decision was painted as a heroic act that ensured the empire's salvation. These works represented the prince as the man at the helm of the ship of state, depicted the adverse situation as an ordeal, and stressed the success of the royal action that resulted in the establishment of a new empire in the tropics.[17]

A pamphlet typical of such praises is the *Reflections on the Conduct of the Prince Regent of Portugal* (1808) by Francisco Soares Franco, professor at the College of Medicine of the University of Coimbra. In this laudatory piece, Franco exalted the actions of the prince, who had liberated the country by fearlessly resisting the aggressor Napoleon, and by establishing the seat of his monarchy in a land far from his native country. Portugal's power would henceforth be in Brazil, as a fortress capable of resisting Europe's threat. "It is in Brazil that, freed from the tyranny of Bonaparte, and from the ignominiousness of Spain, Dom João can punish both, one for his crimes, the other for its weakness, and take revenge on them."[18] Dom João's decision proved to be the correct one, which distinguished him from the other, "effeminate," kings of the rest of Europe. His wise decision demonstrated how the kings are the true defenders of their subjects, and the liberators of their homelands. Only two sovereigns, Dom João of Portugal and Gustaf, king of Sweden, had overcome Napoleon's threat by "animating the hearts with courage and hope for the souls of all peoples."[19]

Most subsequent scholars of the period are surprised that a man of a fainthearted temperament like Dom João organized the escape from Junot's troops and the flight to Brazil. In his *Life of Dom Pedro I*, which was not at all sympathetic to the prince regent, Otávio Tarquínio de Sousa concedes that in 1807, the European context demanded swift decisions and ready resolutions, which Dom João could not offer. But in those stormy times, the circumstances imposed on him the only stance compatible with his personality: neutrality. The prince regent managed to survive the great threats of the time in his hesitant way, by compromising, deceiving, and yielding.

---

*Versailles: Empire, Monarchy, and the Portuguese Royal Court in Rio de Janeiro (1808–1821)* (New York: Routledge, 2001).

[17] For example Antonio José Vaz, *As offerendas pastoris: Idyllio* (Rio de Janeiro: Impressão Régia, s.d.).

[18] Francisco Soares Franco, *Reflexões sobre a conducta do Principe Regente de Portugal, revistas e corrigidas* (Coimbra: Real Imprensa da Universidade, 1808), 7.

[19] Ibid.

According to Tarquínio de Sousa, matters such as honor and dignity did not weigh heavily on Dom João's timorous spirit. If he repeatedly showed himself to be pusillanimous, the sovereign made up for that by being a great strategist.[20]

Among those who judged the decision of the royal family to migrate to Brazil positively, diplomat and historian Oliveira Lima sought to redeem the prince's deeds. He argued that while there were drawbacks – Portugal's decline in Europe – and gains – the new empire that he built for his royal house in America, Dom João became the only concrete threat to Napoleon across Europe by executing what was a "mature idea" of the Portuguese Crown. His decision to move an ocean away should therefore be considered "an intelligent and happy political maneuver [rather] than a cowardly defection."[21]

Desertion or a heroic act, cowardly stampede or sound political judgment, what really matters are the consequences of the flight. A huge entourage of Europeans landed in Brazilian ports. Always prone to recognition and gratitude, it weighed heavily on the prince's mind that all those hundreds of subjects shared with him the challenges of the ocean crossing and remained his loyal companions in exile. The royal entourage reached Brazilian beaches, first in Salvador, in a condition of near-indigence, "deprived of everything except honor." The commoners accompanying Dom João arrived in a condition that was not better, "with their properties plundered, their positions suppressed, the sources of their pensions desiccated and, many of them, literally homeless."[22]

Upon his arrival in Salvador, the prince wanted to win the friendship of the country's upper layers, and he had the power to reward their many favors with hollow honors, as the English merchant John Luccock, an eyewitness to these events, observed.[23] The prince's seat and his Court, at the time of his arrival in Brazil, had no pretension to sumptuousness, quite the contrary. But even so, no matter how prodigal it was, Portugal's dilapidated treasure was not enough to even begin to cover daily expenses. One must remember that Portugal had declared war on France, whose troops invaded the kingdom.

---

[20] Otávio Tarquínio de Sousa, *História dos fundadores do Império do Brasil*, 6 vols. (Belo Horizonte: Itatiaia; São Paulo: Edusp, 1988), vol. 1, 42.

[21] Manuel de Oliveira Lima, *D. João VI no Brasil (1808–1821)*, 2nd edition (Rio de Janeiro: José Olympio, 1945), 5.

[22] John Luccock, *Notas sobre o Rio de Janeiro e partes meridionais do Brasil*, trans. Milton de S. Rodrigues (Belo Horizonte: Itatiaia; São Paulo: Edusp, 1975), 68.

[23] Ibid.

## Conservative Tracks toward Independence

Once the king was installed in Brazil, France remained a real and immediate threat to the north, where French Guiana bordered Portuguese America, and to the south, always threatened by the Río de la Plata, which took the side of the French enemy. Along with the installation of the Portuguese imperial state in Rio de Janeiro, the settlement and maintenance of the immense Court on tropical soil, with its expensive rituals around births, military conquests, deaths, and weddings[24] also generated large expenses. The resident upper classes of Rio de Janeiro enter the scene here, as we will see below.

## Housing the Court in the Tropics

Having evaded Napoleon's troops during the hasty escape from the Tagus harbor in the last days of November 1807, the fleet carrying the prince regent, his family, and part of the Portuguese nobility and bureaucracy set sail, under the protection of the British navy. A storm dispersed the fleet close to the equator. The ships carrying the queen mother D. Maria, D. Carlota (Dom João's wife), and the princesses went directly to Rio de Janeiro, where they had to wait on board for the regent, who first arrived in Salvador on 22 January 1808, after almost two months at sea. João de Saldanha Guedes Brito, count of Ponte and governor of Bahia, was in charge of welcoming the royal party with countless festivities, ringing of bells, cannon fire, and bands.

The royals stepped into their domains in America for the first time after 300 years of colonialism. Eyewitnesses report the perplexity of the residents of the former capital of the viceroyalty at the unusual spectacle, marked by the deplorable condition of the gentlemen, who were exhausted and ragged.[25] The region's authorities sprang into action. As soon as he was informed of the arrival of the distinguished visitors, the governor of Pernambuco sent a shipment of tropical fruits, vegetables, and fresh greenstuff, a relief for those who had spent weeks on salted meat and stale bread.[26]

The prince regent began to make political arrangements during his short stay in Salvador. He visited plantations and engaged with the local elite. Parties, masses, and balls in honor of Prince Dom João were held in the

---

[24] The most conspicuous wedding was that between the Prince heir Dom Pedro and Princess D. Leopoldina of the Austrian Habsburg family.

[25] Kenneth Light, *A viagem marítima da família real: A transferência da corte portuguesa para o Brasil* (Rio de Janeiro: Zahar, 2008).

[26] Antonio Risério, *Uma história da cidade da Bahia* (Rio de Janeiro: Versal, 2004).

streets and main squares of Salvador. The Bahians tried unsuccessfully to convince the prince to make Salvador the seat of the Crown. Nevertheless, the prince followed the original plan to establish his residence in Rio de Janeiro, the economic and political center of the viceroyalty, militarily very well guarded and at a very safe distance from the French threat.[27]

During the brief stay of four weeks in Salvador, Dom João launched a set of administrative measures that would have a decisive impact on the Portuguese overseas empire, among which the opening of Brazilian ports to friendly nations and the foundation of the Medical-Surgical School of Bahia stood out. The royal edict of 28 January, which decreed the opening of the ports, was issued in order to guarantee the survival of the Court because of the loss of Portugal's European trade. The decree effectively suppressed Portugal's commercial monopoly, which had characterized the relations between metropole and colony for three centuries, and thereby the so-called "old colonial system."[28] This measure had lasting consequences for the relations between Portugal and Brazil in the following thirteen years and impacted the very designs of independence.

From Salvador, the royal entourage sailed to Rio de Janeiro. "Never did any mail bring sadder, and at the same time more flattering news!"[29] These words of chronicler Luís Gonçalves dos Santos express with rare accuracy the spirit that marked the landing of the royal family on 7 March 1808 in Rio, an unusual event for both those who arrived and those who watched it. While the prince sojourned in the city of Salvador, the *fluminenses* (the residents of Rio de Janeiro) endeavored to prepare the city for a warm reception of the prince regent and his Court, under the auspices of Viceroy Dom Marcos de Noronha e Brito.[30]

Rio de Janeiro, Brazil's main port and capital of the viceroyalty since 1763, underwent a rapid transformation, suddenly becoming too small to house an entire Court and state apparatus, an entourage estimated at more than 10,000 newcomers.[31] Adaptations were inevitable: the Carmelites were removed to

---

[27] Pedro Calmon, *O rei do Brasil: Vida de D. João VI*, 2nd edition (São Paulo: Companhia Editora Nacional, 1943), 128.

[28] Pinto de Aguiar, *A abertura dos portos do Brasil: Cairu e os ingleses* (Salvador: Progesso, 1960); Rubens Ricupero, *A abertura dos portos* (São Paulo: Senac, 2007).

[29] Luís Gonçalves dos Santos, *Memórias para servir à história do Brasil* (Belo Horizonte, Itatiaia; São Paulo, Edusp, 1981), vol. I, 168.

[30] Alexandre de Mello Moraes, *Historia da trasladação da corte portugueza para o Brasil em 1807–1808* (Rio de Janeiro: E. Dupont, 1872); Ângelo Pereira, *João VI Príncipe e Rei: A retirada da Família Real para o Brasil* (Lisbon: Empresa Nacional de Publicidade, 1953).

[31] Thomas O'Neil, *A vinda da família real portuguesa para o Brasil* (Rio de Janeiro: José Olympio, 2007); Lília Moritz Schwarcz, *A longa viagem da biblioteca dos reis: Do terremoto*

the Capuchin convent, while the Capuchins were transferred to the house of Our Lady of Glory. Connected by means of an improvised walkway to the former viceroy's palace, the Carmelite convent was turned into the royal palace, which housed the queen and her ladies-in-waiting. Other rooms of the convent were occupied with the royal pantry, the kitchen, and various workshops; the convent church was arranged to be the royal chapel. As soon as the royal stewards were transferred to the consistory of the Our Lady of Rosary church and the prisoners to the Aljube prison, the town hall and jail were also attached to the palace and came to house the maids, after extensive renovation to erase the sad memories of its original function. The new stables barely fit in the barracks of the cavalry squad, which moved to Rossio square, and new buildings had to be erected close to the former Dom Manuel beach,[32] where the royal coaches would be installed.[33]

Housing for so many newcomers could not be found overnight in a city whose population was estimated at 60,000 "souls," including Blacks, who made up two-thirds of that figure.[34] The prince regent instituted a notorious lodging system (*aposentadorias*), which greatly contributed to wear out the bonds between the two kinds of Portuguese: the newcomers and the "Brazilians." While it lasted, it provided the Portuguese nobles with some comfort in enjoying the best buildings in town, from which their legitimate owners were deprived until 1818, when the king put an end to the accommodation system. Long after that, disputes were still fought out over the matter.

While these conflicts were barely evident in those early days, they would later get out of hand. Everything was overshadowed by the unprecedented situation, especially in the eyes of the upper classes of Rio de Janeiro, fascinated by the brilliance of the Court. With the exception of a few heirs of wealthier families who had been to Portugal in search of education, the presence of the royal family was an absolute novelty for the *fluminenses*.

---

    *de Lisboa à Independência do Brasil* (São Paulo: Companhia das Letras, 2002); Light, *A viagem marítima da família real*.

[32] The old D. Manuel beach was subsequently destroyed during the early twentieth-century urban reforms in Rio de Janeiro and no longer exists.

[33] Changes in the urban environment of Rio de Janeiro at the time of Dom João were meticulously detailed by Noronha Santos in his notes as the introduction to the *Memórias*, by Father Perereca: Gonçalves dos Santos, *Memórias para servir à história do Brasil*, vol. 1, 66–194; see also Jurandir Malerba, *A corte no exílio: Civilização e poder no Brasil às vésperas da Independência*, 2nd edition (São Paulo: Companhia das Letras, 2018), Chapter 3.

[34] There are no accurate censuses of the population of Rio de Janeiro during the period.

Besides the lodging system, the installation of the royal court demanded drastic measures from the Crown. The creation of a general police department, responsible both for public security and urban improvements, and for the dissemination of more civilized and polished habits through the "moral education" of the population and especially of the local elite, is worth mentioning. Among the most emblematic measures of this civilizational effort were the suppression of lattice or shutter (*gelosias* or *rótulas*, a type of well-sealed trellis window),[35] the revamping of cemeteries, hospitals, and pharmacies based on "European standards," as well as the regulation of behavior in public places such as the theater. Despite such measures, a major obstacle to Europeanizing and civilizing remained, according to the Portuguese authorities: the massive presence of Africans.[36] Although local elites expressed an aversion to slavery, their alleged fear of the negative impact that the immediate abolition of slavery could have on the Brazilian economy made them resigned and tolerant of the enslavement of Africans and their descendants. Thus, while lamenting the "vices" of slavery, the expansion of the use of slave labor was tolerated and even encouraged. If many Africans forcibly brought to the port of Rio de Janeiro were sent to the southern plantations, a large number of them remained in the city. In 1818, the quartermaster reported that, in order to meet the requirements of the "thirty thousand whites who suddenly arrived here" with the prince regent and the royal family, the population of "Blacks" in the city had increased from around 60,000 to 80,000 individuals.[37]

## The Codes of Life at Court

The logic of life at Court, with its codified rituals, symbology, hierarchies, and formulas of sociability, all revolving around the figure of the king, constituted the environment and provided the set of rules for the relationship in Rio de Janeiro between the immigrant Portuguese nobility and the local upper classes, who bore the maintenance costs of the royal house and the

---

[35] Paulo Fernandes Viana, "Registro do Edital (. . .)," 11 June 1809, ANRJ, Codex 323, vol. 1, f. 88–88v; Gonçalves dos Santos, *Memórias para servir à história do Brasil,* vol. 1, 237.

[36] As Russell-Wood notes, while the emancipation of native people was ensured in 1755 and 1758, Brazil lacked proper legislation exclusively addressing African slavery. See A. J. R. Russell-Wood, "Iberian Expansion and the Issue of Black Slavery: Changing Portuguese Attitudes, 1440–1770," *American Historical Review* 83:1 (February 1978), 16–42: 40–1.

[37] Viana to His Royal Highness, 10 August 1818, ANRJ MNB, box 6J 81.

Portuguese state in Brazil. Neither of the two groups would come out of this experience unscathed.

Among the elements that provide a better understanding of Dom João's politics in Rio, the ancient conceptions of the king as patriarch of the royal house and the sacred foundations of royalty must be highlighted. The Portuguese monarchy was still strongly rooted in time-honored foundations, among which the principle of the monarch's liberality stands out, that is, the sovereign's power of distributing graces, honors, and favors – an expedient abundantly used as a means of political patronage in exchange for financial salvation. The monarch's "liberality" guaranteed the king enough symbolic capital to remain at the heart of power relations in the new tropical scenario.

Hierarchical distinctions at Portuguese court society already constituted the main capital available to the Portuguese monarchy in the second half of the seventeenth century. In the past, the granting of honorific graces, such as titles and places in military and religious orders, had been widely used by Portuguese monarchs to repay their vassals for allegiance. Of course, this "gift economy"[38] varied widely over the centuries. Therefore, by profusely distributing favors to his subjects, Dom João did not introduce a practice in Brazil that was not already known back in Portugal. He paid with honors and distinctions everyone who helped him. In order to recognize and compensate for the services of those who ventured with him on the Atlantic crossing, he revived the Order of the Cross and Sword, instituted by Dom João V (1706–1750), with its grand master – always the king of Portugal – its grand crosses, its major and minor commanders, and its special treatment of "deserving" people employed in the royal service, all of whom were, of course, worthy of generous favors.[39] In addition to honors, housing, meals, driving, distinguished forms of treatment, and servants for the higher-ups, the sacrifice of the immigrant vassals, it is worth remembering, guaranteed them symbolic capital of real "value" in a society in which somebody's position was established by criteria of honor and prestige.

The continuation of such practices at the royal court is reflected in contemporary documents such as the *Gazeta do Rio de Janeiro*, the *Memoires*

---

[38] António Manuel Hespanha, ed., *O Antigo Regime* (Lisbon: Stampa, 1993); Maria Eduarda C. M. Marques, "O 'soldado prático' e a lógica da economia do dom," *Revista USP [São Paulo]*, 83 (2009), 126–35.

[39] Mello Moraes, *Historia da trasladação*, 211.

of the legendary chronicler Padre Perereca, Rio's almanacs, and any of the countless dispatch reports issued at Court on royal birthdays, at births, and weddings, or other occasions reason for rejoicing, when the king generously awarded benefits to his subjects. Dom João granted such honors particularly to residents of Rio de Janeiro, surpassing his predecessors in lavishness. The list of cavalry knights distinctions reinforces these numbers. According to historian Sérgio Buarque de Holanda, more than 6,000 insignia of knights, commanders, and grand crosses of the Orders of Christ, São Bento de Avis, and São Tiago were distributed in Brazil under Dom João.[40]

In addition to devaluating the distinctions, the abundant award of favors gave rise to vanity, intrigues, and conflicts among natives or immigrants who considered themselves deserving of benefits. Expectations of promotion at every royal anniversary, public festivity, or military victory made tempers rise, as we learn from the letters of librarian Joaquim dos Santos Marrocos to his father in Lisbon, in which he claimed to have been passed over for a long time while less qualified, but better sponsored, contenders did receive recognition.[41]

Attracted by favors bestowed by the royal court – a legacy of the *ancien régime* – financially powerful individuals came to the rescue of the state. Distinction was granted by the king, and whoever answered his call was rewarded. British trader John Armitage witnessed how upon the arrival of the Court, the leading merchants and landowners gave up their own houses for the accommodation of the royal party; they sacrificed their private interests for the sake of the distinguished guests; and, as far as their means allowed, they donated large sums of money. In recognition, they were decorated with the various orders of chivalry. "Individuals," Armitage wrote, "who never used spurs were confirmed knights, while others who ignored the most trivial doctrines of the Gospel were transformed into Commanders of the Order of Christ."[42]

---

[40] Sérgio Buarque de Holanda, ed., *História geral da civilização brasileira* (São Paulo: Difel, 1982), vol. II, Part 1: 32; Alan Manchester, "A transferência da corte portuguesa para o Rio de Janeiro," in Henry Keith and S. F. Edwards, eds., *Conflito e continuidade na sociedade brasileira*, trans. José Lourenço de Melo (Rio de Janeiro: Civilização Brasileira, 1970), 177–217: 203.

[41] João Armitage, *História do Brasil* (São Paulo: Martins, 1972); Luís Joaquim dos Santos Marrocos, "Cartas de Luiz Joaquim dos Santos Marrocos," *Anais da Biblioteca Nacional*, 56, separate issue (1939); José da Silva Lisboa, *Memória dos benefícios políticos do Governo de ELREI Nosso Senhor Dom João VI* (Rio de Janeiro: Impressão Régia, 1818): 13.

[42] Armitage, *História do Brasil*, 9.

## Circulation of People

The opening of Brazil's ports to international trade after three centuries of Portuguese commercial monopoly lured legions of businessmen, adventurers, and artists to Rio de Janeiro. From different parts of Brazil, they flocked to the capital in search of social ascent and benefaction. No region in Brazil experienced the impact of the arrival of the Portuguese royal family as dramatically as Rio. Capital of the viceroyalty since 1763 and the main export center in south-central Brazil since the time of the gold rush – which had begun in the 1690s – the city became the seat of the entire Portuguese empire, and its administrative, political, and commercial functions expanded significantly.[43]

Daily life in the city changed dramatically as a result of the presence of thousands of newly arrived foreigners of all kind (traders, explorers, scientists, diplomats, artists, adventurers) who in the past had not been admitted to Portuguese America. Cultural life was enriched, in part due to the demands of the royal family. A royal library and printing press were installed in 1811. The first newspapers then began to circulate, anticipating a public sphere that would soon play a fundamental role in political emancipation.[44] Also in 1811, the composer Marcos Antônio Portugal disembarked in Rio, escorted by several singers and musicians, to serve the king as master of the royal chapel and the chamber orchestra; to the same end, Dom João appointed Joseph Haydn's disciple Sigismund Neukomm as chapel master. Opening its doors in 1813 under the auspices of Rio's elite, the Royal Theater of São João, with its 112 boxes and accommodation for 1,020 people, became the epicenter of social and political life during Dom João's reign. The efforts made by the influential minister Antonio de Araújo e Azevedo, count of Barca, also enabled the arrival of a French artistic mission in 1816 – gathering together masters such as the painter Jean-Baptiste Debret, the architect Grandjean de Montigny, Joachim Lebreton (head of the delegation), the Taunay brothers (Nicolas Antoine, painter; and Auguste Marie, sculptor), and the Ferrez brothers (Marc and Zepherin, both sculptors) – whose achievements did not match up with their intentions.[45]

---

[43] Nireu Cavalcanti, *O Rio de Janeiro setecentista: A vida e a construção da cidade da invasão francesa até a chegada da Corte* (Rio de Janeiro: Jorge Zahar, 2003); Armelle Enders, *Histoire de Rio de Janeiro* (Paris: Fayard, 2000).

[44] Marco Morel, *As transformações dos espaços públicos: Imprensa, atores políticos e sociabilidades na Cidade Imperial (1820–1840)* (São Paulo: Hucitec, 2005); Schwarcz, *A longa viagem da biblioteca dos reis.*

[45] Afonso d'Escragnole Taunay, "A missão artística de 1816," *Revista de Instituto Histórico e Geográfico Brasileiro* 74:1 (1911), 5–202; Lilia M. Schwarcz, *O sol do Brasil: Nicolas-Antoine Taunay e as desventuras dos artistas franceses na corte de Dom João* (São Paulo: Companhia das Letras, 2008).

However, not only Europeans circulated there in these troubled times. Many characters coming from the lower strata circulated on the banks of the Atlantic Ocean but studies on such people as the *pardo* Emiliano Felipe Benício Mundurucú are still lacking.[46] A militant active in the 1817 revolution and especially in the Confederation of Ecuador,[47] Mundurucú was arrested along with the legendary Frei Caneca and another free *pardo*, Agostinho Cavalcante e Souza in December 1824. Sentenced to death in 1825, like his two companions who were executed, Mundurucú succeeded in fleeing to Boston and from there to Haiti. Finally, in 1826 he moved to Puerto Cabello, in Bolívar's "Gran Colombia," where he joined the troops of another *pardo* general, José António Páez, and was active until his return to Pernambuco in the 1830s.[48] He extolled in verse Henri Christophe, the "black emperor of Haiti," during his activism in the Confederation of Ecuador. In 1827, he returned to the United States, where he married for the first time. In 1831, he remarried his second African American wife, Harriet, and had children born in Boston and in Recife.[49]

If the circulation of Europeans and North Americans fascinated the native upper classes, who imitated their manners, the presence of people like Mundurucú terrified the city's authorities, for whom a slave revolt remained a specter. In the first year of the Court's stay in Rio de Janeiro, police quartermaster Paulo Fernandes Viana claimed that a slave rebellion in the capital would encourage the French, "well-known enemies" of the Portuguese monarchy. Even after the end of the Napoleonic Wars, Viana asserted "that there has been an insubordinate spirit in the slavery of Bahia," although Napoleon's defenders believed that they should be welcomed there.[50] For many of Dom João's advisers, inspecting and arresting any individual, Black or white, suspected of connections to the Caribbean was

---

[46] I learned about the existence of Mundurucú through the research of Luiz Geraldo Silva.

[47] The Confederation of Ecuador was a revolutionary movement with republican leanings in northeastern Brazil in 1824. It was a reaction to the Constitution granted by Dom Pedro I in the same year. This Constitution kept Brazil under Portuguese rule and retained a centralized government. The movement was triggered in Pernambuco, but quickly spread to other northern provinces.

[48] Vamireh Chacon, *Da Confederação do Equador à Grã-Colômbia* (Brasília: Senado Federal, 1983), 198.

[49] Luiz Geraldo Silva, "Africanos e afrodescendentes na América portuguesa: Entre a escravidão e a liberdade (Pernambuco, séculos XVI ao XIX)" (Full Professor Thesis, Universidade Federal do *Paraná*, 2018), 16–18, 22, 500–1.

[50] Paulo Fernandes Viana, "Registro do Oficio expedido ao Ministro e Secretário da repartição da Guerra," 23 May 1808, ANRJ, Códice 318, f. 16–16v; Viana, [Letter to D. João], 24 November 1816, ANRJ, box 6J 83.

imperative. In 1816, "a black man from the French nation named Carlos Romão" was arrested and jailed, in order to find out if he was a native of "the island of Saint-Domingue, or had arrived from there ... if there are others like him, or mulattoes, if he has ever been to Bahia, or knows people who are there, having come from Saint-Domingue." Such measures had precisely the opposite effect of what was intended, since they could stir up the lower classes.[51]

## Institutional Shifts in the Luso-Brazilian Empire

Is it possible to establish a direct link between Dom João's rule and independence? It depends. Some historians claim that Dom João and his government had no relevant role in the construction of independence, which they portray as the result of the initiatives of the liberal *vintistas*, as the revolutionaries of Porto and Lisbon who established the general and Extraordinary Cortes in 1820 were called. From a strictly political point of view, that makes sense. On the other hand, it is not unreasonable to attribute an important role to Dom João in the independence process, when one considers that, willingly or not, by co-opting Brazilian upper classes through his patriarchal and enticing policy, the sovereign helped decisively define the profile of the new elite that was formed in Brazil during the thirteen years he spent in Rio de Janeiro.

Although many historians refrain from fusing the transfer of the Court and independence, there is no way to untie that bond. The presence of the Court in Rio de Janeiro drew local elites toward a project aimed at preserving their economic hegemony and social status by maintaining territorial integrity and, in particular, by continuing slave-based cash crop production. In exchange, local elites consented to the preservation of a unitary, monarchical political body, which kept an heir of the House of Braganza as its figurehead.[52]

Another decisive aspect of the transfer of the Court that influences the formation of the Brazilian state was the shift in the axis of power: The Crown was no longer an abstract entity, its operations were no longer felt as

---

[51] Paulo Fernandes Viana, "Registro do Ofício expedido ao Juiz do Crime do Bairro de Santa Rita", 11 April 1816, ANRJ, Codex 329, v. 3; Viana, "Registro do Ofício expedido ao Ministro de Estado dos Negócios de Guerra", 8 July 1808, Codex 318, f. 38.

[52] Calmon, *O rei do Brasil*; J. F. de Almeida Prado, *D. João VI e o início da classe dirigente no Brasil* (São Paulo: Companhia Editora Nacional, 1968); Schultz, *Tropical Versailles*; Malerba, *A corte no exílio*.

something coming from abroad.[53] The sudden royal presence provoked an inescapable change in the colony's status, which was formally recognized in 1815, when Brazil's position was elevated from viceroyalty to autonomous kingdom, as an equal partner with Portugal and Algarve.[54]

## The Porto Revolution and the Meeting of the Lisbon Cortes

If the establishment of the Portuguese state and the transfer of the Court to Rio de Janeiro had a decisive impact on Brazilian political emancipation, the role played by the liberal revolution in Portugal in this same process cannot be underestimated. Instigated by the liberal revolution in Spain, this revolutionary movement broke out in the Portuguese city of Porto on 20 August 1820. The "General, Extraordinary Cortes of the Portuguese nation," a body that had been inactive since 1698, soon met in Lisbon with the manifest objective of endowing Portugal with a Constitution, by which the liberals hoped to put an end to the Old Regime's monarchy of divine right. Apart from a Constitution, its initial objectives also included the immediate return of the king. *Vintismo*, as the movement became known, aimed at messianic goals such as the "regeneration" of the kingdom, a dubious notion that implied a desire to return to the glorious past of the nation by establishing a political regime with its center in Lisbon.

In April 1821, yielding to the pressure of the Cortes, Dom João left Rio de Janeiro for Lisbon, designating his first-born son Dom Pedro as prince regent of the Kingdom of Brazil. The old king emptied the public treasury on his return to Portugal, leaving Brazil in a dire condition. In addition, decrees issued by the Cortes in September 1821 changed the organization of the Kingdom of Brazil. Received in Brazil only at the turn of the year, these edicts created provinces directly linked to Lisbon, reducing the power of Rio de Janeiro as the capital of Brazil. The immediate return of Dom Pedro to Europe was also decreed. Most of the Brazilian provinces accepted these measures, but the southern elites loudly expressed their annoyance. They began to mobilize on behalf of the prince regent, who suddenly became the protagonist in a political drama. Dom João initially resisted the demands of

---

[53] Raimundo Faoro, *Os donos do poder: Formação do patronato político brasileiro*, 7th edition (Porto Alegre: Globo, 1987), 249.

[54] Ana Cristina Araújo, "O 'Reino de Portugal, Brasil e Algarves': 1815–1822," *Revista de História das Ideias* 14 (1992), 233–60.

the *vintistas*, but was eventually forced to swear an oath to the Constitution, which was yet to be written in Portugal.[55] The conflict was about the political hegemony of the empire, both with regard to the administrative framework of the Kingdom of Brazil and the question which should be the decision-making center of the Portuguese monarchy.

The captaincies of Brazil, which had been made provinces, sent delegates to the Cortes, not as representatives of Brazil, but as deputies from individual provinces. Prior to their arrival, the debates had focused on an ambiguous transoceanic "dual monarchy," but that notion proved to be a dead end as interest groups in Brazil stressed the need for the prince to stay in Rio de Janeiro, to which the Lisbon Cortes was fiercely opposed. This moment was a turning point for Portugal and Brazil, because from then on, any chance of understanding was lost. From this point on, too, José Bonifácio de Andrada e Silva's leadership helped unite interest groups in south-central Brazil, while the prince took on a political role that until then had been totally alien to him – as symbolized by the events of 9 January 1822 (*"Dia do Fico"*). Designated by the nationalist historiography of the nineteenth century as "patriarch of Independence," José Bonifácio played a lead role in the campaign for the prince regent Dom Pedro to remain in Brazil in January 1822, contrary to the determination of the Cortes of Lisbon. He became Dom Pedro's trusted man and the main head of the Brazilian Party, which politically articulated Brazil's independence. Bonifácio also organized the first independent Brazilian state ministry, at the request of the prince regent.

If one accepts that the *vintistas* challenged Dom João's power, Brazil's independence can be framed as his answer. The liberals of 1820 launched a genuine *coup d'état* against the king, by imposing on him the acceptance of a constitution yet to be written and his unconditional return to the kingdom. In response, the king outflanked the Cortes by accepting the Constitution, but keeping the crown prince in Brazil. He thereby signaled that the cost of the coup would be the definitive loss of the colony, a very high price to pay. Likewise, since Dom Pedro was heir to Dom João, Portugal ironically ran the risk of being recolonized by Brazil upon the father's death. The old king knew very well what he was doing. Days before embarking back to Portugal, he left this clever advice to his son: "Pedro, if Brazil has to break free from

---

[55] Alexandre, *Os sentidos do Império*; Márcia Regina Berbel, *A nação como artefato* (São Paulo: Fapesp/Hucitec, 1999); Lúcia M. B. Pereira das Neves, *Corcundas e constitucionais – A cultura política da independência (1820–1822)* (Rio de Janeiro: Faperj/Revan, 2003).

Portugal, let it be under your guidance, because you will always respect me; and not under any adventurer who despises me."[56]

## The Political Rupture between Portugal and Brazil

In December 1821, José Bonifácio de Andrada e Silva wrote a manifesto on behalf of São Paulo's delegation to the Cortes, which he had spread around São Paulo with the prince's consent. This bombastic document was Brazil's first open affront to the Cortes. The succession of events in the clash between Dom Pedro and the Constituent Assembly of the Kingdom is well known. A whole mythology surrounding the "Cry of Ipiranga"[57] as the foundational event of Brazil as a nation was later carefully constructed by intellectuals linked to the state. Still, the formal proclamation of independence did not end the process of Brazilian political emancipation. Soon the Portuguese party would rise up vehemently in Rio and reveal its conservatism by adhering to absolutism and pinning their hopes on Emperor Dom Pedro I to serve their interests.

In the heat of the events of 1822, Dom Pedro recognized the signal sent by the elites from the center-south of the country, who summoned him to act as the condottiere of their political movement. However, the impetuous prince would soon show signs of his true character. He had championed the movement more because of his hatred for the insolence of the Cortes than out of conviction. At the end of the day, he was a Portuguese by birth and sympathetic to his countrymen. Furthermore, he was seduced by the absolute power with which the conservatives beckoned him. Likewise, Dom Pedro has been deceived by popular campaigns in Rio de Janeiro, São Paulo, and Minas Gerais that asked him to remain in Brazil. Like most representatives of Brazil in the Cortes, it is possible that the young prince regent never desired the outcome of secession. Nevertheless, he defended independence, whose ideals he pursued in name of liberal institutions and a monarchical tradition.

Dom Pedro's overall policy as regent is hard to characterize, although his first measures were liberal in nature. Despite financial difficulties, he abolished taxes, cut government spending, leveled salaries of Portuguese and

---

[56] Cited in Tarquínio de Sousa, *História dos fundadores*, vol. 1, 144.
[57] On the banks of the São Paulo stream, D. Pedro supposedly responded with the cry of "Independence or death!" to the decrees emanating from Lisbon.

Brazilian officials, allowed the expropriation of private property while protecting the right to property, and decreed that individual freedom was guaranteed. His steady hand was manifested on several occasions, such as on 5 June 1821, when he personally neutralized rebellious Portuguese troops in Rio de Janeiro. He was extremely sympathetic to the various elements that made up the Constitution: popular sovereignty, the installation of a parliament, inviolability of royalty, individual and property guarantees, freedom of the press, and the right to petition.[58]

Portugal finally recognized Brazil's political autonomy in 1825, preceded only by the United States (1824) and succeeded by Britain (1827). British diplomatic tutelage was decisive in the negotiations. Under the deal signed, Brazil agreed to pay Portugal a compensation of £2 million sterling. Commercial treaties drawn up with Brazil were financially profitable for Britain; the new country's commitment to abolish slavery, however, was successively delayed by Brazilian elites until the late 1880s.[59]

From then on, Brazil came into existence as an autonomous political body, although Dom Pedro's reign was a disappointment. Between 1826, when the first legislature of the Chamber of Deputies began, and 1831, the year of his abdication, the emperor's popularity declined as rapidly as the lower house gained prestige. Nor could the senators and conservative ministers handpicked by the monarch count on popular support. The ministers were actually prosecuted on various charges, ranging from embezzlement of funds to the unconstitutional installation of military commissions.[60] As his own support continued to diminish, Dom Pedro abdicated his title on 7 April 1831, yielding as he did to his youngest son. After he left for Portugal to fight for the throne against his usurper brother in favor of his daughter, Princess Maria da Glória, he died of tuberculosis three years later, worn out by the war against his brother.

---

[58] Tarquínio de Sousa, *História dos fundadores*, vol. 1; Roderick J. Barman, *Brazil: The Forging of a Nation (1798–1852)* (Stanford: Stanford University Press, 1988).

[59] Manuel de Oliveira Lima, *História diplomática do Brasil: O reconhecimento da independência* (Rio de Janeiro: Garnier, 1901); Francisco Adolfo de Varnhagen, *História da independência do Brasil* (Rio de Janeiro: Imprensa Nacional, 1917); Leslie Bethell, "The Independence of Brazil," in Leslie Bethell, ed., *The Cambridge History of Latin America*, vol. v: Part III, *From Independence to c. 1870* (Cambridge: Cambridge University Press, 1985), 157–96.

[60] Tarquínio de Sousa, *História dos fundadores*, vol. 1; Iara Lis Carvalho Souza, *Pátria coroada: O Brasil como corpo político autônomo (1780–1831)* (São Paulo: Unesp, 1999); Isabel Lustosa, *D. Pedro I: Um herói sem nenhum caráter* (São Paulo: Companhia das Letras, 2006).

## Conclusions

The transfer of the Portuguese court and state apparatus to Rio de Janeiro in 1808 can be seen as a major factor in Brazil's independence process. The smooth transition to independence hinged on two elements. In the first place, Dom João's transfer to Rio of the empire's administrative machine, with its bureaus, secretaries, offices, and military forces, meant that upon gaining independence,[61] Brazil had a fully operational state apparatus that underwent few adjustments. As in all matters, the final decision to go ahead with the transfer was that of the king, but he did avail himself of the counsel of numerous great statesmen, including the counts of Linhares, Barca, the viscount of Anadia, the duke of Palmela, and also João Paulo Bezerra de Seixas, baron of Itaguaí, Tomás Antônio Vilanova Portugal, and José Joaquim de Azevedo, viscount of Rio Seco. Secondly, and just as importantly, the prince regent Dom João and his Court approached the elites residing in Rio de Janeiro in a way that enabled them to help shape the new regime. As a consequence, the elites from the center-south, who backed independence, played a leading role in the construction of the monarchical state throughout the nineteenth century.

The experience of the transfer of the Portuguese royal family and the headquarters of the Portuguese overseas empire to Brazil was decisive for the policies adopted by the elites in charge of Brazilian political emancipation. In fact, profound changes had taken place in Brazil between 1808 and 1822, paving the way for independence. In the context of the Age of Revolutions, Brazil's independence process represented the only successful conservative alternative to the republicanism that characterized political emancipation both in North America and Spanish America.[62]

During 300 years of colonialism, a social class was in the making composed of creole landowners and slaveholders who benefited most from

---

[61] Istvan Jancsó, ed., *Independência: História e historiografia* (São Paulo: Hucitec; Fapesp, 2005); Jurandir Malerba, ed., *A independência brasileira: Novas dimensões* (Rio de Janeiro: Editora FGV, 2006).

[62] Comparative studies on the independence process in the Spanish and Portuguese Americas include Anthony McFarlane, "Independências americanas na era das revoluções: Conexões, contextos, comparações," in Malerba, ed., *A independência brasileira*; and Istvan Jancsó, "A construção dos Estados nacionais na América Latina – apontamentos para o Estudo do Império como projeto," in Tamás Szmrecsányi and José Roberto do Amaral Lapa, eds., *História econômica da Independência e do Império*, 2nd edition (São Paulo: Hucitec; Edusp; Imprensa Oficial, 2002). See also João Paulo Pimenta, *A Independência do Brasil e a experiência hispano-americana (1808–1822)* (São Paulo: Hucitec, 2015).

colonial conditions. This class showed an elastic political allegiance. When expecting honorary nominations and distinctions from Lisbon, its members were devoutly monarchist, but they became republican as a way to challenge the Crown's taxes, which threatened their business (as was the case in *Inconfidência Mineira*). The Haitian Revolution convinced them that a country mostly populated by Black people should not become a republic, because that would jeopardize their own privileges. The elite therefore reconciled itself to the Crown. In the independence period, this creole-born elite joined the monarchy again, when it realized that the Crown would be a safeguard for its commercial connections to Europe and a powerful ally against domestic enemies. It embraced independence conservatively, when the metropole, instead of a driving force, proved to be an obstacle to its interests. Once a rural aristocracy forged in human trafficking and slavery, the elite gradually manifested itself as a social class while taking the reins of Brazil's colonial government for its own benefit.

The price paid by the Brazilians for exiting colonialism was to submit to this landowning and slaveholding class, guarantor of the monarchical state. This state was guided by a select group of "enlightened people" who never hesitated to use all available means, including violence, to defend their class privileges and keep the lower strata under control. When slavery was finally legally abolished in Brazil in 1888, the monarchical state no longer served the interests of that class, which dissolved the empire with a *coup d'état*. But the new republic of Brazil, controlled by the heirs of the slave owners of the past, remained elitist, aimed at ensuring the concentration of land, income, and power in the hands and for the benefit of the same upper strata, while excluding the majority of the population from citizenship. It was only in the twenty-first century that the subaltern classes managed to gain state power democratically and institute a legitimate and representative government. But even then, the upper classes really ruling the country did not accept it.

## 19

# Building New Brazilian Institutions

### JEFFREY D. NEEDELL

### The Decision for Brazil, 1807–1816

For three centuries, his ancestors had looked to the sea – for spreading the faith, for wealth, and for the power that wealth brought. Now, Dom João, prince regent of Portugal, looked to the sea for succor. The kingdom was menaced and then invaded by the French. His allies, the English, had threatened his overseas commerce if he succumbed to French demands. So he looked to the South Atlantic and to Brazil to salvage his position, his possessions, and his power. He left Portugal in 1807, putting the sea between the throne and the dangers of Europe. Moreover, once the French were defeated in 1814, he refused to accept Portuguese or English pressure to return; indeed, in 1815 he raised the State of Brazil to the status of a coequal realm with Portugal. In 1816, upon the death of Maria, his mad mother, it was in Rio de Janeiro that he ascended the throne, as king of Brazil and of Portugal, and lord of what else remained of his ancestors' vast overseas conquests – from the South Atlantic to the Timor Sea.[1]

The decision to relocate to Brazil partly derived from long-term trends associated with Brazilian primacy in Portuguese economic affairs. Since the late seventeenth century, with the collapse of the Portuguese trade monopolies in Asia and Africa due to Dutch, English, and French successes there, the significance of Brazil to Portuguese political and economic survival was clear. Indeed, by the end of the eighteenth century, the monarch was advised to make such a move to place the political center directly over its economic base. It was not only the continued strength of Brazilian cane sugar, which characterized the northeast and had taken on new force in the lowlands near

---

Note that the accepted spelling of Portuguese has varied over the last two centuries. Here, all citations of sources published in Portuguese retain the spelling of the original.

[1] Roderick J. Barman, *Brazil: The Forging of a Nation, 1798–1852* (Stanford: Stanford University Press, 1988), Chapter 2, esp. 42–8, 52–3.

Rio de Janeiro, but alluvial gold found in the vast hinterland stretching into the interior, north and northwest of Rio. Even after the gold began to play out, by 1750, the sugar did not, and both had strengthened, and continued to strengthen, the Atlantic trade in captives drawn from West and West Central Africa (particularly after 1790, given the surge in sugar production throughout the Americas that followed the impact of the Haitian Revolution on Saint-Domingue's former sugar exports to North Atlantic markets). In addition, the English alliance and the Methuen Treaty (1703) had facilitated a great volume of contraband trade between Britain and Portugal and its possessions, in which Portuguese merchants abroad sold English goods (brought by their English partners to Portugal itself) in both Brazil and the Platine region.[2]

The crisis of the French War (1807–1814) simply reinforced the logic of setting up the court in what had become the single greatest source of Portuguese strength. By doing so in an era in which whatever independence the Portuguese monarch still had by 1807 was threatened by both enemy French invasion and allied British threats, Dom João took a critical step at both enhancing that independence and ensuring a greater exercise of it in the future. Who knew what future infelicities the greater European powers might experience and impose upon poor Portugal in years to come? The decision was also strengthened by the ways in which the monarch had founded and built up the military and political institutions in Brazil to sustain the war efforts in Europe. Whatever his promises or assumptions about returning to Lisbon, Dom João had had to face the facts of defeat, of invasion and of possible territorial loss to the greatest military power on the continent. This had meant both rebuilding an army and scrambling to increase revenue through increased trade, leading to the decisions to end Portuguese mercantilist restrictions, set up schools to train new soldiers and physicians, and create a botanical garden to research other tropical export possibilities. So it was that in a few years the prince regent's decisions had created new wealth,

---

[2] Ibid., 42–3; Jeffrey D. Needell, *The Party of Order: The Conservatives, the State, and Slavery in the Brazilian Monarchy, 1831–1871* (Stanford: Stanford University Press, 2006), Chapter 1, esp. 11–18. On Platine and other contraband trade, see Dauril Alden, *Royal Government in Colonial Brazil: With Special Reference to the Administration of the Marquis of Lavradio, Viceroy, 1769–1779* (Berkeley: University of California Press, 1968), 67–8, 388–92; on English commercial relations, Frédéric Mauro, "Political and Economic Structures of Empire, 1580–1750," in Leslie Bethell, ed., *Colonial Brazil* (Cambridge: Cambridge University Press, 1987), Chapter 2; Andrée Mansuy-Diniz Silva, "Imperial Re-organization, 1750–1808," in Bethell, ed., *Colonial Brazil*, 241–2; Kenneth R. Maxwell, *Conflicts and Conspiracies: Brazil and Portugal, 1750–1808* (Cambridge: Cambridge University Press, 1973), Chapters 1 and 2, esp. 8, 11, 42.

new economic and political integration and interests, and some of the critical institutions suitable to a new polity. In 1816, he graced the new kingdom with a core faculty capable of fostering the arts, recruiting practitioners from restoration France. No kingdom could do without civilization, after all.[3]

While the Portuguese commercial and political interests which had suffered from the exile of the court and the end of mercantilism, as well as the direct costs of war, clamored for his return, the exiled Portuguese now in Rio, wealthier, more powerful, and closer to hand, pressed hard to maintain and strengthen the new status quo. The English, critical to Portuguese independence since the late seventeenth century, and the strongest economic actor in Portuguese overseas commerce, pressed in vain for the prince's return to Lisbon (the better to reassert their role in Portuguese affairs in Europe and overseas). The shock, the trauma, and the success of forced exile and then triumph in the tropics, founded upon a flourishing economy, were wonderfully convincing. The establishment of Brazil as a kingdom was simply the most significant, crowning step in the process. Brazil was to remain what it had become, the empire's center, with political and commercial primacy in what remained of Portuguese overseas possessions.

## The Nature of the Monarchy, 1815–1824

It is clear that the king had no sympathy for the revolutionary ideas which were transforming the Atlantic World. Until 1820, he ruled in Brazil as he had ruled in Portugal – as an absolute monarch. The power and preferment and patronage in his hands made his presence desirable in both kingdoms and helps to explain both the Brazilian elite's interest in his staying and the Portuguese elite's interest in his return. Access to the monarch meant appointments, wealth, titles, and greater security to either elite. Absolutism's attractions for the monarch are self-evident and those, as well as the destabilization, violence, and disintegration clear in the revolutionary Atlantic, were persuasive to João VI and to many in the elite. His continued concern to repress or contain any stirrings of liberalism makes sense. Moreover, it is clear that his councilors, even the most enlightened, supported the maintenance of the old ways – they provided the councilors with power personally and seemingly ensured the stability of the sociopolitical

---

[3] Barman, *Brazil*, 42–8, 52–3; Jeffrey D. Needell, *A Tropical Belle Epoque: Elite Culture and Society in Turn-of-the-Century Rio de Janeiro* (Cambridge: Cambridge University Press, 1987), 146–9, 179–81.

order. There was no interest in innovation, even when new circumstances suggested it. Nor was faith in the established monarchy common in the royal court alone. Unlike some fractions of the creole elite in Spanish America, particularly in the newer, frontier viceroyalties (let us not forget the staunch royalism of the majority of elite creoles in the realms of New Spain and Peru), the most powerful families of Brazil had good reason to support the institution. The country's elite was made up of two levels: the great coastal export planters and merchants and the interior's great landholders and merchants, critical to domestic agriculture, ranching, and trade. While the effective impact of the Crown over their local affairs was weak, its charismatic guarantee of the established order over which they presided at that local level was clear, as was its support for the export elite's continued expansion, now free of mercantilist restraints.[4]

Nonetheless, Brazil was a half-continent, and the attractions of the monarch's sway varied enormously, particularly at its further reaches or among those interested in new possibilities and political participation. While much of the elite supported the king and his new presence, other elite fractions further away from the royal court or people further down in the hierarchy did not. They were less likely to benefit from either their new king's presence or patronage. Elements in the local elites, particularly in the far south and the northeast, knew little of the new opportunities of the court in exile and fretted at new revenue demands and greater political centralization. They thirsted to maintain or increase greater local power, a thirst whetted by some of the liberal notions of the era. The same was so in the great port cities among more middling elements or even among the free poor, all of whom had come to learn of popular sovereignty, meritocracy, and social mobility from the revolutionary liberalism that had erupted in the North Atlantic World and lapped the ocean's southern coasts. In 1817, a northeastern captaincy underwent a republican revolution that spread nearby. This rebellion was rapidly quashed by local elite and royal forces. However, this did little to slow or prevent the spread of liberal ideas in Brazil; they were evident in the ongoing successes of the United States, the Spanish American struggles after 1808, and, particularly, the adoption of Spain's 1812 constitution. These events and the ideas associated with them, particularly the idea of popular sovereignty, seemed to presage a new age and affected urban popular discourse. Indeed, throughout the kingdom, the urban middling

---

[4] Needell, *Party of Order*, 31; Barman, *Brazil*, 48–9, 53–5, 60, 61–3.

ranks envied the greater freedoms and political participation signified by liberal constitutionalism.[5]

Beyond these, the great masses of the free and enslaved, as well as their masters, knew of the revolutionary example of Saint-Domingue. Haiti was an issue taken seriously in Brazil, and for good reason. Roughly between a third and a half of the population was enslaved; most of these captives had been born free in Africa. Indeed, the dramatic increase in tropical exports to the Atlantic market since the mid-eighteenth century had led to the greatest increase in Brazil's share (always the largest) in the Atlantic slave trade. Despite the English decision to end its own slave trading in 1807 and its consequent pressure on other kingdoms to put an end to theirs, slave trading to Brazil in the early nineteenth century was unprecedented. It was the result not simply of higher labor demand as sugar production expanded, but the British threat to the trade and the increasing export of cotton, cacao, and, increasingly, coffee (which would dominate exports in quantity and value by the 1830s).[6]

Slaveholding since the sixteenth century had also led to an overwhelming majority of the free being people of color – ranging from freedmen, their descendants, and Indigenous peoples to Brazilians of mixed-race descent and culture, in positions ranging from dependent poverty to the highest ranks of society. Race and class distinctions were generally conflated and hierarchical, but, over time, miscegenation, manumission, and further mobility were constant and obvious facts of life. Moreover, particularly among the urban masses and middling ranks, there were traditional resentments toward the Portuguese immigrants, who dominated the monarchy's institutions, most of its Atlantic trade, and a great portion of local domestic commerce. For the fraction of the population comprising the elite, a largely and putatively white group of intermarrying new Portuguese and long-established planting families, then, the new era was one of threats and

---

[5] Barman, *Brazil*, 56, 59–60; Jeffrey C. Mosher, *Political Struggle, Ideology, and State Building: Pernambuco and the Construction of Brazil, 1817–1850* (Lincoln: University of Nebraska Press, 2008), Chapter 1, esp. 20–9.

[6] Stanley J. Stein, *Vassouras: A Brazilian Coffee County, 1850–1900: The Roles of Planter and Slave in a Plantation Society* (Princeton, NJ: Princeton University Press, 1985 [1958]), 294; Leslie Bethell, "1822–1850," in Leslie Bethell, ed., *Brazil: Empire and Republic, 1822–1930* (Cambridge: Cambridge University Press, 1989), 86. For ongoing data collection and analysis of the Atlantic slave trade, see the Emory University website on slave voyages at www.slavevoyages.org/voyage/database#tables.

opportunities, from within and without. Depending upon one's position, one might want to contain the threats or pursue the opportunities or, in the case of the elite, both.[7]

Thus, when Portugal's liberal Porto Revolt (1820) remade the Lisbon Cortes and called for a constituent assembly, there was no difficulty in getting representatives of Brazil's local oligarchies and the urban middling sorts to move forward and support such novelties as the local election of representatives to attend that assembly. After all, they would dominate both the elections and the delegations – it was a spectacular chance at new power, particularly at the local level. The export elite had significant interests to promote and protect and their allies in the urban elite, exposed to the new ideas, saw new opportunities. Both, sensitive to the revolutionary ideas circulating among the urban middling strata and masses, faced peril and possible opportunity.[8]

The ideas of the era, derived from French and English liberal theory and practice, Spanish liberalism as expressed in the Cádiz Constitution of 1812, and what they had inspired, had been harshly and successfully repressed in Brazil since the 1780s. There had been a conspiracy in the mining captaincy of Minas Gerais then, explicitly linked to the United States example (Figure 19.1). There had been the short-lived "Tailors' Rebellion" in Salvador in 1798, inspired by Saint-Domingue. The Pernambuco rebellion in 1817, noted earlier, drew upon Atlantic republicanism. Similar responses in this era in Spanish America had spiked dramatically after 1808, with the crippling of the legitimate political authority associated with the Spanish monarch's captivity that year; by the late 1810s, royal authority in the region was challenged and even overthrown.

In Brazil, one must assume that this republican destabilization had been, to a very great extent, avoided by the continued sway of the legitimate monarch, emphasized by his presence in Brazil itself. The absolute monarch, if anything, was more powerful and prestigious in Brazil than had ever been the case. His physical presence, in an immemorial patriarchal political culture, associated with divine, unshaken authority and royal justice, must have

---

[7] Needell, *Party of Order*, 39–40, 96, 143–9; Jeffrey D. Needell, *The Sacred Cause: The Abolitionist Movement, Afro-Brazilian Mobilization, and Imperial Politics in Rio de Janeiro* (Stanford: Stanford University Press, 2020), Chapter 1.
[8] Barman, *Brazil*, 67, 69–72, 73, 75, 77–8.

Figure 19.1 Transportation of slaves into Brazil. Universal Images Group / Getty Images.

counted for a very great deal. Now, all of that was clearly undercut: in Portugal itself, the Porto Revolt, inspired by the 1812 Spanish Constitution and the associated 1820 Riego Revolt, struck a great blow. Porto gave liberalism and revolution new strength – even in Brazil's capital, royal seat of the new king. Between 1820 and 1821, the Porto Revolt's promotion of a constituent assembly (and its explicit associations with popular sovereignty, elections, representative government, and a constitutional balance of power) were no longer beyond the pale. They were part of the Portuguese Cortes' demands upon both the king and the kingdom of Brazil. They prefaced a political era of varied interests and groups, which conflicted on some points and united on others, reflecting the contingencies and the possibilities of the revolutionary storms that roiled the Atlantic World at the time.[9]

Suddenly, João VI faced the necessity of retaining what he could of his power and protecting the interests of his family. He demonstrated a pattern

---

[9] See ibid., passim; Maxwell, *Conflicts and Conspiracies*, 218–28, 237–38; Kirsten Schultz, *Tropical Versailles: Empire, Monarchy, and the Portuguese Royal Court in Rio de Janeiro, 1808–1821* (New York: Routledge, 2001), Chapter 7, e.g., 235–6; Jurandir Malerba, *A corte no exílio: Civilização e poder no Brasil às vésperas da independência (1808 a 1820)* (São Paulo: Companhia das Letras, 2000), Chapter 4, e.g., 206–12.

of response that would characterize his and his son's actions over the next decade. When directly threatened by unprecedented revolutionary mobilization, he sought containment and even agreed to demands. Afterward, if he could, he would either repress such threats or, at least, seek a way to shape the revolutionary process. Thus, in 1820–1821, when threatened with dispossession by the Cortes if he did not return to Portugal, he did so (in the latter year). He acted to contain the threat to both kingdoms by participation and intervention in the revolutionary process itself. He would live out his reign, first, as a constitutional monarch within the parameters set by the Cortes, and then (after the 1823 Vilafrancada reactionary, restorationist coup in Portugal) as a "constitutional" monarch attempting to find a balance between the violent factionalism that characterized relations between the Porto Revolt's adherents and their reactionary opposition. The point was to survive and to dominate.[10]

Something of this was demonstrated in Brazil, even before Dom João's departure. In 1820, the various factions in Rio and elsewhere in Brazil, mobilized by the Porto Revolt and its subsequent demands, squabbled between themselves and with the monarch in regard to the electoral process, representation, the role of Brazil in the empire, and the embrace of the Spanish constitutional model. In Rio, the king initially yielded (in the 1821 February constitutionalist rebellion and the April mobilization that followed there) and then revoked his agreements and repressed the movement. He then left for Portugal, assigning his heir, Dom Pedro, to confront the tide in Brazil as prince regent. The king's purported advice to his heir makes perfect sense. As Dom Pedro recalled, when Dom João departed, he advised him to act decisively to maintain control, rather than allow an "adventurer" to take their place. The idea, again, was to secure the dynasty's role – to maintain or to restore the linkage between the two Braganza kingdoms under the royal family in time to come.[11]

The Cortes' threat to Brazil's new position in the Portuguese world and, as part of that, to the prince regent became clear over 1822, and stoked the prince's new defiance and concern, particularly in response to the Portuguese

---

[10] Gabriel Paquette, *Imperial Portugal in the Age of Atlantic Revolutions: The Luso-Brazilian World, c. 1770–1850* (Cambridge: Cambridge University Press, 2013), 179–80, 183, 184–7, 193, 197.

[11] Barman, *Brazil*, 69–72, 74–6; Schultz, *Tropical Versailles*, 236–47; Andréa Slemian, *Vida política em tempo de crise: Rio de Janeiro: 1808–1824* (São Paulo: Hucitec, 2004), Chapter 5, esp. 115–23, 125–8, 131, 132, 133, 135; Isabel Lustosa, *Dom Pedro I: Um herói sem nenhum caráter* (São Paulo: Companhia das Letras, 2006), Part IV, Chapter 2.

JEFFREY D. NEEDELL

empowerment of provincial governments throughout Brazil and in response to the new limits imposed upon Dom Pedro in Rio. The hope that the two kingdoms might remain linked by the same monarch, with Brazil retaining its status, faded. It was claimed, particularly by the elite and the liberals of the south-central provinces, that the Portuguese were determined to restore some kind of domination over Brazil; it was argued that this was behind their policies strengthening provincial self-government and links to Lisbon at the expense of Rio's domination of the kingdom. Many, both in Rio and in the provinces, who had favored working within the Constituent Assembly in Lisbon, now reconsidered. They had initially favored the Cortes as a way to help construct a constitutional government in which their local interests were represented and protected. Now, many became unsure. Along with those more linked to Rio's recent domination of the kingdom, some began to emphasize a constitutional monarchy under Dom Pedro.[12]

In the early 1820s, Dom Pedro moved decisively to demonstrate that he stood for the enhanced position Brazil had had since 1815. He was a key figure among Rio's mobilized factions in the events of 1821, acting to secure his position and maintain a role in the process. As part of this, he had come to associate himself with the ideas of popular sovereignty, constitutionalism, and local governance. He also demonstrated a decisive penchant for personal domination. Against the advice of his closest councilors, he had agreed with and called for a constituent assembly for Brazil itself, as part of this. Again, as with his father, rather than stand aside, he was acting within the revolutionary process to dominate and to contain it. In the end, this was the key to Brazilian independence. Rather than accept a passive role in the face of the increasing dictates of the Cortes to accept a limited mandate in Brazil and, then, their demands to return and to adhere to the constitutional regime now established in Lisbon, he refused. Over 1822, when the very legitimacy and nature of his regency were explicitly challenged, he made a

---

[12] For this paragraph and the following, see the sources cited in note 11 above and Neil Macaulay, *Dom Pedro: The Struggle for Liberty in Brazil and Portugal, 1798–1834* (Durham, NC: Duke University Press, 1986), 77–8; Iara Lis Carvalho Souza, *Pátria coroada: O Brasil como corpo político autônomo, 1780–1831* (São Paulo: UNESP, 1999), 112–42, esp. 115, 116, 118–9, 134–42; Cecilia Helena de Salles Oliveira, "Teoria política e prática de governor: O delineamento do Estado Imperial nas primeiras décadas do séc. XIX," in Cecília Helena de Salles Oliveira, Maria Ligia Coelho Prado, and Maria de Lourdes Monaco Janotti, eds., *A história na política, a política na história* (São Paulo: Alameda, 2002), 48–54. On the debates in Lisbon, see George C. A. Boehrer, "The Flight of the Brazilian Deputies from the Cortes Gerais of Lisbon, 1822," *Hispanic American Historical Review*, 40:4 (1960), 497–512.

formal break with Portugal, declaring Brazil's monarchy an independent one, and raising it from the status of kingdom to that of empire.

In the end, Pedro did this with the manifest support of various elements in Brazil. His strongest support came from the southeastern region dominated by the port and politics of Rio. There, the Portuguese crown elite who had accompanied his father into exile and integrated their interests with those of the local elite were strongly supportive of the status quo established between 1808 and 1820, as were the local elite, which had benefited enormously. The local elites in the provinces of the northeast and the north, as well as that of Rio Grande do Sul, were divided. Most remained monarchist, but there were serious issues in regard to the nature and site of that monarchy. As suggested just above, some were concerned with the newly enhanced power of the Crown in Rio and its demands, and some even preferred the more distant (and therefore less effective) rule of Lisbon. The strongest support for maintaining Portuguese rule, however, came from the Portuguese troops and established Portuguese commercial interests, high and low, in the port cities of the northeast and north. Among the local landholding elite, Brazilian-born middling urban groups and the mobilized urban masses, however, support for an independent Brazilian monarchy seems to have grown over this tumultuous era, stoked by traditional lusophobia, concern for a reassertion of Portuguese interests, and the hope that the Constituent Assembly called for by the prince regent might establish and protect a growing sense of local governance and popular sovereignty, both of which had quickened over 1821–1822. Within a very short time, by mid-1823, an alliance of local land forces and a small navy, cobbled together rapidly and led by postwar British mercenaries, did away with the port city resistance of the northeast and north.[13]

Pedro's 1822 decision to call for the Constituent Assembly, whatever the risks feared by his councilors, was an astute move. It furthered his post-1820 position of containing potential threats to the legitimacy of his position by taking the lead in promoting demands for a constitutional monarchy (with the associated idea of popular sovereignty). In effect, rather than face the fragmentation and republican potential of the various regions' radicals, struggling for independence against the Portuguese monarchy or his own,

---

[13] On the various elements in play, see nn. 4–7. On the events of 1821–1822, see Barman, *Brazil*, 72–107; Slemian, *Vida política*; Lustosa, *Dom Pedro I*, 98, Part IV, Chapters 2, 5, and 6, esp. 108–9, 112, 116–7; Souza, *Pátria coroada*, Chapter 3, esp. 68–99, 104–6, 131–5.

Figure 19.2 Emperor Pedro I. Alamy

he acted quickly to control and shape popular sovereignty by adapting it to the cause of a national monarchy, which had so much to offer the local and provincial elites, in terms of maintaining the strength and order of the status quo. In a phrase, he successfully strengthened the appeal of his charismatic, dynastic role by identifying it with an independence movement, legitimized by the country's elected representatives (Figure 19.2).[14]

In the end, Dom Pedro's success was terribly marred by his unwillingness to accept partnership, compromise, or serious limits to his power. This became clear almost immediately after independence itself. He had

[14] Barman, *Brazil*, 67, 92–5, 100–1. The assembly idea had little support from Dom Pedro's most powerful advisor, José Bonifácio de Andrada e Silva; see Barman, *Brazil*; Emilia Viotti da Costa, *The Brazilian Empire: Myths and Histories* (Chicago: University of Chicago Press, 1985), 17–9; Lustosa, *Dom Pedro I*, 143–5.

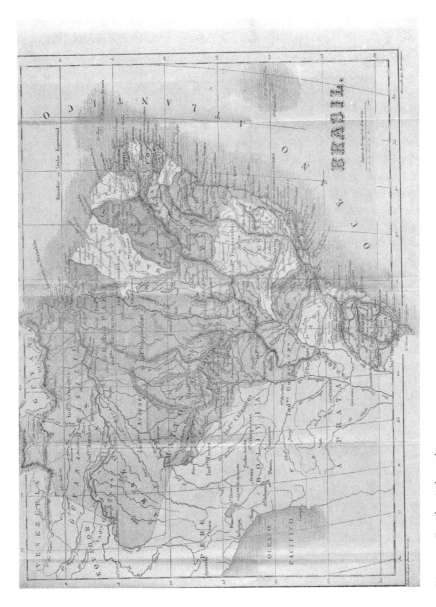

Map 19.1 Brazil at independence

successfully garnered liberal support and used his leadership of Brazilian independence to ascend to the new imperial throne, complete with a staged popular acclamation in Rio and a Church anointment in late 1822. However, matters did not go so well after the Constituent Assembly (1823) met; it was far more liberal than Dom Pedro had anticipated. It comprised highly educated, eloquent representatives elected by the country's local elites. They soon divided into two camps – one, a minority of those closest to the Rio elite (often Portuguese or closely connected to the Portuguese court and commercial notables), associated with crown patronage and office, favoring the monarch's domination (and, thus, their own), and another, a majority (mostly Brazilian-born) made up of various factions, representing the various regional oligarchies and urban, middling sorts, some committed to more radical positions, and all allied to set up a counterweight to the monarch. They looked to make a constitution that would legitimize their ruling in partnership with the Crown, so as to protect the local interests that they presumed to represent and to promote the more enlightened, liberal society of which they dreamed. Divisions were exacerbated by the 1823 absolutist triumph in Portugal, the Vilafrancada, and rumors of interest in reunion between the two monarchies. As the debates became increasingly acrimonious and deadlocked over the monarch's role in the constitution being drafted, and the question of his sanctioning that charter, the assembly's majority did not hesitate to mobilize lusophobia in the streets to force their position upon the emperor and his following. Dom Pedro I, failing at containment, chose repression. He had the assembly closed down (November 1823), and arrested his leading opponents. The rest, shocked and frustrated, retreated to their provinces.[15]

The emperor's Council of State was then pressed into service. Although he publicly claimed authorship of the resulting constitution himself, it was the Council that put it together, one legislating his domination of all three of the traditional powers. Much of this was done through establishing a fourth, so-called "moderating" power, invested with oversight of the three other powers, and advised (not limited) by a new Council of State (which he appointed). He swore to uphold the Constitution on 25 March 1824, and had it published. It would remain the monarchy's constitution (albeit with significant modification, which further strengthened the executive

[15] Barman, *Brazil*, 98, 107–18; Macaulay, *Dom Pedro*, 152–62; Needell, *Party of Order*, 39–41; Lustosa, *Dom Pedro I*, Part v, Chapter 6, esp. 159–60, 160–2, 166–70.

branch, centralized authoritarianism, and undercut parties and parliament) until 1889.[16]

This legal entrenchment of the emperor's preponderance did little to endear the monarch to the various constituencies involved in the liberal mobilizations of the past four years – except for his own minority elite constituency, which was thoroughly identified with his role. Liberal leaders in the northeast, particularly, were shocked by the coup against the assembly and rapid, successive affronts to their hopes for more local governance. They saw all of this as a return to a centralizing, absolutist tyranny dominated by Portuguese. They revolted in early 1824 and, by mid-year, established the Confederation of the Equator (centered in Pernambuco, but involving other provinces of the northeast and north). To no avail; the emperor's forces on land and sea repressed them violently between September and November of the same year; the principal leaders were then tried and executed.[17]

## The Challenges of the Monarchy in Brazil:
### 1824–1831

While violence in the street, and even provincial revolts, would still be a very significant factor for many years, the focus of the struggle over political power and over the nature of the new institutions in which that power was sheathed was the parliament set up by the Constitution of 1824. Parliament was made up of two houses, the Chamber of Deputies (provincial delegations of deputies were elected by provincial electors who themselves were elected by those qualified to vote) and the Senate (each provincial senator was appointed by the monarch from the three candidates garnering the most votes in a provincial election, managed in the same, indirect way that deputies were elected). Those eligible to vote in the elections involving representatives to the Portuguese Cortes or the Constituent Assembly had been a relatively restricted group. That was not the case under the new constitution, which apparently sought to provide at least a façade of inclusion. Indeed, those eligible to vote were, for the times, very liberally defined (by gender, by age, by independence, and by a very minimal income limit).

---

[16] Macaulay, *Dom Pedro*, 160–4; Barman, *Brazil*, 123–6; Needell, *Party of Order*, 34–5; Cecília Helena de Salles Oliveira, "Contribuição ao estudo do poder moderador," in Cecília Helena de Salles Oliveira, Vera Lúcia Nagib Bittencourt, and Wilma Peres Costa, eds., *Soberania e conflito: Configurações do Estaco Nacional no Brasil do século XIX* (São Paulo: Hucitec, 2010), 185–235.

[17] Macaulay, *Dom Pedro*, 165–7; Barman, *Brazil*, 121–3; Mosher, *Political Struggle*, 64–77.

Nonetheless, it was well known that most of the voting public over the years to come voted as they were directed by the local "influences" (the great landholders, merchants, etc.), most particularly in the rural sector, where most Brazilians lived. So, while many of those making up the majority in the Constituent Assembly had ably represented the minority views and interests of their provinces' elite and urban middling interests, nothing much had effectively changed in the first elections under the Constitution; unsurprisingly, many of the very same representatives elected to the Assembly of 1823 were elected provincial deputies to the first legislature (1826–1829).[18]

That being said, it is clear that their views were often liberal. The veterans of the Assembly, or others with similar views, formed the majority which made up the "liberal opposition" in the Chamber of Deputies of the following years. This opposition ranged from a minority of would-be republicans to a majority of moderate monarchists. What they had in common was the interest to limit the monarch's power and to compel him to govern with them, not over them. The Constitution held that the emperor represented the nation in his person, and ruled directly by way of two of the four powers. On the one hand, he did so as the fourth, "moderating" power (the "key of the whole political organization") designed to oversee the harmony, balance, and function of the three traditional powers. Advised by his Council of State (which he appointed), the moderating role allowed him among other things to appoint and dismiss cabinets, dissolve the Chamber and call for new elections, and sanction legislation after it was passed by both houses of parliament. On the other hand, he did so as the head of the executive power. As such, he ruled through his Council of Ministers (his cabinet); but there was no doubt who was in charge. He appointed and dismissed them at his pleasure and headed up their regular meetings. Altogether, these two constitutional roles made for an overwhelming combination.[19]

[18] For voters' and electors' qualifications, see Barman, *Brazil*, 75, 123–4; Needell, *Party of Order*, 34–5, 64; Jeffrey D. Needell, "The Brazilian Election of 1884," in Eduardo Posada Carbó, ed., *The Oxford Handbook of Revolutionary Elections in the Americas, 1800–1910* (Oxford: Oxford University Press, forthcoming); Richard Graham, *Patronage and Politics in Nineteenth-Century Brazil* (Stanford: Stanford University Press, 1990), Part II.

[19] On the Constitution of 1824, see Needell, *Party of Order*, 34–5. The classic analyses include Joaquim Rodrigues de Sousa, *Analyse e comentario da Constituição política do Imperio do Brazil ou theoria e pratica do governo constitucional brazileiro*, 2 vols. (São Luís: B. de Mattos, 1867); Visconde do Uruguay, *Ensaio sobre o direito administrative*, 2 vols. (Rio de Janeiro: Nacional, 1862); Visconde do Uruguay, *Estudos practicos sobre a administração das provincias no Brazil*, 2 vols. (Rio de Janeiro: Nacional, 1865); José

To challenge the monarch, then, the "liberal opposition" dominating the Chamber of Deputies decided to use what they understood of English parliamentary precedent to obstruct as best they could the emperor's cabinets. They did so repeatedly, in the hope that they could thus compel Pedro I to work with them. For the most part, he refused, deepening his unpopularity, increasing the brevity of administrations, and undercutting support for his policies. In Brazilian popular perception, he was criticized for three basic reasons: his authoritarian domination, his promoting and losing war in the Platine region (he maintained the Portuguese colonial strategy designed to guarantee riverine commercial and political access to the Platine and Brazilian interior), and his flagrant disregard for personal propriety, signaled by his scandalous treatment of his first empress, Leopoldina, and his flaunting a mistress, the marquise of Santos.

Clearly, the first reason was the critical one. In regard to the brevity of his cabinets, it suffices to note that, between 1826 and 1831, the emperor appointed six cabinets; most of the ministers in these were successfully confronted by the opposition, which garnered popular support not only for their arguments condemning cabinet policies but because of popular lusophobia. The cabinets, after all, were largely made up from a pool of the exiled Portuguese statesmen of 1808–1821. How could the emperor of Brazil claim to represent and promote Brazilian interests, given his own Portuguese birth and authoritarian direction, and his being served by Portuguese who owed everything to him and had no organic link to the myriad local interests which dominated local affairs across a half-continent? It is noteworthy that the monarch was so insensitive to this issue – which would have been easy to remedy given the number of very capable Brazilian-born statesmen available, Brazilians who actually supported his position – that, in fact, only one "Brazilian" cabinet was appointed by the emperor during these years. Given his personal views and his constitutional position, he apparently thought such criticisms did not count for much. He seems to have thought that what did count was what he thought best for the new nation.[20]

The issue of the monarch's domination is, thus, central to our discussion of new institutions. It was made painfully clear in a critical matter which preceded the first legislature (1826–1829) but would be taken up among the

---

Antônio Pimenta Bueno, *Direito público brasileiro e análise da Constituição do Império*, 2nd edition (Brasília: Senado Federal, 1978 [1857]).

[20] Barman, *Brazil*, 115–1, 130–1, 135–6, 143–4, 146–7, 149–50, 151, 152; Needell, *Party of Order*, 39–42; Macaulay, *Dom Pedro*, 213–4, 228–30, 231–53.

monarch's opposition with vigor before and afterward. It has to do with the diplomacy concerning recognition of Brazilian independence. This depended upon the British. Britain had hoped to maintain the unity between the two kingdoms; it suited them, since the British wanted a strong and loyal Portugal as part of their treaty obligations and their European policies and since Brazil traditionally offered special access to British commerce in South America. Indeed, British commerce with Brazil was very significant and owed much to maintaining special treaty privileges. However, once Portuguese-Brazilian unity was irreparably sundered by Dom Pedro's declaration of independence, the British sought to mitigate the damage by helping to arrange a rapid, amicable peace, in the obvious hope of maintaining as much of their former relations as they could with both monarchies. For their part, Portugal and Brazil had a great deal to gain, as well. Portugal had initially asked for British diplomatic support, in the hope of reconciliation and possible reunion with Brazil. When these proved impossible, Portugal still had an interest in accepting British diplomatic efforts to end the conflict with Brazil. The kingdom remained, in effect, a client state of Britain, particularly in European affairs, something strengthened by the very loss of Brazil; the Portuguese could not really afford to put off the English by refusing to accept the new realities. Brazil's need for British support was also critical. Britain remained its major trade partner, as well as the leading power in the post-Napoleonic world, so that their support for independence meant a very great deal to the new monarchy in terms of both commerce and legitimacy. The new emperor himself asked for British support in the independence negotiations.[21]

As British diplomats moved slowly through discussions with both monarchies, however, one particular issue came into play. As noted earlier, the British decision (1807) to end their part in the booming trade in African captives had led to the British decision to promote such a policy among other slaving kingdoms, particularly in the diplomatic agreements ending the Napoleonic Wars. The two kingdoms with most at stake in this regard were Spain and Portugal, and both, conveniently for Britain, had been and continued to be very beholden to the British. Spain had become something of a client state due to its dependence upon Britain during the war against the French (1808–1814); Portugal's dependency upon Britain was far more

---

[21] Barman, *Brazil*, 95, 103, 107, 126–9; Valentim Alexandre, *Os sentidos do império: Questão nacional e questão colonial na crise do Antigo Regime português* (Porto: Afrontamento, 1993), 738, 753–64.

traditional and far greater, as indicated above. Both were thus in a poor position to defy British policy on the matter, despite the fact that African slavery was critical to their overseas commerce and royal revenue. While the Portuguese remained the single most important suppliers of African slaves in the Americas, the Spaniards had become increasingly important, particularly because of the post-1760s advance of Cuba as a major producer of cane sugar, coffee, and tobacco. Portuguese interest in slaving had (as noted earlier) expanded still further in the eighteenth century as the North Atlantic market for sugar, coffee, tobacco, cotton, and cacao grew dramatically – Brazil produced a great deal of all of them, particularly sugar and coffee. British pressure on Portugal had some early success. Following the 1808–1810 concessions to the British after the beginning of the French War, Dom João had also recognized (1810) the inhumanity of slavery and agreed to some limitation on the slave trade in Africa and the idea of its eventual end. In the discussions at the Congress of Vienna in 1815 to establish postwar relations, matters went differently. Spain and Portugal, while still forced to deal with British pressure on the slave trade, allied in opposing Britain's more radical goals. They blunted these demands while accepting some relatively insignificant limits on the African trade and a vague promise to see to its eventual end. Afterward, in 1817, the Portuguese triumphed with yet another treaty that effectively left them free to trade between Africa and Brazil without restriction. As the South Atlantic aspect of the trade was the critical one for Portuguese interests, this was a triumph, indeed.[22]

Afterward, Brazil had continued its voluminous slave trade with Africa. The Brazilians viewed the trade as indispensable to maintain and to expand the labor critical to their export production. The United States, alone among slaveholding nations in the Americas, maintained and expanded slavery through natural reproduction – because it was practical and possible. In Latin America and the Caribbean, where more than 9 million of the 10 million captives of the Atlantic slave trade were actually sold between the 1500s and the 1800s, natural reproduction occurred but not in sufficient quantities to meet demand.[23] For the most part, given the killing nature of plantation

---

[22] Leslie Bethell, *The Abolition of the Brazilian Slave Trade: Britain, Brazil and the Slave Trade Question, 1807–1869* (Cambridge: Cambridge University Press, 1970), Chapter 1, esp. 29–31, 32–9; cf. Rafael Marquese, Tâmis Parron, and Márcia Berbel, *Slavery and Politics: Brazil and Cuba, 1790–1850* (Albuquerque: University of New Mexico Press, 2017), 85–9.

[23] See, for example, Herbert S. Klein, *African Slavery in Latin America and the Caribbean* (New York: Oxford University Press, 1986), 154–7.

labor conditions, gender disparity, child mortality, the tropical lowland disease environment, and the financial parameters, it was thought cheaper to buy slaves than support their reproduction, so labor requirements were met by the constant importation of Africans.[24]

The matter of the trade came up again after Vienna and the 1817 treaty because of independence. In effect, British diplomatic frustrations in 1815 and 1817 could be reversed once Brazil needed British political recognition and economic relations as an independent monarchy. Now, the British could successfully insist that Brazil accept not only Portugal's past commitments on the trade's geographical limitations and eventual end, but that it move forward considerably – to ending the slave trade with Africa completely in a matter of a few years.[25]

What does all of this have to do with our central issues of Brazil's new institutions and the monarch's domination? Dom Pedro I was personally opposed to slavery and the trade, while few free Brazilians shared such a position. Thus, while it was the British who now introduced the issue of abolishing the Atlantic slave trade into the negotiations over Brazil's independence and recognition, the emperor's role in accepting and promoting the trade's abolition became a critical component in his relations with Brazilian citizens and their elected representatives. Let us see how. In Brazil, as noted above, a real end to the trade was thought to be economic suicide. Moreover, slaveholding was hardly the preserve of planters and merchants alone; it was widespread among all of the free (including the more successful freedmen), both as a status marker and as the means and the goal of social mobility. In sum, when the emperor accepted the idea of an end to the slave trade with Africa, he did so despite the fact that the treaty undercut dramatically the economic, social, and political realities and traditions accepted by the elite and poorer free strata of Brazil.

Indeed, the emperor's diplomats began discussing the slave trade's abolition with the British early on after the 1822 break with Portugal. During the Constituent Assembly of 1823, the British position and the emperor's response were known; despite general Brazilian support for slavery, the need for British support was critical and immediate; somehow, a resolution had to be found. The Assembly, forced to act, put forth two proposals, one for ending the slave trade over a period of four years, the other for the gradual

---

[24] See the summary and citations in the first part of Needell, *Sacred Cause*, Chapter 1. Cf. Bethell, *Abolition*, 41–2.

[25] Bethell, *Abolition*, esp. 29, 31, 32–6, 44–5, 47, 48, 50–1.

end of slavery itself. They also delegated authority to the executive power to negotiate with the British on the matter. Even after the Assembly's dissolution, its position may have had some impact; the emperor's ongoing diplomacy with the British continued and, there, Brazilian diplomats pressed for a minimum four years' delay in any treaty ending the trade. If this were a concession to his citizens' interests, it was the emperor's only one on this issue.

The monarch was well aware of the Brazilian commitment to slavery; indeed, his representatives proposed that the British support him against a possible domestic overthrow in reaction to the treaty's successful settlement (the British refused). Nonetheless, diplomacy continued. So did the elite's concerns. In 1826, with the first session of the first Chamber legislature, the issue was taken up again. The deputies, mindful of the monarch's ongoing diplomacy, began debates on the issue, proposing a much more gradual end to the trade. The challenge to the British position was clear. In the intersession months in 1826 and 1827, then, while the Chamber was not sitting, the British pressed hard to complete the negotiations with the emperor, and succeeded. The emperor's representatives only managed a postponement of four years on practical grounds. The Chamber, when it did meet, was thus forced to recognize the treaty as a fait accompli. It did its best, at least, to maintain Brazilian sovereignty and avoid as much as possible British meddling in the actual implementation of the treaty. They passed final legislation in 1831, draping the treaty with enabling laws emphasizing Brazilian responsibilities and limiting, to the extent possible, British intervention.[26]

Given the organic relationship between the deputies in the Chamber and their elite and middling constituencies, this initial remedial response makes sense. However, the response to the emperor's role was not limited to this. The emperor's post-1823 decision to move forward independently to abolish the slave trade was a significant issue in the 1827 debates of the first Brazilian legislature and was an important step in the careers of the "liberal opposition" deputies who began to emerge as leaders at the time. First of all, the emperor's decision, taken while the Chamber had not yet completed its own deliberations and taken without consultation with the duly elected representatives of the nation was widely considered an egregious example of his "absolutism." Second of all, later, the more reactionary faction of the 1820s

---

[26] Ibid., 41–8, 56, 65, 66–7, 68, 69; Barman, *Brazil*, 147; cf. Tâmis Parron, *A política da escravidão no Império do Brasil: 1826–1865* (Rio de Janeiro: Civilização Brazileira, 2011), 58–64, 85–90; Marquese et al., *Slavery and Politics*, 121–7.

"liberal opposition" leaders would, by the mid-1830s, call for the treaty's revocation. In both instances, their general position against the emperor's abuse of his role and their personal status among their voters and their peers were seriously fortified. Slavery, however old, was critical to the new institutions that comprise our concerns here. The treaty ending the slave trade undercut the monarch's position and strengthened the position of his opposition and their use of parliament to make that opposition count.

The most illustrative example of slavery's relationship to the post-1826 parliamentary opposition and its leaders is telling: Bernardo Pereira de Vasconcelos. Vasconcelos' constituency was the province of Minas Gerais, whose economy depended entirely upon slave labor. Since the mining days of the eighteenth century, *mineiros* had also become critical suppliers of food to their own highland captaincy and to the lowlands extending beyond Rio. They fed slaves and free people in the mines and the established sugar-export plantations; later, they fed the new, highland coffee plantations of the Province of Rio de Janeiro. Indeed, by the 1820s, southern Minas would participate in planting coffee for export as well. Vasconcelos was a magistrate in Minas, with strong links to its planters and merchants. Given that and his outstanding eloquence, legal acuity, and political prowess, Vasconcelos had emerged in the post-1826 Chamber as the principal spokesman for the dominant faction within the "liberal opposition" to the emperor. As part of this, he argued for the slaveholding interests against the emperor's actions on the slave trade and other issues. By 1836, he came to explicitly champion the very revocation of the treaty. While there had been a glut in new African slaves by 1830, anticipating the legal end to the trade after 1826, that had dissipated rapidly over the few years since, and the threat to the economy and the society over which Vasconcelos' supporters presided had become immediate. Hence, the explicit condemnation of the treaty.

Vasconcelos would move on from leading the 1820s "liberal opposition" to a leading position among the *moderados* (moderates) who dominated parliament after 1831 and most of whom formed the kernel of the key evolving party (the reactionary parliamentary majority of 1837, the Party of Order of the 1840s, and, finally, the Conservative Party, c. 1848–1889) which dominated the politics and the changing nature of the monarchy. Two essential components of every successive phase of the party with which Vasconcelos and men like him were associated were a constitutional, representative, parliamentary government, opposed to the personal aggrandizement and abuse of the monarch, and the protection and support of slaveholding, as the fundamental basis for the economy and society over which his constituency presided. In sum, while

Building New Brazilian Institutions

slavery was certainly no new institution, the new monarchy and its institutions that were being debated and constructed in the 1820s and 1830s cannot be understood without a grasp of the role of the slavery central to the interests, debates, and society which that monarchy was designed to maintain and protect. Slavery was assumed and promoted by the statesmen who refashioned the new monarchy's institutions between 1826 and 1840. That put them in direct conflict with the first emperor.[27]

Dom Pedro I's evolving political isolation, fostered by his mixed results in successive attempts to contain or repress challenges to his position, has been signaled already. The attempt to dominate the Constituent Assembly over 1822–1823 failed and led to violent repression (1823), followed by the quashed revolts associated with the imposed Constitution of 1824 and the Confederation of the Equator. In the aftermath of these "absolutist" acts, the emperor, empowered by his dominant position, negotiated an amicable independence from Portugal and recognition by Britain (1825), at the cost of a treaty intended to end the African slave trade (1826). With the first elected legislature (1826–1829), the "liberal opposition" majority in the Chamber pushed back with attacks on his abusive "absolutism" (in which the 1826 slave trade treaty figured prominently) and began a successful campaign of public character assassination and parliamentary obstruction, both fed by the emperor's failures in the Platine region and his highly publicized personal peccadillos.

By 1831, successful parliamentary opposition and a cultivated, lusophobic popular mobilization had undercut the emperor's position dramatically. His attempts at containment had failed; his immediate response was the traditional one. As violence in the streets began to erupt in early 1831, he summoned his most trusted general. The officer could not even assure him of the troops' loyalty; increasingly, the rank and file had been attracted to the lusophobic liberalism of the opposition. Rather than attempting containment through compromise, which was what most of the moderate majority in the "liberal opposition" hoped for, Pedro I abdicated.

It was an unexpected crisis. The most radical leaders of the "liberal opposition," however, saw it as an opportunity, and pressed the *moderado* parliamentary leadership to move immediately to proclaim a republic. That leadership, interwoven with the families and interests of the elite, balked.

---

[27] Bethell, *Abolition*, 80, 84; Macaulay, *Dom Pedro*, 195, 216; Barman, *Brazil*, 93, 147; Needell, *Party of Order*, Chapters 2 and 3, esp. 31–5, 42–3, 61–2. Cf. Parron, *A política da escravidão*, 72–80; Marquese et al., *Slavery and Politics*, 130–42.

Instead, they chose, again, to support the vision of a constitutional monarchy that they had been trying to force upon Dom Pedro since 1823. Faced with radical republicanism, with its associated, clear threat of socioeconomic and national destabilization, they chose, again, the hope of constitutional, balanced partnership with a unifying, charismatic national leader. They accordingly responded within the parameters of the Constitution of 1824. They embraced the constitutional, imperial heir, Dom Pedro II, immediately and, given his temporary incapacity (he was aged five), went through the constitution's steps to elect the three-person regency that the constitution spelled out.[28]

## Legacy

In sharp contrast with the debates of the Constituent Assembly of 1823 and the parliamentary debates of 1826–1831, the debates of the regency (1831–1840) would make it clear why such representatives of the elite acted this way. Let us recall the concerns at play. In the critical surge of liberalism that was plain in the Assembly's 1823 debates, more cautious colleagues, explicitly thinking of the revolution that had transformed Saint-Domingue, cited the threats posed by the ideas of *philosophes* when it came to the free and the enslaved masses. Moreover, during the early regency, when the racial aspect of lusophobia was burnished by some radicals, who called for national solidarity against whites, most free persons recoiled. This appeal to the majority's Afro-Brazilian racial solidarity, with its potential for dividing the free by phenotype and mobilizing the Afro-Brazilian masses, free and slave, along racial lines, came to be called *haitianismo*. It was an occasionally explicit, but generally implicit, issue in Brazilian political discourse until the mid-nineteenth century. The elite and middling ranks of society knew full well what was at stake; better not to quicken the most divisive issue of all, and to rely upon status hierarchy to keep everyone in place. After all, many, perhaps most of the middling strata and some of the elite themselves were of mixed racial descent – their status depended upon maintaining a hierarchy in which race could be ignored or, when noted, undercut by status. Over the decades to come, in political discourse, all of the free would often be referred to as "white," in public debate, if color were noted at all.[29]

---

[28] Barman, *Brazil*, Chapter 5, esp. 158–63; Needell, *Party of Order*, 31–2, 33, 35–6.

[29] *Assembléia geral constituente e legislativa do Imperio do Brasil: Diario da Assembléia Geral, Constituente e Legislativa do Brazil 1823* (Rio de Janeiro: Nacional, 1823–1824), for example, Muniz Tavares, 30 September, A V 258; Silva Lisboa, 30 September A V 261; Maciel da Costa, 30 September A V 264; Needell, *Party of Order*, 39–40, 143–5, 148; Jeffrey D. Needell,

In the great, critical debates of the early regency, where the very nature of, and preference for, the monarchy were debated again, these fears and concerns were clear. The majority who came to dominate the Chamber by the mid-1830s perceived decentralized, democratic, and popular government, the republic, as the door to disaster – a Brazil destabilized, impoverished, and broken apart. These fears, of racial division, of mass mobilization, of social destabilization, of the crippling of Brazilian strength through regional division, all of these had to be muted and managed, and a highly centralized monarchy seemed the obvious solution. The hope was that the abuses of the monarch could be and would be curtailed and balanced out by a Chamber representing the qualified electorate. So, over the 1830s, this Chamber majority worked hard to yoke the two (prince and parliament) together, again, as they had in the 1820s. The parliamentary majority over 1835–1841 would establish the formulas and the usages that would bring them what they had argued for since 1823: an imperial state providing the charismatic, stabilizing impact of a royal dynast, guaranteeing the traditional order and interests over which the Brazilian oligarchies presided, in a governing partnership between Chamber and Crown in the imperial capital.[30]

It was not to be. The struggle between that vision and the practice of the second emperor underlie the larger political drama of the Second Reign (1840–1889). Dom Pedro II, a master at cultivating support, supporting compromise, and restrained, limited intervention, successfully dominated, even when challenging slavery itself. He was aided immeasurably by the memory of the monarchy's first two decades, when parliamentary discord and the weakened crown of 1831–1840 threatened the stability and strength of the new nation. In the end, the resulting, gradual aggrandizement of the emperor's role would prevail over the representative, constitutional aspirations of the old "liberal opposition." Old regime continuities (a charismatic, dominating dynast) and the revolutionary Atlantic World's new possibilities (a constitutional, representative government and a balance of powers) made for an inherently unstable mix. Fear triumphed over hope.

---

"Percepções sobra raça no debates abolicionistas no Brasil (1870–1888)," *Escritos*, 4:4 (2010), 7–21: 11–13; Needell, *Sacred Cause*, Chapter 1; Barman, *Brazil*, 37.

[30] Needell, *Party of Order*, Chapters 2 and 3, esp. 51–72 and 73–80.

20

# Slaves, Indians, and the "Classes of Color": Popular Participation in Brazilian Independence

### HENDRIK KRAAY

In 1888, Pedro Américo Figueiredo de Melo unveiled his spectacular painting commemorating Emperor Pedro I's proclamation of Brazil's independence, the so-called *Grito do Ipiranga*, which took place outside São Paulo on 7 September 1822 (Figure 20.1). It is a sweeping, dramatic work, with an arc of cavalrymen in full dress uniform filling the viewer's right. In the center, on a small rise, Pedro raises his sword as he proclaims that, henceforth, "Independence or Death" would be his watchwords. The riders acclaim him and wave their hats. On the extreme left, a solitary driver leads a team of oxen down the Ipiranga River's bank. Wearing tattered shirt and pants and an unmistakably plebeian straw hat, he glances over his shoulder at the emperor high above him. While his face is obscured, he is disengaged from the action and appears baffled by the scene. Pedro Américo's inclusion of only a single member of the *povo*, the ordinary people or the popular classes, in his now iconic representation of independence visually stresses their marginalization from the process.[1]

Such a view of independence was, by then, well established. Already in 1830, in an official history commissioned by Pedro, José da Silva Lisboa, the viscount of Cairu, declared that "the Brazilian nation's complete independence" derived from the emperor's act, which created a "free state out of

---

Research for this chapter has been supported by the Social Sciences and Humanities Research Council (Canada). I thank Wim Klooster and the participants in the January 2020 Yale University workshop for their comments on an earlier draft, as well as Lloyd Belton for his discussion of Emiliano Felipe Benício Mundurucú.

[1] On the painting, see Cecília Helena de Salles Oliveira and Claudia Valladão de Mattos, eds., *O Brado do Ipiranga* (São Paulo: Editora da Universidade de São Paulo, 1999).

## Slaves, Indians, and the "Classes of Color"

Figure 20.1 *Independência ou Morte*, painting by Pedro Américo Figueiredo de Melo. Museu Paulista, São Paulo, Brazil.

chaos."[2] The influential mid-nineteenth-century historian, Francisco Adolfo de Varnhagen, hailed Pedro for placing himself at the head of Brazil's independence movement; he thereby preserved Brazil's unity and saved the country from anarchy.[3] While Cairu and Varnhagen alluded to challenges to the imperial project, if only to condemn the "false revolutionary dogmas of jacobinican [*jacobínica*] liberty and equality" with which some seduced the *povo* or the "French revolution's incendiary flames," Pedro Américo painted over the uncertainties, fears, and contingencies that emerge from independence-era documents.[4]

Brazil did not, of course, succumb to revolution in the early 1820s, and the country's independence came in the form of a constitutional monarchy that preserved, and for a time, significantly expanded slavery. However, Brazilians and foreigners alike fretted about the possibility of slave revolt and feared the mobilization of the rapidly growing free population of color. By contrast, twentieth-century historians rarely considered the popular classes in their accounts of independence. In his 1975 nationalist interpretation, José

---

[2] José da Silva Lisboa, Visconde de Cayrú, *Historia dos principaes sucessos políticos do Imperio do Brasil dedicada ao Senhor D. Pedro I* (Rio de Janeiro: Typographia Imperial e Nacional, 1830), Part X, Section III, 52.
[3] Francisco Adolpho de Varnhagen, *Historia geral do Brazil* . . ., 2 vols. (Rio de Janeiro: E. & H. Laemmert, 1854–57), vol. II, 438.
[4] Cayrú, *Historia*, Part X, Section III, 95n*; Varnhagen, *Historia geral*, vol. II, 292.

Honório Rodrigues portrayed the Brazilian *povo* as patriotic defenders of national unity but also (and somewhat contradictorily) suggested that they were defeated, for the "counterrevolution" triumphed.[5] The persistence of slavery, monarchy, and latifundia made it look like nothing had changed in Brazil since the colonial period and more than a few students of the period claimed, as did Leslie Bethell, that "an extraordinary degree of political, economic, and social continuity" characterized the "transition from colony to independent empire," during which there was "no major social upheaval."[6]

In the late 1990s and early 2000s, a wave of new scholarship on independence focused on reconstructing the political process, tracing the history of ideas (including radical ones), and elucidating the changing nature of politics and the emergence of a public sphere, but the popular classes were not one of its central concerns.[7] The authors of a 2003 survey advised that readers would find no detailed analysis of Indigenous people or people of African descent in their book, for insufficient research had been done on them.[8] By this time, historians had begun writing about popular participation in Brazil's independence struggle, but no one has attempted a synthesis that assesses its significance and even historians sympathetic to the *povo*'s struggles admit that they ended in defeat.[9] Defeat does not, however, mean that these struggles were unimportant; rather, they were what made independence such an uncertain and contingent process and these years such a dynamic period in Brazilian history.

To make this discussion manageable, I focus on the short period from late 1820, when news of the Portuguese constitutionalist revolution reached the Brazilian provinces, to the end of 1824, when the defeats of a popular

---

[5] José Honório Rodrigues, *Independência: Revolução e contra-revolução*, 5 vols. (Rio de Janeiro: Francisco Alves Editora, 1975), vol. IV, 123–4, 130.

[6] Leslie Bethell, "The Independence of Brazil," in Leslie Bethell, ed., *The Cambridge History of Latin America*, 11 vols. (Cambridge: Cambridge University Press, 1983–2008), vol. III, 196.

[7] István Jancsó, ed., *Brasil: Formação do Estado e da nação* (São Paulo: Hucitec; Ijuí: Editora Unijuí, 2003); István Jancsó, ed., *Independência: História e historiografia* (São Paulo: Hucitec, 2005); Jurandir Malerba, ed., *A Independência brasileira: Novas dimensões* (Rio de Janeiro: FGV Editora, 2006).

[8] Andrea Slemian and João Paulo G. Pimenta, *O nascimento político do Brasil: As origens do Estado e da nação (1808–1825)* (Rio de Janeiro: DP&A, 2003), 10.

[9] See, for examples, Marcus J. M. Carvalho, "Os negros armados pelos brancos e suas independências no Nordeste (1817–1848)," in Jancsó, ed., *Independência*, 881–2; Hendrik Kraay, "Muralhas da Independência e liberdade do Brasil: A participação popular nas lutas políticas (Bahia, 1820–1825)," in Malerba, ed., *Independência brasileira*, 322–30. Continuing popular struggles are emphasized by João José Reis, "O jogo duro do Dois de Julho: O 'Partido Negro' na independência da Bahia," in João José Reis and Eduardo Silva, *Negociação e conflito: A resistência negra no Brasil escravista* (São Paulo: Companhia das Letras, 1989), 97–8.

insurgency in Pará, the Confederação do Equador in Pernambuco, and the Periquitos' Rebellion in Bahia, as well as the overthrow of a radical-liberal government in Maranhão, signaled Pedro's victory over those who challenged his authoritarian, centralist, but constitutional project. This outcome did not seem inevitable to contemporaries. At the time of Pedro's Grito do Ipiranga, constructed as the new nation state's founding moment by the end of the 1820s, large parts of Portuguese America had not joined the emerging polity; one of the new emperor's major tasks was to aid those in the northern provinces who were willing to accept rule from Rio de Janeiro.

Brazilian independence, like independence movements elsewhere in the Americas, cannot be reduced to an anticolonial struggle for national liberation. It is by now a well-established proposition that no Brazilian nation chafed under a Portuguese colonial yoke; rather, it emerged under the auspices of the imperial state, which "forged" the nation, as Roderick J. Barman puts it.[10] Identities emerged out of political struggle over the familiar issues of the Age of Revolutions. Who could be citizens of the new state? What was the proper balance of power between the monarch and the nation's representatives? Where did sovereignty lie? How should power be shared between the central state and its constituent parts (or, better, those who held power in the provinces)? Popular participation in politics during these years was rarely, if ever, about independence narrowly defined; rather it was about the big questions that the Age of Revolutions posed in a society highly dependent on the slave trade (imports averaged nearly 50,000 per year in the 1810s and 1820s), close to 30 percent of whose population was enslaved, and in which free people of color were the most rapidly growing segment of the population.[11]

Regionalism still hampers scholarship on Brazilian independence. Historians in what Brazilians call the "Rio [de Janeiro]–São Paulo axis" – the country's cultural and intellectual center – produce what is considered national history, while those in other states write the histories of their regions in dialogue with the national narrative. Varnhagen's *História da Independência do Brasil*, written in the 1870s, but not published until the 1910s, adopted this

---

[10] Roderick J. Barman, *Brazil: The Forging of a Nation, 1798–1852* (Stanford: Stanford University Press, 1988).

[11] Herbert S. Klein, *The Atlantic Slave Trade* (Cambridge: Cambridge University Press, 2010), 217; Maria Luiza Marcílio, "The Population of Colonial Brazil," in Bethell, ed., *Cambridge History*, vol. II, 63; Herbert S. Klein, "Nineteenth-Century Brazil," in David Cohen and Jack P. Greene, *Neither Slave nor Free: The Freedmen of African Descent in the New World* (Baltimore, MD: Johns Hopkins University Press, 1972), 312, 316.

approach: The book contains a national narrative from the 1820 Portuguese constitutionalist revolt to the recognition of independence in 1825, followed by chapters on eight provinces from Bahia to Pará (Piauí and the southern provinces did not rate separate discussions), a pattern followed by the organizers of edited books on independence.[12] Acknowledging local and provincial structures and conjunctures, this approach obscures common patterns. While Rodrigues castigated provincial leaders for failing to align themselves with Rio de Janeiro and threatening Brazilian unity, historians of Pernambuco now emphasize that their province was the center of a radical-liberal and federalist national project that, since the brief 1817 republican rebellion against João VI, amounted to what Evaldo Cabral de Mello calls "the other independence [movement]."[13] Likewise, Bahian patriots have long held that the independence war in their province and the 2 July 1823 expulsion of Portuguese troops from Salvador should be considered the culmination of Brazilian independence.[14] That many of the more radical popular movements took place far from Rio de Janeiro has tended to marginalize them from the central narrative of Brazilian independence. To be sure, few today still dismiss them as anarchical or separatist movements that threatened a predestined Brazilian national unity, and most scholars recognize that they embodied a combination of local elite grievances (or rivalries) and popular political engagement, but they have still not been effectively incorporated into the narrative of Brazilian independence.

Sources remain a challenge. The popular classes, often illiterate (but not disengaged from literate culture), generated few documents; much of what they thought or did must be inferred from what their opponents said about them. Worried local officials had many incentives to exaggerate threats when they sought aid from provincial capitals or from Rio de Janeiro. Indeed, the boldest claims attributed to members of the popular classes come from their enemies' pens, and one may reasonably suspect a degree of embellishment or a selective citation of the most radical elements; likewise, radical statements attributed to members of the popular classes by later chroniclers often served reactionary purposes. Time and again, fear of a repeat of the Haitian

---

[12] Francisco Adolpho de Varnhagen, *Historia da Independencia do Brazil* (Rio de Janeiro: Livraria Castilho, 1919). For examples, see Carlos G. Mota, ed., *1822: Dimensões* (São Paulo: Editora Perspectiva, 1972); and Jancsó, *Independência*.

[13] Rodrigues, *Independência*, vol. 1, 301–59; Evaldo Cabral de Mello, *A outra Independência: O federalismo pernambucano de 1817 a 1824* (São Paulo: Editora 34, 2004).

[14] Hendrik Kraay, *Bahia's Independence: Popular Politics and Patriotic Festival in Salvador, Brazil, 1824–1900* (Montreal: McGill-Queen's University Press, 2019).

Revolution cropped up in elite rhetoric but this does not mean that slaves or free people of color were plotting a repeat of the August 1791 rebellion around Cap Français, or even that elite divisions were so severe that they might enable such a rebellion. To be sure, there are a few allusions to the Haitian Revolution in unmistakably popular rhetoric, but as students of the revolution's impact in Brazil conclude, "more than nourishing dreams of freedom in the slave quarters and proposals for racial equality among free Afro-Brazilians, Haiti was the stuff of nightmares in the mansions and government palaces."[15]

This chapter begins with a survey of the broad changes in Brazilian society that contributed to popular politicization and a brief overview of the political narrative. Elite divisions opened spaces for popular political actors, slave and free alike. So did militarization and the closely related increased mobility of the free lower classes. Portuguese constitutionalism or *vintismo* produced an expanding public sphere, not just a bourgeois one but also a less genteel public sphere of the streets. I then turn to slaves and the three distinct ways in which they became political actors during these years. In 1821–1822, a wave of "slave constitutionalism" swept Portuguese America as slaves concluded that the Constitution and the associated talk of liberty meant that they would soon be freed. Divisions among the free – sometimes armed conflict for which some recruited slaves – facilitated traditional forms of slave resistance and slaves took advantage of the new opportunities.

The rest of this chapter examines politics among the free. Legally free since the late eighteenth century, Indians constituted a large proportion of the population in the north, but they were still subject to coercive militia and labor service. Elsewhere, small numbers of Indian villages descended from missions maintained a precarious autonomy threatened by Luso-Brazilian settlers who sometimes coveted their lands. Both groups engaged dynamically with the opportunities and threats posed by both *vintismo* and Brazilian independence. The final section focuses on what contemporaries called the "classes of color," the rapidly growing freed and free population of African

---

[15] João José Reis and Flávio dos Santos Gomes, "Repercussions of the Haitian Revolution in Brazil, 1791–1850," in David Geggus and Norman Fiering, eds., *The World of the Haitian Revolution* (Bloomington: Indiana University Press, 2009), 293. See also Marco Morel, *A Revolução do Haiti e o Brasil escravista: O que não deve ser dito* (Jundiaí: Paco Editorial, 2017), 22–4, 28; Rafael Marquese, Tâmis Parron, and Márcia Berbel, *Slavery and Politics: Brazil and Cuba, 1790–1850*, trans. Leonardo Marques (Albuquerque: University of New Mexico Press, 2016), 62–3, 68–70.

descent. The object of much worry since the late colonial period, this group was far from homogenous and its members engaged in strikingly different ways in the politics of these years. Some embraced radical liberalism and virulent anti-Portuguese nativism, while others sought modest change and a greater place for themselves in a reformed order.

## General Contexts

Brazil's independence period, narrowly defined, began in late 1820 with the arrival of news about the Porto Revolution and the convocation of a Cortes (parliament) for the Portuguese nation, which prompted a new, and for some, deeply worrisome politicization. Starting with Pará in January 1821, Brazilian provinces gradually adhered to the constitutional regime. In some, like Pará and Bahia, patriots deposed colonial governors and immediately formed governing juntas; in others, like Maranhão and Pernambuco, governors accepted the constitutional regime and remained in power, in Maranhão's case, until the Cortes ordered elections for new provincial juntas in early 1822. Well before then, most provinces had elected deputies to this parliament. In February 1821, King João VI accepted the new regime. He departed for Lisbon in April but left his son, the future Pedro I, to govern in Rio de Janeiro. The Cortes' vision of a unitary government for the Portuguese nation led it to dismantle the institutions of governance created in Brazil since João had transferred his court to Rio de Janeiro in 1808 and to subordinate provincial military administration to Lisbon through the direct appointment of garrison commanders. Some Brazilians denounced these efforts as "recolonization." Coordinated by José Bonifácio de Andrada e Silva, those interested in preserving a governing apparatus in Rio de Janeiro, especially economic elites in neighboring Minas Gerais and São Paulo, prevailed upon Pedro to defy the Cortes and to proclaim his intention to stay in Brazil (9 January 1822). By the middle of the year, Pedro was rapidly consolidating his government in defiance of the Cortes and some provincial juntas recognized his authority. He convened a council of delegates from the provinces to advise him, and on 13 May, took the title of "permanent defender" of Brazil; on 3 June, he convoked a Constituent Assembly. The 7 September declaration immortalized by Pedro Américo was quickly followed by his acclamation as emperor on 12 October and his coronation on 1 December. The Constituent Assembly convened in May 1823, but Pedro forcibly closed it in November and promised to grant a charter, which he did in March 1824.

At the end of 1822, however, Pedro's writ did not extend far into the northern provinces. Bahia hung in the balance, divided between a patriot government, led by local sugar planters, that recognized Pedro and Portuguese troops besieged in Salvador. With some aid from Rio de Janeiro, Pernambuco, and elsewhere, the patriots would force the Portuguese to evacuate Salvador on 2 July 1823, but many were deeply suspicious of what they perceived as the new emperor's authoritarian proclivities, and demobilizing the patriot troops was a difficult task. Not until the October 1824 defeat of the Periquitos Rebellion (a mutiny of the most radical elements of the patriot forces) could Pedro's supporters consider themselves victorious in Bahia. Pernambuco remained deeply divided between elite factions, one of which sought greater provincial autonomy and would lead the 1824 Confederação do Equador, which formally proclaimed an alliance of northern provinces against Rio de Janeiro and called for a more liberal, decentralized regime. Its defeat marked the end of "the other independence."

Until mid-1823, Maranhão and Pará remained loyal to the Lisbon Cortes, although pro-Pedro patriots from Ceará and Piauí had improvised forces that were advancing against pro-Portuguese troops from Piauí that eventually retreated to Caxias, Maranhão. An improvised navy commanded by British mercenaries played a major role in isolating the Portuguese troops in Salvador, securing the adherence of the capital cities of Maranhão (São Luís) and Pará (Belém) to Rio de Janeiro in mid-1823, and eventually quashing the Confederação do Equador and the radical-liberal government of Miguel dos Santos Freire e Bruce in Maranhão in late 1824.

These political changes and conflicts opened spaces for popular engagement in politics. The constitutional regime lifted press censorship and pamphlets and periodicals proliferated. This new public sphere extended beyond the bourgeois space envisioned by Jürgen Habermas, and in late 1823, one contemporary recalled that João's acceptance of the constitutional regime meant that people could finally "say in the streets what they used to say only at home."[16] Public discussion of political issues was noted throughout Brazil, while news and political ideas circulated through a mix of oral and literate channels.[17] Manuscript and printed *pasquins* (placards) proliferated

---

[16] Quoted in Andréa Slemian, *Vida política em tempo de crise: Rio de Janeiro (1808–1824)* (São Paulo: Hucitec, 2006), 138–9; see also 154–8.

[17] Flávio José Gomes Cabral, *Conversas reservadas: "Vozes públicas," conflitos políticos e rebeliões em Pernambuco no tempo da Independência do Brasil* (Rio de Janeiro: Arquivo Nacional, 2013), 228; Marco Morel, *As transformações dos espaços públicos: Imprensa, atores políticos e sociabilidades na cidade imperial* (São Paulo: Hucitec, 2005), 205, 209,

and observers regularly noted their often-incendiary nature or claimed that they were written in language accessible to the *povo*.[18] One from Sergipe in mid-1824 was but a small slip of paper (7 by 10 cm), with a crudely-written text that called for the death of Portuguese and Brazilian whites.[19] Others were not so radical, but demonstrate that a broad range of issues was up for public discussion.

Songs, shouts, cheers, jeers, and gestures were ephemeral, but meaningful, forms of political discourse that rarely went recorded.[20] In September 1823, the wife of a Bahian sugar planter lamented the "furious language" that poured "from the mouths of Blacks [*negros*]," without noting what they said other than that it expressed "their rage against us."[21] Some later memoirists also recalled especially radical or threatening speech. In Ceará, the "rabble" reportedly dared tell white women in their homes that, "you [who] have borne white children will next year give birth to *cabras* [dark mulattoes]," threats of inter-racial rape that emasculated these women's male protectors.[22] Statements reported by often white witnesses in investigations whose outcomes were never in doubt likely exaggerated popular radicalism (or at least selectively focused on it), but the sheer quantity of these denunciations clearly indicates that something new was afoot.

The traditional practice of petitioning also gained new significance as large, collective petitions became ways of mobilizing and demonstrating support. The January 1822 petition urging Pedro to remain in Rio de Janeiro reportedly bore more than 8,000 signatures, and it took only five days in May to collect 6,000 signatures for a petition calling for a Constituent

---

224; Mark Harris, *Rebellion on the Amazon: The Cabanagem, Race, and Popular Culture in the North of Brazil, 1798–1840* (Cambridge: Cambridge University Press, 2010), 208; José Murilo de Carvalho, Lúcia Bastos, and Marcello Basile, "Introdução," in *Às armas, cidadãos! Panfletos manuscritos da Independência do Brasil (1820–1823)* (São Paulo: Companhia das Letras; Belo Horizonte: Editora UFMG, 2012), 16, 22, 23, 30, 31; Kirsten Schultz, *Tropical Versailles: Empire, Monarchy, and the Portuguese Royal Court in Rio de Janeiro, 1808–1821* (London: Routledge, 2001), 237–59.

[18] Morel, *Transformações*, 223–38; Slemian, *Vida*, 156, 158; João José Reis and Hendrik Kraay, "'The Tyrant Is Dead': The Revolt of the Periquitos, Bahia, 1824," *Hispanic American Historical Review* 89:3 (2009), 399–434: 416.

[19] Luiz R. B. Mott, *Sergipe del Rey: População, economia e sociedade* (Aracaju: Fundesc, 1986), 192.

[20] Morel, *Transformações*, 224.

[21] Maria Bárbara Garcez Pinto de Madureira to Luis Paulino, n.p., c. September 1823, in António d'Oliveira Pinto da França, ed., *Cartas baianas, 1821–1824* (São Paulo: Companhia Editora Nacional, 1980), 122.

[22] Quoted in Tyrone Apollo Pontes Cândido, "A plebe heterogênea da Independência: armas e rebeldia no Ceará (1817–1824)," *Almanack* 20 (2018), 194–215: 212.

Assembly.[23] In February 1822, 848 and 425 people signed two petitions in Salvador for and against the appointment of Luiz Inácio Madeira de Melo as provincial military commander.[24] The complaints from Pernambuco about "three insignificant men of color" who "forged a petition with six hundred signatures" demanding the Portuguese troops' expulsion in January 1822 reveal growing popular engagement in political questions (and efforts to disqualify it).[25]

Independence-era politics cannot be understood without a consideration of the armed forces. The military generated some of the most radical movements during these years and control over the armed forces was essential to securing power. The army, the militia, and the *ordenanças* (a sort of reserve militia) nominally enrolled most of the free and freed male population in distinctively Old Regime ways. In principle, Black men and Indians were excluded from the regulars, whose ranks were supposed to consist of white men. Some Portuguese troops were brought to Brazil after the end of the Napoleonic Wars to pursue the monarchy's expansionist goals in the Río de la Plata. The 1817 republican rebellion in Pernambuco prompted the deployment of Portuguese regiments to Recife and Salvador, where their presence would become deeply controversial (hence the petitions for their removal). Nevertheless, most army units were raised locally; officers and soldiers normally served their entire careers in a single garrison and army regiments were deeply rooted in local society. Mobilizations for the occupations of French Guiana (1809) and Montevideo (1816) prompted authorities to cast their recruitment nets more widely and to overlook colonial racial preferences. The independence conflicts accelerated this process, and by the 1820s, men of color predominated in the enlisted ranks. Campaigns increased mobility among this important sector of the free population, simultaneously disrupting soldiers' and officers' lives and broadening their horizons.[26]

---

[23] Barman, *Brazil*, 83; Rodrigues, *Independência*, vol. 1, 205; Renato Lopes Leite, *Republicanos e libertários: Pensadores radicais no Rio de Janeiro (1822)* (Rio de Janeiro: Civilização Brasileira, 2000), 125–30, 159, 306–8.

[24] This appointment was the flashpoint for fighting between Brazilian and Portuguese troops that marked the start of the independence war in Bahia. Petition of "Negociantes, Proprietários, Militares e mais Cidadãos," 22 February 1822, *Anais do Arquivo Público do Estado da Bahia* 27 (1941), 2.

[25] Quoted in Iara Lis Carvalho Souza, *Pátria coroada: O Brasil como corpo político autônomo, 1780–1831* (São Paulo: Editora UNESP, 1998), 167–8. On petitions, see Vantuil Pereira, *Ao soberano congresso: Direitos do cidadão na formação do Estado imperial brasileiro* (São Paulo: Alameda, 2010).

[26] Shirley Maria Silva Nogueira, "A 'soldadesca desenfreada': Politização militar no Grão-Pará da era da Independência" (Ph.D. dissertation, Universidade Federal da Bahia,

Before independence, Black men (*homens pretos*) served in segregated militia regiments that dated back to the seventeenth century, the so-called Henriques or Henrique Dias regiments, named after a Black hero of the wars against the Dutch in Pernambuco. These were most prominent in older areas of plantation settlement where manumission and natural growth had created significant free populations of African descent; they were less well established in provinces like Maranhão and Pará where slave plantation agriculture had only developed in the second half of the eighteenth century (there, Indians filled the militia and *ordenanças* ranks). The creation of militia regiments restricted to *pardos* (mulattoes) in the last decades of the eighteenth century seemingly sought to divide men of color. Both the Henriques and the *pardo* regiments had officers drawn from their respective "racial" groups, but their position remained precarious, for some officials sought to subordinate these regiments to the regular army by appointing white professional officers to train and command them. Luiz Geraldo da Silva has characterized the Black officers' worldview as "baroque," given their expectation that loyal service to the monarch would secure them reward and protection of their status. New liberal ideas offered opportunities, but also challenged their worldview.[27]

While political horizons expanded, much politics turned on questions of local power. Everywhere in Brazil, the independence conflicts provided the occasion to settle scores or to dislodge rivals. Different regional economic interests in provinces frequently gave rise to competing elites whose members struggled over control of provincial governments and sought support from Lisbon and Rio de Janeiro. They mobilized clients and dependents, free and slave alike, but such mobilizations often escaped elite control.

## Slaves

Independence undermined slavery. João José Reis has emphasized that the patriot rhetoric that equated Brazil's status with slavery resonated among slaves who interpreted it in their own ways.[28] Gladys Sabina Ribeiro further

---

2009), 120–3, 144–55; Hendrik Kraay, *Race, State, and Armed Forces in Independence-Era Brazil: Bahia, 1790s–1840s* (Stanford: Stanford University Press, 2001), 75–7, 126–33.

[27] Luiz Geraldo Silva, "Negros patriotas: Raça e identidade social na formação do Estado nação (Pernambuco, 1770–1830)," in Jancsó, *Brasil*, 500–7; and "Aspirações barrocas e radicalismo ilustrado: Raça e nação em Pernambuco no tempo da Independência (1817–1823)," in Jancsó, *Independência*, 915–34; Kraay, *Race*, Chapter 3.

[28] João José Reis, "'Nos achamos em campo a tratar da liberdade': A resistência negra no Brasil oitocentista," in Carlos Guilherme Mota, ed., *Viagem incompleta: A experiência brasileira (1500–2000), formação, histórias* (São Paulo: Editora SENAC, 2000), 250–2; João

Slaves, Indians, and the "Classes of Color"

claims that "slaves and freedpeople understood perfectly what was going on in the country," surely an exaggeration given the uncertainties of the time, but there is no denying the repeated expressions of concern about slave unrest.[29] From one end of Brazil to the other, slaves thought that the Portuguese constitution's adoption would lead to their freedom. Such slave constitutionalism was but a short-lived phenomenon, and slaves quickly learned what their constitutionalist masters stood for. More generally, the disruptions of the independence conflicts opened new spaces for traditional forms of slave resistance like flight. So did patriot efforts to recruit slaves for their forces and the more sporadic attempts of the Portuguese or conservative groups to employ slaves in military capacities.

Widespread slave constitutionalism demonstrates slaves' engagement with *vintismo*. In 1824, a resident of Marajó island (Pará) lamented that, since early 1821, "Black slaves [had] understood" *vintismo* as "the publication of their freedom and were constantly expecting their masters to release them."[30] Twenty-five hundred kilometers to the south, in Itu (São Paulo), a local judge reported that the August 1821 ceremonies of adhesion to the constitutional regime had been disrupted by news that the slaves were plotting to "regain their freedom, convinced that, because of the constitution, their freedom would be given to them." In an echo of the common trope of royal manumission decrees hidden by local officials, the Itu slaves believed that "their masters and public authorities were hiding the order for this."[31] In the immediate aftermath of Maranhão's adhesion to the constitutional regime, placards in São Luís called slaves to arms to win "liberty" and to put whites to death.[32] The *Correio do Rio de Janeiro* reported in April 1822 that a certain priest (then under arrest) had told a slave shoemaker that the Cortes had decreed the slaves' freedom, but that Prince Regent Pedro was hiding the decree.[33] At about the same time, a Black man claiming to be the King of

José Reis, "Quilombos e revoltas escravas no Brasil," *Revista USP* 28 (December 1995–January 1996), 14–39: 27–8; Reis, "Jogo Duro," 92–3.

[29] Gladys Sabina Ribeiro, *A liberdade em construção: Identidade nacional e conflitos antilusitanos no Primeiro Reinado* (Rio de Janeiro: Relume-Dumará, 2002), 320.

[30] Quoted in Nogueira, "Soldadesca," 213.

[31] Quoted in Magda Ricci, *Assombrações de um padre regente: Diogo Antônio Feijó (1784–1843)* (Campinas: Unicamp, 2001), 312–3.

[32] Souza, *Pátria*, 150–2.

[33] *Correio do Rio de Janeiro*, 24 April 1822. Lúcia Maria Bastos Pereira das Neves considers it an "implausible" story and suggests that it was part of a plot to discredit a faction, *Corcundas e constitucionais: A cultura política da Independência (1820–1822)* (Rio de Janeiro: Faperj and Revan, 2003), 334.

Kongo was arrested in Minas Gerais; like so many others, he had concluded that slaves would soon gain their freedom thanks to the Constitution.[34]

The transatlantic rumor mill transformed these small-scale but widespread incidents into "revolution" and one Lisbon periodical reported a thousand deaths during an alleged constitutionalist slave rebellion in Minas Gerais. No such revolt took place, but the province saw several other conspiracies connected to Portuguese constitutionalism.[35] As Matthias Röhrig Assunção explains, "slave and free black artisans were already imagining abolition as a possible outcome of independence."[36] Throughout Brazil, local officials blamed agitators or emissaries who allegedly told slaves that they were free "by virtue of the constitutional system, or by the king's decrees," as Madeira put it in March 1822; similar reports came from Maranhão and Pará.[37] To attribute slave unrest to outside agitators was, of course, an ideologically acceptable way to deny slave agency and political engagement.

It did not take long for slaves to learn that Portuguese constitutionalism was no abolitionist movement (and that no emancipation decree existed). By the time that the Brazilian Constituent Assembly convened in May 1823, there were no more indications of this kind of slave unrest, and no slaves mistook Brazil's 1824 Constitution for a liberating document. Nevertheless, masters and authorities regularly complained of increased resistance, indications that slaves recognized that, even if constitutions were not meant for them, circumstances had changed and there were now new opportunities for resistance. Quilombos (maroon communities) in Pernambuco and Maranhão grew in size and assertiveness, while masters lamented increased slave

---

[34] Elizabeth Kiddy, *Blacks of the Rosary: Memory and History in Minas Gerais, Brazil* (University Park: Pennsylvania State University Press, 2005), 141.

[35] Emilia Viotti da Costa, *The Brazilian Empire: Myths and Histories*, revised edition (Chapel Hill: University of North Carolina Press, 2000), 56, 140; Slemian and Pimenta, *Nascimento*, 63. For the evidence that this revolt was merely a rumor, see Ana Rosa Cloclet da Silva, "Identidades políticas e a emergência do novo estado nacional: O caso mineiro," in Jancsó, *Independência*, 539–40.

[36] Matthias Röhrig Assunção, "Elite Politics and Popular Rebellion in the Construction of Post-Colonial Order: The Case of Maranhão, Brazil (1820–1841)," *Journal of Latin American Studies* 31:1 (1999), 1–38: 25–6 (quote, 26).

[37] Quoted in Reis, "Quilombos," 28; João José Reis, *Rebelião escrava no Brasil: A história do levante dos Malês em 1835*, revised and expanded edition (São Paulo: Companhia das Letras, 2003), 95; Matthias Röhrig Assunção, *De caboclos a bem-te-vis: Formação do campesinato numa sociedade escravista: Maranhão, 1800–1850* (São Paulo: Annablume, 2015), 341; Adilson Júnior Ishihra Brito, "'Viva a Liberté!': Cultura política popular, revolução e sentimento patriótico na independência do Grão Pará, 1790–1824" (M.A. thesis, Universidade Federal de Pernambuco, 2008), 154–5, 158–60, 163, 257.

Slaves, Indians, and the "Classes of Color"

flight.[38] In May 1823, the editor of a pro-Portuguese periodical in Salvador complained that the rebels besieging the city (the patriots) were stealing slaves or encouraging them to flee; he claimed to have lost seven.[39]

Disruptions to slavery also derived directly from efforts to enlist slaves in masters' conflicts. Sometimes these were private initiatives, which we know about from denunciations that individuals armed their slaves to pursue political conflicts, as did one Pernambucan *corcunda* (absolutist) who, accompanied by five slaves with blunderbusses, pistols, and swords, challenged constitutionalists to repeat their shouts of "death to corcundas."[40] Others were official or semi-official initiatives. Mobilizing forces to aid the patriots in Bahia in late 1822, Rio de Janeiro's government resorted to recruiting freedmen and slaves (who would be freed) for the navy. At least some of those recruited had been freedmen before enlistment, as opposed to slaves freed to serve, but such finer points were often lost on contemporaries, including the navy commander, Lord Cochrane, who lumped the "hundred and thirty black marines just emancipated from slavery" with the "vagabondage of the capital" that, he lamented, comprised his flagship's crew.[41] These recruitment efforts prompted slaves to run away to join the armed forces; one such fugitive was not discovered until 1833.[42]

The most systematic and controversial slave recruitment effort took place in Bahia, where the patriot commander appointed by Pedro, Pierre (Pedro) Labatut, began enlisting abandoned slaves (whose Portuguese masters had fled) into a special battalion. He also tried to convince the civilian patriot junta to levy slave manpower from local planters, but this prompted widespread opposition, which eventually contributed to the May 1823 coup that removed him from command. A significant number of runaways also ended up serving in other units and Labatut's successor reported that the slave-soldiers had always demonstrated "valor and courage, and a decided enthusiasm for the cause of Brazil's independence."[43] He recommended after the patriot victory that these men be freed, and Pedro encouraged owners to do

---

[38] Marcus J. M. de Carvalho, "O outro lado da Independência: Quilombos, negros e pardos em Pernambuco (Brasil), 1817–23," *Luso-Brazilian Review* 43:1 (2006), 1–30: 2, 7–8, 13–23; Assunção, *De caboclos*, 340.

[39] *Semanario Civico* (Salvador), 23 May 1823.

[40] Cabral, *Conversas*, 190. See also Assunção, *De caboclos*, 349.

[41] Thomas Cochrane, Earl of Dundonald, *Narrative of Services in the Liberation of Chili, Peru and Brazil, from Spanish and Portuguese Domination* (London: J. Ridgway, 1859), 27.

[42] Ribeiro, *Liberdade*, 270, 321; Carlos Eugênio Libano Soares, *A capoeira escrava e outras tradições rebeldes no Rio de Janeiro (1808–1850)* (Campinas: Editora da Unicamp, 2001), 293–4, 340, 416 n. 32.

[43] José Joaquim de Lima e Silva to Minister of Empire, Salvador, 16 July 1823, Biblioteca Nacional, Seção de Manuscritos, II-31, 35, 4.

so voluntarily; his government offered compensation to those unwilling to grant manumission. The complex process of clarifying the lines between slaves and soldiers dragged on through most of the 1820s; unfortunately, the legalistic documentation offers no indication of the slaves' motives, other than their overwhelming desire for freedom. The novelty of Labatut's efforts was, however, clear to both masters and slaves.[44]

Neither the Confederação do Equador nor the Periquitos' Rebellion sought to mobilize slaves in the same way that Labatut tried in Bahia in 1823 (although the Confederação did announce its intention to end the slave trade). However, in Pernambuco, both parties accused each other of attempting to free slaves, thereby seeking support from slaveholders by portraying their enemies as the greater threat.[45] The Periquitos' Rebellion's defeat and the Confederação leadership's retreat toward Ceará (where they were soon captured) may have contributed to a slave conspiracy in Maranhão. In 1827, a slave in Iguará told others that "soon the time would come when they would free themselves. The English would on behalf of the king of Congo protect their freedoms, and their allies had already taken Bahia and Pernambuco, and were on their way to Maranhão by land and by sea. They should join them to exterminate all the whites who would oppose them." Evidently, word of British opposition to the slave trade contributed to this plot, while the references to Pernambuco and Bahia may be belated news of the two rebellions.[46] Although this conspiracy lies just outside of the immediate independence period, it connects many of the changes that had taken place since 1820: increased and sometimes politicized slave resistance, news and rumors about faraway political changes with local implications, and distinct slave (and lower-class) understandings of these changes' significance.

## Indigenous Peoples

Decades of scholarship have pointed to the continuing importance of Indigenous peoples in nineteenth-century Brazil. Those under Luso-Brazilian rule in the north were known as Tapuios and Caboclos; there, they constituted the majority of the population. Outside the Amazon region,

---

[44] Kraay, *Race*, 216–33.
[45] Glacyra Lazzari Leite, *Pernambuco 1824: A Confederação do Equador* (Recife: Fundação Joaquim Nabuco, Editora Massangana, 1989), 67, 166 n. 43; Reis and Kraay, "The Tyrant Is Dead," 424.
[46] Quoted in Assunção, "Elite Politics," 23; Assunção, *De caboclos*, 343–4. The suggestion of a connection of the Pernambuco and Bahia revolts to the one in Maranhão is mine.

Figure 20.2 Indian soldiers fighting Botocudos in São Paulo, c. 1820.
Source: "Sauvages civilisés/Soldats indiens de Mugi das Cruzas (province de St. Paul) combatant des Botocudos," Jean Baptiste Debret, *Voyage pittoresque et historique au Brésil* (Paris: Firmin Didot Frères, 1834–1839), vol. 1, plate 21.

smaller numbers of Indian villages existed alongside Luso-Brazilian settlements. Most descended from the early colonial missions that had been secularized and placed under civil administration (the so-called Directory) in the 1750s. This regime's 1798 abolition left these communities in legal limbo. The mid-century reforms had sought to integrate Indians into Luso-Brazilian society equal subjects of the Crown, but in practice, especially in the Amazon region, they remained subject to private and public labor drafts implemented through the militia; Luso-Brazilian colonists regularly encroached on Indian villages' lands.[47] Large numbers of Indigenous people remained effectively outside of Luso-Brazilian control, and it appears that independence little affected them; hostile relations punctuated by occasional periods of peaceful contact would continue to characterize frontier interactions for decades to come (Figure 20.2).[48]

---

[47] André Roberto de A. Machado, *A quebra da mola real das sociedades: A crise política do Antigo Regime português na província do Grão-Pará (1821–1825)* (São Paulo: Hucitec, 2010), 63–73; Harris, *Rebellion*, 104–41.

[48] Hal Langfur, "Cannibalism and the Body Politic: Independent Indians in the Era of Brazilian Independence," *Ethnohistory* 65:4 (October 2018), 549–73.

Pernambuco's few Indian villages tended to monarchism; they had supported the royalists in 1817 and had received reward for their services. By 1824, they had transferred their loyalty to Pedro and fought against the Confederação do Equador.[49] After the constitutional regime's adoption in Ceará, there were fears that the colonial governor (who had remained in office) was insufficiently committed to the new regime and that he would mobilize Indian villages to restore absolutism, as he had done in 1817, when 300 Indians joined the forces that destroyed a short-lived republic aligned with Pernambuco.[50]

Indigenous people's royalism derived from their calculation that they were best served by supporting monarchical authority as a counterweight to the local elites who had embraced republican ideas or were empowered by liberal regimes. Some sought to access new sources of power. Five Indian "nations" from the borderlands of Maranhão, Pará, and Minas Gerais petitioned the Cortes for measures to demarcate their lands, secure their personal liberty, and protect their commerce, framing this request within a Catholic context (they also sought funds to build "a majestic temple dedicated to St. John the Baptist").[51] The Indians of Maranguapé (Ceará) wasted no time in transferring their loyalty to "The King Defender of Brazil [*El Rey Defensor do Brasil*]" and used nativist rhetoric to justify their September 1822 attacks on two local officials, Portuguese-born men who had led settler encroachment on their lands. At that time, the Ceará junta was still loyal to Lisbon and news of the Grito do Ipiranga had not yet reached the province, but Maranguapé's leaders had evidently heard of the title of "permanent defender" that Pedro had taken on 13 May. The junta quickly arrested the ringleaders, but when Fortaleza acclaimed Pedro's government in January 1823, they regained their freedom, for the new government looked sympathetically on their complaints against the "enemies of the Brazilian cause," an example of how independence reshaped a local land conflict.[52]

Portuguese constitutionalism and Brazilian independence also gave Indians new language with which to challenge their subjection to militia

---

[49] Mariana Albuquerque Dantas, "Os 'índios fanáticos realistas absolutos' e a figura do monarca português: Disputas políticas, recrutamento e defesa de terras na Confederação do Equador," *Clio* (Recife) 33:2 (2015), 49–73.

[50] João Paulo Peixoto Costa, "Não deixam suspirar pela sua liberdade: Motins de índios no Ceará e a formação do Estado no Brasil," *Almanak* 21 (April 2019), 484–528: 490–2; Cândido, "Plebe," 200–1.

[51] Julio Sánchez Gómez, "Invisibles y olvidados: Indios e Independencia de Brasil," *Studia Historica* 27 (2009), 235–77: 250 (quote), 268–71.

[52] Costa, "Não deixam suspirar," 496–514. The connection to Prince Pedro's title is mine.

service and forced labor. In November 1823, the captain commander of Oeiras (Pará) complained that local Indians refused to do their duty as members of the *ordenanças*. They declared that "they were not Indians, and that they were Citizens, and if any officer turned up in their settlement, they had plenty of powder and shot" to deal with him.[53] Residents of Alter do Chão (Pará) refused customary labor drafts in 1824 and complained of harassment by people from Santarém: "To those who say that Independence is only for them, and not for Indians: we who have [been granted] freedom by our august Emperor, would say that even though we are Indians, we are baptized as well as they are."[54]

These concerns underlay the insurgency centered on Cametá that swept the lower Amazon from late 1823 to mid-1824. Sparked by the brutal murder of over 250 soldiers who had mutinied calling for a new junta in mid-October 1823 (they were forcibly confined to a ship's airless hold and only one man survived the night), the movement quickly spread through networks of Tapuio deserters. André Machado sees this movement as a radical independence project. Tapuio leaders claimed to support the "true cause of independence," which they closely connected to freedom from labor service; they cheered Pedro and imagined him as defender of the rights that they had gained under the Portuguese constitutional regime (and which they expected the Brazilian empire to secure). A provisional military junta in Santarém managed to block their advance upriver, and with reinforcements from Rio Negro, dispersed the Tapuio patriots.[55]

More generally, local authorities throughout the north repeatedly complained about Indians' greater resistance and assertiveness. In this respect, Tapuios and Caboclos resembled the slaves whose efforts to take advantage of new opportunities to resist slavery were the subject of the previous section. There were, of course, enormous differences in legal status between Indians (nominally free) and slaves (property), but they often made common cause, especially when it came to individual resistance, as they had long done.[56]

---

[53] Quoted in Brito, "Viva a *Liberté!*," 199. For similar incidents, see Nogueira, "Soldadesca," 216; Matthias Röhrig Assunção, "Miguel Bruce e os 'horrores da anarquia' no Maranhão, 1822–1827," in Jancsó, ed., *Independência*, 358; Machado, *Quebra*, 107–8.

[54] Quoted in Harris, *Rebellion*, 193–4.

[55] Machado, *Quebra*, 225–64; Harris, *Rebellion*, 189–93; Nogueira, "Soldadesca," 207–21; Brito, "Viva a *Liberté!*," 173–9, 221–49. On the massacre, see Machado, *Quebra*, 183–95.

[56] Nogueira, "Soldadesca," 217; Brito, "Viva a *Liberté!*," 228.

## The Classes of Color

While slave conspiracies, revolts, and other forms of resistance had long been inescapable facts for Brazilian masters and Indigenous resistance was likewise familiar to elites in Brazil's north, political engagement and mobilizations among the free and freed were perhaps even more troubling because of their novelty. In summarizing the intelligence that he had received from Bahia, a police spy reported in January 1821 that, "unfortunately," talk of constitutions amounted to "placing the dagger in the hands of people of color [*gens de couleur*] against all whites, both Europeans and Brazilians."[57] Reports like this, with or without the added warning that Brazil might go the way of Haiti, poured from the pens of Brazilian and foreign observers, and it would be easy to cite scores of additional examples. They speak volumes about elite fears, but only offer limited insights into the aspirations of the classes of color. By contrast, Labatut complained in 1823 that "rich men" were unwilling to send their sons to Bahia's patriot army, which "generally consisted of the people, commonly called 'of color,' who always comported themselves on all occasions with a remarkable valor."[58] Tension between fears of the mixed-race free lower classes – whom, echoing contemporaries, Reis calls the "Black party" – and the need to mobilize them in the struggle for independence (as well as recognition of their patriotic service) recurs in the documentation of these years.[59]

That contemporaries also spoke of plural classes of color underscores the category's diversity, ranging from recently freed slaves to people many generations removed from slavery who had won greater or lesser social positions; some were on the way to whitening themselves and their families. Terminology also poses problems. *Preto* and *pardo* are often translated as *Black* and *mulatto*, or lumped together under the category of *afrodescendente* (people of African descent) in contemporary scholarship, but these glosses do not do justice to contemporary understandings (although *classes de cor* comes close to the modern North American expression, *people of color*). In addition to their racial connotations, *preto* and *pardo* also signaled, respectively, greater or lesser proximity to slave status.

---

[57] Cailhé de Geine to Intendente Geral da Polícia da Corte, Rio de Janeiro, 2 January 1821, Biblioteca Nacional, Seção de Manuscritos, II-33, 22, 54. This report was written in French.

[58] Pedro Labatut to Minister of War, n.p., 26 February 1823, in Ignacio Accioli de Cerqueira e Silva, *Memorias historicas e politicas da provincial da Bahia*, ed. Braz do Amaral, 6 vols. (Salvador: Imprensa Official do Estado, 1919–1940), vol. IV, 2, n. 2.

[59] Reis, "Jogo duro," 90.

Slaves, Indians, and the "Classes of Color"

Historians have thoroughly documented episodes during which the classes of color expressed radical ideas, often framed in racial terms. In February 1823, Captain Pedro da Silva Pedroso, a Pernambucan army officer who had been deeply involved in the 1817 republican rebellion, briefly overthrew a conservative provincial government closely connected to the most reactionary faction of sugar planters. This faction had sought to take advantage of Pedroso's discontent with the previous liberal junta and his popularity among the troops and the lower classes (since his return to Recife, he had identified as a *pardo* man and had cultivated support among the Afro-Brazilian populace). Pedroso effectively held power for a week (21–28 February 1823), from which period dates an oft-cited anti-Portuguese verse attributed to his supporters: "Sailors [*Marinheiros*] and the whitewashed [*caiados*] / All should be finished off / Because only mulattoes [*pardos*] and Blacks [*pretos*] / Will inhabit this country." *Sailor* was one of the many pejorative nicknames for Portuguese, while *whitewashed* alluded to Brazilian elites' pretensions to whiteness, despite traces of African ancestry. During the investigation into Pedroso's actions, witnesses reported numerous declarations that Blacks and mulattoes were Brazil's rightful owners, praise for Saint-Domingue, and assertions of popular sovereignty (that "peoples were free to overthrow and elect the governments that they wanted"). Pedroso capitulated on the last day of February, and the junta packed him off to Rio de Janeiro, where he managed to ingratiate himself with the emperor and secure a pardon.[60]

In Bahia, the months after the patriot victory were tense, amid conflicts between locally raised troops and forces from outside the province, anti-Portuguese nativist agitation, rumored republican conspiracies, and disorderly conduct among what were perceived as especially dangerous nonwhite regular soldiers. Here, as in many other provinces, news of Pedro's closure of the Constituent Assembly prompted opposition, for this action looked like a Brazilian Vilafrancada (the May 1823 restoration of absolutism in Portugal). Under intense popular pressure, Salvador's city council vigorously protested the measure in December, while proclamations called on Brazilians to take up arms against the tyrannical emperor and members of the lower classes

---

[60] On the Pedrosada, see Silva, "Negros," 515–20; Carvalho, "Os negros," 898–9; Leite, *Pernambuco 1824*, 93; Wanderson Édipo de França, "Pedro da Silva Pedroso: Entre ser um déspota desvairado ou um imortal e pai da Pátria – Pernambuco, 1823," *Revista Tempo Histórico* 5:1 (2013), 1–18. Jeffrey C. Mosher downplays Pedroso's radicalism: *Political Struggle, Ideology, and State Building: Pernambuco and the Construction of Brazil, 1817–1850* (Lincoln: University of Nebraska Press, 2008), 43, 62.

manhandled Portuguese nationals. In early 1824, when Pedro submitted the draft constitution for approval by provincial capitals' municipal councils, "the manipulators [*diretores*] of public opinion among the class of *pardos* and *pretos*, as well as [among] the poor and scoundrels [*canalhas*] of all colors," proposed numerous amendments. His supporters quashed this public debate and the city council recorded only two minor reservations about the new charter.[61]

By then, the central political question in the provinces was whether to acquiesce to Pedro's power to appoint provincial presidents (governors) instituted by the Constituent Assembly in October 1823. The dominant elites in Bahia accepted Pedro's appointment, while in Pernambuco, the Assembly's dissolution prompted an improvised assembly to elect Manuel de Carvalho Paes de Andrade as head of a new junta. Carvalho's government rejected Pedro's appointment of a conservative sugar planter, Francisco Paes Barreto, as provincial president, and on 2 July 1824, he proclaimed the Confederação do Equador in defense of Brazil's "constitutional system."[62] In Bahia, the provincial government prevented supporters of the Confederação from acting, but Paraíba, Rio Grande do Norte, and Ceará joined Pernambuco. In Maranhão, Miguel Bruce's government declined to support the Confederação, but struggled against Itapicuru Valley planter elites whose members saw his reliance on lower-class support in São Luis as dangerous radicalism.[63]

Resisting Rio de Janeiro required mobilizing popular support, which cast into sharp relief the political complexities of these years, for the lower classes often took matters into their own hands. In late June 1824, one of the *pardo* battalions, commanded by Major Emiliano Felipe Benício Mundurucú (or Mundrucu), allegedly planned to sack Recife's commercial district in response to the naval blockade instituted by Pedro's government. Mundurucú reportedly incited his men with an incendiary proclamation and distributed a printed verse that called on them to "imitate Christophe / This immortal Haitian / Hear! Imitate his people / Oh, my sovereign people." Major Agostinho Bezerra Cavalcante and the Henriques dissuaded their *pardo* comrades and continued to police Recife during the Confederação. After his arrest, Mundurucú managed to escape to the United States. (He also spent time in Haiti and Caracas before returning to

---

[61] Kraay, "Muralhas," 326–7 (quote 327).

[62] For surveys of Pernambucan politics during this period, see Mosher, *Political Struggle*, Chapters 1 and 2; Leite, *Pernambuco 1824*; Mello, *Outra Independência*, Chapters 4 and 5.

[63] Assunção, "Miguel Bruce," 352–5; Assunção, *De caboclos*, 311–21.

## Slaves, Indians, and the "Classes of Color"

Brazil in the mid-1830s.) Cavalcante and several other Confederação leaders were executed.[64] The allusions to Haiti were out of date and perhaps misplaced in a movement that many characterized as republican (King Henri Christophe had committed suicide in 1820, and by 1824, Haiti was a unified republic under Jean-Pierre Boyer), but the invocation of a Black ruler points to the ways that the Haitian Revolution may have appealed to free men of color as an example of Black leadership, popular sovereignty, and antiracism. However, in 1837, Mundurucú denied that he had encouraged the sack of Recife and claimed that he and Cavalcante had closely collaborated to keep order in the city. The accusations against him, Mundurucú explained, derived from Cavalcante's defense lawyer, who sought to cast blame on him to exculpate the Black major; the lawyer admitted that he had done so.[65]

Days after the alleged confrontation between Mundurucú and Cavalcante, the military commander in the small province of Sergipe received an anonymous denunciation of a gathering of "killers of the whitewashed [*mata-caiados*]" at which Antônio Pereira Rebouças had allegedly "praised the King of Haiti, and because they did not understand him, spoke more clearly – Saint-Domingue, the great Saint-Domingue." He was further accused of indoctrinating "men of color" and "convincing them that any Black or mulatto man could be a general."[66] Rebouças, a self-taught lawyer from Bahia, son of a Portuguese man and an African freedwoman, had recently arrived in the province as secretary to the newly appointed provincial president. Rebouças' biographer doubts that he had openly expressed such admiration for Haiti, and instead attributes the accusations to a nasty, racist campaign to discredit him, but the liberal emphasis on equal opportunity for the free would be a central plank in his later careers as a journalist, parliamentarian, and jurist.[67]

Regardless of the truth of the accusations against Mundurucú and Rebouças, or the justice of Cavalcante's execution, these men's actions point

---

[64] This episode is widely cited in the literature. The most thorough analysis (and critique of the limited sources for it) is Morel, *Revolução*, 200–20, esp. 201, n. 165. Mundurucú settled permanently in Boston in the 1840s and was active in Black abolitionist circles, Lloyd Belton, "Emiliano F. B. Mundrucu: Inter-American Revolutionary and Abolitionist (1791–1863)," *Atlantic Studies* 15:1 (2018), 62–82.

[65] Emeliano Felippe Benicio Mundurucú, "Correspondência," supplement to *Diario de Pernambuco*, 11 April 1837, esp. Atestado 4; Morel, *Revolução*, 200–4.

[66] Mott, *Sergipe*, 28, 47, 60, 192.

[67] Keila Grinberg, *A Black Jurist in a Slave Society: Antonio Pereira Rebouças and the Trials of Brazilian Citizenship*, trans. Kirstin M. McGuire (Chapel Hill: University of North Carolina Press, 2019), 30–4.

to the complexity of racial politics. Elite fears notwithstanding, there was no unified "Black party" in Portuguese America. Bahia's Black and *pardo* militias were some of the first to join the patriot cause in 1822; they fought well in 1822–1823 and this cemented among their officers and men a strong sense of loyalty to Pedro. After the war, when Bahian governments reorganized Salvador's militia, men of color far outnumbered white men among these part-time soldiers. They showered the imperial government with petitions for promotion and other rewards in recognition of their service. At the end of November 1824, amid the Periquitos Rebellion's chaotic collapse, Lieutenant Colonel Joaquim de Santana Neves, of the Henriques, was the most senior loyalist officer left in Salvador. He rounded up what he could of his men and set up guards around public buildings, for it was feared that the mutinous Black regular soldiers of the Periquitos battalion would sack the city.[68] Santana and his fellow officers could thus present themselves as patriotic defenders of the monarchy and use this service to claim a greater role for themselves in the new nation, something that was more difficult for Pernambuco's nonwhite officers, given their involvement in defeated rebellions against Rio de Janeiro.

The anti-Portuguese rhetoric and violence in so many of the popular movements were not simply about place of birth, but also about political choices such as support for or rejection of a continuing tie to Portugal, or support for or rejection of absolutism (associated with Portugal after the Vilafrancada), class (given the prominence of Portuguese nationals in retail commerce), or local power and land conflicts (as in the case of the Maranguapé Indians). Brazilian and Portuguese became opposed political and social identities amid these struggles.[69] Expelling Portuguese-born office holders also conveniently opened up spaces in the civil and military bureaucracy for Brazilian patriots. The radical-liberal Miguel Bruce began his presidency in Maranhão (July 1823–November 1824) with the expulsion of seventeen Portuguese men. In April 1824, his government ordered the deportation of all unmarried Portuguese men, but soon limited the order to those who were "vagrant and idle," a common pattern as the initial expulsion orders were watered down.[70] After rejecting demands from

[68] Kraay, *Race*, 133–9, 220–2; Reis and Kraay, "The Tyrant Is Dead," 423–5.

[69] Ribeiro, *Liberdade*, Chapter 1; João Paulo Garrido Pimenta, "Portugueses, americanos, brasileiros: Identidades políticas na crise do Antigo Regime luso-americano," *Almanach Brasiliense* 3 (2006), 69–80.

[70] Assunção, "Miguel Bruce," 372–3. For similar instances, see Nogueira, "Soldadesca," 210, 228; Machado, *Quebra*, 204–10; Kraay, *Race*, 118–19.

Slaves, Indians, and the "Classes of Color"

soldiers and the populace to expel Portuguese in October 1823, the provisional junta of Pará attempted to placate the Cametá rebels by expelling more than 200 Portuguese, but this measure was annulled in 1825.[71] In January 1823, Pedroso attempted to arrest 162 Europeans (Portuguese) and the December 1823 protests in Salvador and Recife also included calls to expel them.

Lusophobia frequently turned violent as political questions, class conflict, disputes over government posts, and local feuds merged in complex ways. Sacking Portuguese properties and roughing up their owners were common occurrences in periods of unrest. In Maranhão, such acts of violence were known as *lustros* and Bruce's critics claimed that he encouraged them.[72] In remote Rio de Contas (Bahia), conflicts over local power in 1822–1823 were quickly defined as a struggle between Brazilians and Portuguese, but they had little to do with the war then raging around Salvador. The alleged Portuguese party had no links to Madeira's forces and one eyewitness testified that a leader of the Brazilian party had declared "that poor Europeans [Portuguese] were Brazilians and rich Brazilians were Europeans."[73] As this witness made clear, anti-Portuguese violence and the seizure of Portuguese-owned property could easily turn into a broader class struggle. Such conflicts were often also framed in racial terms and extended from Portuguese to all whites, as we have already seen in the radical rhetoric from Pernambuco and in the elite fears of a repeat of the Haitian Revolution. A soldier arrested in Pará made this threat explicit when he told a captain that, "if he had forty men with him, he would put all the little whites [*branquinhos*] to the sword," for they did not support Cametá; there, the "rustic *povo*" reportedly understood nothing but calls to "finish off all who are white."[74]

From the police spy's worries about placing daggers in Blacks' hands to reports of calls for racial war in Cametá, the documentation of these years amply reveals elite fears of a mobilized and politically active racialized lower class. Such fearful accounts may have exaggerated the classes of color's radicalism, and can lead us to miss the diversity of political views among its members, which ranged from the Bahian Black officers' monarchism (with

---

[71] Brito, "Viva a *Liberté!*," 171–2; Nogueira, "Soldadesca," 210, 228.

[72] Assunção, "Miguel Bruce," 367–71; Assunção, *De caboclos*, 330–2.

[73] Quoted in Moisés Amado Frutuoso, "'Morram os marotos!' antilusitanismo, projetos e identidades políticas em Rio de Contas (1822–1823)" (M.A. thesis, Universidade Federal da Bahia, 2015), 12, 86, 89.

[74] Quoted in Nogueira, "Soldadesca," 214; and in Brito, "Viva a *Liberté!*," 247.

its implicit demand for a greater role in reformed Old Regime–style institutions), to Rebouças' defense of legal rights (and its ultimately radical demand for equality among the free), and to the much more violent race and class conflicts embodied in lusophobia.

By early 1825, the popular challenge and the radicalism among members of the elite had been defeated. Bahia and Pernambuco were under martial law. After blockading Recife, Lord Cochrane sailed for Maranhão where he removed Bruce from the presidency, while the Cametá insurgency was crushed. Rafael Marquese, Tâmis Parron, and Márcia Berbel suggest that the *povo* had nevertheless won a signal victory. The Constituent Assembly defined Brazilian citizenship broadly, granting it to all free-born Brazilian males, as well as to freedmen, and the 1824 Constitution enshrined this principle in law but excluded the African-born from citizenship. Marquese, Parron, and Berbel cite the Pernambucan deputy, Venâncio Henriques de Resende, as evidence for the Assembly's consciousness of the popular demand for citizenship: "In this day and age, so much importance is given to this word that there would be great jealousy, and displeasure, if a class of Brazilians believed that this title was exclusive. In this they do not want to claim all political rights, because they recognize that not everyone is capable of everything; they do want, however, to be recognized as Brazilian citizens."[75] In the same vein, the 1824 Constitution's remarkably liberal bill of rights – to be sure, honored more in the breach than in practice – became a touchstone for popular politics.[76]

By the 1830s, when a new wave of radical-liberal mobilization prompted Pedro's abdication (7 April 1831) and sparked revolts that reprised many of the issues of 1820–1824, the memory of independence was also up for grabs. In contrast to Cairu's portrayal of independence as Pedro's achievement, the wily Pedroso published a letter in a Recife periodical in 1834 in which he denied that José Bonifácio had been the first to call for independence. He boldly declared that "this glory belongs solely to me, because I was the first who, in the city of Recife, on 6 March 1817 at 2:00 p.m., uttered this magic word, which was echoed on 7 September 1822 by José Bonifácio."[77] In this way, he reduced Pedro to his adviser's mouthpiece and claimed the 1817 republican rebellion as a first step to independence, something that

---

[75] Quoted in Marquese et al., *Slavery*, 126.
[76] Art. 179, "Constituição Política do Império do Brasil," 25 March 1824, *Coleção das Leis do Brasil*.
[77] Quoted in Silva, "Negros," 519–20.

Slaves, Indians, and the "Classes of Color"

radical liberals would argue decades later. Joaquim Cândido Soares Meirelles, a mulatto doctor accused of fomenting Haitianism (racial conflict) in 1830–1831, declared that the patriot army in Bahia had been composed "of mulattoes and Blacks" who had fought courageously to "liberate the pátria in the hope that they would be able to aspire to something more than master tailor, carpenter, or stonemason."[78] In 1836, Salvador's *O Defensor do Povo* denied that "men of color" were plotting "to do away with the white race" and rather emphasized that they had been "the bulwarks of Brazil's independence and liberty." They were not advocates of disorder; rather, they sought full equality before the law, as the 1824 Constitution in fact prescribed.[79] While in Caracas in 1826, Mundurucú published a manifesto in which he proclaimed that he had been "one of the first . . . to raise the banner of liberty" in Recife back in 1817; in 1837, when the provincial president blocked a patronage appointment that he had somehow wrangled from allies in the imperial government, he invoked the constitution and accused his enemies of racism, for they would not tolerate "a *pardo* officer in a post of distinction."[80]

These assertions reveal popular understandings of independence that differed dramatically from Pedro Américo's painting or the histories by Cairu and Varnhagen, as well as the continued struggle to make effective the Age of Revolutions' promises. However, they do not exhaust the range of political ideas circulating in independence-era Brazil. The two allusions to the Kongolese monarch cited in this chapter point to African political ideologies that may have shaped how some understood the Age of Revolutions. Likewise, Indigenous concepts surely influenced political actions and ideologies in the north, but the existing scholarship on the region does not offer explicit indications of this.

It is difficult to discern how the rank-and-file participants in the independence struggle subsequently perceived their actions. In 1834, one Antônio Benguela was arrested in Rio de Janeiro and threatened with impressment. He declared that he was exempt, for he had already served. Back in 1822, on his owner's death, he had been sent to the navy. He fought in the "wars of

---

[78] *Sentinella da Liberdade no Rio de Janeiro*, 20 December 1832. On Meirelles, see Morel, *Revolução*, 258–303.
[79] *O Defensor do Povo* (Salvador), 13 February 1836.
[80] Emiliano Felipe Benício Mundurucú, *Manifiesto que hace a la nación colombiana . . .* (Caracas: Imprenta de Tomás Antero, 1826), 1, reprinted in Vamireh Chacon, ed., *Da Confederação do Equador à Grã-Colômbia* (Brasília: Senado Federal, 1983), 194; Mundurucú, "Correspondência," *Diario de Pernambuco*, 11 April 1837; Morel, *Revolução*, 220–4.

545

Bahia and of Rio Grande do Sul [the Cisplatine War]" and was subsequently "freed by the ex-emperor."[81] Antônio's surname indicates that he was an African, but he implicitly claimed Brazilian citizenship by virtue of his service to the state; for him, Brazil's independence marked a major life change. It also did so for a Mina slave by the name of Francisco in Pernambuco. Marcus Carvalho traces how, conditionally freed in 1811, he constructed a new persona for himself as Francisco Antônio da Costa, a married man running his own small shop, increasingly distant from his former owner; at some point in the early 1820s, he enlisted in the Henriques. He fought valiantly in the Confederação do Equador's final battle, and was covered in artillery powder burns when taken prisoner. His former owner immediately launched an ultimately successful lawsuit to revoke his freedom on the grounds of ingratitude.[82] That Benguela might still be impressed, that Costa was returned to slavery, and that Mundurucú and so many other free men of color still had to fight for equality underscore how effectively the popular challenge had been defeated, how precarious freedom still was for those close to slavery, and how many resources the master class had to maintain its position, but defeat does not lessen their struggles' significance for our understanding of Brazil in the Age of Atlantic Revolutions.

[81] Quoted in Soares, *Capoeira*, 287, 318, n. 140.
[82] Marcus J. M. de Carvalho, "De cativo a 'famoso artilheiro' na Confederação do Equador: O caso do africano Francisco, 1821–1827," *Varia História* 27:1 (2002), 96–116: 111, 113–6.

21

# Brazil and the Independence of Spanish America: Parallel Trajectories, Linked Processes (1807–1825)

JOÃO PAULO PIMENTA

## Introduction

The current view of Brazil's independence as an atypical process in the early nineteenth-century American political context began to be forged between the years 1820 and 1822, i.e., in the midst of the process itself. This view served the immediate political interests of some of its protagonists, who defended their own actions as positive and beneficial to Brazil and the rest of the world because they supposedly showed the possibility of making a revolution without major conflicts, violence or the spilling of blood. According to this view, Brazil's independence was superior to those of the countries of Spanish America because it was peaceful, which should make Brazil more deserving of international respect than its continental neighbors.

This view, purposely distorted and politically connected to specific interests, would become a veritable myth of the foundation of the Brazilian nation. According to this myth, Brazil was an exemplary case of a nation that, throughout its history, had been able to control and even eliminate conflicts, and was characterized by internal stability and political conservatism, which helped establish a social pact. Emerging during the independence process, this myth would be reworked by historians of independence and would become popular in general, despite sustained criticism. Thus, the mythicized premise of Brazilian national conservatism would erase the wars that effectively occurred during independence. It also exaggerated the continuities between colonial and national history, separating Brazil's history from that of other American countries, although Brazil's monarchy, slavery,

Translated by Robert Sean Purdy.

and territorial boundaries from colonial times did not simply continue in the national period, but were actually reinvented. There is no doubt that in many ways the historical processes of Brazil and Spanish America differed sharply, both in terms of origins as in developments and results, revealing parallel trajectories. In other respects, however, these processes demonstrated similarities: in their time, they were interrelated and influenced each other reciprocally. The linkage of parallel trajectories – which in many moments ceased to be parallel – is obscured by the still dominant view of Brazil's independence as a contrasting and exceptional case.

The independence of Brazil, achieved in 1822, was a process partly determined by the history of three centuries of Portuguese colonization of America. But at the same time, it broke with part of this history, and had profound and lasting results. The most important, probably, was the emergence of a Brazilian nation, state, and identity that did not exist before independence, and which still bore the marks of colonization. In this sense, the depth of these transformations implies a true revolution, witnessed and elaborated by many of its observers and participants. As historians well know, a revolution is never absolute, and it is never capable of suddenly changing all the structures of a society. All revolutions imply strong ruptures, but they also have continuities, reworking ideas of past, present, and future. In this sense, Brazil's independence is closer to contemporaneous revolutions in other parts of the world, such as the independence of the British colonies of North America, the French Revolution, and the emergence of Haiti. None of them was taken as a simple model, accepted or rejected by the people who in many ways shaped Brazil's independence. All of them, however, suggested possible plans and actions, provided parameters for worldviews, and helped to elaborate collective experiences in which the idea of a political separation between Brazil and Portugal gained momentum until it finally became a reality. Among these various revolutions, those of Spanish America, precipitated by the same European upheavals that hit Portugal and Brazil in the early nineteenth century, proved especially important. This is because Spanish American events occurred closer to Brazil than the others, both spatially and temporally. These events led to practical measures in relation to the borders of Brazil at the same time that they influenced the main political decision-making centers of Portuguese America and Portugal.

It is therefore necessary to balance the analysis of how Brazil's independence was unique with what it had in common with Spanish America. The emphasis of this chapter is on the latter point, since the historiography of independence leans largely on the side of the affirmation of its uniqueness.[1] Complementarily, it is also necessary to outline the opposite movement: how parts of Spanish America were influenced by what was happening at the same time in Brazil.

## Portugal, Brazil, and the Start of Independence in Spanish America (1807–1815)

Between the end of 1807, when the French army invaded Portugal, and the beginning of 1808, when Spain also began to be dominated by the French, the political circumstances of the Iberian empires began to differ widely. In Spain, King Fernando VII and the entire court commanded by the Bourbon dynasty, were barred from ruling, and their principal members were imprisoned on Napoleon's orders, which immediately led to the beginning of armed resistance against the French and the formation of juntas that governed autonomously. The purpose of these juntas was to preserve the authority of the imprisoned king. The confusing Spanish events of March, April, and May 1808 became known sooner in Brazil than they did in some important regions of Spanish America. By sea, sometimes supplemented by land, news from Spain took approximately two months to reach the Caribbean, New Spain, and Venezuela; news arrived in Bahia and Rio de Janeiro in three months, as it did in Montevideo and Buenos Aires; but the same news took four or five months to arrive in Chile and Peru. Thus, in 1808, while subjects of the Spanish king in Lima celebrated his alliance with Napoleon, which they believed had brought Fernando VII to power, at the American headquarters of the Portuguese court in Rio de Janeiro it was already known that war had broken out between Spain and France. More generally, the power vacuum in the Spanish Empire between 1808 and 1810 provoked numerous reactions in Europe and the Americas.

In the short term, the transfer of the Portuguese court to Brazil under British military protection between late 1807 and early 1808 led to the preservation of the unity of the Portuguese Empire; however, important changes took place: Lisbon was no longer the metropolis; Portugal lost its status as the center of the empire; and for the first time in the history of modern European empires a colonial territory became the seat of central power. This new situation would create novel conflicts and, in the medium

[1] Wilma Peres Costa, "A independência na historiografia brasileira," in István Jancsó, ed., *Independência: História e historiografia* (São Paulo, Hucitec/Fapesp, 2005), 53–118.

term, would contribute significantly to the end of the Portuguese empire in America. And this occurred more or less simultaneously with the demise of the Spanish empire. Immediately, however, the transfer of the Court proved to be a great geopolitical success: The fear that Portugal would meet the same fate as Spain in the European wars was dispelled, and in Rio de Janeiro, Prince Regent Dom João was able to strengthen the new foundations of his empire.

By mid-1808, the Iberian empires found themselves in a completely dissimilar situation: as one began to fragment, the other managed to survive and strengthen itself. But the fate of the Portuguese empire seemed increasingly tied to that of the Spanish empire. This is why, for years to come, the notion of a historical interrelationship between the two empires would not escape many of the observers of the time, and was subtly implied in the analyses of the London newspaper *Correio Brasiliense*, published by the Portuguese Hipólito José da Costa and widely read at the time, including by the Portuguese court. In February 1809, the editor feared that because the legitimate government of Spain was suddenly gone, "the Spanish colonies in America would fall into a fatal anarchy." Shortly thereafter, in July, da Costa expressed his conviction that "the total separation of America, as far as Europe is concerned, is an event that must inevitably happen more or less in months."[2]

If the events in the Iberian Peninsula of 1807 and 1808 paved different paths for the independence of Brazil and Spanish America, it must be pointed out that these paths had a common origin: the Napoleonic Wars and the determined reactions of Portugal and Spain. These responses, especially the transfer of the Portuguese court, meant that the Iberian Americas, which were never completely isolated from each other during the colonial centuries and always maintained many points of contact and entanglement, began to experience new conditions that would reciprocally influence each other.

In the sixteenth, seventeenth, and eighteenth centuries, contact between parts of Brazil and Spanish America was diverse and often intense, including the movement of people and news, and involved both conflict and harmony. The borders of the vast region of the Luso-American Amazon and Mato Grosso with the Venezuelan captaincy general and the viceroyalties of New Granada and Peru had always been active sites of diverse exchanges. From the mid-eighteenth century onwards, however, the most important borders

---

[2] João Paulo Pimenta, *La independencia de Brasil y la experiencia hispano-americana (1808–1822)* (Santiago: DIBAM, 2017), 79.

were those between Brazil and the Viceroyalty of the Río de la Plata. In addition to the trade in livestock between the Banda Oriental and Rio Grande de São Pedro – the southernmost part of Brazil, now Rio Grande do Sul – several ports in Brazil had direct contact with Montevideo and Buenos Aires. To these ports, Brazil exported African slaves, cotton, sugar, coffee, brandy, timber, shipbuilding materials, cassava flour, tobacco, indigo, yerba mate, and rice, as well as smuggled gold. In the opposite direction, Brazil received meat, leather, wheat flour, live animals, and fur. For this reason, the Portuguese population of Montevideo and Buenos Aires was quite considerable at the beginning of the nineteenth century, as was the Spanish American populations in parts of Brazil such as Rio de Janeiro, Bahia, Recife, Santa Catarina, and Rio Grande. The re-exports and the flow of people involved in this trade also connected Brazil and the Río de la Plata with many other regions of America, Europe, and Africa. Between 1808 and 1810, as political turmoil in Spanish America grew, these economic ties between Brazil and Spanish America intensified. First, Brazil opened its ports to foreign trade, as decreed on 28 January 1808; then, customs tariffs for Brazilian products entering the port of Buenos Aires were reduced, as decreed on 13 July of the same year; and finally, the Río de la Plata's ports were opened to foreign trade, as decided on 2 November 1809.

As soon as it arrived in Brazil, the Portuguese court developed a special policy regarding its new neighbors. Because of the war waged against France in Europe, the instability it caused in Spanish America, and the uncertainty produced by the new alliance between Portugal and Great Britain – which for several Portuguese statesmen was not a totally reliable partner – D. João's government sought to militarily strengthen Brazil's borders. To the north, the border with the French colony of Cayenne was an old concern, which led D. João to turn toward military action, forcing the French government of Cayenne to capitulate on 12 January 1809. Portugal would only restore it to France through a treaty on 28 August 1817. To the south, the government of Rio de Janeiro sent letters to the Buenos Aires town council on 13 March 1808, offering it protection against the French threat, but at the same time asserting that the Portuguese court would intervene, if necessary, in the region in defense of its own interests. Portuguese representatives were sent to Montevideo and Buenos Aires, while Spanish agents were allowed to settle in Rio de Janeiro and other cities in Brazil, accentuating an intelligence and spy network that already existed on the border of the Rio de São Pedro with the Banda Oriental, which even involved Viceroy Santiago Liniers and the governor of Montevideo, Francisco Javier Elío. These measures, combined with Portuguese trade in the Río de la Plata, formed an Americanist foreign policy on the part of D. João's government that was both aggressive and a product of fear.

Carlota Joaquina's claims to be recognized as Princess Regent of the Americas can be understood as part of this foreign policy. The wife of D. João of Portugal and sister of Fernando VII of Spain, Carlota was at the center of a political project that emerged from the power vacuum in the Spanish empire. Supported by some members of the Portuguese court, the British cabinet, and the Portuguese political press, Carlota addressed all the viceroys, captains general, and other Spanish political authorities and subjects, in a manifesto of 19 August 1808. In it she called for the unity of the Spanish Empire and called for the recognition of her person as the center of Spanish royal authority, given the absence of her brother. Her claims found significant support in Buenos Aires itself among merchants who traded with Brazil and who were increasingly involved in political issues.[3] In Upper Peru, the backlash against Carlota's project was violent, accentuating local conflicts, and precipitating the formation of a governing junta in Chuquisaca on 25 May 1809. And while it is certain that Carlota's manifesto also arrived in New Spain, New Granada, Quito, Peru, Venezuela, Chile, Cuba, Guatemala, and the Philippines, almost nothing is known about its reception in those regions. Even if the project weakened with the opposition it encountered everywhere, it would be revived on many occasions in the years ahead when the trajectories of the Portuguese and Spanish empires intersected, serving as a kind of dynamo for common political projects.[4]

An essential component in this intersection of the trajectories between Brazil and Spanish America was the gradual growth across the continent of the newspaper press and the expansion of other public spaces of political discussion. In Rio de Janeiro, the creation of the Royal Press in 1808 initiated the circulation of texts, pamphlets, and laws printed in Brazil, as well as the first newspaper, the *Gazeta do Rio de Janeiro*. The *Gazeta*, together with the *Correio Brasiliense* and the *Idade do Ouro do Brasil* (started in Bahia in 1811), would publish content dealing with Spanish American events. Some of these newspapers began to stress that violent upheavals, civil wars, and bloodshed such as allegedly occurred in Spanish America should be avoided in Brazil.

---

[3] Tulio Halperín Donghi, *Revolución y guerra: Formación de una élite dirigente en la Argentina criolla* (Buenos Aires: Siglo XXI, 1972), 9.

[4] Sara Marques Pereira, *D. Carlota Joaquina e os "espelhos de Clio": Actuação política e figurações historiográficas*, 2nd edition (Lisbon: Horizonte, 2008), 75–127.

Through these newspapers, as well as diplomatic reports, official and private correspondence, and the circulation of people, rumors, and news, Spanish America became increasingly familiar in Brazil, arousing interest, fears, and expectations, and provoking reactions. Some of these reactions were later boosted by the alliance between Portugal and Great Britain, signed on 19 February 1810. This alliance allowed the government of Rio de Janeiro to incisively advance its interests on the American continent.

In 1811, the Court of D. João considered an armed intervention in Paraguay or Upper Peru. According to Portuguese minister Rodrigo de Sousa Coutinho, in a letter to the prince regent on 16 January, the government of Buenos Aires – a revolutionary junta since 25 May 1810 – was doubtlessly acting to "revolutionize the borders of the neighboring countries of Your Royal Highness with the intention of attacking the States of Your Royal Highness." He therefore recommended urgent measures to "prevent revolutionaries from dominating your frontier."[5] It was in the Banda Oriental that this intervention materialized. Since 1810, D. João's government had supported Governor Elío in his resistance against the revolution in Buenos Aires. After the declaration of war between the governments of the two main Spanish ports of the Río de la Plata, a Portuguese army crossed the Rio Grande de São Pedro and in August 1811 joined the Spanish royalist forces of Montevideo. The war ended with the armistice of 20 October 1811 between Montevideo and Buenos Aires, shortly afterwards endorsed by Rio de Janeiro, but not by one of the military commanders in the service of Buenos Aires, José Gervasio Artigas. From then on, Artigas would become an important radical political leader, enemy of the governments of both Buenos Aires and Rio de Janeiro. For Brazil, the 1811 intervention was the first of many in the region in the years to come.

The entanglement of the trajectories of Brazil and Spanish America would continue to be stimulated by events in Spain as well. The meeting of the Cortes of Cádiz in 1810 resulted in the promulgation of the Cádiz Constitution in 1812, which also applied to the overseas territories. The weakening of absolutism in Spain worried the Portuguese court in Rio de Janeiro, while it offered the opportunity to strengthen itself as a bastion of royalism in America, especially as more and more independent governments were forming on the continent, some of which were republican. This strengthening would take place mainly from 1814, with the end of the

---

[5] Valentim Alexandre, *Os sentidos do império: Questão nacional e questão colonial na crise do Antigo Regime português* (Porto: Afrontamento, 1993), 248–9.

Napoleonic Wars in Europe and the triumph of the absolutist reaction at the Congress of Vienna. Absolutism was restored in Spain with the return of Fernando VII to power, who abolished the Cádiz Constitution and intensified conflicts with the former colonies. In Portugal, there was more and more talk of the court returning to Lisbon. But in Brazil and elsewhere, the perception grew that if that happened, revolution would also come to Portuguese America. This possibility was publicly debated. Tomás Antônio Vilanova Portugal, minister of D. João, proposed the expulsion from Rio de Janeiro of all Spanish American officials and political immigrants who were deemed dangerous because of their participation in American revolutions.[6]

Under these circumstances, not only did the Portuguese court not return to Lisbon, but Brazil was elevated to the status of kingdom, equal to Portugal. The creation of the United Kingdom of Portugal, Brazil, and the Algarves on 16 December 1815 had been an idea of French Minister Talleyrand, who recommended it to the Portuguese representatives at the Congress of Vienna.[7] As a royalist and conservative polity, Brazil could not risk following the same steps as Spanish America.

## Articulated Independences (1816–1825)

In 1816, the court of Rio de Janeiro decided on a new invasion of the Banda Oriental, justifying it as a move to pacify the region and restore its economic prosperity, which was threatened by continuing conflicts. One political argument used was that the mouth of the Río de la Plata would be a "natural frontier" for the Portuguese domains in America, which was evidently not accepted by the outside forces. On 20 January 1817 Portuguese troops entered Montevideo, where they were favorably received by various local authorities involved in business with Brazil. With their support, a formal Portuguese government was installed that would rule the city and parts of the interior of the Banda Oriental. At the same time, Artigas' "Liga de los Pueblos Libres" gained strength in various regions of the former viceroyalty,[8] just as the opposition of the Buenos Aires government to Portuguese policies

---

[6] *Política lusitana en el Río de la Plata – Colección Lavradio, III* (Buenos Aires: Archivo General de la Nación, 1964), 328.

[7] Ana Rosa C. da Silva, *Inventando a nação: Intelectuais ilustrados e estadistas luso-brasileiros na crise do Antigo Regime português* (São Paulo: Hucitec/Fapesp, 2006), 250 ff.

[8] Ana Frega, *Pueblos y soberania em la Revolución Artiguista: La región de Santo Domingo Soriano desde fines de la colônia a la ocupación portuguesa* (Montevideo: Ediciones de la Banda Oriental, 2007), 167–252.

grew. And in Europe, where absolutism once again reigned supreme, Madrid contemplated sending a Spanish military expedition to reconquer Montevideo and Buenos Aires, and possibly also attack Brazil.

According to José Luiz de Souza, a diplomat serving Portugal in Spain in 1817 and 1818, "the circumstances of Brazil, surrounded by countries in revolt, require certain precautions not to provoke the rest of the insurgents against us." The invasion of the Banda Oriental would supposedly bring security not only to Brazil, but also to Spain's American colonies.[9] The entanglement between Brazil and Spanish America was thus further complicated.

According to a French military officer passing through Pernambuco, in February 1817 there was disturbing unrest in the province, whose inhabitants were following "with particular interest the progress of the Spanish insurgents, with the government itself aware that there was correspondence with them through the maritime route."[10] The republican revolution that occurred in Pernambuco between March and May of that year, under the leadership of Domingos José Martins, Father João Ribeiro, and others, cannot be considered a direct consequence of the Spanish American revolution of independence, although several of its participants effectively followed rumors and news concerning Brazil's continental neighbors, and were even inspired by them (the revolutionaries of Pernambuco asked the United States for support and even considered an expedition to St. Helena to free Napoleon). The Pernambuco revolution shows that the process of strengthening the Portuguese empire, initiated by the move of the court in 1808, was stagnating. One of the reasons for the outbreak of the movement – which ended in brutal military repression commanded by the court of Rio de Janeiro, with the support of the Bahian government – was the heavy taxation that the court had imposed on regions of Brazil with which it had little contact and shared few interests.[11] Moreover, the revolution showed that the situation of Portuguese America was neither unconnected to nor different from that of Spanish America: both produced (successfully or not) governmental juntas, ruptures with the metropolises, constitutions, and republican governments. The paths of Brazil and Spanish America, partially separated in 1807 and 1808, intersected again in 1817, and with special intensity.

[9] Pimenta, ed., *La independencia de Brasil*, 291.
[10] Oliveira Lima, *D. João VI no Brasil*, 3rd edition (Rio de Janeiro: Topbooks, 1996), 509–10.
[11] Denis Bernardes, *O patriotismo constitucional: Pernambuco, 1820–1822* (São Paulo: Hucitec/Fapesp, 2006), 204–18.

Meanwhile, Portugal witnessed the harsh repression of a conspiracy in 1817 directed against Marshal Beresford's government, and strongly critical of D. João's policy in Brazil, which prioritized American issues over European affairs. The Portuguese court's resistance to return to Lisbon, its constant interventions in the Banda Oriental, and its apparent focus on Brazil and disregard for the affairs of Portugal led to a new revolution, unleashed in the city of Porto on 24 August 1820. It was only at this juncture that Brazil's independence ceased to be merely something expected – or feared – to occur in the future, and became reality in a process in which Spanish America would continue to be active.

The Portuguese revolutionaries of 1820 imposed a limitation on the authority of King D. João VI (who had been crowned in 1818, two years after the death of his mother, D. Maria I) through the formation of a legislative and Constituent Assembly, which would meet for the first time on 26 January 1821, without the presence of representatives of the provinces of Brazil. The movement was politically based on constitutional liberalism, which had been present in the western world since the late eighteenth century, and although it was now fought by the Holy Alliance and the other European absolutist powers, it was still alive in some parts of the Atlantic World such as Naples and Spanish America. In fact, the Porto Revolution was directly inspired by the Spanish anti-absolutist uprising that had taken place in January 1820, and its protagonists adopted Spanish criteria for the election of deputies from all over the United Portuguese kingdom who were to make up the Constituent Cortes. The Spanish constitution was even provisionally adopted, since the Portuguese one was not ready. In the following months, one of the leaders of the revolution, Manuel Fernandes Tomás, would not tire of denouncing D. João's policy in Brazil as harmful to the interests of the Portuguese nation, since it had reversed roles and turned Portugal into a kind of colony of Brazil; he denounced, in particular, the actions of D. João VI in relation to Spanish America.

In southern Brazil, the confrontation on 22 January 1820 between Portuguese armies and Artigas' forces at Tacuarembó in the Banda Oriental forced Artigas to withdraw from the political scene (as he would spend his last thirty years in exile in Paraguay) and paved the way for the consolidation of Portuguese power over the region. However, this power would increasingly bring more problems to the Rio de Janeiro government. The Portuguese commander of Montevideo, Carlos Frederico Lecor, manipulated a Congress of representatives of the Banda Oriental that met from 15 July through 8 August 1821. In doing so, contrary to the provisions passed to him by D. João VI and his minister Silvestre Pinheiro Ferreira, he made Portuguese domination official, and formally created the Cisplatine Province, which he integrated with Brazil. Officials at the court had expected that the Congress would decide for the return of the Banda Oriental to Spain, for its union with the other provinces of the Río de la Plata or even for outright independence. What mattered was that the Banda Oriental should cease to serve as a pretext for attacks by the Constituent Cortes in Lisbon and as a factor of instability in the already shaky United Kingdom of Portugal, Brazil, and the Algarves.

Support for the constitutional liberalism of the Porto Revolution came from many parts of Brazil, where new provincial governments were formed between January 1821 and February 1822.[12] Political upheaval grew further with the election of the provincial representatives to the Constituent Cortes. The years 1821 and 1822 witnessed profound political instability in Brazil and Portugal, with a rapid succession of dramatic events amid increasingly politicized social contexts. One of the most important indications of this situation is the dizzying growth of the newspaper press in Brazil, made possible by the decrees of the Constituent Cortes of 21 September and 13 October 1820, as well as by the formal abolition of censorship, effected by D. João VI on 2 March 1821. Whereas three newspapers were published in Brazil in 1820, by 1821 there were twenty-six, and one year later thirty-eight.[13] Debates and attacks by editors on each other, as well as discussions about Brazil's future, became commonplace.[14] Newspapers continued their vast coverage of events in Spanish America, where almost everywhere Spain's power seemed to be waning rapidly. They also brought news from other parts of the world, especially legislative and constituent matters in Portugal. And increasingly, commentators publicly expressed the view that Brazil could – or even should – follow in the footsteps of its neighbors, separating itself from Portugal and declaring its independence.

A significant example of a man moving between Brazil and Spanish America at this time is the Spanish-Cuban lawyer Joaquín Infante. Accused of a conspiracy in Cuba in 1810, author of a constitutional project for that

[12] Márcia R. Berbel, *A nação como artefato: Deputados do Brasil nas Cortes portuguesas 1821–1822* (São Paulo: Hucitec/Fapesp, 1999), 57–81.

[13] Andréa Slemian and João Paulo Pimenta, *Naissance politique du Brésil: Origines de l'État et de la nation* (Paris: L'Harmattan, 2019), 73–4.

[14] Marco Morel, "La génesis de la opinión pública moderna y el proceso de independencia (Rio de Janeiro, 1820–1840)," in François-Xavier Guerra and Annick Lémperière, eds., *Los espacios públicos en Iberoamérica: Ambigüedades y problemas: Siglos XVIII–XIX* (Mexico City: FCE, 1998), 301–6.

island published in Venezuela in 1812, and member of the anti-Spanish expedition of Javier Mina to New Spain in 1817, Infante was arrested and remained incarcerated in a Spanish prison in Morocco between 1818 and 1820. In the latter year, he returned to the Americas, where he would practice law first in Mexico between 1823 and 1825, then in Colombia between 1826 and 1828. Infante perfectly embodies the Atlantic dimension of the era of revolutions, including Brazil: one of his most important political writings, *Solución a la cuestión* (1820), was partially translated into Portuguese (1821), and published and commented on in Brazil. In the pages of the newspaper *Revérbero Constitucional Fluminense*, Infante's arguments for the independence of Spanish America served as a perfect example for Brazil.[15] The publishers of *Revérbero*, Joaquim Gonçalves Ledo, José Clemente Pereira, and Januário da Cunha Barbosa, would soon become key characters in Brazil's independence, and also featured prominently in the first months of the new empire that was created at the end of 1822.[16]

The Constituent Cortes did not want Brazil to be independent, and the intention of the vast majority of the deputies assembled in Lisbon was, in effect, to maintain and reform the bases of the Portuguese nation, including Brazil and the Portuguese colonies of Africa and Asia. However, the work of the Cortes accentuated antagonisms between Portuguese from Europe and American Portuguese, and unintentionally contributed to the emergence of projects that aimed at a complete separation between Brazil and Portugal. Before 1821, this option, it should be repeated, did not have support from a majority, and was not even clearly formulated, despite the writings of outside observers, such as the celebrated and influential Abbé de Pradt. These antagonisms grew with the return of D. João VI to Lisbon on 21 April 1821 in response to orders from the Constituent Cortes. Afraid of the detrimental effects this return could have on the United Kingdom of Portugal, Brazil, and the Algarves, the king kept his son, Prince D. Pedro, in Brazil, a measure that would prove crucial to the future development of events. From 29 August, the elected deputies from Brazil began to take their seats in the Cortes, and on 29 September and 1 October, decrees were issued that abolished institutions that had been created in Brazil since 1808. Such decrees provoked a broad negative reaction, both among Brazil's deputies as

---

[15] Priscila Ferrer Caraponale, "Joaquín Infante e as independências ibero-americanas: Uma biografia política (1775–1827)" (Ph.D. dissertation, São Paulo, FFLCH-USP, 2019), 63–194.

[16] Cecília de S. Oliveira, *A astúcia liberal: Relações de mercado e projetos políticos no Rio de Janeiro (1820–1824)* (Bragança Paulista: EdUSF, 1999), Chapter 2.

well as in public political discussions across the ocean, where the measures were viewed as part of a supposed plan for the "recolonization" of Brazil by the Cortes. Although it is very difficult to prove the existence of such a plan, or even to interpret these decrees as an expression of it, the impact on the American provinces of the idea that the courts wanted to recolonize Brazil was so strong and so negative that it would pass into posterity, contaminating many historians of independence who came to believe in what in 1821 and 1822 had been just powerful political rhetoric.

The arrival at the Cortes on 11 February 1822 of the representatives elected in São Paulo – a well-articulated group – accentuated the growing antagonism between Brazil and Portugal. In Rio de Janeiro, meanwhile, Prince D. Pedro disobeyed the order of the courts to return to Portugal, and on 9 January 1822, he publicly announced his decision in a demonstration of his capacity for political leadership. To reorganize his American government, he involved José Bonifácio de Andrada e Silva, who would assume the status of one of the protagonists of independence, which was being prepared in the following months. On 16 February, D. Pedro convened a Council of Attorneys General of the provinces of Brazil, and on 3 June announced his intention to form a constituent assembly for Brazil. On 6 August, D. Pedro issued a manifesto to "friendly nations," calling for outside recognition of his government as separate from Portugal. The deepening of the divisions took place on two fronts: in Brazil, several provinces experienced political and armed conflicts between groups loyal to the Cortes and those loyal to the ruling prince; in Portugal, some of Brazil's deputies left Lisbon and returned to Brazil, while others would refuse to sign the new constitution, approved on 22 September, and which, incidentally, was intended to apply to Brazil and its inhabitants.

The date 7 September 1822 would later be converted into a founding moment of Brazilian nationality, a landmark of independence and a central symbol of its memory. But it is not at all certain that a formal declaration of independence of Brazil was made by Prince D. Pedro near the village of São Paulo. The fact is that the prince regent was there, in the midst of a trip to increase his political support in a region that was rumored to challenge his rule. The documents that should attest to the historical character of the alleged statement of 7 September are flawed and inconclusive. On 12 October the prince was hailed as D. Pedro I, emperor of Brazil, and he was crowned on 1 December. By the end of that year, Brazil was joining more than a dozen American countries that had likewise broken with their old metropole and began the establishment of new states and new nations whose existence virtually no one could have imagined before 1808.

After 1822, Spanish America, now mostly a mosaic of new countries, would continue to be present in the Brazil that it had helped to create. Wars of independence similar to those in Spanish America also occurred in Brazil, as the new empire was not immediately accepted everywhere. There were wars between adherents and opponents of the imperial project, and if they were not as massive and destructive as those in other parts of the continent, they nevertheless involved a significant number of people in violent episodes that left deep marks on Brazilian society. The most striking wars occurred between 1822 and 1823 in Pará, Maranhão, Piauí, and Bahia. In order to defeat the opposition to his government and finally make these important provinces part of the Brazilian Empire, D. Pedro I had to mobilize armed forces that did not yet form a cohesive and efficient national army. To assist him in this task, he hired the Scottish mercenary Thomas Cochrane, a veteran of the naval wars in Chile and Peru.

There was also conflict in the Cisplatine Province, before it joined the empire of Brazil in 1824. The wounds of the conflict, however, remained open, and on 14 June of the following year, a military force led by Juan Antonio Lavalleja, known as Los 33 Orientales, arrived in La Florida, north of Montevideo. With the support of the government of Buenos Aires, he began to articulate an opposition to the Brazilian government of the Cisplatine Province, called the Eastern Province by its opponents. The province declared its independence from the empire on 25 August, as well as its adhesion to the United Provinces of the Río de la Plata. In response, the government of Rio de Janeiro declared war on Buenos Aires in December 1825, starting a confrontation that would not end until 1828, when both the Cisplatine Province and the Eastern Province were dissolved and the Eastern Republic of Uruguay was created. The war would have a major impact on the formation of national states in South America, helping to overthrow the centralizing government of Buenos Aires, and exacerbating the political and economic crisis in the Brazilian Empire that would end with the abdication of D. Pedro I in 1831. Throughout the nineteenth century, two other great wars would involve Brazil, Argentina, and Uruguay.

In the years immediately after independence, the Brazilian Empire would not only relate to its American neighbors through war, but also through diplomatic relations. The first foreign government to recognize independence was paradoxically that of Buenos Aires in June 1823. In 1824 it was the turn of the United States and the African kingdom of Benin. The recognition by Portugal and Great Britain occurred in treaties on 29 August and 10 October 1825, respectively, and that same year came recognition by

France and the Austrian Empire. In 1826, it was the turn of Sweden, the Holy See, Switzerland, the Netherlands, and Denmark, as well as three other countries in Spanish America: Chile, Peru, and Colombia.[17] The history of formal political, economic, and cultural relations between Brazil and the new countries of Spanish America began amid mutual see-sawing between understanding and conflict, rapprochement and fear.

Strictly speaking, it cannot be said that Brazil simply inherited the monarchy, slavery, and territoriality from Portuguese America. With the death of D. João VI in 1826, D. Pedro I of Brazil also became D. Pedro IV of Portugal, and after his fall as emperor in 1831, he returned to his native country, engaging in a war against his brother D. Miguel for the Portuguese throne. In Brazil, abdication was considered tantamount to the nationalization of the monarchy, which would not be Brazilian for good until the beginning of the young king Pedro II's reign in 1840. Portuguese colonial slavery, based on the slave trade with Africa, had significantly increased since 1808. In Brazil, the Portuguese court resisted British pressures to abolish human trafficking, so that slavery became a Brazilian national institution from 1822, leaving the new nation with a powerful social structure that would remain intact until slavery's formal extinction in 1888, although the slave trade was abolished in 1850. Finally, the expansion and maintenance of a large territory was, as we have seen, accomplished in an arduous process by the Brazilian Empire, which only achieved its continental dimension through the use of massive violence and after internal wars. And even as the nineteenth century advanced, Brazil's central government had to confront in several provinces more than a dozen serious rebellions, some of which challenged the territorial unity of the state and nation (Figure 21.1).[18]

In the new scenario opened up by the independence of the Americas, the presence of a lasting territorial and monarchical giant on a largely republican continent – by comparison, the Mexican empire, which shared key features with Brazil, lasted only from 1821 to 1823 – would be a source of tension between states. On 23 January 1825 – a few weeks after the famous Battle of Ayacucho, which practically ended Spanish royalism in America – Simón Bolívar wrote to Colombian President Francisco de Paula Santander: "Unfortunately Brazil limits all our states; it therefore has many facilities to

---

[17] Rodrigo Wiese Randing, "Argentina, primeiro país a reconhecer a independência do Brasil," *Cadernos do CHDD*, 16:31 (2017), 499–524.

[18] For example, the *Cabanada* (in Pernambuco and Alagoas, 1832–1835), the *Cabanagem* (in Pará, 1835–1840), the *Sabinada* (Bahia, 1837–1838), the *Balaiada* (Maranhão, 1838–1841), and the *Farroupilha* (Rio Grande do Sul, 1835–1845).

Figure 21.1 Slave market in Rio de Janeiro. Getty Images.

wage war on us successfully, as the Holy Alliance wants. And I think it will be very pleasing to the entire European aristocracy that the power of the royal prince [D. Pedro I] extends to the destruction of the germ of revolution."[19] A few months later, a misunderstanding between authorities in the Brazilian province of Mato Grosso and the Upper Peruvian province of Chiquitos about the possibility of incorporation of this border by the empire of Brazil caused a serious political tremor on the continent, and raised the possibility of the kind of war that Bolívar had feared. In 1826, Brazil was already at war with Buenos Aires, and both governments were notoriously absent from the Congress of Panama, which in June and July of that year introduced a system of diplomatic relations between the new American states.

Even so, Spanish America would never be a distant neighbor of Brazil: not only would its affairs continue to arouse interest in the empire's press, politics, and public opinion, but those same affairs would offer new opportunities for Brazil to intervene directly in the business relations of America. Radical political leaders who, after 1822, became opposed to D. Pedro I, such

[19] Arnaldo Vieira de Melo, *Bolívar, o Brasil e os nossos vizinhos do Prata: Da questão de Chiquitos à guerra da Cisplatina* (Rio de Janeiro: Gráfica Olímpica, 1963), 19.

as Cipriano Barata, Frei Caneca, and João Soares Lisboa, were interested in Spanish America, with whom they maintained business ties – in the case of Soares Lisboa – and evoked its events on key moments of the empire's nascent political life. In 1823, amid rumors that D. Pedro I intended to close the Brazilian Constituent Assembly, Cipriano Barata threatened the emperor by referring to the recent case of Mexico's emperor Iturbide. On 4 October Barata wrote in his newspaper, *Sentinela da Liberdade*: "We know for sure, and it is public knowledge, that our Sovereign Congress was about to be dissolved in early September, as happened in Mexico during the time of the infamous usurper Iturbide." In the same newspaper, he added on 29 October: "It is good that our Emperor has the picture of Mexico before his eyes, to see that Iturbide's recklessness led to his fall, like the fall of Daedalus."[20] In his own way, D. Pedro I listened to Barata: not only did he not close the assembly on 12 November – the first Brazilian constitution would be imposed in 1824 – but he also put Barata in prison along with some deputies, learning from the very "examples of Iturbide and Charles I [of England],"[21] who were deposed after defamatory public campaigns.

## Impact of Brazil on Spanish America

There is as yet no general, systematic, and detailed interpretation of the impact that the events of Brazil and Portugal had on the independence of Spanish America. What the historiography has provided so far has been some preliminary interpretative schemes,[22] and a number of careful and enlightening studies of specific regions. Together, they all support the view that the entanglement of the two historical processes is rooted not only in the many important ways in which Spanish America influenced the history of Brazil's independence, but also, in reverse, in the impact of Brazil on its continental neighbors.

In addition to the interrelated circumstances Brazil and Spanish America shared between 1808 and 1825 – trade, war, diplomatic relations – there are

---

[20] Marco Morel, ed., *Cipriano Barata: Sentinela da Liberdade e outros escritos (1821–1835)* (São Paulo: EDUSP, 2009), 481–2, 518.

[21] João Paulo Pimenta, *Tempos e espaços das independências: A inserção do Brasil no mundo ocidental (c. 1780–c. 1830)* (São Paulo: Intermeios, 2017), 127.

[22] Ron L. Seckinger, *The Brazilian Monarchy and the South American Republics 1822–1831: Diplomacy and State Building* (Baton Rouge: Louisiana State University Press, 1984); Thomas Millington, *Colombia's Military and Brazil's Monarchy: Undermining the Republican Foundations of South American Independence* (Westport, CT: Greenwood, 1996).

also a number of others that help complete the picture outlined here. A first set concerns bilateral political and economic relations in the context of independence. The arrival of D. João's court in Brazil in 1808 soon raised the fear of potential Portuguese and British military expansion on the continent, especially in Montevideo and Buenos Aires, cities that still lived under the specter of the English invasions of 1806 and 1807. Carlota Joaquina's project raised such fears, which were confirmed by the Portuguese invasions of the Banda Oriental in 1811 and 1816. In Cuba, the opening of Brazil's trade decreed in 1808 and the British expansion in the continent were seen as opportunities to be tapped by the island's producers, slaveholders, and traders, according to one of its leading informal spokesmen, Francisco de Arango y Parreño.[23] Expectations were also awakened by the *Plan de las Operaciones*, drawn up around 1810 by the radical revolutionary leader Mariano Moreno or someone affiliated with his ideas. It proposed a series of measures to destabilize Brazil, including fomenting slave revolts, promoting civil wars, and the invasion of the Portuguese territories of America.[24] Although today it seems an unrealistic plan, in 1810 it was based on a diagnosis of the unstable political situation in Brazil, and the close resemblance of its trajectory to that of parts of Spanish America, especially the Río de la Plata.

Further north, in 1814 and 1815, Spanish royalist authorities from Upper Peru, fleeing persecution by revolutionaries, crossed the border and sought asylum from Portuguese authorities in Brazil. On the border of Venezuela and the Rio Negro, Spanish American revolutionary leaders made regular contacts with Portuguese royalist authorities between 1817 and 1819, with whom they even signed an informal friendship treaty.[25] The border between the Luso-Brazilian region of the Rio Negro and the province of Maynas in Peru had experienced an intense exchange of activity since the late eighteenth century, extending through the first decades of the nineteenth century.[26] Besides, from 1822, the empire of Brazil had to deal with escaped

---

[23] Rafael de Bivar Marquese, "1808 e o impacto do Brasil na construção do escravismo cubano," *Revista USP* 79 (2008), 118–31.

[24] Noemí Goldman, "Utopía y discurso revolucionario (El plan de operaciones de M. Moreno)," *Espacios [Buenos Aires]* 6 (1987), 52–6.

[25] Adilson Júnior Ishihara Brito, "Insubordinados sertões: O Império português entre guerras e a fronteira no norte da América do Sul – Estado do Grão-Pará, 1750–1820" (Ph.D. dissertation, São Paulo, FFLCH-USP, 2016), 502–42.

[26] Carlos Augusto Bastos, *No limiar dos impérios: A fronteira entre a capitania do Rio Negro e a província de Maynas: Projetos, circulações e experiências (c. 1780–c. 1820)* (São Paulo: Hucitec/Capes, 2017), 368–511.

slaves who fled to territories beyond Brazil's far west border where, in 1825, the Republic of Bolivia would be created.[27] All these situations make up a mosaic whose general contours are not yet sufficiently known. The unstable economic and territorial arrangements existing between Brazil and Spanish America built an entangled mesh of relationships.

A second set of situations concerns the area of political culture, and the experiences and expectations which the events in Brazil introduced to Spanish America. Between February 1819 and March 1820, the newspaper *Correo del Orinoco*, mouthpiece for the revolution in Venezuela, discussed with the *Correio Brasiliense* the 1817 Pernambuco Revolution and the meanings of the independence of the Americas in an eloquent demonstration of how the written word was seen as a fundamental political weapon in the context of independence movements that, by the end of the decade, already involved North and South America.[28] The unfolding of Brazil's independence process was followed with interest in many parts of Spanish America, including New Spain and Peru, where newspapers had provided documents, analyses, and information about it.[29] On 10 June 1822, the *Gazeta del Gobierno* of Lima stated, for example, that "much of Brazil is in a state of great anarchy. Bahia has become a theater of civil war, where much blood has been spilled. Pernambuco has also risen, and even in Rio de Janeiro it is likely that independence will be declared. And many people think that the Royal Prince [D. Pedro] will take that side."[30] It is quite true that the mere publication of news does not mean that it had an impact in the environment where it was received. However, it is also true that newspapers respond not only to their own agendas, but also to the interests of their readers. In fact, through a profusion of texts in newspapers and pamphlets, as well as political statements concerning Brazil, readers in Spanish America could follow the Portuguese interventions in the Banda Oriental in 1811 and from 1816, not to mention the war against the empire of Brazil between 1825 and 1828. The press was, therefore, one of the many ways in which Brazilian independence

---

[27] Newman Caldeira, "À margem da diplomacia: Fugas internacionais de escravos do Brasil em direção à Bolívia (1822–1867)," *Outros Tempos* 8 (2010), 146–62.

[28] Ana Cláudia Fernandes, "Revolução em pauta: O debate *Correo del Orinoco–Correio Brasiliense* (1817–1820)" (M.A. thesis, São Paulo, FFLCH-USP, 2010), 115–59.

[29] Camilla Farah Alves, "Na América, dois impérios: Os encontros entre o Brasil e o México na imprensa periódica (1808–1822)" (M.A. thesis, São Paulo, FFLCH-USP, 2015), 82–169.

[30] Maria Julia Neves, "O Peru lê o Brasil: O mundo luso-americano na imprensa e na política peruana, 1808/1822" (M.A. thesis, São Paulo, FFLCH-USP, 2014), 117–18.

entered Spanish America in the early nineteenth century, rendering the two processes of independence inseparable from each other.

Today's historians must bear this in mind and, while respecting perceptions of the interplay between processes at work at the time, challenge some of the foundational myths of Latin American states and nations, which have ended up distorting our perception of American independence.

22

# Waves of Sedition across the Atlantic: Liberal Politics in Angola in the Wake of Brazilian Independence (c. 1817–1825)

ROQUINALDO FERREIRA

## Introduction

In early 1823, a black commander named Domingos Pereira Diniz presided over an emergency meeting with top military subordinates in Benguela, a city in the Portuguese colony of Angola. Diniz was the highest military authority in town as well as the head of Benguela's provisional junta, a governing body established following Portugal's liberal revolution in 1820. Benguela had been engulfed in chaotic politics since the beginning of the Black man's tenure almost one year earlier. Now, Diniz was frantically seeking to circumvent Portuguese wrath, after being accused of being one of the leaders of a movement to turn Benguela into an overseas province of Brazil, which had just cast off the colonial yoke. In survival mode, the shrewd leader oriented his peers to swear loyalty to Portugal and its recently passed constitution, seeking to diffuse a crisis that would nonetheless land him into a two-year exile in Luanda on suspicion of secessionism.[1]

This chapter pieces together Domingos Pereira Diniz's career to chart the African ramifications of Portugal's Porto Revolution from 1820 as well as how Brazil's independence impacted Portuguese territories in West Central Africa (Angola). I begin by examining how the circulation of news across the South Atlantic through Brazilian newspapers created a single political space that effectively straddled two continents. By braiding together events unfolding in Angola and Brazil, I argue that liberal reforms enacted in the

---

[1] "Termo feito pela Corporação Militar de Benguela," 4 January 1823, Arquivo Histórico Ultramarino (henceforth AHU), Angola, cx. 142.

wake of the Porto Revolution brought about a period of deep instability in Angola and across the South Atlantic by empowering local elites not always aligned with Portugal's strategic goals.[2] I then examine how Portugal's grip over its cities like Luanda and Benguela was deeply shaken by Brazil's break from Portugal in 1822.

By seeking to join independent Brazil, Benguela elites implicitly challenged the political and institutional order created by the 1820 liberal revolution in Porto, which gave birth to the so-called *vintismo* movement. The Oporto movement ushered in an era of constitutional power at the expense of Portugal's *ancien régime*, reflecting a wider revolutionary wave that swept across the Iberian Peninsula. Although a French invasion arrested the rise of liberal politics and restored absolutism, constitutionalist forces in Spain regained momentum by 1820. Together with the British occupation and Portugal's diminished standing after the royal family's relocation to Brazil in 1808, this worked as a catalyst for the Porto Revolution, prompting the establishment of a legislative body known as the Cortes, which brought to Lisbon representatives of Portugal and its empire to write its first constitution (1822).[3]

From classic studies by R. R. Palmer and Jacques Godechot, studies of the Atlantic Revolutions have undergone considerable changes over the past twenty years.[4] While decentering this scholarship away from Europe and the United States, scholars have explored multiple forces that drove movements that altered the landscape of politics in multiples sites in Latin America and across the globe.[5] Yet, even though people of African descent have now

---

[2] Cristina Nogueira da Silva, "Da Carta de Alforria ao Alvará de Assimilação: A Cidadania dos 'Originários de África' na América e na África Portuguesas, Séculos XIX e XX," in Cecília Helena Salles de Oliveira and Márcia Berbel, eds., *A experiência constitucional de Cádis – Espanha, Portugal e Brasil* (São Paulo: Editora Alameda, 2012), 109–37.

[3] See Gonçalo Monteiro, Chapter 17 in this volume.

[4] R. R. Palmer, *The Age of the Democratic Revolution: A Political History of Europe and America, 1760–1800* (Princeton, NJ: Princeton University Press, 2014); Jacques Godechot, *France and the Atlantic Revolution of the Eighteenth Century, 1770–1799* (New York: Free Press, 1965).

[5] Sinclair Thomson, *We Alone Will Rule: Native Andean Politics in the Age of Insurgency* (Madison: University of Wisconsin Press, 2002); Jane Landers, *Atlantic Creoles in the Age of Revolutions* (Cambridge, MA: Harvard University Press, 2011); Clare Anderson, "The Age of Revolution in the Indian Ocean, Bay of Bengal, and South China Sea: A Maritime Perspective," *International Review of Social History* 58 (2013), 229–51; Ada Ferrer, *Freedom's Mirror: Cuba and Haiti in the Age of Revolutions* (New York: Cambridge University Press, 2014); Marcela Echeverri, *Indian and Slave Royalists in the Age of Revolution: Reform, Revolution and Royalism in the Northern Andes, 1780–1825* (New York: Cambridge University Press, 2016); Ali Yaycioglu, *Partners of the Empire: The Crisis of the Ottoman Order in the Age of Revolutions* (Stanford: Stanford University Press,

become important actors in the historical narrative of the Atlantic Revolutions, Africa itself still remains relatively understudied.[6] This chapter seeks to make a contribution to efforts currently under way to redress this lacunae by bringing Africa into the mainstream of the Era of Atlantic Revolutions scholarship.[7]

By weaving together micro and macro histories, the chapter seeks to understand how conflicts over political representation and constitutional rights – two crucial principles of liberalism – played out on the ground across the South Atlantic, particularly in Angola.[8] What made the Angolan case unique was its status as part of a continuum of social, cultural, and economic relations connected to Brazil, where the Porto Revolution catalyzed anti-colonial sentiments that had been brewing since at least 1817, if not earlier. That Brazil's breakup from Portugal strained Portuguese grip over Angola provides an unique case of a Latin American independence that resonated powerfully in Africa. Scholars have recently taken steps toward probing deeper into the place of Angola in the waves of sedition and political instability that swept the Atlantic World around the time of Brazilian independence.[9] This chapter is inspired by their efforts.

Diniz enjoyed unparalleled power in Benguela's politics, with "so much influence in this city that nothing (even orders from governors) is executed

---

2016); Sujit Sivasundaram, *Waves across the South: A New History of Revolution and Empire* (Chicago: University of Chicago Press, 2021). See also Clément Thibaud, "Pour une histoire polycentrique des républicanismes atlantiques (années 1770–années 1880)," *Revue d'histoire du XIX$^e$ siècle* 56 (2018), 151–70; Peter Hill, "How Global Was the Age of Revolutions? The Case of Mount Lebanon, 1821," *Journal of Global History* 16:1 (2021), 65–84.

[6] Joseph Miller, "The Dynamics of History in Africa and the Atlantic 'Age of Revolutions,'" in David Armitage and Sanjay Subrahmanyam, eds., *The Age of Revolutions in Global Context, c. 1760–1840* (Basingstoke: Palgrave Macmillan, 2010), 101–24; Pernille Røge, "Rethinking Africa in the Age of Revolution: The Evolution of Jean-Baptiste-Léonard Durand's *Voyage au Sénégal*," *Atlantic Studies* 13:3 (2016), 389–406.

[7] Paul Lovejoy, *Jihād in West Africa during the Age of Revolutions* (Athens, OH: Ohio University Press, 2016); Toby Green, *A Fistful of Shells: West Africa from the Rise of the Slave Trade to the Age of Revolution* (London: Allen Lane, 2019).

[8] For methodological insights, see John-Paul Ghobrial, "Moving Stories and What They Tell Us: Early Modern Mobility between Microhistory and Global History," *Past & Present*, 14:242 (2019), 243–80.

[9] Gabriel Paquette, *Imperial Portugal in the Age of Atlantic Revolutions: The Luso-Brazilian World, c. 1770–1850* (New York: Cambridge University Press, 2013). See also Gilberto da Silva Guizelin, "Província (de) um Grande Partido Brasileiro, e mui pequeno o Europeu: A repercussão da independência do Brasil em Angola (1822–1825)," *Afro-Ásia* 51 (2015), 81–106.

without his approval."[10] In 1824, Portuguese authorities praised him for helping to obtain food supplies for an expedition of 400 soldiers dispatched from Lisbon to crush secessionism in Angola and defend the African colony from a possible attack from Brazil.[11] Yet they were often suspicious about his political ambitions as well as the fact that he was a Black man. Likely channeling fears sparked by the Haitian Revolution as well as episodes of racial disputes in Brazil, the governor of Angola, Nicolau de Abreu Castelo Branco, once pointedly remarked: "The fact that this individual was the commander of a troop comprised of individuals of his color immediately caught my attention."[12]

Portuguese suspicions about Diniz were mostly fueled by his actions as head of Benguela's provisional junta, when the Black commander lent support to an extraordinary petition in which fifty-five Benguela residents – including the city's most prominent merchants – stated that "the general aspiration of the inhabitants of this province [Benguela] is to pledge obedience" to Brazil.[13] After endorsing the document, Diniz forwarded it to Rio de Janeiro, where Brazilian officials published it in its official gazette with thinly disguised rejoicing. They added: "What is remarkable is how the people of the African coast, in another continent, wish to profit from uniting with a center [Rio de Janeiro] that is closer to them" than Portugal.[14]

Benguela's secessionist petition instantly turned Angola into a battlefield of Brazil's independence from Portugal. As though Benguela was already a Brazilian province, Rio de Janeiro officials – whose grip over Brazil itself was still very much uncertain – began shipping official documents to the African city, including a decree "from 10 December [of 1822], which marks the [celebration of] the independence of Brazil [sic] and its elevation to the category of empire [sic]."[15] Diniz would later defend himself by saying that receiving the Brazilian decrees did not constitute a crime or betrayal of Portugal because no document issued by the Brazilian government was ever enforced in Benguela. However, this line of reasoning did not persuade

---

[10] "Oficio do Governador de Benguela," 14 November 1824, AHU, Angola, cx. 146.
[11] "Oficio do Governador de Benguela," 26 June 1824, AHA, cód. 448, fs. 65v–66.
[12] "Oficio do Governador de Angola," 23 November 1824, AHU, Angola, cx. 152. See also João José Reis (with Hendrik Kraay), "'The Tyrant Is Dead': The Revolt of the Periquitos, Bahia, 1824," *Hispanic American Historical Review* 89:3 (2009), 399–434; Marco Morel, *A Revolução do Haiti e o Brasil Escravista: O que não deve ser dito* (Jundiaí: Paco Editorial, 2017).
[13] *Gazeta do Rio,* n. 120, 5 October 1822, 603.
[14] *Gazeta do Rio,* n. 120, 5 October 1822, 603.
[15] "Oficio de Luiz da Cunha Moreira," 2 January 1823, AHU, Angola, cx. 142.

Portuguese authorities in Luanda. While accusing the Benguela Junta of reducing to a minimum official communication with Luanda, they also claimed that Benguela secessionists had dispatched a man named Ezequiel Carvalho – Diniz's closest ally – to Rio de Janeiro on a secret mission to request military support from the Brazilian government.

## An Integrated South Atlantic

In many ways, the Benguela secessionist petition reflected the deeply symbiotic and multilayered relationship that Benguela had with Brazil, particularly Rio de Janeiro, which was the primary destination of the thousands of enslaved Africans shipped from the city during the era of the transatlantic slave trade. Benguela's Atlantic community stretched well beyond the brutal and dehumanizing business of slavery. To educate their offspring, the Benguela elite – mostly comprised of individuals who had enriched themselves in the slave trade – would turn to Brazil, which was also the place of choice for accessing Western medicine unavailable in Benguela as well as food supplies in times of drought or to feed the city's military. Now, with the city's elite boldly enunciating its intention of joining Brazil against Portugal's colonial power, Benguela's ties with Brazil had taken a menacingly political turn.

Strikingly, Angola's Atlantic community was also informed by Brazil's newspapers, which circulated in Luanda and Benguela and disseminated news that deeply shook the African colony as Brazil made its way toward political independence from Portugal. In 1824, Luanda authorities reported that four ships recently arrived from Brazil had brought newspapers.[16] Tellingly, Luanda officials learned about Benguela's alleged secessionism through the *Gazeta do Rio*, which was one of the at least eleven newspapers in Rio in 1822.[17] Although this newspaper had been created as a platform for Portugal's *ancien régime*, it had become fully aligned with Brazilian independentist forces by the time it published the Benguela petition.[18] In addition to circulating in Brazil, copies of the *Gazeta* made their way to England and,

---

[16] "Oficio do Governador de Angola," 1824, AHA, cód. 7183, fs. 24–25v.

[17] Tereza Fachada Levy Cardozo, "A *Gazeta do Rio de Janeiro*: Subsídios para a *História da Cidade* (1808–1821)," *Revista do Instituto Histórico e Geográfico e Brasileiro* 371 (1991), 341–436: 397.

[18] Marco Morel, "Da gazeta tradicional aos jornais de opinião: Metamorfoses da imprensa periódica no Brasil," in Lúcia Maria Bastos Neves, *Livros e impressos: Retratos do setecentos e do oitocentos* (Rio de Janeiro: Eduerj, 2009), 153–84: 168–70; Marco Morel, "Independência no papel: A imprensa periódica," in István Jancsó, ed., *Independência: História e historiografia* (São Paulo: Hucitec, 2005), 617–36: 630.

chiefly, Portugal, where several newspapers reprinted articles that the *Gazeta* had previously published in Rio.[19]

The birth of the Brazilian press dated back to the arrival in Rio de Janeiro of the Portuguese royal family in 1808, which led to the establishment of a vibrant political press and the dissemination of pamphlets that played a key role in debates prior to and around the time of Brazilian independence.[20] Already in its first issue, in 1811, the Salvador-based *Idade d'Ouro* published news about political events in Europe.[21] In 1821, with the advent of free press after the constitutional revolution in Porto, several political newspapers were created across Brazil. As early as 1822, Pernambuco's *O Conciliador Nacional* and *O Maribondo* pushed for political emancipation from Portugal, which was then a far from consensual idea, while another Pernambuco newspaper (*Segarrega*) challenged Rio de Janeiro's centrality in Brazil's body politics.[22] In Bahia, political agitation through newspapers was so intense that a few publications were banished in 1821.[23]

As these newspapers – particularly those from Rio – made their way to Luanda and Benguela, the cities' residents closely followed the political turbulence in Brazil. It was from Rio's newspapers, for example, that

[19] Juliana Meirelles, "A *Gazeta do Rio de Janeiro* e o impacto na circulação de idéias no Império Luso-Brasileiro (1808–1821)" (M.A. thesis, Unicamp, 2006), 68–9, 93–5, 97. For further information about the *Gazeta*'s place in the cultural politics of the Portuguese court in Rio de Janeiro, see Juliana Meirelles, "Política e cultura no Governo de D. João VI (1792–1821)" (Ph.D. dissertation, Unicamp, 2013), 264–79.

[20] Marco Morel, *As transformações dos espaços públicos: Imprensa, atores políticos e sociabilidades na Cidade Imperial, 1820–1840* (São Paulo: Hucitec, 2005), 200–39. For Salvador, see Marcelo Siquara Silva, "A cultura letrada na Bahia (1821–1823): A experiência da independência Brasileira" (Ph.D. dissertation, Universidade Federal da Bahia, 2018), 52. See also Hendrik Kraay, Celso Thomas Castilho, and Teresa Cribelli, "Introduction: From Colonial Gazettes to the Largest Circulation in South America," in Hendrik Kraay, Celso Thomas Castilho, and Teresa Cribelli, eds., *Press, Power, and Culture in Imperial Brazil* (Albuquerque: University of New Mexico Press, 2021), 1–31.

[21] Argemiro Ribeiro de Souza Filho and Maria Aparecida Silva de Souza, "A Bahia na crise do Antigo Regime: Aprendizado político, conflitos e mediações (1808–1823)," in Cecília Helena de Salles Oliveira, Vera Lúcia Nagib Bittencourt, and Wilma Peres Costa, eds., *Soberania e conflito: Configurações do Estado Nacional no Brasil no século XIX* (São Paulo: Hucitec, 2010), 239–86: 280. See Maria Beatriz Nizza da Silva, *A Primeira Gazeta da Bahia: Idade d'Ouro do Brasil* (São Paulo: Editora Cultrix, 1978). For an overview of press and political ideas after the arrival of the Portuguese royal family in Brazil, see Andrea Slemian, *Vida política em tempo de crise: Rio de Janeiro (1808–1824)* (São Paulo: Hucitec, 2006), Chapter 3.

[22] Mário Fernandes Ramires, "Palavras impressas em tempos de luta: Periódicos pernambucanos e os debates políticos ocorridos entre 1821 e 1824" (M.A. thesis, Universidade Federal de São Paulo, 2014), 10, 40, 152.

[23] Siquara Silva, "A cultura letrada na Bahia (1821–1823)," 53.

Luanda officials learned that the Confederação do Equador had been crushed in 1824.[24] To prevent the flow of information and political ideals across the Atlantic, Luanda authorities put a ban on newspapers such as the *Estrela*, which held "demagogic principles" and apparently published fictional news of the death of Portuguese officials.[25] In sharp contrast, Luanda officials complained about not receiving official correspondence from Lisbon, nor did they feel confident about the integrity of outbound correspondence shipped to Portugal via Brazil.[26]

Tellingly, the Benguela secessionist petition contained an explicit reference to a Brazilian newspaper named *A Malagueta*, Rio de Janeiro's most popular newspaper with 500 subscribers.[27] It had been created by a Portuguese national named Luis May, who wrote incendiary articles favoring Brazilian independence and in support of constitutionalism. While praising the "provocative and erudite Malagueta, which has brought to live that kingdom [Brazil]," the petition's writers openly stated their hope that the newspaper would give them inspiration to fight for "sacred rights" of independence by following "Brazil's steps." Unsurprisingly, though to no avail, Luanda officials sought to ban *A Malagueta* from Angola.[28]

While eradicating absolute royal power in Portugal, the Porto Revolution sought to reaffirm Lisbon's place as the center of Portugal's empire by demanding the return of the Portuguese royal family to Portugal and the reversal of free trade policies in Brazil. These policies ran counter to the status quo born out of the French invasion of Portugal in 1808, which had forced the Portuguese royal family to escape to Rio de Janeiro – an unprecedented moment in the history of European colonialism.[29] Rio's role as the

---

[24] "Ofício do Governador de Angola," 23 February 1825, AHU, Angola, cx. 147. Interestingly, due to the relative proximity of Angola and Brazil and the frequency of maritime exchanges, the two cities might have received news about key events in Brazil's political history earlier than far-flung Brazilian provinces did. In 1822, for example, it took about one month – about the length of the maritime crossing from Rio de Janeiro to Benguela – for the population of Caetité to learn that D. Pedro I had been proclaimed emperor of Brazil. See Argemiro Ribeiro de Souza Filho, "As juntas governativas e a independência: Multiplicidade de poder na Bahia," in Teresa Malatian, Marisa Saenz Leme, and Ivan Aparecido Manoel, eds., *As múltiplas dimensões da política e da narrativa* (São Paulo: Olho D'Água, 2004), 51–63: 57, 59.

[25] "Ofício do Governador de Angola," 6 August 1824, AHU, Angola, cx. 145.

[26] "Ofício do Governador de Angola," 14 October 1823, AHU, Angola, cx. 143.

[27] Isabel Lustosa, *Insultos impressos: A guerra dos jornalistas na independência (1821–1823)* (São Paulo: Companhia das Letras, 2000), 155–61.

[28] "Ofício do Governador de Benguela," 24 August 1824, AHA, cód. 449, fs. 12v.–13.

[29] Lucia Maria Bastos Pereira das Neves, "Against the Grain: Portugal and Its Empire in the Face of Napoleonic Invasions," in Ute Planert, ed., *Napoleon's Empire: European*

seat of the Portuguese empire profoundly impacted Portugal's relationship with its colonies in Asia and Africa. Instead of Lisbon, colonial administrators, merchants, and military personnel from places as far away as Maputo (Mozambique) and Goa (India) turned to Rio de Janeiro to deal with administrative and legal matters. As the Benguela Junta wrote in its secessionist petition, by attaching themselves to Rio instead of Lisbon, "we can deal with [administrative, commercial, and legal issues] in less than three months and return to our homes [in Benguela]," thus avoiding the complications of having to navigate imperial bureaucracies in Lisbon.[30]

The trajectory of a merchant named Manoel Antonio da Costa Guimarães illustrates how Benguela merchants profited from Rio's status as the seat of the Portuguese empire. As the holder of Benguela's *almoxarife* office (i.e. as customs officer), Guimarães relocated to Rio in 1809, even though he had not regularized the accounts under his supervision. He then visited Benguela several times, likely to carry out his slave trading activities, before settling in the city again in 1814. Three years later, to avoid judicial procedures against him and after clashing with a Benguela governor, he sought refuge in Rio. In early 1819, however, Rio's Junta do Comércio had issued a royal provision that allowed Guimarães to return to Benguela to collect funds the city's merchants had lent to a Benguela merchant who had recently passed away. Instead of returning to Brazil with the funds, however, Guimarães headed off to the Benguela backlands, where he likely used them to invest in the slave trade.[31]

Beyond the intricacies of imperial bureaucracies, the Portuguese revolution also profoundly impacted the body politic at home and abroad through the creation of governing bodies known as provisional juntas, which embodied constitutional power. While undermining or eliminating the power of Lisbon-appointed governors of captaincies, provisional juntas enfranchised a limited number of members of colonial society, which participated in elections that selected members of juntas. In Benguela, for example, about two dozen individuals seem to have participated in the election that

> *Politics in Global Perspective* (New York: Palgrave, 2015), 101–14. For the court's transfer to Rio, see Malerba, Chapter 18 in this volume.

[30] *Gazeta do Rio*, n. 120, 5 October 1822, 602. For the establishment of state institutions in Rio de Janeiro after the arrival of the Portuguese royal family in 1808, see Maria de Fátima Silva Gouvêa, "As bases institucionais da construção da unidade dos poderes do Rio de Janeiro Joanino: Administração e governabilidade no Império Luso-Brasileiro," in Jancsó, ed., *Independência*, 707–52.

[31] "Ofício do Governador de Benguela," 26 November 1819, AHA, cód. 447, fs. 90v.–91v.; "Ofício do Governador de Benguela," 3 July 1820, AHA, cód. 447, fs. 132–132v.

voted Diniz into power in 1822. By creating these governing bodies, Portugal apparently sought to bypass Rio de Janeiro, then viewed as a locus of monarchic power that stood in opposition to Portugal's liberal revolution, and establish a direct communication with provincial governments in the colony.[32]

Yet the creation of provincial juntas had a number of unintended consequences. In Brazil, the governing bodies channeled and catalyzed a nascent political culture in which elite and nonelite political groups not always aligned with Lisbon's interests felt emboldened to voice their views. An unprecedented era of participatory politics ensued. In Bahia, supporters of absolutism dominated the first junta but social pressure eventually led to the election of individuals committed to constitutionalism and mostly born in Brazil.[33] While Salvador's junta pledged obedience to Lisbon, other juntas in the Recôncavo (the area around the Bay of All Saints) advocated loyalty to Rio de Janeiro – then viewed as a standard bearer of constitutionalism – in opposition to Portugal.[34] In Pernambuco, three members of the 1817 anticolonial revolt became members of a provisional junta, which voiced opposition to the presence of metropolitan troops in the province, undercutting Portugal's interests.[35]

In Benguela, which had always been prone to volatile politics, the establishment of a provisional junta provided an opportunity for members of the local elite, such as Domingos Pereira Diniz, to consolidate their already considerable power in colonial affairs. Born in Luanda in 1775, the Black man had been recruited into the military at the age of thirteen and participated in military campaigns against coastal rulers accused of engaging in commerce with foreign merchants north of Luanda. These operations were deemed strategic due to the risk of foreign trade for the commercial stakes of the Luanda merchant community and the city's economy writ large. Diniz's military commanders praised his "value and honor" in battles as well as

---

[32] Andrea Slemian, "Portugal, o Brasil e os Brasis: A diversidade dos territórios e as disputas pela soberania na construção de um novo império monárquico na América," *Claves* 1 (2015), 91–120: 107.

[33] Souza Filho, "Confrontos políticos e redes de sociabilidade," Chapter 2; Siquara, "A cultura letrada na Bahia," 57, 94.

[34] Souza Filho, "As juntas governativas e a independência."

[35] Denis A. M. Bernardes, "Pernambuco e o Império (1822–1824): Sem constituição soberana não há união," in István Jancsó, ed., *Brasil: Formação do estado e da nação* (São Paulo: Hucitec, 2003), 379–409; Cláudia Maria das Graças Chaves and Andréa Slemian, "Memorial às Cortes de Lisboa de Manoel Luís da Veiga (1821): Constitucionalismo e formas de governo no Brasil," *Análise Social* 218 (2016), 122–44.

"prudent and accurate" leadership in military operations. Afterwards, he worked mostly in the military administration.[36]

The first breakthrough in Diniz's career came when he was transferred to Benguela in 1800.[37] In 1806, while promoting him to lieutenant, Benguela officials described him as an "officer who has served satisfactorily for 19 years, of which six or seven in this city as an alferez (ensign)."[38] His duties were then mostly related to issuing *bandos*, or licenses for slave ships departing for Brazil, a coveted job that allowed him to profit from Benguela's slave trade economy.[39] By then, he also owned a number of captives, a few of whom were employed as part of a personal militia.[40] Another way in which he benefited from the Benguela slave trade was by renting out buildings he owned to the city's highly transient population of merchants, the vast majority of whom were slave dealers.[41]

Diniz's transfer to Benguela occurred at a time when colonial officials argued over the place of Black people in the military, shedding light on dueling views on race that suggests that his social ascent would not have been possible if he had not been deployed to Benguela. In Luanda, governor of Angola, Miguel Antonio de Mello, had once defended the appointment of mixed-race officials to regular forces, invoking legislation that specifically precluded the use of race in Angola's military. According to Governor Mello, "it was wrong to exclude men from honors and assignments because they were not white."[42] However, this attitude was at odds with policies recently implemented by Luanda's military commanders, which reserved top positions in the city to white individuals and marginalized nonwhite officers.

Significantly, Diniz himself accused Luanda officials of holding racial prejudice against him. "One of my sins or shortcomings in the eyes of [Governor of Angola Nicolau Castelo Branco] is without a doubt the fact that I am a native of this country and a lack of white skin."[43] One incident demonstrates how his racial identity set him back. In 1823, although his seniority and leadership position made him eligible to become the commander of Luanda's infantry, the city's officials voiced concern about

---

[36] "Carta do Coronel do Regimento de Infantaria de Luanda," 2 January 1800, AHA, cód. 258, fs. 120v–121v.

[37] "Ofício do Governador de Angola," 4 January 1800, BNRJ, doc. 22-2-59, f. 35.

[38] "Promoção para postos Vagos em Benguela," 25 June 1806, AHA, cód. 275, fs. 85–85v.

[39] "Bando do Bergatim Paquete Infante," 13 August 1810, AHA, cód. 519, f. 48.

[40] "Requerimento de Mahori," 31 August 1812, AHA, cód. 440, f. 26v.

[41] "Portaria do Governador de Benguela," 5 September 1816, AHA, cód. 519, f. 207.

[42] "Carta do Governador de Angola," 31 July 1800, AHA, cód. 152, fs. 1v–8.

[43] "Requerimento de Domingos Pereira Diniz," 1 February 1827, IHGB, Dl. 125, 11. 02.

how other infantry officers would react to having him as their commander. In their view, "being a black man, his presence would provoke dissatisfaction among other officials of the same branch of the military." To avoid this outcome, they then appointed him as a commander of one of Luanda's forts, a relatively minor position in the city's military hierarchy.[44]

While Diniz's blackness was clearly a problem in Luanda, likely due to the larger concentration of European officials there, it did not seem to constitute a major impediment in Benguela. Two years before his arrival, fifty-two Black individuals and eight mixed-race officers served in Benguela's eighty-five-individual infantry regiment. The number of white officers stood at only ten.[45] More importantly, nonwhite individuals held high profile positions not only in military but also in society at large. In 1798, while the number of Benguela's white merchants stood at thirty-one, thirteen were nonwhite individuals, including Nazário Marqués da Silva, a wealthy Black merchant who had been born in Bahia. Da Silva was once described as a "forty-six years old [man] who was married to Domingas Maria, a thirty-year-old black woman, and [who] owned twelve slaves."[46]

Diniz's professional turning point came in 1811, when he was appointed commander of an expedition dispatched to the Benguela backlands to punish African rulers who had rebelled against the Benguela government.[47] During the expedition, which lasted about one year, he commanded about sixty professional soldiers and a fifty-five men locally recruited militia (*guerra preta*).[48] He engaged in several military operations. When a soba (African ruler) prevented one of the soldiers from entering his territory, Diniz ordered an attack that led to the seizing of sixty-six cattle and the enslavement of three African women and their children.[49] On another occasion, he directly interfered in the internal affairs of an African fiefdom by siding with two sobas who had requested support against another ruler.[50]

---

[44] "Oficio do Governador de Angola," 22 June 1823, AHU, Angola, cx. 142.
[45] "Mapa da Companhia de Infantaria de Benguela," 1796, AHA, cód. 441, f. 10.
[46] "Testemunho de Nazário Marques da Silva," 31 May 1796, AHU, Angola, cx. 84, doc. 9, fs. 29–30.
[47] "Portaria do Governador de Benguela," 21 March 1811, AHA, cód. 519, f. 71; "Oficio de Domingos Pereira Diniz," 10 September 1811, AHA, cód. 445, f. 96v.; "Oficio do Governador de Angola," 20 June 1812, AHA, cód. 507, fs. 4v.–5.
[48] "Instrumento em pública forma," 18 June 1825, AHU, Angola, cx. 149, doc. 32.
[49] "Carta do Capitão Domingos Pereira Diniz," 3 February 1812, AHA, cód. 445, fs. 124–125v.
[50] "Oficio de Domingos Pereira Diniz," 6 November 1811, AHA, cód. 445, fs. 109v.–110v.

Another incident sheds further light on Diniz's role as the expedition's leader. A soba named Mulundo turned to Diniz for help to release a subject named Sungo, then being held as a slave in Benguela for shipment to Brazil. According to Mulundo, who found out about the subject's plight through another subject who had just returned from Benguela, Sungo had been sold into slavery by another African ruler, likely after being made a prisoner in a war. Through Diniz, who wrote a letter to the Benguela administration on behalf of the African ruler, Mulundo asked the Benguela administration to hold his subject in Benguela until he could return to his village and obtain the means to rescue him.[51]

In the wake of the expedition, Diniz wrote a report that displayed the extent of his knowledge about the province's African population while assessing the Benguela government's plans to use the military to strengthen its power vis-à-vis African rulers. In his view, Africans had long mastered the use of firearms, possessed significant gunpowder, and could easily mobilize a significant army. Unlike Portuguese forces, which often relied on unreliable *guerra preta* recruits who were known to defect from the colonial army, seasoned warriors who had fought in several wars comprised their armies. To stand a chance of success, according to Diniz, any military operation by the Benguela government would require at least 600 armed men.[52]

In fact, the Portuguese waged several wars against Africans near Benguela either on their own or as supporters of powerful African rulers from the interior. In 1814, the Socoval ruler asked the Benguela government for approval to take on Africans known as Muquanzo. According to the ruler, an attack was warranted because the Muquanzo had robbed cattle and murdered one of his subjects. To obtain military support and effectively prosecute the war, the Socoval then asked the Benguela government to mediate contacts with a ruler allied to the Portuguese who lived in Dombe Grande.[53] Yet the Benguela government was clearly also able to wage wars with Africans on their own, and at least once did so by deploying troops from Luanda, including African soldiers led by African allies.[54]

Diniz's performance in the expedition was not uncontroversial. In 1814, while complaining about disruption of trade caravans with the backlands, which was the lifeblood of the city's economy, Benguela merchants urged

[51] "Ofício de Domingos Pereira Diniz," 16 September 1811, AHA, cód. 445, f. 97; "Ofício de Domingos Pereira Diniz," 23 September 1811, AHA, cód. 445, f. 97.
[52] "Ofício de Domingos Pereira Diniz," 26 February 1812, AHA, cód. 445, fs. 135–7.
[53] "Ofício do Governador de Benguela," 27 August 1814, AHA, cód. 446, fs. 5–5v.
[54] "Carta do Governador de Angola," 8 May 1819, AHA, cód. 155, fs. 52v.–53v.

the government to organize another expedition. However, they made a point of criticizing Diniz's expedition as an example of a poorly managed operation. In their view, the campaign had amounted to "nothing more than a chain of disorders, without any practical result than giving Africans certainty of [Benguela's] lack of forces to punish them. As a result, they became bolder and more imperious."[55]

Despite the criticism, it was certainly Diniz's performance as the expedition's commander that earned him a promotion to sergeant mor of Benguela, which placed him at the very top of the city's military regular forces.[56] In this capacity, he often conferred with Benguela governors on military matters. In 1813, for example, governor João de Alvelos Leiria forwarded him a petition by a soldier seeking release from the military. The soldier had defected from the military and sought "refuge" in Bié, where he had married the daughter of José de Assunção Mello, a *sertanejo* born in Brazil who had long established himself in the Benguela backlands (*sertões*) to trade in captives and ivory. In the petition, while seeking an official discharge from the military, the soldier asked to be forgiven for his defection.[57]

By several accounts, Diniz was not shy about leveraging his military position to challenge the authority of Lisbon-appointed officials, including governors of Benguela. In a relatively minor incident, he once objected to the deployment of Benguela's militia to perform nocturn patrolling in the city. In his view, this task should be carried out by the professional military men under his command.[58] In another incident, Diniz was said to spread lampoons (*pasquims*) against a governor of Benguela.[59] He also sided with local elite against a Lisbon-appointed judge who had constrained Benguela's commerce with the *sertões* by determining that African traders would have to appear before him three days after arriving in the city. To avoid "commotion" in Benguela, the Portuguese Crown ordered the judge removed to Rio de Janeiro.[60]

These disputes took place during the administration of Benguela governor Manoel de Abreu de Mello e Alvim, who once felt slighted after Diniz used

---

[55] "Carta do Governador de Angola," 24 May 1814, AHA, cód. 323, fs. 105v.–106v.

[56] "Portaria do Governador de Benguela," 14 May 1812, AHA, cód. 519, fs. 106–106v.; "Portaria do Governador de Benguela," 9 July 1812, AHA, cód. 519, f. 109.

[57] "Portaria do Governador de Benguela," 11 January 1813, AHA cód. 519, f. 122.

[58] "Portaria do Governador de Benguela," 5 September 1816, AHA, cód. 519, fs. 201v.–202.

[59] "Oficio do Governador de Benguela," 7 January 1819, AHA, cód. 447, fs. 46–53.

[60] "Oficio do Governador de Benguela," 27 September 1816, cód. 446, f. 89; "Carta Régia," 13 December 1816, AHA, cód. 361, fs. 39v.–40.

one of Benguela's public parades – at which most of the city congregated to celebrate religious or secular holidays – "to show that he was the governor and commander of the parade."[61] The bickering escalated when Alvim accused Diniz of plunging Benguela into a crisis by refusing to enforce an order to arrest Antonio Ezequiel de Carvalho, an officer in the city's militia.[62] The incident resulted in Diniz being arrested at his home and eventually taken to Luanda to face military trial.[63] Although Luanda officials reprimanded him for disrespecting superiors, he was exonerated from accusation of insubordination and allowed to return to Benguela.[64]

This crisis marked the first documented occasion on which Diniz associated with Ezequiel Carvalho, who would become perhaps his primary ally in Benguela's politics. When Diniz resigned in 1822 from his position as head of the Benguela Junta, Carvalho took a group of soldiers to the city council to intimidate its members to vote Diniz back into power.[65] Later, Carvalho was accused of traveling to Rio de Janeiro on a secret mission to request Brazilian military support for Benguela secessionism. He was also accused of plotting to place Diniz as governor of Benguela and participate in a meeting in which one of his subordinates was apparently overheard saying that "if the governor continued to persecute individuals from Rio de Janeiro, he would be assassinated."[66] Carvalho wound up deported to Portugal in 1824 and metropolitan authorities later ordered him dismissed from Benguela military forces.[67]

By early 1822, following orders from Lisbon and Luanda, Benguela officials had established an elected provisional junta in the city, signaling their alignment with the 1820 Porto Revolution's liberal principles while opening the door for Diniz's election as the head of the governing body. How exactly Diniz came into power is not clear. In his telling, he was first elected not only

---

[61] "Portaria do Governador de Benguela," c. 10 December 1817, AHA, cód. 519, fs. 256 v.–257.

[62] "Portaria do Governador de Benguela," 11 November 1817, AHA, cód. 519, fs. 251 v. – 252; "Carta do Governador de Benguela," 8 March 1818, AHU, Angola, cx. 152.

[63] "Portaria do Governador de Benguela," 10 November 1817, AHA, cód. 519, fs. 251–251v.; "Carta do Governador de Angola," 18 December 1817, AHA, cód. 155; "Portaria do Governador de Benguela," 15 November 1817, AHA, cód. 519, f. 255.

[64] "Carta do Governador de Angola," 21 November 1818, AHA, cód. 155, fs. 41–41v.; "Oficio do Governador de Angola," 23 November 1818, AHA, cód. 507, fs. 126v.–127; "Carta do Governador de Angola," 11 March 1819, AHA, cód. 155, f. 57.

[65] "Certidão passada por Bernardino Dias Barboza," 10 January 1823, AHU, Angola, cx. 143.

[66] "Oficio do Governador," 13 May 1823, AHU, Angola, cx. 142.

[67] "Carta do Conde de Subserra," 18 October 1824, AHU, cód. 542; "Oficio vindo de Lisboa," 30 October 1824, AHA, cód. 7183, f. 27v.

as the representative of the military but also the junta's vice-president. Turmoil ensued after Benguela governor Antonio Guedes Quinhones, then the junta's president, refused to swear an oath to the Portuguese Constitution, prompting a new election that resulted in Diniz emerging as the junta's president.[68] According to Quinhones, Diniz orchestrated a military coup that gave him control of the junta but plunged the city into political chaos.[69] The clash neatly illustrates how Portugal's liberal revolution further empowered local elite men such as Diniz.

In many ways, the circumstances surrounding Diniz's political ascent mirrored the destabilizing impact of the Porto Revolution across the broader Portuguese empire. In Bahia, where a declaration of official support for the Portuguese revolution was slightly delayed due to the fear of slave revolts, the initial news of the liberal revolution elicited calls for immediate separation from Portugal.[70] Soon, Bahian elites had formed a government that broke ties with Rio de Janeiro and declared allegiance to the Portuguese Cortes. Political infighting, social unrest, and military clashes gripped the province. In Salvador, street clashes pitted groups in favor of constitutional power against absolute power supporters, turning violent and costing lives or wounding 200 people.[71] Portuguese troops occupied Bahia's capital city, yet independentist forces, in part led by provisional juntas, remained strong in the Recôncavo.[72]

The Porto Revolution also destabilized Rio de Janeiro's political fabric. According to Manoel Patrício Corrêa de Castro, an Angolan representative to the Lisbon Cortes then passing through Rio on his way to Portugal, a deep divide separated supporters of "democracy" from those who "desired [the

---

[68] "Representação de Domingos Pereira Diniz," 9 November 1822, AHU, Angola, cx. 143.

[69] "Extrato de Oficio do Governador de Benguela," 11 July 1822, AHU, Angola, cx. 141, doc. 60; "Oficio do Governo Provisório do Governo de Benguela," 30 March 1822, AHA, cód. 448, fs. 16v.–17v.; "Oficio do Governo Provisório do Governo de Benguela," 22 April 1822, AHA, cód. 448, fs. 18v–21.

[70] Siquara, "A cultura letrada na Bahia," 55; Souza Filho and Silva de Souza, "A Bahia na crise do Antigo Regime," 263. See also Lucia Maria Bastos Pereira das Neves, *Corcundas e constitucionais: A cultura política da independência (1820–1822)* (Rio de Janeiro: Revan, 2003).

[71] Siquara, "A cultura letrada na Bahia," 75–84, 133–4. For the participation of enslaved and nonelite people in Salvador's conflicts, see Hendrik Kraay, "Em Outra Coisa não falavam os Pardos, Cabras, e Crioulos: O 'recrutamento' de escravos na guerra da independência na Bahia," *Revista Brasileira de História* 22:43 (2002), 109–26.

[72] Siquara, "A cultura letrada na Bahia," 124; Souza Filho and Silva de Souza, "A Bahia na crise do Antigo Regime," 267–8.

adoption] of the Portuguese constitution."[73] As early as February 1821, street protesters had forced the Portuguese monarch to embrace the principles of the liberal constitution then being written in Lisbon.[74] Violent repression followed after protesters called for the adoption of the Cádiz Constitution as well as legislation backing up press and individual freedom. In mid-1821, as a new wave of street protests again shook Rio, the regent ruler of Brazil had been forced to declare support for the liberal principles underpinning the constitution still being crafted in Portugal.[75]

Likewise, political and social unrest broke out in Pernambuco, which had already been the epicenter of an anticolonial revolt in 1817.[76] Soon authorities faced a military sedition in favor of an immediate alignment with the liberal revolution.[77] An officer who had presided over the repression of the 1817 revolt became the leader of Pernambuco's first junta, stoking significant tension that eventually led to his dismissal. A new junta was then elected with an unprecedented level of participatory politics.[78] Pernambuco elites remained skeptical if not altogether hostile to Rio de Janeiro's central role in the independentist movement. After it had become clear that Brazil would split from Portugal, Pernambuco's constitutional forces called for an autonomous status for their province.[79]

Against this backdrop, the deeply convulsing impact of the Porto Revolution on Angola should not be surprising. In Luanda, where authorities

---

[73] *Diario das Cortes Geraes e Extraordinarias da Nação Portugueza* (henceforth DCGENP), session of 21 September 1822, 43, 535.

[74] Márcia Berbel, "Os apelos nacionais nas Cortes Constituintes de Lisboa (1821/1822)," in Jurandir Malerba, ed., *A Independência Brasileira: Novas dimensões* (Rio de Janeiro: FGV Editora, 2006), 181–208; Alexandre Bellini Tasca, "Enredamentos: O constituir nacional entre Portugal e Brazil nas Cortes de Lisboa (1820–1822)" (M.A. thesis, Universidade Federal de Minais Gerais, 2016), 87.

[75] Vera Lúcia Nagib Bittencourt, "De Alteza Real a Imperador: O governo do Príncipe D. Pedro, de abril de 1821 a outubro de 1822" (Ph.D. dissertation, Universidade de São Paulo, 2006), 104–34.

[76] Luiz Carlos Villalta, "Pernambuco, 1817, encruzilhada de desencontros do Império Luso-Brasileiro," *Revista USP* 58 (2003), 58–91; Flavio José Gomes Cabral, "A linguagem política oitocentista: Cartas, panfletos, versos e boatos no norte da América Portuguesa," *História Unisinos* 21:2 (2017), 259–69.

[77] Flavio José Gomes Cabral, "Os efeitos da notícia da Revolução Liberal do Porto na Província de Pernambuco e a crise do sistema colonial no nordeste do Brasil (1820–1821)," *Fronteras de la Historia* 11 (2006), 389–413: 396–8.

[78] Denis Bernardes, "A gente ínfima do Povo e outras gentes na Confederação do Equador," in Monica Duarte Dantas, ed., *Revoltas, motins, revoluções: Homens livres pobres e libertos no Brasil do século XIX* (São Paulo: Alameda, 2011), 131–66: 139.

[79] Andréa Lisly Gonçalves, "As várias independências: A contrarrevolução em Portugal e em Pernambuco e os conflitos antilusitanos no período do constitucionalismo (1821–1824)," *Clio* 36 (2018), 4–27: 7.

initially opposed the establishment of a provisional junta, supporters of constitutionalism called for the removal of Angola governor Manoel Vieira Tovar de Albuquerque. In an anonymous letter, a constitutionalist sympathizer stated: "After the news from Portugal, many have said that [Angola] should follow Portugal and change the government. Some have wanted to arrest your excellency [governor of Angola] and send you to Rio de Janeiro, as those from Pernambuco had done with a general [who was their governor]."[80] By October 1821, the "people" of Luanda had sent two petitions to the Cortes in Lisbon to denounce that the then governor Joaquim Inácio de Lima had neither embraced the project of a new constitution being discussed in Lisbon nor had taken steps to elect Angola's representatives to the Cortes.[81]

Lisbon authorities learned from Governor Lima himself about the specifics of the establishment of the Luanda governing junta. According to Lima, who had returned to Lisbon in early 1822 due to health reasons, a provisional junta made up of nine members (including the governor) had been elected in December 1821.[82] By then, the city had already been engulfed in a political crisis strikingly similar to the ones then unfolding in Brazilian cities such as Salvador and Recife. Like in Salvador, the election of Luanda's provisional junta drew strong opposition from constitutional power sympathizers, including members of the military establishment, who called for a do-over election based on voting rules used in Pernambuco.[83] Luanda officials reported "nightly gatherings to discuss several events in Europe and the fact that the captaincies of Bahia, Pernambuco, Maranhão and Pará had decided to follow the same [political] path." They also wrote that "once news of the revolution in Pernambuco became known in this city [Luanda], small gatherings took place by people wishing to travel there."[84]

Although it is difficult to pinpoint who exactly participated in political agitation in Luanda, Manoel Ferreira de Lima illustrates the profile of a possible Brazilian participant. De Lima had first settled in Luanda in 1818,

---

[80] "Carta de Anônima," 26 March 1821, AHU, Angola, cx. 140, doc. 46.
[81] DCGENP, session of 22 July 1822, n. 63, 911; DCGENP, session of 12 December 1821, n. 248, 1.
[82] Diário do Governor n. 103, 3 May 1822, 725; "Oficio da Junta Provisória do Governo de Angola," 2 January 1822, AHU, Angola, cx. 141, doc. 1.
[83] DCGENP, session of 11 July 1822, n. 53, 769. See also "Proclamação aos soldados do Regimento de Linha e Esquadrão de Cavalaria de Luanda," 8 February 1822, AHU, Angola, cx. 141, doc. 9; "Extrato de Oficio da Junta Provisório de Angola," 22 February 1822, AHU, Angola, cx. 141.
[84] "Oficio do Governador de Angola," 17 February 1822, AHU, Angola, cx. 140.

perhaps as an exile of an anticolonial and republican revolt that occurred in Pernambuco in the previous year, which had prompted thousands of individuals to leave or be sent into exile. In Luanda, de Lima worked for a while as the city's *vedor* (comptroller) of water supply and later applied for the position of lieutenant in the city's militia.[85] More importantly, he was later described as "radical liberal and restless rebel from Pernambuco." De Lima had then returned to Recife, where he presumably took part in the Confederação do Equador, but clearly remained still connected to Luanda. According to the city's authorities, his legal representative in Luanda had "proved himself to possess similar character and sentiments."[86]

It was against this backdrop that Luanda authorities received the news that Benguela was well on its way to break off from Portugal and become an overseas province of Brazil. "Through newspapers and private letters [from Brazil], we have come to learn about the secret maneuvering to make this province join the Brazilian cause, completely splitting from the obedience of the courts, the king, and this city [Luanda]." While reaffirming allegiance to Portugal's Cortes, Luanda authorities observed that "Rio de Janeiro cannot fulfill this city's request because it belongs in Africa, not in Brazil, nor can this city sever ties [with Portugal] on its own volition and without orders from the Cortes." According to them, nothing except a "spirit of novelty" could explain the Benguela junta's actions.[87] After considering sending troops to Benguela, they wound up dispatching two envoys to the city, both members of Luanda's provisional junta, who were put up at Diniz's house and carried copies of the *Gazeta do Rio de Janeiro* with the petition that the Benguela junta had sent to Brazil.

In response to the envoys' query, Diniz rebuffed claims of secessionism by stating that not only had the Benguela junta not concealed its petition but had also shared it with Luanda's authorities. According to him, the junta did not even know that Brazil had become independent when it sent the document to Rio de Janeiro in September 1822. At face value, Diniz's claims were perfectly plausible given the fact that Brazil's breakup from Portugal was by no means certain by then. On one hand, Prince Regent Pedro I refused Lisbon's orders to return to Portugal in January 1822 and five

---

[85] "Requerimento de Manoel Ferreira de Lima," 25 November 1823, AHU, Angola, cx. 143.

[86] "Ofício do Governador de Angola," 16 October 1824, AHU, Angola, cx. 143, doc. 44.

[87] "Carta da Junta de Governo de Angola," 13 December 1822, AHA, cód. 156, fs. 62v.–64; "Ofício da Junta Provisória de Luanda," 13 December 1822, AHA, cód. 507, fs. 218v.–219v.

months later openly defied the Lisbon Cortes by calling for the establishment of a legislative body to write a constitution. These steps suggested that Brazilian independence was no longer a far-fetched prospect. Yet the vast majority of Brazilian representatives in the Lisbon Cortes signed the Portuguese Constitution in September 1822, which suggests that the idea of a complete breakup from Portugal might not yet have crystalized.

From the viewpoint of the governor of Benguela, João Antonio Pussich, however, not only did the Benguela junta know that Brazilian independence was inevitable but the prospect of an independent Brazil was precisely what motivated the governing body to reach out to Rio de Janeiro. Pussich claimed that the Brazilian government acted in a way that suggested that it already considered Benguela as its overseas province. Particularly suspicious, according to Pussich, was the fact that the Brazilian government had "declared war on subjects of the kingdom of Portugal, confiscated their assets, and banned navigation to ports where the authority of the king was recognized," yet it still allowed the continuation of trading connections with Benguela.[88]

Although the governor's claims might sound exaggerated, perhaps reflecting more deep anxiety among Portuguese officials than reality, the Portuguese were not alone in viewing rumors of Angola's annexation to Brazil as credible. British authorities, then deeply implicated in negotiations for Portugal's recognition of Brazilian independence, went as far as officially broaching the subject with the Brazilian government. The Rio de Janeiro government hired foreign mercenaries to fight on its behalf in several Brazilian provinces and actively sought to shore up its sympathizers in Pernambuco. However, influential politician José Bonifácio categorically denied plans to annex Portuguese territories in Africa. "With regards to colonies or the coast of Africa, we want none, nor anywhere else. Brazil is quite large enough and productive enough for us, and we are content with what Providence has given us."[89]

At the heart, rumors of secessionism were fueled by the multiple ways that Angola interacted with Brazil. Individuals who had previously served in or were born in Brazil occupied positions both in the city's civilian and military administrations. In 1817, Antonio José da Fonseca Pinto Lemos de

---

[88] "Oficio do Governador de Benguela," 8 May 1823, AHU, Angola, cx. 142.
[89] Kenneth Maxwell, "Why Was Brazil Different? The Contexts of Independence," in Carlos Guilherme Mota, ed., *Viagem incompleta: A experiência brasileira (1500–2000)* (São Paulo: Senac, 2000), 177–95.

Lacerda, previously an *alferes* (second lieutenant) in the colonial army in Rio de Janeiro, served in one of Benguela's military companies.[90] To find personnel for Benguela's chronically understaffed hospital, the city officials turned to slave ships' crewmembers. In 1816, one crewmember, named Raimundo Mendes de Oliveira, was enlisted to serve in Benguela's hospital due to the "urgent needs that currently exist (in Benguela) as a result of personnel with his specialty."[91] In another example, José Joaquim, a surgeon on the *Galera Felix Eugenia*, was hired by "the clergy, nobility and people of this city to stay here for one year."[92]

While these ties had been part and parcel of the very integrated world of slavery in the south Atlantic, the prospect of Brazilian independence had given them a menacingly political twist. Luanda officials were well aware that Brazil itself remained convulsed politically as it made its way toward independence. In their minds, however, once the newly independent nation achieved political stability, it would inevitably stake out territorial claim in Portuguese Africa. According to Angola governor Nicolau Castelo Branco, "there is no question that once the government now in power [in Brazil] has stabilized the internal situation, it will stage some form of attack on Angola." In Castelo Branco's view, Portugal should consider its relationship with Brazil as it decided the number of soldiers deployed to Angola. "If Brazil remains as our enemy, it would be indispensable to have between five to six hundred European soldiers" in Angola. If that is not the case, the number could be dropped by half.[93]

Castelo Branco's fears were not isolated. Newly appointed governor of Benguela João Antonio Pussich had actually become convinced that Benguela was a hotbed of secessionism even before setting foot in the city. According to him, if not for the soldiers that accompanied him, he would not even have been allowed to disembark to take up his position as governor.[94] His encounter with Diniz, then at the apex of power as the head of the Benguela junta and the city's military commander, made a deep impression on the newcomer governor. One anecdote is illustrative. According to the naval commander who had escorted Pussich to Benguela, "three or four days after coming to power governor João Antonio Pussich came onboard to say that although he had no complaint about lieutenant colonel Diniz, he was afraid of him and

---

[90] "Portaria do Governador de Benguela," 30 January 1817, AHA, cód. 519, f. 220v.
[91] "Portaria do Governador de Benguela," 23 January 1816, AHA, cód. 519, fs. 187v.–188.
[92] "Portaria do Governador de Benguela," 28 February 1816, AHA, cód. 519, f. 190v.
[93] "Ofício do Governador de Angola," 13 July 1825, AHU, Angola, cx. 149.
[94] "Ofício do Governador de Benguela," 8 May 1823, AHU, Angola, cx. 142.

demanded that [Governor of Angola] Avelino removed him to Luanda."[95] Soon, Pussich accused the Black man of being the leader of "Brazilian party" that had "plotted revolutions against Europeans and in favor of Brazil."[96]

Pussich then took actions to quash what he viewed as Benguela's secessionist forces. First, he ordered the seizing of "all merchandise in the custom house of this kingdom that belonged to the subjects of the Empire of Brazil; all merchandise and funds held by merchants of this kingdom as well as their representatives; all buildings in the city and country as well as all vessels that belonged to their merchants of that empire."[97] By doing so, the governor sought to cripple what he rightly saw as the lifeblood for the city's economy and its increasingly politically active merchant community. Yet, although he blocked the slave trade to Rio de Janeiro and Pernambuco, Benguela merchants bypassed that prohibition by declaring their ships would leave for Salvador.[98]

Pussich's actions mirrored steps to weaken secessionism in Luanda, where governor of Angola Cristovão Avelino Dias also saw the seizing of Brazilian merchants' assets as a way of retaliating against anti-Portuguese forces in Brazil. According to Dias, "it would be shameful if this country traded with a city whose troops are battling against the heroic defenders of Bahia."[99] In contrast to Benguela, however, the governor ran into opposition. After reminding the new governor that "the supreme law of Luanda clearly mandated free trade of slaves with those ports of Brazil where there is peace and friendship," Luanda merchants adamantly opposed the seizing of assets of Pernambuco merchants.[100]

Second, under circumstances not entirely clear, Pussich somehow managed to remove Diniz to Luanda. To return to Benguela, the Black man first wrote a petition in which he claimed that his wife was sick and tried to dispel allegations of secessionism that had dogged him for years. Interestingly, he began by admitting that the Benguela junta had indeed "petitioned her majesty to become part of Brazil" three years earlier. Yet he downplayed the significance of the petition, arguing that "they [the petitioners] had soon changed their minds" and lacked local support to sever ties to Portugal. Any realistic attempt to break the Portuguese grip over the city would require

---

[95] "Oficio do Governador de Benguela," 19 January 1826, AHA, cód. 449, fs. 70v.–71.
[96] "Oficio do Governador de Benguela," 13 May 1823, AHU, Angola, cx. 142.
[97] "Decreto da Junta Provisório de Benguela," 2 June 1823, AHU, Angola, cx. 142.
[98] "Oficio do Governador de Angola," 11 April 1824, AHU, Angola, cx. 144.
[99] "Carta do Governador de Angola," 26 June 1822, AHU, Angola, cx. 142.
[100] "Representação do Corpo de Comércio e Cidadãos de Luanda," 21 June 1823, BML, cód. 44, fs. 35v.–39.

backing from the military, which was under his command. In his words, "how would it be possible to make Benguela become part of Brazil" without support from the city's military establishment?[101]

## Conclusion

Domingos Pereira Diniz's career provides insights into the rapidly changing political environment ushered in by the Porto Revolution and the rise of liberalism in the Portuguese South Atlantic. That the Black man was already on a socially upward trajectory before he became the head of Benguela junta illustrates how the colonial army provided opportunities of social mobility for locally born individuals. In the army, Diniz likely seized upon his status as a locally born individual to position himself as a dependable point person for the Portuguese establishment, both in making alliances and in taking on local populations. Diniz's bitter complaints about being stigmatized and marginalized due to his blackness suggest tantalizing differences in attitudes toward race between Luanda and Benguela which merit further research.

A turning point in Diniz's life came about after the Porto Revolution paved the way for liberal reforms in Portugal and its sprawling empire. While encapsulating these reforms, the Black man's trajectory shows how they enfranchised local elites and also unleashed forces that the Portuguese could not entirely sway. Mirroring the case of provisional juntas across Brazil, the Benguela provisional junta became a hotbed for the most fractious politics of the time. As a military man, Diniz's voice was obviously never inconsequential, yet it is undeniable that the position of president of the Benguela junta turned him – and his often opaque politics – into the center of gravity of Benguela's power at a critical juncture.

What dramatically raised the stakes, of course, was that Diniz's rise happened just as Brazil became an independent nation, which sent powerful ripples across the Atlantic and seriously destabilized Portugal's grip over the coastal enclaves of Luanda and Benguela. Due to the transatlantic slave trade, both cities had long gravitated toward Brazil. Their elites felt less attached to Portugal than to the newly independent nation, with which they had long developed commercial, social, and cultural ties. The disputes that ensued brought Portuguese rule in Angola almost to the brink of collapse, marking the onset of decades of geopolitical rivalry between Portugal and its former colony over influence in West Central Africa.

---

[101] "Requerimento de Domingos Pereira Diniz," 14 July 1825, AHU, Angola, cx. 151.

# Index

**Introductory Note**

References such as "178–79" indicate (not necessarily continuous) discussion of a topic across a range of pages. Wherever possible in the case of topics with many references, either these have been divided into sub-topics or only the most significant discussions of the topic are listed. Because the entire work is about "Latin America," the use of this term (and certain others which occur constantly throughout the book) as an entry point has been restricted. Information will be found under the corresponding detailed topics.

Abascal, José Fernando de, 70, 121, 209–15, 227, 285–6, 290, 294, 295, 357
abdications, 232, 493, 560–1
abolition decrees, 43, 314
abolition of slavery, 284, 312, 382, 384, 387, 392, 396, 416, 441, 448
  gradual, 122, 264
  immediate, 374, 384–5, 398, 484
abolitionism, 44, 312, 322
abolitionist movement, 414, 532
abolitionists, 44, 322, 399, 407, 414, 424
absolute monarchy, 315, 461
absolute power, 124, 141, 492, 581
absolutism, 170, 173–4, 279–80, 290, 292, 295, 296, 515, 517, 553–5
  and royalism, 279–92
  enlightened, 62, 185, 190–1
  return to, 295–8
absolutists, 118–20, 127, 139, 172, 290, 302, 533
abuses, 167, 243, 318, 341, 516, 519
Acapulco, 164, 169
active citizenship, 12, 274, 362, 374, 381, 395, 460, 467
active urban pardos, 233, 236
activism, 124, 131, 139, 488
Aculco, 160–1
Adams, John, 20, 325

administration, 97, 116, 191, 195, 200, 210, 450, 469, 475, 511
adventurers, 45, 246, 426, 487, 492, 503
*afrancesados*, 125, 130, 455
Africa, 13, 85, 87, 425, 476, 496, 500, 513–14, 569, 584, 585
  *see also* Angola.
  West, 35, 309
  West Central, 497, 567, 588
African descent, 228–31, 233–7, 282–4, 287–9, 294–5, 300, 306, 394, 396–7, 398
African rulers, 577–8
African slave trade, 312, 313, 391, 406, 517
African slaves, 79, 84, 230, 253, 414, 513
African women, 309, 577
Africanization, 312, 319, 387
Africans, 230, 254, 283, 289, 304, 308–9, 369, 390, 484, 578–9
  and their descendants, 304–24
  enslaved, 49, 304, 319, 405, 415, 432, 446, 571
agents, 16, 19, 31, 47, 131, 144, 348, 422, 426
  French, 33, 42, 47, 187
agrarian seigneurial rights, 464–5
agriculture, 85, 90, 116, 237, 406, 447, 451–2, 464
*aguardiente*, 88, 192, 218
Aguilar, Manuel, 193

## Index

Aguirre, Matías Martín de, 169, 329
Alamán, Lucas, 420–3
*alcabala*, 88, 312, 376
Alcobaça, 465
Alegre, Magaly, 358
Alexander I, Tsar, 137, 148, 414
Algarve, 456, 460, 466, 490, 554, 557, 558
Alicante, 150, 207
allegiance, 13, 37–8, 108, 166, 171, 187, 198, 233–4, 311, 313
Allende, Ignacio, 161–2
alliances, 96, 99, 107, 172, 214, 220, 281, 310, 549, 553
Althaus, Clement de, 366
Álvarez de Toledo, José, 385–6
Álvarez Thomas, Ignacio, 214, 216–17
Alvear, Carlos de, 263, 268–70, 408
American representatives, 106, 109, 118, 188
American Revolution, 1, 3, 10, 13, 16, 21, 25, 29–30, 40–1, 43
American Revolutionary War, 14, 97
Americanism, 206, 215–19, 220
Américo, Pedro, 521, 526
amnesties, 150, 165, 176
anarchists, 43, 47, 390, 467
anarchy, 10, 23, 37, 39, 50, 266, 370, 383, 389, 521
Anchoriz, Ramón Eduardo, 408
*ancien régime*
    Portugal 20, 436–8, 443–7, 476–7, 490–2, 501–5, 512–14, 548–52, 556–9, 567–73, 580–5 *see* Portugal, *ancien régime.*
    Spanish, 122
Andean region, 76, 295, 331, 378
Andes, 91–2, 94–6, 99, 214, 218–21, 224–5, 230, 301–2, 396, 400
Andrada e Silva, José Bonifacio de, 491–2, 526, 544, 559
Angola, 13, 430, 446
    *see also* Benguela.
    liberal politics in the wake of Brazilian independence, 13, 567–88
Angostura, 74, 346, 387, 414, 423
Angoulême, duc d', 149–50
antagonisms, 139, 215, 284–5, 558
Antepara, José María de, 407
Antioquia, 43, 289, 295, 379, 386–7, 396
Anti-Slavery Society, 321
Apartado, Marqués del, 407–8
Apodaca, Juan Ruiz de, 171, 296, 316
Aponte, José Antonio, 100, 307, 314–15
appointments, 196, 200, 434, 498, 529, 576

Aragua, 242
Aranda, Conde de, 63, 98, 342
Arango, Francisco de, 99, 564
Araújo e Azevedo, Antônio de, 477, 487, 494
archbishops, 140, 155–6
Areche, José Antonio de, 91–2, 96
Arequipa, 20, 358, 366
Argentina, 35, 74, 206, 220, 225, 275, 318, 412, 420, 448
Argentines, 274, 402, 413, 424
Argüelles, Agustín de, 111, 115, 128, 130, 135, 138, 385
Argüello, José, 169
aristocracy, 25, 125, 129, 424, 452–3, 461–2, 468, 470
aristocrats, 15, 140, 237, 301, 461, 471–2
Arizpe, Ramos, 111, 118
armies, 124–7, 140–1, 160–9, 210–15, 217–25, 258, 267–70, 292–6, 355–6
    British, 21, 30, 40, 124
    counterrevolutionary, 21, 31, 36–40, 132, 141, 148, 152, 211, 227, 262, 463, 522
    French, 44, 102–4, 106, 110, 124, 149–50, 430–1, 433, 439, 441
    insurgent, 160–1, 163, 165, 195
    Portuguese, 104, 134–5, 147–8, 270, 272, 436–7, 446–7, 456, 496, 508–9, 524, 527, 529, 541–3, 553–4, 556, 558, 581
    regular, 158, 211, 293–4, 530
    revolutionary, 71, 260–1
    royal, 162, 358, 359
    royalist *see* royalist army, 158
Armijo, José Gabriel de, 169
armistices, 144, 146, 171, 173, 262, 553
Army of the Faith, 150
Arocemena, Pablo, 248
Arredondo, Joaquín de, 169
Arriaga, Julián de, 84, 94
Artigas, José Gervasio, 26, 73, 261–2, 265–6, 268, 271–2, 553–4, 556
Artiguist Confederation, 268–9, 272
Artiguists, 262, 265–7, 268, 271
artillery, 139, 161–2, 163
artisans, 231, 252, 255, 308, 320, 430, 467, 469
Asia, 425, 467, 476, 496, 558, 574
*asiento*, 80, 83, 86
assassinations, 29, 39, 168
Asunción, 258, 264
asylum, 300, 410, 564
Atlantic slave trade, 49, 500, 513
Atlantic World, 50, 177, 179, 184, 187, 281, 300, 311–12, 321, 323
atrocities, 391–2

590

## Index

*audiencia*, 66, 91, 155–6, 157, 195, 200, 212, 297
Austria, 47, 80, 148, 440
  intervention, 19, 147–8, 149, 152, 201, 385,
    455, 503, 553
autonomous provinces, 272–3
autonomy, 6, 13, 67–8, 108, 116–17, 258,
    343–4, 351, 429, 437
  local, 20, 190, 430
  political, 106, 119, 181, 201, 203, 493
Ayacucho, 15, 225, 272, 372, 561
Aycinena family, 176, 181–2, 189, 191–3, 196,
    198, 199–200, 421
Aymara, 254, 331
*ayuntamientos*, 109, 119, 155, 187, 192, 196–7
Azeredo Coutinho, J.J. Cunha, 389, 392
Azores, 457

Badajoz, 207, 476
Bahia, 379–80, 432, 481–2, 488–9, 523–4,
    526–7, 533–4, 539–46
Bajío, 293, 296
Banda Oriental, 73–4, 261–2, 265–6, 270–4,
    276, 551–7
banditry, 36–40
Barata, Cipriano, 563
Barba, Gabriel Dorotea, 307, 309, 314–15
Barbosa, Januário da Cunha, 558
Barcelona, 125, 150, 152, 240–3
Barclay, Herring, Richardson, 419
Bardají, Eusebio, 137, 145
Barinas, 240–1
Baring Brothers, 418
barracks, 414, 439, 483
Barras, Paul, 477
Barry, David, 416
Basadre, Vicente, 146
Basel, Treaty of, 63, 100, 311
Bastille, 18, 45, 97
Batavian Republic, 15, 22
battles, 83, 161–4, 168, 171, 213–14, 233–4,
    241–3, 244, 273, 359–60 *see also*
    *individual battle names*
Bayamo, 314
Bayonne, 27, 32, 65, 177–9, 187, 205–6,
    330
Beard, Mary, 368
Becker, Carl, 325
Beira Alta, 466
Belém, 478, 527
Belgrano, Manuel, 214–15, 217, 262–4, 267,
    270–1, 409, 424
Bello, Andrés, 347, 407, 408, 423
Bello, Carlos, 423

Benguela, 13, 546, 567–8, 570–80, 584–8
  *see also* Angola.
  backlands, 574, 577, 579
  elites, 13, 19–20, 32–3, 90–1, 181–3, 262–4,
    270–1, 494–5, 498–501, 514–15,
    517–18, 568, 571
  governors, 215–16, 218, 222, 269–70, 481,
    574, 576, 579–80, 583, 586–7
  junta, 571, 574, 577–8, 580, 584–8
  merchants, 13, 80, 411–12, 418–19, 461–3,
    499, 514, 516, 574, 576, 578, 587
Bentham, Jeremy, 407
Beresford, William Carr, 401–3, 556
Bethell, Leslie, 61, 522
BFBS (British and Foreign Bible Society), 421–2
BFSS (British and Foreign School Society),
    421–2, 425
Biassou, Georges, 310–11
Bight of Biafra, 87
Billaud-Varenne, 25
Bío-Bío river, 416
bishops, 136, 170, 253, 392, 454, 466
Black militias, 307, 310, 315
Black officers, 99, 530, 543 *see also individual*
  *names*
Blacks, 44, 230, 232, 234, 310, 323–4, 379–80,
    385–6, 483–4, 539
  free, 26, 294, 301, 307–8, 314, 315–17, 323,
    374–6, 380
Blanco Encalada, Manuel, 221
Blanco White, José María, 111, 386
Blaufarb, Rafe, 27
Blonde, José Manuel, 319–20, 323
Bogotá, 19, 178, 372, 408, 423
Bolívar, Simón, 74, 228, 240–2, 244–9, 300–1,
    349, 358–9, 387–9, 407, 421
Bolivia, 15, 76, 92, 211, 253, 273, 275, 349,
    360, 389
Bonaparte, Joseph, 65, 105, 115, 133, 139,
    155, 186–7, 256, 279, 404
Bonapartes, 47, 125, 155, 257, 262–4, 267,
    358, 479 *see also* Napoleon
Bonavía, Bernardo, 169
bondage, 44–5, 387, 445
bonds, 49, 417, 434, 483, 489
borders, 36, 98, 239, 276, 431, 440, 548,
    550–3, 562, 564
Borges de Barros, Domingos, 461
Boston, 321, 443, 488
Bourbon, 63, 80, 85, 115, 213, 285, 362, 368,
    439
  *see also* individual *family members.*
  Family Compact, 96, 98

591

## Index

Bourbon (cont.)
reformers, 86–90, 305, 362, 365, 367, 371
reforms, 63, 67, 85, 89, 90, 91–2, 130–1,
142, 179, 183–4, 227, 285, 329, 352–5,
367–8, 376, 455
Spanish, 65, 176, 186
Boves, José Tomás, 39, 241, 242–3, 244, 247
Boyacá, 74, 423
Boyer, Jean-Pierre, 388, 541
Braganzas, 404, 431, 432–4, 436, 443, 453, 455,
489
Brazil, 404–6, 431–47, 449, 454–7, 477–82,
489, 503–5, 512–14, 546, 584–8
1807–1816, 496–8
1815–1824, 498–506
1824–1831, 509–18
and independence of Spanish America,
547–66
and Robespierre, 389–91
at independence, 507–9
building new institutions, 496–519
circulation of people, 487–9
codes of life at court, 130, 141, 330, 332, 484
conservative tracks toward independence,
474–95
Constituent Assembly, 532, 563
Constitution, 16, 457, 460
elites, 434, 437, 493, 539
Empire, 272, 391, 415, 537, 560, 562,
564–5, 587
Franco-British War and escape of royal
family, 476–8
housing the court in the Tropics, 481–4
impact on Spanish America, 563–6
independence, 443, 445–7, 456, 494, 504,
508, 522–5, 545, 565–6, 569–73, 585–6
and Angola, 567–88
and classes of color, 538–46
conservative bias, 476
Indian participation, 534–7
popular participation, 520–46
proclamation, 520
recognition, 444, 512
slave participation, 530–4
institutional shifts in Luso-Brazilian
empire, 489–90
newspapers, 43–4, 190, 206, 232, 255–8,
319, 534, 549, 565–6, 567, 573, 583–4
political rupture with Portugal, 32, 37, 78,
204, 233, 235, 237, 472, 492–3, 571
ports, 81, 84–6, 173, 216, 319, 402, 411,
456, 477–8, 480, 551, 587
provinces, 490, 522, 526, 556, 559, 562,
570, 585

relationship with Portugal and Africa, 449
royal family on the run, 478–81
slave trade, 86–8, 100–1, 318–19, 383–5,
390, 412–16, 433, 446–7, 513–16
south-central, 487, 491
Southern, 446, 556
Brazilian Party, 434, 437, 442, 456, 480, 491,
493, 539, 543, 587
Brazilians, 443–4, 474–5, 492, 494–5, 510–11,
521–2, 523, 538, 542–4, 561
Breña, Roberto, 7, 102
Bridge of Calderón, 162
Brion, Luis, 245
*Bristol Mercury*, 415
Britain, 28, 47–50, 79–80, 82–3, 96–7, 148,
399, 400, 411–14, 476–7, 512–13
1808–1814, 404–9
1814–1824, 409–16
and Latin American independence, 399–426
armies, 21, 30, 40, 124
background and early emancipation
schemes, 399–404
Bill of Rights, 113, 265
client states, 512
colonies, 44, 400, 548
diplomats, 33, 133, 134, 147, 263, 267, 451,
463, 480, 487, 512
education and culture, 19, 23, 113, 309,
314–15, 317, 363–5, 372, 420, 423–4
government, 7, 385, 401, 403, 406–7, 412,
415–16, 425
invasions, 206, 258, 401–4
miners, merchants, and money in the
1820s, 88–9, 154–6, 416
politicians, 16, 23, 30, 112, 210, 216–17,
223, 345, 350, 399, 407, 409–10, 412
Royal Navy, 49, 400–1, 406, 415, 425,
481
support, 247, 315, 425, 512, 514–15
British and Foreign Bible Society (BFBS),
206, 258, 399, 401–4, 407, 412, 421–2
British and Foreign School Society *see* BFSS, 421
British Arch, 418
British Empire, 97, 154, 402, 433
British West Indies, 84, 416
Brown, Howard, 20, 30
Brown, Matthew, 352, 354
Bruce, Miguel, 540
Buenos Aires, 205–12, 214–21, 253–62,
264–6, 268–76, 378–9, 401–4, 551–5
capture from British troops, 257
government, 221, 379, 553, 560
junta of, 210, 261, 289
bureaucrats, 66, 90, 95–6

592

## Index

Burgos, Francisco J. de, 317
Bustamante, Carlos María, 413
Bustamante, José de, 176, 191–201
Butterwick-Pawlikowski, Richard, 9

*cabildo abierto*, 208, 256, 258
*cabildos*, 207, 253, 255–8
Cabildos, Santiago, 208
cabinets, 510–11
Caboclos, 534, 537
Cabrera de Nevares, Miguel, 146
cacao, 232, 500, 513
caciques, 35, 92, 291–2, 359
Cadalso, José, 363
Cádiz, 14–16, 102–3, 105–11, 113–15,
    119–23, 126–30, 232–3, 282–4,
    295–6, 336–8
  Constitution, 104–6, 113–16, 119–20,
    126–7, 134, 147, 167, 282–4, 288–9,
    299, 331–2, 440–1, 456, 502, 556
  Cortes 7, 116–18, 120–2, 135–8, 144–6,
    150–3, 490–2, 503–4, 558–9 *see*
    Cortes, of Cádiz
Cairu, viscount, 520–1, 544–5
California, 400, 416
Callao, 2, 301
Calleja, Félix María, 158–68, 293, 296
Cametá, 537, 543–4
Campeche, 84, 87, 156, 305
Campillo y Cosio, José del, 89–90
Campo Grande, 460
Campomanes, Pedro Rodríguez de, 342,
    356, 369
Canarians, 241–2
Canary Islands, 87, 332
Cancelada, Juan López, 391
Caneca, Frei, 488, 563
Canga-Argüelles, José, 128
Canning, George, 399, 411–13, 415
cannons, 163, 172–4, 481
*capelas*, 452
captaincies general, 91, 173, 229, 236, 240,
    289, 307, 491, 574, 583
captives, 87–8, 357, 497, 500, 513, 576,
    579
captivity, 136, 236, 256, 343, 436
Capuchins, 483
Carabobo, 242, 300
Caracas, 11, 110, 117, 176, 228–9, 231,
    233–42, 289–90, 406–8
Carache, 241
careers, 234, 325, 515, 529, 541
Caribbean New Granada, 231, 239–41, 247
  population, 231

Caribbean South America, 45, 228–51, 287
  Caribbean connections, 244–9
  demographics, 229–35
  military strategies, 240–4, 302, 355
  political experiments, 229, 235–40, 325–7,
    345, 346, 348
Carlo Alberto, 147
Carlo Felice, 147–8
Carlos II, 305
Carlos III, 63, 83–4, 88, 91, 94, 97, 184, 210
Carlos IV, 47, 63, 97–9, 104–5, 154–5, 185–6,
    206, 310, 314, 357
Carlota, 187, 256, 481, 552
Carmelites, 482
Carneiro, Manuel Borges, 461
carrera de Indias, 81
Carrera, José Miguel, 213–17
Carta, 444–5, 460
Cartagena, 83–4, 228–31, 233–41, 243–9, 250,
    285, 287, 289–90, 305, 377–8
  exiles, 124–5, 150–3, 244–6, 271, 272, 440,
    469, 498, 499, 584
  independent, 239, 245, 249
  siege, 228, 243, 245
Carvalho Paes de Andrade, Manuel de, 540
Carvalho, Ezequiel, 571, 580
Carvalho, Manuel de, 447–8, 456
*castas*, 180, 298, 365, 369–70, 391
Castelli, Juan José, 261, 402–3
Castelo Branco, Nicolau de Abreu, 570, 576,
    586
Castlereagh, Lord, 399, 409, 411
Catalonia, 86, 140, 142
Catholic Church *see* Church, 7
Catholic religion, 6–9, 75, 104, 113, 136, 170,
    308, 338, 350
cattle, 167, 218, 267–9, 577
*caudillismo*, 351, 358
caudillos, 26, 39, 242, 354, 358–9, 365,
    371
Cavalcante e Souza, Agostinho, 488
Cavalcante, Agostinho Bezerra, 540–1
cavalry, 74, 162–3, 165
Cavero, Ignacio, 248
Cayenne, 551
Ceará, 527–8, 534–6, 540
cemeteries, 168, 423, 484
censorship, 7, 201, 314, 321, 451, 455, 557
Central America, 75–6, 176–204
  1750–1796, 179–85
  1796–1811, 185–91
  1811–1814, 191–9
  1814–1818, 199–200
  1818–1821, 200–2

593

*Index*

Central American Federal Republic, 345
Central Americans, 19, 97, 177, 179–84, 188,
  189–90, 198–9, 202–3, 286
central junta, 65–7, 232, 235, 258
centralism, 10, 265, 271, 273, 346
Césaire, Aimé, 375
Chacabuco, 219
Chaco, 253, 254
Chamber of Deputies, 493, 509–10
Chamber of Peers, 469, 472
Chambers, Sarah, 352, 354, 358, 367
chaos, 10, 167, 305, 319, 431
Charcas, 92–3, 210, 212, 285, 358, 404
charters, 197, 202, 283–4, 298, 330, 346, 457,
  460, 465–6, 470–1
Chaves, María Eugenia, 387
Chávez, Hugo, 54
Chayanta, 92–4
Chiapas, 179, 184
Chihuahua, 163, 420
Chilavert brothers, 408
children, 4, 23, 26, 306, 309, 318, 369–70,
  414, 421, 424
Chile, 72–5, 211–25, 286–7, 293–4, 384–5,
  403–4, 408–9, 416–18
  captaincy general, 91, 382
  reconquest, 69, 75, 160, 216–19, 220, 256, 296
  treasury, 216
Chilean émigrés, 215, 219
Chilean politics, 212–13, 218
Chilean revolutionaries, 212, 213–14, 215
Chileans, 210, 214, 218–20, 225, 418
Chiloé, 213, 417
Chirino, José Leonardo, 312
Christophe, Henri, 314, 381, 392, 395,
  414–15, 488
Church, 107, 113, 118, 124–5, 129, 136, 138,
  182, 190, 291
Cisneros, Baltasar de, 258
Cisplatine Province, 557, 560
citizenship, 12, 132–3, 233–4, 236–7, 283–4,
  317, 326–7, 334, 335, 336, 337, 338,
  390–1, 544
  active, 12, 274, 362, 374, 381, 395, 460, 467
  concept, 333–8
city councils, 68, 176, 253, 540, 580
Ciudad Real, 181, 184, 187
civil equality, 42, 341, 462
civil liberty, 114, 341, 386
civil rights, 58, 60, 132, 194, 337
civil wars, 137–8, 140, 143, 154, 210–11,
  213–14, 444, 445, 564–5
  Mexico, 28–9, 75–6, 88–9, 157–68, 172–3,
  318–19, 332, 384, 412–14, 419–20

Southern Cone, 210–15
Spain, 138–42
civilians, 125, 130, 160, 161, 163, 167, 242–3,
  244
Clarkson, Thomas, 414
classes, 158, 166, 279, 281, 324, 461–3, 467–8,
  494–5, 538, 540, 542–4
  lower, 71–2, 194, 229, 310, 489, 539–40
  middle, 127, 131, 134, 418, 453, 462–3,
  467–8
  of color, 520, 525, 538–46
  popular, 20, 263, 274, 294, 295, 299,
  520–2, 524
  privileged, 38, 461–3, 464, 470
  upper, 33, 70, 76, 443, 476, 489, 495
Clemente Pereira, Jose, 558
clergy, 7, 30, 33, 159, 282, 290–1, 452, 465, 586
  high, 157, 461, 463
  regular, 129, 452, 459, 470
  secular, 466–7, 469, 471
clergymen, 118, 129, 136, 157–8, 163, 471
client states of Britain, 512
climate, 90, 365, 369
clubs, political, 12, 47, 131, 135
Coahuila, 163, 169
coca, 88
Cochrane, Lord, 221, 533, 544
codes, 130, 141, 330, 332, 484
Código Carolino, 376
coffee, 500, 513, 551
Coimbra, 430, 457, 461, 476, 479
Colegio de San José de la Habana, 309
Collins, Juan Bautista, 308
Colombia, 143–5, 146, 225, 229, 231, 313,
  317, 318, 346, 558
  Greater *see* Gran Colombia, 74
colonialism, 57, 395, 449, 481, 494–5
color, 42, 101, 231, 306, 308–10, 320–2,
  379–80, 523–5, 529–30, 538–42 *see*
  *also classes, of color*
Colored American, 322
Comayagua, 181, 184
commanders, 256, 261, 464–5, 471, 486, 570,
  576–7, 580
  *see also individual names.*
  royalist, 16, 77, 162, 214, 241–2, 256, 293,
  296, 299
communities, 35, 40, 92–3, 261, 275, 279,
  283, 291, 294, 330
  Indigenous, 92, 95–6, 154, 185, 252, 260,
  267, 275, 291, 338
compensation, 384, 456, 471–2, 493, 534
competition, 181, 182, 274, 400, 411, 476
composite monarchy, 343, 441

594

*comuneros*, 136, 137, 149, 340
Concepción, 211, 219, 379
Concha, Manuel de la, 169
Condorcanqui, José Gabriel, 94
Confederação do Equador, 381, 488, 523, 527, 534–6, 540, 546, 573, 584
confederations, 148, 265–6, 272–3, 345, 381, 447–8, 509, 517
Congress of Verona, 142, 148
Congress of Vienna, 124, 271, 513–14, 554
congress, Sovereign, 460, 563
conscription, 34, 139, 384
consensus, 34, 36, 72, 177, 204
conservatism, 277, 475, 492
conservatives, 37, 75, 118, 135, 492
conspiracies, 124–6, 138, 140, 358, 360, 379–80, 382–3, 437, 438–9, 447
conspirators, 45, 134, 140, 147, 380, 439
constituent assemblies, 501–10, 514, 517, 518, 526, 528, 539, 556–8, 559
Constituent Cortes, 556–8
Constitutional Charter, 138, 197, 330, 457, 460, 466, 470–1
constitutional experiments, 198–9, 288–9, 326, 349
constitutional liberalism, 556–7
constitutional monarch, 124, 439, 441, 503
constitutional monarchy, 33–4, 119, 123, 139, 143, 282, 284, 504, 505, 518
constitutional reforms, 138, 197
constitutional regime, 128, 130–1, 133, 135–6, 138, 146–7, 153, 526, 527, 531
constitutional rule, 298–9
constitutional Spain, 134
as sanctuary for European liberals, 150–3
constitutional triennium *see Trienio*, 34
constitutionalism, 197, 203, 347, 445, 504, 573, 575, 583
liberal, 130, 190–1, 287, 290, 500, 567, 588
slave, 525
constitutions, 112–14, 119–22, 126–35, 139–43, 147–50, 290–1, 295–6, 298–9, 329, 330, 331, 332, 333, 335, 336, 337, 338, 490–1, 508–10
and war, 287–90
Cádiz, 104–6, 113–16, 119–20, 126–7, 167, 282–4, 288–9, 331–2, 440–1
concept, 329–33
French, 15, 113
liberal, 59, 68, 189, 197, 284, 292, 298, 313, 316
new, 10, 43, 313, 331, 349, 386, 443–4, 509, 559, 583
written, 330, 333, 440, 443, 456–8

containment, 503, 508, 517
continuities, 107, 226, 276, 351, 354, 473, 547–8
contraband, 80, 83, 86–8, 186
control, royalist, 239, 240, 243, 246, 294
convents, 154, 163, 352, 372, 483
Coquimbo, 216, 219
Coram, Robert, 25
Cordillera, 216–17, 219
Córdoba, 171, 258, 269, 401
Cornish, Reverend S.E., 323, 416
Coro, 228, 232, 233–4, 238, 312, 376, 394
Corrêa de Castro, Manoel Patrício, 581
*corregidor*, 92–4
Correio Brasiliense, 408, 552, 565
Correo del Orinoco, 565
Corrientes, 262, 265
corruption, 23, 93, 351, 370, 420
Cortes, 105–12, 127–31
Constituent, 556–8
Lisbon, 490, 491, 501, 527, 581, 585
of Cádiz, 14, 102–23, 128, 282–3, 385
from Atlantic perspective, 102–4
Spanish American deputies, 106, 109–10, 116, 118
swearing in of deputies, 107
Portuguese, 134, 509, 581
corvée, 45, 465
Costa Rica, 179, 305
costs, 117, 118, 192, 432, 438, 491, 517
cotton, 90, 417, 432, 500, 513, 551
Council of Regency, 67, 188, 232, 261
Council of State, 144–5, 199, 454, 510
councilors, 472, 498, 504–5
councils
city, 68, 253, 540, 580
town, 119, 155, 181, 189, 194, 207, 344
counterinsurgency, 159, 195, 200, 293
counterrevolution, 21, 31, 36–40, 132, 141, 148, 152, 211, 227, 262, 463, 522
counterrevolutionaries, 37, 39, 131, 137, 140, 152, 170
counterrevolutionary armies, 132, 148, 211, 262
coups, 47, 125, 137, 140, 155–6, 171, 372, 388, 491, 495
Court of Mixed Commission, 415
court of Rio, 474–6, 478, 490, 526, 549, 553
codes of life, 484–6
creole juntas, 66, 183, 185–6, 188–90, 191, 193, 196–7, 199–200, 203, 236, 240, 406

595

## Index

creoles, 64–72, 73, 75–6, 94–6, 158–9, 181, 182, 188–94, 364, 376
  autonomy in Central America, 200–2
  elites, 183, 185–6, 188–90, 191, 193, 196–7, 199–200, 203, 236, 240
  establishment, 181, 187, 195, 200–1
  loyalty, 155–6, 188–9, 192–4, 195, 197–8, 278, 280–1, 284–8, 291–2, 536
crimes, 38, 320, 355–6, 361, 479, 570
*crisis hispánica*, 108, 110, 119
Crosbie, John and Joseph, 417
Cruz, José de la, 169
Cruz, Luis de la, 221, 224
Cuautla, 163–6, 168–9
Cuba, 98–101, 174, 244–7, 286–7, 300–1, 307–8, 312–19, 321–4, 415–16
  planters, 7, 28, 312–13, 319, 393, 514, 516
Cuban officials, 305, 309, 312–13, 315, 319
Cuban slaves, 100, 307
Cubans, 83, 99, 100, 317, 319
Cúcuta, 346, 387, 414
Cuenca, 285
Cumaná, 238, 240–3, 309
Cundinamarca, 288, 330, 336
Curaçao, 234, 244–6
Cuyo, province, 215–16, 218
Cuzco, 73, 94–5, 222, 224, 255, 271

da Costa, Francisco Antônio, 546
da Costa, Hipólito José, 408–9, 550
da Costa, João Maciel, 390
da Silva Lisboa, José, 390, 520
Dade Massacre, 322
Dávila, José, 169
Davis, John A., 12, 46
Davison, H.W., 321, 323
Davison, Jorge, 321–3
de Abreu de Mello e Alvim, Manoel, 579
de la Cruz, José, 169
de Montigny, Grandjean, 487
de Pradt, baron, 341, 389, 558
de Sartiges, viscount, 366
de Sousa Coutinho, Rodrigo, 451, 477, 553
Debret, Jean-Baptiste, 487
debts, 154, 223, 419, 469, 472
declarations of independence, 5, 60, 68, 110, 210, 225, 238, 263–4, 271, 330
decrees, 22–4, 113, 121, 423, 464–5, 471, 482, 490, 557, 558–9
Defoe, Daniel, 400
delegates, 12, 16–18, 222, 334, 336, 491, 526
demagogues, 37, 237
democracy, 2, 15–21, 31, 37, 50, 326, 340, 378
  representative, 16–18

democratic revolution, 1, 6
denunciations, 241, 262, 528, 533
deputies, 106–16, 144–7, 264–5, 390, 458–65, 509–11, 558–9
  elected, 109, 111, 460, 466, 526, 558
  peninsular, 104, 108–9, 112, 116, 118, 120–2, 189, 191, 200, 330–2
  Spanish American, 106, 109–10, 116, 118
  substitute, 109
desertion, 40, 174, 213–15, 243, 480
despotism, 115, 341
Dessalines, Jean-Jacques, 9, 32, 380, 391
destabilization, 33, 138, 279, 498, 501, 518, 519
diamonds, 432, 502
Diario de la Habana, 309, 316, 321
Dias, Cristovão Avelino, 587
dictatorship, military, 167–8
dignity, 166, 341, 356, 480
Diniz, Domingos Pereira, 567–81, 584, 586–8
diplomacy, 512, 515
diplomatic relations, 142, 148, 560, 562–3
diplomats, 33, 133, 134, 147, 263, 267, 451, 463, 480, 487, 512
diputaciones provinciales, 119
Directory, 31, 57, 383, 477
discontent, 47, 65, 92, 117, 127, 155, 430, 437, 439, 447–8
disease, 243, 304, 400
dissent, 34, 177, 404, 438–9, 440
diversity, 290, 326, 347, 460, 543
Dolores, 157, 160
dos Santos, marquis, 381, 527
Drescher, Seymour, 44, 49
drought, 139, 571
Dutch Republic, 11–13, 79–80

Earle, Rebecca, 243, 352–3, 367, 371
Echávarri, José Antonio de, 172–3
economic crisis, 134, 154, 170, 526, 560
economic elites, 170, 526
economic equality, 23–7
economic growth, 100, 255
economic power, 203, 210
economic prosperity, 432, 434, 554
economy, 139, 231, 237, 265, 267, 272–4, 318, 382, 432, 516
Ecuador, 77, 488
Edinburgh, 410, 412
editors, 369, 383, 391, 408, 468, 533, 550, 557
education, 19, 23, 113, 309, 314–15, 317, 363–5, 372, 420, 423–4
  mutual, 19, 421, 423–4
  national, 113
  public, 7, 113, 422–3

596

# Index

effeminacy, 355, 360–5, 479
eighteenth century, 62, 84–5, 86, 96, 181,
    361–2, 430–2, 446, 450–1, 530
*El Negrito*, 317
El Palmar conspiracy, 126
El Pardo Treaty, 476
El Salvador, 179, 184
Eldon, Lord, 412
elected deputies, 109, 111, 460, 466, 526,
    558
elections, 66–7, 68, 75, 106, 109, 121–2, 270,
    501–2, 556–7, 574–5
Elío, Javier, 139, 551
elites, 19–20, 32–3, 90–1, 181–3, 262–4,
    270–1, 494–5, 498–501, 514–15,
    517–18, 568, 571
  Benguela, 13, 568, 571, 574, 578, 587
  Brazilian, 443–4, 474–5, 492, 494–5,
    510–11, 521–2, 523, 538, 542–4, 561
  creole, 64–72, 73, 75–6, 94–6, 158–9, 181,
    182, 188–94, 364, 376
  divisions, 525
  economic, 170, 526
  enlightened, 327
  fears, 41–2, 47, 119, 387, 389, 395–6, 445,
    519, 538, 542, 543, 552–3, 564
  Guatemalan, 120–1, 176, 177, 185, 187,
    196, 198, 201, 202–3, 408
  local, 176–7, 193, 194, 481, 484, 489, 499,
    505, 508, 575
  political, 47, 207, 456
  provincial, 182, 184, 201, 203, 354, 443,
    506
  revolutionary, 19, 26, 30, 60
emancipation, 22, 27, 42, 44, 50, 314, 318,
    337, 341, 349
  political, 474–5, 487, 490, 492, 494, 572
émigrés
  Chilean, 215, 219
  patriotic, 245–6
  Portuguese, 153
emphyteusis, 452–3
empire of Brazil, 560, 562, 564–5, 587
enlightened absolutism, 62, 185, 190–1
Enlightenment, 4, 6, 11, 19, 317, 362–3,
    369–70, 451, 468, 475
  Spanish, 103, 114, 183
enslaved Africans, 49, 304, 319, 405, 415,
    432, 446, 571
enslaved people, 42, 252, 263, 275, 429
enslavement, 43, 313, 484, 577
entailed estates, 452–3, 464
entanglements, 58–60, 172, 550, 553–5, 563
Entre Ríos, 262, 265, 271, 272, 274

envoys, 248, 407, 412, 584
Equador, Confederação do, 381, 488, 523,
    527, 534–6, 540, 546, 573, 584
equal pay, 315
equal rights, 5, 22, 29, 66, 132, 189, 192, 261,
    337
equality, 24–6, 42, 45, 58–60, 67, 143, 145,
    380, 391–2, 545–6
  civil, 42, 341, 462
  economic, 23–7
  legal, 38, 233–4, 237, 238
  political, 112, 122
  racial, 45, 284, 317, 525
Escamilla, Juan Ortiz, 29, 38, 154
España, José María, 312
Espoz y Mina, Francisco, 125, 141, 149
Esquilache, marquis, 84
estates, entailed, 452–3, 464
ethnicities, 158, 279, 281, 291, 302, 308
*exaltados*, 130–8, 140–3, 146, 148–9, 151
exclusion, 236, 368, 388, 395, 463
executions, 29, 63, 155, 163, 168, 242–4, 245,
    262, 380, 383
executive powers, 138, 207, 448, 510, 515
exiles, 124–5, 150–3, 244–6, 271, 272, 440,
    469, 498, 499, 584
  Italian, 152
  political, 112, 122
expenses, 166, 192, 197, 221, 223, 333, 405,
    437, 504, 568
experiments, 226, 295, 310, 322, 325–7, 346,
    399
  constitutional, 198–9, 288–9, 326, 349
  republican, 47, 189, 228, 240, 325
exports, 431, 432, 446, 476, 500, 516
expulsion, 145, 255, 524, 529, 542, 554
Extraordinary Cortes, 106, 108, 113, 137,
    142, 489–90

Fagoaga, José María, 384
Fajardo, Manuel Palacio, 409
families, 22–3, 27, 30, 182, 188–9, 198,
    199–201, 306, 308, 371–3
farmers, 11, 14, 25, 154, 464–5, 468
fathers, 4, 97, 104, 306, 315, 357–8, 366, 486,
    504–5
fears, 41–2, 47, 119, 387, 389, 395–6, 445,
    519, 538, 542, 543, 552–3, 564
federalism, 119, 325, 326–7, 344–5, 347
  concept, 343–7
federalists, 10–11, 273, 345, 524
federalization, 343–4
federations, 76, 265, 345, 438
Feijoó, Father Benito Jerónimo, 362, 368–9

## Index

Fernando VII, 72, 103–5, 116, 124–5, 138–41, 148–50, 186–7, 207–10, 292–6, 316
  restoration and liberal opposition, 124–6, 176–8, 199–201, 202, 278, 279–80, 292, 295–8, 299, 391–2, 439
Ferrer, Ada, 99, 100
Ferrez, Zepherin, 487
feudalism, 27, 30, 45
Figueiredo de Melo, Pedro Américo, 520–1
first Spanish liberalism, 108, 112, 114–15, 120
fleets, 82, 89, 316, 405, 481
Flinter, George D., 301
Flón, Manuel de, 159
Flórez Estrada, Álvaro, 130, 334
Florida, 84, 97, 305, 307–8, 311, 314–15, 322, 560
Floridablanca, Conde Moñino de, 36, 97–8
*forais*, 452–3, 464–5, 471
forced labor, 434, 537
foreign trade, 84, 551, 575
foreigners, 9, 48, 79, 81, 86, 151, 328, 366, 390, 404
former slaves, 44, 99–100, 304, 308, 310–11, 313, 317, 376, 379
*foros*, 452–3
Forster, Georg, 25
fortresses, 164, 172, 173–5, 479
France, 36, 44–5, 59–64, 79–80, 98–9, 148–9, 382–4, 392–5, 468–70, 476–7
  armies, 44, 102–4, 106, 110, 124, 149–50, 430–1, 433, 439, 441
  colonies, 376–7, 382, 386, 389–91, 394
  constitutions, 15, 42, 113
  Convention, 44, 98, 385
  Directory, 31, 57, 383, 477
  Four Sergeants of La Rochelle, 139
  invasions, 46, 47, 66, 68, 232, 235, 277–8, 282, 285, 454, 456
    Portugal, 102, 313, 430, 454–6, 549
  Vendée, 28, 31, 36, 38, 47
Franklin, Benjamin, 342
free Blacks, 26, 294, 301, 307–8, 314, 315–17, 323, 374–6, 380
free people of African descent/origin, 229, 287, 317, 429
free people of color, 37, 42, 228, 231, 308, 313, 320, 432, 523–5 *see also classes, of color*
free trade, 70, 86, 186, 190, 201, 258, 405, 417–18
free-womb laws, 264, 275, 318, 324, 379, 384, 397
  Gran Colombia, 74, 77, 354, 377, 386–9, 413

freedmen, 381, 387, 390–1, 394–5, 460, 500, 533, 544
freedom, 39–40, 45–6, 58–9, 71–2, 234, 302–3, 339, 340, 385–6, 531, 536–7
  of opinion, 341
  of worship, 9, 333
  realm of, 50
Freemasonry, 136, 141, 408–9, 439, 456, 457
French agents, 33, 47, 187
French Antilles, 375, 377, 384, 394–5
French Caribbean, 100, 374–5, 378–9, 385
  revolutions, 380, 396
French Jacobins, 25, 139
French Republic, 46, 185, 311
French Revolution, 1, 3–4, 29, 41–2, 44–5, 47–8, 57–60, 62–3, 65, 130–1
French revolutionaries, 24, 27, 42, 50, 139, 349
French-Caribbean revolutions, 374–5, 380, 384, 389, 391–2, 396–8
Fronteira, marquis of, 457, 470
*fuero militar*, 306–7, 317

*Gaceta de Buenos Aires*, 385
*Gaceta de Guatemala*, 185
*Gaceta de Lima*, 370
*Gaceta de Madrid*, 143
*Gaceta de México*, 391
Gainot, Bernard, 29
Galiano, Antonio Alcalá, 130, 342
Galicia, 135–6, 169
Gallum, Ana, 309
Gálvez, Bernardo de, 97
Gálvez, José de, 97
Gamboa, Francisco Xavier de, 88
García de Toledo, José María, 237–8
García Rebollo, Ignacio, 169
García, Joaquín, 99, 310
Garibay, Pedro, 156
*Gazeta de Caracas*, 407
*Gazeta del Gobierno*, 565
*Gazeta do Rio de Janeiro*, 485, 552, 584
Geggus, David, 45, 312
gender, 281, 351–3, 356, 361, 368, 373, 509
Geneva, 41
geography, 179, 184, 253, 285, 295, 430
geopolitical literacy, 308, 319
George IV, 411–12
Gibbs, Wiiliam A., 322–3, 417
Gibraltar, 80, 83–97
Gil de Castro, José, 359
Goa, 430, 574
goals, political, 11, 71, 221, 229–30
Godoy, Manuel de, 63, 97–8, 154, 186

598

# Index

Goldschmidt & Company, 419
Gonçalves dos Santos, Luís, 482
Gonçalves Ledo, Joaquim, 558
González Bravo, Juan Gualberto, 200
Gonzalez, José Caridad, 312
goods, 36, 78, 81, 84, 92, 98, 157, 173, 452–3, 470
Görres, Joseph, 50
governance, 68, 97, 423, 476, 526
governing juntas, 69, 187–8, 233, 526, 552, 583
governors, 215–16, 218, 222, 269–70, 481, 574, 576, 579–80, 583, 586–7
gradualism, Thermidorian, 383–4
Grafton Street Symposium, 406, 410
Graham, María, 417
Gran Colombia,
   free-womb laws, 386–8
Gran Oriente Americana, 408
Gran Reunión Americana, 408
Granada, 178, 195, 197, 207
grandeeship, 454, 461, 463, 466, 469, 472
Great Britain *see* Britain, 28
Greater Caribbean, 3, 248
Greater Colombia *see* Gran Colombia, 74
Green, Jacob, 25
Grégoire, Abbé Henri, 392–3
grievances, 13, 30, 38, 92, 93, 192, 193, 202
Grimaldi, marquis, 84
Grito do Ipiranga, 520–3, 536
Guadalajara, 159, 161–2, 170
Guadalupes, Los, 408
Guadeloupe, 45, 374, 376, 382–3, 396, 397
Gual, Manuel, 312, 383
Guanajuato, 157, 159, 162–4, 169, 293, 420
Guaraní, 254
Guatemala, 168
Guatemala City, 176, 178, 181–4, 188–9, 191–201, 203
Guatemala, oligarchy, 189–91, 196–200, 203
Guatemalan elite, 202–3
Guayana, 234, 238, 242
Guayaquil, 14, 37, 76, 88, 224
Güemes, Martin Miguel de, 269, 270, 272
Guerrero, Vicente, 299, 324, 388
guerrillas, 38, 104, 142, 211, 267, 269, 293–4
Guimarães, Manoel Antonio da Costa, 574
Guiror, Manuel de, 92
Guitán, Alejandro Álvarez, 169
Guridi y Alcocer, José Miguel, 111, 118, 346
Gutiérrez, Daniel, 246, 384
Gutiérrez, Nicolás, 169

Habsburgs, 114–15
Haiti, 43–5, 228, 244–9, 377–8, 381, 385–9, 393, 540–1
   king of, 43, 314, 381, 541
Haitian Republic, 45, 246, 388
Haitian Revolution, 3, 28, 39, 42, 44–5, 495, 497, 524–5, 541, 543
*haitianismo*, 396, 518
Hall, Francis, 423
Hamel, Joseph, 422
hard labor, 314, 387
harmony, 192, 379, 462, 510, 550
Havana, 82–4, 156, 174, 307–9, 313, 314, 316–17, 319–20, 322–3, 332
Helvetic Republic, 6, 8, 46
Henri Christophe, King, 385, 541
Henriques regiments, 530, 540–2, 546
heterogeneity, 55–6, 58, 62, 291
Hidalgo Revolt, 176, 190, 286, 293
Hidalgo y Costilla, Miguel, 117, 157, 160
hidalgos, 8, 14, 70, 161–3, 179
hierarchy, 27, 171, 471, 484, 499, 518
high clergy, 157, 461, 463
high nobility, 452, 454, 461, 463
High Peru, 72, 76
Hispanic liberalisms *see* Spanish
   liberalism, 111, 282, 289, 338, 342, 348
Hispanic revolutions, 282–4, 289, 338, 342, 348
Hispaniola, 63, 305
*historia patria*, 53
historic constitution, 114
historic nationalism, 114–15
historicism, nationalist, 115
historiography, 54–9, 68, 120, 288, 339, 346, 352, 358, 361
   revisionist, 54–5, 57
Holguín, 314
Holy Alliance, 104, 116, 173, 274, 300, 411, 440, 441, 556, 562
homes, 3–4, 45, 50, 80, 84, 320–1, 323, 527–8, 574, 580
homosexuality, 352, 360–1, 364, 373
Honduras, 87, 178, 179, 184, 193–4
honor, 76, 311, 315, 322, 353–4, 359, 361, 480, 481, 485–6
hospitals, 154, 174, 484
households, 23, 238, 367, 373, 461
houses, 30, 83, 320, 370, 381, 448, 453–4, 482–3, 486, 509–10
Huanta, 301
Hungary, 42

599

# Index

Idade do Ouro do Brasil, 552
ideas
  political, 13, 58, 374, 430, 437, 527, 545
  revolutionary, 42, 101, 140, 203, 498, 501
identities, 69, 284, 287, 353, 361–2, 523, 548
ideologies, 10, 29, 36, 40, 45, 338, 358, 394, 545
Iguala, Plan of, 33, 75, 166, 168–71, 202, 299, 384
illiteracy, 132, 309, 394, 460, 524 *see also*
  *literacy*
imperial crisis, 176, 179, 197, 210, 226, 252,
  256, 287, 326, 327
  Central America, 185–91
  South American reactions, 206–10
imports, 81, 86, 122, 239, 476, 523
imprisonment, 155, 192, 195, 378, 408
incomes, 17–18, 125, 186, 453, 460, 495
Inconfidência Mineira, 430, 450, 495
independence
  *see also* Introductory Note.
  Brazil 21 *see* Brazil, independence.
  declarations, 5, 60, 210
  movements, 41, 67, 69, 72–5, 76, 108, 214,
    316, 436, 442
  political, 106, 119, 181, 201, 203, 493
  process, 32–3, 44, 48, 56, 143, 205, 251,
    291, 299, 340, 489, 547
  total, 233, 236–7, 240, 259
  wars, 54–6, 228–9, 243–4, 249–50, 270,
    272–3, 278, 280, 281, 292–3
independentists, 234, 267, 272
Indians, 33–5, 94–5, 231, 264, 266, 289–90,
  294, 301–2, 529–30, 535, 536, 537
  participation in Brazilian independence,
    534–7
  villages, 13, 35, 264, 266, 275, 293–4, 465,
    525, 535–6, 559, 578
Indigenous communities, 92, 95–6, 154, 185,
  252, 260, 267, 275, 291, 338
Indigenous groups, 40, 64, 71, 253, 261, 275
Indigenous people/populations, 89, 92, 94,
  229–30, 283, 286, 294, 300, 301–2,
  534–5
individual liberty, 112–13, 122
inequality, 8, 23, 45, 351, 367
  *see also* equality
  juridical, 8, 35, 275
Infante, Joaquín, 557–8
Inquisition, 37, 72, 98, 107, 113, 125, 127,
  299, 356, 361
insubordination, 93, 465, 580
insurgency, 145, 168, 292–3, 295–9, 357–8, 537
insurgent armies, 160–1, 163, 165, 195
insurgents, 142, 144, 160–5, 167, 170–1,
  241–2, 247–8, 284, 292–3, 298–9

insurrection, 4, 41, 47, 134, 137, 157, 158–60,
  377, 379, 382
integrated South Atlantic, 571–88
intellectuals, 23, 45, 152, 301, 329, 345, 375,
  475, 492
intendants, 91, 95, 157–9, 184, 193
Internal Provinces, 159, 169
international dimension of revolutions,
  40–50
interpretations, Spanish Empire, 54–60
intervention,
  Austrian, 147–8, 152
invaders, French, 38, 46, 149, 232, 357, 359,
  440
invasions
  British, 97, 154, 402, 433
  Napoleonic/French, 42, 46, 47, 66, 67,
    232, 235, 277–8, 282, 285, 454–6
Ireland, 6, 28–9, 49
Irisarri, Antonio José de, 409, 417
Isla de Sacrificios, 174
Isla del Carmen, 169
isthmus, 176–82, 184–5, 189–90, 193–202,
  305
Italy, 12, 26, 46, 80, 104, 148, 152
Iturbide, Agustín de, 33, 75–6, 166, 169–73,
  177, 202, 293, 299, 419–21, 563
Iturrigaray, José de, 155–6
Ixtlahuaca, 169

Jabat, Juan Gabriel de, 156
Jacobinism, 383, 396
Jacobins, 19, 25, 48, 139, 409, 467
Jalisco, 420
Jamaica, 84, 228, 244–9, 321, 323, 395
Jáuregui, Manuel Francisco de, 155
Jerez, Bishop García, 194
Jesuit Missions, former, 255
Jews, 7, 8, 467
João VI, 135, 457, 459, 466, 498, 502, 524,
  526, 556–8, 561
João, Dom, 436, 438–40, 442, 478–82,
  485–91, 496–7, 503, 553
journalists, 120, 131, 147, 328, 338, 348, 440,
  541
Jovellanos, Gaspar Melchor de, 114–15,
  329–30, 342
Junín, 15, 225
juntas, 65–6, 68–9, 71–3, 155–6, 207–9, 233,
  236–7, 257–61, 287–90, 574–5
  Buenos Aires, 210, 261, 289
  Caracas, 117, 238
  central, 105–6, 117, 121, 187, 188, 279,
    343

600

## Index

creole, 66, 406
  governing, 69, 187–8, 233, 526, 552, 583
  local, 68, 257
  provisional, 155, 316, 543, 567, 570, 574–5, 581–4, 588
  Santa Fe, 110, 117, 265, 271, 274, 295
juridical inequality, 35, 275
justice, 1, 8, 22, 44, 46, 93, 116, 223, 538, 541

Katari, Tomás, 92–3
kings *see individual ruler names*, 105
Kingsley, Anna Madgigine Jai, 309
Kongo, 35, 43, 314, 531, 545
Kramer, Lloyd, 23
Kwass, Michael, 12

La Aurora de Matanzas, 319
La Bisbal, Count, 126, 149
La Coruña, 125–6
La Guaira, 232, 241, 376, 382, 396
La Paz, 29, 95, 255, 257, 261
La Pola, 372
La Serna, José, 222, 224
La Victoria, 242
Labatut, Pierre, 239, 241, 533–4, 538
labor, 90, 238, 267, 318, 320, 363, 513
laborers, 158, 255, 266, 269, 434
ladinos, 180–1, 185, 203
Lafayette, Marquis of, 139
Lamport, William, 400
Lancaster, Joseph, 19, 407, 421, 424
Lancasterian schools, 415, 421–5
Larrazábal, Dr. Antonio de, 118, 189
Las Cabezas de San Juan, 124
Lautaro Lodge, 214, 219, 220, 264, 265, 267–8, 270, 408
Lavradio, count of, 468, 470
lawyers, 39, 68, 129, 181, 354, 356, 457, 541
Lee, Wayne, 30
legal equality, 37, 233–4, 237, 238
legislators, 7, 12, 20, 24, 333, 387
legitimacy, 67–8, 69, 122, 155–6, 188, 206–7, 225, 227, 284, 504–5
  political, 122
Leleux, Pierre Antonine, 248
Lemaur, Francisco, 172–4
León, 169, 178, 181, 184, 193–4, 317
Leopoldina, 511
Lequerica, José Mejía, 111, 118
Les Cayes, 246, 248
liberal constitutionalism, 190–1, 500
liberal constitutions, 59, 68, 189, 197, 284, 290, 292, 298, 313, 316

liberal discourse, 119, 132, 280, 462, 464, 468
liberal opposition, 33, 152, 445, 510, 516–17, 519
  and restoration of Fernando VII, 124–6
liberal party, 338, 341, 463
liberal reforms, 130, 287, 290, 567, 588
liberal revolution, 77, 302, 469, 490, 567–8, 575, 581–2
  Spanish, 102–23, 134, 147
liberalism, 130, 278, 279, 282, 290–1, 295, 326–7, 338, 339, 340, 341, 461–2, 472–3
  and royalism, 279–92
  concept, 338–43
  constitutional, 556–7
  Portuguese, 135, 455, 472
  revolutionary, 333, 499
  Spanish, 111, 139, 145, 342, 455, 501
    first, 108, 112, 114–15, 120
liberality, 340, 485
liberals, 104–5, 118–20, 124–5, 127–9, 135–7, 139, 148–50, 338–9, 461–2, 466–7
  European, 147, 150–1
  peninsular, 116, 119
  Portuguese, 134, 148, 442, 445, 457
Liberating Army, 221, 222–4
liberation, 41, 74, 149, 358, 460
liberators, 47, 72, 76–7, 179, 217, 273, 317, 320, 372, 421
liberty, 2–3, 11, 36–7, 42–5, 48, 110, 112, 114–15, 312–13, 545
  individual, 112–13, 122
  recovered, 114
Lima, 73, 205, 206, 209–12, 219, 222, 224, 364–5, 370–2, 583–4
Liniers, Santiago, 64, 256–8, 551
Linton, Marisa, 29
Lisboa, João Soares, 563
Lisbon, 431, 439, 441–3, 453–4, 456–60, 472, 491, 504–5, 573–5, 579–83
  Cortes, 490, 491, 501, 527, 581, 585
literacy, 308
  geopolitical, 308, 319
Llano, Ciriaco de, 169
loans, 270, 416–19
local authorities, 69, 265, 314, 336, 394, 537, 554
local elites, 176–7, 193, 194, 442, 481, 484, 489, 499, 505, 508, 575
local officials, 92, 524, 531–2, 536
local populations, 149, 255, 259, 293–4, 297, 588
local power, 345, 499, 530, 542–3
London, 7, 384–6, 392, 402, 406–10, 412, 417–26, 456, 463
López de Santa Anna, Antonio, 424

# Index

López, Jorge, 320, 323
Louis XVI, 32, 63, 98, 155
Louis XVIII, 139, 141, 148
Louverture, Toussaint, 9, 100, 310–11, 377, 382, 392, 395–6
Lovejoy, Paul, 35
lower classes, 71–2, 194, 229, 310, 489, 539–40
loyalists, 14, 34, 40, 190, 203, 261–2, 267, 269–70, 272, 276
loyalty, 155–6, 188–9, 192–4, 195, 197–8, 278, 280–1, 284–8, 291–2, 536
Luanda, 13, 567–8, 571–2, 575–80, 582–4, 587–8
  authorities, 571–3, 584
  officials, 571–3, 576, 580, 583, 586
Luna Pizarro, Arequipan Francisco-Xavier, 345
lusophobia, 448, 518, 543–4

Mably, Gabriel Bonnot de, 48, 342
Macha, 92–3
Madeira de Melo, Luiz Inácio, 529
Maipú, battle of, 220, 270
*Malagueta, A,* 573
Mamatoco, 302
manifestos, 314, 359, 492, 545, 552, 559
Mântua, Medeiros, 464
manumission, 304, 318, 385, 448, 500, 530
Maracaibo, 228, 233–4, 238–9, 242, 285, 377
Marajó island, 531
Maranhão, 443, 523, 526–7, 530, 532–4, 536, 540, 542–4, 560, 583
Marcantoni, Marco, 248
Maria da Glória, Princess, 493
María Luisa, Queen, 97–8
Maria, Dona, 444–5
*maricones,* 364–5
Mariño, Santiago, 241–2, 245
Marion, Ignace, 248
markets, 79, 81, 84, 89, 90, 415, 417, 446
maroons, 39, 306, 532
Marquese, Rafael, 396, 544
Márquez, Remigio, 245
martial law, 167, 544
Martín, Juan, 214, 217, 359
Martínez Marina, Francisco, 115, 329
Martínez, María Elena, 361
Martinique, 40, 395
Martins, Domingos José, 555
masculinities, 353–4, 360–1, 365–6, 373
masses, urban, 19, 71, 201, 204, 500
masters, 21, 28, 266, 268, 318, 384, 394, 447, 487, 531–4

Matanzas, 319–23
Mato Grosso, 550, 562
Maturín, 241–3
Mawe, John, 406
May Revolution of 1810, 48, 418
McFarlane, Anthony, 20, 231
Medellín, 44, 386, 395
Medina, Manuel, 307
Mello, Evaldo Cabral de, 524
Mello, Miguel Antonio de, 576
Méndez, Luis López, 407, 408, 410
Mendoza, 215–18, 219, 265, 270, 379, 394, 425
merchants, 13, 80, 411–12, 418–19, 461–3, 499, 514, 516, 574, 576, 578, 587
  Benguela, 574, 578, 587
Mercurio Peruano, 73, 364
Mercurio Venezolano, 383
merit, 205, 226, 261, 317, 355, 588
mestizos, 88, 94, 166, 229, 254, 269, 337, 378, 382, 391
Metapán, 193
Mexican Empire, 170–2, 173, 300, 561
Mexicans, 75, 172, 174–5, 384
Mexico, 28–9, 75–6, 88–9, 157–68, 172–3, 318–19, 332, 384, 412–14, 419–20
  1808–1825, 154–75
  civil war, 157–66, 210–15
  military dictatorship, 167–8
  Plan of Iguala, 33, 75, 166, 168–72, 202, 299, 384
  political crisis of 1808, 154–7
  start of war of independence, 168–72
Mexico City, 14–16, 154, 160, 164, 168–71, 172, 290, 293, 391, 400
Michelena, José Mariano, 419
Michoacán, 157, 159, 163, 420
middle classes, 127, 131, 134, 418, 453, 462–3, 467–8
Mier, Servando Teresa de, 331, 393, 408
Miguel, Dom, 457, 459, 466–9, 472, 561
Milan, 46–7, 83
military confrontations, 219, 238–9, 241, 284, 455 *see also* battles
military dictatorship, 167–8
military forces, 158, 162, 197, 256, 266, 292–3, 494, 560 *see also* armies
military officers *see* officers, 124
military operations, 160, 212, 576, 577–8
military orders, 452, 464, 469–71
military reforms, 302, 355
military service, 218, 231, 306, 310, 314
military tribunals, 196, 356

602

## Index

militias, 30, 258, 267, 280–2, 286, 292–4, 305, 309, 529–30, 535
   Black, 307, 310, 315
Mina, Francisco Xavier, 410
Mina, Javier, 558
Minas Gerais, 430, 432, 492, 501–2, 516, 531–2, 536
miners, 88–9, 154–6, 416
mines, 87, 89, 212, 253, 267, 294, 416, 420, 431, 516
Minho, 466
mining, 88–90, 406, 417–20, 516
Minorca, 80, 83, 97
minorities, 55, 106, 136, 146, 181, 198, 230, 233, 508, 510
Miranda, Francisco de, 60, 71, 237, 238, 383–4, 393, 397–8, 401, 402, 407–8
Miranda, M.G., 462, 464
Miranda, Pedro Machado, 392
misogyny, 351, 368, 369
mobilizations, 11, 202, 232, 294, 466–7, 521, 529–30, 538
   plebeian, 20, 260
*moderados*, 130–2, 135–6, 138, 141–2, 516–17
moderates, 118, 130, 132, 138, 214, 260, 516
Mompox, 377
monarchical crisis, 278, 280–1, 291
monarchical restoration *see* restoration, 6
monarchical state, 46, 475, 494–5
monarchies, 31–3, 104–6, 124–6, 279–83, 300–3, 343–4, 433–7, 441–3, 448
   constitutional, 33–4, 119, 123, 139, 143, 282, 284, 441, 504, 505, 518
   Portugal, 272, 488, 491, 505
monarchism, 32–3, 224, 227, 277, 291, 300, 351, 447, 536, 543
monarchists, 75, 271, 301, 313, 495, 505
   moderate, 510
monarchs, 155, 157, 282, 285, 496–7, 498, 503–4, 508–11, 515, 516
   *see also individual ruler names.*
   constitutional, 69, 124, 439, 503
money, 76, 90, 215, 223, 370, 416, 418, 477, 478, 486
monitorial method, 421, 424–5
Monroe Doctrine, 412
Montalvo, Francisco de, 297
Monte de las Cruces, 160, 166
Monteagudo, Bernardo de, 56, 223–4, 423
Montesquieu, 338, 342, 363
Monteverde, Domingo de, 238–9, 241, 244, 247
Montevideo, 253, 255–8, 261–2, 264–5, 267, 270, 285, 549, 551, 553

Montilla, Mariano, 245
Mora, José María Luis, 35
Morales, Francisco, 242
Morelos, José María, 70, 160, 163–6, 168, 198
Moreno, Mariano, 208, 210, 259, 564
Moreno, Ysidro, 315
*morgados*, 452–3, 464, 471
Morillo, Pablo, 72, 74–5, 149, 228, 240, 243–4, 247–8, 296–7, 316
Morro Castle, 83, 307
motivations, 55–6, 99, 203, 226, 401, 449
Mounted Lancers of Jaliscoya, 306
Mouzinho da Silveira, José Xavier, 457, 462, 469–71
Moxó de Francoli, Archbishop Benito María, 404
Mozambique, 446, 574
mulattoes, 164, 166, 172, 234, 294, 299, 305, 337, 378, 380, 381, 386, 396, 489, 530, 538, 539, 541
Mulundo, 578
Mundurucú, Emiliano Felipe Benício, 381, 395, 488, 540–1, 545–6
municipal governments, 17, 184, 198, 286, 472
Muquanzo, 578
mutinies, 3, 29, 87, 527
mutual education, 19, 421, 423–4

Naples, 47, 133–4, 147, 332, 441, 556
Napoleon, 47, 65, 104, 110–11, 116, 124, 150, 186–7, 205–6, 213, 248, 342, 357, 360, 366, 382, 407, 430, 455, 478, 480, 549
   *see also* Bonapartes
Napoleonic invasions *see* invasions, Napoleonic/French.
Napoleonic Wars, 128, 152, 410, 414, 441, 454, 488, 512, 550, 554
Nation, the, 3, 112, 282–3, 292, 458, 466, 467
National Assembly, 5, 8, 12, 14, 38
national education, 113
national militia, 131–2
national representation, 112, 336
national sovereignty, 27, 112, 129, 333
nationalism, historic, 114–15
nationalist historicism, 115
nationality, 5, 309, 335
nationalization, 329, 561
natives, 41, 48, 92, 257, 486
natural law, 43, 114
natural rights, 5–6, 23, 207, 376
navies, 49, 319, 400–1, 403, 406, 411, 415, 425, 431, 481

## Index

negotiations, 144, 145, 149, 267, 268, 295, 299, 477, 514, 515
"negroes," 33, 415, 467, 528
neutrality, 28, 45, 96, 99, 218, 246, 248–9, 477, 479
new citizens, 376, 382
  as in Guadeloupe, 382–3
New Granada, 10, 74, 230–2, 238–9, 241, 243–4, 246–8, 285–6, 291–7, 386–7
  Caribbean *see* Caribbean New Granada, 231
  viceroy, 19, 297
new man, 353–60, 362, 367
New Orleans, 307–9, 321
New Spain, 74–5, 117–18, 120–1, 143, 154–7, 166–71, 285–6, 293–6, 331–2
  viceroy, 14, 305
New York, 26, 30, 321–2
newcomers, 181, 474, 482–3
news, 43–4, 190, 206, 232, 255–8, 319, 534, 549, 565–6, 567, 573, 583–4
newspapers, 11, 12, 357, 377–86, 455–6, 552–3, 557, 563, 565, 571–3 *see also* individual titles
Nicaragua, 178, 179, 184, 193–6, 305
Niquitao, 241
nobility, 27, 129, 264, 431, 434, 439, 452–3, 463, 469–70, 478
  high, 452, 454, 461, 463
North America, 28, 31, 34, 39–40, 80, 83–4, 97, 494, 548
North Americans, 16, 25, 31, 96–7, 342, 345, 348, 440, 488
Nuestra Señora de Guadalupe de Amapa, 306
Nueva Galicia, 159
Núñez de Cáceres, José, 388
Núñez, Antonio, 302

Ó Barbosa, José do, 381
oaths, 155, 290, 298, 409, 464, 491, 581
Oaxaca, 160, 169, 173, 296, 420
O'Donojú, Juan de, 171
officers, 124, 129, 132, 221–2, 354–5, 356, 410, 529–30, 580, 582
  Black, 99, 530, 543
  white, 315, 577
O'Higgins, Bernardo, 213–21, 223, 224, 408, 417, 421, 425
Olavide, Limeño Pablo de, 342, 356
old regime, 13, 21, 70, 125, 292, 429, 447 *see also* ancien régime
oligarchy, Guatemala, 189–91, 196–200, 203
Oporto *see* Porto, 134

opposition, liberal, 33, 124, 152, 445, 510–11, 516–17, 519
*ordenanças*, 466, 471, 529–30, 537
Ordóñez, Cristóbal, 169
Orinoco, 231
Osorio, Mariano, 214
Ossa, Juan Luis, 402
owners, 32, 208, 253, 268, 309, 318, 461, 539, 543

Pachuca, 169, 420
Padilla, José Prudencio, 234–5, 245, 249
Páez, José António, 488
Paine, Thomas, 18, 24, 31, 265, 349, 383
*país*, 185, 192
Palmela, duke, 494
Palmela, marquis, 470
Palmer, R.R., 1, 6, 568
Pampas, 253, 254
pamphlets, 12, 14, 321–2, 347, 355, 463, 469, 479, 565, 572
Panama, 77, 88, 231, 305, 311, 345, 388, 393, 400, 562
  Congress, 413
Pan-Americanism, 413
Pando, José María de, 391–2, 398
Papillon, Jean-François, 99, 310–11
Pará, 400, 443, 523–4, 526–7, 530–2, 536–7, 543, 560, 583
Paraguay, 16, 74, 143, 264, 268, 269, 272, 275, 553, 556
Paraíba, 540
*pardo* coast, 229–35, 243, 244–7, 249–51
pardocracy, 388
*pardos*, 231, 232–7, 249–50, 289, 375–7, 380, 386–8, 395–7, 538–40
  active urban, 233, 236
  northeastern, 380–2
Paroissien, James (Diego), 402–3
Parron, Tâmis, 396, 544
parties, 218–19, 339, 466, 481, 516, 534
Party of Order, 516
Pasto, 291, 301
pater familias, 354
*patria*, 69, 192, 254, 334–7
patriarchy, 33, 351–4, 358, 361, 368, 373, 489
patriotic societies, 131–2, 134–5, 144, 221, 263
patriotism, 191, 229, 250, 335
patriots, 13–14, 38–40, 48, 55, 205, 209, 242–3, 245, 526–7, 533
peace, 3, 49, 63, 77, 83, 129, 187, 193, 254, 365

604

# Index

peasants, 2, 11, 14, 20, 37–8, 45, 252–3, 266, 269, 272
Pedro I, 33, 381, 479, 506–8, 511, 514, 517, 520, 526, 559–63
Pedro II, 33, 448, 518, 519, 561
Pedro IV, 460, 561
Pedro, Dom, 33, 442–5, 447–8, 457, 469–70, 490–3, 503–5, 508, 531–3, 558–63
Pedroso, Pedro da Silva, 539, 543, 544
Peel, Sir Robert, 410
peers, 351, 356, 469, 472, 516, 567
Peinado, José María, 176, 189–90, 193
Pelegrín, López, 146
peninsular deputies, 109, 116, 118–20
peninsular liberals, 116, 119
peninsular Spain, 104, 108–9, 112, 116, 118, 120–2, 189, 191, 200, 330–2
peninsular Spaniards, 102, 111, 118, 122, 441
Peninsular War, 28, 125, 409, 438
Pennsylvania, 6, 30
Pensacola, 97, 308
pensions, 306, 410, 480
people of color, 101, 310, 316–17, 321, 375, 500, 538
perceptions, 38, 375, 394, 438, 554, 566
Pérez de Castro, Evaristo, 128
Pérez de Tudela, Manuel, 349
Pérez Morales, Edgardo, 248–9
Pérez, Benito, 248
Pérez, Domingo, 218
Periquitos Rebellion, 527, 534, 542
Perl-Rosenthal, Nathan, 13
Pernambuco, 380–1, 447–8, 523–4, 526–7, 529–30, 532–6, 540, 542–4, 555, 582–4
revolution, 555, 565
personal interest, 37, 424
Peru, 72–3, 88–9, 91–2, 212–13, 221–4, 270–1, 285–6, 294–6, 357–60, 365–6
capital, 219, 222
High, 72, 76
independence, 222, 224
Upper, 40, 41, 76, 209–12, 253–5, 257–8, 260–2, 267–70, 552–3
viceroy, 212, 214, 272, 285
viceroyalty, 20, 37, 73, 120, 353, 355, 357, 361, 364, 369
Peruvian–Bolivian Confederation, 345, 360
Peruvians, 92, 221, 225, 283
Pétion, Alexandre, 32, 45, 246, 248–9, 388, 395
petitions, 20, 22, 93, 386–7, 455, 460, 528–9, 579, 583–4, 587
petrimetres, 362
Pezuela, Joaquín de la, 217, 222, 298–9

Philadelphia, 105, 321, 339, 385, 408
Constitution, 342, 344
Philippines, 154, 166, 287, 300, 316, 552
Piar, Manuel, 234–5
Piauí, 524, 527, 560
Pimenta, João Paulo, 41, 547
Piñeristas, 237
Pinheiro, Silvestre, 148
Pisco, 221–2
Pitt, William, 399, 401, 411
Plack, Noelle, 20
Plan of Iguala, 33
plantations, 39, 232, 294, 309, 481
planters, 7
Cuba, 100
Platine region, 497, 511, 517
plazas, 43, 136, 313, 315, 433
plebeians, 2, 11, 19, 27, 90, 260, 264, 357, 468–9
mobilization, 20, 260
plots, 139–40, 376, 382, 534
plunder(ing), 29, 30, 39, 168
political autonomy, 106, 119, 201, 203, 493
political clubs, 12, 47, 131, 135
political culture, 7, 250, 393, 430, 501, 565, 575
political elites, 32, 78, 235, 472
political emancipation, 474–5, 487, 490, 492, 494, 572
political equality, 112, 122
political experiments, 229, 235–40, 325–7, 345, 346, 348
political goals, 11, 71, 221, 229–30
political ideas, 13, 58, 374, 430, 437, 445, 527, 545
political independence, 37, 204, 233, 237, 571
political legitimacy, 122
political power, 5, 10, 119, 181, 182, 186, 237–8, 509
political revolutions, 78, 102–4, 112, 122–3, 205, 235, 240, 276
political rights, 23, 136, 336, 544
political sovereignty, 207, 219, 225, 227
political transformation, 123, 277, 280
politicians, 16, 23, 30, 112, 210, 216–17, 223, 345, 350, 399, 407, 409–10, 412
see also individual names.
British, 97, 154, 402, 433
politicization, 12–13, 43, 78, 206, 274, 526
politics, 20, 23, 262–3, 351–3, 357–8, 361–2, 371–3, 403–5, 522–3, 525–6
Chilean, 212–13, 218
new, 288, 352–4, 359, 361, 368, 373
popular, 131, 544

605

# Index

Pombal, marquis, 429, 475
Ponte, José Tovar, 407
Popayán, 284, 294, 301
Popham, Sir Home Riggs, 401
popular classes, 20, 263, 274, 294, 295, 299, 520–2, 524
popular politics, 131, 544
  under Spanish constitutional regime, 131–3
popular sovereignty, 10, 131, 136, 225, 493, 499, 502, 505–6, 539, 541
popular support, 134, 140, 187, 257, 493, 540
populations of color see people of color, 101
Porro, Miguel, 315
porteños, 212, 221, 257, 260–1, 266–7, 418
Porto, 134, 332, 441, 455, 456–7, 468, 472, 489–90, 568, 572
  revolution, 441, 474, 490, 503, 526, 556–7, 568–9, 573, 581, 588
Portobelo, 80, 239, 243, 246
ports, 482
  Brazil, 323
Portugal, 439–40
  1820, 456–9
  ancien régime, 20, 450, 452, 453–4, 472, 486
  and start of independence in Spanish America, 549–54
  French invasions, 102, 313, 430, 454–6, 549
  intercontinental monarchy and reforms, 450–2
  monarchy, 272, 485, 488, 491, 505
  political rupture with Brazil, 492–3
  social and political change from ancien régime to liberalism, 450–73
  social categories and political discourse, 460–9
  war and change, 470–3
Portugal, Marcos Antônio, 487
Portuguese, 104, 134–5, 147–8, 270, 272, 436–7, 446–7, 456, 496, 508–9, 524, 527, 529, 541–3, 553–4, 556, 558, 581
Portuguese armies/troops, 104, 270, 272, 524, 527, 529, 553–4, 556, 581
Portuguese Atlantic World, 429, 435, 441, 444, 450
Portuguese Constitution, 444, 456, 581–2, 585
Portuguese court, 134, 416, 431, 475, 485, 494, 549–52, 554, 556, 561
  in Rio see court of Rio, 474
Portuguese liberalism, 135, 455, 472

Portuguese liberals, 134, 148, 442, 445, 457
Potosí, 92, 210, 212, 253, 274
power, 9–10, 103–4, 147, 188–9, 353–5, 357–9, 495, 506–10, 523, 574–5
  absolute, 124, 141, 492, 581
  economic, 203, 210
  executive, 138, 207, 448, 510, 515
  local, 345, 499, 530, 542–3
  monarch's, 279, 510
  political, 5, 10, 119, 182, 186, 237–8, 445, 509
  vacuums, 78, 206, 224, 226, 343, 448, 549, 552
pragmatism, 346, 348
presidents, 45, 166, 212, 259, 273, 325, 336, 360, 388, 409
  for life, 273, 389
prestige, 129, 140, 327, 343, 436–7, 485, 493
priests, 8, 37, 111, 118, 136, 157, 158, 163, 168, 291
primary schools, 95, 185, 424
prisoners, 93, 168, 197, 200, 242, 244, 468–9, 483, 546, 578
prisons, 128, 137, 139, 245, 311, 468, 563
privileged classes, 38, 461–3, 464, 470
privileged positions, 210, 425
privileges, 5–6, 14, 32, 35, 129, 158, 170, 315, 323, 462
proclamations, 12, 192, 221, 334, 337, 452, 458, 466, 474, 478
profits, 81, 85, 92, 416, 452, 570, 576
progressive reforms, 183, 185, 189
prohibitions, 9, 262, 275, 309, 456, 587
pronunciamientos, 124–6, 130, 134, 139, 298, 342
property, 23–7, 154, 159, 306, 309, 453, 460, 493, 537, 543
proprietors, 19, 157, 159, 461–3
prosperity, 310, 333, 342, 437, 462
Protector, 76, 146, 222, 224
Protectorate, 223
provinces, Brazil, 490, 522, 526, 556, 559, 562, 570, 585 see also individual province names
provincial elites, 182, 184, 201, 203, 354, 443, 506
provincial governments, 504, 530, 540, 575
provincial presidents, 540, 545
provisional juntas, 155, 316, 543, 567, 570, 574–5, 581–4, 588
Prussia, 148
public offices, 199, 337, 380, 381

606

## Index

public opinion, 9–15, 292, 298, 303, 328, 540, 562
public sphere, 60, 298, 302, 329, 371, 487, 522, 525
Puebla, 160, 169, 170, 173, 286
*pueblos*, 10, 163, 343–4, 347
Puerto Cabello, 228, 234, 241–2, 488
Puerto Principe, 314
Puerto Rico, 59, 76, 101, 109, 143, 247, 249, 286–7, 300–1, 305
Pueyrredón, Juan Martín de, 214, 217–20, 270–1
punishments, 195, 244, 245, 355
  exemplary, 29, 162, 168
Pussich, João Antonio, 585, 587
Pyrenees, 37, 98, 139–40

Quakers, 413
quartermasters, 160, 484
Quechua, 95, 254, 331
Queen Anne's War, 305
queer history, 360–1
Querétaro, 169, 286, 420
quilombos, 532
Quintana, Hilarión de la, 111, 221
Quito, 20, 72, 74, 76, 143, 178, 188, 285, 552

racial equality, 45, 284, 317, 525
radical republicanism, 33, 374, 383–4, 397, 518
radicalism, 57, 132, 138, 350, 439, 528, 540, 543–4
radicalization, 66–7, 147, 237, 269
radicals, 208, 260, 263, 270, 433, 437, 505, 518
Ramírez, José Miguel, 145
Ramos Arizpe, José Miguel, 111, 118, 145
Ramos de Arizpe, Miguel, 346
Rancagua, 214, 215–16, 220
Rayón, Ignacio, 163, 165
Real, José María del, 409–10
rebellions, 2, 28, 92, 93–6, 98–100, 158–9, 394, 396, 499, 525
rebels, 30–2, 92, 94, 96, 158, 160, 312, 314, 439, 441
Rebouças, Antonio Pereira, 381, 395, 541, 544
Recife, 437, 488, 529, 539, 541, 543, 544–5, 551, 583–4
Recio, Tiburco, 315
recolonization, 526, 559
Recôncavo, 575, 581
reconquest, 69, 75, 160, 216–19, 220, 256, 296

*Reconquista*, 228–9, 240, 243–4
reformers, 86–90, 305, 362, 365, 367, 371
  Bourbon, 67, 85, 88–92, 183–4, 227, 285, 305, 329, 362, 376
reforms, 63, 67, 85, 89, 90, 91–2, 130–1, 142, 179, 183–4, 227, 285, 329, 352–5, 367–8, 376, 455
  Bourbon, 67, 85, 88–92, 183–4, 227, 285, 305, 329, 362, 376
  constitutional, 138, 197
  liberal, 130, 287, 290, 567, 588
  military, 302, 355
  progressive, 183, 185, 189
regencies, 105, 109, 117, 140–2, 149, 157, 188–9, 232, 445, 448
regeneration, 134, 357, 446, 490
regionalism, 70, 72, 184, 200, 202, 523
regular army, 158, 211, 258, 293, 530
Reign of Terror, 374, 383, 397
*reino unido*, 436–8, 440
religion, 6–8, 49, 113, 136, 275, 423, 458, 466
  Catholic, 6–9, 75, 104, 113, 136, 170, 308, 338, 350
religious toleration/tolerance, 9, 409, 426
relocation, 311, 405, 416, 437, 439, 441, 496
Renovales, Mariano, 410
*reparto de comercio*, 92–3, 95
representation, 15, 18, 55, 236, 240, 274, 277, 282, 344, 347
  national, 112, 336
representative democracy, 16–18
representative government, 340–1, 457, 495, 502, 519
representative system, 19, 462, 468
repression, 29, 116, 125–8, 139, 142, 255, 261, 312, 323, 508
republican experiments, 47, 189, 228, 240, 325, 443, 499, 555
republicanism, 221, 225, 227, 229, 233, 240, 276, 300–2, 441, 447
  radical, 33, 374, 383–4, 397, 518
republicans, 35, 39, 139, 238–41, 242, 244–8, 271, 340, 342, 439–40
Resende, Venâncio Henriques de, 544
resentment, 20, 143, 255, 260, 438
resources, 89, 154, 156, 209, 212, 215, 219, 221, 267, 270
restoration, 124–6, 176–8, 199–201, 202, 278, 279–80, 292, 295–8, 299, 391–2, 439
Restrepo, José Félix, 387
Restrepo, José Manuel, 411
return to nature, 10
revenue, 406, 451, 453–4, 472, 497

607

# Index

Revérbero, 558
Revolt of the Tailors, 379
Revolução Anticonstitucional em 1823, 463
revolution, social, 57, 75, 252
revolutionaries, 3–4, 13–15, 37, 57–8, 133–5,
185, 208–9, 211–14, 225–6, 268–9
Haitian, 100
revolutionary elites, 19, 26, 30, 60
revolutionary ideas, 42, 101, 140, 203, 498,
501
revolutionary liberalism, 333, 499
revolutionary movements, 133, 187, 310,
441, 490
revolutionary processes, 53, 208, 225, 277,
303, 344, 375, 503, 504
revolutionary upheavals, 54, 59–60, 133
revolutions
  see also Introductory Note and individual
  countries.
  democratic, 1, 6
  French-Caribbean, 398
  Hispanic, 348
  imperial, 37
  Oporto 441 see Porto, revolution,
  republican, 214
  Spanish, 183
rhetoric, 14, 30, 67, 223, 307, 312, 335
Ribeiro, Father João, 555
Riego, Rafael del, 126, 135, 137–8, 150, 298,
342, 502
Rieti, 147
rights, 4–9, 20, 22, 42, 43, 112–13, 288–90,
312, 334–5, 340–1
  civil, 58, 60, 132, 194, 337
  equal, 5, 22, 29, 66, 132, 189, 192, 261, 337
  individual, 112, 190, 197
  natural, 5–6, 23, 207, 376
  new, 22, 335
  of man and citizen, 5, 8, 42, 330, 331
  political, 23, 136, 336, 544
  seigneurial, 129, 451–4
Rio de Janeiro, 405–6, 431–2, 442–4, 481–94,
523–4, 526–7, 551–5, 570–5, 579–86
  slave market, 562
Río de la Plata, 73–5, 210–11, 214, 217–18,
221–3, 252–76, 285–6, 401–3, 551–2
  aftermath, 273–6
  British invasions and metropolitan
  collapse, 256–9
  from independence to crisis, 268–71
  many endings, 272–3
  revolution, 259–63
  rival projects, 263–8

slave insurrection, 378
young viceroyalty, 252–5
Rio Grande, 505, 540, 546, 551, 553
Rio Negro, 537, 564
Riohacha, 228, 231, 246, 249
rioplatenses, 217, 223–5
Riordan, Liam, 28, 38
Rivadavia, Bernardino, 409, 419–21, 424–5
Robertson brothers, 248, 419
Robespierre, Maximilien, 48, 383, 389–91
Robinson, Maria, 421
Rocafuerte, Vicente, 346, 421
Rodney, T.M., 323
Rodríguez Peña, brothers, 402–3
Rosas, Claudia, 367, 370
Rousseau, J.-J., 17, 24, 48, 208, 259, 338
Rowe, Michael, 14
royal donations, 454, 471
royalism, 31–6, 250, 277–82, 288, 289, 290,
293, 296, 300, 304, 553
  between absolutism and liberalism,
  279–92
royalist army, 163–5, 167–8, 212–15, 243,
245, 289, 293–4, 297, 299
  in wars of independence, 292–4
royalist commanders, 77, 162, 214, 241–2,
293, 296, 299
royalist control, 239, 240, 243, 246, 294
royalist diaspora, 300
royalists, 38–40, 161–7, 216–17, 234, 238–48,
277–81, 284, 294–5
Rozas, Juan Martinez de, 208
Rozas, Senator José María, 223
rumor syndrome, 394–5
rumors, 42, 135, 195, 255, 301, 386, 388, 394,
400, 585
rural areas, 13, 21, 126, 130, 132, 139, 265,
271, 274, 294
Russia, 104, 148, 400, 440

Sáenz, Manuela, 372
sailors, 60, 316, 411, 434, 539
Saint Thomas, 245
Saint-Domingue, 29–31, 32, 39–41, 44–5,
99–100, 312–13, 377–8, 383–6, 391–2,
394–7
  destruction, 390
  revolution, 374, 378
Salamanca, 356, 363
salaries, 91, 267, 378, 410, 459
Salta, 255, 269, 424
Salvador, 379–80, 432, 480–2, 524, 527, 529,
533, 542–3, 545, 581–3

# Index

Salvador, José, 194
Salvadoran uprising, 178, 193
San Carlos, 182, 184, 411
San Diego, 163, 169
San Francisco, 169, 402
San Juan de Ulúa, 172–4
San Juan del Río, 169
San Luis Potosí, 159, 160, 169, 420
San Martín, José de, 72, 74, 76, 214–24, 263, 270, 300–1, 358–9, 408, 421
San Miguel, Evaristo, 141–2, 149
San Salvador, 176–8, 181, 184, 192–4, 198
cathedral, 178
San Severino Castle, 321
Santa Ana, 193
Santa Cruz de la Sierra, 210
Santa Cruz, Andrés de, 359–60
Santa Fe,
junta, 117
Santa Marta, 228, 231, 233–4, 238–41, 243, 246, 285, 297, 302
Santana Neves, Joaquim de, 542
Santander, Francisco de Paula, 421, 561
Santarém, 537
Santiago, 178, 205, 206–7, 209–11, 213, 215, 220–1, 223, 378, 385
Santo Domingo, 99–100, 163, 300, 310–11, 316, 377, 379, 381, 385, 388
Santo Ildefonso Treaty, 476
Santos Marrocos, Joaquim dos, 486
Santos, Joaquim dos, 381
São Luís, 527, 531
São Paulo, 430, 461, 492, 520–1, 523, 526, 531, 559
Saravia, Gonzalo Quintero, 97
Sarmiento, Domingo Faustino, 358
Sarratea, Manuel de, 409
Schafer, Daniel, 310
Schlemmer, Joseph, 46
Schlesinger, Arthur, Jr, 326
schools, 53, 309, 406, 421–5, 497
Lancasterian, 415, 421–5
primary, 95, 185, 424
Scott, Joan, 353, 360
secessionism, 567, 584–7
second slavery, 312, 318
secular clergy, 466–7, 469, 471
security, 232, 341, 439, 498, 555
seigneurial rights, 129, 451–4
agrarian, 464–5
self-government, 9, 68, 72, 167, 259, 276, 344
*Semanario Crítico*, 369
*señorito afeminado*, 360–6

Seo de Urgel, 140–2
separation from Spain, 202, 235, 437
separation of powers, 331
Sergipe, 381, 528, 541
servants, 163, 366, 431, 460, 485
Seven Years' War, 9, 83–4, 97, 252, 306, 327, 355
Sevillán, Bernardo, 320, 323
Seville, 138, 149–50, 156, 328
ships, 80, 82, 87, 117, 431–2, 433, 479, 481, 586, 587
British, 174, 316
sieges, 2, 164, 166, 172, 228, 243–5, 261–2, 264–5, 282
Sierra Leone, 313
Sieyès, abbé, 17
Silva Lisboa, José da, 391, 398, 520
Silva Maia, J.J., 468–9
silver, 89, 167, 253, 267, 417, 419
slave constitutionalism, 525, 531
slave market, 405
slave rebellions, 99, 287, 313, 380, 387, 389, 488
slave revolts, 3, 177–9, 312, 323, 430, 488, 521, 581
slave ships, 100, 576, 586
slave trade,
Atlantic, 49, 500, 513
slaveholders, 76, 98–100, 494, 534, 564
slavery, 44, 99–100, 263–4, 312–13, 318, 321–2, 324, 513–17, 546, 561
abolition, 284, 312, 382, 384, 387, 392, 396, 416, 441, 448
*see also* free-womb laws
immediate, 284, 375, 384–5, 398, 484
second, 312, 318
slaves, 86–8, 98–101, 229–34, 309–10, 312–14, 377–9, 385–7, 394–5, 525, 530–4
African, 79, 84, 230, 253, 414, 513
Cuban, 100, 307
former, 44, 99–100, 268, 304, 308, 310–11, 313, 317, 376, 379
participation in Brazilian independence, 530–4
Smythe, Percy Clinton Sydney, 406
Sobremonte, Rafael de, 256, 401
social classes *see* classes, 2
social groups, 35, 55, 204, 462
social hierarchies, 116, 158
social revolution, 57, 75, 252
social status, 37, 231, 306, 489
social transformations, 266, 289, 327
Sociedad Constitucional, 136
Sociedad de Caballeros Racionales, 408

# Index

Sociedad Patriótica de Agricultura y de Economía, 237
societies, patriotic, 131–2, 134–5, 144, 221, 263
Society of the Ring, 136
Sola, Pablo Vicente, 169
soldiers, 26, 161–2, 165–6, 174, 355, 439, 529, 543, 577–9, 586 see also armies
Soriano, Cristina, 8, 42
Soublette, Carlos, 245
South Atlantic, 59, 416, 496, 513, 567–9
integrated, 571–88
Southern Cone
1808–1824, 205–27
Americanism to national states, 219–25
Americanist strategy, 215–19
civil war, 444
Southern Europe, 348
Spanish model, 133–5
Souza, José Luiz de, 555
Sovereign Congress, 460, 563
sovereign states, 222–3, 345
sovereignty, 9–15, 17, 69, 70, 205, 207, 210, 212, 285, 432–3
national, 27, 112, 129, 333
political, 219, 225, 227
popular, 10, 131, 136, 225, 493, 499, 502, 505–6, 539, 541
Spain
see also Introductory Note
1820 liberal programme, 129–30
1820 revolution, 126–8
American question, 143–6
civil war and King's coup d'état, 138–42
coup d'état of July 1822, 141, 148
exaltados, 130–8
foreign intervention and fall of constitutional regime, 147–50
liberal struggles and reactionary conspiracies, 135–8
many faces of liberalism, 130–1
moderados, 130–2, 135–6, 138, 141–2, 516–17
national militia, 131–2
peninsular, 109
Royal Guard, 140
ultra-royalists, 34, 137–40, 150
Spaniards, 64, 66–7, 74–5, 90–1, 143, 173–4, 260, 309–10, 317, 337–8
Spanish American deputies, 106
Spanish authorities, 88, 176, 187–9, 191, 193, 195, 197–8, 245–6, 320, 321
Spanish constitution 7 see Cádiz, Constitution
Spanish Cortes 14 see Cortes, of Cádiz

Spanish Empire
interpretations, 54–60
overview, 53–78
Spanish governments, 33, 48, 144, 147–8, 152, 279, 310, 404
Spanish Liberal Revolution, 102–23
application of Constitution in America, 120–1
prelude, 102, 104–8
Spanish liberalism, 111, 139, 145, 288, 295, 342, 455, 501
first, 108, 112, 114–15, 120
Spanish model in Southern Europe, 133–5
Spanish officials, 45, 71, 83, 99, 181–3, 187–8, 193, 311–12, 319
Spanish troops, 36, 83–4, 98, 171–2, 174, 228, 240, 255
speeches, 42, 322, 381, 385–6, 426, 468, 528
spies, 96, 381
St. Augustine, 308–9
stability, 147, 191–2, 221, 367, 420, 436, 498, 519
status, 4–7, 181, 184, 283, 301, 308, 315, 370–1, 381–2, 518
status quo, 13–14, 28, 34, 125, 258, 439, 441, 505–6, 573
status, social, 37, 231, 306, 489
Stirling, Charles, 248
succession, 34, 79–80, 97, 305, 354, 476, 492
Sucre, Antonio José de, 76, 245, 272
sugar, 99, 218, 389, 431, 432, 461, 497, 500, 513, 551
Sungo, 578
Supreme Directors, 216–18, 220, 224, 265, 268–70, 272
Suriname, 313
surrenders, 95, 171, 175, 239, 242, 402, 431
Sussex, duke of, 221–2, 408, 424
Sweden, 479, 561
Switzerland, 14, 45, 561
symbols, 70, 135, 150, 274, 371, 455, 467

Tabasco, 169
Taber, Robert D., 32
Tacna, 358
Taguanes, 241
Talca, 219
Tampico, 169, 174
tapadas, 370–1, 372
Tapuios, 534, 537
Taunay, Auguste Marie, 487
Taunay, Nicolas Antoine, 487

## Index

taxes, 20, 89, 159, 167, 199, 239, 275, 312, 471, 472
Tegucigalpa, 194–5
Ten Years' War, 324
Terralla y Landa, Esteban, 357, 365, 370
terror, 43, 99, 160, 242–3, 374, 383, 397
terrorism, 212
Texas, 169, 322
Texcoco, 169, 413
Thermidorian gradualism, 383–4
Thermidorian Reaction, 374, 398
Thibaud, Clément, 10, 42, 45, 235, 238, 389
Thomson, James, 423
Thornton, John, 35
Tierra Firme, 296, 298, 316
tithes, 45, 129, 451–3, 465, 471
tobacco, 13, 218, 376, 432, 513, 551
Toledo, 237, 245
tolerance, 6, 8
Tomás, Manuel Fernandes, 556
Toreno, count, 111
Torre Tagle, marquis, 221–2, 408, 424
Torre, Miguel de la, 301
Torres, Manuel María de, 169
Totonicapán, 202
town councils, 119, 155, 181, 189, 194, 207, 344
towns, 10, 13–14, 157–61, 253, 254, 264, 285, 293–4, 343–4
trade, 79, 81–2, 85–8, 399–400, 462, 464, 499, 500, 513–16, 551
  foreign, 84, 551, 575
  free, 70, 86, 186, 190, 201, 258, 405, 417–18
Trafalgar, 63, 234, 256
trained, 359
transformations, 13, 265, 326, 332, 432, 548
  political, 123, 277–303
  social, 266, 289, 327
transition, 2, 50, 127–8, 133, 233, 236, 250, 359, 447, 522
treason, 140, 193, 197, 200, 215, 403, 410
treaties, 63, 80, 84, 86, 97, 100, 146, 311, 319, 513–17
Treaty of Basel, 63, 100, 311
Treaty of Córdoba, 146
Treaty of Córdoba, 171
Treaty of Madrid, 476
Tribunal of Loyalty, 189, 192
tribute, 35, 91–3, 201, 267, 275, 289–90, 292, 298, 306, 312
*Trienio*, 34, 104, 116, 124–53, 340, 463
Trinidad, 228, 244–6, 249, 415

Tristán, Flora, 365–6
Triumvirate, 260, 262, 265
troops 30 *see* armies
Trujillo, 222, 241
Tucumán, 210, 215, 217–18, 262, 269, 271
Tupac Amaru, 35, 92, 94–5, 98, 255, 378, 382, 396, 400
Tupac Katari, Julian, 95, 255
Two Sicilies, 133
typhus, 166
tyranny, 3, 34, 259–60, 314, 389, 410, 479

ultra-royalists, 457
United Kingdom of Portugal, 460, 485, 554, 558
United Provinces of the Río de la Plata, 218, 262, 266, 268, 269–73, 560
United States, 40, 44, 59–60, 163, 166, 319, 321, 325–6, 340, 342, 346
  liberal spirit, 342
unity, 53, 193, 198, 285, 344, 512, 549, 552
upper classes, 33, 70, 76, 443, 476, 489, 495
Upper Peru, 40, 41, 76, 209–12, 253–5, 257–8, 260–2, 267–70, 552–3
urban masses, 19, 71, 201, 204, 500
Urrutia, Carlos de, 200
Uruguay, 41, 255, 273, 275, 318, 418, 560
Usulután, 193
Utrecht treaties, 80, 476

Valdivia, 212–13
Valençay, 105
Valencia, 126, 139, 207, 238, 241–2
Valladolid, 159–60, 161, 169, 207
Valle, José Cecilio del, 349, 420
Valle, Narciso del, 376, 395
Valongo slave market, 405
Valparaíso, 221, 417–18
Vargas, Tomás, 320
Varnhagen, Francisco Adolfo de, 521, 545
Vasconcelos, Bernardo Pereira de, 516
vassals, 92, 280, 315, 485
Vendée, 28
Venegas, Francisco, 166, 293
Venezuela, 74, 228–32, 238–47, 286, 293–7, 312–13
  captaincy general, 91, 229
  eastern, 234, 245
  population, 231
Veracruz, 80, 84, 164, 166, 169, 170, 171, 305–6, 308, 420
Verna, Paul, 245

611

## Index

Verona, Congress of, 142, 148
veterans, 15, 130, 218, 410, 510, 560
Viana, Paulo Fernandes, 488
viceroyalties, 73, 84, 154–6, 167, 170–1, 210, 212, 252–8, 285–6, 481–2
    former, 260, 273, 386, 554
    New Granada, 91, 117, 120, 229
    New Spain, 117, 120, 155, 391
    Río de la Plata, 252–6
viceroys, 73, 156, 167, 168, 209–10, 212–13, 222, 257–8, 286, 290 see also individual names
Victoria, Guadalupe, 166, 173
Vienna, Congress of, 124, 271, 513–14, 554
Vila Real, 467
Vilafrancada, 508, 542
Vilanova Portugal, Tomás Antônio, 485, 494, 554
villages, 11
villas, 158–9, 163–5, 167, 170
Villèle, Joseph de, 139–40
vintismo, 459, 461, 464, 490, 525, 531
Vinuesa, Matías, 137
violence, 27–31, 239, 241–4, 292, 295, 367, 372, 495, 498
Virginia, 6, 26
virtue, 8, 317, 323, 335, 340, 343, 354–5, 359, 361, 368
Vittorio Emmanuelle I, 147
volunteers, 152, 246, 268, 292–3
voters, 17, 516

War of Jenkins' Ear, 82, 305
War of the Austrian Succession, 306
War of the Spanish Succession, 79–80, 97, 305
war to the death, 29, 240–1
Warsaw, 46, 455

wealth, 24–5, 90, 159, 184, 210, 231, 431, 470, 496, 498
weapons, 4, 99, 158, 163, 244, 246–9, 316, 467
Wellesley, Richard Colley, 407
Wellington, duke of, 106, 124, 411
Whatmore, Richard, 41
Wheatley, Phyllis, 322
white officers, 315, 577
White, Blanco, 111, 342
Whitelocke, Lieutenant-General John, 403
Wiggins, Nansi, 309
Wilberforce, William, 319, 384, 393, 398, 407, 414, 424
Windham, William, 403
women, 5, 20, 21–3, 158–60, 260, 263, 309, 320, 352–3, 365, 366–73, 460–1
    African, 577
    American, 21, 369
    useful mothers and deceitful women, 367–73
written constitutions, 330, 333, 440, 443, 456–8

Yrigoyen, Matías de, 407
Yucatán, 284

Zacatecas, 159, 169, 420
zambos, 254, 266, 289, 294, 375
Zapiola, Carlos, 408
Zapiola, José Matías, 408
Zavitz, Erin, 32
Zea, Francisco Antonio, 144
Zegarra, Margarita, 367
Zepherin, Marc, 487
Zitácuaro, 163, 166, 169
Zuazola, 242